4–5 billion years ago

After the Bauhaus, Before the Internet:

Sun starts to produce energy

A History of Graphic Design Pedagogy

EDITED BY GEOFF KAPLAN

no place press

3.5 million years ago

first tools from stone, wood, antlers, and bones

FOREWORD

TIM BARRINGER

Yale has trained artists since Colonel John Trumbull founded a gallery at the university in 1832. The present Yale School of Art dates from 1864. Pedagogy in the visual arts has taken its place alongside teaching in humanities and sciences here for a quarter of a millennium. Makers, theorists, and historians—all of them pedagogues—have long formed an uneasy alliance in which each constituent provides an irreducible contribution. When leading practitioner and teacher in the field Geoff Kaplan proposed a conference and, later, a book on the history of pedagogy in graphic design in the postwar period that would bring together prominent designers, instructors, and historians, it seemed appropriate that this should be a joint endeavor of the History of Art Department and the Yale School of Art (with the collaboration of the dean at the time, Marta Kuzma) and that it should take place in the lecture hall we share with the Yale School of Architecture (led by Dean Deborah Berke). The physical proximity of artists, architects, and art historians at the junction of Chapel and York Streets in New Haven (with the Yale University Art Gallery just steps away) can yield startling synergies, even as it forcefully reveals our disciplinary limitations. For the art historian, it always looks more interesting across the street.

The conference was held in May 2019, in what now seems a long-ago pre-COVID utopia of cordial interaction, free circulation, and open discussion. It was a rich and multifaceted convening about graphic design discourse, education, and practice over the postwar decades. The same spirit of constructive exchange can be found in the pages of this book. Design pedagogy of the 1950s, '60s, and '70s was a topic that, positioned in plain sight between the vast historiography of the Bauhaus and the lived experience and memory of the present generation, had never adequately been examined. The essays gathered here—some developed from conference papers that have been reworked over the past two years, and others that are new and significant contributions—constitute a vivid seminar in the relevance of that defining moment in visual culture and global history to graphic design practice and pedagogy today. Reflecting on the conference's themes, we can connect the abiding motifs of the postwar era to the wrenching dramas of race, class, and identity and the environmental crisis that are being played out in real time around us.

If *disegno* is a practice reaching back to the studios and academies of the Renaissance, with a cool practicality to counter the sensuous allure of *colore*, modern design originated in the industrial revolution, an emanation of the primal scene of the modern capitalist world amid the steam and gaslight of the factories of Arkwright and Wedgwood in the English Midlands. A product of that first machine age, design has played a key role in shaping the cultural, visual, and material forms of modernity in ways both transformative and catastrophic. In the mid-nineteenth century, provoked by the material excess and dizzying stylistic mélange of the exhibits at the Great Exhibition of 1851 at London's Crystal Palace, theorists such as Gottfried Semper, Augustus Pugin, and Henry Cole sought the "true principles" of design. These they attempted to express in printed books, manifestos, teaching materials, and leaflets. Though the term was not coined until William Addison Dwiggins uttered it in 1922, these printed materials were early manifestations of "graphic design."

In an important chapter of this book, Deborah Littlejohn points out that "graphic design education is dominated by a practically oriented self-concept, despite being situated within academic universities where scholarly inquiry is the predominant value." While this is undoubtedly true in many instances, personal experience at Yale has suggested the contrary. Art history seminars, including my own, have benefitted from the active contribution of generations of MFA students of Sheila Levrant de Bretteville, Caroline M. Street Professor of Graphic Design, who has headed Yale's Graphic Design program since 1990. Sheila describes her "person-centered" approach as "emphasizing the students' desire to communicate, and focusing on what needs to be said and to whom they want to say it." Such focus and articulacy of purpose moves beyond the practical sphere and invites students to participate actively not only in humanities classes but in the wider culture.

Many of the contributors to this volume find graphic design as an academic subject inchoate, a topic of rich possibility but not yet a clearly formed discipline. It is, in Littlejohn's vivid characterization, "a mushy territory intersecting art, advertising, communication and rhetoric, cognitive psychology, linguistics, media studies, and computer science." Writing from the *terra firma* of art history, I find this lack of definition appealing. It contrasts with the dead hand of patrilineal inheritance in my discipline, as portrayed in the recent influential account *A History of Art History,* by Christopher S. Wood, where adherence to a circumscribed male Eurocentric tradition is offered in preference to professional diversity, interdisciplinary creativity, or political commitment.

We are what we read. The character of graphic design as a subject depends, as does that of art history, upon the texts chosen to exemplify it on student reading lists. Bibliographies, discussed in several essays, can serve as institutional manifestos, such as those compiled by Katherine McCoy, who taught at Cranbrook Academy of Art from 1971 to 1995, as "a cross-disciplinary guide to history, theory, methodology, practice, and process in graphic design, industrial design, interior design, and architecture." But they can also be highly personal, formative constructions based on individual experience and epiphany. For Geoff Kaplan, it was the very act of reading, as an integral part of training in design, that enabled graphic design to move beyond practical and professional preparation to become an academic discipline after World War II. Kaplan and Rachel Churner explore these questions in a remarkably frank and vivid interview, published here for the first time, with one of the mainstays of the student bibliography since the 1980s, Hal Foster. If *The Anti-Aesthetic* (1983) and *Recodings* (1985), articulating a postmodernist social and intellectual critique, were on every design student's shelf for a generation or more, *Design and Crime* (2000) diagnosed contemporary design as being inalienably corrupted by its imbrication with consumerism.

In her gripping "autoethnography" articulated through reflections on a lifetime's bibliographic explorations, Audrey G. Bennett reveals the significance of "peripheral texts," including theory, poetry, and fiction, from Benjamin and Borges to bell hooks, that were included in eclectic student reading packets at Yale in the mid-1990s. Such collections, she notes, "can simultaneously evoke resonance and dissonance in each reader." Recalling her experience as the only Black student in her cohort, Bennett purposes the term "minor literature" to signify the writings missing from the assigned bibliographies—writings that speak from a minority community, writings by Black designers. In a persuasive call to action, with implications well beyond the particular field, she demands "a more integrative approach to graphic design pedagogy, in which major and minor literatures come together to form a de-canon—a fractalized coalescence of cross-disciplinary texts that originate from the Global South and attempt to bring about the end of marginalization and the beginning of consciousness about the contributions of 'others' to the discipline."

If the books on a student's shelf charted a visual and conceptual landscape for their explorations, a map marked out both with possibilities and restrictions, current periodicals could exemplify ways to proceed. In an eloquent tribute, Gail Swanlund recalls the arrival of an edition of the magazine *Emigre*, one of the first fruits of the new Mac design technology of the early 1980s. Her account of a first encounter with the printed publication is, however, embodied—visceral, even: "I held it to my nose to sniff the oily printer ink, then I sat down and opened to the first page. The magazine was so big I could set my forearms on a spread, and I had to bend in to examine every detail, to read blocks of sometimes teeny type. In these pages, I saw Zuzana [Licko]'s typefaces in performance; the issue's content percolated through her work." The essays collected here add many vivid testimonials to the contribution to debate in classrooms and design studios of such periodicals, eagerly consumed each month.

While this book is strictly focused on the period *after* the Bauhaus, that foundational institution is a presence on almost every page. Indeed, essays by J. Dakota Brown and Juliet Koss demonstrate that, however seductive the utopian and interdisciplinary visions and ambitions laid out by its founders and leaders, the Bauhaus was firmly enmeshed in the contradictions of Weimar Germany. The recent historiography has, as Colin Fanning notes, moved to denaturalize its mythologies, noting that student experience, fractured along lines of class, gender, race, and religion, drastically differed from the institution's expressed ideals of collectivity and universality. And while there was no term equivalent to "graphic design" in use among the overlapping circles of designers and architects at the Bauhaus, by the mid-1920s the heritage of the Arts and Crafts movement was being replaced by a distinctively new approach. László Moholy-Nagy proposed applying to book and poster design the lessons of photographic communication in the age of mass media, while, as Koss recalls, Josef Albers demanded that "We have to be able to register a poster's message as we speed past in our car or in the tram." Such a sentiment would have been anathema to William Morris.

One of the many significant revisions proposed here is an insistence on recognizing female agency, against the grain of the modernist historiography. Jordan Troeller, for example, reveals the crucial contribution of photographer Lucia Moholy to the distinctive Bauhaus graphic aesthetics associated with her husband Moholy-Nagy. Maria Gough adds a salutary reminder that the Bauhaus should not be considered the sole font—pun intended—of later developments in typography and book design, making a convincing case for the impact of Soviet avant-garde practice, especially that of El Lissitzky, on the generation of American designers of the 1960s.

Similar revisionist revelations lie in store for the reader keen to learn about the major foci of discussion in the conference—graphic design pedagogy at Ulm, in Germany, and at Cranbrook, in the US, among others, whose methods are subjected to a crisp and provocative comparison in a chapter by Hugh Dubberly. The essays gathered here are exemplary models in how to assess the strengths and weaknesses of pedagogy—curriculum and practice—but also how to research student experience. To read these analyses is an important, if often humbling, experience for those of us who devote our time to teaching and leave too little time for self-reflexive critique.

Pedagogical practices at the short-lived but hugely influential Hochschule für Gestaltung at Ulm are examined by Craig Buckley. Ulm has long been admired for its fearless engagement with various forms of scientific and cultural theory, principally the critical theory of the Frankfurt School, and relative lack of interest in mundane questions of fabrication. Buckley draws a firm distinction between the "Visual Communication" department at Ulm (which used the English term in preference to German not-quite-cognates) and the Bauhaus, where designs were licensed to companies who mass produced and sold the products. The Ulm school's faculty and students, by contrast, became transformational consultants to Braun, Lufthansa, BASF, and Olivetti, and were involved in production processes, supply chains, and market identities that remain instantly recognizable today.

We were privileged to have as a keynote speaker at the conference Gui Bonsiepe. Born in 1934, Bonsiepe studied at Ulm from 1955 to 1959 in the "Information" department and taught there from 1963 until the institution's closure in 1968. He lamented in 1995 that "design is a foreign body in the realm of traditional higher education institutions," and in the current essay he adds: "The design disciplines stress the formation of nondiscursive intelligence, including aesthetic or sensorial competence understood as the capacity to make perceptual, particularly visual distinctions." Yet his genial presentation at the conference, amplified in the chapter given here, indicated a profound understanding of the mission of the university. Design, for Bonsiepe, cannot be assimilated into theory, psychology, technology, or the rarefied sphere of aesthetics. Intersecting with each, it belongs to none. Serving in this book as an authoritative primary source, eyewitness, and actor,

Bonsiepe taught at Ulm during its final flowering and played a role in defining projects at Cybersyn, the pioneering digital center of Salvador Allende's Unidad Popular government in Chile. But more importantly perhaps (as Pamela M. Lee notes in her response to his plenary contribution), Bonsiepe serves the role of a timely and authoritative commentator on the tectonic shifts of the present. Viewing the globalized world from Brazil, he is well placed to call attention to the profound destruction wrought by the pursuit of economic growth at any cost, a process in which "design" has been complicit. Fred Turner and Annika Butler-Wall amplify this point in their sobering chapter "Designing for Neoliberalism," with its chilling vision of a new, shape-shifting "upper class" of patrons. In his ninth decade, however, Bonsiepe is willing to offer fragments of hope for a return to a more idealistic conspectus: "The disposition to consider how to change existing social relations," he avows, "remains not only desirable but necessary."

Bonsiepe's association with both Europe and the Americas is emblematic of the transregional reach of design pedagogy and the shifting global currents within design itself. To take just a handful of examples among many in this book, Silvia Fernández offers a—to this reader—revelatory account of the emergence of modern graphic design in Latin America, focusing on Argentina. Wael Morcos's interview with Basma Hamdy and Yara Khoury offers critical perspectives from Egypt and Lebanon. Ian Lynam's essay on graphic design educator and graphic designer Kōhei Sugiura 杉浦康平 reveals a significant relationship between Ulm and graphic design practice and pedagogy in Japan. This book reveals a global story—but one in which every local and regional instantiation is marked by difference.

Thomas Ockerse, born in 1940 and thus Bonsiepe's near contemporary, tells by contrast an American story that is a palimpsest of the development of the field. Ockerse first heard the phrase "graphic design" in 1963, the year he enrolled in Yale's new BFA in the subject. His chapter offers an eye-witness account of the early struggle of graphic design in the US to distinguish itself from advertising and "commercial art": Moving from student to professor via commercial practice, Ockerse was buffeted by the winds of ideological change, eventually becoming the leader of a "laboratory for typographic experiments" at Indiana University in the late 1960s. In the '70s, with new colleagues at RISD, he produced *Graphic Design Education: An Exposition*, a significant short book strongly influenced by semiotic theory. In a final pivot, Ockerse has embraced the concept of design as both a practical and reflective practice, a distinction he has chosen to impart, he reveals, through pedagogy rather than through publications or manifestos.

What Ockerse learned early on is still true. As Lauren Williams reminds us in a powerful intervention, design and its pedagogy "cannot escape unblemished from its entanglements with capitalism." Hal Foster agrees: "Part of my suspicion about design is that, historically, it has often tended to recoup artistic experiments for capitalist ends." But perhaps this is true not just of design but of the larger project of the modernist avant-garde, which art historian Tom Crow memorably described (in "Modernism and Mass Culture in the Visual Arts") as the "research and development arm" of the culture industry, of capitalism itself. Crow's position perhaps undermines a viewpoint in which (to quote Foster's gentle self-parody) "art [is] positioned as the good object, and design as the bad." Postmodernist scholarship drew attention to the cultural effects of what Fredric Jameson long ago termed "late capitalism"; but Williams makes a crucial further move, situating design, and design pedagogy, within a history of *racial* capitalism reaching back to the early modern period, a history whose elemental trajectories are only now being widely understood and contested. As Williams insists, design and design pedagogy's "complicity with capital, neoliberalism, and white supremacy calls for close examination." In a lively chapter that opens with a richly theorized meditation on cave painting but jolts us suddenly into an uncomfortable present, Ignacio Valero further reminds us that we are now "confronted with the simultaneous and intertwined acceleration of crises at the ecological, economic, and political levels globally." Under these circumstances, questions of capitalism's planetary impact must lie at the core of design pedagogy, as they do in a compelling syllabus he developed at the California College of the Arts in 2014, entitled "Media Matters: A Semiotics, Ecology and Political Economy of the Image and the Commons."

Despite its intersections with the major intellectual questions of the day, the historiography of graphic design constantly threatens to default to normative hierarchies—the intellectual equivalent of factory settings. In a sharply focused assessment, Chris Lee points out that graphic design history "has privileged a narrative of design's progressive orientation toward mass production and mass communication, implicitly normalizing the values of a Western colonial/statist/capitalist order" and in doing so it has "glossed over the significance of labor, particularly gendered labor and instead fetishized technological progress and individual (male) genius as the drivers of history." While the rich multiplicity of voices represented in this collection lend it the character of a significant revisionist intervention, the wholesale disavowal of these heroic narratives remains a work in progress.

The chapters in this book have subjected the practices of education in graphic design—legacies and inheritances; bibliographies and curricula; practices and aspirations—to rigorous analysis and critique. But what of the future? As Williams notes: "Educators, the canon, the monographs, and—to a lesser extent—the student bodies are not inclusive with respect to gender or race, and so the schools are sites that reproduce oppressions that intersect and amplify each other along lines of race, gender, sexuality, ability, and citizenship." Her call to transform the demographics and discourses of design education resonates with the demand of Yasmine Gibson and Jessica Wexler for a dramatic expansion of the purview of the field: They call for "a new design pedagogy that expands the narrative work of the design educator to embrace the structural, financial, and administrative," claiming persuasively that "equity, pluralization, greater agency, and access are only possibly through changes at the level of the structural, where the hierarchies and pathways that determine access to knowledge can be reimagined."

Any substantive change in pedagogy requires self-reflexive analysis on the part of the teacher, often a practice accompanied by sobering, humbling realizations. Returning to the opening of this introduction, Williams's and Lee's remarks prompt me to revisit my citation of John Trumbull—a name so often rolled out when art at Yale is mentioned. As the creator, in works like *The Signing of the Declaration of Independence* (1818), of a foundational iconography of an American continental empire that permitted slavery, this is a patriarch who casts a dark shadow. That Trumbull's corpse is buried under the Yale University Art Gallery may stand as a nice gothic symbol of the continuing authority of white patriarchy—still present after two centuries, difficult to remove, and rotten. Significant efforts for change are underway at Yale, precipitated in large measure by student activism, but profound transformation cannot be achieved by administrative fiat or by a single individual or isolated group. Rather, it is through fundamental shifts in every classroom, in each curriculum, in the pages of every bibliography, in the daily work of the design studio and the art history seminar, that large-scale change is ultimately precipitated.

I recall, in my own sphere, the transformative effect of a compilation of texts titled *Race-ing Art History: Critical Readings in Race and Art History* when it appeared twenty years ago, offering the possibility of dispelling art history's silence on the question of race in classroom discussion. The editor of that book, Kymberly N. Pinder, was announced as the new dean of the Yale School of Art as of 2021, the first woman of color to occupy that role. I have every reason to believe that the kind of generative shared endeavor of historians, critics, and practitioners represented by this book will be continued and redoubled under her leadership. Finally, all the contributors, I know, will join me in offering thanks to Geoff Kaplan for his vision in convening a generative event and shaping from it a book as compelling to the mind as it is to the eyes and hands.

A HISTORY OF GRAPHIC DESIGN PEDAGOGY, OR SO THEY TELL ME

GEOFF KAPLAN

A History of Graphic Design Pedagogy begins with a statement by Katherine McCoy with whom I studied while at Cranbrook Academy of Art in mid-1990s. I do not recall exactly when Kathy made the statement, but it would have been a few years after graduate school, when I was establishing my studio practice and teaching at ArtCenter, CalArts, and Otis. I am certain it was communicated over the phone when I asked for teaching advice. Kathy said: "Graphic design moves from a professional practice to a discipline when design writes its own histories and theories." Over the years, as I lived in Los Angeles and then in San Francisco, I've considered the historicity of her pronouncement. Even as the parlance shifted from that of LA Valley Girls to that of Silicon Valley brogrammers, from "Dude, this is like totally awesome" to "design thinking, interdisciplinary, and problem-solving," I frequently toyed with the terms by which we describe design, especially as they relate to McCoy's statement on the "discipline" of graphic design.

Today, when design calls for inter-, trans-, and multi-disciplinary strategies, I continue to explore when, and if, graphic design was, is, or could become a discipline. Spurred on by this phone call and by years of teaching, I set out to understand how we tell these stories and how we transmit this history to our students. The following, then, is structured as a conversation between myself and my peers.

As McCoy explained in one of our many follow-up conversations:

> When professional practice led education, graphic design was a professional orientation at best. When graphic design education started breaking new ground, it became more like a discipline. The first part of our history there was the service industry, also called "commercial art." The sense of graphic design professionalism arrived in the early to mid-'60s, when it split from advertising, with the rise of corporate identity. That lasted to the late '60s and early '70s before education started taking the ascendancy. I do think there was at least a ten-year period where design had become a profession, where we left behind the service-to-industry model. At that point design moved in a disciplinary direction.

But what does the term discipline mean in light of graphic design history? And what does discipline mean relative to practices of reading as well as writing?

•

In any discussion of discipline, references to Michel Foucault's *Discipline and Punish: The Birth of the Prison* are unavoidable. The French title of the book, *Surveiller et punir*, telegraphs the interests of surveillance in the notion of disciplinarity—the sense of watching and being watched and the sense of control that stems from both. Foucault argues for the historical rise of what he will call disciplinarity or control society: Namely, how populations are managed within the modern West. Foucault describes changes in penal systems in

Western society after the democratic revolutions of the eighteenth century, from a mode of punishment related to the power of the sovereign—a spectacle for all his subjects—to forms of control involving self-policing, self-regulation, and the internalization of disciplinary power.

The classic example of modern discipline is that of the panoptic prison where guards are stationed in a central watch tower. The tower's design renders the presence of the guards invisible; they can at any time observe and regulate the actions of the prisoners from within this centralized structure. Because the prisoners never know when they are being observed, they internalize the power dynamics and assume that they are always being watched.

Foucault provides the foundational statement on control society—a useful way of thinking about how we self-regulate within our own disciplinary homes. But there are far less theoretical ways to approach the question of design discipline. A contemporary form of disciplinary control comes to us by way of Yelp or other user-generated content platforms and in the form of reviews, ranked lists, and judgments of our peers and audiences. The scrutiny of the other disciplines keeps us in order. The scrutiny of the institution produces discipline. To return to McCoy's statement one could say: As designers construct their histories and theories they, in turn, discipline themselves.

The cover images throughout these pages offer a proposed library as determined by the terms and voices of the essay

But the term discipline need not be punitive; it can also be a "shared commitment." Deborah Littlejohn draws a distinction between practice and discipline, with recourse to Thomas Kuhn, by suggesting that a discipline is a set of shared "beliefs, values and techniques." In a footnote to her dissertation, "Building a Theory of Relationships among Academic Culture, Professional Identity and the Design of the Teaching Environment," she states:

> Practice refers to the "design industry" and the activities associated with professional services (advising clients, creating concepts and producing prototypes). In a second sense, practice is a "coordinated effort formed around a particular activity," as in "the carrying out of some action." A discipline is defined as a set of shared commitments to patterns of thinking and behaviors common to an academic community in a given field (Kuhn, 1970).

Littlejohn continues:

> Based on the assumption that design's beliefs, values and techniques . . . are very different from other fields with established cultures of inquiry and bodies of knowledge . . . the components of . . . what defines those beliefs, values and techniques . . . in non-design disciplines manage domain-specific knowledge internal to a profession, in the design professions the same components of the . . . beliefs, values and techniques . . . orient externally towards the larger culture, precisely because of the absence of explicit bodies of design knowledge. The result is that the

components of the disciplinary . . . beliefs, values and techniques . . . act as a kind of "sociological wrapping" around the design professions to, as it were, hold them together to achieve social identity and standing (Wang and Ilhan, 2009, p. 5).

Kuhn's model describes "how scientific communities manage knowledge" (ibid, p. 5). Following Kuhn, however, the . . . beliefs, values and techniques . . . "govern not a subject matter, but rather a group of practitioners, not knowledge" (Kuhn, 1970, p. 180).

•

Typically, one would start a history of graphic design pedagogy with the Bauhaus because those who attended the school are thought to have held a set of shared practices and commitments—and there has been extensive research in this field. But as Argentine painter Tomás Maldonado explained in *Ulm* 8/9 in 1963:

> The Bauhaus didactics, particularly its preliminary course, was a question of exaltation of expression, intuition, and action, above all of "learning by doing" . . . but this educational philosophy is in crisis. It is incapable of assimilating the new types of relations between theory and practice, engendered by the most recent scientific developments. We know now that theory must be impregnated with practice, practice with theory. It is impossible to act today without knowledge, or to know without doing.

Following Maldonado, I situate the historical concerns of this study in a postwar moment in which theory was as important as practice—the period after the Bauhaus, as the title makes clear. The pedagogy of the Ulm School of Design, Germany, among the most important post-Bauhaus design programs, would become instrumental in disseminating its ideas within the US and internationally after the war. The Hochschule für Gestaltung, Ulm (HfG) was established in 1950 with the private funds of Inge Scholl as a memorial of sorts to her brother and sister who were murdered by the Nazis in 1943. Additional funding came from American foundations, a Cold War–narrative in the making, no doubt. Max Bill, an alumnus of the Bauhaus, was appointed the first director of the Hochschule which opened its doors to students in 1955 and closed in 1968.

The mission statement of the school appeared in the first *Ulm* journal from October 1958:

> The Hochschule für Gestating educates specialists for two different tasks of our technical civilization: **1.** The design of industrial products; **2.** The design of visual and verbal means of communication. The school thus educates designers for the production and consumer goods industries as well as for present-day means of communication: press, films, broadcasting, television, and advertising. These designers must have at their disposal the technological and scientific knowledge necessary for collaboration in industry today.

Classes offered in the foundation course included a range of topics including: methodology (introduction to mathematical logic, permutations and combinations, topology); sociology (changes in the social structure since the Industrial Revolution); perception theory (introduction to the main theories and problems of visual perception); cultural history of the twentieth century (painting, sculpture, architecture, literature); and mathematics, physics, chemistry. And in the Visual Communications department classes were taught on technology (typesetting, process reproduction, printing, paper); semiotics (introduction to the modern theory of signs, social psychological basis of the use of signs, analysis of signs, symbols, signals, emblems); history of typography, exhibition design, and film; theory of science (epistemological foundations of modern science, history of the idea of experiment, theory of machines, behavior theory); and optional courses in operational research (group theory, set theory, statistics, linear programming, standardization).

What this list of course offerings demonstrates is a radical shift away from the "sense-based" craft pedagogy of the Bauhaus toward a pedagogy based on science, history, philosophy, and modern production technologies. The shift was in part due to the influence of Maldonado. In the second issue of *Ulm*, 1958, the painter wrote:

> The ideas which supply the basis for what might be called the Bauhaus ideology are today, a quarter of a century after that institution closed, difficult to translate into language of our present-day preoccupations. Furthermore . . . some of these ideas must now be refuted with the greatest vehemence as well as with the greatest objectivity.

In a 2012 interview with Isabel Clara Neves and João Rocha, Maldonado elaborated:

> We were living in another time. There was the onset of a conflict in which young professors understood that it was no longer possible to continue with Bauhaus traditions; because Max Bill proposed the same exercises they did at [the] Bauhaus, it was a near repetition of the same ideas. It was a difficult conflict to manage because there were Bill's ideological characteristics and ours, and the conflict grew worse with time. I am talking about 1955. For example, [the] Bauhaus was known for not having a library, there was distrust for all that could be considered philosophical and scientific literary culture.

•

To further home in on Ulm's pedagogical concerns, consider the position of Gui Bonsiepe, who studied at Ulm in the Information department from 1955 to 1959 and taught there from 1963 until the school's closing. "The Invisible Facets of the HfG Ulm" is the title of a lecture Bonsiepe redrafted as an essay for *Design Issues* (summer 1995), where he elaborated on the history and influences of Ulm:

> Design opposes the cognitive ideal and the understanding of practice in universities. Design opposes the interoperation of technology prevailing in technical institutions. Design opposes the ideal of aesthetic experience of artistic institutions.

Bonsiepe goes on to state: "Design has no place in any of these institutions; and if it did, it would just be tolerated as a foreign body."

Bonsiepe addresses a problem critical to my project through the metaphor of design as a "foreign body." His statement implicitly complicates McCoy's insistence that graphic design has or even could satisfy the conditions of disciplinarity. Bonsiepe tells us

that design as it relates to the academy produces a number of structural discontinuities. The academy is not capable of providing an institutional home for design within either the sciences or the arts. If for Littlejohn "design is pre-disciplinary," for Bonsiepe it is "anti-disciplinary" by default. Bonsiepe offers some historical remedies for the formation of design discourse and its bearing on design education and professional practice:

> The HfG reclaimed and instituted design as an autonomous discipline, which couldn't be allowed to serve as an agency for other disciplines. Thus, it was neither an appendage of, nor a supplement to, mechanical engineering; nor submissive to marketing; nor a variant of the fine arts in the form of applied arts; nor a subcategory of architecture. Design is neither art nor technology nor science since none of these realms of knowledge provides the distinctions necessary to grasp the concept of design. . . . The HfG used education, with its programmatic disposition, to build a bridge to the scientific disciplines. The HfG broke with the long tradition of the skill-oriented instructional program of the craft schools. Design was demystified; and treated as a teachable and learnable discipline, with methods whose application made superfluous the recurrent communication between master and student through osmosis.

Putting an even finer point on Littlejohn's characterization of design as "pre-disciplinary," Bonsiepe, in a somewhat exaggerated tone, continues: "design is still in its prehistoric stages . . . [and] we find ourselves at a historical moment in relation to the advent of universal digitation."

•

For the purposes of this project, we might replace the notion of *writing* our own histories to *reading* them, and instead chart the literature that was taken up by generations of graphic designers after the Bauhaus. Rephrasing McCoy's statement, one could say: Graphic design moves from a professional practice to discipline when design *reads* its own histories and theories.

We start with Bonsiepe's recollections of the Ulm library:

> The list of books held in the small HfG library . . . in the mid-1950s included the first Amsterdam edition of Horkheimer and Adorno's

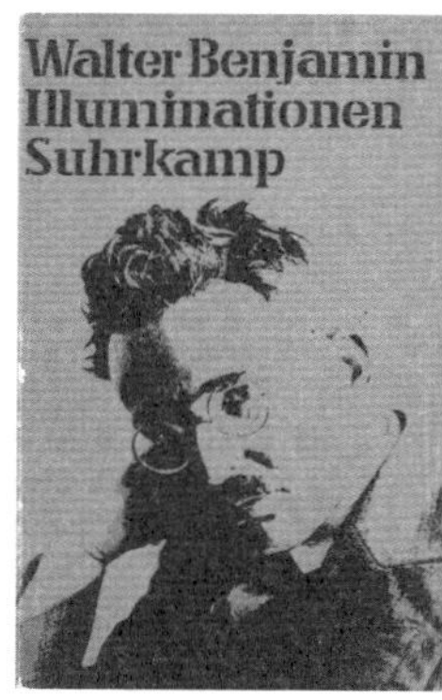

> *Dialectic of the Enlightenment*; the first, two-volume edition of Walter Benjamin's writings; and the two-volume edition of D'Arcy Thompson's ground-breaking work, *On Growth and Form*.

The books Bonsiepe says were noticeably absent are equally interesting, especially considering the date—1968—when, in major metropolitan areas around the globe, areas of concentrated intellectual and labor union activity were ablaze in fervent protest by those who were demanding the halting of war and the liberation of the underserved global masses.

> . . . Nor would Derrida's writings have found much approval with the HfG—although they certainly would have been discussed had they been better known before 1968. Postmodernism, which Lyotard aptly identified as the "loss of faith in meta-narratives," also didn't coincide with the HfG's program.

Is it safe to say, based on the above, that Bonsiepe, at least in the mid-'90s when this statement was penned, is a proponent of master-narratives?

Shelia de Bretteville was in Italy working at the pivotal moment of 1968. The formation of her political views was constructed by large degree by the actions on the streets of Europe and the books she was reading. De Bretteville recalls:

> Anyone who lived through the prior two years was not untouched by the Civil Rights Movement and the revolution in Paris. . . . I was fascinated with the revolution in May in Paris in the streets and the graphic output during that time. I was reading Franz Fanon . . . and Paulo Freire's *Pedagogy of the Oppressed*. Those books and the times had a huge impact on me when I began to teach because, from Freire, the whole idea that the role of the teacher is to help the student become themselves, I took to heart. Certainly Franz Fanon's attitude toward institutionalized racism was part of what was installed in my sensibility. . . . It just had a big effect on the way I thought about people, in how I cared about individuals, and certainly Freire gave me a way of teaching: that every student has a body of knowledge of their own that they bring.

•

Now let us compare the Ulm reading list to what Jeffrey Keedy has to say about his reading habits in the early '80s. Keedy plays a significant role in any narration of contemporary design history, particularly related to the institutionalizing impact of the act of reading on design discourse. Following is an excerpt from a conversation I had with Keedy in 2016 about what he was reading as graduate student and how reading influenced his pedagogical formation as a young teacher:

> Keedy: It wasn't until 1984, my first year at Cranbrook when I started reading the journal *Visible Language* and Tom Ockerse, who had published all this stuff about semiotics—the Rhode Island School of

Design was big into semiotics. I remember that was the current academic material that was available, that was the most theoryish theory, it was straight Charles Peirce's theory of the sign.
I remember starting off with that—reading it, thinking about it, and saying, okay, I guess this stuff makes some sense—the science of signs, but it also seemed fairly patched together, and therefore not very interesting. Simultaneous to that, all the deconstruction stuff hit seemingly everywhere in art and architecture: Everyone started being interested in the French material.

Kaplan: The story I heard is that at Cranbrook you were hanging out with architecture students and cherry-picking their reading. Is this true?

Keedy: Partially. Actually, it was the presence of Daniel Libeskind, head of the architecture department—he was a big influence—he brought all those people in. Zaha Hadid came . . . all the big-name architects came through. Also, some art critics and art theory people visited, so it was in the air—but not for the graphic design people. My first year at Cranbrook I met Hani Rashid, in architecture; we would talk and then I would hang out in the architecture department. The industrial design student Allen Cooper read a lot, and he started being interested in theory. Also, since we were right next to Ann Arbor, I used to go over to Borders Books, and there was this whole row, basically a section in the bookstore, that contained all the French stuff including Derrida and semiotics. The University of Michigan humanities programs were starting to pick all that stuff up, and I'm like, oh, what's this Roland Barthes stuff? It was picking up steam, and it was big, it was the thing.

Kaplan: You brought these books and their influences into the studio, and from there they found their way into form?

Keedy: The reason I'm mentioning Tom Ockerse and *Visible Language* is that the poststructuralist stuff made more sense to me. It seemed to pick up and push farther the theory that was most influential at that time. In the '70s it was about design methodologies and semiotics and rhetoric. Rhetoric was always the big thing with Ockerse and so if you were there and exposed to all these more advanced psychoanalytic-influenced notions of language that we were getting from the French writers, it just made sense to me and felt relevant at the time. Peirce seemed too structuralist and out of date. Everyone else realized, wait a minute, look at what Derrida has to say about how language works, and how language is basically used as a cultural construct. Immediately I thought, gosh, that makes a ton of sense for graphic design, because that's what we are doing. We're making cultural constructs. It was a big deal. Although there were whole bunch of people who hated it, others thought it was great. . . . It was a certain moment when there was energy in thinking, in critical thinking and in theory. Because I was young and dumb, I naively thought that this was what design really needs to help make it and establish it as a cultural practice, not just a bunch of hacks that help people get things printed and sold. I thought, this theory is the thing that will cement it and make it a part of broader cultural practice. I thought, this is going to catch on!

And for a while it was part of the fight of design as not just greasing the wheels of capitalism with style and taste but as being a cultural practice. Everyone accepts that now. That fight has been won. . . . Design as a cultural practice or as an art practice is now accepted, which in my undergraduate [days] was not the case. Everyone still had that Paul Rand mentality; "This is not art, don't think you're an artist, sonny."

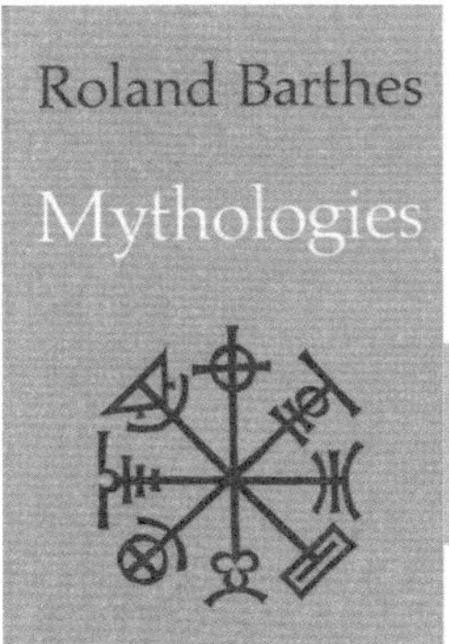

•

To continue the journey through the literary turn within the field of graphic design, we turn to design educator Meredith Davis, who outlines the formalization of a reading list for graphic designers. In the mid-'90s Davis asked a few of her colleagues from various related disciplines for their reading lists in the form of annotated bibliographies, which went onto becoming a publication supported in part by a grant from the National Endowment for the Arts.

Davis recalls:

I was really trying to reorient things in terms of graduate education here at North Carolina State, and Andrew Blauvelt was a colleague, so it was helpful to have someone else that was reading. I was interested in specific people's bibliographies. What did somebody who has a particular point of view read? I choose people who were known for a particular perspective, Andrew being one, Liz Saunders in cognitive science, from Ohio State; Jessica Helfand, from Yale, on new media;

Ewan Duncan, from Illinois Institute of Technology, on design planning and business. I pickd people that had enough visibility and had a teaching role of a particular kind. Then the question in my mind was, What do those people read? . . . I asked them to annotate their lists, so that people had some idea about how to enter those readings. Each of those bibliographies had a little matrix along with it, so that you could cross-reference what topics were covered by a particular book.

Kaplan: It sounds like your annotated bibliography project is more than reading prescribed by a list of books. It also projects an attitude about reading, an attitude about how one goes about developing habits of knowledge production. If there's a group of educators and designers that embrace books, it would also seem true that there's another camp that rejects the significance of reading.

Davis: Oh, absolutely, yeah. And there's another thing: Students would come and say, "What should I read?" None of the people that compiled these bibliographies ever asked that question of somebody else. They learned by going through libraries and reading and rejecting and reading again and again. That's the kind of inquiry that I fear we lose too often. . . . It's the kind of thing that you want an inquiring mind and an educated person to continually do.

I find these stories of individual reading habits enlightening evidence that allows us to trace a narrative path when examining McCoy's statement that self-historization and theorization are disciplinary acts. On the relationship between design and reading, Andrew Blauvelt points out that the first canonical graphic design text, *History of Graphic Design,* was published by Philip B. Meggs in 1983. To put this publication date into perspective, Janson's *History of Art* had been widely distributed as the "go to" text over twenty years previous (and of course Vasari's *The Lives of the Artists* was by then over four centuries old).

Blauvelt: As an undergraduate I had type history class at the Herron School of Art and Design. I didn't have graphic design history. Every Tuesday there was an instructor who ran the typographic workshop and classes in type history. The program offered graphic design history from within the modern art

> history context, and typography history classes. The theory came from photography, not graphic design, mostly literary theory, structuralism, and poststructuralism.

To return to the conversation with Keedy, who went from Michigan to California, library in tow, shortly after graduating a few years in advance of Blauvelt:

> Keedy: At CalArts we offered a design history class that Lou Danziger was teaching, and then Lorraine Wild also wanted to teach her own version of design history so they were both teaching design history simultaneously—fighting design histories. There was no idea for a design theory course yet at that point. . . . Sheila de Bretteville said I could teach a theory course at Otis and I got to put it together the way I wanted. It was a lot of Barthes and some Derrida, with some design theory mixed in. It wasn't until several years later that I started teaching design theory at CalArts. It was a straight-up theory class. I taught two theory courses over two semesters.
>
> Theory 1 was a history of design theory. I started at the end of the nineteenth century with William Morris, then I went all the way through to *Émigré* and the *Looking Closer* books. That was the history overview, and then Theory 2 was strictly contemporary stuff.
>
> Kaplan: Did you make a distinction in these classes between the history of design and the theory of design?
>
> Keedy: Yeah. The first one is the history of theory. It was more like, here are the theories, here's how people theorize design historically. Here's how they did it in the end of the nineteenth century, and here's how they did it in the early twentieth century, here are the early modernists. . . . Here's what they thought at the Bauhaus, and then here's what they thought at Bauhaus Chicago. It was a history of theories in one semester. It must have been twelve lectures and each one would have included two or three handouts that would start with Ruskin. . . . Theory 2 goes from the '80s to present (I think I stopped teaching by 2007).

•

In the postwar American and European contexts, the introduction of comparative literature, history, and the rhetoric of postmodernism into graphic design led to the creation of a historically specific design discourse: a disciplinary act of self-theorization. But what about now, at a moment in which seemingly everyone is a designer, where all our choices and behaviors are "curated," and where the notion "design thinking" is recruited to solve problems across the economic and disciplinary spectrum? Foucault diagnosed a shift from the disciplinary to the control society as populations self-regulated and self-policed their behaviors and activities. But if the language of graphic design has been generalized to those well outside the field, what are the current prospects of design as a discipline? Does graphic design possess the necessary autonomy to be a discipline? Or, is graphic design, as if by definition, a thing that fills space between autonomous disciplines?

Some within the academy pushed to theorize the activity of graphic design in attempts to evolve graphic design beyond simply a service industry model. In so doing they mobilized the postmodern ideas of anti-mastery, anti-grand-narrative, the birth of the reader, and allegory. Writing in 2002 in the "ABCs of Contemporary Design," Hal Foster proclaimed:

> Contemporary design is part of a greater revenge taken by advanced capitalism on postmodernist culture—a recouping of its crossings of arts and disciplines, a routinization of its transgressions. We know that autonomy, even semi-autonomy, is a fiction, but periodically this fiction is useful, even necessary, as it was at the high-modernist moment of Loos and company one hundred years ago.

But what happens now, when postmodernism itself seems at some kind of end? Can we as designers carry on with this fiction of semi-autonomy? And most importantly, once or if graphic design has congealed into a discipline, can we then suggest that it, too, could harness at least partial autonomy?

In response, I offer a provocation from Keedy. His comments dramatize our situation as both practitioners and educators. To the notion of design as a contemporary discipline, he opines:

> Everyone accepts that design is a cultural practice, but what didn't get established is, *who* is the designer and *what* is it to be a designer—that just disappeared into the vapor. That's why, to me, the issues of criticism and theory (and the more in-depth dialogue about what design is and what its history and its practice are) are so hard. But also, I thought, essential. The thing is, that has all evaporated. There's just this very loosey-goosey idea that design is whatever you make it. You can make something with Adobe products, and you are a designer. It's a weird thing where now designers have that cultural permission. I think everyone simultaneously got the same cultural permission, because now the guy at Subway is an artist, a sandwich artist. Everyone now is like, "Oh yeah, we got permission."

•

I could have chosen to start this introduction not with McCoy's proclamation on a disciplinary shift in graphic design but instead with a statement, made in passing, by Anne Burdick. Anne and I were on a break from our respective classes on a February afternoon in the mid- to late aughts at ArtCenter where I was a guest lecturer and Anne was the chair of the Media Design Program. Anne said: "Graphic design belongs in the house of the humanities." As the newly minted chair, she was fresh from presenting her vision for the MFA design department to the administration, hence her epigraphic statement. It struck me as both obvious (due, of course, to my own predilections) and profound. Since my undergraduate training in graphic design in the early to mid-'80s, when graphic design was only and always described as a "problem-solving" activity, I have been suspicious of this characterization. What problems? And if design is about solving problems, then why do so many persist (war, hunger, income inequality and homelessness, racism and antisemitism . . .)? The problems that we graphic designers are attempting to "solve" must not be too difficult or "wicked." Burdick's blunt statement made clear to me the possibility that "problems" could be thought of and acted upon as philosophical ones as opposed to, say, mathematical; as sociological, not scientific; as historical, not purely technological.

•

In 2016 I delivered a talk about my project at the AIGA Educator's Conference in which I considered McCoy's prognosis for the potentialities of graphic design within the academy and its role within culture at large. Over the past few years, it has occurred to me that the condition McCoy has been anticipating is in fact present—but with a twist. The call for a disciplinary move cannot come from within graphic design by practicing graphic designers (or, as Lorraine Wild says, as "expert witnesses"); we cannot write our own histories and theories. The disciplinary act must be formally instantiated by a discipline that is already institutionally recognized, such as art history or visual and critical studies.

With this in mind, when developing the contents for this book and the proceeding Yale conference upon which it is founded, I invited, in addition to design professors and practitioners, art historians Maria Gough, Juliet Koss, Pamela M. Lee, and Sydney Skelton Simon, and Professor of Communication Fred Turner precisely because their working methodologies demonstrated a path toward disciplinarity. To find those with a PhD in Design, however, proved more complicated, as if to prove Bonsiepe's provocation that the history of graphic design will always be rejected by the academy. Deborah Littlejohn was an exception. After obtaining her MFA in graphic design from CalArts in the early 1990s, Littlejohn received a PhD in Design at North Carolina State University in 2011. Here we witness a graphic designer who had ventured beyond the institutional boundaries of the practice of graphic design to continue her design studies and in effect push the practice closer to a discipline by shifting her institutional setting outside, or adjacent, to graphic design—and who then returned as a professor in the graphic design program at NC State (of note, in 2019, Burdick received a PhD from Carnegie Mellon's School of Design).

Two additional contributors to the book, Colin Fanning and J. Dakota Brown, who studied interior design and graphic design respectively, are currently PhD candidates focusing on graphic design history. Fanning planned on practicing interior design but was stymied due to the recession. Serendipitously, he landed an internship at the Denver Art Museum in the curatorial department of architecture and design. The experience radically changed his career path away from form-making toward a pursuit of a PhD from the Bard Graduate Center, where his emphasis is on design history and material culture, specifically the pedagogical history of Cranbrook during McCoy's tenure from 1971 to 1995. Fanning's coursework offers a particularly striking example of contemporary design pedagogy: He works with professors of the history of art and design *and* philosophy/intellectual historians *and* anthropologists *and* materials scientists. Bard's program takes seriously the possibility of a trans-disciplinary teaching approach that yields the ground for an institutionally legitimatized historian of graphic design.

Graphic Design Book List cont'd. Yale, Paul Rand '74

Individual Artists and Monographs:		
Gablik, Suzi	Magritte	
• Gilot	Life with Picasso	
Herbert, R. L.	Modern Artists on Art	Spectrum
Herron, Patric	Braque, Challenge of Modern Art	
Kahnweiller	Juan Gris	
Klee, Paul	Vol. 2, The Nature of Nature	
• Kueppers	El Lissitzky	NY Graphic Soc.
• Leger, Fernand	Functions of Painting	Doc. of 20 C Art Viking
• LeCorbusier	City of Tomorrow	
"	Towards a New Architecture	
"	Modulor 1-2	
" (Jenks, J. C.	LeCorbusier	
Malevich, K.	Essays on Art	
• Rubin, Wm	Picasso in the Collection of MOMA	MOMA
• Schmalenbach, W.	Kurt Schwitters	
• Seuphor	Mondrian	Abrams
Van Doesburg	Bauhaus Edition in English	
Van Gogh	Van Gogh Letters	NY Graphic Soc.
Schapiro, Meyer	Nature of Abstract Art	Marxist Quarterly, 1937

Design Theory:		
Wengler, Hans	Bauhaus	
• Banham, Reyner	Theory & Design in the First Machine Age	Arch Press
Giedion, Siegfried	Mechanization Takes Command	
Kouenhowen	Made in America	Doubleday
• Moholy-Nagy	The New Vision	Wittenborn
Mumford, Lewis	Technics and Civilization	Harcourt Brace
Ruder, Emil	Typography	

Gestalt		
Arnheim, Rudolf	Art and Visual Perception	U. of Cal.
Koffka	Gestalt Psychology	Harcourt, Brace
Wertheimer	Laws of From	

Rand, Paul:		
	Thoughts on Design	Wittenborn, 1946; Studio Vista, 1970
	Black in the Visual Arts	Graphic Forms- Harvard, 1949
	The Trademark as an Illustrative Device	Trademark Design Theobold, 1952
	Ideas About Ideas	Industrial Design Mag. 8.55
	The Art of the Package	Print Mag. Jan/Feb 1960
	Advertisement Ad Vivum Ad Hominum?	Daedalus Winter, 1960
	The Trademarks of Paul Rand	Wittenborn, 1960
	Design and the Play Instinct	The Education of Vision-Braziller 1965

Brown received a BFA from NC State in the mid '90s and practiced design with Rick Valicenti at Thirst before venturing back to school in pursuit of an advanced degree with the goal of historicizing graphic design pedagogy between the late '80s and mid-'90s as a corrective to his experiences studying and practicing design during those moments. Brown's research, as he describes it, "connects a longer labor history, the history of capitalism, and technology to theoretical disagreements within design history that have a direct bearing on everyday experiences of the designer and their audiences . . . including attempts at understanding the experience of work within certain structural constraints as foundational to what design *is* and what design even *means* (my emphasis)." Which is to say, he attends specifically to the essential questions as named by Keedy.

To finish with the proposed alternate beginning, then: Burdick's domicile metaphor implies that one could always return home and as such a return would require first leaving. Although be forewarned, upon returning, home may not look the same as before.

Yale University
Graphic Design Book List
Paul Rand - 1974

Those who cannot remember the past are condemned to repeat it." Santayana

General Theory:

Bell, Clive	Art	
Biederman, Ch.	Art as the Evolution of Visual Knowledge	
Collingwood	Principles of Art	
Dewey, John	Art as Experience	
Eisenstein, S.	Film Sense	Harcourt-Brace
" " "	Film Form	
" " "	Film Essays	
Eisner	Educating Artistic Vision	Macmillan
Fry, Roger	Vision and Design	
Goodman, Nelson	Languages of Art	Bobbs Merrill
Malraux	Museum Without Walls	
Panofsky	Meaning in the Visual Arts	Princeton U Press
Wolfflin, H.	Principles of Art History	
	Sense of Form in Art	
	Renaissance & Baroque	

General Modern:

Apollinaire	Apollinaire on Art	D/20C Art-Viking
Barr, Alfred	Cubism & Abstract Art	MOMA
urnham, Jack	Beyond Modern Sculpture	Braziller
hipp	Theories of Modern Art	U. of Cal. 168
Ozenfant, A.	Foundations of Modern Art	
Richardson & Stangos	Concepts of Modern Art	Icon
Villier, Dora	Abstract Art	

Cezanne:

Badt, K.	The Art of Cezanne	Faber & Faber '56-'65
Loren, Earl	Cezanne's Compositions	U of Cal Press
Fry, Roger	Cezanne	
Rewald, John	Cezanne's Letters	

Modern Art Movements:

Cooper, Douglas	The Cubist Epoch	
Gaunt, Wm.	The Aesthetic Adventure	
Gauss, C. E.	Aesthetic Theories of French Artists	John Hopkins
Gray, Camilla	The Great Experiment:Russian Art	
Jaffe, H. L.	De Stijl	Studio Vista
Kozloff	Dadaism & Futurism	Charterhouse, NY
Rewald, John	Impressionism	MOMA
Scharff	Constructivism	
Shattuck, Roger		

After my presentation in 2016, Geoffry Fried, who teaches graphic design at Lesley University, introduced himself. Fried studied graphic design at Yale in 1980–82, and he wanted to "correct the record" about Paul Rand's rumored distaste for reading and its intellectual role within the studies of graphic design. As can be seen from the Rand's "Graphic Design Book List," dated 1974, the record has been corrected. Rand's list appears very similar to an undergraduate general art history course reader with a bonus overdose of self-promotion. Of note, Rand's reading list is predictive, yet more limited in scope to that of McCoy's reading lists from a decade later, as detailed in Andrew Blauvelt's essay (images on pages 185–86).

DESIGN PEDAGOGY'S TRACES: NOTES ON EVIDENCE AND METHOD

COLIN FANNING

Our conceptions of pedagogy and its constituent components (ideas, processes, prescriptions) might tend toward the abstract, thanks in part to the long shadow cast over Western models of education by Enlightenment notions of reason. If pedagogy as a historical subject usually falls under the umbrella of intellectual history, such framing leaves out important questions about the material means by which these abstractions are communicated, carried out, and more widely circulated—in short, made concrete. Prompted by scholars who have worked to recover the importance of tangible objects as well as ideas to the history of education, my curiosities as a design historian lean in exactly this direction.[1] What kind of a *thing* is design pedagogy? Can we touch it, hold it, taste it? How might we recover such dimensions in historical terms and in their complex temporal and cultural specificities? If the broad-strokes narrative of design between the Bauhaus and the Internet is one of increasing specialization, theorization, and dematerialization—dynamics that only accelerated with the digital turn of the late twentieth century—how can we get access to these striking technological and conceptual transformations through design pedagogy's stubbornly material traces?

This question seems particularly relevant when studying the educational history of a field like graphic design, where *making* is the primary aim and where what is made straddles a delicate line between object and image. It's no secret that design history has a general bias toward professional contexts and design objects successfully brought to market, although numerous critiques of and expansions upon this model have argued for addressing contexts of

1. As part of the broader material turn in the humanities, the history of the "object lesson" as a pedagogical technique has seen a growing interest in recent years, as has its contemporary application as both model and metaphor in scholarship. See, for example, Sarah Anne Carter, *Object Lessons: How Nineteenth-Century Americans Learned to Make Sense of the Material World* (New York: Oxford University Press, 2018); Lorraine Daston, ed., *Things That Talk: Object Lessons from Art and Science* (New York: Zone, 2004); and Laurel Thatcher Ulrich, Ivan Gaskell, Sara J. Schechner, and Sarah Anne Carter, *Tangible Things: Making History through Objects* (New York: Oxford University Press, 2015).

2. On issues of consumption and mediation, see John A. Walker, *Design History and the History of Design* (London: Pluto Press, 1989), esp. chaps. 5 and 9; and Grace Lees-Maffei, "The Production—Consumption—Mediation Paradigm," *Journal of Design History* 22, no. 4 (2009): 351–76. On the significance of vernacular and amateur design, see, among others, Judy Attfield, *Wild Things: The Material Culture of Everyday Life* (Oxford: Berg, 2000); and Teal Triggs, "Alphabet Soup: Reading British Fanzines," *Visible Language* 29, no. 1 (1995): 72–87. On the theory and practice of speculative design, see Tony Fry, *Design Futuring: Sustainability, Ethics, and New Practice* (Oxford: Berg, 2009); Jamer Hunt, "Prototyping the Social: Temporality and Speculative Futures at the Intersection of Design and Culture," in *Design Anthropology: Object Culture in Transition*, ed. Alison Clarke, 2nd ed. (London: Bloomsbury, 2017), chap. 6; and Anthony Dunne and Fiona Raby, *Speculative Everything: Design, Fiction, and Social Dreaming* (Cambridge, MA: MIT Press, 2013).

consumption, vernacular and amateur making, speculative or unrealized designs, and so on.[2] As a result, the specific history of design education is comparatively less well developed, aside from an ever-dominant focus on the Bauhaus and its diaspora. Even those pedagogical histories that do exist tend to emphasize prominent individual educators and high-level conceptual shifts while struggling to integrate student perspectives and material practices.

While the preference to focus on established professionals over yet-to-be designers and the labor of educators is partly a matter of priorities, it is also one of evidence and survival bias. An archive, we know well, is never neutral; the various kinds of documentation that form our research material are subject to many of the same hierarchies and processes of selection that play out in other social spheres.[3] In design (speaking very broadly), this means that well-known individuals and institutions, and their most highly valued works, have left more complete records and have been given greater historical attention than those that fall afoul of changing regimes of value.[4] For graphic design specifically, the gaps and erasures of this process are compounded by the ephemerality of so much of what graphic designers produce—especially the unfinished or provisional work done in educational settings.[5]

This is where the tangibility of design pedagogy represents an intriguing, if difficult, prospect for historical research. Sometimes the best way to get at the subject may look very little like "graphic design" as we usually understand it, but this can help foreground education as a lived phenomenon, a type of everyday experience, rather than a rarefied intellectual exercise—the product of bodies as well as minds. Shifting the frame of reference also raises the question of where, precisely, design pedagogy's histories are located: in institutions? Individuals? Objects? In this essay I attempt to lay out some of the key forms of evidence when working across these scales and discuss the challenges and opportunities of working with their variable traces.

3. A rich vein of scholarship across discipline grapples with the contingencies and constructedness of archives. Theoretical classics include Michel Foucault, *The Archaeology of Knowledge and the Discourse on Language*, trans. A. M. Sheridan Smith (New York: Pantheon Books, 1972); and Jacques Derrida, "Archive Fever: A Freudian Impression," *Diacritics* 25, no. 2 (1995): 9–63. See also Carolyn Steedman, *Dust: The Archive and Cultural History* (New Brunswick: Rutgers University Press, 2002); or Antoniette Burton, ed., *Archive Stories: Facts, Fictions, and the Writing of History* (Durham, NC: Duke University Press, 2005).

4. On "regimes of value," see Arjun Appadurai's introduction to *The Social Life of Things: Commodities in Cultural Perspective* (Cambridge: Cambridge University Press, 1986); see also Attfield, *Wild Things*, 27.

5. Bridget Wilkins, for example, discusses the low value assigned to graphic design based on its ephemerality—but argues that the mechanisms of collectability and aesthetic value should be secondary to understanding graphic design's wider cultural relevance—in "No More Heroes: Why Is Design History So Obsessed by Appearance?" *Eye* 2, no. 6 (Spring 1992), reprinted in *Graphic Design: History in the Writing, 1938–2011*, ed. Sara De Bondt and Catherine de Smet (London: Occasional Papers, 2012), 69–71.

The Institution

Of the many possible scales of analysis, institutions are one of the most prevalent frames of reference for thinking historically about design education—think about how easily we use phrases like "the Ulm approach" or "the Cranbrook spirit," for example. This makes sense in many ways: Much design training takes place *in* institutional settings, and institutions often possess the administrative structures and resources to organize, preserve, and grant access to useful archives of primary material. But educational institutions can also be slippery subjects for historians to grasp; we have to stay attentive to the differences between an institution's public face and the actual actions or lived realities of those who populate it.

The Bauhaus, with its privileged position in the history of design, is a clear example of how this can play out. A large (and growing) body of literature has attempted to denaturalize the school's immense historiographic presence, uncovering the extent to which its oft-preached precepts of rationality and functionalism were ideologically motivated, unstable in their meanings, unevenly applied in practice, and rooted in an elite social stratum of interwar Germany. Despite the image of universality and collectivity the school's advocates strove to cultivate, the vaunted "objectivity" of interwar modernism was always a deeply subjective affair. Careful archival work has gradually cracked open the smooth facade of the Bauhaus to show how multiple concerns, strategies, and identities were at play within the seeming monolith—particularly among its students, whose experience of the school's utopic ambitions differed greatly across the intersecting axes of gender, class, nationality, and religion.[6] To point this out is not to diminish the real and important contributions of the Bauhauslers, but rather to underscore the fact that

Teaching Fellowship **IN GRAPHIC DESIGN**

For the academic year 1952-53, a teaching fellowship is offered to men and women especially qualified in the graphic arts. The recipient will act as an assistant in instruction on the faculty of the Department of Design, and will in addition to his teaching duties receive credit toward the degree of Master of Fine Arts. His teaching duties will include responsibility for one of the introductory courses in the department.

THE PROGRAM IN GRAPHIC DESIGN AT YALE

This program, established in the fall of 1950, offers advanced professional training in the field of graphic design. The graduate program, leading to the degree of Master of Fine Arts, is open to qualified graduates of liberal arts colleges who have majored in art, and to graduates of art schools. This is normally a program of two years duration.

The undergraduate program, normally of four years duration, leads to the degree of Bachelor of the Fine Arts. The first two years are spent in the basic program of the Department of Design, and the last two in the graphic design major.

The equipment of the department includes a typographic workshop, a photographic studio and darkroom, drafting rooms, and a graphic arts workshop equipped for lithographic, intaglio, letterpress and silk screen printing.

In addition to the courses offered within the Division of the Arts, students may elect courses given elsewhere in the university.

The faculty members who are responsible for the work of the majors in graphic design include Alvin Lustig, Herbert Matter, and Alvin Eisenman.

Applications for admission to the school, as well as applications for the Teaching Fellowship, should be made not later than June 1, 1952. Both men and women are eligible. Requests for information and the necessary blanks should be addressed to JOSEF ALBERS, *Chairman,*

Alvin Lustig, detail of a 1952 announcement for a teaching position at Yale University

institutional agendas often mask a more complex reality inside the walls that can take significant work to recover.

Physical records in institutional archives are a crucial tool in reconstructing those complex inner workings (with the caveat, of course, that the absences within an archive speak as loudly as its presences). Tracking the development of policies and positioning can provide important corroboration of or correction to our received images of design schools and illuminate the role of sometimes contentious, often dry institutional protocols in design education. Though administration is not synonymous with pedagogy, it structures and mediates the development and delivery of instruction in ways that a straightforward "history of ideas" approach might not capture: how resources were apportioned, what standards or policies educators were held to, what internal power struggles shaped the wider terrain of graphic design, which discussions were given over to public view and which remained undisclosed.[7] Documents revealing these kinds of parameters aren't just textual evidence in the usual sense but can also be understood as specific tools within a larger apparatus of control—material means by which institutions claim and exercise power over educators' and students' experiences.[8]

Additionally, archival research sometimes helps to unearth those activities and concerns of educators and students that never found "official" visible form as posters or other promotional materials. Mundane but revealing debates about departmental budgets, changing curricular emphases, students' financial struggles or acclimation to the demands of studio work, and other day-to-day dimensions of education can help us understand how people negotiated the institutional frameworks that surrounded them. The interaction *between* educators at different institutions made evident in an archive is also useful in getting away from fuzzy notions of "influence" toward more concrete exchanges and networks. Finding the actual letters, faxes, or emails that show who talked to whom, who sent what where, who was at the table and who was left outside, can be a monumental, time-consuming task of research—sometimes impossible, if records are destroyed or inaccessible—but such documents are key material traces of the too-often invisible labor of education and collaboration. Their stubborn persistence from the past into the present can help us

6. A few examples (among many potential others) include Gillian Naylor, *The Bauhaus Reassessed: Sources and Design Theory* (London: Herbert Press, 1985); T'ai Smith, *Bauhaus Weaving Theory: From Feminine Craft to Mode of Design* (Minneapolis: University of Minnesota Press, 2014); and Elizabeth Otto, *Haunted Bauhaus: Occult Spirituality, Gender Fluidity, Queer Identities, and Radical Politics* (Cambridge, MA: MIT Press, 2019).

7. Particularly given the long struggle for legitimacy within the academy that many graphic design educators describe, it is crucial to understand the larger institutional forces at play in the university as a cultural form and to interrogate the narrative of legitimization in more detail.

8. I borrow this line of thinking from Lisa Gitelman, who writes that "documents are important not because they are ubiquitous . . . but rather because they are so evidently integral to the ways people think and live"; see Lisa Gitelman, *Paper Knowledge: Toward a Media History of Documents* (Durham, NC: Duke University Press, 2014), 4.

cut through the layers of interpretation that accrue in secondary literatures or even contemporaneous criticism and press coverage. A useful model for corralling these messy types of evidence is Paul Stirton's piecing together of Jan Tschichold's correspondence with (and learning from) his modernist peers across Europe as he moved through multiple institutions and developed his work as a theorist, pedagogue, and amateur archivist of graphic design.[9]

As in any predominantly institutional perspective of history-writing, we should maintain a degree of skepticism toward prescriptive rather than descriptive understandings of design education, acknowledging forms of learning that fall outside institutional frameworks and understanding the limits of any particular organization's impact on larger processes of cultural production.[10] It is also important to set institutional histories within wider frames of reference by using other kinds of evidence that may initially seem to have little to do with design. Thinking through how the legal and policy landscape of a given time and place might affect design training, for example, or tracking broader shifts in expectations and attitudes toward higher education can help contextualize and complicate the structures of late capitalism, nationalism, and globalization that tightly grip pedagogy during the period under discussion.[11] Connecting these rather abstract notions

Invitation ticket for a 1930 public program about poster and leaflet design sponsored by the Bolshevik Party's printing arm

9. Paul Stirton, *Jan Tschichold and the New Typography: Graphic Design Between the World Wars* (New Haven: Yale University Press, 2019).

10. On the limitations of institutional histories, see Walker, *Design History and the History of Design*, 65–67. Such skepticism might productively extend to professional organizations and societies as well; see, for example, Dora Souza Dias, "International Design Organizations and the Study of Transnational Interactions: The Case of Icogradalatinoamérica80," *Journal of Design History* 32, no. 2 (2018): 188–206. Public design workshops and initiatives are one form of pedagogy not captured in the institutional frame; see Jennie Klein, "Doin' It in Public: Feminism and Art at the Woman's Building," *Frontiers: A Journal of Women Studies* 33, no. 2 (2012): 129–36; or several of the contemporary projects discussed in Cynthia E. Smith, *By the People: Designing a Better America* (New York: Cooper Hewitt, Smithsonian Design Museum, 2016).

11. For example, Carma Gorman, "The Role of Trademark Law in the History of US Visual Identity Design, c. 1860–1960," *Journal of Design History* 30, no. 4 (2017): 371–88. Fred Turner and Annika Butler-Wall in this volume explore the dynamics of late capitalism and neoliberalism with great insight; see 300–15. On the nation as an organizing category in the history of design education, see Paul Betts, *The Authority of Everyday Objects: A Cultural History of West German Design* (Berkeley: University of California Press, 2004), esp. chap. 4; reconsidering nationalism and globalism more generally, see Jonathan M. Woodham, "Local, National and Global: Redrawing the Design Historical Map," *Journal of Design History* 18, no. 3 (2005): 257–67.

to the most visible *stuff* that design schools leave behind—posters, pamphlets, newsletters, conference proceedings, and so on—is one of the important interpretive tasks of a history of design pedagogy. While institutional rhetoric and promotional materials should not be conflated with the actual experience in the studios, when viewed critically these material traces help us understand how institutions position themselves in relation to multiple publics and mobilize the accomplishments of their faculty and students to different ends.

The Individual

Institutions, of course, are made up of people, and the biographical dimension is perhaps the most attractive scale of analysis for histories of design pedagogy—but this too comes with perils. From design history's very beginnings as a distinct academic field, the question of the individual designer's proper place in historical method has been a source of constant debate. Many of the field's methodological texts demonstrate a decided ambivalence toward the individual designer as the prime locus of history and history-writing, but it is hard to deny that monographic studies appealingly humanize the larger themes of the field.[12] We are, after all, people ourselves, and setting out to understand the past through a person or people whose activities we can trace and whose thoughts and feelings we hope to infer is an understandably common path. On a practical level, one's research is nicely bounded by the span of a human life, and the archival search is (in many cases) reduced to a manageable number of specific collections in institutional and personal hands.

Still, critiques of the individual creator as a primary design-historical focus (which form an extensive and varied literature in their own right) make some important points about the nature of evidence when working in a personal or biographical mode. By over-privileging the notion of authorial intent, we run the risk of undercutting the distributed, intensely collaborative nature of design and design education. If, as Jeffrey Meikle puts it, "we tend too quickly to accept the opinions of designers and promoters about the meanings of their creations," we then might struggle to bring into focus how design works are procured or commissioned, consumed and used, caught up in larger systems of value, and reinterpreted in contexts far beyond the originator's control.[13] Moreover,

12. See the oft-cited Clive Dilnot, "The State of Design History, Part I: Mapping the Field," *Design Issues* 1, no. 1 (1984): 4–23; and the same author's "The State of Design History, Part II: Problems and Possibilities," *Design Issues* 1, no. 2 (1984): 3–20. See also Walker, *Design History and the History of Design*, 45–47; and Kjetil Fallan, *Design History: Understanding Theory and Method* (Oxford: Berg, 2010), esp. 8–11.

13. Jeffrey L. Meikle, "Material Virtues: On the Ideal and the Real in Design History," *Journal of Design History* 11, no. 3 (1998): 149. See also Victor Margolin, "Narrative Problems of Graphic Design History," *Visible Language* 28, no. 3 (1994): 233–43.

a heavy focus on authorship can overlook the many ways in which individual action is conditioned by social, political, or economic formations (which, of course, are themselves historically contingent and ideologically inflected), or how such processes perpetuate inequities in both the design professions and the writing of their histories.[14] This caution toward human agency, it should be said, is not an attempt to remove individual subjectivity from the equation altogether. Rather, it serves to remind us that (to paraphrase art historian Nicos Hadjinicolau) the history of design is more than a history of design*ers*.[15] What evidence we find when looking closely at an individual's work and life is enriched when we place it in conversation with the larger cultural and discursive constructions of their time. In his study of the polymath educator Gyorgy Kepes, for example, John R. Blakinger models a skillful speculative reconstruction of Kepes's lines of thought and ways of working from scattered, fragmentary notes in the archive, careful to situate these more personal insights within the institutional and political contexts that greatly shaped Kepes's world: the Massachusetts Institute of Technology and the Cold War United States.[16]

In addition to these epistemological issues, a curious category error can crop up when examining design education primarily through the frame of authorship. On occasion, educators' work for professional clients is mobilized as a direct stand-in for their pedagogical methods.[17] While we can expect an educator's ideas about design training to inform their professional work in some sense, using that work as a shorthand for their teaching actually

14. Some important early examples of scholarship grappling with these issues include Cheryl Buckley, "Made in Patriarchy: Toward a Feminist Analysis of Women and Design," *Design Issues* 3, no. 2 (1986): 3–14; Cheryl D. Miller, "Black Designers: Missing in Action," *Print* (September/October 1987): 58–65, 136–38; Ellen Mazur Thomson, "Alms for Oblivion: The History of Women in Early American Graphic Design," *Design Issues* 10, no. 2 (1994): 27–48. Recent contributions offering further models for deeply contextualizing graphic design as part of cultural history and cultural studies include, for example, David Raizman, *Reading Graphic Design History: Image, Text, and Context* (London: Bloomsbury Visual Arts, 2021); and Grace Lees-Maffei and Nicolas P. Maffei, *Reading Graphic Design in Cultural Context* (London: Bloomsbury Visual Arts, 2019).

15. See Nicos Hadjinicolaou, *Art History and Class Struggle* (London: Pluto Press, 1978), one of the paradigmatic texts in advocating a social history of art. While the Marxist approach has in turn been critiqued for its uneven attention to visual and material evidence—the actual stuff of art and design history—it productively reshaped the kinds of questions such histories ask. See also Fallan, *Design History*, 11.

16. John R. Blakinger, *Gyorgy Kepes: Undreaming the Bauhaus* (Cambridge, MA: MIT Press, 2019).

does a double disservice. On the one hand, it overlooks the significant co-producing roles of other entities (clients, institutions, vendors, tools, materials) in the realization of design objects; on the other, it risks implying that there's nothing more to design education than producing work and expecting students to follow by example. While that might indeed be the tack some educators have taken, such a conclusion must be argued, not assumed; we should no more suggest a pedagogue's professional portfolio corresponds exactly with their approach to instruction than we would imply their teaching methods are a direct cognate for their client relationships. However, drawing stark lines between the categories of "educator" and "professional" is likewise counterproductive; the ways in which these fluid identities inform, enrich, or grate against one another in the everyday practice of design pedagogy are exactly what make the work of teacher-practitioners of interest.

But there is a clear difficulty when it comes to understanding design education from the opposite side of the studio crit, as it were. Histories that foreground the student's perspective are rare compared to those that focus on educators—whose circumstances of employment facilitate the production and preservation of records. Autobiographical contributions in the broader literature partially address this imbalance when authors discuss their student experiences and convey firsthand microhistories of graphic design pedagogy at specific institutions in certain moments.[18] Yet once again, survival bias is an operative concern. Many such authors write from the position of their noteworthy careers in the academy and the profession—theirs are the *success* stories of graphic design education. This by no means invalidates their contributions to writing the history of

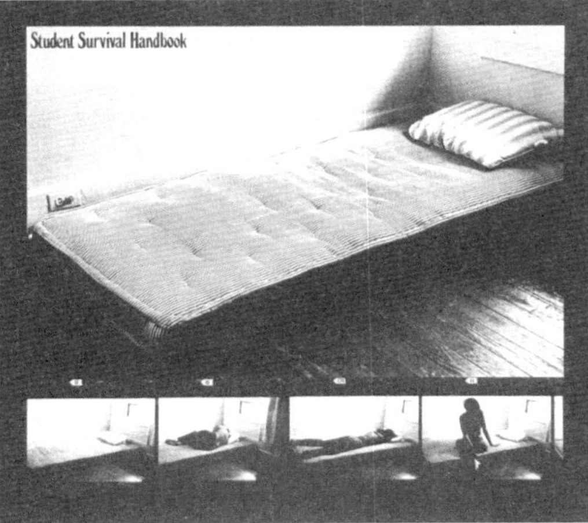

Frances Greenberg, detail of "Student Survival Handbook," 1972–73, part of a series produced by Cranbrook Academy of Art Design Department students during the 1970s and early 1980s

17. Though groundbreaking surveys in their time, both Philip B. Meggs's *A History of Graphic Design* (New York: Van Nostrand Reinhold, 1983) and Richard Hollis's *Graphic Design: A Concise History* (London: Thames and Hudson, 1994) fall prey to this conflation at several points. For more on the intellectual underpinnings of both texts, see Johanna Drucker, "Philip Meggs and Richard Hollis: Models of Graphic Design History," *Design and Culture* 1, no. 1 (2009): 51–77.

18. For instance, students (or students-turned-faculty) of the Ulm school have written fairly extensively on their experiences; see Heiner Jacob, "HfG Ulm: A Personal View of an Experiment in Democracy and Design Education," *Journal of Design History* 1, nos. 3–4 (1988): 221–34; or Gui Bonsiepe, "The Invisible Facets of the Hfg Ulm," trans. John Cullars, *Design Issues* 11, no. 2 (1995): 11–20. Several contributions to this volume provide additional examples, as well as many of the contributions to Steven Heller, ed., *The Education of a Graphic Designer*, 3rd ed. (New York: Allworth Press, 2015).

the field; indeed, the trajectories of their respective careers provide enormously illustrative examples of how individual work and personal networks intersect with institutional contexts. But alongside voices like these, a deeper history of design pedagogy should strive to recover the perspectives, experiences, and contributions of others who aren't able to look back on the field's development from pedagogic spaces they themselves have helped construct.

When considering more recent generations of design educators and students, oral history offers an immensely valuable tool for recovering firsthand experience from a broader range of individuals than those with privileged presences in the archive. Time- and resource-intensive to conduct (as so much of the research process is), oral history comes with some unique challenges of interpretation. Memories are fallible; it's human nature to retroactively cast events as part of a tidier narrative than perhaps existed in the moment; and the interview process itself can reshape an interviewee's thoughts and self-awareness in unpredictable ways. These particularities do not diminish oral history's usefulness—in many ways, their very subjectivity is precisely what makes them valuable complements to the much less vocal materials of the archive, lending a more visceral sense of texture to what we can glean from documents and objects. Oral histories, as Alessandro Portelli reminds us, "are credible but with a *different* credibility."[19] They are no more inherently biased than ostensibly "official" documentary sources—and in fact allow us to get closer to understanding what particular events *meant* to those who were involved, rather than hewing to top-down interpretations that tend to accrue around archives and institutional settings.[20] While building trust with interviewees and crafting interview structures that acknowledge the researcher's own biases and preconceptions require considerable care, the process of oral history can get at the social terrain of an institution or profession—daily habits, political undercurrents, interpersonal rapports or struggles—and bring the past into something much closer to living color, where it might be most possible to touch, smell, and taste design pedagogy.

The Object

In a 1994 article introducing a three-issue series for the journal *Visible Language* on critical histories of graphic design, Andrew Blauvelt laid out an agenda for integrating discursive understandings of graphic design into the writing of its history, articulating a healthy skepticism of object-based analyses.[21] The field's object bias, he rightly pointed out, tended toward a narrow focus on canonized "good design," leaned heavily on the methodological tool of formal

19. Alessandro Portelli, "What Makes Oral History Different," in *The Oral History Reader*, ed. Robert Perks and Alistair Thomson, 3rd ed. (London: Routledge, 2016), 53.

20. Ibid., 52–54. See also Linda Sandino, "Oral History and Design: Objects and Subjects," *Journal of Design History* 19, no. 4 (2006): 275–78; and Valerie Yow, *Recording Oral History: A Guide for the Humanities and Social Sciences*, 3rd ed. (London: Rowman and Littlefield, 2015).

21. Andrew Blauvelt, "An Opening: Graphic Design's Discursive Spaces," *Visible Language* 28, no. 3 (1994), esp. 208–09.

analysis, and too readily fell into the linear narration of successive styles—art-historical tropes that design historians have contested in various ways since the field's early days. But looking specifically at the history of graphic design pedagogy, thinking through and with its objects *as* objects (not just visual data) presents some intriguing possibilities for further contesting the teleological inclinations Blauvelt warns against.

Publications are a chief means of access for historic student graphic design work, whether in academic journals; anthologies of pedagogic techniques; or school profiles, contests, and other features in the design press.[22] In complement to widely read manuals like Josef Müller-Brockmann's *Grid Systems in Graphic Design* (1961) and Emil Ruder's *Typographie* (1967), such reportage captures a broader range of thinking and illustrates the direct and indirect forms of collaboration between educators and students that shaped the culture of design pedagogy. Dan Friedman's "Weather Project" exercise is one well-known example; other documents by American educators who have had a major impact on the field include Tom Ockerse's *Graphic Design Education: An Exposition* and *Projects and Processes* by Katherine McCoy.[23]

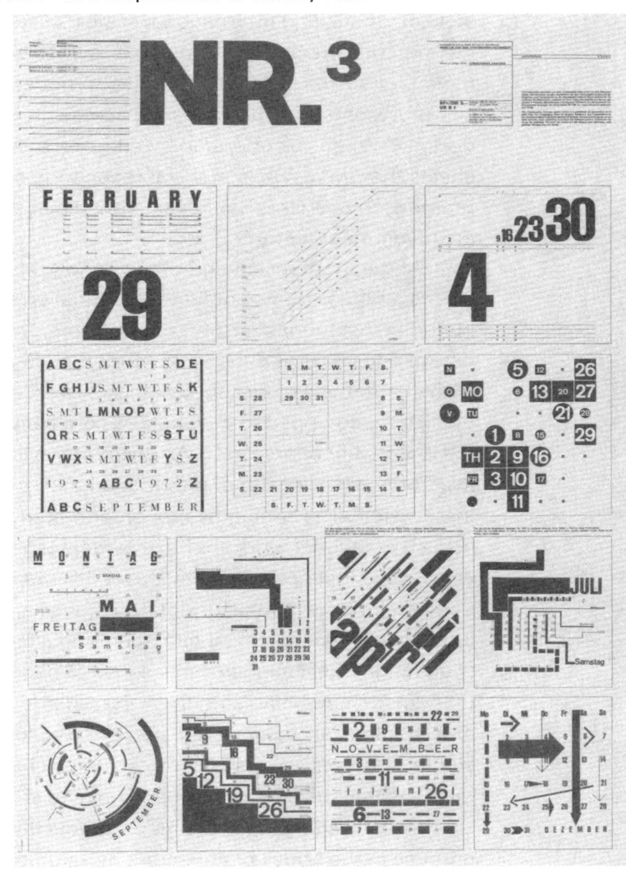

Wolfgang Weingart, poster illustrating calendar designs by Basel Kunstgewerbeschule students, 1974

22. Anthologized publications on this topic are legion; as one example, Igildo G. Biesele, *Graphic Design International: Creative Work of Selected Colleges of Design from 12 Countries* (Zurich: ABC, 1977).

23. Daniel Friedman, "A View: Introductory Education in Typography," *Visible Language* 7, no. 2 (1973): 129–44; see also Brian Johnson and Silas Munro in this volume, 163–71. Tom Ockerse, *Graphic Design Education: An Exposition* (Providence, RI: Rhode Island School of Design, 1977); and Katherine McCoy, *Projects and Processes 6/75: Cranbrook Graduate Design* (Bloomfield Hills, MI: Cranbrook Academy of Art, 1975).

Small-scale reproductions in the pages of these texts might seem to offer limited interpretive value, perhaps supporting a basic analysis of the formal strategies at play in different pedagogic settings. But of greater interest and salience are the facts of *mobility* and *exchange* these texts represent. As opposed to object histories that aim to assign graphic design objects a proper place in a narrative of progress—giving them a kind of historical and semantic fixity—thinking about pedagogical exercises and their textual representations as designed objects, alongside other highly mobile forms like the poster, usefully reframes them as portable things with a rhetoric of their own that operates across local, national, and international scales. Elizabeth Guffey's work on the material circulation of posters provides one methodological model for such a reframing, helping to understand conditions of self-representation and exchange across the wider landscape of design.[24] When corroborated by educators' syllabi and assignment sheets that *do* reside in archival repositories, even nonchalantly reproduced exercises can reveal how the abstractions of pedagogy are given material form.[25]

At the more recent end of the period this volume covers, there's a higher chance of finding original student work, whether buried in institutional archives or secreted away in the files of design educators and the (now-former) students themselves. One of the limitations of discourse analysis, as Kjetil Fallan notes, is that it's "ill equipped to encounter a core concern of design history: the materiality of objects."[26] An encounter with the physical thing itself provides a wealth of information that might otherwise remain inaccessible. The sometimes rough-and-ready quality and clever ad hocism of student work are most evident when you can hold it in your hands, get up close, turn it over. It's much easier in this way to understand how graphic design is as much an embodied practice as a visual and intellectual one, requiring a tacit knowledge of a wide range of techniques and a series of negotiations across multiple kinds of intractable matter.[27] Particularly in relation to periods of technological change, the persistence of "old" techniques in studio exercises can also counteract technologically deterministic readings that prize innovation and novelty at the expense of continuity (readings that design programs themselves sometimes produce in the hopes of appearing more up-to-date than their competitor institutions).

24. Elizabeth E. Guffey, *Posters: A Global History* (London: Reaktion, 2015).

25. For an in-depth study of how representations of making and made things are imbricated with skill and knowledge, see Ann-Sophie Lehmann, "Showing Making: On Visual Documentation and Creative Practice," *Journal of Modern Craft* 5, no. 1 (2012): 9–23. Andrew Blauvelt's own contribution to this volume is a fruitful consideration of a different kind of archival object, the bibliography; see 182–96.

26. Fallan, *Design History*, 33.

Every design student who has labored overnight to perfect a studio exercise in time for the morning crit knows in their bones that these things are not just the background radiation of some intellectual abstraction we call education, but important objects of labor and skill in their own right. While it might be tempting to view them as prototypes pointing toward some future moment of "real" production, or as simple rehearsals for professional practice, I prefer to see them as essential instruments of mediation between the abstract and concrete in design pedagogy—tools for a process of becoming, as well as documents of students' understanding (or misunderstanding) of their teachers' aims and their own positionality within larger networks of design. Their intentionally provisional status—explicitly meant to be supplanted by subsequent versions or surpassed by a student's continually advancing skills—is itself

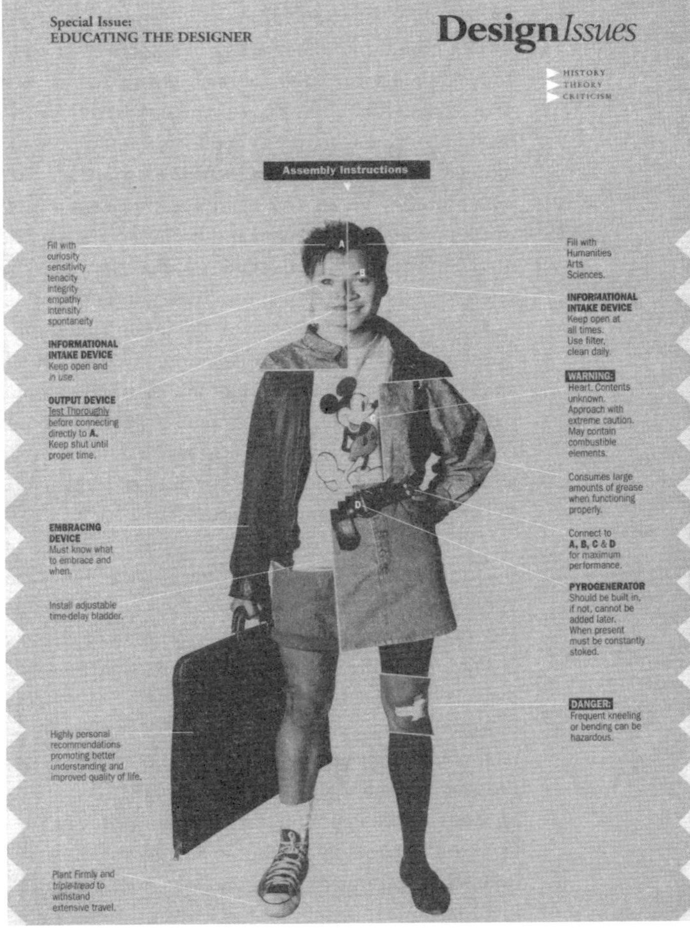

John Greiner, cover for "Educating the Designer," a special issue of the journal *Design Issues* (7, no. 2, [1990])

27. The relatively recent historical focus on embodiment as a nondiscursive dimension of the past has a complex intellectual genealogy: Maurice Merleau-Ponty's *The Phenomenology of Perception* (London: Routledge, 2002 [1962]) is often named as a foundational text, which is later taken up widely in queer and disability studies, anthropology, and archaeology, intersecting with various aspects of cognitive science and sociology as well.

meaningful, distinguishing them from other kinds of "finished" design objects and inviting a different kind of interpretation.

In pointing to these kinds of objects as evidence, I have in mind Judy Attfield's formative work stressing design as an integral part of everyday life rather than as the sole province of a privileged professional class. One of her key aims was to "expand the definitions of design so as not only to include its more usual role of 'things with attitude' but also to include a consideration of it as a process through which individuals and groups construct their identity, experience modernity and deal with social change."[28] These questions are particularly potent for understanding design pedagogy's history. If design-historical scholarship maintains its ambivalence about the dominance of professional designers in the field's literature, a more specific and critical understanding of the everydayness and embodied quality of design training itself—gleaned from engaging the messy and mundane means by which designers are made—might serve to better integrate non- or not-yet-professional designers in the larger historiographic picture.

A great deal of writing about graphic design is rooted in the logocentrism of literary criticism and theory, paying careful attention to signs, symbols, and their contingent meanings. But learning *how* to mobilize these elements of visual communication is as much the work of the body as it is of the mind. A trope in discussions of compositional choices—"it just feels right"—and designers' habituated preferences for certain materials, tools, and techniques are clues pointing to the embodied nature of the design process, reflecting what Gail Weiss calls "the interrelationship between bodies and the technologies which are addressed to/made for them."[29] Looking at graphic design objects (even born-digital ones) through this more haptic lens opens up an expanded set of historical questions about the kinds of sensory knowledge students develop in the studio, distinct from but complementing the discursive dimension of their education.[30] If we understand graphic design pedagogy primarily as a delivery of conceptual frameworks and a space to debate the various "rules" of typography, layout, color, and so on, we risk overlooking opportunities to better understand how the corporeal experience of *making* leads to *knowing*—and how the lens of embodiment might expand the interpretive range of design history writ large.[31]

Retracing Evidence

As histories of graphic design and its pedagogy continue to grapple with the formalist legacies of art history and bend toward the kinds of nuanced and contextual interpretations advocated by many historians and practitioners alike, methodological challenges multiply as wider numbers and types of actors, objects, and

28. Attfield, *Wild Things*, 11.

29. Gail Weiss, *Body Images: Embodiment as Intercorporeality* (New York: Routledge, 1999), 4.

30. A brief but insightful contribution to such a project, focusing on the print trades, is Christine Percy and Teal Triggs, "The Crafts and Non-Verbal Learning," *Oral History* 18, no. 2 (1990): 37–39.

agendas come into the frame. Given the biased and fragmentary nature of the evidence across the history of design education, it can be terribly easy to see historical consensus where none truly existed. Close attention to what does survive, though, can reveal important disunities lurking below tidy received narratives.[31] Seemingly dominant ideas can be imperfectly transmitted, strategically adapted, contested both overtly and covertly, and just plain misunderstood—sometimes by their staunchest adherents. Retroactive reputation management and the layering of successive interpretations can warp our impression of the importance, coherence, or even the basic facts of chronology of institutions, ideas, and careers. In the face of these historical (and historiographic) challenges, the material evidence of graphic design pedagogy and its legacies becomes all the more crucial to the tasks of reconstruction and contextualization. Although archives and objects introduce their own ambiguities into any analytical project, they are key markers of the essential tensions—between the theoretical and the practical, the prescriptive and the descriptive, the individual and the collective—that histories of design pedagogy should embrace and explicate rather than attempt to resolve.

31. A considerable body of work approaches this task in the histories of science, art, and industry in the early-modern period; as one example, see Pamela Smith, Amy R. W. Meyers, and Harold J. Cook, eds., *Ways of Making and Knowing: The Material Culture of Empirical Knowledge* (Ann Arbor: University of Michigan Press; New York: Bard Graduate Center, 2014). For more on the intersections of knowledge production, vision, and embodiment, see Johanna Drucker, *Graphesis: Visual Forms of Knowledge Production* (Cambridge, MA: Harvard University Press, 2014); and Jennifer Anna Gosetti-Ferencei, *The Life of Imagination: Revealing and Making the World* (New York: Columbia University Press, 2018), chap. 5, "The Embodied Life of Imagining."

32. Audrey G. Bennett in this volume provides a pointed example; see 247–58.

DESIGNING A DISCIPLINE

KATHERINE MCCOY

Design history is still young, having begun about thirty-five years ago, propelled by the 1983 publication of Philip Meggs's landmark book, *A History of Graphic Design.* To date, graphic design's history has focused mainly on the canon of design practice—a chronology of groundbreaking work by influential professionals. There has been far less research on the origins and trajectory of the academic discipline of design: what has been taught where and by whom; how it has been taught; and the educational outcomes of students' work and graduates' professional contributions. When design history does touch on design pedagogy, it is typically to celebrate a design educator's individual design work.

The Bauhaus curriculum is one of the few academic programs that have been fairly well documented; most designers and design educators can at least envision the Bauhaus curricular diagram. Yet even the iconic Bauhaus work we revere is mainly that of Bauhaus masters, rather than their students and graduates. Later in the twentieth century, the Arts and Crafts department of Basel's Allgemeine Gewerbeschule (which would be renamed the School for Design in 1980) would be another important contributor to the history of design education. Armin Hofmann's *Graphic Design Manual* (1965) and Emil Ruder's *Typography* (1967) featured student work and included some basic design pedagogy. However, these Swiss "bibles" contain predominantly visual material with minimal text, and there remains much to be researched, documented, and evaluated.

What other design programs have been adopted into the design-history canon? Among the historic avenues of design education, there are some heroic episodes and some regrettably mediocre ones, all of which need examination.

Terminology

As we launch our discussion of design pedagogy, defining our terms is essential, and there are many: pedagogy, of course, but also curriculum, discipline, profession, industry, applied art. We will have to define practice, method, theory, research, and criticism. Even our discipline's name needs clarification. Is it graphic design, visual communication, communication design, or something else? (A note: Although "communication design" now seems a better name for the discipline, this essay will use "graphic design," given the focus on the period from the Bauhaus to the Internet.)

Pedagogy and Profession

The very idea of pedagogy is relatively new in graphic design. Even today, it is likely that many design educators would not be able to define the word, and do not think of pedagogy as related to their teaching. But whether they use the term or not, every design educator employs some sort of pedagogy, and our graphic design discipline *does* have a chronology of educational pedagogies, from the rudimentary to the more developed.

This book title uses the term "pedagogy." But the broader history of graphic design education and the "discipline" of graphic design are at stake. An educational discipline encompasses a specialized body of knowledge and leads to the systematic production of new knowledge. A discipline contains technical terminologies, theories, methods, and research transmitted in academic institutions.[1]

"Pedagogy" is a close neighbor of "curriculum," which also enters this discussion. Meredith Davis, one of the key authors of the National Association of Schools of Art and Design (NASAD) Communication Design accreditation standards, defines pedagogy as "how we teach" and curriculum as "what we teach"—parallel partners. And the "discipline" of graphic design is the educational partner of the "profession" of graphic design.

Graphic design's historical trajectory has been an evolution toward a profession, away from a trade, a craft, an art, a business, or an industry. Although graphic design does contain elements of some or all of these, essentially graphic design is—or is becoming—a profession.

One of the essential elements of a profession is an academic discipline with an accepted body of knowledge and expertise, communicated through specialized education and regulated by accreditation. Other elements of a profession include a professional-client relationship, an expected quality of practice, service for the greater good, and ethical standards. Fortunately, graphic design now generally meets these basic criteria, although it has taken years to reach this level.

Now Let's Discuss What Graphic Design Is NOT

Graphic design is *not* an "industry," as so many practitioners like to call it. Despite how often we hear and read this term in communications from the American Institute of Graphic Arts, the usage is mistaken. Graphic designers do not sell products to customers; graphic designers provide specialized professional services for clients. Comparisons are helpful. Architecture is well established as a distinct profession and is not confused with industry, although an architect often partners with industrial affiliates, such as contractors and window manufacturers. A medical doctor may work closely with pharmaceutical companies and healthcare equipment manufacturers, but the MD is a professional, while their affiliates are industries and businesses.

And graphic design is *not* an "applied art," as described by so many university art departments and NASAD policies through the years. Indeed, graphic design is neither "applied" nor "art." Like other design fields, it is a distinct profession and discipline, not

1. Armin Krishnan, "What Are Academic Disciplines? Some Observations on the Disciplinarity vs. Interdisciplinarity Debate," *National Centre for Research Methods Working Papers* (January 2009), http://eprints.ncrm.ac.uk/783/1/what_are_academic_disciplines.pdf, 10.

a commercial subset of fine art practice and art education. Yet, "applied art" is how early graphic design practice and academic study were defined for much of the twentieth century, and this heavy baggage continues to weigh us down even today. Few communication design programs exist outside of university art departments or independent art colleges. This proximity to the arts has been problematic in many ways, including art-oriented foundation years, underdeveloped design curricula, lack of design course prerequisites, and sketchy design faculty qualifications. Even today, underutilized and unqualified fine arts faculty can be found teaching graphic design courses, in spite of NASAD accreditation standards. And many art school programs' faculty members are predominantly adjunct practicing professionals with limited academic qualifications. The academic degrees of Bachelor of Fine Arts and Master of Fine Arts reflect this fine art presumption in their names.

The association of graphic design with art practice originated in the late nineteenth and the early twentieth centuries, when advertising demanded eye-catching imagery and typography. Clever ideas and a talent for drawing could launch a man (and it was nearly always a man in that era) into a proto-design career. Until the 1970s one could become a commercial artist or advertising designer through on-the-job apprenticeship training in advertising agencies or the typesetting and printing trades, honing one's drawing technique and acquiring graphic arts skills. These skills were sometimes polished in rudimentary art schools but more often were acquired informally. Fine art painters frequently turned to commercial illustration and advertising layout for income—think Frederick Remington, Maxfield Parrish, and Maynard Dixon—further blurring the distinction between fine and commercial art.

After the difficult years of the Depression and World War II, commercial art evolved a vigorous branch of advertising design and illustration, sometimes referred to as the "New York School." Here, art directors and illustrators employed the "Big Idea"—brilliant flashes of intuition—to create clever combinations of text and image. This working method relied on individual talent rather than didactic method. Yet as independent art colleges grew rapidly after World War II, particularly in New York City, art schools developed advertising design and commercial art programs focused on the Big Idea. They employed renowned East Coast designers and illustrators as faculty, usually on an adjunct basis. Studio courses, the main educational format, cultivated creative intuition through an "a-ha!" conceptual approach. In classes, the faculty illustrated this conceptual process with examples of their own work, and "samples and examples," as described by one of our important educational thinkers, Sharon Poggenpohl, at a Society of Typographic Arts conference in Chicago in the late 1970s.

Graphic design magazines and design competition annuals were students' reading material, given the paucity of graphic design books in the 1950s through the 1970s. Learning was based on student emulation of their faculty's personal intuition and compelling personality, with no codified and repeatable design methods. Educational success was limited to the level of brilliance in both teacher and student. Pedagogy and curricula (if those terms can even apply) typically relied on the individual faculty member's unique assignments that simulated professional practice. Courses were mostly "studio," mainly differentiated by year (Sophomore Studio, Junior Studio, Senior Studio) with projects of increasing difficulty. The Foundation course quickly became the standard first-year experience, required of both art and design students in nearly all US art schools—Bauhaus-inspired but decidedly art-oriented. This inappropriate and wasted first year continues up until today in a majority of Communication Design programs.

However, it is important to note that, at its best, the New York School made eloquent use of rhetorical images and the text-image relationships. Think of Doyle Dane Bernbach's Volkswagen ads of the mid-1960s and the best of Pushpin Studio. These provide eloquent examples of semiotic and rhetorical principles: icon, index, symbol; and pun, paradox, antithesis, periphrasis, metaphor, oxymoron. They even demonstrate some poststructuralist strategies, such as open meaning. In fact, many New York School classics are important elements in my own communication theory lectures. Ironically, in art schools through the years, this sort of work has been intuitively conceived by students and critiqued by faculty with virtually no knowledge of any communication theory.

Professionalization

Also in the 1960s, American graphic design began to define itself as a separate practice, rather than a subset of advertising or fine art. Advertising and design diverged as consulting design firms and corporate design groups pursued projects that were more criteria-driven, including corporate identity systems, signage systems, annual reports, and exhibition design. These focused on information rather than persuasion. The term *graphic design* came into more general use, likely influenced by Alvin Eisenman's naming of the Yale graduate program in the 1950s. And practicing designers were more often design program college graduates—for instance, the outstanding mid-1950s Yale MFA classes that included Ivan Chermayeff, Tom Geismar, Burton Kramer, and Rob Roy Kelly.

In the late 1960s, a European element arrived in the U.S that further defined this fledgling professional identity. The Swiss school of graphic design—the close relative of the Bauhaus (1919–33) and the Hochschule für Gestaltung Ulm (1953–68)—stressed rationalism, some systems methods, and the formal minimalism of European "constructive art." Swiss graphic designers were teaching in several American art schools by the mid-1960s. The first to introduce Swiss school graphic design was the Kansas City Art Institute from 1964 to 1974, under department chair Rob Roy Kelly. Hans Allemann, Inge Druckrey, and their faculty colleagues produced numerous influential graduates, including April Greiman and Jerry Herring. The Swiss method was furthered in 1966 by Ken Hiebert's new Philadelphia College of Art program, soon followed by Gordon Salchow's University of Cincinnati program. Concurrently, a number of Swiss-trained designers joined prominent American and Canadian design firms and corporate design groups. Unimark International promoted

"European" systems design and an Americanized Swiss-school graphic vocabulary, led by Massimo Vignelli. The MIT publications group and Muriel Cooper's MIT Press adopted Swiss method and form. And Expo '67 built a Swiss modernist environment in Montreal.

This new European modernist approach included functionalist problem-solving and teamwork—previously found only in industrial design education, inspired largely by George Nelson's writings. It also included some repeatable methodology. The grid system and the hierarchical interpretation of verbal messages organized clients' messages into logical spatial compositions. Typography began to be taught as a conceptual method, as well as an art and a craft. And it came with a professional ethic and idealism; an ambition to improve people's everyday experience and to upgrade the visual environment. This movement also gave us some of the first graphic design books containing a bit of conceptual and form-giving method—the Swiss graphic design "bibles" by Müller-Brockmann, Karl Gerstner, Emil Ruder, and Armin Hofmann.

In the same period, both industrial design and counterculture conceptual methods became popular. Brainstorming and conceptual blockbusting introduced repeatable problem-solving methods not dependent on an individual designer's brilliance. And the very first glimmers of communication theory came to light—semiotics and rhetoric—via the Unimark publication *Dot Zero* and Germany's Ulm school. (It should be noted that most American designers and design educators had only the dimmest knowledge of Ulm's work during or following the school's existence. Even now American designers and design educators have a limited understanding of Ulm's fifteen years of contributions.)

A Profession

Through these years, graphic design began to take its place as a design profession, as had architecture, industrial design, interior design, and landscape architecture. At the 1978 Chicago ICOGRADA conference, Jay Doblin, the distinguished seminal industrial design educator, writer, and practitioner, argued that a profession is defined by three interdependent components: practice, education, and research. In the 1960s, it is notable that professional practice introduced and developed most of the important new design methods, including teamwork, corporate identity systems, and environmental signage systems. Design schools lagged behind, and research and its publication were virtually nonexistent.

In the earlier years of design education, from early commercial art onward, emulation of professional practice was the norm. Throughout the 1960s, school projects continued to simulate professional practice and new graduates' portfolios showcased hypothetical professional projects as so many "samples and examples." Then design education, via the Swiss, introduced the grid system and information design and began to raise the standard of professional practice rather than merely emulate it. In the 1970s, the balance between practice and academia shifted further. With academic postmodernist formal experiments, education began to lead the profession. Students innovated form languages and visual content beyond professional practice norms, responding to postmodernist interests in commercial vernaculars and syntactic form experiments. Wolfgang Weingart's graphic form and typography experiments at the Basel school became a major influence, as did Cranbrook Academy of Art's explorations. A few schools, such as Illinois Institute of Technology's Institute of Design and Stanford University, began to develop new conceptual design methods, sometimes computer-supported. Many of these contributions came from graduate design programs. Graduate design degrees began to be valued in professional practice for the first time, whereas in preceding years graduate school had been viewed as remedial and of limited value. An example: In the mid-1980s a rising young designer said to me, "Why go to grad school? I already have a job!" These newly rigorous academic explorations quickly found their way into professional practice, initiating a two-way street of influence. More recently, with the robust research of PhD communication design programs, Jay Doblin's cycle may be completing itself—a serious shift toward true professionalism.

Pedagocial Historical Research, Documentation, and Interpretation

So now the time is ripe for some historical research, documentation, and interpretation. What questions should be asked? Some possibilities:

- What have been the groundbreaking programs? Who were their originators, what were their curricula and didactic methods? What norms did they reject? Who were their influential graduates?
- What was being read? A history of books published on graphic design would reveal much, as well as a collection of bibliographies by prominent design faculty through the years.

Other topics include:

- conceptual design methods, repeatable design processes, and design research
- communication theory in graphic design curricula
- teaching methods for form, typography, and imagery
- pedagogical formats: studio, critique, and project assignment traditions and newer innovations
- educational objectives, learning outcomes, and syllabi
- MFA and PhD programs' development through the years

And a *history* of graphic design history is needed. Perhaps the development of design history was delayed by a modernist idealization of perpetual newness and the rejection of history's relevance, as well as a conflation of history with stylistic eclecticism.

These are just some elements of design pedagogy in need of documentation and analysis. The design of the discipline of graphic design is well underway. Now it is time to design the critical frameworks for the history of our discipline. Let us get to work!

SUSPENDED BETWEEN DISCIPLINE AND PROFESSION: A HISTORY OF PERSISTENT IMMATURITY AND INSTABILITY IN THE GRAPHIC DESIGN FIELD

DEBORAH LITTLEJOHN

In my research, I have studied how graphic design occupies an ambiguous disciplinary position: Is it a profession or an academic field? Such a question expands to encompass other themes, including graphic design's current position within academies of higher learning; social, technical, and professional shifts underway in all areas of design practice; and a mandate for disciplines from all fields to become more interdisciplinary.[1] If the history of graphic design can be understood as a story about its uneasy relationship with commerce, the history of graphic design education is a story of its uneasy relationship with the profession—a tale that often finds one faction pointing to the other as the culprit. Debates over problems in graphic design education and the profession are conspicuous for their failure to examine the links between what students are taught, on the one hand, and the skills and competencies needed to perform a particular job well, on the other. The premise of this paper is that the shifting landscape of the graphic design field has been persistently suspended between the ideals of modernism's discipline builders and the existing realities of institutional structures, professional identities, the professional labor market, accreditation processes, discursive constructs, and technological developments.

Debates promoting (as well as questioning) the status of graphic design as a profession and a discipline have cyclically surfaced since the early twentieth century and continue today.[2] Disagreements often ensue when I suggest that graphic design is not a discipline, and understandably so: Any debate that raises questions about legitimacy will be sensitive. In stating that graphic design is not a discipline, I am not making a claim about the rigor of design programs or the quality of those who teach therein. Rather, I want to establish clarity as to what "being a discipline" means in

1. See my "Becoming a Discipline: Problems in the Emergence of Design Criticism as a Field of Inquiry," *Design and Culture* 5, no. 1 (2013): 29–32; and "Disciplining the Graphic Design Discipline: The Role of External Engagement, Mediating Meaning, and Transparency as Catalysts for Change," *Art, Design and Communication in Higher Education* 16, no. 1 (2017): 33–51. See also Meredith Davis and Deborah Littlejohn, "Accountability for Anticipating Design Outcomes," *AIGA Design Futures* (2019), https://www.aiga.org/aiga-design-futures/accountability-for-anticipating-design-outcomes/.

Nazca people of Peru are believed to have experimented with balloon flight

order to demonstrate why graphic design remains an immature field with an unstable identity—and why this "betwixt and between" condition persists. The field of graphic design is characterized by differences, contradictions, and ambivalences between professional self-concepts and the discipline of inquiry and teaching in the academy. To name a few: **1.** The professional practice of graphic design is not a science. The disciplinary study of academic subjects,

2. Alvin Lustig, "Designing, a Process of Teaching," in *The Collected Writings of Alvin Lustig* (New Haven: Holland R. Melson Jr, 1958), 9–25; Ken Garland, "Here Are Some Things We Must Do" (1967), in *Looking Closer 3: Classic Writing on Graphic Design*, ed. Michael Bierut (New York: Allworth Press, 1999), 43–44; Ron Levy, "Design Education: Time to Reflect," *Design Issues* 7, no. 1 (1990): 42–52; Paul Rand, "Confusion and Chaos: The Seduction of Contemporary Graphic Design," *AIGA Journal of Graphic Design* 10, no. 1 (1992); Gui Bonsiepe, "A Step Towards the Reinvention of Graphic Design," *Design Issues* 10, no. 1 (1994): 47–52; Michael Sullivan, "The Sorry State of Design Education," *How* 11, no. 4 (1996); Ann Schoenfeld, "Educators Seek the Higher Ground," *Eye* 25 (1997); Ralph Caplan, "Designer, Heal Thy Self," *Print* 10, no. 10 (1999): 40; Allan Davies and Anna Reid, "Uncovering Problematics in Design Education: Learning and the Design Entity," in *Re-Inventing Design Education in the University: Proceedings of the International Conference*, ed. Cal Swann and Ellen Young (Perth: School of Design, Curtin University, 2001), 178–84; Geoffry Fried, "Defining the Discipline of Graphic Design," in *Echo: A Response to HearSay, 10 Conversations on Design* (Philadelphia: University of the Arts, 2002), 4–13; Cal Swann, "Nellie Is Dead,'" *Art, Design and Communication in Higher Education* 1, no. 1 (2002): 50–53; Robin Landa, "A Cold Eye: 'No Exit' for Designers," *Print* 56, no. 2 (2002), 22; Kelvin Browne, "School Daze: Design Education Ain't What It Used to Be," *Applied Arts* 18 (2003): 3, 10; Ken Friedman, "Design Curriculum Challenges for Today's University" (2004), https://www.academia.edu/311100/Friedman._2002._Design_Curriculum_Challenges_for_Todays_University; Sharon Poggenpohl, "Language Definition and Its Role in Developing a Design Discourse," *Design Studies* 25, no. 6 (2004): 579–605, and "Musings about Design," in *The Designer: Half a Century of Change in Image, Training, and Techniques*, ed. Rosemary Sassoon (Chicago: University of Chicago Press, 2008), 51–64; Anne Burdick, "Graduate Education: Preparing Designers for Jobs That Don't Exist (Yet)," *Core77.com* (2007), https://www.core77.com/posts/8266/Graduate-education-Preparing-designers-for-jobs-that-dont-exist-yet; Erik Stolterman, "The Nature of Design Practice and Implications for Interaction Design Research," *International Journal of Design* 2, no. 1 (2008): 55–65; Meredith Davis, "Why Do We Need Doctoral Study in Design?" *International Journal of Design* 2, no. 3 (2008): 71–79; Don Norman, "Why Design Education Must Change," *Core77.com* (2010), https://www.core77.com/posts/17993/why-design-education-must-change-17993; Helen Walters, "Design and Business Education: The System Is Not Good Enough," *DesignObserver.com* (2011), http://yeah.winterhouse.com/feature/design-and-business-education-the-system-is-not-good-enough/27658.

by contrast, is. **2.** Graphic design education is dominated by a practically oriented self-concept, despite being situated within academic universities where scholarly inquiry is the predominant value. **3.** In what has been called a "problem of expectation," graphic design education teaches a range of skills and knowledge that address competencies beyond the merely vocational, even though the graphic design profession generally understands the core mission of educational programs to produce a steady stream of talent.[3] **4.** Disciplines do not emerge in isolation; they build upon and adapt knowledge from preexisting fields, so-called reference disciplines. Yet the history of the graphic design field reflects periods where it seeks to differentiate and bifurcate itself from—as well as align and attach itself to—other reference disciplines and practices (e.g., fine and applied arts, advertising, marketing, and interaction design, social design, cultural anthropology, among others). **5.** Since the establishment of doctoral design programs in the 1990s, there has been a process of transformation of scholarly design research to other disciplines outside of "graphic design" proper. But there remains an absence of graphic design research practice located within the general design knowledge domain. **6.** With regard to self-concepts of graphic design, we find rhetoric dealing with the instability and crises of disciplinary structure. Yet this rhetoric of crisis corresponds, in many ways, to the alternate performance standards for scholarly achievement that academic design faculty are beholden to. **7.** The recent programmatic concept of "interdisciplinarity" defines graphic design as a field in "plurality." Design research, however, shows an astonishing continuity and uniformity of a traditional, practice-oriented kind of thinking. **8.** Finally, graphic design subdisciplines require ideas of open, relatively autonomous realms of multidisciplinary intersections and references. Accreditation bodies, however, require that the terminal professional MFA design degree in the US offer a curriculum dominated by studio-based coursework.

Graphic design education became a formal subject taught in the American higher education system following a much larger, nationwide professionalization process that began in the mid-nineteenth century and took place in other fields such as medicine, engineering, business, and law.[4] This effort was part of the establishment of the modern research university with its various disciplinary "tribes and territories," as Tony Becher has characterized it.[5] As institutional subdivisions of the various activities making up a university, "disciplines" emerged as an organizational, bureaucratic idea determined by political constraints. In this sociological sense, we could just as well understand a discipline as a "social network," a "clique," or a "gang," and as Becher points out, gangs operating in the academy are not much different from those out on the street—and it is often easier to join an existing one than start a new one.

3. Bryan Lawson and Kees Dorst, *Design Expertise* (Burlington, MA: Elseveir, 2009), 214.

4. Julie Thompson Klein, *Interdisciplinarity: History, Theory, and Practice* (Detroit: Wayne State University Press, 1990).

5. Tony Becher and Paul R. Trowler, *Academic Tribes and Territories: Intellectual Enquiry and the Cultures of Disciplines*, 2nd ed. (Buckingham: Open University Press, 2001).

Academic institutions are both a reflection and reinforcement of knowledge classifications, and they therefore influence processes of establishing and maintaining expertise within disciplines.[6] To understand what university structure and disciplinary practices bring to bear on the persistent instability of graphic design's academic identity, it is useful to recall how the modern research university came about in the United States. Following the end of the Civil War, American scholars who had gone abroad to study in Germany brought back the idea of the university as a place to do research that creates fundamental knowledge (preferably using the scientific method). This notion was contrary to the established model of the university as a refuge for the liberal arts.[7] Faculty were still expected to teach and serve their institutions; however, in this new model, leading universities expected them to obtain specialized training in a discipline. Over time, research in a field of specialization became important to a successful academic career—a system that was reinforced by the emergence of formally organized disciplines, the American Association of University Professors, independent sources of funding by the federal government and others, demand for faculty with visibility and national reputations, and increasing competitiveness among institutions for recognition and prestige.[8] Notably, the legitimacy and survival of disciplines now depend on their ability to produce knowledge that advances their field, while organizational context plays a role in determining what comes to count as true disciplinary knowledge.[9]

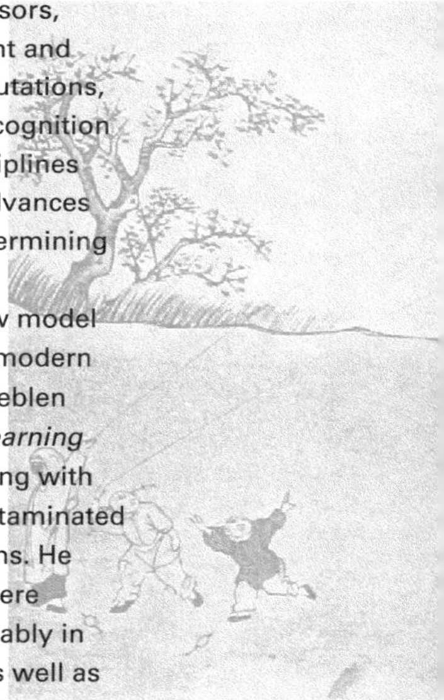

How did the professional schools compare to the new model of higher education during this formative moment of the modern university? Economics scholar and sociologist Thorstein Veblen provided a scathing critique of the former in his *Higher Learning in America*, which opens with a lament of all that was wrong with higher education. Veblen argued that universities had contaminated their hallowed halls by admitting schools of the professions. He insisted that professional schools rendered universities mere technical programs, and that their faculty would fail miserably in their attempts at scholarship, embarrassing themselves as well as the true scholars in the university. For Veblen, there must be firm separation between the research universities, whose work is true scholarship, and the schools of the professions, whose charge is the preparation of individuals through practical vocational training.[10] Indeed, the research-intensive model of the new university that became the norm in the twentieth century created existential problems for professional schools. The reason is that much of the knowledge essential to professions is not what the university would call "fundamental knowledge," and professional practitioners are

6. Patricia J. Gumport and Stuart K. Snydman, "The Formal Organization of Knowledge: An Analysis of Academic Structure," *Journal of Higher Education*, 73, no. 3 (2002): 375–408.

7. Magali S. Larson, *The Rise of Professionalism: A Sociological Analysis* (Berkeley: University of California Press, 1977).

8. David W. Leslie, "Resolving the Dispute: Teaching Is Academe's Core Value," *Journal of Higher Education* 73, no. 1 (2002): 49–73.

not, as a rule, trained to be scientists or scholars. As Veblen makes clear, when professions joined the modern academy, it was, in a palpable sense, as second-class citizens.

Prior to graphic design's own professionalization effort, students learned their craft through apprenticeship. In the 1940s, prominent designers of the time, who included Bauhaus faculty recently immigrated from Europe, declared the traditional apprenticeship model "inadequate to the task" of professional preparation.[11] As graphic design education entered higher education, it was typically housed in the schools of fine art. Where a design program calls "home" determines the kinds of turf wars it deals with—whether exclusively arts-focused private institutions or within public multidisciplinary universities where, more than likely, the STEM fields dominate. Wherever it may be located, graphic design education remains rooted in studio arts, where a so-called art hierarchy[12] reigns — a system that, in many graphic design schools, serves to reify the identity crisis at the core of the field.[13] As Katherine McCoy recalled, one outcome of the decision to locate design programs in schools of fine art was that faculty trained in subject specialties such as painting, drawing, and sculpture, teaching graphic design as a commercial—i.e., "tainted"—application of the fine arts.[14] Hinting at the disciplinary battles I suggested previously, McCoy pointedly notes how art faculty were slow to realize that graphic design was not simply a commercial application of "pure" fine art ideologies and processes.[15]

What Does It Mean to Be a Discipline?

Is graphic design a discipline? The answer is that "it's complicated," and the reason is that "discipline" is a complex, multifaceted construct. A simple yes or no will not suffice. In some ways, graphic design is a discipline, but there are also important ways in which it fails to live up to this description. To understand why, a few definitions are necessary: **1.** A discipline is a group of people involved in the study of something with a goal of creating new knowledge, where "knowledge" is justified true belief. **2.** Science is the pursuit and application of knowledge about the natural and social world following a systematic methodology with a goal of describing and explaining phenomena.[16]

The purpose of a discipline is to produce and validate knowledge. The discipline of graphic design would then involve the study *of* graphic design as a phenomenon—graphic design exists, it

9. Louis Menand, *The Marketplace of Ideas: Reform and Resistance in the American University* (New York: Norton, 2010).

10. Thorstein Veblen, *The Higher Learning in America: A Memorandum on the Conduct of Universities by Business Men* (New York: Sagamore, 1957).

11. Ellen Mazur Thomson, *The Origins of Graphic Design in America, 1870–1920* (New Haven: Yale University Press, 1997), 86.

12. Milton Glaser, *Art Is Work: Graphic Design, Interiors, Objects and Illustration* (Woodstock, NY: Overlook Press, 2000), 263.

13. Roy R. Behrens, "The Hole in Art's Umbrella: Graphic Design Faculty at Art Schools Still Don't Get No Respect from their Fine-Arts Colleagues," *Print* 54, no. 4 (2000), 24–26.

14. Katherine McCoy, "Education in an Adolescent Profession," in *The Education of a Graphic Designer*, ed. Steven Heller (New York: Allworth Press, 1998), 3–13.

happens, and we want to make sense of it. For that to happen, there must be a critical mass of "disciples" trained in the practices of knowledge production whose task is to publish, debate, organize, distribute, and publish knowledge anew. A discipline has both a cognitive as well as a *social* dimension in that it is structured by beliefs and values that help determine what work is most important, identify exemplary practitioners, and prescribe the proper knowledge, discourses, methods, and problems.[17] For example, one way that disciplines structure practice is through establishing a canon of standardized texts that provide symbolic meanings and common narratives for what the field does. To accomplish its knowledge-generating mission, a discipline also relies on methodologies and critical analyses of knowledge. In short, a discipline is also defined by its knowledge system (or epistemology) that guides its practices. A knowledge system is characterized by: **1.** the methodologies informing the study of something, including the current explanatory goals and repertory of concepts and procedures; **2.** the way the discipline defines terms such as "proof," "evidence," and "argument"; **3.** a tradition of criticism and validation as to whether certain claims count as knowledge.[18]

Each of these collections of features defining the objects, practices, and values of a discipline presents fundamental implications for graphic design education, particularly with regards to the curriculum and how it needs to imbue students with a "disposition" for disciplined inquiry—understanding the boundaries of different knowledge systems and the means to appropriately select and apply methods. Thus, the research mindset involves a set of informed assumptions about causality and complexity and how we can know things about the way the world works, in that what is

15. Ibid., 3–13.

16. I use the term "science" here in a general sense—i.e., as a systematic activity of building and organizing knowledge. This meaning is not the same as the "scientific method," i.e., the approach used in the design of quantitative research, also referred to as the "experimental method." Although the scientific method is often promoted as a necessity of "doing science," it is not. If science (in the general definition) were solely a method, then it would not be very useful—the scientific method is not an end unto itself, it is a means to an end.

17. Lee S. Shulman, "Signature Pedagogies in the Professions," *Daedalus* 134, no. 3 (2005): 52–59.

18. Thomas S. Kuhn, *The Structure of Scientific Revolutions*, 2nd ed. (Chicago: University of Chicago Press, 1970), 181.

"knowable" about the world adheres to a reality that can be "discovered." A research disposition also emphasizes the use of empirical data to develop explanations and predictions; the possibility and appropriateness of "objectivity" (i.e., independent from the bias of the observer-researcher); logical coherence; and finally, the belief that people can build systems of knowledge that correspond to the way the world actually works.[19]

The ultimate outcome of disciplined inquiry is a cumulative body of knowledge that offers an approximate description about how the world works. In physical terms, disciplinary knowledge is represented in the published body of peer-reviewed journals, textbooks, conference proceedings, curricula and academic courses, and domains of inquiry. Ideally, the body of knowledge will have a center that experts in the field agree upon, and then peripheral domains that represent the edges of inquiry where there is much debate, innovation, and difference of opinion.[20]

Because they are cumulative and self-defined, disciplines have clear distinctions in the knowledge systems that they use to guide the knowledge-building process. Take the concept of "proof." For physicists, proof requires a process of empirical observation and statistical induction; for historians, proof rests on the interrogation of testimony. A physicist would not attempt to prove something by finding out what someone said about it a hundred years ago any more than a historian would seek to explain the causes of the Civil War by recreating it in a controlled experiment.

Consider, then, these topical claims about graphic design: **1.** W. A. Dwiggins coined the term "graphic design" in 1922. **2.** Graphic design improves businesses' "bottom line." **3.** A serif font is more readable for long texts than a sans serif font.

Each of these statements can be analyzed, its meaning and truth discovered, and its implications considered—but to do that, we need a set of methodological tools, and the tools required are different in each case. The claim about Dwiggins, for example, is a historical claim. We can establish the truth of it by using the tools of the historian, i.e., looking at the archival record and drawing on available source material.

Rather than seeking to make sense of the human past as history does, sociology seeks to understand the nature of the social world and the relationship between people and sociocultural structures. To find out if graphic design improves business, we might collect several years of data on business expenditures for graphic design services and then look for a positive correlation in the data on profit margins.

Cognitive psychology is the study of human thinking and understanding. The tools of cognitive psychology often, though not always, involve creating experimental situations. To test which typeface is more readable, we might set up a quasi-experiment to measure variables associated with reader content comprehension for texts set in each typeface.

19. Ibid., 183–85.

20. Ibid., 187.

An understanding of disciplinary boundaries matters because certain disciplines let us reach some conclusions but not others—and the methods we choose are based on the questions we pose. In studying graphic design as a phenomenon, we need to know how to use tools that fit the purpose. Clarity as to the disciplinary nature of our claims, with their corresponding notions of "evidence" and "proof," lets us make convincing arguments (with evidence that backs up our claims) and have richer discussions about that fascinating thing we want to study.

Is Graphic Design a Discipline?

Graphic design values and aspires to be a discipline, calls itself a discipline, and, in some ways, acts like a discipline. Most of the major graphic design organizations define graphic design using the word "discipline." Furthermore, graphic design has a home in the academy, largely as a branch of the broader discipline of fine arts. So why the skepticism? Why does graphic design have such a long period of criticism, from both inside and outside the academy, claiming there is a crisis at its core? It is not because graphic design is a young field; there are many true disciplines much younger than graphic design. The reason for doubt about the field's status as a true discipline is because we cannot identify a set of methods, concepts, and traditions of criteria for what counts as "graphic design knowledge" that are specific to it. Let me be clear: Graphic design has failed to produce a cumulative body of knowledge that has a clear conceptual core that is consensually agreed upon by mainstream graphic design experts. One scholar of the field (who hails from sociology) captured this condition perfectly when describing that a critical voice in graphic design, which started to surface in the 1990s, is a:

> very busy, multi-vocal conversation, comprised of hundreds and hundreds of exceedingly short essays, interviews and opinion pieces [where] particular issues, concerns and themes recur time and time again, but rarely are they clearly debated, let alone resolved.[21]

The core problem of why graphic design cannot be considered a discipline is that it is, in technical terms, "pre-paradigmatic": It lacks agreement from the field's experts about what it is and what it is about; what its foundational texts, theories, and frameworks are; what its key findings are; and how it fits with the rest of the body of disciplinary knowledge.[22] The facts that: a) the term "graphic design" is not widely understood beyond the confines of the field itself; and b) graphic design has existed in the academy (under an umbrella of different degree titles and program labels) for over seventy years and is still pre-paradigmatic are strong arguments challenging the field's status as a true discipline.

21. Matthew Soar, "Graphic Design/Graphic Dissent: Towards a Cultural Economy of an Insular Profession" (PhD diss., University of Massachusetts Amherst, 2002), 53.

22. Kuhn, *The Structure of Scientific Revolutions*, 182.

To get a sense of what a paradigmatic discipline is, we can once again consider physics. Sir Isaac Newton created a paradigm for understanding matter in motion that remains a monument of intellectual achievement to this day. Newton's single paradigm was replaced by two paradigms in the early twentieth century, quantum mechanics and general relativity; nevertheless, physics remains paradigmatic in the sense that its two paradigms are foundations providing knowledge about how the world works upon which mainstream physicists agree. Likewise, chemistry is paradigmatic in that it has the periodic table and the laws of molecular forces to describe how matter changes chemically. Moreover, these broad domains of inquiry create a cohesive network of understanding that gives us knowledge about energy and matter that is both generalizable and verifiable (i.e., tested and confirmed across multiple situations and found to hold true consistently)—at least until new paradigms emerge that falsify the old ones.

In contrast to these established domains, graphic design has no consensually agreed upon definition. Study any book about graphic design or skim any basic intro to the field and readers will find a summary of major, competing, incommensurate approaches that spell out a mushy territory intersecting art, advertising, communication and rhetoric, cognitive psychology, linguistics, media studies, and computer science. In addition, each of these major approaches has its own merit and is a different and competing perspective on the graphic design subject (however it may be defined). Indeed, we are not even able to define what our field is about. Thus, the reason graphic design fails to be a discipline is because it fails as a coherent system of knowledge that maps the relevant portion of the world. To ascertain if this assumption is correct, ask ten design academics which portion of the world they are trying to map when using the term "graphic design" and you will get ten different answers. If a key feature of true "disciplined" knowledge is a clear, consensual center that provides a foothold to describe how portions of the world actually work, it is here that graphic design fails in ways that chemistry, history, and physics do not—and it is in this manner that graphic design is not a true discipline.

Conclusion

The tension between scholarly work, on the one hand, and an education for professional practice, on the other, is a main factor keeping graphic design in a state of persistent immaturity as a discipline. The histories of the modern university and of graphic design education outlined here reflect a long-standing and conflicted relationship between discipline and profession, which, in turn, we can interpret as a rearticulation of the traditional "theory vs. practice" or "ivory tower vs. the real world" dichotomy.

Let me conclude by bringing to bear two issues that seem to emerge from these "theory/practice" debates, wherever they arise. Firstly, the reality is that "discipline" and "profession" are necessarily intertwined. Without a profession to use and improve the knowledge of the discipline, the field, as a whole, will not advance,

Sumerian use abacus to count

nor will it change—and ultimately, it will cease to exist. In other words, knowledge has little value without people to use it, indicating that knowledge—created, perpetuated, and disseminated—has an inherently *social value* (i.e., to develop a field's knowledge, it must be made public). Teaching students how to *study* something, instilling the requisite researcher mindset, is an entirely different pedagogy than teaching them how to *do* something—i.e., producing good graphic design (and notably, this is the primary mission of any graphic design program in this country, at the bachelor's or the master's level). Our venerable Bauhaus-inspired curriculum is well suited to the latter, and it has (at least until very recently) enabled graphic design education to prepare successful professional practitioners. It is, however, ill-suited for teaching designers the emergent competencies that are increasingly necessary for succeeding in twenty-first century markets, and it is especially deficient when the mission is to prepare advanced researchers with the disciplinary skills necessary to produce new knowledge for the field.[23]

Whether consciously or not, graphic design education has become an insular academic area of study within its university context. The curriculum—and the pedagogy through which it is delivered—is isolated from other knowledge communities, as many faculty are suspicious of and tend to shun the theories and knowledge from other fields.[24] As graphic design programs are essentially professional schools, there is a dilemma in being a school both of practice and of scholarly research—a "twofold relationship to the worlds of the practice and the larger university mirrored in the relationship of discipline- and practice-oriented components of the school."[25] Graphic design programs ignore their academic surrounding at their own peril, as the philosopher Donald Schön warns:

> Just to the extent that a reflective [design] practicum succeeds in creating a world of its own, it risks becoming a precious island cut off both from the world of practice to which it refers and from the world of academic courses in which it resides. If it is to avoid this fate, it must cultivate activities that connect the knowing- and reflection-in-action of competent practitioners to the theories and techniques taught as professional knowledge in academic courses.[26]

Secondly, "interdisciplinarity" has become a buzzword—if not a mandate—throughout the entire US academic university enterprise.[27] Meanwhile, the self-proclaimed interdisciplinary nature of

23. Meredith Davis offers a thorough discussion on the differences in graphic design professional curricula vs. academic research curricula. See Davis, "Confronting the Limitations of the MFA as Preparation for PhD Study," *Leonardo* 53, no. 2 (2020): 206–12.

24. Andrew Blauvelt, "Disciplinary Bodies: The Resistance to Theory and the Cut of the Critic," *Visible Language* 28, no. 3 (1994): 196–202.

25. Donald A. Schön, *Educating the Reflective Practitioner* (San Francisco: Jossey-Bass, 1987), 306.

26. Ibid., 312.

27. Diana Rhoten, "Interdisciplinary Research: Trend or Transition," *Items and Issues* 5, nos. 1–2 (2004): 6–11.

design presents real difficulties for the discipline-specific structures that characterize universities. *Interdisciplinary work, however, is logically prior to, and predicated upon, the existence of disciplines.* We cannot do interdisciplinary work unless we understand what the different disciplines can and cannot do.

Inquiry	Character of the Designer	Character of the Discipline
Disciplinarity	Individuals demonstrate understanding of one set of concepts and one methodological approach. They are able to generate unique questions and contribute new research in this field.	An understanding is demonstrated of one set of conceptions and one methodological approach from field to practice. Able to tolerate questions and contribute new designs in this field only.
Multidisciplinarity	Individuals demonstrate disciplinary competence and understand that their endeavors must be related to the endeavors of others in surrounding disciplines.	An understanding is demonstrated of disciplinary difference and shows ability to learn from other disciplines.
Crossdisciplinarity	Individuals demonstrate disciplinary competence and know how concepts from other disciplines relate to their own, having mastered some of those concepts. They are able to constructively communicate with those from other disciplines.	An understanding is demonstrated of disciplinary difference and the problem-focus of other disciplines.
Interdisciplinarity	Individuals demonstrate at least two disciplinary competences. One is primary, yet they are able to use the concepts and methodologies of another discipline well enough to contribute to its questions and findings. New understandings of the primary discipline result.	An understanding is demonstrated of at least two disciplinary competencies. One is primary, yet it is able to employ the concepts and methodologies of another discipline. Strengthens understanding of the primary discipline.
Transdisciplinarity	Individuals demonstrate at least two disciplinary competences, neither of which is primary. They work in and contribute to both and generate unique conceptions and artifacts as a result of an emergent transdisciplinary perspective. They are able to communicate with individuals from a variety of disciplines in a synoptic manner.	An understanding is demonstrated of at least two disciplinary competencies, neither of which is primary. Abstracts disciplines to bridge new problems.
Pluridisciplinarity	This problem-solving mode combines disciplines that are already related, such as design and engineering. Some of the various domains in design itself involve pluridisciplinarity.	An understanding is demonstrated of a combination of disciplines that are already related in the various domains within design itself.
Metadisciplinarity	This mode connects history/theory and practice so as to overcome specialization; it seeks to develop an overarching framework that differs from disciplinarity in that it does not address single problems.	An understanding is demonstrated that shows an effort to overcome disciplinarity by using methods to construct overarching frameworks to connect practices and their histories to new problems.
Alterdisciplinarity	Globalization and the proliferation of the digital results in connections that are no longer "amid" systems, cannot be measured "across" systems, and do not encompass a "whole" system. Instead, the digital has generated an "other" dimension so that we might now need to consider "alter-disciplinarity."	An understanding is demonstrated that shows an ability to make connections that generate new methiods to identify "other" dimensions of design activity and thought.

Undisciplinarity	Practice shifts from being "discipline-based" to "issue- or project-based." "Undisciplined" research straddles the ground and relationships between different idioms of distinct disciplinary practices. Here a multitude of disciplines "engage in a pile-up of jumbled ideas and perspectives. Undisciplinarity is as much a way of doing work as it is a departure from ways of doing work." It is an approach to creating and circulating culture that can go its own way without worrying about what histories-of-disciplines say is "proper" work. In other words, it is "undisciplined."	An understanding is demonstrated that purposely blurs distinctions and has shifted from being "discipline-based" to "issue- or project-based"; an ability to mash together jumbled ideas and methods from a number of different, distinct disciplinary practices that can be brought together to create new, unexpected ways of working and new projects. Displays an anything-goes mindset that is not inhibited by well-confirming theories or established working practices.[28]

The graphic design field is losing intellectual and professional ground to other, more established disciplines that are better positioned to claim our expertise.[29] If we do not develop a consistently active, intellectually robust research culture for the field that lets us bring deep, *disciplined* knowledge to the interdisciplinary table, do we seriously imagine that others will hold off from doing so? Or that we will be pleased with the results?

28. This chart comes from Craig Bremner and Paul Rodgers, "Design Without Discipline," *Design Issues* 29, no. 3 (Summer 2013): 4–13.

29. Take, as an example, results of a quick search of offerings at a large public Research I institution: Visual Interface Design for Mobile Devices (Computer Science major); Visual Rhetoric, Multimedia Development (Communications major); Visual Thinking (Graphic Communication major); Designing Web Communications, Online Information Design and Evaluation (English major); Data Visualization (Statistics major); Advanced Visual Analytics (Business Management major); Human Information Processing, Psychology of Human-computer Interaction (Systems Engineering major); and Scientific and Technical Visualization: Theory and Practice (Education major).

PUTTING MODERNISM ALL OVER THE MAP: THE BAUHAUS AND WEIMAR POLITICS

J. DAKOTA BROWN

In countless ways, the Bauhaus gave form to the modern experience—from the shapes of the letters we read to the arrangement of the cities we inhabit. Its canonical status has made it an object of both praise and scorn. As its admirers argue, the school synthesized novel aesthetic and technological developments into an approach whose longevity proves its enduring relevance. To its detractors, the Bauhaus represents the origin-myth of "objective" design, whose apparent universalism conceals the narrow particularity of its time and place. Discussions of the Bauhaus legacy quickly become not just formal or methodological arguments but *political* ones. Such debates threaten, however, to inflate the Bauhaus's political effects while effacing the political conditions in which it was formed. The life span of the Bauhaus is coextensive with that of the German Weimar Republic; as I hope to demonstrate, the former makes little sense in abstraction from the latter.

Atmospheres

The Weimar period begins with the German Revolution of 1918–19, which deposed Kaiser Wilhelm II and brought World War I to a halt. With Berlin still engulfed in political unrest, a new constitution was announced from Weimar on August 11, 1919.[1] The young republic was founded by the Social Democratic Party (SPD) in a coalition with the moderate Democratic and Catholic Center parties.[2] Responding to significant pressure from the extra-parliamentary Left, the SPD went on to win several measures that we now take for granted as the baseline for liberal democracy: It extended voting rights and gender equality, and guaranteed legal protections for unions and an eight-hour working day.[3] Nominally socialist, the SPD framed postcapitalist society as a compelling but distant goal, one that could only be reached after a long period of peace and recovery.[4] This, in turn, relied upon restarting the capitalist economy. But that economy, already burdened by harsh postwar reparations agreements, proceeded to lurch from one disorienting crisis to the next. Wartime debt produced inflation, which spiraled into

1. Eric Weitz, *Weimar Germany: Promise and Tragedy* (Princeton: Princeton University Press, 2007), 32.

2. Ibid., 84.

3. Ibid.

4. Ibid., 85.

5. Ibid., 103.

6. Adelheid von Saldern, "The Workers' Movement and Cutural Patterns in Urban Housing Estates and in Rural Settlements in Germany and Austria during the 1920s," *Social History* 15, no. 3 (October 1990); Susan R. Henderson, *Building Culture: Ernst May and the New Frankfurt Initiative, 1926–1931*, ed. Frank J. Coppa (New York: Peter Lang, 2013).

hyperinflation by 1923. The economy was stabilized the following year, but mostly on the backs of the workers: High unemployment and deteriorating working conditions were the necessary side effects of a five-year boom.[5] During this period, cities spent massive sums—often lent by American banks—on new housing developments (many of which employed modernist architects and designers).[6] The links to US finance, however, meant that the Depression of 1929 had a direct and devastating effect on Germany's economy.[7] By 1932, a third of the national population was unemployed, and the legitimacy of the republic was seriously in question.[8] The Weimar period ends with Hitler's consolidation of dictatorial powers in 1933, at which point the SPD was immediately banned.

The origins of the Weimar-era Right can be traced to paramilitaries like the *Freikorps*, populated by nationalist veterans. But its more respectable wing extended from the traditional classes of the countryside to the large capitalists of the cities. Prominent figures in parliament, the churches, and the courts shared a resolve to overturn the gains of the revolution.[9] Respected military officers secretly funneled arms and training to paramilitaries.[10] The Right was broadly united by the *Dolchstosslegende*, or "stab-in-the-back myth," which held that the German army had not been defeated abroad, but rather undermined at home by Jews, the Left, and other "degenerates"—all of whom were to blame for Germany's humiliating terms of surrender.[11] Such groups were depicted as parasites in a discourse that increasingly resorted to a language of racial hygiene.[12]

To the left were the communists, whose opposition to World War I had provoked a traumatizing split with the pro-war SPD. Throughout the unrest of 1918–19, their aim was to push the social-democratic revolution toward a more fundamental upheaval: the German contribution to an international revolution, of which the Russian Revolution was but the first successful act.[13] The Left's base of power was in massive street demonstrations, as well as widespread strikes and mutinies. From occupied factories and armories, workers' and soldiers' councils proposed an immediate socialization of productive relations; they largely rejected invitations to enter government and negotiate with the representatives of property and power.[14] For communist theorists like Rosa Luxemburg, World War I represented the ultimate—and, potentially, the final—catastrophe of

7. Harold James, "Municipal Finance in the Weimar Republic," in *The State and Social Change in Germany, 1880–1980*, ed. W. Robert Lee and Eve Rosenhaft (New York: Berg, 1990).

8. Weitz, *Weimar Germany*, 122.

9. Ibid., 82, 365–66.

10. Ibid., 114–16.

11. Ibid., 95–98.

12. Ibid., 98.

13. Pierre Broué, *The German Revolution, 1917–1923*, ed. Ian Birchall and Brian Pearce, trans. John Archer (Leiden: Brill, 2005).

14. Weitz, *Weimar Germany*, 90–91.

Western capitalism. Gesturing mockingly at the grand promises of "our lofty European civilization," Luxemburg depicted the wartime crisis as a crossroads: The choices were "socialism or barbarism."[15]

The SPD's support for the war made it many enemies on the left, while its signature on the peace treaty cemented the hostility of the right.[16] Taking fire (sometimes literally) from both sides, the SPD ordered a crackdown. Given the conservatism of the institutions of law and order, this was destined to fall much harder on the left.[17] In early 1919, the SPD dispatched *Freikorps* units to put down a communist uprising.[18] The paramilitaries then launched a brutal campaign of repression against strikers and militants, culminating in the assassination of Luxemburg and fellow communist leader Karl Liebknecht.[19] In a bid to establish stability, in short, the governing social democrats wiped out their erstwhile comrades on the left, while empowering a radicalized Right that had no intention of returning the favor.[20]

During the Weimar years, an unbroken mood of crisis translated to continuing appeals from both ends of the political spectrum: those who desired a complete break with capitalism (even in this more "democratic" guise) and those who wished to violently reassert pre-democratic hierarchies and exclusions (or far worse).[21] For most of the 1920s, decisive and stable victories for the right, left, or center were elusive; communists and fascists alike alternated between electoral politics and street confrontations.[22] In the 1928 election alone, forty-one separate parties participated, with fourteen of those achieving some level of representation in the Reichstag.[23] Accelerating political fragmentation, combined with the unprocessed trauma of the war, left many with the impression of a social world in which everything was up for grabs. For many historians and theorists, this provides some explanation for the interwar period's experimentation and innovation, which extended well beyond questions of economic or political organization.[24]

Foundations

The Bauhaus existed in three different forms: It was first a multidisciplinary art and craft school in Weimar (1919–25), then a production-oriented "Institute of Design" in Dessau (1925–32), and finally a private architecture school in Berlin (1932–33). Over the course of its brief and turbulent life, interpretations of the institution's politics varied widely. Under Walter Gropius, the eclectic

15. Rosa Luxemburg, "The Crisis of German Social Democracy" (The Junius pamphlet), 1915, https://www.marxists.org/archive/luxemburg/1915/junius/.

16. Weitz, *Weimar Germany*, 31–32, 37. The parties of the Right had resigned ahead of the signing of the 1919 Treaty of Versailles, so they could claim with some truth that the socialists had betrayed them.

17. Ibid., 82, 99–101.

18. Ibid., 30–31, 97. In Eastern Europe, *Freikorps* divisions were also implicated in anti-Jewish pogroms. Ibid., 38.

19. Ibid., 97–99.

experimentation of the Weimar period gave way to a more practical footing in Dessau. During the final, crisis-wracked years in Dessau and then Berlin, the Bauhaus swung from an overt engagement with Marxism under Hannes Meyer to an attempted coexistence with National Socialism under Ludwig Mies van der Rohe. But even as some Bauhaus designers acquiesced to right-wing pressure, their embrace of geometric abstraction and machine rationalism met passionate resistance. Flat roofs, bare industrial materials, and sans serif typography were read by nationalist commentators as irredeemably un-German and internationalist—or, in less restrained language, as inherently "Jewish" and "cultural-Bolshevist."

The Bauhaus was chased across three cities by a metastasizing fascist movement, and the last options for negotiation evaporated in spring 1933 when the Gestapo seized the Berlin campus. A century since its founding, the legend of the Bauhaus remains overshadowed by the circumstances of its closure. Due to its long struggle with threats from the right, the school is often remembered as a left-leaning and progressive project, destroyed by an enemy that was always external. However, a closer look at the political alignments of Bauhaus professors and students (collectively, *Bauhäuslers*) reveals a much messier picture—itself characteristic of the ideological chaos that reigned in the Weimar years.

Although the Bauhaus quickly became synonymous with rootless internationalism in Germany, wartime nationalism played an important role in the school's founding. When the Belgian architect Henry van de Velde, director of the Weimar School of Arts and Crafts, was forced to resign amid mounting anti-foreigner sentiment in 1914, he named the young architect Walter Gropius as a potential successor.[25] Weimar's Academy of Fine Art also had its eye on Gropius, who had recently distinguished himself with the Fagus factory in Alfeld, the first building wrapped in a multi-story "curtain wall" of glass and steel.[26] While still an officer at the front, Gropius

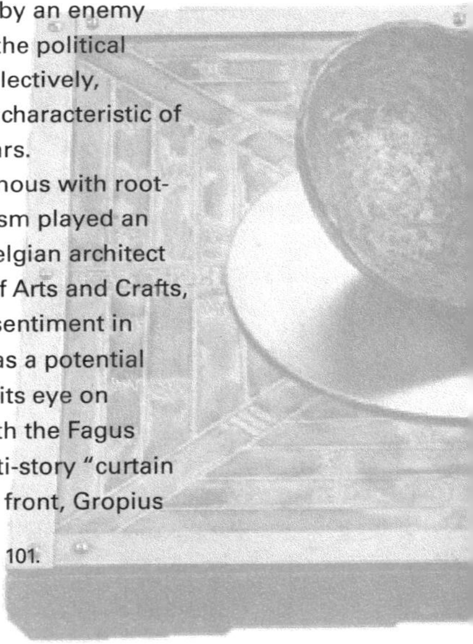

20. "The old elites and the Social Democrats . . . ran toward one another and embraced, but only temporarily. Once the sense of panic had passed, once officers, civilian officials, and capitalists felt the balance of power shifting in their direction, they would look for other allies, which they found, ultimately, in the Nazi Party. The Social Democratic unwillingness, in the winter of 1918–19, to break the powers of their longtime adversaries would come back to haunt them from 1933 to 1945, the twelve long years of the Third Reich." Ibid., 28.

21. Here, the National Socialists should be distinguished from mainstream conservatives. Nazis often positioned themselves as a "New Right" opposed not just to the republic but to the old order as well. Contemporaneous photomontages by John Heartfield skewered the Nazis' attempts at anti-aristocratic and even anti-capitalist messaging.

22. Ibid., 101.

23. Ibid., 104.

24. Ibid., 39, 361–64.

25. Magdalena Droste, *Bauhaus 1919–1933* (Cologne: Taschen, 2015), 16.

drew up plans for a new type of school, and he received approval for a merger of the two institutions in 1919.[27]

Given the Bauhaus's later reputation for machinelike abstraction, Gropius's introductory "Program" of 1919 is a rather jarring document. On the cover, where one might expect a bold composition of abstract forms, we instead find Lyonel Feininger's ragged woodcut of a cathedral rising into a turbulent sky, beset by shafts of light.[28] Such was the international influence of British Arts and Crafts: an early aesthetic confrontation with industrial capitalism that called for the reform of everyday objects and spaces. Uniting art and labor under this evocative medieval imagery, Gropius calls for a return to "the crafts":

> For art is not a "profession." . . . Let us then create a new guild of craftsmen without the class distinctions that raise an arrogant wall between craftsman and artist! Together let us desire, conceive, and create the new structure of the future... which will one day rise toward heaven from the hands of a million workers like the crystal symbol of a new faith.[29]

The Bauhaus's pedagogical sequence even maintained the categories of medieval guilds: Students were "apprentices" working under "masters" rather than professors, and those who passed the initial coursework became "journeymen" eligible for paid work in the workshops. Many later became "young masters"—junior teachers—themselves.[30]

At the Bauhaus, each apprentice worked with two masters: a "master of craft" (a skilled artisan) and a "master of form" (an avant-garde painter). This dialectical approach aimed to educate a new type of creative agent. Here, the Bauhaus mission was particularly successful. This new, hybrid producer—the modern designer—would go on to transform the profession of architecture and to usher in wholly new specializations in the furniture, textile, printing, and advertising industries. It is emblematic of the Bauhaus's contradictory legacy, however, that this occurred not through a revolutionary transformation of class relations but rather through the invention of new professional distinctions.

Qualified masters of craft could be difficult to find, but the criteria for masters of form were much less straightforward: Gropius

26. Ibid., 16–17.

27. Typical of the Bauhaus's vaunted minimalism, its name was whittled out of the much more cumbersome "State School of Building [*Staatliches Bauhaus*] in Weimar, United former Grand-Ducal Saxon Academy of Fine Art and former Grand-Ducal Saxon School of Arts and Crafts." Ibid., 17.

28. Ibid., 17–18.

29. Walter Gropius, "Program of the Staatliche Bauhaus in Weimar" (1919), in *The Industrial Design Reader*, ed. Carma Gorman (New York: Allworth Press, 2003), 98.

30. Droste, *Bauhaus 1919–1933*, 22.

wrote of a "duty . . . to enlist powerful, famous personalities wherever possible, even if we do not yet fully understand them."[31] They were drawn from an international cohort of expressionist painters: The US-born Feininger was among the first hired, and the Swiss painter Paul Klee followed in 1920. Wassily Kandinsky joined the following year. Already a renowned painter and theorist, Kandinsky had recently left the USSR after his idiosyncratic spirituality came into conflict with the materialist emphases of postrevolutionary art.[32] The Swiss painter Johannes Itten, who devised the Bauhaus's influential foundation course (*Vorkurs*), wielded the strongest initial influence on Bauhaus pedagogy.

Though they differed in important respects, each of these men shared a search for "cosmic unity," which was thought to be accessible through the exploration of basic forms.[33] Itten's interpretation of this theme, however, dipped the furthest into the territory of magic. His teaching ranged across botanical studies, color theory, art history, and mysticism; each class opened with movement and breathing exercises.[34] A disciple of the Mazdaznan sect, Itten kept his head shaved and wore a monk-like outfit; his most devoted students wore matching robes.[35] The sect practiced strict sexual and dietary discipline, and briefly convinced the school's canteen to expressly serve what one visitor described as "uncooked mush in garlic."[36] Itten's focus on the awakening of individual potentials would later come into conflict with the Bauhaus's emphasis on mass production. Like the pottery workshop master Gerhard Marcks, Itten's premodern nostalgia was also linked to right-wing myths of national, racial community.[37] As former Bauhaus Archive curator Magdalena Droste summarizes, Bauhaus culture was constituted by a volatile mix of "highly contradictory ideas."

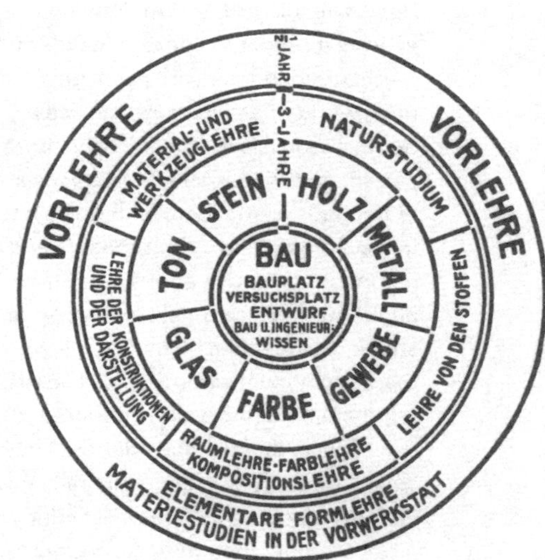

Diagram of the Bauhaus curriculum, Walter Gropius, 1922.

> At the beginning, German nationalists and anti-Jewish students tried to gain the upper hand. Messianic visionaries . . . were allowed to

31. Ibid.

32. Ibid., 66.

33. Ibid., 65.

34. Ibid., 24–31.

35. Ibid., 31–32.

36. Nikil Saval, "How the Bauhaus Redefined What Design Could Do for Society," *New York Times*, February 4, 2019.

speak and Itten and [George] Muche to canvass for their vegetarian Mazdaznan beliefs. Anarchist, socialist, conservationist, life-reformist, and esoteric schools of thought all found support at the Bauhaus.[38]

Systems

Admission to the Bauhaus reflected Weimar's progress on equality of access to education and training. But while women actually outnumbered men in the first class of students, they were immediately segregated into a weaving workshop (later home to the Bauhaus's only female master, Gunta Stölzl).[39] Gropius publicly affirmed gender equality, but privately commented that the masters should not undertake unnecessary "experiments" with "the fairer sex."[40] As Droste points out, this was one of the Bauhaus's deepest ironies. Textile production drew on deep traditions of craft knowledge, even as it prepared apprentices for one of Germany's most heavily mechanized industries.[41] Far from a marginal adjunct to the "real," male world of architecture, the activity of the weaving workshop established a clear model for the more industrial focus of the Dessau period. Anni Albers's textile designs are particularly sharp specimens of Bauhaus abstraction, with grid systems that reveal, upon closer inspection, dynamic asymmetries and unexpected rhythms. Among her most innovative efforts was a fabric designed for a trade school auditorium, which reflected light on one side while absorbing sound on the other.[42] While some women eventually moved beyond the weaving workshop, inflated admissions standards kept their numbers hovering around a third of the student body.[43]

Dance, theater, and sports at the Bauhaus were co-ed, and sexual morality was generally relaxed and bohemian. As Elizabeth Otto has documented, feminist critique and queer expression were also common, though these currents mostly flew under the radar of official production.[44] Right-wing pressure on the school's existence was fueled, in part, by provincial shock at the nontraditional lifestyles and androgynous dress of the apprentices. Fittingly, many of these objections crystallized around a single design project. In 1922, apprentice Peter Keler produced a baby cradle using the elementary forms that had become de rigueur in Kandinsky's courses. The

37. Droste, *Bauhaus 1919–1933*, 32, 68. In an essay, Itten once argued "that the white race represented the highest level of civilization."

38. Ibid., 50.

39. Ibid., 72; Elizabeth Otto, *Haunted Bauhaus: Occult Spirituality, Gender Fluidity, Queer Identities, and Radical Politics* (Cambridge, MA: MIT Press, 2019), 99.

40. Droste, *Bauhaus 1919–1933*, 40.

41. Ibid., 72.

42. Ibid., 184.

43. Otto, *Haunted Bauhaus*, 100.

44. Ibid., 10, 137–38. Though Berlin was known for the innovative early research into gender and its embodiment at Magnus Hirschfeld's Institut für Sexualwissenschaft, sexual minorities remained criminalized during the Weimar period.

suspended platform on rockers was formed from three interlocking shapes: a yellow triangle, a red rectangle, and a blue circle. When the crib appeared in the Bauhaus's inaugural exhibition of 1923, news began to spread that it had been a gift for a pregnant apprentice. A contemporaneous newspaper editorial seized upon this apparent celebration of a "fallen girl" as "evidence for the destructive methods of teaching and education practiced at the Bauhaus."[45]

Aside from their origins in Bauhaus coursework, the basic shapes of Keler's cradle also reflected a turn toward design for mass production. The 1923 exhibition had opened at the height of Germany's postwar inflation, and many of its displays were explicitly framed as solutions to housing and materials shortages. The school's own finances, meanwhile, were in dire shape, and the staging of the exhibition itself was a stipulation in a loan agreement.[46] Motivated, in part, by the need to raise funds, Gropius began pushing a more industrial focus. This move precipitated the departure of Itten, and the *Vorkurs* was divided between the recently arrived Hungarian painter László Moholy-Nagy and the young master Josef Albers.[47] Gropius had, in the meantime, revised the school's motto: "A Unity of Art and Handicraft" became "Art and Technology—a New Unity." As theater director Oskar Schlemmer had remarked a few years earlier, the dominant spirit of the Bauhaus was split between "Indian cult" and "Americanism," the latter a shorthand for a fascination with assembly lines and automation.[48]

After a right-wing electoral victory in 1924, the Bauhaus's funding was slashed in half. In response, the masters closed the school and weighed their options. Among many offers for a new location, Gropius chose the manufacturing center of Dessau, which was home to large factories for IG Farben and the engineering firm Junkers. Just as importantly, the ruling coalition of liberals and social democrats in Dessau were receptive to Gropius's plans for standardized developments of workers' housing.[49] Relocating also provided an opportunity to build a new campus from scratch. Gropius planned discrete structures for workshops, studios, apartments, and offices, all of which were linked by a floor that gathered collective activities: meals, performances, and intricately conceptualized parties. The structure literalized pedagogical ideals of transparency, openness, and collaboration. Gazing at the giant curtain wall that ran the length of the workshop wing, the art theorist Rudolf Arnheim marveled at the structure's blunt statement of its own construction: "No screw is concealed, no decorative chasing hides the material being worked. It is very tempting to see this architectural honesty as moral, too."[50]

Bauhaus pedagogy and production underwent several important transformations in Dessau. Bauhaus GmbH, a retail business for the products of the workshops, was founded in 1925.

45. *Bauhaus: Model and Myth*, directed by Niels Bolbrinker and Kerstin Stutterheim (Germany, 2009), DVD.

46. Droste, *Bauhaus 1919–1933*, 105.

47. Ibid., 46, 140.

48. Quoted in ibid., 101.

49. Ibid., 120.

50. Quoted in ibid., 122.

The workshops also formed partnerships with manufacturers: Young master Marcel Breuer's tubular steel chairs, for example, were adapted as lightweight seating for the nearby Junkers aviation factory. Though "building"—*Bau*—had always been planned as the school's spiritual center, it was only in 1927 that an architecture department was founded. By this time, the old guild categories were mostly dropped: Apprentices became students.[51] The school was now on the same institutional footing as traditional art and technical academies.

At Weimar, the rudiments of what we now recognize as Bauhaus graphic style were scattered across the workshops and even the city; it was only at Dessau that this approach became more systematic. The *Vorkurs,* as we have seen, acclimated students to the use of elementary shapes and colors—an influence that blended readily with samplings of Dutch De Stijl and Russian Constructivism. De Stijl founder Theo van Doesburg even set up a competing course in Weimar, where he took to heckling Itten for his undisciplined "expressionist jam."[52] Later, Joost Schmidt's short-lived "free sculpture" workshop staged experimental studio photographs, some of which found their way into Bauhaus publications.[53] Moholy-Nagy—technically the master of the metals workshop—then began to fuse photography and print production with a hybrid practice he called "typo-photo." As a student in Weimar, Herbert Bayer had first merged texts with planes of color in the mural-painting workshop. At Dessau, he took charge of the new advertising workshop, which combined the resources of the photography, sculpture, and art-printing workshops and added typesetting equipment.[54] Printing workshops had survived in varying incarnations because they were consistent moneymakers for the school. At Dessau, portfolios of art prints gave way to a book series, an intermittent journal, and assorted advertising and marketing materials.[55] The workshop doubled as a public relations center for the Bauhaus's expanding catalog of products.

The Bauhaus was on relatively secure footing in 1928 when Gropius—worn down by political conflict and frequently called away from campus for architectural commissions—announced his intention to step down.[56] He chose Hannes Meyer, head of the new architecture department, as his successor. To some *Bauhäuslers* this seemed an odd choice: Meyer was an outspoken critic of what he saw as the school's vague (and bourgeois) rhetoric of spiritual revolution. He planned to replace this "bogus-advertising-theatricalness"[57] with a new, "functional-collectivist-constructive" direction.[58] The Bauhaus would now be oriented toward "necessities" rather than "luxuries," centering the needs of the working class.[59] Design problems would take their cues less from formal exercises directed by painters and more from current research in the natural and social

51. The original Weimar professors usually retain the title "master" in the historical literature of the Dessau period and after. I follow that convention here.

52. Ibid., 54.

53. Ibid., 156.

54. Ibid., 135, 148.

55. Ibid., 137–39, 180.

sciences. Bayer and Moholy-Nagy—whom Meyer once called a "painting journalist"—soon resigned.[60]

Tensions

Departing from the Bauhaus's official position that it was engaged in "objective, entirely non-political cultural work," Meyer was open in his communist sympathies.[61] Aiming for a "proletarianized" Bauhaus—where atomized individuals were united into cooperative teams—he rearranged the class schedule to more closely approximate an industrial workday.[62] A growing body of communist students understood the Marxist worldview to be the only consistent outcome of a Bauhaus education.[63] Trade union facilities and workers' housing completed under Meyer, after all, had clear precedents in projects initiated by Gropius—who once defended his own generous master's quarters by saying, "What we today consider luxury will tomorrow be the norm!"[64] Kandinsky and Josef Albers, meanwhile, had begun sending alarming reports of student radicalization to the liberal mayor, Fritz Hesse.[65]

Meyer's political sympathies naturally attracted controversy. Bauhaus students were overheard singing communist songs at a 1930 party, which produced a feeding frenzy in the right-wing press. Later, it came to light that he had donated to a student group's mutual-aid effort for a communist-led miners' strike.[66] Attempting to stem the formation of a full-fledged "communist cell" at the Bauhaus, the masters dismissed twenty in a move that made Meyer himself a target of the students' ire.[67] Hesse, however, was as intent on removing Meyer as he was on winning his impending reelection.[68] When it became apparent that no amount of protest would reverse the decision, Meyer boarded a train for Moscow with a "Red Bauhaus Brigade" of his closest students.[69] Stalinist design policy, however, would prove hostile to Meyer, who rounded out the rest of his career as a city planner in Mexico.[70] His directorship was all but erased for decades as Bauhaus alumni, led by Gropius, worked to actively suppress his contributions.[71]

Gropius had meanwhile contacted the talented and rigorously apolitical architect Ludwig Mies van der Rohe. Though Mies's Bauhaus directorship is mostly remembered for his efforts to

56. Éva Forgács, "Between the Town and the Gown: On Hannes Meyer's Dismissal from the Bauhaus," *Journal of Design History* 23, no. 3 (2010).

57. Droste, *Bauhaus 1919–1933*, 170.

58. Ibid., 166.

59. As Droste perceptively argues in the case of the German Trades Union building, however, Meyer-era Bauhaus projects never completely escaped his own diagnosis of formalism. Ibid., 195–96.

60. Ibid., 60.

61. So reads a 1924 letter of protest from the Bauhaus masters, announcing the Weimar campus's closing. Quoted in ibid., 113.

62. Ibid., 171, 196.

63. Ibid., 198.

64. Quoted in ibid., 130.

65. Ibid., 189.

66. Ibid., 199.

67. Ibid.

keep the school open, his first act as director was to shut it down. Bauhaus students had called a strike to protest the underhanded manner of Meyer's dismissal, and a communist student paper published searing accusations against Gropius and Kandinsky.[72] When the masters demanded the names of its authors, they were met with silence.[73] Backed by Hesse, Mies responded with a police raid targeting Meyer's remaining foreign students, who were then expelled.[74] Others, like the Croatian graphic designer Ivana Tomljenović—producer of the only known experimental film made at Dessau—quit in solidarity.[75]

The next month, all students who had survived the purge were ordered to reapply. New enrollees were required to sign a revised constitution that affirmed a more purely aesthetic program of study, ended shared governance by students and professors, and even banned smoking.[76] In an attempt to reduce expenditures, Mies increased tuition even as he slashed support for the workshops that provided advanced students with a wage.[77] But the onset of a global depression in 1929, followed by a substantial electoral breakthrough for the Nazis in 1930, signaled the beginning of the end for the Dessau Bauhaus. Local National Socialists circulated a flyer ahead of the 1931 elections demanding a cessation of the school's funding; the cover of a protest against frivolous spending was belied by an accompanying demand for the campus's immediate demolition.[78] The Nazis later converted the complex into a home-economics school for women.[79]

During the Bauhaus's last days in Weimar, Social Democratic and Communist politicians had been united in attempts to defend the school. But this time, the SPD abstained in the final vote.[80] Mies rented a vacant telephone factory in Berlin, and the Bauhaus began its final incarnation as a small private school. Writing from Dessau in late 1931, one student reported that only a few of his colleagues did not identify as communists; a year later in Berlin, he noted that this balance had completely flipped.[81] The anticommunist contingent grew to include a number of Nazi Party members, including the professor Friedrich Engemann. Weaving master Gunta Stölzl—a socialist married to a Jew—had already been forced out following a campaign of personal harassment that included swastika graffiti.[82]

None of this stopped the Gestapo from locking down the Berlin campus for three months in 1933. During this time, the remaining *Bauhäuslers* attempted to persuade the party of the value of their work.[83] Students wrote personal letters to propaganda minister

68. Forgács, "Between the Town and the Gown," 267.

69. Otto, *Haunted Bauhaus*, 187.

70. Saval, "How the Bauhaus Redefined What Design Could Do for Society."

71. Droste, *Bauhaus 1919–1933*, 166.

72. Ibid., 204.

73. Ibid.

74. Ibid.

75. Otto, *Haunted Bauhaus*, 180–84.

76. Droste, *Bauhaus 1919–1933*, 204.

77. Ibid., 206.

78. Ibid., 226–27.

79. Otto, *Haunted Bauhaus*, 192–94.

Joseph Goebbels; among Mies's many entreaties, he argued that the Bauhaus's closure would by now affect "people with almost exclusively nationalist beliefs."[84] In the end, the state canceled its obligations to pay professor salaries and presented a list of demands—including the dismissal of the relatively conservative Kandinsky—that Mies rejected. With an informal vote and a champagne toast, the Bauhaus closed for good on July 19, 1933.

Afterimages

The Bauhaus inspires enduring interest due in part to the remarkable personal trajectories of its alumni. *Bauhäuslers* with Jewish heritage or leftist affiliations had begun to emigrate even before the school's closure, but its final end accelerated the globalization of modernist forms and concepts. Anni and Josef Albers landed at Black Mountain College in North Carolina, where they taught alongside John Cage, Merce Cunningham, and Elaine and Willem de Kooning. Moholy-Nagy continued his work at Chicago's "New Bauhaus"—later the IIT Institute of Design—thanks to the funding of the industrialist (and Bauhaus fan) Walter Paepke. In West Germany, Bauhaus alumnus Max Bill cofounded the Ulm School of Design in 1953 along with Inge Aicher-Scholl, who dedicated the school to the memory of her siblings, Sophie and Hans Scholl, executed ten years earlier for their work with the resistance group the White Rose.

During the war, Bauhaus graphic designer Moses Bahelfer forged identification papers for the French Resistance, while photographer Irena Blühová published underground newspapers from Nazi-occupied Czechoslovakia.[85] But there were also many who never got out. In 1932, photographer Gertrud Arndt captured a forlorn image of weaver Otti Berger in the raking light of the abandoned Dessau canteen.[86] Berger later fled Germany, but was recaptured and killed at Auschwitz, where her former classmate Fritz Ertl—now a Waffen-SS officer—had designed barracks, gas chambers, and crematoria.[87] The coexistence of such extremes should make it clear that the Bauhaus was less a singular political project than a microcosm of the social forces then tearing German society to shreds. Across the careers of three prominent Bauhaus masters, one glimpses a bizarre montage of political impulses.

One of the most controversial projects of the Weimar period was the *Monument to the March Dead*, a memorial for workers killed during a right-wing putsch in 1920.[88] Commissioned by a local trade union syndicate, the jagged concrete bolt was a project

80. Droste, *Bauhaus 1919–1933*, 113, 200.

81. Ibid, 208.

82. Otto, *Haunted Bauhaus*, 191.

83. Droste, *Bauhaus 1919–1933*, 234.

84. Ibid., 235.

85. Darran Anderson, "How the Bauhaus Kept the Nazis at Bay, Until It Couldn't," Bloomberg CityLab, March 11, 2019, https://www.bloomberg.com/news/articles/2019-03-11/100-years-later-how-the-bauhaus-resisted-nazi-germany.

of Gropius's architecture studio, built with the assistance of the Bauhaus workshops. Thirteen years later, Gropius was compiling an exhaustive proposal for the German Reichsbank, which spliced the open geometry of the Bauhaus complex to the bombastic, hulking style increasingly demanded by Hitler himself.[89] Though Gropius was a finalist, opportunities in Germany were drying up, and he quietly emigrated to England in 1934. As Jonathan Petropolous has documented, however, Gropius hesitated to burn bridges. In 1936, he formally requested the party's permission to accept a position at Harvard—in a letter that argued for the propaganda value of his appointment.[90] That same year, Nazis demolished the *Monument to the March Dead*.[91] Though Gropius spent the remainder of his career obscuring the details of his Berlin years, he also made several attempts to secure visas for endangered architects and designers.[92]

Walter Gropius, *Monument to the March Dead* (completed 1922, destroyed 1936)

In 1926, Mies designed a monument to Rosa Luxemburg and Karl Leibknecht: an uneven block of rough brick evoking the walls against which countless socialist militants were shot in the unrest of 1919.[93] Luxemburg and Liebknecht were, as we have seen, victims of the SPD's haphazard policy of appeasing the far Right, only to be betrayed in turn—a pattern that repeated itself, in miniature, under Mies's Bauhaus directorship. He would later join Gropius as a finalist for the Reichsbank competition in 1933; a submission for the Third Reich's pavilion at the Brussels World's Fair followed in 1935. As Tom Dyckhoff has suggested, it is easy to picture Mies's hesitation as he added a stone eagle and swastika flags to his sketches—though less for their content than for their status as external, decorative embellishments. In 1937 he emigrated to the US, having realized that, as Dyckhoff writes,

> his future patron would be no government, no political system, but the economic system that was emerging triumphant in the US.

86. Otto, *Haunted Bauhaus*, 190–91, 194.

87. Ibid., 199.

88. Saval, "How the Bauhaus Redefined What Design Could Do for Society."

89. Jonathan Petropoulos, *Artists under Hitler: Collaboration and Survival in Nazi Germany* (New Haven: Yale University Press, 2014), 74–77.

90. Ibid.

91. Saval, "How the Bauhaus Redefined What Design Could Do for Society."

92. Petropoulos, *Artists under Hitler*, 86.

93. Saval, "How the Bauhaus Redefined What Design Could Do for Society."

> Modernism, the International Style, would succeed as the landscape not of communism, bolshevism or nazism, but of international capitalism.[94]

The case of Herbert Bayer, as recently documented by Patrick Rössler, reveals an exceptionally high degree of collaboration by a *Bauhäusler* with no known Nazi sympathies.[95] After leaving the Bauhaus in 1928, Bayer established a successful advertising practice in Berlin. Despite the danger faced by his many Jewish friends (including his estranged wife, Irene Hecht), he stayed on well after the Nazi takeover. Bayer contributed design and illustration to three prominent efforts of Nazi propaganda; in his work on the 1934 exhibition *German People, German Work*, he was joined by Gropius and Mies.[96] But even Bayer's 1936 pamphlet for the Hitler Youth provided insufficient cover for his association with the Bauhaus; he fled the next year after one of his paintings was included in the Nazi-sponsored *Degenerate Art* exhibition.[97] In the 1940s and '50s, Bayer would play a central role in the consolidation of corporate modernism in the United States. He joined New Bauhaus patron Walter Paepke in founding the International Design Conference in Aspen, a meeting-ground for design and corporate management that would establish the model for the modern design conference.

Political zigzags like those of former Bauhaus masters were not unheard of in a period of capitalist crisis met by rising challenges from the left and the right. However, the shifting commitments of its most prominent alumni underline the ambiguity of the Bauhaus's politics of form. A century since its founding, it is commonplace to say that the Bauhaus was neither a school nor a style but a utopian idea. This was, however, a utopia founded under the sign of barbarism. The Bauhaus idea convinced a number of influential designers that their practice held an inherent life-reforming potential: one that could be actualized above or beyond the existing relations of social power. But because the *Bauhäuslers* nonetheless remained entangled in those relations, they frequently stumbled into affirming or even intensifying them. The modernist approaches developed at the Bauhaus showed themselves equally adaptable to socialism, fascism, and capitalism. That they became the face of the latter owes more to the contingencies of a failed socialist revolution—and a successful fascist counterrevolution—than to any timeless political essence embedded in those forms.

94. Tom Dyckhoff, "Mies and the Nazis," *The Guardian*, November 29, 2002, https://www.theguardian.com/artanddesign/2002/nov/30/architecture.artsfeatures.

95. Anja Neidhardt, "Herbert Bayer and the Ethics of Design," *Fictional Journal* 2 (April 2017), https://www.fictional-journal.com/herbert-bayer-ethics-design/.

96. Petropoulos, *Artists under Hitler*, 78.

97. Neidhardt, "Herbert Bayer and the Ethics of Design."

DURING THE BAUHAUS

JULIET KOSS

In recent decades, "Bauhaus" has served as a form of shorthand as slippery as it is useful. As Barry Bergdoll noted in 2019, on the centenary of the school's founding, the term "has become . . . a catchall synonym for modernism in architecture and design," generally concealing the extraordinary diversity of achievements, opinions, identities, behaviors, politics, and pedagogies among those enrolled or teaching at the school.[1] On occasion it stands for a domesticated avant-gardism, or for Weimar design in general, since the school's life span, 1919 to 1933, precisely matches that of the Weimar Republic. Sometimes it suggests a joyful, creative internationalism that, at long last, included women within its ranks, with new forms of art-school socialization incorporating these New Women, along with the New Objectivity (*neue Sachlichkeit*) and the New Vision (*neues Sehen*) of the Weimar era. At other times the label covers all twentieth-century flat-roofed, white-box architecture in Europe and beyond. In the field of graphic design, "Bauhaus" often appears as a stand-in for the New Typography of Weimar Germany, later disseminated around the world, although the school's typographic innovations were often primarily theoretical. As Paul Stirton has argued, "developments in cities such as Berlin, Bielefeld, Essen, and Magdeburg suggest that the Bauhaus was more of a symbol of progressive theories of design than a model of design education."[2]

Cynics may justifiably insist that the term "Bauhaus" now provides, above all, a useful marketing tool. Since 2019, for example, it has been possible to purchase, among many other gems, the self-described "beautifully re-created" Bauhaus typography from Adobe Inc., available "exclusively to Creative Cloud members, so *you* can design with a piece of living history." In fact, the Bauhaus label was always a useful marketing tool, and it was one that Walter Gropius, the school's founding director, was careful to develop and maintain during his tenure there from 1919 to 1928 and for decades afterward—long after his departure from Germany in 1934, until his death in 1969. "From the very beginning," Annemarie Jaeggi has written, "the word 'Bauhaus' was used as a trademark: Bauhaus Evenings, Bauhaus Teas, and Bauhaus Festivals were organized; the relaxed 'Bauhaus Dance' was danced to music performed by the Bauhaus Band; Bauhaus products, Bauhaus Books, and Bauhaus buildings were prepended with the distinguishing name as a verbal seal of quality."[3] From 1919 onwards, the school was enmeshed in reputation building and cultural politics, often guided in this activity by Gropius himself.

Such guidance took place most prominently in 1938, with the opening of the exhibition at the Museum of Modern Art in New York showcasing Bauhaus achievements—or, at least, certain

1. Barry Bergdoll, "What Was the Bauhaus?" *New York Times*, April 30, 2019.

2. Paul Stirton, *Jan Tschichold and the New Typography: Graphic Design Between the World Wars* (New Haven: Yale University Press, 2019), 113.

3. Annemarie Jaeggi, "Bauhaus: A Conceptual Model," in *Bauhaus: A Conceptual Model* (Ostfildern: Hatje Cantz, 2009), 13.

objects that had been created in the school's first nine years, under Gropius's leadership.[4] Designed by Gropius and Herbert Bayer, with assistance from Ise Gropius, the exhibition and its attendant catalog solidified the school's international reputation. Yet in capping the story in 1928, the exhibition and catalog also laid the foundations for some of the central misrepresentations of the school that remain in circulation today—especially, but not only, in the popular imagination—despite any number of corrective analyses that have since appeared in monographs, edited volumes, and subsequent exhibitions at MoMA and around the world.[5] Remarkably, the exhibition carefully omitted the work carried out under the aegis of its second and third directors: Hannes Meyer, who ran the school from 1928 to 1930; and Ludwig Mies van der Rohe, in charge from 1930 until its closure in 1933. In this way, MoMA solidified the school's identification with its founding director and his friends and acolytes, presenting a distorted version of Bauhaus history and either minimizing or erasing a range of artistic and pedagogical efforts and achievements.

Persistent among the distortions is the belief that architecture and design were central to the Bauhaus pedagogical structure and that courses in these fields encouraged a particular style of two- and three-dimensional work at the school. While its three directors were all architects by profession, architecture was taught there only after 1927, with Meyer's arrival, and it was never a required course.[6] The formal study of graphic design likewise arrived late to the school, with the establishment in 1928 of a course in Advertising

4. The exhibition ran from December 7, 1938, to January 30, 1939. On how "Gropius and Bayer designed an exhibition that was itself symbolic of exile" (288), see Karen Koehler, "The Bauhaus 1919–1928: Gropius in Exile and the Museum of Modern Art, N.Y., 1938," in *Art, Culture, and Media under the Third Reich*, ed. Richard Etlin (Chicago: University of Chicago Press, 2002), 287–315. Three decades later, Bayer designed *50 Jahre Bauhaus* (*50 Years of the Bauhaus*), which opened at the Württembergischer Kunstverein in Stuttgart before traveling through Western Europe and North America to close at the Pasadena Art Museum in 1970; the exhibition was accompanied by the immediately canonical volume *The Bauhaus: Weimar, Dessau, Berlin, Chicago*, ed. Hans M. Wingler, trans. Wolfgang Jabs and Basil Gilbert (Cambridge, MA: MIT Press, 1969).

5. In Anglophone scholarship, one early marker of scholarly revisionism was *Bauhaus Culture: From Weimar to the Cold War*, ed. Kathleen James-Chakraborty (Minneapolis: University of Minnesota Press, 2006); such efforts intensified in the years leading up to the school's centenary. Notable contributions include *Bauhaus 1919–1933: Workshops for Modernity*, ed. Barry Bergdoll and Leah Dickerman (New York: Museum of Modern Art, 2009); *Bauhaus Construct: Fashioning Identity, Discourse, and Modernism*, ed. Robin Schuldenfrei and Jeffrey Saletnik (New York: Routledge, 2009), and Elizabeth Otto, *Haunted Bauhaus: Occult Spirituality, Gender Fluidity, Queer Identities, and Radical Politics* (Cambridge, MA: MIT Press, 2019).

6. See Wallis Miller, "Architecture, Building, and the Bauhaus," in James-Chakraborty, *Bauhaus Culture*, 63–89. Meyer's work appeared in the MoMA catalog only in the shadow of Gropius's achievements: "In 1927 Gropius succeeded in bringing the Swiss Hannes Meyer to the Bauhaus as instructor in Architecture. Hannes Meyer became head of the Architecture Department and, after Gropius left in 1928, Director of the entire Bauhaus for a short period." *Bauhaus 1919–1928*, ed. Herbert Bayer, Walter Gropius, and Ise Gropius (New York: Museum of Modern Art, 1938), 112.

Design taught by Joost Schmidt, whom Meyer appointed Junior Master of Typography and Advertising.[7] While formalizing the school's commitment to the emerging field of graphic design, this course also confirmed that field's fundamental orientation toward commercial application and, specifically, that most modern mode of media communication: advertising. "If the Bauhaus started out offering instruction in the craft of the artistic print," Frederic J. Schwartz has written, "it ended giving professional education in the field of advertising. Affinities and involvement with the advertising trade were neither coincidental nor accidental, for advertising was, in many ways, central to the activities of the Bauhaus."[8] Regardless of what commodities or events were advertised by means of these designs, moreover, the enterprise being promoted was always the school itself.

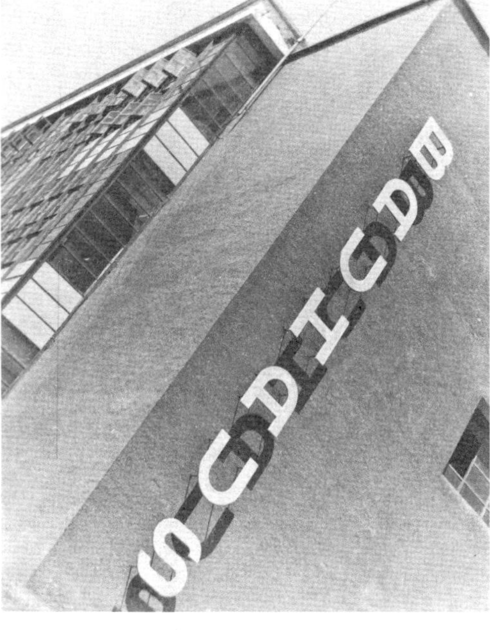

Iwao Yamawaki, *Bauhaus-Dessau*, 1930/32, vintage print. Galerie Berinson, Berlin

•

Like the Weimar Republic, the Bauhaus was founded in 1919 in the town of Weimar, the erstwhile home of Goethe, Schiller, and Nietzsche in the center of Germany. In the contemporary popular imagination, however, the school is best known for the building it moved to seven years later in the growing industrial city of Dessau, halfway between Weimar and Berlin. Designed by Gropius to house and educate its

7. Schmidt, who had studied at the Bauhaus from 1919 to 1925, taught Lettering (*Schrift*) in the Preliminary Course from 1925 to 1932 while also overseeing the technical arrangements for the Bauhaus Theater. In addition to being in charge of the Workshop for Advertising, Typography, and Printing (*Reklame, Typografie und Druckerei*) and its affiliated photography division from 1928 to 1932, he also ran the Sculpture Workshop for two years (1928–30) and taught nude drawing and figure drawing in 1929–30. See Anne Monier, "Printing, Bookbinding, Typography, and Advertising," in *The Spirit of the Bauhaus*, ed. Oliver Gabier and Anne Monier, trans. Ruth Sharman (New York: Thames and Hudson, 2018), 136–45.

8. Frederic J. Schwartz, "Utopia for Sale: The Bauhaus and Weimar Germany's Consumer Culture," in James-Chakraborty, *Bauhaus Culture*, 123.

Roman engineer Vitruvius perfects the modern, vertical water wheel

students, the Dessau Bauhaus building became something of a calling card for the school as well as for its architect. It also, literally, turned the Bauhaus name into the Bauhaus logo, with its capital letters designed by Bayer descending along its photogenic edge, as seen in a photograph that was made by Iwao Yamawaki after his move from Japan in 1930 to study at the school. Endessly pictured and disseminated in photographic form, the building quite literally spelled out on its façade how architecture and graphic design could work together to advertise and celebrate the creative and pedagogical labor taking place at the school.

Dessau had been chosen as a venue primarily because its mayor, Fritz Hesse, offered funding for the construction of the new building as well as for a series of nearby houses, also designed by Gropius, for the school's masters; these economic incentives were reinforced by the possibility of relationships with local industry, especially with Junkers Aircraft and Motor Works. The establishment and development of such relationships to industry, with all the potential commissions and commercial entanglements these might entail, were fundamental to the school's business and cultural plan in 1926; in keeping with this orientation, one central aim of the course in Advertising Design initiated two years later was to professionalize this field of study at the Bauhaus in order to strengthen potential commercial ties. Graphic design helped develop and promote the institution's corporate identity—what we might now somewhat anachronistically call the Bauhaus brand—and not only on the building's exterior. Just as crucially, graphic design work provided a lucrative and necessary means of support for the institution and for its masters and students, both during and after their time there.

Das Endziel aller bildnerischen Tätigkeit ist der Bau! Ihn zu schmücken war einst die vornehmste Aufgabe der bildenden Künste, sie waren unablösliche Bestandteile der großen Baukunst. Heute stehen sie in selbstgenügsamer Eigenheit, aus der sie erst wieder erlöst werden können durch bewußtes Mit- und Ineinanderwirken aller Werkleute untereinander. Architekten, Maler und Bildhauer müssen die vielgliedrige Gestalt des Baues in seiner Gesamtheit und in seinen Teilen wieder kennen und begreifen lernen, dann werden sich von selbst ihre Werke wieder mit architektonischem Geiste füllen, den sie in der Salonkunst verloren.

Die alten Kunstschulen vermochten diese Einheit nicht zu erzeugen, wie sollten sie auch, da Kunst nicht lehrbar ist. Sie müssen wieder in der Werkstatt aufgehen. Diese nur zeichnende und malende Welt der Musterzeichner und Kunstgewerbler muß endlich wieder eine bauende werden. Wenn der junge Mensch, der Liebe zur bildnerischen Tätigkeit in sich verspürt, wieder wie einst seine Bahn damit beginnt, ein Handwerk zu erlernen, so bleibt der unproduktive »Künstler« künftig nicht mehr zu unvollkommener Kunstübung verdammt, denn seine Fertigkeit bleibt nun dem Handwerk erhalten, wo er Vortreffliches zu leisten vermag.

Architekten, Bildhauer, Maler, wir alle müssen zum Handwerk zurück! Denn es gibt keine »Kunst von Beruf«. Es gibt keinen Wesensunterschied zwischen dem Künstler und dem Handwerker. Der Künstler ist eine Steigerung des Handwerkers. Gnade des Himmels läßt in seltenen Lichtmomenten, die jenseits seines Wollens stehen, unbewußt Kunst aus dem Werk seiner Hand erblühen, die Grundlage des Werkmäßigen aber ist unerläßlich für jeden Künstler. Dort ist der Urquell des schöpferischen Gestaltens.

Bilden wir also eine neue Zunft der Handwerker ohne die klassentrennende Anmaßung, die eine hochmütige Mauer zwischen Handwerkern und Künstlern errichten wollte! Wollen, erdenken, erschaffen wir gemeinsam den neuen Bau der Zukunft, der alles in einer Gestalt sein wird: Architektur und Plastik und Malerei, der aus Millionen Händen der Handwerker einst gen Himmel steigen wird als kristallenes Sinnbild eines neuen kommenden Glaubens.

WALTER GROPIUS.

Lyonel Feininger, woodcut; and Walter Gropius, text for the program of the State Bauhaus in Weimar, 1919

Yet the justified block of text presenting Gropius's foundational manifesto and program for the school in 1919 appears far from what the phrases "Bauhaus graphic design" and "Bauhaus typography" now usually evoke: asymmetrical layouts, sans serif type, bright primary colors, and a proliferation of lowercase letters. The woodcut by Lyonel Feininger gracing the pamphlet's cover shows a building that likewise flouts standard ideas of "Bauhaus architecture," a phrase that generally conjures up visions of prefabricated, machinic cubes—understood also as abstract white cubes, often because they had been strikingly photographed in black and white by Lux Feininger (Lyonel's son) or Lucia Moholy. By contrast, this fantasy Gothic cathedral is surmounted by three shining stars, their light blazing forth from its symmetrical spires, with bold, expressionist lines radiating vertically from earth to heaven in the background like a gathering of nearby skyscrapers. Equally foreign to received notions of Bauhaus design is the fact that image and text remain wholly separate: woodcut on the cover; manifesto and program inside.

"Architects, sculptors, painters, we all must return to the crafts [*Handwerk*]!" Gropius famously announced within this text.[9] "For there is no such thing as 'art as a profession,'" he explained. "There is no essential difference between the artist and the craftsperson [*Handwerker*]. The artist is an enhancement [*Steigerung*] of the craftsperson." No mention was made of the German word *Gestaltung*, let alone anything that might be translated more specifically as "graphic design," a phrase that would be coined in the United States three years later, in 1922, by William Addison Dwiggins.[10] And yet, by placing art and craft—aesthetic practice and utilitarian functionalism—on a continuum, and by gathering a range of artistic practices under the protective roof of architecture (or "building"), Gropius articulated a vision of creative activity that was at least nominally communal and collaborative, laying the groundwork to develop the idea of design, including graphic design, at the Bauhaus. This vision was utopian and interdisciplinary; the school would be a *Gesamtkunstwerk*, or total work of art, fostering collaboration in the glorious future that its inhabitants would, together, create.[11]

9. Walter Gropius, "Program for the Staatliche Bauhaus in Weimar" (April 1919), in Wingler, *The Bauhaus*, 31; translation slightly modified.

10. "*Gestaltung* today is usually translated as 'shaping, forming, design or arrangement,' but in the 1920s it was a charged word, meaning 'form creation.' The term was used as a reference by the avant-garde, specifically by the journal *G: Materials for Elemental Form-Creation*, to describe a post-representational form, and the process of its creation." Morgan Ridler, "The Bauhaus Wall Painting Workshop: Mural Painting to Wallpapering, Art to Product" (PhD diss., CUNY Graduate Center, 2016), 23–24.

11. On the significance of the *Gesamtkunstwerk* at the Bauhaus, see Juliet Koss, "Bauhaus Theater of Human Dolls," *The Art Bulletin* 85, no. 4 (December 2003): 724–45; reprinted in Juliet Koss, *Modernism after Wagner* (Minneapolis: University of Minnesota Press, 2010), 207–43.

As with any attempted incarnation of the *Gesamtkunstwerk*, the Bauhaus negotiated with some difficulty the relationship between individual fields of specialization and their overall integration. Gropius's schematic representation in 1922 of the school's course offerings shows something of the tricky relationship of its various elements, with the notion of building, or *Bau*, at the project's heart.[12] This was to be the symbolic goal throughout the course of study, which would proceed downwards from the top of the circle, along the descending vertical line. But with "building" unavailable as a course offering in 1922, architecture existed, essentially, as an ideal. Students began with the *Vorlehre*, or Preliminary Course; this was taught by Johannes Itten from 1919 to 1923, led jointly by Josef Albers and László Moholy-Nagy from 1923 to 1928, and overseen by Albers alone for the next five years. Oriented around a playful, hands-on exploration of materials, this course also incorporated the study of color theory (with lectures on composition by Paul Klee and Wassily Kandinsky) and life drawing (also sometimes taught by Klee).[13] Following the required Preliminary Course, the last two years of study at the Bauhaus were to be taken up with students' individually chosen (or, more often, carefully encouraged) areas of specialization engaging particular materials: stone, wood, metal, glass, etc. In between the general and specific courses students were to study more amorphous or theoretical topics, such as space, color, material, nature, construction, and composition.

Notably absent from Gropius's schematic drawing in 1922, and from the school's pedagogical framework more generally, was the history of art, architecture, or design—indeed, any historical study whatsoever. Also missing were typography and *Gestaltung*, in part because such work was not defined by its physical materials: ink and paper, or a printing press made of metal and wood. But while not initially articulated as Bauhaus disciplines, typography and graphic design became increasingly important at the school, owing partly to the presence in Weimar of Theo van Doesburg (and, occasionally but influentially, Kurt Schwitters) and, after 1923, the arrival of Moholy-Nagy, whom Gropius had hired to take over the Preliminary Course. This pivotal Bauhaus year also brought, from July through September, the Bauhaus Exhibition, which, among other things, constituted a major publicity coup for the institution and marked a shift in emphasis away from crafts and toward what Gropius called "art and technology: a new unity."[14]

12. In his English-language version of the schema in 1938, Gropius updated this central area to include both "BUILDING: practical building experience—building experiments" and "DESIGN: Building and Engineering Sciences." See Bayer et al., *Bauhaus 1919–1928*, 25.

13. "The nucleus of this basic course . . . consisted of studies on [*sic*] materials (play with various materials, from paper, plaster of Paris, wood, to glass, cane, and even briquettes, to develop a feeling for and an understanding of their specific qualities." Hans M. Wingler, "Origin and History of the Bauhaus," in Wingler, *The Bauhaus*, 4.

14. On the Bauhaus Exhibition in 1923, see Anne Monier, "The 1923 Bauhaus Exhibition: Four Years of Creativity," in Gabier and Monier, *The Spirit of the Bauhaus*, 201.

The catalog for the Bauhaus Exhibition, produced in an edition of 2,000, boasted a cover designed by Bayer and a title page by Moholy-Nagy, who was responsible also for the book's interior pages. It was here, in the first official Bauhaus publication, that Moholy-Nagy announced the existence and goals of "the New Typography," which he defined as "clear communication in its most vivid form."[15] But if the primary goal was to communicate, such communication would be more than semantic and its recipient a viewer as much as a reader; the printed page was to convey a sense of liveliness as much as any literal textual content. "A new typographic language must be created, combining elasticity, variety, and a fresh approach to the materials of printing, a language whose logic depends on the appropriate application of the processes of printing," Moholy-Nagy explained. Following the approach of the Preliminary Course, that is, the New Typography would entail a playful engagement with movable type and make use of creative methods unique to the medium of printing. But just how was "clear communication in its most vivid form" supposed to appear on the page?

Herbert Bayer, cover; and László Moholy-Nagy, title page, *Staatliches Bauhaus in Weimar 1919–1923*. Weimar and Munich: Bauhausverlag, 1923

The signature Bauhaus achievements in the realm of graphic design were the fourteen Bauhaus Books, each just over nine-by-seven inches in size, that Gropius and Moholy-Nagy conceived of in 1923 and produced with Albert Langen Publishers from 1925 to 1930, in both cloth- and paperbound editions and with print runs between 2,000 and 3,000.[16] Employing text for visual as well as semantic effect, the series made judicious use of bold graphic elements and asymmetry to formulate a new typographic language; the covers, especially, galvanize the fundamental building blocks of the centuries-old system of movable type—punctuation symbols, capital letters—to invoke not only the authors' ideas but also the works of art for which they were already well known. Meaning was also produced in hybrid form inside each book, with graphic elements producing their own insistent visual language. By aligning the school with their authors' advanced ideas—regardless of whether each author was, in fact, teaching there—the Bauhaus Books operated as a form of marketing for the institution, and it was this achievement, as much as the visual appearance of each book, that brought the series most firmly in line with the emerging notion of graphic design.

Hero of Alexandria, a Greek scientist, pioneers steam power

15. László Moholy-Nagy, "Typography as a Means of Communication," reprinted in Bayer et al., *Bauhaus 1919–1928*, 80.

16. See Adrian Sudhalter, "Walter Gropius and László Moholy-Nagy: Bauhaus Book Series, 1925–1930," in Bergdoll and Dickerman, *Bauhaus 1919–1933*, 196–99.

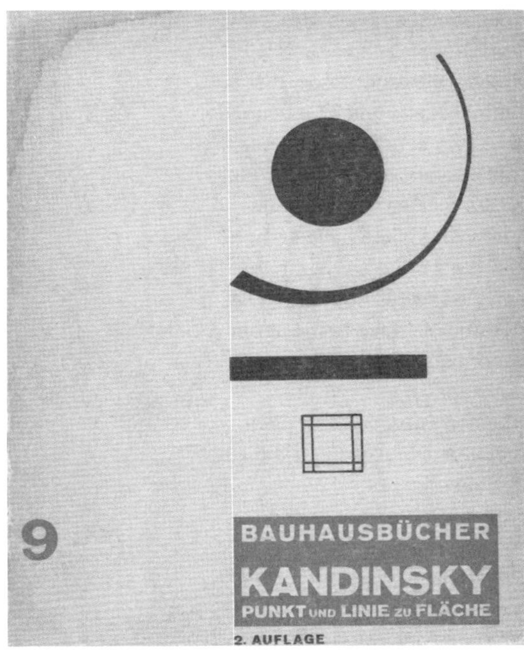

9
BAUHAUSBÜCHER
KANDINSKY
PUNKT UND LINIE ZU FLÄCHE
2. AUFLAGE

Herbert Bayer, cover for Wassily Kandinsky, *Punkt und Linie zu Fläche*, Bauhaus Book no. 9. Munich: Albert Langen Verlag, 1926

Visual and verbal communication are fused with particular elegance in Bayer's 1926 design for the cover of Kandinsky's *Point and Line to Plane* (*Punkt und Linie zu Fläche*), the ninth of the Bauhaus Books and the only one for which Bayer was fully responsible for both interior and exterior design. Four vertically stacked elements pretend to a symmetry that they do not, in fact, possess—nothing, here, is centered—to create, instead, a design of exquisite visual balance conflating representation (both figurative and symbolic) and abstraction while also testing the limits of two-dimensionality. Three elements are easily explained: the point, line, and plane of the book's title appear as a large black circle, a curved line, and a horizontal bar, respectively, with the most visually forceful placed emphatically at the top. Were it not for the fact that the curved line is thicker at one end than the other, as if gradually receding into the distance, the shapes could be considered out-of-scale punctuation marks: a period, a parenthesis, and a dash. Or, to borrow Kandinsky's words, they may represent the three building blocks of artistic creation: a "geometric point," understood as "the ultimate and most singular union of silence and speech"; a "geometric line," or "the track made by the moving point" conveying tension and direction; and a "basic plane . . . which is called upon to receive the work of art."[17] Whether viewed as a creative trio of mark making, movement, and platform or as an artistic triad of expression, tension, and background, together the marks reflect the broad continuum of literal and symbolic visual meaning discussed within the book.

Kandinsky himself might well have called the curved line on his book's cover, as he described a similar line inside its pages, "a geometric curve in ascent . . . with uniformly decreasing emphasis whereby heightened tension of ascent is attained."[18] The variation in the weight of this curve, suggesting movement as well as shifting tension and emphasis, allows Bayer's otherwise two-dimensional design to flirt with the possibility of spatial depth, as if a wayward punctuation mark had somehow slipped momentarily onto the

17. Wassily Kandinsky, *Point and Line to Plane* (1926), trans. Howard Dearstyne and Hilla Rebay (New York: Solomon R. Guggenheim Foundation, 1947), 25, 57, and 115.

18. Ibid., 89.

Bauhaus dance floor. This subtle suggestion of a raised arm, perhaps, or of the point's planetary trajectory, is echoed below by a fourth element, smaller and slighter than the other three, that initially seems too weak to support them visually and also bears no relation to traditional punctuation. Here, two concentric squares are reinforced at their corners by four smaller ones, hinting at a certain three-dimensional stability. This might be read as a tiny picture frame from which Kandinsky's point, line, and plane have escaped. Or, perhaps, the three pictographic elements are hovering in the two-dimensional air above an abstracted pedestal. Following the visual logic of the twenty-five diagrams included in the appendix of Kandinsky's book, the four components could also be seen as charting the movements of a figure in space.

In *Painting, Photography, Film* (*Malerei, Photographie, Film*), published in 1925 as the eighth of the Bauhaus Books and designed by its author, Moholy-Nagy presented what might be taken as a general theory of graphic design. Promulgating what he termed the "typophoto," an amalgam of "typography" and "photography," he suggested that printed text and printed image were both forms of writing that aimed, above all, at clear visual communication. "Typography is communication composed in type," Moholy-Nagy declared; "photography is the visual representation of what can be optically apprehended. **Typophoto is the visually most exact rendering of communication**."[19] In other words, designers should do more than integrate photographs into the layout of a page of text, something that had been possible since the 1870s with the incorporation of the photosensitive process block (or line block) technique and that, with the introduction of the halftone process in the 1880s, had become affordable for the purposes of mass circulation. Following on the development of such early twentieth-century technologies as the automatic typesetting systems that made generating and circulating mass-market publications far more economical, the aim of typophoto, Moholy-Nagy asserted in 1925, was to absorb and convey the lessons of photographic communication in the age of mass media.

Albers, too, advocated for absorbing the lessons of industrialization into the design of the printed page. The lengthy tomes of the previous century had long since given way to the telegraphic communications of the machine age, he explained in "On the Economy of Lettering Form [*Zur Ökonomie der Schriftform*]" (1926), and the printed page should likewise break free of outmoded conventions. "We have to read quickly," he insisted,

> just as we speak tersely. (Today only schools forbid students—wrongly—to speak in incomplete sentences.) Therefore flowing script can no longer dominate. Accentuated, emphasized, underlined, abbreviated,

19. László Moholy-Nagy, "Typophoto," in *Malerei, Photographie, Film* (Munich: Albert Langen, 1925); trans. Janet Seligman in Moholy-Nagy, *Painting, Photography, Film* (Cambridge, MA: MIT Press, 1969), 39; boldface in the original.

> illustrated writing will prevail. Just as in speech the message, the explanation, the exclamation, the program, the acronym, the key word, prevail. We have to be able to register a poster's message as we speed past in our car or in the tram.
> So we are distancing ourselves from the book and, accordingly, from the kind of typeface used in books. Most printed matter no longer consists of books.[20]

Oriented equally to visual and semantic communication, graphic design should in its creation, distribution, and perception reflect the twin ideals of standardization and rationalized labor.

Such an argument provided the framework for the various experimental designs Bayer produced for a purportedly universal lettering system (albeit only with the Roman alphabet); without the visual friction of serifs and capital letters, the new design would, at least in theory, convey meaning more effectively. "By working with a small number of interchangeable elements," Ellen Lupton has written, Bayer "sought to automate the design process, taking as his model the production of industrial goods."[21] Following the logic of the assembly lines that were being used for the production of Ford Motor cars, or that of the modular housing design of Gropius's Dessau-Törten Housing Estate, which began construction nearby in 1926, the "universal" lettering was intended to suggest a certain efficiency in production. It also promised a more accessible reception experience.

Herbert Bayer, design for "universal" lettering, ink and gouache on paper, 1927. Harvard Art Museums/Busch-Reisinger Museum. Gift of the artist

In 1925, the Bauhaus Printing Workshop, which for the school's first six years in Weimar had been led by Walther Klemm and Lyonel Feininger, became the Printing and Advertising Workshop [*Druck und Reklame*]. It kept this title for the duration of its years in Dessau, where it was run by two junior masters: Bayer from 1925 to 1928 and Schmidt from 1928 to 1932. Both commercially and otherwise, the workshop was one of the more successful Bauhaus endeavors; portfolios were printed there for fundraising purposes, invitations

20. Josef Albers, "Zur Ökonomie der Schriftform," in *Offset: Buch- und Werbekunst* no. 7 (1926), 395; slightly modified English version from "On the Economy of Typeface," trans. Russell Stockman, in *Josef Albers: An Anthology, 1924–1978*, ed. Laura Martínez de Guereñu, María Toledo, and Manuel Fontán (Madrid: Fundación Juan March, 2014), 209.

21. Ellen Lupton, "Herbert Bayer: Designs for 'Universal' Lettering, 1925 and 1927," in Bergdoll and Dickerman, *Bauhaus 1919–1933*, 200. "Several letterheads he designed for the Bauhaus actually deliver arguments for single-case text along their bottom edges, such as 'we write everything small in order to save time.'" (200).

to the Bauhaus parties were produced, and a range of other advertising and marketing materials were made on the premises for Bauhaus (and other) products, including for the Bauhaus Books. Both pedagogically and in relation to the creative output and professional identities of its students and masters, this work was often carried out interstitially, in that amorphous area where—increasingly with every passing decade—pedagogical vision overlaps with public relations. Interdisciplinarity and commercialism were enmeshed at the Bauhaus and, functioning essentially as the school's publicity division, the Workshop became central to its operations, both literally and symbolically, even as advertising itself came to be understood ever more broadly.[22]

Inaugurated in December 1926, Gropius's Dessau Bauhaus was forced to shut its doors less than six years later. Under the direction of Mies van der Rohe, who had taken on this leadership role in 1930, the school reopened in Berlin in October 1932, but only for a semester; teaching ceased in early April 1933 and the Bauhaus was officially dissolved that July. With the photographer Walter Peterhans taking the reins of the Printing and Advertising Workshop for these final months, the possibilities of "typophoto," Moholy-Nagy's ideal synthesis of typographic and photographic imagery carried out for the purposes of effective communication, could be explored only briefly in Germany's media capital before the establishment of the Third Reich in late March 1933. But for more than a dozen years in Weimar and in Dessau, the Bauhaus enterprise had been sustained and celebrated by a broad range of promotional material produced by Bauhäuslers who, while they would not have identified themselves as graphic designers, worked with increasing professionalism in the emerging field of graphic design.

22. "In 1927, the 'advertising department' became, along with architecture, theater, and free painting/sculpture, one of the four major areas in which instruction was offered. In the Hannes Meyer era, this instruction included lectures on economics and advertising psychology." Schwartz, "Utopia for Sale," 123.

MOHOLY'S "QUESTIONS OF INTERPRETATION"

JORDAN TROELLER

"Questions of Interpretation," published in 1971, was among the last of several texts that the Prague-born Lucia Moholy wrote on the Bauhaus in the decades following her brief affiliation with the school (1923–28). Neither student nor instructor nor staff member, Moholy belonged to the all but forgotten group of *Meisterfrauen*, as she put it, "those wives of the Bauhaus masters [in her case, László Moholy-Nagy] who had no official status and yet crucially participated in the history and reception of the Bauhaus."[1] In Moholy's case, that role was especially significant. As the school's official photographer in all but name, she helped to craft the photographic language that became vital to its public presentation: a tightly cropped, undramatic, *sachlich* portrayal of its members, objects, and architecture. Both during the school's existence and in the decades after its closure in 1933, when many in the West could no longer travel to Dessau, her photographs substituted for the absent architecture, laminating space and image in a way that profoundly shaped the writing of the building's history.

Whether Moholy knew of the historiographic weight of her images is unknown; she certainly understood photography's close relationship to the written word. She was as much a writer as she was a photographer, publishing two books, one of which was the first mass-market history of the medium, *A Hundred Years of Photography 1839–1939* (1939), and numerous articles and reviews, as well as pioneering early efforts in the field of information science. Photography was, for her, indivisible from the medium of print and transcription. She was one of the few at the Bauhaus in the early 1920s who had any training in the graphic arts, having taken classes at the Akademie für Graphische Künste und Buchgewerbe in Leipzig.[2] Such knowledge proved essential as the Bauhaus, around 1922, began incorporating images into its publicity materials. Not long after, the school published the first of the Bauhausbücher, a series edited by Moholy's husband. Given Moholy's integral role in all of László Moholy-Nagy's endeavors during their marriage, from editing his texts to fabricating his photograms,[3] it is all but fact (had anyone kept track) that Moholy shaped the designing, editing, and publishing of this book series.

Unlike many of her male colleagues at the Bauhaus, Moholy believed in the power of legibility. This marked her distance from, say, her husband's approach to graphic design. On one occasion, Moholy-Nagy even embarrassed her in front of a printer for a comment in which she espoused clarity as a design goal, responding, "One doesn't need to recognize it, it should just look good."[4] While for such artists, photography served as a means of asserting

1. Lucia Moholy, "Zur Zeit als ich mein Elternhaus verließ . . ." (Zurich, after 1974), 16–17, Lucia Moholy Papers, Bauhaus-Archiv, Berlin; all translations mine.

2. Lucia Moholy, *Marginalien zu Moholy-Nagy: Dokumentarische Ungereimtheiten / Moholy-Nagy, Marginal Notes: Documentary Absurdities* (Krefeld: Scherpe, 1972), 61.

3. Jordan Troeller, "Lucia Moholy's Idle Hands," *October* 172 (Summer 2020): 80–86.

artistic originality, for Lucia Moholy it was first and foremost a *replicative* medium, one defined by its shifting meaning in relation to a material support; the difference, for instance, between a photograph printed on gelatin silver paper versus in the context of a book. To give just one example: In reviewing Hans Maria Wingler's *Das Bauhaus*—a formative volume for the school's history and one that in Muriel Cooper's English edition would become a milestone in graphic design history—Moholy observed:

> Most of the illustrations are familiar from earlier publications. Excessive retouching, though, has changed some of them considerably: furniture that used to stand on the ground and vessels that once occupied tabletops now float in the air; lamps have left the ceiling without a trace. Cast shadows are all but gone and vibrant highlights replaced by the dull stroke of the retouching brush. One is almost compelled to forget that the Bauhaus had also accomplished something in the realm of photography![5]

Moholy's typically distanced voice here belies the fact that many of these photographs were *hers* or, in the cases in which they were taken by others, followed principles of photographic arrangement that she had developed.

As her most programmatic text on the Bauhaus's reception, "Questions of Interpretation" reflects on such photographic arrangements as not only a question of visual design but one applicable to the writing of history as a series of inclusion and exclusions. The essay deconstructs the various myths of the school as they were in the process of being formed, paying close attention to vehicles—like graphic design—which others took for granted. She paves the way for a more diversified understanding of the school's activities, dislodging an overemphasis on architecture and pointing to the school's afterlife in contemporary art, particularly through the preliminary course's integration into art school education. She also emphasizes the variety of Bauhaus photography and graphic design, correcting a historical record that for decades had equated that development solely with the work of Moholy-Nagy. "Interpretation" for her, in other words, was a question to be asked of both the written word and visual representation.

4. Lucia Moholy, "Notiz über ein Gespräch," December 16, 1927, Lucia Moholy Papers, Bauhaus-Archiv.

5. Lucia Moholy, "Hans Maria Wingler: Das Bauhaus," *Du: Kulturelle Monatsschrift* 23, no. 8 (1963): 74.

QUESTIONS OF INTERPRETATION

LUCIA MOHOLY

Some colleagues are of the opinion that the history of the Bauhaus can only begin to be written once the last of its members has passed away. I, however, hold the opposing position; that we who are still here are obligated to share as much as possible of our knowledge, our experiences, our memories, and our own questions and provisional answers, in an effort to spare those who follow from groping in the dark. What follows, then, are a few key terms that by no means lay claim to completeness.

We are still far from a single clear, encompassing picture of the situation; as one former Bauhaus member said in Berlin in 1967, "There are so many versions of the Bauhaus circulating that one is tempted to believe that there was not one but seven or eight Bauhauses."

In an effort to compare these various versions by placing them in relation to one another, I have taken several examples from the press which address the subject of the Bauhaus. In doing so, I came across widely different meanings. One finds—among headlines like "The Fanfare of the Bauhaus Has Faded Away" (*Schweizer Werkbund Kommentare*), on the one hand, and "The Bauhaus Idea Is as Timely as Ever" (*Stuttgarter Zeitung*), on the other hand—the sober assertion that "the Bauhaus has shifted from being viewed in a vaguely romanticist light to an historically factual [*sachlich*] one" (*Schwäbische Donauzeitung*).

In many circles, the notion that the Bauhaus was a school of architecture still persists. The name itself may have in part projected (or even still projects) this power of suggestion; another reason for it may lie in the school's founding manifesto, which implored a "new guild of craftsmen [*Handwerker*]" to erect "the building of the future." The collection of documents published in 1962 by Hans M. Wingler and titled *The Bauhaus* has revived the memory of that manifesto. "Gropius builds his last cathedral," read accounts of the opening of the Thomas Glassworks in Amberg, Oberplatz, in summer 1970.[1]

That the initial concept found a strong resonance, albeit one that could not be quickly realized, was due to the nature of the situation at the time. But who (except perhaps those immediately concerned) was (or even could have been) in a position to grasp the manifold forces of the post–World War I period, which would come together to shape the school's everyday existence? Quite a few may have been astonished to read Otto Stelzer writing in 1968: "At that time, Gropius had acted tactfully, and he was the man for it. The whole world spoke of *Handwerk* and of the spirit of the architectural collectives [*Bauhütte*]; that was the fashion of the day, and such language especially found favor among the conservatives within the

1. The Glassworks in Amberg was Walter Gropius's last built work, designed with his Boston architectural firm The Architects Collaborative (TAC) and completed in 1970, one year after his death.—*Trans.*

finance ministries. It was actually the conservatives who applauded the founding manifesto's sentence: 'Architects, sculptors, painters, we must all return to the crafts [*Handwerk*]!'"[2] Such a reading must have been authorized, for soon thereafter one could hear Gropius saying similar things on television. A tragic legacy in the last year of his life? To this, Stelzer offers the answer: "It is easy to establish that a man like Gropius never had such a 'return' in mind, for in 1916 there already existed a draft of the manifesto and it by no means concerns a revival of *Handwerk*."[3]

Faith in the manifesto was so firm and sure that soon thereafter the Sommerfeld House in Berlin-Dahlem, built in 1921 by Walter Gropius and Adolf Meyer in a prairie style with abundant ornamental wood carvings, was praised as a "document of the Bauhaus doctrine" (G. C. Argan). The same author, in advancing the opinion that industrial design confers "mythical significance" upon an object, wrote in 1951 that Bauhaus wallpaper was to be understood as the "bearer of the new conception of space [*Raumidee*]" and Bauhaus lamps as "an absolute identification of light and space." Much clearer was Walter Gropius's own formulation, as reported from Argentina in 1960: "Architecture should be in everything,

2. I have left "*Handwerk*" in the original, because "craft" does not connote the range of activity signified by the term, which includes the industrial trades. Bakers and bricklayers, for instance, were also considered *Handwerker*, along with artisans, painters, and architects. For an expanded discussion, see Stefan Muthesius, "*Handwerk/Kunsthandwerk*," *Journal of Design History* 11, no. 1 (1998): 85–95.—*Trans.*

3. One could have added here: "as the conservatives understood it," which is the subtext of Stelzer's quote (and what Moholy means by "tragic" in the preceding sentence). To understand this better, one would need to go back to Gropius's drafts for the founding manifesto, which can be found in Volker Wahl, ed., *Das Staatliche Bauhaus in Weimar: Dokumente zur Geschichte des Instituts 1919–1926* (Cologne: Böhlau, 2009). To read these texts, it is crucial to grasp that although the far left and the conservative right in Germany at this time both invoked the term "*Handwerk*," each side had a very different conception of what this meant—whether it would be used to stoke the resentment of small tradesmen who had been left behind in an industrializing Germany, or whether it would be used in a revolutionary sense, as it was in the case of the Arbeitsrat für Kunst (in whose journal Gropius's draft appeared), as the basis for a whole-scale transformation of labor (from alienated to unalienated) as part of a Communist reorganization of everyday life.—*Trans.*

from a teacup to a city plan."[4] Myth and reality [*Sachlichkeit*] often compensated for one another's shortfalls.

In circles further afield, the Bauhaus embodies today, as it did then, "the advent of modern architecture" (*Nationalzeitung Basel*), even though it is well known that during its first eight years it had no architecture program. All that it had were lectures on statics and the history of architecture, and Gropius's architectural firm offered students bits of information and, now and again, the possibility of collaboration on his private architectural projects. The designation "Architectural Department of the State Bauhaus in Weimar," in volumes 1 and 3 of the Bauhaus Books, which were assembled in 1924 and published in 1925, is to be attributed to the anticipatory character [*Ungereiftheit*] of the terminology back then.

The first regular department of architecture and planning was established in 1927. To lead it, the Swiss architect Hannes Meyer was appointed. Meyer continued to direct the workshop when he led the school from 1928 to 1930, just as Mies van der Rohe did in his role as the Bauhaus's third director. As such, the assertions often made about the Bauhaus with respect to housing construction and urban planning, as well as architectural efficiency and industrialization, are at best descriptions of the later Bauhaus—if one can ascribe them at all to a single site. A more accurate picture, though, is that they were part of an incredible movement, propelled on many sides and coming into being in numerous places almost simultaneously.

What also remains little known today is that the photography course at the Bauhaus was first established only in 1929. And yet one often hears it mentioned with reference to Moholy-Nagy. That does not correspond to the facts. What is correct is that, as Müller-Brockmann put it, at the Bauhaus Moholy-Nagy "promoted an engagement with typography and photography as a medium for both artistic and commercial statements," and also that, as Wingler writes, "Moholy-Nagy's photographic experiments characteristic of the Dessau period precipitated similar endeavors." But Moholy-Nagy neither established nor headed the photography course. Indeed, at the time of its founding, he, along with Gropius and others, had already left the Bauhaus. It was Walter Peterhans who oversaw the photography course from 1929 until 1933. And those are not the only inaccuracies and contradictions that ought to be set straight.

In early 1928, Gropius resigned his position as director. It is erroneous to speak of a resignation in 1925 (*Stuttgarter Zeitung*) or a "dismissal" in 1933 (*Zeitgemäße Form*). Before he came to Harvard in 1937, he was in England from 1934 to 1937—not from "1937 to 1940," as the Sunday *Times* quoted him as claiming. But even at Harvard, in his immediate proximity, the publication *Building Harvard* appeared in 1964, which described him as the director of the Bauhaus in the 1920s and early '30s (". . . the famous Bauhaus in Germany which Gropius led in the 1920s and early 1930s"). It is quite likely that a measure of uncertainty here played a role, one that concerned the dates of the Bauhaus's duration, and

4. Gropius's quote is in English in the original.—*Trans.*

was triggered through the title of the book that was published in the US in 1938: *Bauhaus 1919–1928.*

Apart from that, unconfirmed interpretations circulate as to who among those involved "belong to some extent to the group of founders" (Grohmann); who occupied the position of assistant director at any given point; which teachers were "discovered" by whom; and who was "accepted" or "rejected" by whom (Schreyer). There are voices that count El Lissitzky and Theo van Doesburg among the Bauhaus Masters (Farner); and others that as well regard Malevich and Mondrian as affiliated members, "combatants that stood in close relation to the Bauhaus" (Stelzer). In contrast, there is a tendency among former members of the Bauhaus to underestimate the influence of the Russians and the Dutch. Also underestimated is (and has been) the role of Hannes Meyer, even though his name has resurfaced through the books by Wingler and Schnaidt.[5] In the entry on the Bauhaus in the *Encyclopedia of the Arts* of 1966, the second director goes unnamed—an omission that is, of course, mimicked by the press.

Even though systematic instruction in the field of architecture was not practiced until the late Bauhaus period, it has become routine to use the phrase "Bauhaus architecture" with reference to the Bauhaus before and during 1928. The tendency that appeared on the part of the public to group together all products developed at the Bauhaus—including dishware, lamps, fabric, wallpaper, furniture, printed matter, etc.—as "Bauhaus style" met the subsequent retort that there was not and could not be a single Bauhaus style; such a style, it was believed, would have meant a "return to academic stagnation, into the very state of inertia that is inimical to life and against which the Bauhaus was called into being" (volume 12 of the Bauhaus book series).[6]

The use of the expression "Bauhaus architecture," however, has remained unchallenged, even though—or perhaps because—it lends itself to various meanings. From the start, the very concept "Bauhaus" has been open to interpretation. Even to the initiated, it could be an idea, a program, a method, an institute, and/or a building. How, then, should the outsider be expected to differentiate the various meanings? Even back then it seems to have been tempting to replace an idea or program, whose meaning was not clear, with the realized building, the B a u h a u s—as it read in large letters, visible from a distance—and to allow oneself to be lulled by the belief that the "building of the future" had already been erected. It

5. Claude Schnaidt, ed., *Hannes Meyer: Bauten, Projekte, und Schriften/ Buildings, Projects, and Writings* (Teufen: Niggli, 1965). Hans M. Wingler's *Das Bauhaus: Weimar, Dessau, Berlin, Chicago* (1969), published in an English edition by the MIT Press that same year, includes a section of documents relating to Meyer's tenure.—*Trans.*

6. Walter Gropius, *Bauhausbauten Dessau* (Munich: Albert Langen, 1930). Fifty-four of Moholy's photographs appear in this book.—*Trans.*

may also be that the confident tone of Walter Gropius's resignation letter to the magistrate of the city of Dessau was meant to portray the matter in a positive light. Gropius went; the building remained.

The press later granted a substitutive role to the Gropius-designed buildings in Dessau, which were carried out as private commissions by his firm (the workshops were involved only in the interior furnishings), a role that lives on in the description "Bauhaus architecture" and one that "lends its name to an entire direction in architecture" (*Tagesanzeiger*). In his account "The Dessau Bauhaus Today" (*Der Monat*), James Marston Fitch wrote that his "perception of the Gropius architecture" (note that he did not say Bauhaus architecture) "was formed through a specific selection of original photographs"—he called them "classical views"; one with which the "Bauhaus of today" was no longer identical.

The misguided notion of the primacy of architecture—"architecture was the dominant motive" (*Paris This Week*)—was somewhat reined in by the traveling exhibition of 1968, *Fifty Years of Bauhaus*. This resulted from the fact that many of the architectural photographs on display represented works from the post-Bauhaus period and often had little to do with the years between 1919 and 1933. With this section, as well as several others, an effort had to be made to justify the exhibition's title. This in turn led some journalists to give more weight to the exhibition that represented "the work and accomplishments of the Bauhaus in the period from 1919 to 1969" (*Neue Zürcher Zeitung*), or the "fifty-year existence of the Bauhaus" (*Die Zeit*). The exhibition's title was neither correct nor even felicitously chosen; it suggested a continuity that did not correspond to the actual given facts. In Germany, there were years included, which had prompted Bauhaus members— and for some even forced them—to abandon what had once been "Bauhaus" and, sooner or later, to search for a new homeland. Whether one can claim, as happened at the opening in Stuttgart, that under these circumstances the Bauhaus represents "the German contribution to the culture and civilization of the world in this century" (*Staatsanzeiger für Baden-Württemberg*) is questionable.

The recent press on the Bauhaus has also overemphasized the fine arts. At times the Bauhaus has been portrayed in such a way that one might think it was first and foremost a meeting place for painters, who had retreated to an environment in which they were able to live their art undisturbed, not unlike artist colonies such as Worpswede. At its inaugural exhibition in 1962, the Museum of the Twentieth Century in Vienna [today the MUMOK] described the position of artists at the Bauhaus as follows: "With their work, the Bauhaus masters demonstrated that no damage can be done to the 'pure and eternally artistic' [*Rein- und Ewig-Künstlerischen*] when it renounces its isolated genius. . . . and admits objective laws."[7] Within the sphere of these objective laws, artists found themselves

7. The speaker refers to Kandinsky's phrase in his 1911 treatise *Über das Geistige in der Kunst* (*On the Spiritual in Art*).—*Trans.*

together "in the camaraderie of the Bauhaus" (Haftmann); in their studios they remained, each to his own, a solitary actor [*Einzelgänger*]. They had brought with them that which made them artists; they did not develop it at the Bauhaus, even if the relative security of existence and, above all, the shared pedagogical ideas within the group proved to be of great significance for their personal development.

Among the champions of the "isolated genius," there was, however, no shortage of bemoaning that the artists had shifted from their own (fine art) work to collaboration in the Bauhaus experiment. The opposite has also been insinuated; that the Bauhaus's pedagogical success is due to the fact "that artists with great teaching abilities were at the same time able to render their own art teachable" (*Werk*). Here lies a fundamental misunderstanding.

The oft-encountered description "Bauhaus painters" is also misleading, for it attempts to place a number of disparate artistic personalities under a single integer and thus define the Bauhaus in terms of painting. At times, Bauhaus masters are mentioned in the same breath as the "Blue Rider" (*Pictures on Exhibit*); and on occasion one also comes across the set phrase "Mondrian and the Bauhaus" (*Kunstnachrichten*).

In connection with an exhibition in London, the press reported on the "romantic trait in Bauhaus art" (*National Zeitung Basel*) and saw the "Periclean power of this modern Weimar classicism" (*Frankfurter Rundschau*), while *The New Statesman* wrote, in a cool, considered voice: "What have such things to do with the Bauhaus . . . whose main achievement *qua* school was not in the field of painting at all."[8]

Instead of mitigating this tendency to emphasize the fine arts at the Bauhaus, the traveling exhibition effectively intensified it. A comparison of works by the relevant masters makes sense, of course, and it was understandable that one also wished to exhibit works of their students there. Important here was the relationship between the fine arts, on the one hand, and instruction plus workshop training, on the other hand. The relatively large number of fine-art works on display (in Stuttgart) could have led to a shift in emphasis regarding this relationship. But because a portion of the critique was a priori inclined to focus on the painting, it led—as it had already on earlier occasions—to debates on whether the pedagogical methods at the Bauhaus had been devised to train a new generation of painters. "Of course not," declared Reyner Banham, already in 1962, "that was not the intention."[9] But in 1968, the question was again of interest for many, for it allowed one to make conclusions about why the traveling exhibition was presented the way it was.

Yet, in a completely different sense, one can credit the exhibition for having made clear the difference between art and work done as part of the workshop training [*Werklehre*]. Proponents of the Primary Structures, Minimal Art, Art of the Real, Land Art, and

8. Statement left in English in the original.—*Trans.*

9. Statement left in English in the original.—*Trans.*

the like have repeatedly positioned these experiments as derived from the Bauhaus or "those affiliated with the Bauhaus"—a misconstruction that has been partly corrected through the thorough study of the preliminary course at the Bauhaus. Characterized by Gropius as the "artery of the Bauhaus's collective work" and demonstrated by the exhibition (in reference somewhat to contemporary pedagogy), the preliminary course undertook experimentations, studies, exercises, "études," all aimed at an engagement with form and color, structure and texture, surfaces and materials, fabric and interior space, balance and tension, without by any means claiming to produce art. "Investigation and not creation," as a lecture on the BBC put it, and "a shaking sifter [*Schüttelsieb*] of talent, a trial that determined the right choice of workshop," read the *Stuttgarter Zeitung*.[10]

Whether folded or bent, stretched or crumpled, cut up or perforated, transparent or opaque, colored or pale, layered or in rows, floating, static, or in motion, that which yesterday and today seeks to address the viewer as art is often guided by the achievements of the 1920s, which, for completely different ends, grew out of the preliminary studies from both the early and late Bauhaus. "It is most interesting," read an opinion in the *Frankfurter Allgemeine Zeitung*,

> that this part of the Bauhaus, the preliminary course, notably took on a life of its own in Paris. Op art, Schöffer, Vasarély, Agam, Takis (one should also add here Bridget Riley)—they all have elevated that transitional point as the end goal. They have made an Absolute of what in Weimar and Dessau was mere pedagogy.

An English cynic said: "That Op is op no one can doubt; but is Op art?"[11]

According to the Stuttgart catalog, the exhibition planners allowed for nearly 300 works of fine art by Bauhaus members; that number was later reduced. Works listed as "Bauhaus graphics" were grouped together in a separate catalog. "But why?" asked a London critic. The answer can be deduced from H. M. Wingler's introduction to the newly published portfolio of works. Although an exhibition prospectus from 1963 spoke of "works from the graphic workshop of the Staatliche Bauhaus," clarifying who belonged in which group, two years later, one read that "technical realization in the printing workshop is regarded . . . as a criterion of membership in Bauhaus graphics . . . To include 'foreign' works as Bauhaus graphics is legitimate, because by accepting any artistic sketch for printing, one is always making an ideological decision." Thus, on the walls of the Stuttgart exhibition, among the familiar Bauhaus names, one could find prints by Archipenko, Baumeister, Beckmann, Boccioni, Carrà, Chagall, Chirico, Goncharova, Grosz, Heckel, Jawlensky, Kirchner, Kokoschka, Léger, Larionov,

10. The BBC lecture topic and the list of art movements in the 1960s earlier in the paragraph are all in English in the original.—*Trans.*

11. Again, quote in English in the original. It is worth underscoring that the interjection on Riley—the only woman named in the list—is from Moholy (and not the cited author).—*Trans.*

Marcoussis, Mondrian, Pechstein, Pampolini, Rohlfs, Schmidt-Rottluff, Severini—all of whom never belonged to the Bauhaus community. It then becomes clear why these names necessitated their own catalog.

It would seem that, apart from all else, the magic of major names had proved irresistible. On the occasion of a 1964 show in Frankfurt, one spoke of Dexel, Michel, and Molzahn as "devotees [*Zugewandten*]," and on one page of the previously mentioned publication of the Harvard University Information Center, under the section "From the Bauhaus," artistic contributions by Arp and Mirò were named along with those by Albers and Bayer.

Notwithstanding the fact that the press has done everything conceivable to render accessible the "legendary idea that goes by the name Bauhaus" (*FAZ*), it has remained, to this day, essentially impossible to grasp. The role of design, too, which had a clearly practical function as craft [*Handwerk*] and as industrial design, has suffered a loss in conceptual clarity over the years. What has endured is the summary formula: "The cradle of all that today purports to be super-modernist lies with the Bauhaus."

A consciousness of the meaning and significance of this prehistory has hardly surfaced. Those who might have shed light on the matter or themselves espoused similar ideas are sometimes named but often overlooked. Julius Posner, professor at the Hochschule für Bildende Künste, Berlin [today the Berlin University of the Arts—*trans.*], has expressed himself on various occasions with respect to the subject of historical relationships, especially on the Werkbund and the Bauhaus, and has incited controversy with such remarks. Significant for these connections were the exhibitions of the Neue Sammlung in Munich in 1969 and 1971, where one could see impressive examples of functional design from the nineteenth century. In a 1966 lecture on "Education through Manual Making [*Erziehung durch manuelles Tun*]," sponsored by the Bauhaus-Archiv, Otto Stelzer said that the Bauhaus was "not so much the birthplace of entirely new, revolutionary ideas as it was a kind of gathering receptacle for concepts that were already long in existence." "In fact," he added, "Bauhaus ideas have a long prehistory." Already at the inauguration of the Bauhaus-Archiv in 1960, H. M. Wingler spoke of the "manifestation of a historical development that spans more than a century"; and in his foreword to a 1966 publication of Gottfried Semper's collected writings, he asserted that the journal *Science, Industry, and Art* of 1852 has recently often been viewed "as the incunabulum of pursuits that then peaked in the Bauhaus."

Accompanying these historical events has been the effort to evoke a future. "The Bauhaus lives on, radiantly ascending to the heavens, even at the most magnificent gate that ever admitted entry into a continent, even in New York," wrote Benno Reifenberg in 1965. "One would have to go back to Cluny and the determination of highly educated monks in the tenth century, in order to find parallels to a similar occurrence. They held that next to the salvation of the soul was a secular order, and accordingly they set their aims high, almost as far as the regime of the Church. . . . The fascination of the name Bauhaus stems from faith in a reforming power, one that architecture does not intend to relinquish."

Less "heavens-ascendent" but also professing a vision of an architectural future was the socially critical thesis advanced by Roland Günter that "the single true revolution in architecture, that of the Bauhaus, sought effectively to emancipate man in a world without emblems and not simply to raise him in the social hierarchy, but this revolution in essence has not yet been carried out, because the structure of our society has only become mobile, not anti-hierarchical." Here, too, we see an attempt at equating Bauhaus architecture and architecture in general with one another.

When one speaks of the historical Bauhaus, H. M. Wingler said in Chicago in 1967, one must realize that it can be divided into four stages, each of which came to an end, respectively, in 1923, 1928, 1930, and 1933. The position of anyone conversant on the subject of the Bauhaus, he went on, will be determined by the particular stage on which the person chooses to focus. As a provisional basis for discussion, such a division may be useful. As a point of departure, however, for a more comprehensive evaluation, it is inappropriate; it reinforces the tendency to pit individual phases against one another and to lump the majority of successes that have been attributed to the Bauhaus into one or another of these stages. In this way, one does not even get close to the heart of the Bauhaus phenomenon, which all in all had a total of only fourteen years at its disposal; there can be no question of "twenty-four active years" (*New York Times*).

Debates on the historical Bauhaus, "laboratory and mission in one," are not without tension, pathos, and emotion; traces of esoterica are also to be found. One would have to shake loose from such restrictions if one wants to be in the position to convey objective criteria [*Wertmaßstäbe*].

With this ad hoc selection of quotes from the press, I have tried to demonstrate that there is still considerable work to be done: comparative studies of extant literature; a critical assessment of individual works; a close reading of the manifestos; analyses of environmental conditions, including the personal and interpersonal dynamics—all this and much more, in addition to an estimate of achievements and results, constitute some of the basic prerequisites for a legitimately valid interpretation of the Bauhaus.

The subject of a Bauhaus "succession [*Nachfolge*]" here has remained unconsidered.

—*Translated by Jordan Troeller*

Originally published as "Fragen der Interpretation" in *Bauhaus und Bauhäusler: Bekenntnisse und Erinnerungen*, ed. Eckhard Neumann (Stuttgart: Hallwag, 1971), 169–78. This translation first appeared in *October* 172 (Summer 2020): 125–34.

THE CRUX OF COORDINATION: VISUAL COMMUNICATION AT THE HOCHSCHULE FÜR GESTALTUNG, ULM

CRAIG BUCKLEY

In the half-century since its controversial dissolution, the stories told about the Hochschule für Gestaltung in Ulm, Germany (1953–68), have achieved near-mythic status. Their emphasis has also shifted significantly. Beginning in the 1970s, architectural historian and critic Kenneth Frampton hailed the school not for any particular objects it produced but for its "extraordinarily high level of critical consciousness" regarding design's position in capitalist societies.[1] In the 1980s and '90s, extensively illustrated catalogs edited by former teachers and students advocated for the ongoing relevance of the "Ulm model" to design training by providing a more complete and nuanced picture of the school's teaching and production.[2] More recently, historians have excavated the school's complex financial and political relationships during the Federal Republic of Germany.[3] Historians of graphic design, for their part, have regarded the production of the Ulm school chiefly as a branch of Swiss International–style typography, characterized by asymmetrical layouts, generous use of blank space, and mathematical grid systems.[4] Today, however, the school's legacy is more likely to be gauged through the lens of our digital devices. Such claims hinge on the role of Braun electronics—objects whose design principles were rooted in the Ulm school's teachings—as models for Apple's design program under Jonathan Ive.[5] Thus a review of the most recent exhibition to explore the school's legacy summarized it simply as "the school that linked the Bauhaus and the iPhone."[6]

1. Kenneth Frampton, "A Propos Ulm: Curriculum and Critical Theory," *Oppositions* 3 (1974): 17–36. See also "hfg ulm: ein Rückblick," a special issue of the Swiss journal *Archithese* in 1975.

2. To cite only the major books and catalogs, not the numerous articles: see Herbert Lindinger, *Hochschule für Gestaltung Ulm: Die Moral der Gegenstände* (Berlin: Ernst und Sohn, 1987) [translated as *Ulm Design: The Morality of Objects* (Cambridge, MA: MIT Press, 1991)]; Eva von Seckendorff, *Die Hochschule für Gestaltung Ulm* (Marburg: Jonas Verlag, 1989); and Dagmar Rinker and Marcela Quijano, eds., *Ulmer Modelle, Modelle nach Ulm* (Ostfildern: Hatje Cantz, 2003).

3. See the comprehensive volume by René Spitz, *Hfg Ulm: The View Behind the Foreground: The Political History of the Ulm School of Design* (Stuttgart: Axel Menges, 2002). Most recently, see Peter Kapos, "Art and Design: The Ulm Model," http://www.ravenrow.org/texts/84/.

4. See, for instance, the passing references in Philip Meggs, *A History of Graphic Design* (New York: Wiley, 1980), 320, 323; Stephen Eskilson, *Graphic Design: A New History* (London: Laurence King, 2007), 320; Richard Hollis, *Graphic Design: A Concise History* (New York: Thames and Hudson, 1994).

5. See Jonathan Ive, "Foreword," in *Dieter Rams: As Little Design as Possible*, ed. Sophie Lovell (London: Phaidon, 2011).

While the design of electronic devices played an important role at Ulm, any reading that values the school's legacy solely for its contribution to a genealogy of the iPhone remains utterly reductive. Nor can work that emerged from the school's classrooms and workshops be adequately read on stylistic grounds alone. If the Ulm school was an important relay between the Weimar-era Bauhaus and today's digital design culture, a key place to begin complicating that history is the epistemological shift taking place in its pedagogy, notably the school's turn to formal-mathematical procedures drawn from topology and information theory, a turn that linked student design exercises to emerging network and computer sciences.

The turn to such procedures underpinned a shift from graphic design toward the much broader concept of visual communication. Graphic design was to be but a part of a broader array of visual-communication techniques, which the school understood as a self-critical cultural activity within an industrial mass society. To graphic design's investment in paper-based practices such as typography, layout, and printing, the Ulm school added photography, exhibition design, film, and television, an array of techniques that was to be approached as "unified field."[7] Visual communication marked a new emphasis on the eye, yet this optical orientation did not mean a flattening of design to two dimensions. Increasingly it meant a spatialization of the department's projects, and a refusal to firmly separate work in two dimensions from work in three dimensions. While the school produced compelling typography, books, and posters, its most consequential graphic work was in designs for exhibitions, televised animations, wayfinding systems, computer interfaces, and identity programs. Two key transformations accompany the turn to visual communication. Two- or three-dimensional point grids, or rasters, took on a central role as a means of exerting design control and for

Traveling exhibition of the HfG Ulm, Ulm Museum and Kornhaus Ulm, 1963. Conception and exhibition design: Herbert Lindinger, Claude Schnaidt, Tonci Pelikan

6. See "The School That Linked the Bauhaus to the iPhone," https://www.phaidon.com/agenda/design/articles/2016/october/13/the-school-that-linked-the-bauhaus-to-the-iphone/. For another recent example of this narrative, see Nicholas Fox Weber, *iBauhaus: The iPhone as the Embodiment of Bauhaus Ideals and Design* (New York: Knopf, 2020).

7. See the description of the Visual Communication department in *Ulm: Vierteljahresbericht der Hochschule für Gestaltung, Ulm* 1 (October 1958): 20.

conceptualizing the kind of freedom available to designer and user alike. Along with the raster there emerged a different set of ideas about the designer: He or she was no longer to be understood as an originator of form but as a *coordinator.* As a coordinator, the designer mediated between processes of production and consumption and was positioned in the middle of a complex web of human, material, semiotic, and technical relationships. This rethinking of grid systems on the one hand and the designer's role on the other bears closer examination for the critical questions it raises about the historical intersections of graphic design, architecture, and digital media today.

The Ulm School and the Post-WWII Situation in Germany

The Ulm school was conceived in relation to a central problem facing postwar Germany: the need for a process of cultural reeducation in order for the country to become a stable democratic republic.[8] Led by Inge Scholl and Otl Aicher, the project for the Ulm school grew from Scholl's desire to create an institution in memory of her siblings, Hans and Sophie Scholl, who had been executed by the Nazi regime in 1943 for their role in the subversive publishing and graffiti campaigns of the White Rose resistance group.[9] First active in the reestablishment of Ulm's *Volkshochschule*, Scholl went on to envision a more specialized school devoted to democratic communications, with courses in journalism, radio, and film and additional instruction in photography, advertising, industrial design, and urban planning.[10] Scholl proved adept at securing the support of occupying American forces for the project while deftly positioning the future school not as a branch of the official reeducation initiatives but as an extension of the democratic thinking found in wartime resistance circles.[11] By the early 1950s, the plan for a school devoted to communication with an added interest in design had shifted to one for a school of design with an emphasis on questions of politics and communication. Such a turn, as cultural historians Paul Betts and Hans-Jürgen Sembach have argued, reflected the degree to which everyday objects were infused with sociopolitical significance in post-WWII Germany, a context in which design was understood as part of a project of cultural reparation, or *Wiedergutmachung.*[12]

8. The foundation of the Ulm school has been examined in great detail; this account stresses only the most pertinent concerns. For the most extensive accounts, see von Seckendorf and Spitz.

11. Scholl, who was not quite thirty at the time, persuaded US High Commissioner John McCloy to commit a million Deutschmarks to the school. See Lindinger, *Ulm Design*, 18–19.

9. On the White Rose Group, see Inge Scholl, *The White Rose, Munich 1942–1943* (Middletown, CT: Wesleyan University Press, 1983).

10. Originating in the nineteenth century, *Volkshochschulen* were nonprofit schools for adult and continuing education, an alternative to universities and trade schools. The initial vision for the Ulm school was also informed by the writer Hans Werner Richter, who left the project in 1950 as Max Bill became more involved. For an outline of the initial vision, see the "Yellow Program" reprinted in Spitz, 48–52 and 72–73.

Despite its reputation for rigor, even dogmatism, the school was never monolithic but was animated by internal tensions and contradictions.[13] These tensions remain key to thinking through Ulm's pedagogy in the 1950s and '60s. As a privately managed (yet in part publicly funded) *Hochschule*, or college, the Ulm school was independent from the state university system and was free to determine its teachers and curriculum, yet this autonomy came at the price of continual insecurity about funding. The foundation that oversaw the school was envisioned and directed by a woman, yet the school's teachers and student body were overwhelmingly male.[14] The school's teachers and students were committed to developing models for a democratic, anti-fascist industrial culture, yet the institution was charged with being an elitist cloister detached from everyday life in Germany.[15] The school cultivated working and financial relationships with some of the largest West German corporations, yet its teachers also developed influential critiques of what they termed "neo-capitalism" and its consumer culture.

The creation of the Department of Visual Communication was itself a product of such tensions. Scholl and Aicher had initially recruited the Swiss artist, designer, and architect (and former Bauhausler) Max Bill as director of the school and architect of its campus.[16] Bill saw the Ulm school as a continuation of the Bauhaus project in which the creation of significant form entailed a transformation of patterns of living, making design akin to aesthetic

12. Klaus-Jürgen Sembach, "Heimat—Glaube—Glanz," in *Die Fünfziger Jahre: Heimat Glaube Glanz: Der Stil eines Jahrzehnts*, ed. Michael Koetzle, Klaus-Jürgen Sembach, and Klaus Schölzel (Munich: Callwey, 1998), 8–9. Cited by Paul Betts, *The Authority of Everyday Objects: A Cultural History of West German Industrial Design* (Berkeley: University of California Press, 2004), 5.

13. Reyner Banham recalls a school governed by a "cast-iron set of categorical imperatives"; see "HfG Ulm in Retrospect," in Lindinger, *Ulm Design*, 57–59.

14. Roughly fifteen percent of the student body at Ulm were women. The most comprehensive account can be found at http://www.frauen-hfg-ulm.de/index.html.

15. The national magazine *Der Spiegel* painted an unsympathetic picture of a "Cold War in the design cloister" in "Auf dem Kuhberg," *Der Spiegel* 12 (1963): 71–75. For an analysis that unpacks the relative isolation of Ulm, see Anna-Maria Meister, "Radical Remoteness: The HfG Ulm as Institution of Dissidence," in *Architecture and the Paradox of Dissidence*, ed. Inez Weizman (London: Routledge, 2014), 89–01.

16. Bill brought historic ties to the Bauhaus, but he was also a leading voice in the international Concrete art movement. As a designer and architect associated with the Swiss Werkbund, he played a prominent role in advocating for a renewed link between moral authority and good design through the influential traveling exhibition *Die gute Form* at the end of the 1940s. For a recent overview of his design campaigns, see *Max Bill's View of Things, Die Gute Form: An Exhibition, 1949* (Zurich: Lars Müller, 2015).

self-determination. Bill conceived of Ulm's foundation course in Visual Design along the lines of the one he had experienced at the Bauhaus in the 1920s, and he invited former Bauhaus teachers—including Josef Albers, Helène Nonné-Schmidt, Walter Peterhans, and Johannes Itten—to lead this course in its first two years.[17] In describing his hopes for the new school, whose campus he had begun designing in 1953, he did not hesitate to frame its mission as "turning life into a work of art."[18] Yet disagreements over the curriculum led to Bill's resignation less than two years after the official opening of the school in 1955. A younger generation of teacher-designers—including Aicher, the Argentine painter and theorist Tomás Maldonado, and the Dutch architect and industrial designer Hans Gugelot—fundamentally reorganized the curriculum.[19] The establishment of Visual Communication as a department was part of this reorganization and was bound up with a growing skepticism about the Bauhaus's pedagogical legacy.

Lessons in the Foundation Course at the HfG, 1955.

In choosing the anglophone term *communication* rather than the German term *Gestaltung*, or more professional terms such as *Grafik* or *Gebrauchsgrafik*, the new rectors chose a word that was hardly self-evident to German speakers. In the late 1950s, Aicher recalled, a group of politicians on an inspection tour of the school asked suspiciously whether the term *Kommunikation* was linked to communism or communion.[20] The Dessau Bauhaus had engaged emergent mass media through its Printing and Advertising

17. For a detailed account of the foundation course and the emergence of raster assignments, see William S. Huff, "Grundlehre at the HfG, with a Focus on 'Visuelle Grammatik,'" in Rinker and Quijano, *Ulmer Modelle*, 172–97. On the Visual Communication department and its students, see Barbara Stempel and Susanne Eppinger Curdes, *Rückblicke: Die Abteilung Visuelle Kommunikation an de HfG Ulm 1953–1968* (Ulm: club off ulm, 2010).

18. Max Bill, "Education and Design," in *Architecture Culture 1943–1968*, ed. Joan Ockman (New York: Rizzoli, 1993), 162.

19. Aicher was joined in the Visual Communication Department in 1957–58 by Anthony Froshaug, a typographer trained at London's Central School of Art and Design, and Friedrich Vordemberge-Gildewart, a Dutch painter and designer with ties to the Concrete art movement. In the 1960s the international teaching staff included Herbert Lindinger (Austria), Herbert Kapitzki (Poland), Kōhei Sugiura (Japan), Tomás Gonda (Argentina), and William S. Huff (US).

20. Otl Aicher, "The Eye, Visual Thinking," in *Analogous and Digital* (Berlin: Ernst and Sohn, 2015), 36–46.

Workshop, created in 1925 and headed by Herbert Bayer, but it did not have a theory of visual communication, nor could it have conceived of a department by that name.[21] As a discourse, visual communication emerges at the New Bauhaus founded by László Moholy-Nagy in Chicago in 1937, which became the Institute of Design in the 1940s. The Institute of Design replaced its Visual Design department with the Department of Visual Communication, underscoring its role in training designers who would work in the domain of mass communications, and more particularly advertising, rather than in the production of objects or buildings.[22] As presented by Moholy-Nagy, visual communication made the eye rather than the hand the central concern of design training.[23] More than the physical and material qualities of visible surfaces in the world, the *visual* in visual communication stressed the role of the optical image as a mediator between the eye and the brain. The concept was theorized more extensively by Moholy-Nagy's protegé and colleague Gyorgy Kepes in his best-selling textbook *Language of Vision* (1944). The purpose of visual communication, Kepes argued, was to develop a consciousness of how the mediating process between eye and brain worked, to grasp visual structures that were "universal and international," language-like in their coherence yet able to move across cultures separated by different tongues.[24] On the one hand, the theory of visual communication brought avant-garde painting and photography into a tighter rapport with theories of optical-image formation drawn from Gestalt psychology; on the other, it linked avant-garde techniques with advertising design. Such a reinterpretation, it has been argued, redirected the revolutionary politics out of which much interwar avant-garde work emerged toward commerce and new forms of technocratic pedagogy.[25] For Kepes, the theory of visual communication was never simply a

21. On the Printing and Advertising Workshop, see Gerd Fleichmann, *Bauhaus Typografie: Drucksachen, Typografie, Reklame* (Düsseldorf: Marzona, 1984); and Ute Brüning, ed., *Das A und O des Bauhauses: Bauhauswerbung: Schriftbilder, Drucksachen, Ausstellungsdesign* (Berlin: Bauhaus Archiv, 1995).

22. See Dagmar Rinker, "Industrial Design Is Not an Art," in Rinker and Quijano, *Ulmer Modelle*, 45.

23. See Moholy-Nagy's description of visual communication in "Education of the Eye: Prospect of the School of Design for 1939/40," reprinted in *50 Jahre New Bauhaus: Bauhausnachfolge in Chicago*, ed. Peter Hahn und Lloyd C. Engelbrecht (Berlin: Bauhaus Archiv, 1987), 138.

24. Gyorgy Kepes, *The Language of Vision* (New York: Paul Theobald, 1944), 13.

25. On Kepes's technocratic organicism, see Reinhold Martin, *The Organizational Complex: Architecture, Media, Corporate Space* (Cambridge, MA: MIT Press, 2003), 42–79. For a recent account that resists the reading of Kepes as part of a technocratic institution, see John R. Blakinger, *Gyorgy Kepes: Undreaming the Bauhaus* (Cambridge, MA: MIT Press, 2019).

means for improving "optical sales-talk"; rather, it aimed at reforming a visual environment swamped by the proliferation of billboards, posters, logos, signage, magazines, labels, and shop windows.[26] Visual communication was to counter the "destructive forces" of technological modernization, overcoming what Kepes called the "tragic formlessness" of social existence in the twentieth century.[27]

With the ascendance of visual-communications discourse, it might be said that the legacy of the American Bauhaus overtook that of the German Bauhaus, yet it is important to note how the tenor of visual communications at Ulm differed from the version developed in the United States.[28] Aicher and Scholl had come of age under the Nazi regime, where excessive control, emotional manipulation, and spectacular display were of greater concern than the formless miscommunication characteristic of capitalist mass commerce.[29] As Aicher later explained, the Visual Communication department was meant to situate the problem of design within the broader arena of public discourse, linking problems of form to questions of "propaganda, language, persuasion, and publicity."[30] Under National Socialism all kinds of visual communication, from art to advertising to news, had been subjected to what the Nazis termed *Gleichschaltung*. A Nazi neologism, *Gleichschaltung* implied necessary conversion, a coming-over to the cause that was also a ruthless consolidation, the elimination of any opposition to cultural and political unity.[31] If the American discourse stressed visual communication as a kind of knowledge capable of countering the heteronomy of capitalist mass commerce, teachers and students at the Ulm school in the 1950s were more acutely aware of communication as a means for consolidating social control.

26. Kepes, *The Language of Vision*, 219.

27. Ibid., 12.

28. In public debates over the legacy of the Bauhaus in the Ulm journal, the reference point remained the Bauhaus of Weimar Germany. Eva von Seckendorf has documented how important the legacy of the Chicago Bauhaus and its successor institutions were for the early years of the Ulm school. See von Seckendorf, *Die Hochschule für Gestaltung in Ulm*, 39–40.

29. See Eva Moser, *Otl Aicher, Gestalter*, 146.

30. Aicher, "The Eye, Visual Thinking," 36.

31. The term was originally an electrical-engineering term for switching alternating current to direct current. On the National Socialist redeployment of the term, see Robert Michael and Karin Doerr, *Nazi-Deutsch/Nazi-German: An English Lexicon of the Language of the Third Reich* (Westport, CT: Greenwood Press, 2002), 192; and Claudia Kuntz, *The Nazi Conscience* (Cambridge, MA: Belknap Press, 2003), 72.

In presenting the new curriculum in 1958, Maldonado, Aicher, and Gugelot thus moved away from any grand statements about turning life into art or battling formlessness, emphasizing instead the "education of specialists for two different tasks of our technical civilization: the design of industrial products (industrial design and building departments) and the design of visual and verbal means of communication (visual communication and information departments)."[32] This matter-of-fact outline contained a latent theory of post-WWII, post-Bauhaus design. Design was no longer understood as an effort to reintegrate life, craft, and art into a coherent, beautiful whole; it was a particular kind of *Aufgabe*, a task or duty within a fundamentally industrial civilization. Design came to be conceptualized as a field of activity structured by division. On a pragmatic level, design was a practice situated between production and use, while on a pedagogical level it was split between the conceptualization of objects (industrial design, building) and the shaping of signs (visual and verbal communication).[33] The theory of coordination responded to an industrial society structured by division: searching for a mediation between production and consumption and for a rationally synchronized relation between objects and signs. It was to such an end that the curriculum pursued a general methodology, offering courses in mathematical analysis, theories of perception, semiotics, sociology, and cultural history, subjects that were not offered at the Bauhaus.[34]

Grid Media

The recurrent exploration of grids in the Ulm School's pedagogy, while ostensibly mathematical in their objectives, manifested a latent tension between the search for new means of coordination and Germany's recent historical legacy of totalitarian control. The intellectual and manual work required in the grid exercises central to the school's foundation course called less for invention or expression than for arrangement under severe constraints. Ilse Grubich's "Disturbance of an Isometric Structure," produced for the foundation course taught by Maldonado, was a twenty-two-by-twenty-two-inch grid dominated by cool blue, gray, and purple—a color sequence that repeats regularly in a three-row pattern from top to bottom. The work would be entirely monotonous were it not for occasional flashes of clashing color. Irregularly placed squares of pink, mauve, and green disturb the regularity of this structure,

32. *Ulm* 1 (October 1958): 1.

33. The curricular division thus mirrored Maldonado's larger theorization of design at this moment as an activity within a field divided between direct artifacts, on the one hand ("whose use occurs with the objects themselves"), and indirect artifacts on the other ("that fulfill a function of conveyance"). See Gui Bonsiepe, "On the Heteronomy of Design in a Post-Utopian Age," in this volume, 264–70.

34. *Ulm* 1 (October 1958): 5.

chromatic interruptions that introduce vibration into an otherwise monochrome two-dimensional field. William S. Huff's work in the same course regularly distributed orange, green-gray, and yellow across a tiled geometric surface, contrasting colors that form no easily discernible pattern. The ambiguous surface can be read either as a network of flat diamonds or as the square facets of a field of cubes seen in isometric projection. Flickering between two and three dimensions, the arrangement works to neutralize any domination of figure over ground. More than material specificity or tactile concerns, the format of such problems—grids, tiling systems, various kinds of mathematical curves—shared an interest in a radical equality among different parts. The overriding concern was how to control visual effects when no shape, color, or pattern was larger or more important than any other.

Sumner Fineberg, Collage for Photogram, 1940s. Translucent and patterned plastic film. Art Institute of Chicago

While Gestalt psychology loomed large at both Ulm and the Institute of Design, the differences in how it was mobilized are revealing. The exercises specified by Maldonado were closely related to problems drawn from the Concrete-art movement, of which he had been a leading figure in Argentina.[35] Concrete art, he argued, had at its core a commitment to destroying illusory space in painting, the formal kernel of which was the dominance of figure over ground on a two-dimensional plane.[36] In Kepes's teaching in Chicago, exercises often yielded results that resolved themselves around strong figure/ground contrasts, drawing on a wide range of techniques, from collage and photomontage to drawing, painting, and camera-less photography. Kepes argued that the mind's inability to bear the chaos of light falling on the retina actively molded

35. For a collection of Maldonado's writings, see *Design, Nature, and Revolution: Toward a Critical Ecology* (1972; Minneapolis: University of Minnesota Press, 2019). On Maldonado's career, see Laura Escot, *Tomás Maldonado: Itinerario de un Intelectual Técnico* (Buenos Aires: Patricia Rizzo, 2007), and Mario H. Gradowczyk, *Tomás Maldonado: Un moderno en acción* (Buenos Aires: Editorial de la Universidad Nacional de Tres de Febrero, 2009).

36. Maldonado articulated these ideas as early as 1948 in an illustrated manifesto entitled "El Arte Concreto y el Problema de lo Illimitado; notas para un estudio téorico," now in the collection of the Yale Art Gallery. See Huff, "Grundlehre at the HfG," 190–91.

37. He writes: "We cannot bear chaos—the disturbance of equilibrium in the field of experience. Consequently, we must immediately form light-impacts into shapes and figures." Kepes, *Language of Vision*, 41.

these luminous stimuli into figures, a mental shaping activity that he saw as analogous to design's capacity to work against the forces of dissolution and disequilibrium in modernity.[37] Maldonado's exercises, by contrast, aimed to expunge figural illusion in search of the qualities structuring a ground. In the reorganized pedagogy at Ulm, anti-illusory procedures drawn from international Concrete art dovetailed with a specifically post-fascist suspicion of figuration, monumentality, and populism.

While the prevalence of the grid in student exercises hailed in part from the legacy of abstract painting, theorizations of the grid that draw solely on modernist painting cannot adequately think through its expansive and changing role at Ulm. The exercises deployed at the school can be read in the light of Rosalind Krauss's influential theorization of the grid's role as a mythic structure in modernist abstraction: a flattened geometric surface that covers over a latent contradiction between scientific materialism and aesthetic spiritualism.[38] Yet at Ulm grids played a wider role. The problem was less that of breaking with painting's mimetic relation to the world than it was of structuring a whole host of conventions, from letters, photographs, objects, and diagrams to pages, posters, exhibitions, and buildings. The ability of the grid to translate between these different instances was key. To grasp this role, an account of the grid as media must supplement the formalist-structuralist understanding of the grid as sign. Such an account might begin by recognizing what Bernhard Siegert has theorized as the triple function of the grid.[39] Grid media, he argues, operate as imaging techniques translating between two and three dimensions, as diagrammatic procedures defining addresses in which data can be stored and retrieved, and as "enframing" devices that subject what has been stored to availability and control.[40] More than an element of visual style, then, at Ulm the grid was a medium for thinking: a means by which design exercises were counted, classified, configured and reconfigured.

Such a reading means setting the grids and tiling patterns realized in paint for the foundation course alongside more analytical studies, in which the role of the grid as diagrammatic media becomes particularly evident. Like any number of students around

38. Rosalind Krauss, "Grids," in *The Originality of the Avant-Garde and Other Essays* (Cambridge, MA: MIT Press, 1986), 9–22.

39. Berhard Siegert, "(Not) In Place: The Grid, or Cultural Techniques for Ruling Spaces," in *Cultural Techniques: Grids, Filters, Doors and Other Articulations of the Real* (New York: Fordham University Press, 2015), 98.

40. Ibid. Siegert draws the term "enframing" (*Bestand*) from Heidegger, who described it as nothing less than the essence of technology in his influential essay "The Question Concerning Technology," which was contemporaneous with the formation of the Ulm school. The crucial point for Heidegger (as for Siegert) is that technology should not be confused with the tool or instrument but rather be defined as the manner in which modern Western perception imposes order onto nature so as to make it subject to use.

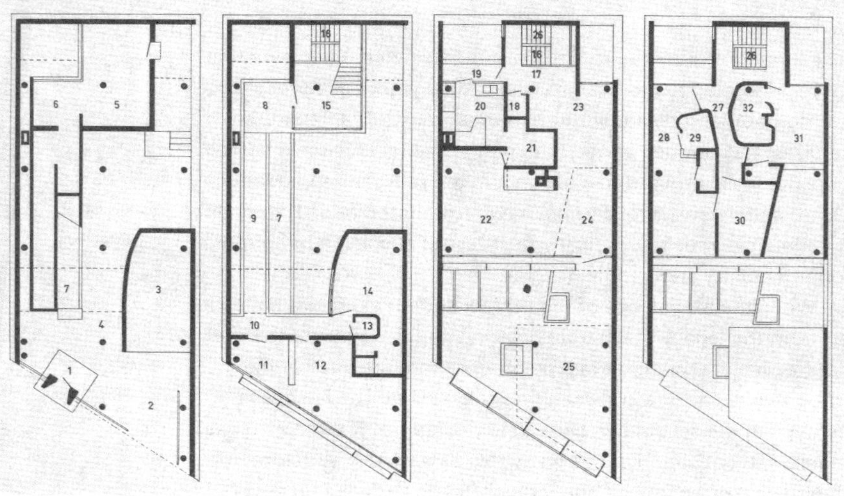

Curutchet House Floor Plans, Visual Methodology Exercise, *Ulm* 4 (April 1959)

the world in the 1950s, those in Ulm's foundation course were asked to study the work of Le Corbusier. Yet rather than treat this living "master" as a precedent to be emulated, students were asked to correct the architect's recently completed Curutchet House in La Plata, Argentina (1949–1953). The assignment began by asserting that "the [architect's] original decisions concerning the arrangements of various rooms were not correct" and asked students to improve the arrangement of entrances, stairs, passageways, and walls by using topological mathematics.[41] Each area on the floor plans was assigned an individual number and then plotted systematically on a graph. By comparing the greatest number of connections on each level as revealed by the graph, students could then identify which among a corresponding catalog of regular and semi-regular grids would have been optimal for solving the circulation needs of the house. If the ostensible universality of a mathematical procedure could correct the failures of a "master" of the modern movement, it could, *mutatis mutandis*, correct other design problems faced by the modern movement as well. The topological mathematics of grids and lattices were offered as heuristic models, helping students to comprehend "complicated relationships between objects . . . relationships [that] cannot be grasped naively and intuitively; and which cannot be mastered merely with the aid of a good 'feeling for form.'"[42] Trained to conceptualize three dimensions from two-dimensional projections and vice versa, students honed a type of spatial-graphic thinking powerful enough to remedy a building on the other side of the planet that none had seen in person.

Such foundation-course exercises were reminiscent of design assignments in Ulm's other departments as well. In the Industrial

41. *Ulm* 4 (April 1959): 62. The circumstances of the house's alteration were far more complex than the exercise acknowledged. For an account, see Alejandro Lapunzina, *Le Corbusier's Maison Curutchet* (New York: Princeton Architecture Press, 1997).

42. *Ulm* 4 (April 1959): 68.

Design department, students were routinely set the task of creating complex three-dimensional lattices by combining blocks of one or two shapes. In the Industrialized Building department, design problems similarly employed a modular-systems approach. In both cases a three-dimensional grid was the necessary background for the definition of elements. Students developed their studies by exploring all of the possible ways in which one or two standard elements might combine, aggregate, and interlock. They produced no shortage of visually arresting results, yet these were not exercises in creating particular, definitive shapes; rather, they were meant to foster a relational awareness of "interconnected forms" and "systems of forms."[43] At the end of a particular assembly exercise, students were asked to tally all of the pieces and their relative frequencies in order to calculate a numerical assessment of an arrangement's "complexity." Such a framework highlights another important facet of communications discourse at Ulm: If an optical understanding of communication had been drawn from Moholy-Nagy and Kepes, the school's teaching also incorporated a mathematical understanding of communication drawn from the founder of information theory, Claude Shannon.[44]

Ana-Maria Rutenberg, *3D Combinations of Two Elements,* Ulm 16–17 (June 1966)

It was Abraham Moles, an engineer who subsequently trained as a philosopher, who framed this mathematical understanding of communication for the Ulm school. Bracketing off qualitative differences such as form, color, and texture, he argued that a notion of complexity drawn from the mathematics of communication was "the only universal dimension" for comparing all objects of industrial design on the basis of structure.[45] Moles distinguished structural complexity—the variety of combinations of physical parts in a given object—from functional complexity, the variety of basic

43. "Results of Teaching: Problem 1," *Ulm* 17/18 (June 1966): 23.

44. Ibid. Shannon's landmark paper was "A Mathematical Theory of Communication," *Bell System Technical Journal* 27 (July and October 1948): 379–423, 623–56. On the permeation of Shannon's information theory in design circles through the work of Charles and Ray Eames, see Orit Halpern, *Beautiful Data: A History of Vision and Reason since 1945* (Durham, NC: Duke University Press, 2015), 79–144.

45. Abraham A. Moles, "Products: Their Structural and Functional Complexity," *Ulm* 6 (October 1962): 9.

operations that a user can employ in using an object.[46] He further distinguished complexity from complication. Whereas complication described relationships between many different kinds of things that were connected in many different ways, complex relationships involved a very large number of elements whose connections were either identical or substantially similar. In complex structures the relations between elements were largely uniform, yielding a condition more readily mastered by the human mind.[47] As an alternative to complication, complexity could thus be seen as a means for conceptualizing design problems in ways that sought to make both differences and connections more uniform.[48]

ulm 2

Vierteljahresbericht
der Hochschule für Gestaltung, Ulm
Oktober 1958

Preis pro Nummer DM 1.–/SFr 1.–/ÖS 7.50
Jahresabonnement DM 4.–/SFr 4.–/ÖS 30
portofrei

Quarterly bulletin
of the Hochschule für Gestaltung, Ulm
October 1958

Price per issue 2s6d/$0.50
Yearly subscription 10s/$2.00 post paid

Bulletin trimestriel
de la Hochschule für Gestaltung, Ulm
Octobre 1958

Prix du numéro 125 frs/L 175
Abonnement annuel 500 frs/L 700 port payé

Tomás Maldonado

Neue Entwicklungen in der Industrie und die Ausbildung des Produktgestalters

Die Anschauungen, die die Ideologie des Bauhauses bestimmt haben, lassen sich ein Vierteljahrhundert nach Schließung dieses Instituts schwer in die Sprache unserer heutigen Problematik übertragen. Mehr noch: wir müssen einige dieser Anschauungen, wie wir sehen werden, mit größter Entschiedenheit, aber auch mit größter Objektivität zurückweisen.

New Developments in Industry and the Training of the Designer

The ideas which supply the basis for what might be called the Bauhaus ideology are today, a quarter of a century after that institution closed, difficult to translate into the language of our present-day preoccupations. Furthermore, as we shall see, some of these ideas must now be refuted with the greatest vehemence as well as with the greatest objectivity.

Les nouvelles perspectives industrielles et la formation du «designer»

Les conceptions qui servirent de fondement à ce que l'on pourrait appeler l'idéologie du Bauhaus, sont aujourd'hui, un quart de siècle après la fermeture de cet institut, difficiles à traduire dans le langage de nos préoccupations actuelles. Plus encore, quelques-unes de ces conceptions doivent être maintenant réfutées avec la plus grande véhémence ainsi qu'avec la plus grande objectivité.

Cover, *Ulm* 2 (October 1958). Anthony Froshaug, designer

From Grid to Raster

These charts and graphs, together with the block assembly and grid exercises, were all presented to the public via the strict typographic framework established for the school's magazine by Anthony Froshaug in 1958. Froshaug, who taught in the Visual Communication department, opted for a square format structured by a four-column grid. Such a design was of a piece, as has often been noted, with the contemporaneous grid-based designs popularized in the influential Swiss magazine *Die Neue Graphik*, founded the same year.[49] Even when redesigned by Tomás Gonda in 1963 to be compatible with standard A4 paper, the layout remained faithful to a rigorous grid-based approach. Despite its unvarying consistency, the grid provided a surprisingly supple

46. Ibid. See also Moles, "Theory and Complexity of Technical Civilization," *Ulm* 12/13 (March 1965): 11–24.

47. Moles, "Products: Their Structural and Functional Complexity," 9.

48. When Maldonado introduced Moles's text in the pages of the *Ulm* journal, he expressed hope that such a system for describing objects could provide a framework for judging which particular design methodology would be most appropriate for any given industrial object.

49. For an overview, see Richard Hollis, *Swiss Graphic Design: The Origins and Growth of an International Style, 1920–1965* (New Haven: Yale University Press, 2006).

matrix, in which the relation of word to image could take on variable asymmetrical configurations. The design thinking behind such a system was expressed by Aicher, in terms reminiscent of Moles, as a search for complexity in design.[50] The key to finding a design lay not in a compositional idea but in developing a "schema that fixes all the elements to be laid out—lines, columns, images, titles, captions, and marginalia—so precisely that they yield interchangeable and freely combinable units. The format is the frame, and the elements should fill the entire frame in any arrangement."[51] The "enframing" role of grid media makes itself palpable here: The frame that elements must "fill entirely" is but the visible manifestation of an underlying schema of measurement that converted words and images into precise numerical units. At the base of such a system is the point, the smallest unit of typographic measurement, the key dimension for converting word and image into units compatible with a gridded frame.[52] Aicher's method, like the broader pedagogy described in the journal, implied a rationality. Counting and classifying would allow one to define elements, yet this precise conversion of language and image into a catalog of elements was not yet a solution to the problem of arrangement. The idiosyncrasy of feeling, sacrificed to counting, was recovered at another level. Schematization, as Aicher explained, was to be the basis for free combination. As a design rationality, Ulm's typographic grids offered a specific idea of freedom that hinged on combination and variability. The open-ended interchangeability and combination of numerically defined elements was a self-reflexive freedom, a set of possibilities immanent to the grid system in which it operated.

From these examples, one can distinguish three levels at which the grid operated as media at Ulm. Grids functioned as visual motifs on pages, posters, objects, building elements, screens, and exhibition systems. Yet they were also the underlying configuration that enabled a given layout, object, or framework to appear otherwise, a general ordering structure organizing the potential for variation. Finally, as in the case of graph theory used to analyze circulation patterns, typographical systems used to quantify text and image, or information theory used to analyze combinations of three-dimensional elements, grids provided the framework for making physical arrangements of things computable and comparable as numerical relations. Together, these three modalities highlight how the grid at Ulm was being linked to a different system of purposes in postwar design discourse, a system that may be more

50. Otl Aicher, HfG Seminar 1962, "Zeitungen, Zeitschriftentypographie," *Entwicklung 5: An der Hochschule für Gestaltung Ulm* (1964), unpaginated.

51. Ibid.

52. As Richard Hollis has noted, Swiss grid systems of the kind developed by Karl Gerstner took units of type as their basis, effectively relating all content through number, in contrast to the grid systems developed by Jan Tschichold, which used proportional division of standard page sizes and were thus linked to material formats. Hollis, *Graphic Design: A Concise History*, 130.

effectively understood through the term used at Ulm: *der Raster*. In addition to grid or pattern, the term *Raster* denotes different kinds of *screen*. The raster was first associated with the glass screens that emerged with the half-tone process in the later nineteenth century. Composed of grids of dots in varying densities, these screens translated photographic negatives into optical patterns reproducible alongside text in newspapers and magazines. By the mid-twentieth century, the raster was defined in reference to television screens: as the "totality of points that make up a television image."[53] The school's foundation course offered a mathematical definition of the

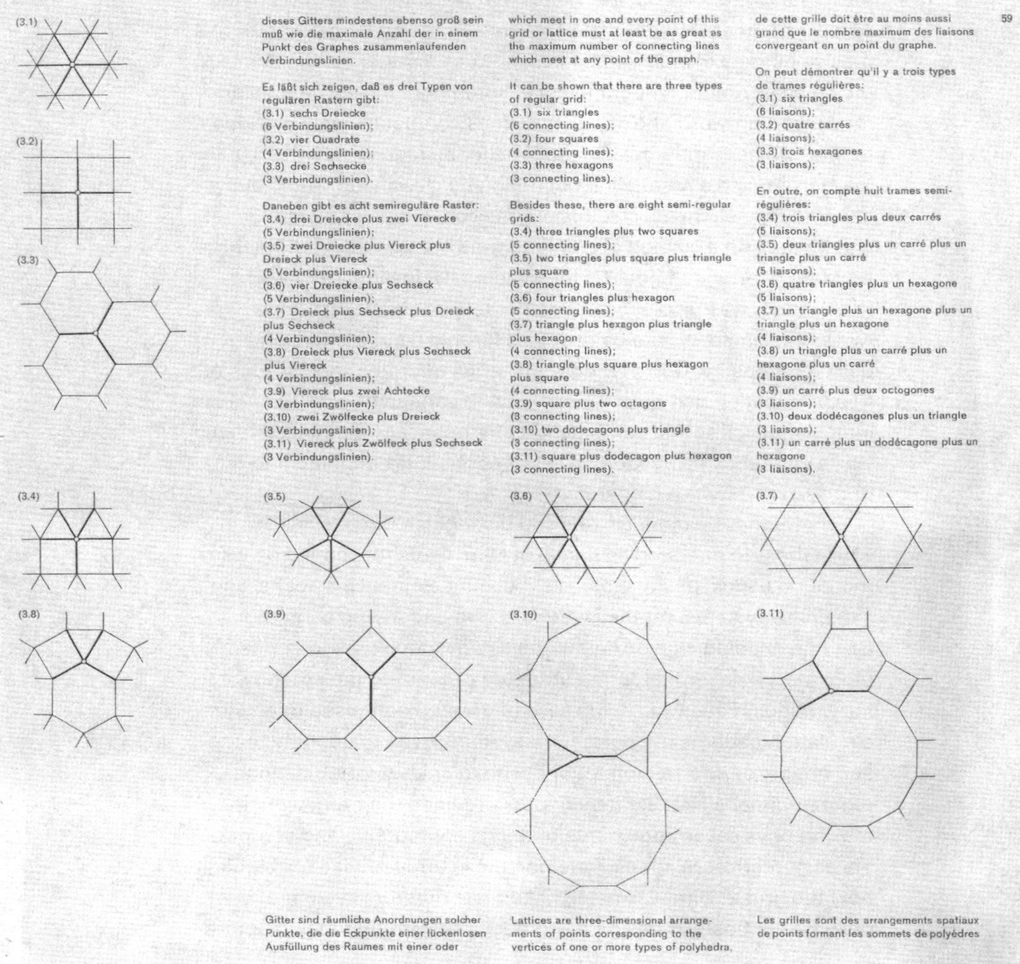

dieses Gitters mindestens ebenso groß sein muß wie die maximale Anzahl der in einem Punkt des Graphes zusammenlaufenden Verbindungslinien.

Es läßt sich zeigen, daß es drei Typen von regulären Rastern gibt:
(3.1) sechs Dreiecke
(6 Verbindungslinien);
(3.2) vier Quadrate
(4 Verbindungslinien);
(3.3) drei Sechsecke
(3 Verbindungslinien).

Daneben gibt es acht semireguläre Raster:
(3.4) drei Dreiecke plus zwei Vierecke
(5 Verbindungslinien);
(3.5) zwei Dreiecke plus Viereck plus Dreieck plus Viereck
(5 Verbindungslinien);
(3.6) vier Dreiecke plus Sechseck
(5 Verbindungslinien);
(3.7) Dreieck plus Sechseck plus Dreieck plus Sechseck
(4 Verbindungslinien);
(3.8) Dreieck plus Viereck plus Sechseck plus Viereck
(4 Verbindungslinien);
(3.9) Viereck plus zwei Achtecke
(3 Verbindungslinien);
(3.10) zwei Zwölfecke plus Dreieck
(3 Verbindungslinien);
(3.11) Viereck plus Zwölfeck plus Sechseck
(3 Verbindungslinien).

which meet in one and every point of this grid or lattice must at least be as great as the maximum number of connecting lines which meet at any point of the graph.

It can be shown that there are three types of regular grid:
(3.1) six triangles
(6 connecting lines);
(3.2) four squares
(4 connecting lines);
(3.3) three hexagons
(3 connecting lines).

Besides these, there are eight semi-regular grids:
(3.4) three triangles plus two squares
(5 connecting lines);
(3.5) two triangles plus square plus triangle plus square
(5 connecting lines);
(3.6) four triangles plus hexagon
(5 connecting lines);
(3.7) triangle plus hexagon plus triangle plus hexagon
(4 connecting lines);
(3.8) triangle plus square plus hexagon plus square
(4 connecting lines);
(3.9) square plus two octagons
(3 connecting lines);
(3.10) two dodecagons plus triangle
(3 connecting lines);
(3.11) square plus dodecagon plus hexagon
(3 connecting lines).

de cette grille doit être au moins aussi grand que le nombre maximum des liaisons convergeant en un point du graphe. 59

On peut démontrer qu'il y a trois types de trames régulières:
(3.1) six triangles
(6 liaisons);
(3.2) quatre carrés
(4 liaisons);
(3.3) trois hexagones
(3 liaisons);

En outre, on compte huit trames semi-régulières:
(3.4) trois triangles plus deux carrés
(5 liaisons);
(3.5) deux triangles plus un carré plus un triangle plus un carré
(5 liaisons);
(3.6) quatre triangles plus un hexagone
(5 liaisons);
(3.7) un triangle plus un hexagone plus un triangle plus un hexagone
(4 liaisons);
(3.8) un triangle plus un carré plus un hexagone plus un carré
(4 liaisons);
(3.9) un carré plus deux octogones
(3 liaisons);
(3.10) deux dodécagones plus un triangle
(3 liaisons);
(3.11) un carré plus un dodécagone plus un hexagone
(3 liaisons).

Gitter sind räumliche Anordnungen solcher Punkte, die die Eckpunkte einer lückenlosen Ausfüllung des Raumes mit einer oder

Lattices are three-dimensional arrangements of points corresponding to the vertices of one or more types of polyhedra,

Les grilles sont des arrangements spatiaux de points formant les sommets de polyèdres

Catalog of Rasters from Foundation course, *Ulm* 4 (April 1959)

raster: "A raster is obtained when a surface is completely covered by one or more types of congruent polygons."[54] Such a definition emphasized the different patterns made by combinations of regular shapes on a planar surface and in particular stressed the lines intersecting at any given point. The catalog of grids presented to the

53. Duden, *das Raster*, def. 1: "Gesamtheit der Punkte, aus denen sich ein Fernsehbild zusammensetzt."

54. *Ulm* 4 (April 1959): 58.

school's students comprised three regular rasters (based on a single shape) and eight semi-regular rasters (based on two or more shapes). A direct extension of the school's interest in topological mathematics, the raster at Ulm differed from the grids of modernist abstraction in emphasizing the point as connective node in a surface pattern or network. In such a definition, the distinction between centrifugal and centripetal grids was of far less interest than the question of how many lines connected to each point in any given pattern.[55] While this topological definition of the raster was indifferent to most of the qualities of the modernist grid in painting, including quality of line, relation of line to frame, color, facture, and density, the distinction between point and line was momentous for understanding the raster as media. As a set of points with a measurable number of relations to other points, it was the means by which different types of grids could be systematically compared and calculated. In supporting such mathematical comparison and calculation, rasters expanded their capacity for translation: Raster systems could describe two-dimensional surfaces and diagrams, three-dimensional assemblages of elements, arrays of dots structuring the light passing through glass, and, increasingly, electromagnetically sensitive points activated by the sweep of an electron beam in a vacuum tube.[56] Combining the function of grid and screen, the raster could be at once a particular surface pattern and a filter capable of translating images and information through different technical channels. Positioned, often invisibly, in the midst of a communication process, the raster was not unlike the mediating role of the designer. It is thus not entirely surprising that the rational procedures associated with different kinds of raster media dovetailed with the emergence of different ideas about the designer's role in the 1950s.

55. Krauss's structuralist reading of the modernist grid distinguished grids formally based on whether the lines remained internal to the grid or extended beyond it. Krauss, "Grids," 9–22.

56. The raster system used for television screens would come to form the basis for today's pixelated computer screens, but not until the 1970s, when raster graphics superseded the linear graphics of random-scan displays used in early computer screens. On this history, see Jacob Gaboury, "The Random Access Image: Memory and the Computer Screen," *Grey Room* 70 (Winter 2018): 24–53. On the *Rasterbilder* of K. O. Gotz, and their influence on early video art, see Christine Mehring, "Television Art's Abstract Starts: Europe circa 1944–1969," *October* 125 (Summer 2008): 29–64. For an incisive account of the dot screen as a transmedial "factory form" shared by modern art and cinema, see Mal Ahern, "Factory Forms: Reproducing Images in the 1960s" (PhD diss., Yale University 2019).

Designer as Coordinator

More than anyone at Ulm, it was Maldonado who theorized this new role of designer as coordinator. What he developed was a meta-theory of design, whose emphasis on production and consumption processes could be applied to architecture, visual communication, and industrial design equally. Historically, the theory proposed a three-stage development. At the turn of the century the designer's work was little differentiated from that of inventor-entrepreneurs like Ford or Edison.[57] With the rise of the Bauhaus and the emergence of automotive styling in the 1920s and '30s, the designer's work was aligned with that of the artist as a creator of forms. In the 1950s, however, the designer's role was to make decisions that would consequentially intervene in a production and consumption process.[58] Training students for this new role meant going beyond the preeminent place Bauhaus pedagogy gave to questions of form. Bauhaus pedagogy, Maldonado argued, had developed much of value when it came to assessing shape, material, color, and texture, yet the overriding emphasis on these concerns had impeded the questioning of how to relate this knowledge to contemporary developments in science and industry.[59]

Tomás Maldonado lecturing at HfG Ulm (preliminary course), 15 March, 1956

Coordination, for Maldonado, engaged in a more horizontal type of mediation and required an ability to move between scientific and industrial knowledge and aesthetic know-how. Coordination was neither a physiological linkage between eye and brain—as it had been for Moholy-Nagy—nor was it a capacity to synthesize technical specializations and raise them to the higher plane of art, as it had been for a historian like Sigfried Giedion.[60]

57. See Tomás Maldonado, "New Developments in Industry," *Ulm* 2 (October 1958): 1

58. The dispute with Bill was implicit in Maldonado's claim that core Bauhaus ideas were to be refuted with the "greatest vehemence" and the "greatest objectivity."

59. Ibid., 39.

60. Moholy-Nagy's prospectus for students at the Institute of Design in Chicago stressed the need to cultivate "coordination between hand and brain," which was in line with the Bauhaus's goal of reconciling the manual training of the crafts with the intellectual work of the fine arts. During the '50s, Giedion stressed that the architect's "future" lay in his or her role as "coordinator"; he saw this action as an integration of specialized forms of technical knowledge into a complete "work of art." See Giedion, "Education of an Architect," in *Architecture: You and Me* (Cambridge, MA: Harvard University Press, 1958), 103.

Sir John Harington describes one of the first modern flush toilets.

The postwar designer was to "coordinate, in close collaboration with a large number of specialists, the most varied requirements of product fabrication and usage; his will be the final responsibility for maximum productivity in fabrication, and for maximum material and cultural consumer satisfaction."[61] Such a theory called on the designer to place divergent concerns and entities on the same level; the consumer's demand for satisfaction was to be equal to the producer's demand for productivity. The task of design was to find out which decisions (formal, logistical, material) might reconcile these not necessarily compatible demands. Maldonado was well aware that designers knew the demands of production far more concretely than the desires of consumers, a predicament revealed in the collision of references throughout his text, in which theories of management and philosophical pragmatism appear alongside Henri Lefebvre's Marxian sociology of everyday life.[62] The user's stake in design was central to Ulm's notion of the designer's role in a democratic public sphere, yet Maldonado could only lament that a theoretical framework for understanding this elusive figure was still to be established.[63]

The theory of coordination was also a skeptical riposte to the growing appreciation of automotive and object styling as a form of popular art in the 1950s. Initially formulated in the writings of Reyner Banham, John McHale, and others associated with the Independent Group, the conception of styling as Pop Art understood industrial design to be a form of symbolic communication.[64] For Maldonado, the continual changes characteristic of styling were only superficial pseudo-communication, modifications designed to promote economic competition rather than make fundamental improvements in the object.[65] Yet Maldonado also rejected the countervailing idea of *Gute Form* advanced by his former mentor, Max Bill. For Bill, the idea that modern beauty emerged almost magically from function was no longer sufficient, as the same functions could be fulfilled by any number of different forms, and functions themselves often changed over time.[66] Only a renewed debate over inherent beauty, he argued, could set adequate terms on which postwar objects could be judged and design education pursued. If Banham's notions were rooted in iconography, Bill's

61. Maldonado, "New Developments in Industry," 34.

62. Maldonado's essay draws both from management theory—notably American "operations research" theorists such as Anatole Rapoport—and the sociologically informed critiques of managerialism advanced by Gregor Paulsson in Sweden and Henri Lefebvre in France.

63. More explicit remarks on the role of consumption are in Tomás Maldonado and Gui Bonsiepe, "Science and Design," *Ulm* 10/11 (May 1964): 10–29.

64. For a collection of Banham's writings on Pop design, see Reyner Banham, *Design by Choice*, ed. Penny Sparkle (New York: Rizzoli, 1981).

65. Maldonado, "New Developments in Industry," 31.

66. See Max Bill, "Beauty from Function and as Function," *Werk* 8 (1949): 272–82.

were rooted in philosophical idealism, which held that beauty was a universal quality of disinterested pleasure that particular forms awoke in the beholder. Maldonado's theory of coordination, by contrast, drew on a strain of philosophical pragmatism. If design was a problem of communication, it hinged neither on the transmission of meaning nor on transfers of feeling; rather, it was as a medium for coordinating actions in a situation subject to conflict.[67] Maldonado's pragmatic notion of coordination returned to the term's etymological roots—to be coordinate as being of equal rank, degree, or importance. As in the grid exercises in the foundation course, coordination implied coordinates. Present at the level of physical objects, at the level of background systems, and at the meta-level of design methodology, the coordinates of the raster were the physical means by which the theory of coordination pursued its work. If the raster was to serve as a framework for equalizing the concerns of producers and consumers, it also operated as an infrastructure through which designers imagined their ability to intervene in the production-consumption process. Yet such a framework came at a price: It required that differences be expressed in formal and quantitative terms.

Coordination Spaces

The raster's role as a medium of translation sustained the expansion of graphic design into three dimensions pursued within the Visual Communication department. A signal instance of this expansion was the work that Aicher and his students did for Braun, at the time a relatively small electronics firm that decided to take a gamble on the new school, asking its Industrial Design professor Hans Gugelot to redesign a few of its radios and record players.[68] The new devices created an

Braun Radios on display, Berlin, 1954

67. Maldonado often cited thinkers associated with philosophical pragmatism like Charles Morris. The foregoing account of philosophical pragmatism's understanding of communication draws on John Durham Peter's account in *Speaking into the Air: A History of the Idea of Communication* (Chicago: University of Chicago Press, 1999), 19–21.

68. Often attributed to Dieter Rams alone, the design of the Braun radios involved a number of people, including Gugelot and Aicher and sometimes others. For an account, see Peter Kapos, "Art and Design: The Ulm Model, Part 2: Contradictions of Utopia," http://www.ravenrow.org/texts/84/.

immediate stir and have since become landmarks of twentieth-century design. Small, muted in color, and insistently geometrical, they combined wood with industrial materials like sheet metal and Perspex in a manner totally at odds with the dark walnut housings and gold trim that had defined the look of radios since the 1930s.[69] Aicher helped Gugelot design the configuration of the buttons and dials that allowed users to operate these machines, and with his students he would also coordinate the manner in which these objects appeared to the public through packaging, posters, booklets, display systems, exhibition stands, and pavilions. Of particular importance was the design of exhibition environments, spaces that stood between corporate management and the production process, on the one hand, and sites of consumption and use on the other. Such environments were designed to operate within temporary exhibitions and trade fairs, a field that exploded in the 1950s.[70] Unlike the large sample fairs of the interwar period, the post-WWII fairs were specialized by market segment (with different exhibitions for electronics, automobiles, apparel, and publishing) and thus required a new emphasis on differentiating brands within a sector. If architects like Henry Van de Velde and Peter Behrens had pioneered what came to be called corporate identity in the first decades of the twentieth century, the expansion of such practices in the postwar decades was led by graphic designers who mobilized a hybrid array of architectural, mathematical, and graphic techniques.[71]

The most extensive feature of this commission was the D55 display system, first used at the 1955 television, radio, and phonograph fair where Braun launched its redesigned offerings.[72] A framework made from standard square metal tubes, the D55 could be configured to create enclosed rooms as well as open display areas, using panels to fashion partitions, backgrounds, and display

69. An overview of Aicher's work for Braun was reproduced in *Entwicklung 5: An der Hochschule für Gestaltung Ulm* (1964). See also Marcus Rathgeb, *Otl Aicher* (London: Phaidon, 2006), 46–54.

70. Johannes Huynen, *Trends in Trade Fairs* (Valkenburg: Uitgeverij Valkenburg, 1973). Tellingly, the most comprehensive record of the exhibition designs from this period was compiled and edited by an Ulm student, Klaus Franck. See Klaus Franck, *Exhibitions: A Survey of International Designs* (London: Architectural Press, 1961).

71. On the history of corporate-image strategies in the US during first half of the twentieth century, see Roland Marchand, *Creating the Corporate Soul: The Rise of Public Relations and Corporate Imagery in American Big Business* (Berkeley: University of California Press, 1998). On IBM and the changes in postwar corporate-identity programs, see John Harwood, *The Interface: IBM and the Transformation of Corporate Design 1945–1976* (Minneapolis; University of Minnesota Press, 2011).

72. The fair was the "Grosse Deutsche Rundfunk-, Fernseh-, und Phono-Ausstellung" (Greater German broadcasting, television, and phono exhibition) in Düsseldorf.

surfaces. Steel sections connected to wood or Perspex elements via regularly spaced slots. The lightly detailed joints were not unlike the rasters in the foundation course, nodes of connection within a three-dimensional lattice articulated by panels in various orientations. More of an open-ended puzzle than a fixed object, the three-dimensional grid system was designed to be put together, disassembled, and reconfigured differently depending on the event.[73] Period photographs typically show it floating in darkness, buoyed by the glow of its own integrated lighting—at once a demonstration of technical coordination and a means for more radically segregating Braun's new designs from other objects at the fair. If the D55 aimed to detach Braun from its immediate context, it also orchestrated a more diffuse sense of atmospheric coordination that arose from internally juxtaposing radios, record players, and televisions with plants, textiles, and Hermann Miller furniture. This type of coordination distinguished Braun by establishing visual connotations between its products and other prestige design objects. As a critic like Jean Baudrillard would argue a few years later, the mathematical and technical aspects of such a systematic approach to design were symptomatic of the increasing pressure to systematize the connotative processes within postwar consumer culture.[74]

"D55" exhibition stand for Braun at the Broadcast Exhibition in Düsseldorf, 1955. Design: Otl Aicher and Hans G. Conrad.

73. The modular and variable nature of the D55 was part of the larger emphasis on "systems design" in the Ulm school, which included Gugelot's M125 modular storage system. See Hans Wichmann, ed., *System-Design Bahnbrecher: Hans Gugelot 1920–65* (Basel: Birkhauser, 1987).

74. The systematization of connotation in an industrial society was central to Baudrillard's critique of the function of atmosphere in his Marxian-semiotic critique of consumption. See *The System of Objects* (London: Verso, 1996 [1968]). Baudrillard was responding in part to the kind of cybernetic thinking advanced by Moles, which became a flash point for leftist and pro-Situationist groups in 1966, when Moles assumed a post in the sociology department at the University of Strasbourg.

William Gilbert publishes *De Magnete* describing how Earth behaves like a magnet

The attention the Visual Communication department brought to designing the middle zone between production and consumption highlights a final historical difference between the Ulm school and the Bauhaus. At the Bauhaus, students and masters designed objects, textiles, furniture, and wallpaper that were licensed to intermediary production companies who provided mass production and marketing.[75] By contrast, students and teachers at the Ulm school operated as consultants to industrial clients. In working for firms like Braun, Lufthansa, BASF, Olivetti, and others, designers like Aicher, Gugelot, and Maldonado engaged corporations with existing production processes, supply chains, and market identities. Design in such a context, as Maldonado noted, was less a question of demiurgic form creation than a process of "redesign."[76] Redesign meant comprehending a firm's established means of production as well as the manner in which its products were perceived by an existing market. This new role for the designer at the Ulm school mirrored the parallel rise of the consultant designer in the US in the 1950s, yet at Ulm the relationship between designer and corporation was mediated by a pedagogical framework.[77] Such corporate relationships had their own structure at the school: the *Entwicklungsgruppen*, or development groups.[78] Work for corporate clients was distinct from work done in particular courses and was supervised by a professor who handpicked the students in the development group. Whereas the Bauhaus workshops were structured around materials, the development groups were organized around a logic that was managerial, serving to organize a professor's relationships both with students and with external clients. In such a context, experimental work moved from the studio to industry and vice versa, as forms of corporate hierarchy and organization were introduced into the workings of the school.

75. On Bauhaus commerce, see Anna Rowland, "Business Management at the Weimar Bauhaus," *Journal of Design History* 1, no. 3/4 (1988): 153–75; and Frederic J. Schwartz, "Utopia for Sale: The Bauhaus and Weimar Germany's Consumer Culture," in *Bauhaus Culture: From Weimar to the Cold War*, ed. Kathleen James-Chakraborty (Minneapolis: University of Minnesota Press, 2006), 115–38.

76. Maldonado, "New Developments in Industry," 37.

77. On the rise of the consultant designer at IBM, see Harwood, *The Interface*, 18–57.

78. The development groups were established as part of the 1957 reorganization of the school under Aicher, Gugelot, and Maldonado. Aicher's group was known as E5. The partnerships also brought in revenue to the school. See René Spitz, "Design Is Not a Science," *Design Issues* 31, no. 1 (Winter 2015): 7–17.

The Crux of Coordination

Returning to where this essay began, how might one reconsider the claim that the Ulm school represents the missing link between the Bauhaus and the design of contemporary digital devices? Reckoning with the school's legacy means more than considering outward resemblances between today's devices and those conceived by Ulm's teachers and students; rather, it calls for putting pressure on the school's effort to universalize mathematical reasoning as a basis for pragmatic, rational communication. This claim to universality was linked to the school's egalitarian idea of the designer as coordinator, a figure who might arbitrate between the demands of producers and consumers in postwar capitalist production. If coordination envisioned a mediating role for designers between consumers and producers, the raster-based design procedures pursued in the Visual Communication department at Ulm provided a framework for synchronizing the appearance of objects, typography, packaging, displays, and exhibition systems. As a strategy for producing a unified brand identity linking products, interface design, advertising, and presentation, techniques of coordination have been foundational to the branding of our era's hegemonic personal-computing firms.[79] The alignment of such corporate-identity programs with Ulm's more egalitarian rationalism was not accidental but rather grounded in the idea of a universal and neutral basis for communication. Pedagogic research combined with corporate patronage provided the leverage needed to universalize these specific design principles, a process that excluded qualitative differences rooted in nationality, ethnicity, gender, culture, or politics.[80] Such a criticism of the universalizing ambitions pursued at Ulm should not erase the recognition, equally central to the theory of coordination, of the manner in which social antagonisms shaped the field of design within capitalism. Rather than style, the themes of variability and complexity within Ulm discourse may be the most potent sites for considering the school's pertinence to contemporary digital transformations of design culture.

The idea that a logic of variability is a hallmark of today's digital design cultures has been influentially argued by a number of critics and historians. One of the most outspoken, Mario Carpo, claims that the digital era is quintessentially about programs and processes capable of authoring variable and nonstandard yet serially produced objects, a mode of design at odds with the mass production of identical and standardized objects under an industrial paradigm.[81] If variability is quintessentially digital, what to make of the importance of variability to industrial theorists and designers like Moles, Aicher, Maldonado, and Bonsiepe? Such a recognition challenges the argument that the digital represents a

79. On the importance of Braun's designs as a model for the Apple Macintosh, see Walter Isaacson, *Steve Jobs* (New York: Simon and Schuster, 2011), 192–205.

80. Joanna Drucker advances a similar critique of midcentury Swiss graphic design in *Graphic Design History: A Critical Guide* (Upper Saddle River, NJ: Prentice Hall, 2009), 264.

fundamental rupture with analog industrial processes. Maldonado, Aicher, and Bonsiepe engaged with coordination as fundamental to the dimensional and procedural organization of industrialized serial production precisely to intervene in the tendency towards homogenization and uniformity latent in such systems.[82] The crux of the school's democratic aspirations was to ask designers to engage with the basic coordinating frameworks of industrial production while simultaneously recognizing that interventions at the level of industrial standards were normative decisions implying forms of aesthetic and social control that could not be democratized.[83]

The discourse of the variable that emerged at the school sought to resolve this conflict by conceptualizing a set of basic elements that left a maximum degree of freedom to an unknown user whose decisions could determine the exact combination and assembly of these elements. Bonsiepe theorized this principle of variability as a *Baukastensysteme* (literally, "building-block system"), a formulation that underscores the affinity of variability with toys and construction kits.[84] A variable system was not a rejection of standardization; it entailed a particular conception of standardized elements. The standardization of dimensions and connections could produce a consolidated, identical series, but they could also yield a system that enabled and encouraged differential forms of assembly. A theorist like Moles heralded this kind of play as offering a new solution to the old problem of "unity in diversity," arguing that the future of industrial design was tending toward a "universal Meccano," a world of technical objects open to variation through recombination.[85] That Moles's vision of variability alluded to a turn-of-the-century children's toy, itself derived from late-nineteenth-century engineering, reveals how a much older vision of prefabrication continued to structure Ulm's midcentury vision of the future. While contemporary techniques

81. Carpo outlines a theory of variability in digital design as a quality of algorithmic differentiation used in online advertising, in the mutability of contemporary finance, and in the promise of nonstandard digital fabrication. See *The Alphabet and the Algorithm* (Cambridge, MA: MIT Press, 2011). Carpo's emphasis on variability represents a dominant motif in a parametric strain of architectural discourse about digitality. See also Bernard Cache, *Earth Moves: The Furnishing of Territories* (Cambridge, MA: MIT Press, 1995); and Greg Lynn, "Architectural Curvilinearity: The Folded, the Pliant, and the Supple," *Architectural Design* 63, no. 3/4 (1993): 8–15.

82. Gui Bonsiepe, "Systems and Variable Systems," *Ulm* 6 (October 1962): 30.

83. The idea of a universal three-dimensional grid capable of standardizing all dimensions across industry was pursued during the Nationalist Socialist period by Ernst Neufert, an architect who had originally trained under Walter Gropius. See Neufert, *Bauordnungslehre*, ed. Albert Speer (Berlin: Volk und Reich Verlag, 1943). On Neufert and the relation between standards and norms, see Nader Vossoughian, "Standardization Reconsidered: *Normierung* in and after Ernst Neufert's *Bauentwurfslehre*," *Grey Room* 54 (Winter 2014): 34–55, and Walter Prigge, ed., *Ernst Neufert: Normierte Baukultur im 20. Jahrhundert* (Frankfurt am Main: Campus, 1999).

for digitally automating variations in form are technically distinct from those envisioned at Ulm, the liberatory and ludic claims made on their behalf are not. The paradox of variability was that while it envisioned systems capable of giving freedom of assembly to the user, it could only do so by defining differences within the formal terms of a cybernetic-industrial paradigm. The claim that today's digital processes enable the triumph of differential variations over standardized repetitions veils the crux of coordination. Techniques for automating the production of differences continue to depend on forms of standardization that have become less apparent, the product of raster systems embedded in software rather than in the matrices of the typecase or the casting mold.[86] The recurrent themes of variability and complexity in Ulm's discourse might be recognized not as ancestors of today's arguments but as sites of struggle, reminders of the fundamental antagonisms shaping the field of design.

84. Ibid. Bonsiepe derived the notion from Karl-Heinz Borowski's dissertation on modular building systems, which argued that toys and construction kits were the prototype of postwar ambitions toward modular building. "From the multiple combinations of blocks made possible by the construction kit," he wrote, "a variety of different structures can be built up. Once dismantled, other buildings can be assembled from the reused blocks." See Borowski, *Das Baukastensystem in der Technik* (Berlin: Springer, 1961), 1.

85. Moles, "Theory of Complexity and Technical Civilization," 12.

86. Friedrich Kittler has argued for the importance of the grid to the simultaneous emergence of perspective and movable type as a foundational technique for digital computing in "Perspective and the Book," *Grey Room* 5 (Fall 2001): 38–53. Recently, Reinhold Martin has mobilized Kittler's insight in his call for a wider genealogy of the grids that structure CAD software and parametric modeling. See "Points of Departure: Notes Toward a Reversible History of Architectural Visualization," in *The Active Image: Architecture and Engineering in the Age of Modeling* (Cham: Springer, 2017), 1–21.

DESIGN IN LATIN AMERICA: MIGRATIONS AND DRIFT

SILVIA FERNÁNDEZ

The process by which graphic design education in Latin America became "modern" can be traced through four distinct phases. In this essay, I will use the case of Argentina as representative example, tracking design education through: **1.** proto-modernity and the influence of the Bauhaus; **2.** "Arte Concreto Invención," Tomás Maldonado, and the Ulm School of Design; **3.** the creation of design careers viewed from the perspective of modernity; and **4.** the current status of graphic design careers in Latin America.

The urban modernity of the 1920s and '30s in Latin America was not the simple effect of industrialization but the result of a complex multicausal process in which political, social, cultural, urban, and technological factors converged. This modernity—or, better, "proto-modernity"—brought the period of "good taste and good speaking" adopted from the Spanish colonizers to an end. Nevertheless, it was connected to Europe, for travelers, immigrants, and exiles carried in their luggage testimonies of modernity in the form of books, magazines, works of art, and above all ideas, which—along with the local "Criolla" culture—formed the new imaginary. It was a precipitated process of building a new cultural identity that would generate a "utopian tension" between the resistance to let go of the past and the rationality proposed by the avant-garde.[1]

Bunge y Bonn grain silo being built in 1903, revised by Le Corbusier in 1919

An early example of proto-modern constructions in Argentina can be found in the grain silos built by the company Bunge and Born in 1904 in the harbor of Buenos Aires. These structures were presented by Walter Gropius in his 1911 article "Monumental Art and Industrial Buildings" as examples of the intersections between monumental art and new industrial constructions.[2]

It was a decade later that the first signs of modernity became visible in literature and in art, with painters like Emilio Petorutti and Xul Solar. In 1920, a major Paul Klee retrospective was held at the Galerie Hans Goltz in Munich. The following year, Solar traveled to Munich and in 1922 he studied at the academy Art Workshops, where Klee had previously taught. During his stay in Munich (1921–23), Solar met "Hans Reichel (a friend of Klee's), his wife Olga and the young Elena Alberti, all three becoming an important nucleus in his circle of friends."[3] Later, he brought Klee's ideas back to Argentina. The critic Mario Gradowczyk maintained that Klee is

1. Joaquín Medina Warmburg, ed., *Walter Gropius proclamas de modernidad (Escritos y conferencias, 1908–1934)* (Barcelona: Reverté, 2018).

2. Beatriz Sarlo, *Una modernidad periférica: Buenos Aires 1920 y 1930* (Buenos Aires: Nueva Visión, 2003), 34.

3. https://www.xulsolar.org.ar/biografia.html.

"the European artist most admired by Xul and with whom he shares affinities in painting, music and spirituality."[4]

But it was in architecture that modernism made the most significant contributions. As early as 1925 the architect Alejo Martínez designed twenty proto-rationalist houses in a city in the interior of Argentina. His colleague Alberto Prebisch wrote the first texts on modern architecture, confronting the academy with the most current theories of Gropius, Le Corbusier, Worringer, and Riegl. Although Prebisch adhered to classicism in some of his architecture, in Buenos Aires he designed the Gran Rex theater, a significant example of modern architecture.

In 1928 the architect Wladimiro Acosta, born in Odessa, emigrated to Argentina. Before arriving, he visited Berlin, where he established links with Erich Mendelsohn and immersed himself in the design trends of the Bauhaus. In Buenos Aires, Acosta worked for a short time in the studio of Prebisch, and in 1932 he developed the "helios" system, a design method that aimed to take full advantage of the benefits of the sun. This impetus would characterize his later projects, both buildings and single-family houses.

But it is Victoria Ocampo who was perhaps the key figure in the modernization of Argentinian culture, albeit always with a connection to classicism. Although not trained as an architect, Ocampo designed two modernist houses. The first, in 1927, was in a seaside health resort. Describing her motivations, she wrote: "At that time I was hungry for white walls, no moldings, no ornaments."[5] In 1928, with the direction of architect Alejandro Bustillo, Ocampo designed a house in Buenos Aires that was a scandal when it was erected in a neighborhood that favored the neoclassical style.

Alejandro Bustillo, house of Victoria Campo, in *Neustra Arquitectura* 2 (October 1929)

In 1931 Ocampo made her most important cultural contribution by founding *Sur*, a cultural, intellectual, and literary magazine of international reference. She designed the cover herself. It was a disruptive element in the graphic landscape of the 1930s, and its modernity is present in the dominant white space that serves not as a background but as a dynamic element of typographic composition.[6]

Ocampo met Gropius in 1929 in Berlin, and from then on the two maintained a relationship. Texts from Gropius were published

4. Mario Gradowczyk, *Xul Solar* (Buenos Aires: Ediciones ALBA, Fundación Bunge y Born, 1994), 100. All translations are by the author unless otherwise noted.

5. Victoria Ocampo, "A propósito de Bauhaus," in *Testimonios, Vol. 9 (1971–1974)* (Buenos Aires: Ediciones Sur, 1975), 148.

6. See Silvia Fernández, *Señal Bauhaus*, part of the collection *Mujeres en el diseño argentino* (La Plata: Ediciones Nodal, 2019).

in *Sur*, the first, with the title "Total Theater," was included in the magazine's first issue. Thanks to the relationship with Ocampo, Gropius founded a studio in Buenos Aires between 1931 and 1934, in association with the architect Franz Möller, who had been a member of his studio in Berlin. Three decades later, Gropius traveled to Buenos Aires to work on the German embassy in a joint endeavor with Amancio Williams, the well-known Argentine architect. Neither the Möller studio's large projects, like housing blocks in Puerto Madero and a neighborhood in the maritime resort nor Gropius's plans for the embassy were ever realized. Nonetheless, his influence was significant: Gropius and Möller built two family houses on the outskirts of Buenos Aires, projects that "had an influence on Wladimiro Acosta, Antonio Vilar and Alberto Prebisch."[7] As Magdalena Faillace notes, the studio also had an impact on the design world in Argentina at the time: "On a small scale, the Gropius-Möller studio designed domestic furniture. They brought to market different types of metal furniture produced in the country under exclusive designs."[8]

Other "Bauhausians" could be found in Argentina. In 1935, Grete Stern traveled as a companion of photographer and filmmaker Horacio Coppola, who had met her in Walter Peterhans's class at the Bauhaus in Berlin.[9] Stern and Coppola would be protagonists of a decisive and consistent Bauhaus influence in photography, graphic design, and art in Buenos Aires. Another Bauhaus alumnus who lived and died in Argentina was Joseph Tokayer. The German artist studied at the Bauhaus in Dessau and graduated in 1931 with a specialization in graphic design. In 1937 he left Marseille for Buenos Aires because of the risk that Nazism presented. (Stern, too, fled Nazi persecution.) According to a local critic, Tokayer would be "the only Bauhausian in Argentina who designed contemporary graphics."[10] He worked for the graphic industry, for pharmaceutical laboratories, and for publishers. Tokayer is an exceptional case in the Argentinian design scene. He was "discovered" in 2018 through a mention of his name in an exhibition about the Bauhaus presented the previous year in Buenos Aires. His daughter, who lives in Buenos Aires, donated the photo album taken during his period in Dessau to the Bauhaus Archive. The research about the works of Tokayer in Buenos Aires is in process.

In the 1940s the foundations of modernity were revised by a new generation of architects, painters, and designers, who emphasized, even more, the utopian possibilities of modernity's ideals. It was through Tomás Maldonado, a mercurial personality, that OAM

7. Magdalena Faillace, ed., *Arquitectura e ingeniería de Alemania en Argentina* (Buenos Aires: Ministerio de Relaciones Exteriores, Comercio Internacional y Culto, 2010), 135.

8. Ibid.

9. Roxana Marcoci and Sarah Hermanson Meister, *From Bauhaus to Buenos Aires: Grete Stern and Horacio Coppola* (New York: Museum of Modern Art, 2015).

10. Sigwart Blum, "In Memoriam: José Tokayer," *Argentinisches Tageblatt*, March 5, 1972.

(Organization of Modern Architecture) and Arte Concreto Invención (Concrete Art Invention) interacted and carried out a radical revision of the status quo.

The year 1948 was decisive for the group. That year, Maldonado left the "splendid isolation" that Argentina had experienced during the war and traveled to Europe. There he made contact with the most advanced representatives of Concrete art and modern architecture and reasserted the radical position of the group.

The magazines published by Concrete Art Invention—*Arturo* and, later on *Nueva Visión*—became an important part of Argentine culture. The editors gave space to artists such as Vordemberge-Gildewart, Vantongerloo, Kandinsky, Gropius, Mies van der Rohe, Moholy-Nagy, Bauhaus alumni and the Allianz group, led by Max Bill, as well as to Swiss concrete painters like Richard Lohse, Verena Loewensberg, and Camille Graeser. The group also established links with graphic and industrial design agencies in Buenos Aires.

Cover of *Arte Concreto Invención,* Buenos Aires, August 1946

In 1954, due to his relationship with Bill, Maldonado went to Germany to teach at the recently inaugurated Ulm School of Design. Postwar Germany had suspended its progressive intellectual production during the early days of reconstruction. Now, almost a decade later, the country was ready for a new design school for democracy. Inge Scholl, Otl Aicher, and others created the Ulm school as part of the Marshall Plan's reeducation program for the German population. Bill devised the pedagogical proposal based on the Bauhaus. Gropius, too, expressed this sentiment in the opening speech in 1955, calling the school the "New Bauhaus." But it was Maldonado who, with his idea of incorporating science into the pedagogical project and of opening the school internationally, gave a special imprint on the courses—not without controversy.[11]

Maldonado left a void in Argentina, and even when he was residing in Europe his stature increased throughout Latin America. (Other important designers in Latin American countries included Anni and Josef Albers in Chile in the 1930s, Hannes Meyer in Mexico at the end of the '30s and throughout the '40s, and Max Bill in Brazil at the beginning of the '50s.) Brazil and Argentina created the first design schools in Latin America under Maldonado's direct influence. He developed the first curriculum of the Escola Superior de Desenho Indutrial (ESDI) in Rio de Janeiro. In Argentina two schools were created in the 1950s: in Mendoza by César Janello, an architect of the OAM group, and in La Plata by professors who consulted Maldonado for the pedagogical program and also visited Ulm. The first curriculum included similar subjects as the Ulm school, including physics, mathematics, and even cultural integration.

In Chile, too, Maldonado was a powerful presence. After a group of students from the University of Chile with a critical attitude

11. Tomás Maldonado, *Disegno industriale: Un riesame* (1976; Milan: Feltrinelli Editore, 2001).

Antoni Van Leeuwenhoek and Robert Hooke independently develop microscopes

toward their study program attended the Education Congress held by the ICSID in Buenos Aires in 1968, they contacted Maldonado, who told them that a former Ulm colleague was arriving in Chile to work on a technical project for the development of small- and medium-scale industries. The students got permission to participate in the Ulm-influenced project, and the university recognized their activities for the final degree. In Mexico, the first graphic design career was created in 1961 at the Universidad Iberoamericana with teachers influenced by Ulm. In 1975 the creation of a design course at the UAM University was heavily influenced by the Ulm experience. In Cuba, the Ulm school and design schools of East Germany had a strong impact on design education.

In the 1970s Venezuela offered the country's first design course at a private institute. Colombia modeled its first course on the Bauhaus Basic Course. The Tadeo Lozano University in Bogotá had academic links to the design school of Offenbach, which was to a considerable degree an heir of the Ulm school. And in the 1980s, Ecuador, Peru, Uruguay, and Paraguay opened schools for careers in design.

•

This brief overview allows us to see that, in general, design education in Latin America has its origins in a late modernity and has accompanied the industrialization processes within these countries.[12]

In the late 1980s, design courses began to be influenced by digital technology, and new positions in the burgeoning field were created, especially in private universities and private institutions. Education became a business. Public universities suffered for years from the lack of resources required to keep up with ever-evolving hardware and software systems. During the 1990s, sweeping privatization of public companies (from energy and communication to oil and banking) led to a heavy demand for designers in the area of corporate identity.

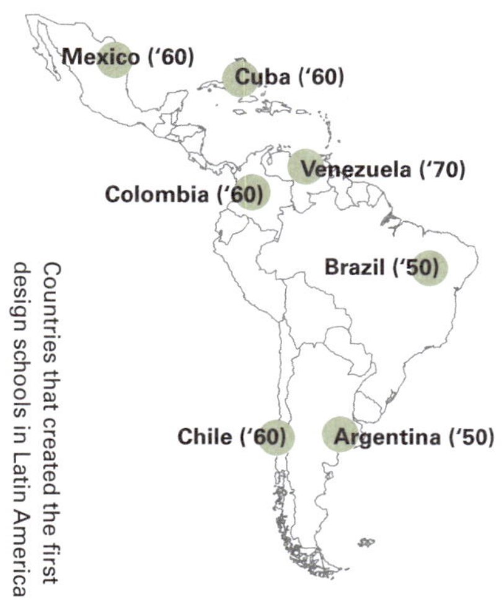

Countries that created the first design schools in Latin America

In the first decade of this century a new phenomenon in Latin American design courses arose: the growing influence of design discourse on design practice. The study of public communications opened the space for corporate identity to be theorized within design programs. The prevalence of design discourse increased academic

12. Silvia Fernández, "The Origins of Design Education in Latin America: From the HfG in Ulm to Globalization," *Design Issues* 22, no. 1 (March 2006): 3–19.

pressure for the creation of postgraduate courses—master's and doctoral programs—that could only be taught by professors with a corresponding degree. As a consequence, graduate programs in Latin America tend to produce theses based only on the discursive domain, applying a standard format of a formalized "research methodology."

Due to the inertia of academic careers in general, the graphic design area of study at the University of Buenos Aires, which was created in 1984, revised its program only in 2018. Despite this academic inaction, a wave of interest in historical studies is currently underway.

In 2007 DISUR (Argentine Academic Network of Design Careers at National Universities) was created, with members only from public and not private universities. This network has expanded throughout Latin America in recent years. The topics of each Congress offer a good opportunity to understand the concerns of the group:

- design for the formation of citizens (2015),
- design in the strengthening and integration of regional development (2016),
- design policy in Latin America (2017),
- design education in discussion (2018),
- design and gender (2019).[13]

There exists some discomfort and limited interest in programmatic questions about the future of design education. Beyond this there are critical voices that propose a fundamental revision of university education (and education in general).[14]

The changes that are generated will certainly accompany far-reaching reviews of public policies, economy, education, health, housing, and the essential political action against the inequality prevailing in a continent where more than 30 percent of the population is poor. In Argentina the latest statistics indicate that 40 percent of children live in poverty.

One can imagine everything that design could contribute to improve equality in the future. In Latin America, apparently, the utopia of modernity is still valid.

13. See DISUR, https://disur.edu.ar.

14. "Líderes de enseñanza firmaron un documento de 'Compromisos para la Educación de Argentina,'" *Perfil* (Buenos Aires), September 11, 2019, https://www.perfil.com/noticias/educacion/lideres-ensenanza-firmaron-documento-compromisos-para-educacion-argentina.phtml?rd=1.

TOWARD DESIGN AS A REFLECTIVE PRACTICE

THOMAS OCKERSE

Having worked as a graphic designer through the particular phase of its history that this book charts—from my first acquaintance with it in 1963, and throughout my career as a practitioner and educator of graphic design—I decided to write this from a reflective perspective, reviewing my history with it even as I continue to work within the field, having substantially contributed to its identity, developments, and articulations. Today I see graphic design as a discipline in its own right—and one that can ultimately contribute substantially to the evolution of humanity and the world we live in.

The development of graphic design from the early 1960s to the 1990s has been well tracked in numerous books, articles, and conferences that provoked debate and critical analysis. Growing out of the more general endeavor of "commercial art," this new field strove to adopt new values of what was seen as more responsible action in order to become a "professional practice" like architecture and product design. Having had an early start at the progressive Ulm School of Design in Germany, where it was called "visual communication design," graphic design took hold in the US in the late 1950s and early '60s. It aimed to solve problems by addressing the ways in which visual systems communicated information, while shunning the limited sensibilities typical of advertising in the commercial world.

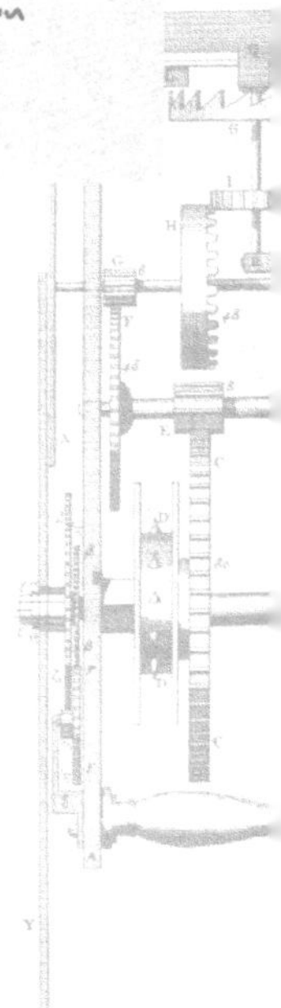

The challenge of establishing graphic design as a "professional practice" was largely the result of its resemblance to the commercial world of advertising, since both use visual language and typography to communicate ideas. But graphic designers seek quality in the communication of ideas, whereas the world of advertising too easily accepts mediocrity in its affinity with quantity and the superficial. Unfortunately, the abundance of commercial mediocrity constantly undermines the design's higher aims of quality and authenticity. This phenomenon continues to interfere with the preparation for and practice of design, tempting many non-designers to call themselves designers.

In 1963, I graduated from Ohio State University's Commercial Art Department. During my time at OSU, the BFA program began to change, implementing a new "visual communication design" program when I was a senior. OSU was increasingly interested in the Ulm School of Design as a model for its graduate program, and the school started hiring faculty from Ulm before the design school closed in 1968.

The first time I heard the term "graphic design" was in 1963, when I enrolled in Yale University's MFA in Graphic Design. That program was the first officially to adopt the name, and other schools eventually followed suit. Despite the fact that few practitioners were able to define its difference from "commercial art" and distinguish it from advertising, the term became familiar. Slowly, the field's special attention to the treatment of visual form and typography for communication needs in objects and systems like books, signage, and corporate identity helped distinguish it from the world of advertising.

Throughout the period of this book's history (late 1950s–1995), I made the practice of graphic design an intimate part of my life. My practice and teaching came to mean more and more to me, and I increasingly saw graphic design as a professional discipline. Over time it became clear to me that the purpose of design was far more expansive than the fulfilling of a "need" or the solution of a communication "problem"; it was, instead, an opportunity to honor the ideal potential for its products to contribute to our world and humanity as incentives to the deepest potentials of our human sensibilities in search of value and truth.

For many years the territory of design practice was relatively simple, consisting of graphic design (the design of visual communication), industrial design (the design of objects), and architecture (the design of spaces). Today that territory often appears to have expanded, with a proliferation of "design" expertise under new labels, such as: information design or information architecture, experience design, interface design, interaction design, interactive design, universal design, service design, ethnographic design, human centered design, user centered design. The new jargon includes terms like persona, stakeholders, usability, scenario, human factors, heuristic evaluation, design thinking, action-centric design, etc.

These new labels may be reminiscent of the emperor's new clothes, but together they remind us that "design" is no longer a limited, specialized skill. Rather, it reflects a democratized practice of implicit, multicentered intelligence. Technology tends to facilitate the democratization of design by incorporating insights from different fields (computer science, engineering, biology, cultural anthropology, behavioral psychology, linguistics, marketing, etc.). Thus, individuals from other fields find their way into design as a new field in which to apply their knowledge.

Of course, this has also confused the field and confused its identity. For example, the relational phenomenon often directly reflects the design of electronic devices as a distinctive endeavor labeled as Experience Design and Interaction Design. However, "experience" and "interaction" remain fundamental to the principles of design, i.e., objects like tickets, posters, books, guides, doorknobs, cell phones, buildings, social environments, and the internet all serve the need for human interaction and human experience. Nothing new, really, since design values were always intended to address human nature, human interests, and human environments—and relational awareness does not change the *principles* of design knowledge and skill. Plus, this multirelational collaboration provides a powerful way of looking at our design future.

Christiaan Huygens develops the pendulum clock

Learning Under the Influence

What design means to me now was fostered early on by the vision of the Yale graduate program and the individuals who taught there, particularly Norman Ives, Herbert Matter, Walker Evans, Alexey Brodovitch, Bradbury Thompson, Paul Rand, John Hill, Polly Lada-Mocarski, John McCrillis, and the leader of the gang, Alvin Eisenman. These teachers encouraged me in a process of search. Eventually I converted *search* to *inquiry*—which is search with intention and purpose. Inquiry, as part of a spiraling process and energy, creates theory. When theory is applied to practice, it leads to further inquiry, and as this reciprocal process continues the mysteries of our work are gradually unveiled. The process reflects the so-called doctrine of shells (i.e., to uncover what lies hidden, within or without) and thereby to also gain an ever-expanding view of relational factors from the invisible and visible worlds we live in). This gathering of perception becomes a conscious building of knowledge and insight that we must share so that others can also continue to build on it.

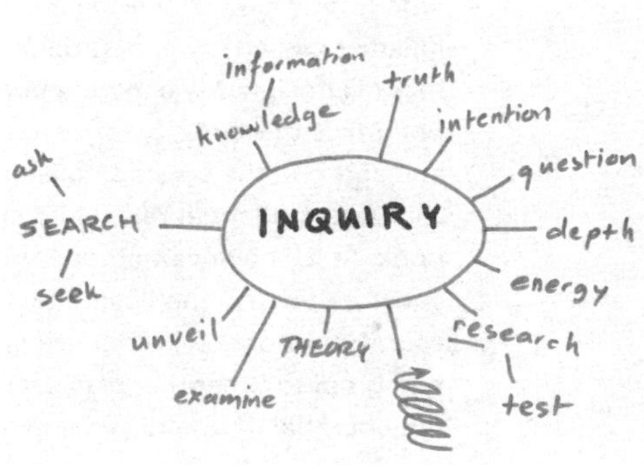

After receiving my MFA in 1965, I began my career as a graphic designer at J. K. Fogelman Associates, a small studio in Morristown, New Jersey. There I worked directly under the direction of Jim Fogelman. Ignorant as I was of the field of "graphic design," and relatively uninformed of "scholarly" interests, I was unaware of Jim's status in the field. Jim's long and illustrious career was pioneering: he was credited by Philip B. Meggs as the originator of "corporate identity design" in America for his work with large companies like CIBA. In Jim's studio I worked for two years on design accounts for CIBA, Hoffman LaRoche, Interchem, Syntex, and others. From his mentorship I gained great insight into this field of practice, which I now identify as a principal practice of Design with a capital D.

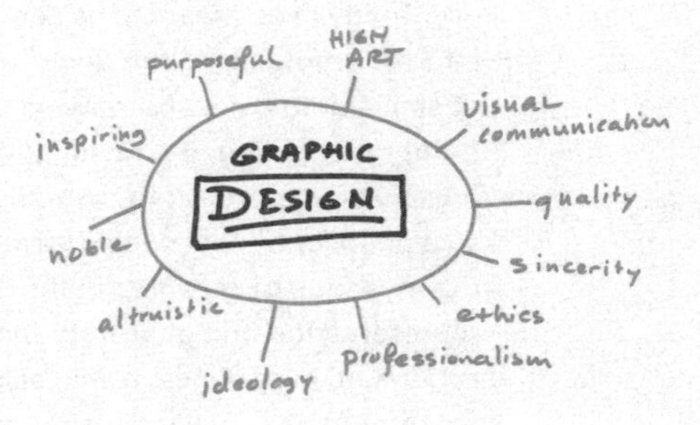

Learning from Teaching

After my two years at J. K. Fogleman I began teaching in graphic design at Indiana University (1967–71). At IU I confidently offered what I had been taught at Yale, often using the same assignments, supplemented with insight from my professional experience. However, a group of MFA students who were also teaching in the Graphic Design program began to question my "practical" approach to teaching as well as my private design practice. Their questions were genuine, stimulated by their educational program, their innate curiosity, and the activism of the '60s. Their friendly confrontation inspired me to reassess my assignments and teaching methods by giving students significant latitude to discover themselves and their own interests while exploring graphic design work. This also brought back fond memories of Norman Ives, whose assignments and manner of teaching were the highlights of my own education.

The dynamic environment at IU included other departments and people, like Mary Ellen Solt, a professor of Comparative Literature, who made "concrete poetry" and sought my advice on typography, and Umberto Eco, who exposed me to semiotics. These ideas provoked my experimentation with the ideas of and means for graphic design. My concrete poetry drove an inquiry into the *poetic* potentials of words, type, visual form, and the experience of time and space in the created objects.

As a student at Yale, I had created the *A-Z-Book* as a children's book. At IU, however, others praised it as a remarkable work of concrete poetry, and I came to see it from a different perspective: as a "bookwork" for a poetic experience. My IU laboratory for typographic experiments essentially gave me fabulous insights into the potential of graphic design as an opportunity for poetics!

Expanding Insight

I came to realize that my experimental work centered on aspects of *meaning* in visual form—an obvious concern for visual communication, but one I had only confronted intuitively. For designers the primary focus was on visual form and aesthetics and their integration with materiality and technology; practical applications came last. I discovered that other designers were unable or even unwilling to address the idea of "meaning," as they were primarily interested in the visual aspects of design. Only faculty from other IU departments, like Solt and Eco, were interested in questions of semantics due to their linguistic interests.

Today I see *meaning* as central to the process of design. My interest unfolded (cf. the doctrine of shells) into a new framework for understanding, the result of my unscholarly approach to *semiotics* as a philosophy that could unwrap the mystique of *meaning* in the representation and interpretation of action and experience. It was also a result of my gradually developing interest in *theosophy* as a source of perennial philosophy and universal metaphysics; and my interest in studying the nature of the mind from scientific and noetic-scientific perspectives.

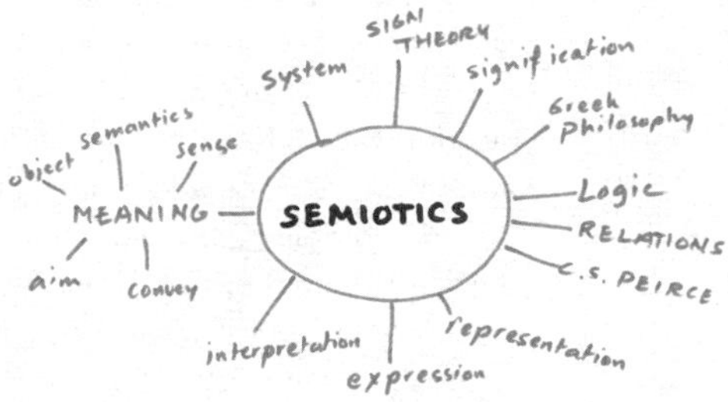

In 1971, after four years at IU, I started teaching in the Graphic Design department at RISD. At the time, the program, albeit heavily influenced by Yale's graduate program, had become too fragmented and disordered and needed attention. The appointed head was a senior professor from the Illustration program who had hoped to combine the two programs into one as Visual Communication. Two years later I became department head. With the goal to help rebuild the graphic design program over the next few years (including the decision to not combine with the Illustration program), I began to understand design and design education in new ways and in more depth. The program's sudden increase in enrollment fostered its growth and forced active discussions among the department's four full-time faculty members (including me) about the nature and purpose of the department.

The faculty members were eager to bring their different experiences and ideas into cohesion for the overall graphic design curriculum. Some of the expertise the faculty brought to this discussion was related to the Ulm school, which expanded our perspectives to make sure it included visual form, systems thinking, semiotics, planning and methodology, and even the business of design. Together we crafted a program that fused the diversity of our experiences into a common overall vision and mission.

That led to a very engaged and dynamic program that attracted more and more students. The department's growth—of both students and faculty members—raised further questions about what and how we taught, with an eye toward relevance for a field that was still young and largely undefined. While we as a faculty felt good about the program we had developed, we also received plenty of criticism, since the external expectations (including from students) did not necessarily match their insistence on seeing the practice of graphic design as a "commercial" art!

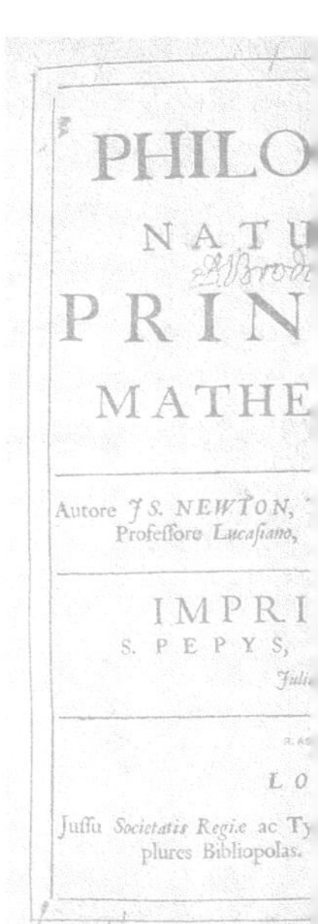

Public Didactics

That criticism was based on the generally established perceptions of graphic design, and it made us decide to share our curriculum publicly to better communicate what it was about. In the fall of 1976, we presented a "didactic exhibition" of the program in the main student gallery at RISD, sharing what the faculty taught and why. Importantly, we decided not merely to present student work as subjective examples of work (typical for such exhibitions at RISD); instead we shared the curriculum as a whole, allowing the faculty to decide how the visual examples of student work could represent their courses and the reasons for assignments. The faculty came together to describe the underlying principles involved in what we shared and envisioned, and how our differences would best contribute to this.

As one might expect from professional graphic designers, we used the information we gathered to create a comprehensive list of words that would reflect the subjects, concepts, and skills of our graphic design curriculum. This list of words was categorized in a somewhat logical manner and organized into a diagram. This diagram was duplicated, and copies were mounted in front of each group of visual samples in the exhibition. The diagrams had red dots placed in front of key words that the faculty member considered most expressive of the images that followed for the assignments and course work.

The diagrams were all that accompanied the huge range of visual examples, excepting a few texts near the entrance that introduced the exhibition by defining graphic design as a practice and 1686 describing its educational objectives. This exhibition proved very successful, not only in terms of attendance but also for stimulating pedagogical debate with other programs in the college. The holistic presentation of the program also helped bring other departments into a process of reexamination of their own programs from a more unified perspective.

Presentations in the student gallery tended to last only one or two weeks. Our exhibition was no exception, which proved very unfortunate considering its popularity and the extensive effort made for it. However, the effort was of immense value for everyone

involved, especially for the faculty member, who gained a much deeper understanding of what it takes to teach, and prepare students for, a field of practice. It strengthened our determination to define the field of graphic design as a *professional discipline*, and thereby work toward the future of the program and its embrace of Graphic Design as a discipline within higher education.

Installation at Wood-Gerry Gallery, RISD, Providence, Rhode Island, 1976 and cover for *Graphic Design Education: An Exposition* (1977)

Graphic Design Education: An Exposition

In 1977 we decided to share the content and methods of our effort with a broader audience. Public awareness had already developed well beyond the lingering notions of the field's "commercial/advertising" emphasis, but we wanted to share with other institutions what a design curriculum should attend to in preparing students for the field. Our efforts resulted in a publication entitled *Graphic Design Education: An Exposition*, a modest, thirty-two-page booklet limited by a tight budget.

As principal author of this booklet's text, I later developed the text as a working paper for the Education Committee of the American Institute of Graphic Arts. At that time, I was an AIGA

Isaac Newton formulates his three laws of motion

board member and founding member of the Education Committee. After many revisions and contributions, the paper was published in 1987 by the AIGA under the title "Graphic Design Education."

While the content of the 1977 booklet was a major guide for the department's undergraduate program at RISD, it also sparked a graduate program. From the inception of the MFA program at RISD in 1978 until 1990, I carried a full teaching load in addition to considerable administrative duties as chair of the department and head of the graduate program. It was only in 1990, when I stepped down as director of the undergraduate program, that I was able to look back at the department's development since 1976—something I had been eager to do for decades. I wanted to document these developments, not only because of my intimate involvement with every phase of the department's birth and evolution but also in order to reaffirm its quality and substance. This project culminated in the 1991 publication of *SPIRALS*.

SPIRALS was first envisioned in the 1980s as an annual publication for the department faculty and students. However, a lack of funds delayed its realization, and when the first issue finally became possible there was already a huge backlog of contributions ready for inclusion. That resulted in an overly ambitious effort that ultimately nixed future issues. This issue was called *SPIRALS'91* and was published as a boxed set of eight booklets totaling 360 pages—and was indeed the last printed publication from the department.

For *SPIRALS'91* I wrote an in-depth essay about the department's graphic design education entitled "Position Paper." It was intended as an objective overview for a general perspective, and therefore purposely avoided any tendencies toward ideology or subjective emphasis. "Position Paper" thus helped frame the contents of other, more subjective articles in *SPIRALS'91*.[1] This text offered definitive statements on the *practice of graphic design as a discipline* as we had come to view it, and the pedagogy required to prepare students for the discipline.

The excerpts from "Position Paper" below demonstrate how well, in my opinion, some of its tenets have held up. By 1990, the field of graphic design had matured a great deal, and the practice had more fully realized its role in culture and society and had accepted professional responsibility for *informational objects or environments*. The excerpts also point to what has changed and what was overlooked, and to that end, I have added a new section on design as a reflective practice.

Graphic Design: The Practice of a Discipline

To appreciate the scope of knowledge and extent of skills necessary for the practice of graphic design we must first understand what "the practice of graphic design" is: or, rather, what it will be ten or fifteen years from now as the practitioner matures and the field develops. Graphic design involves the production of visual "language" to communicate "messages." Through visual communication, the designer purposefully marks, signs, and names thoughts, events, or facts. The designer conveys information with a definite meaning and purpose. As a problem-solver, the designer aids his fellow man in the process of problem analysis and the synthesis of ideas into solutions. The graphic design "product" contains the conscious integration of the human factor, technology, and aesthetics. The development of this product considers "need" as paramount, stresses the primacy of information communication, and measures the utility of solutions by a social gauge. Visual communication in itself covers a vast territory, especially in this age of expanded technology in mass communication. Those who practice visual communication are recognized by many titles: commercial artists, directors of advertising, illustrators, animators, photographers, typographers, or printers—to name a few. The graphic designer also functions within this broad panorama. Yet, since the profession is rather new (the term has only been used in the United States since the late Fifties), there are often misunderstandings about what it entails. For this reason it is necessary to clarify the distinction between graphic design and other visual communication activities, and to clarify the unique function of the graphic designer.

What separates graphic design from other commercial or visual communication practices is its emphasis on a greater understanding of the structural and aesthetic function of form as information; a concern for objectivity in problem solving; and a recognition of the need for socially responsible communication. The products created by graphic designers can appear similar to those of commercial artists as far as their production and use, but the crucial difference lies in the designer's reliance on an underlying value system which has at its core a concern for human need and social value. The designer must always keep the larger social context of his solutions in mind, and, at the same time, define the needs of the

1. A note in the preface of *SPIRALS'91* outlines the evolution of "Position Paper" and the aim to be the starting point for dialogue: "This text in SPIRALS'91 could be considered a third generation of the original text mentioned above (cf. 1977). Improvements upon the use of its written language were made, with some phrasings borrowed from the AIGA publication. Major new segments were added which are based on writings and lectures by Ockerse for other occasions. The author hopes that this document is not merely appreciated as a comprehensive description of the ideological framework of the graphic design program at RISD, but also a document that becomes a basis for on-going discussions among those who are participating in the program, and a reference for those outside RISD who are interested in the promulgation of graphic design education."

client and that client's perspective. The final visual solution is merely the residue of a process which mediates the needs, function, goals, and objectives of the project. [. . .]

"Good design" is a marriage of form, content, and function. In selecting the appropriate language for the solution, the designer must first truly understand the ramifications of the assignment. The response to that problem must be limited, of course, to the operational life of the product. However, as Moholy-Nagy said: "Man. not the product, is the aim." Societal needs are crucial. Therefore, for the designer, "creativity" means the ability to work innovatively within the constraints imposed by the problem, with available technology, and with cognizance of the human social setting.

Advancement in the sciences and a general growing social awareness require that the graphic designer, as an interpreter of human communications, have a thorough understanding of the intricacies of human relationships. As contributor to human communications, the designer must be fully aware of not only what is said, but of how it is said, and must demonstrate sensitivity to what is implied and inferred by others. In meeting these needs, the graphic designer must progress with society rather than perpetuate the past. Moreover, the designer must act as innovator rather than as imitator.

Unlike its many counterparts in visual communication, graphic design does not take a subordinate attitude to the "marketplace." Nor does the designer depend on cosmetic solutions and voguish imitations. The designer will always seek to produce well-designed products which contain a sense of timelessness. Whereas the commercial artist does not need to have a critical appreciation for the social, epistemological, and visual problems involved in forming his products (except, perhaps, cosmetically), this appreciation is essential for the graphic designer. Mediating between client and user (or audience) is a crucial skill for the graphic designer. Clients can be individuals, groups, or institutions, and their needs are: to publicly present, distribute, or promote a name, fact, product, event, or system. Since the term "design" denotes planning and forming, the graphic designer's expertise can be viewed in this way: a. the designer as planner, with particular knowledge and skills in analysis, systematic planning, processes, and the conceptualization of ideas (essential skills for design analysts, planners, project coordinators,and directors): b. the designer as form-giver, with specific knowledge and skills in the production of visual systems and form expression.

The graphic designer must have at least some knowledge and skill in both areas. The distinction serves merely to establish possible extremes of interest or expertise with a single area. Often the scale of a project requires varieties of expertise, and these separate functions may be assumed by many people or by a single person.

The Evolution of Practice and Education in Graphic Design

With [design's] maturity comes knowledge and understanding. But knowledge and understanding increase the depth and complexity of problems and also add to the development of the practice. Practitioners then need to be even more informed and have greater critical skills to deal with these revealed complexities. Such a practice requires a higher level of learning than "training" alone permits; and this higher level is what we refer to as "education." As our knowledge and understanding of basic principles beneath the activity of the practice develops through education, theory is formed. Just as each learning phase brings greater understanding to the field of practice, so does the practice add to the education, each carrying the other into its next level. This is not a cycle, but a spiral, in which ideas evolve to higher planes. It is this evolution which transforms a trade into a profession.

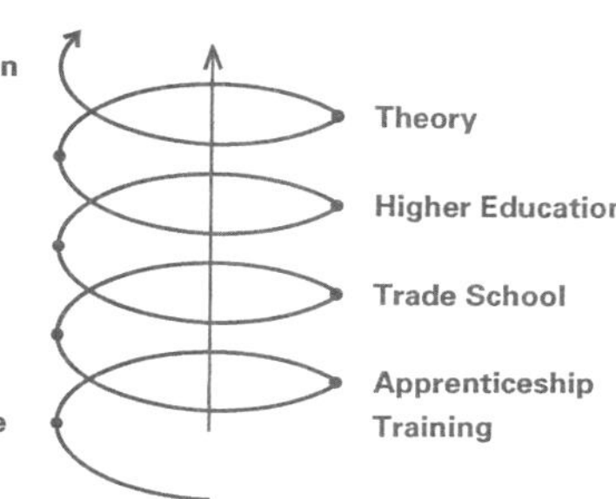

Just as practitioners have come to understand the significance of their service to society, so has the public come to expect practitioners to be effective in their services.

Graphic Design Education

[. . .] Training is concerned with preparing the student for specific tasks: the known. But education concerns itself with preparing for the future: the unknown. To respond to the educational needs of tomorrow's graphic designer, higher education offers undergraduate and graduate programs. This means a specific period of time, generally four to six years, devoted solely to general education and practice related requirements.

How to synthesize general education with a more specific graphic design education is a matter of balancing institutional priorities. We can model this principle as two triangles: the general and the specific. One represents the emphasis of basic education in the beginning years and its decrease over time, while the other triangle demonstrates the concentration in graphic design, which begins slowly and is increased over time. Undergraduate levels should emphasize general education, with the concentration limited to the fundamentals of that field. Over the study years the concentration gradually increases and naturally becomes full concentration in the form of graduate study or practice.

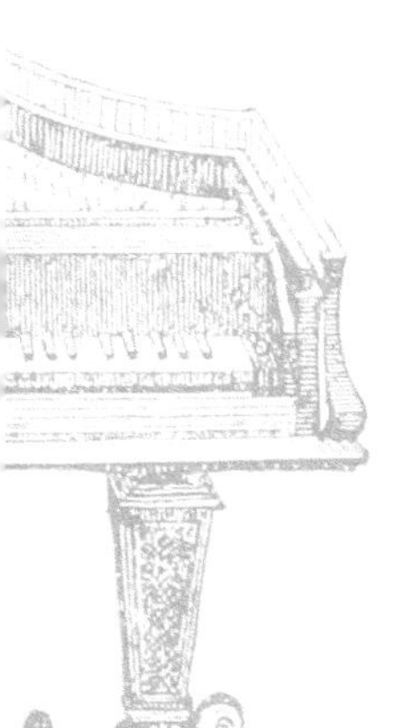

The effect of the Bauhaus on design is still very much with us today, especially in the area of education. And wherever the phrase originated, the form follows function principle or the form follows function myth will surely be debated for some time to come.

Art and design: some definitions. As I indicated earlier, I can't see one without seeing the other. Take either the heart or the mind out of the body and what do you have left?

Design is external, in that its forms and application extend basic human functions and needs. These pertain to three primary areas — messages, as in our need to communicate with each other; products, which enable us to extend the mechanical functions of the body; and environment, or control of conditions around us.

Art is internal, in that its forms affect the senses and thereby influence the psyche, the emotions, the spirit. The fine arts emanate from the area of human messages. They involve the individual, the one whose forming is a singular act. And they involve the individual who may or may not elect to correspond with the maker of that form. This does not rule out the human need on both sides.

Design as a profession today is too generalized at best, and, at worst, it is totally misunderstood. It becomes a catchall for any forming or communicating endeavor which does not bear the label of fine art.

We must clarify and set off the meaning of design — with a small "d." It is the basic, intelligible order of a system or structure evident in any form. The graphic designer, industrial designer, or architect may often use such an order as a vehicle by which other functions or messages are made manifest.

Design with a big "D" — the design profession — is a problem solving activity. The problem or task most often originates with someone other than the designer. This is the client. There is an understanding between the two about the intended objective of the task prior to starting the project. The person who uses or receives the result is neither the client nor the designer, but someone totally outside the design process.

Very often the first responsibility of the designer is to design the problem, for the client can only speak in terms of a need, a result, or an answer. The designer must be objective and not indulge in self-expression at the expense of the intended purpose or function. The designer remains backstage and can change as the problem dictates. The identity of the fine artist too often becomes locked in a singular style or technique.

The designer works in cooperation with others, if not on a design team, then at least in communication with, or as the bridge between, the client and the technical means by which the project is realized.

The designer can affect other levels beyond the project at hand and even beyond the immediate concern or knowledge of the client. For instance, solving a problem to accommodate handicapped persons makes the solution much better for everyone using it.

Design is well done if it does its job. Design becomes an art when it elevates the task to touch the spirit as well.

The place of design (small "d") in the fine arts is important, but I feel it is often misunderstood by those who are either inexperienced or insecure. They have a fear that an evidence of order or purpose will compromise artistic freedom and expression. There is the mystique that artistic truth and fulfillment are only found on the fringe of the unexplained: "if you can't figure it out, it must be art."

The designer or fine artist cannot go very far without assimilating a basic visual literacy necessary for all forming and visual communication, directed or expressed. What experienced dancer, no matter how improvisational the performance, does not know the function and limit of every muscle in the body? The visual artist and the designer must be as prepared.

We will always have with us those engaged in art for art's sake, design for design's sake, and architecture for architecture's sake, each in a closed world. This is where theory and controversy are often incubated. We will also have, on the other end of the scale, compromise and commercialization to test moral standards in each of these professional areas.

I believe that there is a stronger commonality between fine art and design if we laterally cut across these areas. The best fine artist and the best designer share a confidence and an understanding of their own work. They understand and respect those principles inherent in the other discipline. The less accomplished or less confident artist or designer clings to a style or depends on certain rules, is swayed by fashion or fad, and in the end really doesn't offer much to our world.

We must make a difference. If we have a strong idea, a strong form will follow. Consider the Shaker chair; whether it is 100 years old or was carefully hand-crafted last year, we are still drawn to the beauty of the proportion and to the feel of the material. The idea is its strength.
We cannot teach creativity, but if you know your tools well, and you understand the basic language, inspiration will follow. Don't be afraid of a certain discipline, because control of your abilities will give you a freedom of movement to do what you want. Know the past, but don't hide in the closet of history. Your ideas will form the future and these must make a difference. Art and design then become a matter of personal choice and application. The better you are, the less these labels will be a concern.

An Overview of the Practice Related Subjects, Concepts, and Skills in Graphic Design Education
The following classifications and categories review the subjects, concepts, and skills that should be incorporated in the graphic design curriculum in various ways and in varying depth. This list forms the content for a basic graphic design education.

Visual Form, Perception, Configuration, and Aesthetics
Graphic designers must be sensitive to the perceptual and aesthetic functioning of visual forms. In other words, they must be visually literate. These forms make up a language of the visual: that is to say, they produce a grammar or syntactics made up of: point, line, plane, volume, texture, color, figure-ground, juxtaposition, sequence, rhythm, module, proportion, symmetry, gestalt, programming, and hierarchy. Studies and experiences center on visual phenomena and perceptual problems. Since these are elemental, they are studied throughout the curriculum and are found in a broad array of visual art courses. The graphic design curriculum should include course work that leads to concepts and skills in:
Form Analysis, Visual Phenomena, Unity of Form, Perceptual Differentiation
Structure and System
Composition and Visual Framing
Visual Abstraction

Methods, Processes, and Techniques for Visual Forming
Graphic designers must be familiar with the basic tools, techniques, and processes that generate or produce images, sketches, models, and finished objects. They must use hand tools with skill and sensitivity in order to develop craftsmanship, which is integral to the creative process and to the making of objects. It follows that they must also know basic methods to visualize, to develop form, and to practice visual schematics. The graphic design curriculum should include course work that leads to concepts and skills in:
Drawing
Visual Translation
Visualizing Techniques
Model Making
Visual Schematization, Mapping

Technology and Production Systems

Technology plays a constant role in the process of design, in the production of objects, and in the methods for the visual transmittal of information. Graphic designers are responsible for the visual translation of ideas into two and three dimensions as well as into the creation of environments and computerized and projected systems. These designers must be aware of the potential production and communication uses of relevant materials, media, and technologies, and must have the ability to critically judge the quality of craft for other professionals and services used.

The graphic design curriculum should include course work that leads to knowledge and appreciation of concepts and skills in:

Typesetting Technology
Photography and Graphic Arts Technology
Film and Video Graphics
Printing Technology
Paper Making Technology
Binding and other Finishing Systems
Computer Technology Systems

Visual Communication

Graphic designers address communication problems. They interpret ideas and represent them with visual systems. They understand how meaning is formed and how the visual language functions in this capacity. They know how to incorporate expressive qualities in message presentation to achieve a desired effect. In these ways they contribute not only to the advancement of the field but to systems for human communication as well.

The graphic design curriculum should include course work that leads to concepts and skills in:

Visualizing and Expressing Information
Semantics of Form and Structure
Semiotics (Theories of Sign, Language, and Communication)

Strategic Design and Design Process Management

Graphic designers objectively determine design priorities and alternatives: they help clients determine needs. They define strategies for design solutions: they research, define, and evaluate criteria and requirements: they develop and refine concepts; and present these through sketches and models.

Designers coordinate many diverse aspects of projects (including production requirements, design management, and sometimes marketing strategies) to unify results. With the problem-solving essential to any design situation, this task can vary in scope, method, and application.

To manage complexity effectively, the graphic designer needs to understand these processes on many levels, from form creation to professional practice, and create methodologies that serve as guides in these processes.

The graphic design curriculum should include course work that leads to concepts and skills in:

Strategic Planning: Goals, Facts, Needs, Research, Action
Creative and Rational (Methodological) Processes

Computer-Aided Problem Solving
Process and Product Management
Design Evaluation

Communicating Concepts and Requirements

Graphic designers communicate both concepts and requirements to the client: to production specialists; to other professionals who contribute to the design process; and to members of the broader social framework. This communication involves expression and transmittal as well as the reception and evaluation of information. Graphic designers are expected to have the skills to communicate at all stages of the design process.

The graphic design curriculum should include course work that leads to concepts and skills in:
Specifying Technical Instructions
Writing Objectives, Briefs, and Reports
Verbal, Graphic, and Audiovisual Presentations
Listening

Business and Professional Practices

As partners in the world of business and society, graphic designers accept a professional responsibility and ethical stewardship that relates to design practice. They run offices, keep records, and write contracts. They fulfill obligations and contractual responsibilities. They have the skills to work effectively and to negotiate with others. They understand the role of the graphic designer in the process of design production. And they are able to appreciate the contribution of relevant disciplines.

The graphic design curriculum should include course work that leads to knowledge and appreciation of concepts and skills in:
Business Responsibilities and Ethical Stewardship
Lawful Aspects in Design Practice
Accounting and Taxation
Estimation, Valuation, and Budgeting
Contract Writing and Negotiation

History

Graphic designers should have a sense of their work and its relationship to history. In particular they must have a knowledge of facts, trends, and sequences in the historical developments in visual communication design and technology. Exposure to significant contributors and movements provides both a framework within which graphic design can be examined and the work of role models studied.

Specific subjects of study for graphic design in history are:
History of Letterforms and Typography
History of Graphic Arts and Printing
History of Graphic Design / Visual Communication
History of Design Arts (Architecture, Industrial Design)

Critical Thought, Ethics, and Society

Graphic designers, as significant contributors to the products of society and therefore the world we live in, accept a professional responsibility and ethical stewardship as protectors of public and environmental

Jethro Tull invents the horse-drawn seed drill

well-being. For this reason, they must understand the value of their contributions in such contexts as: culture and artifact; aesthetics and exhibition; social purpose and function; economy and technology; human ecology, cycle, and the environment; education and social development; philosophy and ethics. Design criticism provides a framework in which to raise questions concerning such value orientation.

With this overview of subjects, concepts, and skills, the list becomes an instrument for programs to map out the curriculum content: what is taught; where and when in the program items are taught; and the relations courses, projects, or experiences have to each other as building blocks. From the overall picture adjustments can be made as desired, with as much emphasis on a certain item or a lack of attention to others brought in balance, or the reasons of emphasis or de-emphasis merely clarified to position the program from a philosophical basis.

The Learning Environment[2]

To strive for the educational goals of both general education and practice it is necessary to integrate curriculum content with an appropriate learning environment: teachers, teaching methods, environment, equipment, and institutional support systems.

The Faculty

The foremost stimulus in the educational environment is the faculty. It forms the content and makes any curriculum successful, or not. As the primary source for most information, its members stimulate values and appreciations.

The Program

As in most disciplines, a well-coordinated graphic design program provides students with a progression of learning experiences that result in a structured sequence of required and elected courses.

Teaching Methods

A teaching method in graphic design must contain two aspects:

1. Theory and Inquiry: teaching based on (universal) principles, or the "theory" approach (e.g., abstractions for observation and application).
2. Practice: teaching based on the practical information of facts and specifics (e.g., concrete skills that directly relate to techniques and simulated office practices, to "real" problems, to teaching by example).

Both are important since each serves different aspects of graphic design preparation. Indeed, their integration is critical.

Theory and Inquiry

It is important to note that the very nature of inquiry is as natural to the practice as it is to the study of graphic design. Consider the responsibilities designers carry in their practice. The subjects of human communication, visual language, and problem solving are but a few that present this practice with difficult questions. As society develops,

2. Note that the "Position Paper" adds an extensive text for each part, which is not included here.

so does communication practice, and so do our questions expand. The practice itself, by its very nature one of seeking appropriate responses to human problems, contributes considerably to this inquiry. Research and search, analysis and evaluation: these are natural activities in the practice of design, as has been stated. But since its practice is also limited in its ability to delve deeply into this inquiry, higher education can and must absorb the responsibility. Some of this can happen in undergraduate programs, in student projects, but especially through the assignments of an educated faculty. Courses are already abstractions of the subject, and they provide a basis from which to view principles at work without the worry of "practical" matters. At graduate levels of study the process of inquiry becomes a major directive for students: for this reason, theory enters easily and naturally here.

The word "theory" is often a red flag to the very practical people that graphic designers are, but such apprehension stems from a misunderstanding about just what theory is. We know that theory helps to develop a framework for principles: a foundation on which to build. We learn about "visual phenomena" and "contrast" to understand principles that apply to many types of specific situations. (We can never learn all situations, but we can prepare ourselves for them when they arise by learning principles!) Theory demonstrates interrelations and maps the organization of specifics. Theory de-mystifies the complex; and this is essential to education, because to understand means to simplify. And when we are aware and understand, knowledge becomes powerful and generative! Specifics, on the other hand, are limited information and lack generative power. Understanding principles and relations offers new insights and forms the very stimulus for creativity and innovation. In other words, theory simply means to get to the essence of something.

To such an end design theory is developed from practice, for the designer becomes aware of recurring elements, and begins to understand the principles in action beneath the surface of specific design applications. Theory can also be borrowed from other disciplines such as sociology, philosophy, linguistics, or mathematics; however, where possible, it should be incorporated into studio practice. That is, principles should be understood in application rather than in isolation.

The "Position Paper" was later revised to discuss the development of the theory of graphic design, particularly in terms of semiotics.

The Language for Communication

To prepare oneself for the field called graphic design, one has to learn the "parts" as a cohesive "system" of parts. This "system" as a whole is also called the "language" the graphic designer uses to communicate. Moreover, this is a "visual" language, emphasized by the word *graphic.*

This *visual language* can be broken down into its "grammatical" dimensions: the *syntactic dimension*, consisting of the visual forms and structures of the means of communication; the *semantic dimension*, consisting of the semiotics that identifies parts and wholes of meaningful elements; and the *pragmatic dimension*, defining how the parts can be used effectively by the designer to *speak with, for,* and *to* a public in the presentation of ideas and messages. This breakdown, as we know from linguistics, helps us to understand how the result can produce right interpretation.

Designers must have the knowledge and skills of each dimension of the language. The points below are in the "Position Paper," but here noted under the three dimensions.

The Syntactic Dimension:
an understanding of form perception;
an aesthetic sensitivity to visual form and object, and their role in their environment;
a knowledge and skill in visual forming, structuring, and media translations;
an awareness of relevant materials and media, with an ability to choose objectively that which is appropriate.

The Semantic Dimension:
a knowledge of communication and sign theory;
an ability to identify, define, and analyze problems.

The Pragmatic Dimension:
knowledge of concepts and facts from the humanities, social and natural sciences, and technology, and an ability to synthesize them;
an ability to communicate concepts and requirements, verbally and visually;
a knowledge of business responsibilities.

The Language Use

The proficient use of language as a system of parts depends partly on its ability to incorporate forms of expression for holistic perception, and to help mediate the explicit and the implicit. We can identify three types of language uses: the practical, the dialectical, and the poetical.

• The practical is a language-use to communicate information with a singleness of meaning, characteristic of clarity for direct information (as opposed to metaphor and emotional devices). It is in itself indifferent to the indirect, cognitive, or meta-qualities. It is therefore the most useful in daily life. The dictionary is a good example.

• The dialectical is a language-use to communicate with logical argumentation, meaning to encourage, counsel, or persuade. Typically, this includes a mindset to define a position. It often has ulterior motives, as we can see in advertising, propaganda, and political speeches. Characteristically, an argument takes a position, an oblique point of view.

• The poetical is a language-use to communicate by stimulating the imagination and the intelligence—one's higher level of consciousness. A characteristic device is to expect one to "experience" the object of communication, as a participant in the experience to integrate with the object. The intention is to satisfy an inner sense that deepens or broadens one's view or understanding. It evokes principles and values, essence and vitality.

• These three uses of language are not discrete and separate but relate to each other in a dynamic state of relatives that can best be understood in their concentric relations: the simplest and most immediate in the center; the most difficult and abstract on the outside. Although one mode is emphasized according to motive and need, all three are always present. That means the apparently simple or limited still is capable of depth and poetry, while the complex and abstract has an apparent need for more clarity.

Design for Semiosis

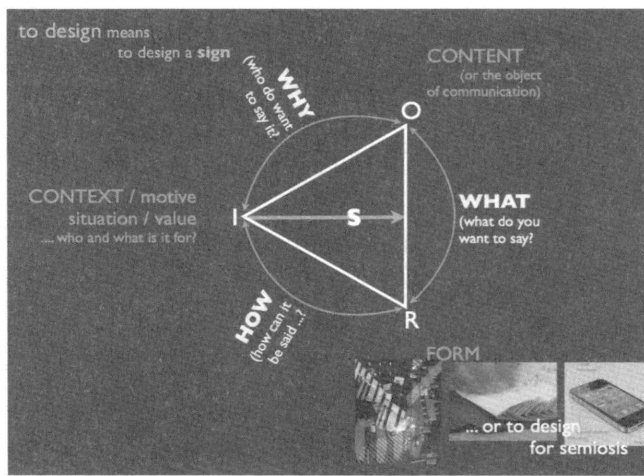

This is the area that had been traditionally covered by so-called communication theory. However, whereas communication theory speaks more to the relationships between *sender* and *receiver*, semiotics expands our understanding of the relationship through the study of sign processes, or *semiosis. Semiosis* involves the inquiries into *what*, *why*, and *how*; but it also brings in the relative meaning of *form* (and all that comes with one's experience with the design that results); *content* (and all that is considered part of the *information* and *message* to communicate); and *context* (with all that can be considered to give particular value to the relationship recipients will have with it as a result, as well as the situation this will relate to, and the motives behind this design). This creates a triangular dynamic for an interaction among the three arts that affect each other constantly.

The "Position Paper" concludes by noting that "the design arts in higher education must address a practical discipline in providing a sound underpinning in a general education that includes the fine arts. The practical and functional requirements of the design product, and of the process entailed in forming it, are by no means divorced from the object's poetic, spiritual potential equal to 'art'! The intuitive faculties of the designer remain just as important for the design arts as they are for the free arts and are as needed in spite of design's more rational appearance. Therefore, if anything is to be said, we can vouch that more is demanded from students in design arts than from students in free arts."

•

I still agree with many of the claims of the "Position Paper," but there are important additional aspects of the theory of graphic design that I have expanded well beyond the moment of the early 1990s: graphic design as a discipline and design as a *practical* and *reflective* practice. I conclude this essay by elaborating on both.

Graphic Design as a Discipline

To underscore the value and meaning of the word *discipline*, we must understand the full meaning of that word. That is partly due to a limited perception of that word that unfortunately carries negative connotations related to punishment. However, to the contrary, discipline simply means to have regulated action in accord with a certain practice—like Design. With discipline one gains control, and with that come structure and stability for actions. And then, and ONLY from discipline, the door to freedom opens!

Jocko Willink describes this well: "While Discipline and Freedom seem like on opposite sides of the spectrum, they are actually very connected. The only way to get to a place of freedom is through discipline. If you want more free time, you have to follow a more disciplined time management system. You also have to have the discipline to say 'No' to things that eat up your time with no payback."[3] Thus, if you want *design freedom*, you must have *design discipline*. Consider this especially for Design, since having freedom in design is truly at the heart of what I have called right motive and right action!

To develop a practice as a *discipline* and move it as such beyond the "commercial" and superficial tendencies of advertising remains critical. Without this, the very notion of Graphic Design remains merely commercial art. I have said this above but feel a strong need to repeat it here because, unfortunately, I have continually seen graphic designers struggle with this throughout its professional history. I have especially seen this in the educational programs of graphic design and slide back into the superficial base for commercial art. That may come from having lost sight of this practice as a discipline, or from not caring what that means; or from never having understood the underlying principle for a practice as a discipline and teaching it. Sadly, I have seen this tendency in many educational programs—including at RISD's Graphic Design program during the past twenty years . . . !

Design as a Practical AND Reflective Practice

At the very heart of this practice called Graphic Design with a capital D is an embrace of a process that is at once *practical* and *reflective*. While I have published short articles on this, over the years I have mainly shared this topic via my lectures in courses and in professional conferences. The lectures proved most appropriate since my personal presence along with many visual examples helped underscore the value of this, versus what might otherwise appear as too vague, theoretical, and abstract.

3. Dan Schwabel, "Jocko Willink: The Relationship Between Discipline and Freedom," *Forbes.com*, October 17, 2017, https://www.forbes.com/sites/danschawbel/2017/10/17/jocko-willink-the-relationship-between-discipline-and-freedom/#39def7b26df8.

Having come to see the central nature of Design with a capital D as a Reflective Design Practice, what does that mean to the process of Design, and what does that mean for the Reflective Designer?

First and foremost, the practice of Reflective Design requires discipline. From discipline emerges order, and when there is order there is harmony. These attributes—order, discipline, and harmony—are recognized factors for any expectation to achieve high quality, including Design with a capital D. Quality can only come from having right motives (from a disciplined perception), and the fallout of action from the premise of right motives is right action.

When a Reflective Design Practice is understood to incorporate right action as a discipline, right action becomes the guiding practice and naturally guarantees an orderly rhythm. The common habits of action, being merely repetitive, diminish. Instead, by becoming fully attentive to the moment of the experience, *reflection* becomes deeper and more meaningful as a result of becoming increasingly alert and meaningful. The means (methods, tools, environments) also become more effective to serve their purpose.

Order also applies to the consciousness of the practitioner involved in this approach to the Design (for the individual or as a team). By becoming attentive, alert, thoughtful, the mind becomes more efficient as a receptive instrument and adaptable to one's inner nature and depth of consciousness. From that the Reflective Design Practice brings about greater harmony in consciousness, wherein the mind can most effectively avoid its ordinary tendencies to take off on its subjective inclinations. This brings about a true sense of union with the tasks at hand.

The Reflective Design Practice as right action also brings about a sense of purification and illumination, along with the attributes of order: refinement, grace, and atonement. Finally, with this comes greater receptivity to Truth, as an illumined state of awareness and consciousness—and with Truth comes Beauty (Plato: "Beauty is the splendor of Truth").

This illumined state of consciousness is one that brings true freedom because the state of mind is then unhampered by the subjective mind (which has been described as a "lower" mind that belongs to the so-called personality or subjective aspects of an individual). The wisdom teachings and modern science explain this lower nature as one that is typically driven by desire and habit through conditioning by the external world. Finally, the subjective mind colors perceptions and facilitates illusionistic tendencies due to its unguided framework.

On the other hand, the mind in a *reflective* state becomes an objective instrument. That mind is naturally a still mind, because it is removed from the "subjective" tendencies of the lower nature. In other words, and necessary for Design with a capital D, *objectivity* is key! In that state of objectivity, the mind itself is able to function holistically, in union with "all that is." That mind draws from the individual's natural "intelligence"—which word refers to that which is deep within each of us. That mind draws the intelligence from the depth of one's nature, one's spiritual center, which is also part of the Spirit of All that is. Such a still mind is beautifully represented by the title of South Korean author Haemin Sunim's book *The Things You See Only When You Slow Down* (a book given to me by one of my past graduate students).

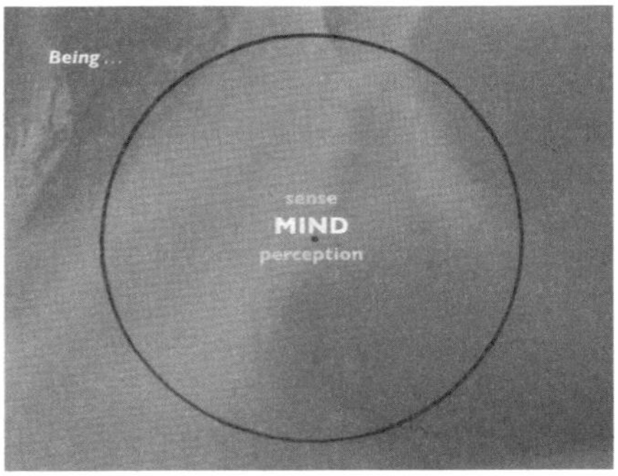

The still mind is not one that can be cultivated. Rather, it comes naturally by virtue of "giving oneself up" (i.e., giving up the "personality" and its subjectivity). Only in that objective state of mind is the true contemplative process possible for a union with essence and universal values.

The great Japanese designer Kenya Hara explains this as well in his book *Designing Design* (represented in his illustration below)—although he uses the image of the brain to represent the idea of consciousness.

In other words, the Reflective Design Practice of Design enables the Designer to generate a *multicentered intelligence for a consciousness* free from the constraints of preconditioned expectations and limited perspectives. Only from this is an enlightened process possible for endless possibilities toward truly CREATIVE results. And from this illuminated state of being, the enlightened actions make it possible for work to end up as the creation of objects that become the *Poetic Pillows* I mentioned early on, that serve as true POETIC enrichments for society and humanity.

Abstract and perhaps eccentric as this may sound to the readers of this, I can only assure you that this idealistic potential for Design has been proven true: first from my very own experiences, which have developed in that direction of depth over my many years as a Reflective Design Practitioner; and secondly from what many, many of my students, after having attended my courses and assignments, have come to practice and have exemplified in their products.

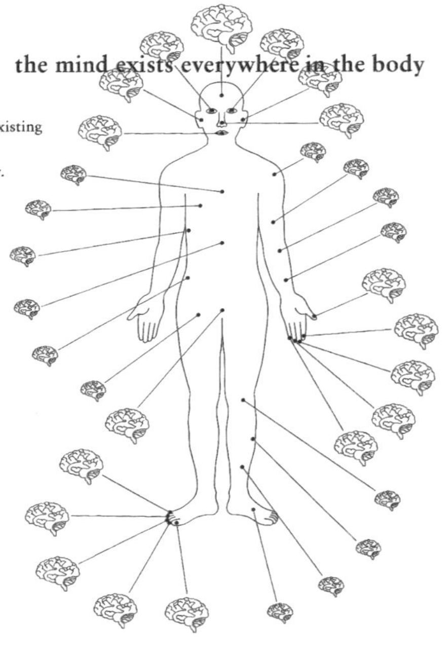

the mind exists everywhere in the body

Let's consider the brain as existing everywhere in the body.
This is a vision, not a theory.

These are simply testaments to the power and success of the true sense of Design Practice derived from a true sense of Discipline.

The following quote came in my view recently, and it perfectly sums up what this Reflective Practice means. The author, Jiddu Krishnamurti, has been one of my most powerful inspirations over many decades. These words (from a public talk he gave in Ojai, CA, 1966) sum up perfectly what the reflective practice truly means:

> The moment the conscious mind is completely quiet,
> without any movement of pleasure,
> experience or knowledge, there is no unconscious.
> You ask how this is to be achieved.
> The "how" is the most mischievous question
> because in asking how, you want a system or method,
> and the moment you follow a system, method or practice,
> you are already caught in that, and so you never discover.
> But if you actually see that only the completely quiet mind
> can observe, if you understand that, see the truth of it,
> then the unconscious is not.

Thomas Newcomen builds the first practical steam engine

AFTER THE GOLD RUSH, AFTER THE PROLOGUE: DESIGN, ENVIRONMENT, AND EXPERIMENTAL PEDAGOGY AT THE CALIFORNIA INSTITUTE OF THE ARTS, 1969–1974

JAMES MERLE THOMAS

If one regards the aesthetic and temporal poles of this volume as, on the one hand, the radical laboratories of 1920s Weimar and Dessau and, on the other, the ideational churn of Silicon Valley some eighty years later, then resting somewhere in between is California at the cusp of the 1970s. This essay concerns itself generally with that transitional moment and specifically with design and pedagogy at the California Institute of the Arts as a broader debate about modernism, postmodernism, art, and education unfolded. I begin by considering the relationship between ecological metaphor and feverish speculation—what comes after the gold rush—and then review a series of documents central to the formation of CalArts as the school opened at the dawn of the 1970s. While the essay ultimately focuses on the development of the School of Design during the early CalArts years—in particular the important role played by Sheila Levrant de Bretteville and the short-lived but influential Women's Design Program—it does so in the spirit less of an authoritative case study than of a Foucauldian assessment of a broader condition that characterized the school at the moment of its inception.[1]

1. This essay is based on research conducted at the California Institute of the Arts Institute Archives in Valencia, California, and a series of exchanges with Sheila Levrant de Bretteville in Los Angeles, New York, and New Haven between 2015 and 2019; and which culminated in a conversation included as part of the symposium that gave rise to the current volume. I thank Geoff Kaplan for inviting me to engage Sheila and her work through the context of this project, and Sheila for warmly receiving my questions. Thanks also to Pamela M. Lee for introducing me to de Bretteville's work, and to Fred Turner, who, along with Pamela, crystallized some of this thinking during seminars held at Stanford University over a decade ago. Finally, I wish to thank Louise Sandhaus, whose friendship and diligent research on the history of graphic design—particularly as it was developed at CalArts during the early 1970s—have proved invaluable to my thinking about this topic.

After the Gold Rush

Beginning roughly with the publication of Rachel Carson's *Silent Spring* in 1962, the terms "environment" and "ecology" proliferated during the 1960s through an endless universe of cultural references: Cold War–era discourses about "man/space systems," Allan Kaprow's intermedial productions, psychedelic happenings, lysergic inner space, and diverse countercultural spheres all trafficked in environmental and ecological metaphors, extending the terms through various media: design, architecture, literature, film, and so on.[2] By the time Reyner Banham's *Los Angeles: The Architecture of Four Ecologies* was published in 1971, California was at the vanguard of this fascination. Stewart Brand's *Whole Earth Catalog*, hatched in Menlo Park and first published in the spring of 1969, drew deeply from the nascent ecological movement, Buckminster Fuller's architecture, and descriptions of various "media environments." Popular culture was no exception: During the first few months of 1970, and shortly after the 1969 Santa Barbara oil spill catalyzed outrage about pollution and lack of federal regulation, Neil Young penned a few paeans to environmental disaster. The timing of his dopey lyrics—"Look at Mother Nature on the run in the 1970s"—underscored the extent to which "ecology" had emerged as *the* cultural metaphor of the moment. And on April 22, tens of thousands of Angelenos joined millions nationwide for a series of parades, public gatherings, and teach-ins to mark the first Earth Day; even Richard Nixon's administration participated. That same spring and some forty miles from Young's Topanga Canyon home, another gold rush was underway at the California Institute of the Arts, a feverish, speculative moment when "some thirty million dollars of conservative Disney money funded an academy devoted to radical cultural innovation."[3]

Incorporated in 1961 after the merger of the Los Angeles Conservatory of Music and the Chouinard Art Institute, and planned throughout the 1960s, CalArts was the vision of Disney brothers Walt and Roy, who initially conceived the school as an educational

2. For a concise summary, see James Nisbet, *Ecologies, Environments, and Energy Systems in Art of the 1960s and 1970s* (Cambridge, MA: MIT Press, 2014).

3. Herbert Gold, "Walt Disney Presents: Adventures in Collegeland!" *Atlantic Monthly*, November 1972, 50. Gold's humorous and incisive account and James Real's "When You Wish Upon a School" (West, 1972) rank among the most informative contemporaneous assessments of CalArts during the moment of its formation. Both are cited throughout Janet Sarbanes, "Radical Pedagogy at CalArts, 1969–72," *East of Borneo*, June 5, 2014, https://eastofborneo.org/articles/a-community-of-artists-radical-pedagogy-at-calarts-1969-72/, which serves as an excellent overview of the early CalArts years.

pipeline for the Disney empire. On its new campus, a massive complex in the Valencia foothills just outside of Los Angeles designed by the Pasadena-based architecture firm Ladd & Kelsey, the school would assume a commanding role alongside other cultural institutions built during the booming 1960s such as the Los Angeles Music Center and the Los Angeles County Museum of Art.[4] The school took shape in earnest after Walt Disney's death in 1966, and within a year, CalArts trustees had appointed Robert W. Corrigan, dean of the NYU Tisch School of Arts, and Herbert Blau, a theatrical director at the Lincoln Center, to serve as the first president and provost, respectively. Corrigan and Blau immediately began securing appointments for forward-thinking artists and scholars from across the country as they developed the school's intellectual and aesthetic orientation.[5] The plan quickly diverged from Disney's earlier vision, luring artists John Baldessari, Allan Kaprow, Nam June Paik, and Judy Chicago, filmmaker Alexander MacKendrick, and composers James Tenney and Morton Subotnick to lead the school's various divisions. Between 1969 and sometime around 1972 or 1973, CalArts realized a radical pedagogical vision, one that emulated the spirit of the Bauhaus and Black Mountain College, while attempting to address student demands, amplified through the cultural upheaval of the late 1960s, that education be less concerned with mechanical preparation and formulaic professionalization. Through an embrace of interdisciplinarity and experimentation, CalArts explicitly channeled the ecological language of the era, directly engaging what the school's new president termed the "expanded environment" of pedagogy and practice.[6]

Despite the influx of cash and creative luminaries, CalArts was off to an uneven start. Even with several rounds of Disney funding, the sprawling Valencia campus was plagued by budgetary and logistical issues, such that the school was forced to hold classes at a former Catholic girls' academy in Burbank for the 1970–71 academic year before formally inaugurating classes on its new campus in November 1971. Almost immediately, the "gap year" at Villa Cabrini assumed quasi-legendary status, sensationalized as an

4. For an excellent critical take on the architectural development of CalArts and its relationship to Valencia, see Craig Hodgetts, "Biography of a Teaching Machine," *Artforum*, September 1973, 61–65.

5. Many of the school's first administrators were hired by H. R. Haldeman (soon-to-be Nixon's infamous chief of staff), who chaired the CalArts board of trustees. Haldeman had cultivated a familiarity with the arts and the American avant-garde during his time at the J. Walter Thompson advertising agency. The list of his hires included Robert Corrigan (president), Herbert Blau (provost, dean of theater), Paul Brach (art), Mel Powell (music), Maurice Stein (critical studies), Alexander MacKendrick (film), and Richard E. Farson (design). See Sarbanes, "Radical Pedagogy at CalArts, 1969–72."

6. Robert Corrigan, "Interoffice Memorandum," *Arts in Society* 7, no. 3 (Fall/Winter 1970): 92. The issue was edited by Sheila de Bretteville, Barry Hyams, and Marianne Partridge.

era of "drugs on campus, erotic posters [of Disney characters], and nude swimming." Blau's first admissions bulletin declared that there would be no fixed curriculum; classes would be held spontaneously. Throughout the early years, a heady (and largely male-centric) institutional posture emerged as Baldessari, Michael Asher, Douglas Huebler, and other West Coast artists led a freewheeling curriculum. As art historian Jenni Sorkin notes, the school was a space of "intensive masculine bravado; the premiere American art school of the 1970s, the place to make a Happening alongside [Allan] Kaprow, the progenitor of the genre."[7]

While CalArts quickly established a reputation for its unconventional approach to teaching art practice, one of the most influential (and ultimately controversial) figures of the school's early years was not an artist but a sociologist: Maurice Stein, who was appointed dean of the School of Critical Studies, and who sought to align critical theory and cultural criticism with the school's studio curriculum. This process was made tangible through *Blueprint for Counter Education*, an experimental publication published in 1970, sold in the CalArts bookstores, and discussed in faculty meetings as a promising curricular tool. Compiled by Stein while he taught sociology at Brandeis (with an assist from Larry Miller, who had cycled through the Students for a Democratic Society and other '60s protest movements after studying at Brandeis before joining CalArts as an associate dean), *Blueprint* consisted of an introductory text ("shooting script") and three large collages rendered in an oversized poster format ("charts"), presenting viewers with an information-laden cross-reference guide of twentieth-century names and cultural touchstones. Influenced by Stein's ties to philosopher Herbert Marcuse and media theorist Marshall McLuhan, the project aligned the Frankfurt School with Bauhaus and Black Mountain values.

Through a style that combined strident Constructivist composition, aleatoric Fluxus tactics, and funky Cooper Black–font nods to the American postwar cultural landscape, *Blueprint* trafficked in modernist visual strategies (experimental photography, collage, radical juxtaposition of text and image) while holding up Marcuse and McLuhan as its twinned spiritual poles—a concept made explicit in one chart through the iconography of a large magnet—for thinking through aesthetics, philosophy, and mass media. At the core of *Blueprint* was an attempt to reframe questions about art, literature, and culture through an experimental and explicitly environmental pedagogical approach. The authors described it as "a portable learning environment," while explicitly parsing modernism as a "meditative environment" and postmodernism

7. Jenni Sorkin, "Learning from Los Angeles: Pedagogical Predecessors at the Woman's Building," in *Doin' It in Public: Feminism and Art at the Woman's Building*, ed. Meg Linton and Sue Maberry (Los Angeles: Otis College of Art and Design, 2011), 40.

as a "participatory environment" and developing the project through a collaborative pedagogical process that employed architectural blueprints, Xerox technology, and extensive photomechanical collage.[8] Although *Blueprint for Counter Education* was conceived at Brandeis at the end of the '60s, Stein understood the School of Critical Studies at CalArts as "the final chapter" of the project, in which the charts were to be put into practice as the new school took shape.[9]

The experiment was short-lived. Within a year of its opening, the school had assumed a less freewheeling approach, as a growing desire for vocational and professional training clashed with Blau and Stein's enthusiasm for unbridled interdisciplinarity. Sensational accounts of nudity and unstructured studio classes notwithstanding, Critical Studies was arguably the site where this battle raged most fiercely. Throughout 1970 and early 1971 Stein attempted to secure a faculty appointment for Marcuse. But the attempt by one of its deans to hire a Marxist philosopher was the final straw for the conservative Disney family and the CalArts trustees, who saw the school in financial and organizational free-fall. Roy Disney agreed to a final endowment of $10 million in September of 1971, committing the enterprise to its brand-new Valencia facilities on the eve of their opening. The funding was conditional, however: Corrigan and Blau were fired, with more layoffs to come. In the spring of 1972, Corrigan was replaced as president by William S. Lund, a real estate investor who happened to be married to Walt Disney's daughter—and whose ties to the Disney dynasty signaled a return to the orderly kind of institute Walt and Roy had once envisioned. Not long after, Lund euphemistically forecasted an "administrative restructuring," and the purges began. Within a month of his appointment as acting president, dozens of faculty and staff had been fired, and over the following months every department of the school began operating under significant budgetary restrictions.

Writing on the impact of *Blueprint for Counter Education*, Paul Cronin has described Critical Studies as the "glue" at CalArts: an analytic and ideological program that linked and reinforced studio work across the experimental school's various clusters.[10] In hindsight, however, the School of Design might be seen as the CalArts division that most successfully (if perhaps briefly) mediated theory and practice during this period, particularly as the controversies surrounding Critical Studies threatened to destabilize the entire institution. First, a concise timeline of the School of Design's leadership helps to orient: In consultation with Corrigan and Blau, psychologist Richard Farson was hired to serve as the inaugural

8. See "Questioning Enlightenment Logic: An Interview with Maurice Stein, Larry Miller, and Marshall Henrichs," in Maurice Stein, Larry Miller, and Marshall Henrichs, *Blueprint for Counter Education Expanded Reprint: Instruction Manual* (New York: Inventory Press, 2016), 58–65.

9. Ibid., 65.

10. Paul Cronin, "Recovering and Rendering Vital," in Stein, Miller, and Henrichs, *Blueprint for Counter Education*, 36–56.

dean of the School of Design when it opened in 1970. As CalArts prepared to relocate to its new Valencia facilities in 1971, Farson resigned and was replaced by designer Victor Papanek, whose controversial tenure as dean lasted for one year. In July of 1972, Papanek was replaced by Paul Maguire, who had previously chaired the design program at Chouinard; Maguire remained in this role through the 1975–76 academic year. In the fall of 1976, the School of Design was absorbed by the School of Art, resulting in the School of Art and Design. Departmental correspondence and course catalog materials illustrate how throughout this period (and particularly between 1970 and 1973), the School of Design developed a robust interdisciplinary curriculum that encouraged students to engage with the themes of environment and ecology as described above. These materials also suggest how, during the same months that Critical Studies served as a lightning rod for controversy, the School of Design balanced philosophical and epistemological approaches to practice and pedagogy while mounting an ambitious program of study (one that was not always universally embraced by its faculty) that linked graphic design to an expansive curriculum that encompassed architecture, planning, computing, film, and video, as well as studies in the social sciences.

The Esalen-CalArts Encounter

Before the Lund purges began in 1972, Blau and Stein found an ideal leader for the School of Design in Farson, whose interests in socially engaged design complemented their general vision for the school.[11] Trained as a psychologist and therapist, Farson had co-founded the La Jolla–based Western Behavioral Sciences Institute in 1958, a nonprofit think tank focused on interdisciplinary social sciences research and field-defining research on group encounters; within a decade he was in Big Sur, leading the Esalen Institute's wide-ranging investigations into human consciousness. Farson's West Coast bonafides and earthy, systems-oriented interest in individual and group dynamics were, according to one review of the nascent program, "just the mix of encounter group, environmental concern, and personal freedom that design students crave." Through an envisioned partnership that Farson planned between the new art school and New Age institute (dubbed by the same journalist as the "Esalen-CalArts Encounter"), Farson espoused a mix of practical and philosophical approaches to design, not as a "spicing up of ailing design disciplines with a pinch of social science," but through an interdisciplinary approach that attempted to rethink the field through a combination of social-science methodologies, DIY sensibility, and an attendant emphasis on "total environments and social architecture." (As expected, Farson endorsed the ethos of the *Whole Earth Catalog*, and Stewart Brand was among those who

10. Ann Ferebee, "Well, They've Got to Start Designing Spaceship Earth Somewhere. It May as Well Be at CalArts," *Design and Environment* 1, no. 2 (Summer 1970): 20–27.

11. Farson initially held two roles at CalArts, serving as head of the School of Design and as vice president of environmental affairs.

were invited to speak at the school.) At CalArts, Farson noted several months before the school opened, "The great environmental problems we now face—congestion, pollution, deception, invasion of privacy—will not be mere conceptual dilemmas but motives and cues for action" requiring "an ecological approach. . . . Taste and style are not enough. The designer must also improve the quality of human life."[12]

A survey of internal correspondence and promotional material created in late 1969 and 1970 reflects the complexity of Farson's duties as he assembled the School of Design. By spring 1970, Farson had successfully negotiated positions for associate deans Peter Pearce and Craig Hodgetts, whose respective backgrounds in structural design and architecture further telegraphed the interdisciplinary perspective of the program. He was also in regular correspondence with Papanek, who aggressively (he was, in his own words, "pushy") sought employment at the school; and was regularly updating Blau on the envisioned activities of the coming academic year. Shaped through early departmental conversations and further honed with input from Pearce and Hodgetts, a May 1970 memorandum to Blau's office functions like yet another blueprint for education, charting the operational scope of the nascent school. The text theorizes the "democratization of design" while reflecting Farson's many administrative duties, outlining the workaday responsibilities of the department over the coming two years. By that spring Design comprised fourteen full-time faculty, a small roster of teaching assistants, and a growing enrollment of graduate and undergraduate students, not to mention a group of visiting faculty whose expertise in psychology, architecture, environmental design, and publishing would further reinforce the wide-ranging, interdisciplinary interests of the program's core faculty.[13]

Although her name was not yet included on the list of core faculty that Farson submitted to Blau, Sheila Levrant de Bretteville was already immersed in the mechanics of the department and working to shape the aesthetic of the entire CalArts enterprise. De Bretteville had studied at Barnard

Sheila Levrant de Bretteville, *taste and style just aren't enough*, 1970. Promotional flyer for the School of Design, California Institute of the Arts

12. Ferebee, "Well, They've Got to Start Designing Spaceship Earth Somewhere. It May as Well Be at CalArts," 20–27.

and trained as a graphic designer at Yale in the 1960s before living briefly in Milan while working as a designer for Olivetti.[14] In late 1969—and owing partly to her affiliation with Hodgetts, with whom she shared a studio in New York—de Bretteville was invited by Farson to create departmental stationery and promotional materials for the school. The most visible of these products was a recruitment flyer for potential students in 1970 that included a shrink-wrapped array of small pine cone, toy jack, and microchip.

To craft the flyer announcing the new school and its ethos, de Bretteville stepped outside of conventional artistic networks, working instead with industrial printers who made products for grocery stores ("I was thinking about Save-On and Ralphs"), a process that ultimately yielded a mass-produced, two-color, three-dimensional shrink-wrapped poster. Through her use of bright color and modernist Helvetica typeface and an explicit nod to technology, de Bretteville's design embodies what Lorraine Wild once termed a "hippie modernist" aesthetic of simultaneously crisp and unruly

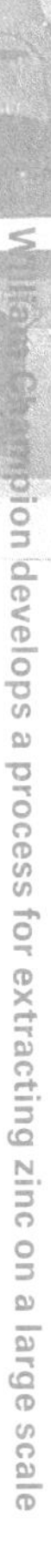

13. *Memorandum*, May 11, 1970, CalArts Archives. Envisioned guest speakers for 1970–71 included Buckminster Fuller, Jane Jacobs, Lawrence Halprin, Stewart Brand, John McHale, and group contributions from Ant Farm, as well as representatives from Esalen, Anna Halprin's San Francisco Dancer's Workshop, and Archigram. Many of these names and groups reinforce existing associations between Design faculty and known figures in architecture, design, planning, and psychology. However, the mention of the south LA Watts Writers' Workshop–affiliated Mafundi Institute invites further research into how CalArts—and specifically the School of Design—operated in relation to a broader network of activist organizations that emerged in the wake of the 1965 Watts uprising. Also of note is the document's timing. On May 11, 1970, artist Robert Irwin and NASA-affiliated psychologist Edward C. Wortz convened a week-long symposium in Irwin's Venice Beach studio. The conference focused on issues of quality of life and "habitability," an interdisciplinary concept Farson repeatedly discusses as a key area of focus at the School of Design for the coming year.

14. In addition to working out of Olivetti's Milan offices, de Bretteville recalls traveling around Europe for trade fairs and promotional events while designing print advertising for the company's business machines and industrial applications. Interview with de Bretteville, Los Angeles, March 2015. For examples of the Olivetti design work, see Rose DeNeve, "A Feminist Option," *Print*, May/June 1976, 54–59. Reproduced in Louise Sandhaus, *Earthquakes, Mudslides, Fires and Riots: California and Graphic Design, 1936–1986* (New York: Metropolis, 2014), 332–38.

design.[15] Through the computer chip, jack, and pine cone, the flyer also alludes to a broader cultural preoccupation with systems-oriented thinking, and (perhaps unintentionally) to the crisp work of Charles and Ray Eames, whose films and exhibition-based studies of IBM computers and children's toys were meant to encourage a sense of purposeful experimentation and play—themes that were central to the newly formed art school's pedagogical stance. Farson's text was reworked to be a beacon for would-be students, who, in eschewing "mere taste and style," would study the interrelations of ecology, technology, and human need.

Although de Bretteville has at times subsequently downplayed the flyer and initially objected to the gendered implications of a solely male-oriented design philosophy ("I was embarrassed for years at the pronoun," she said about her use of "he" for the designer in the flyer's text), her contribution was, in terms of sheer impact (she estimates that more than twenty thousand copies of the flyer were produced and circulated nationally), one of the most consequential, serving as a highly visible recruitment tool. Indeed, the flyer has recently been reproduced in several re-examinations of the aesthetics of the era and enjoys a privileged status within a critical historiography of postwar California design.[16] Like *Blueprint for Counter Education*, the poster can also be interpreted as yet another "founding document" of CalArts—its means of production and dissemination blended vernacular style with an anticipatory mode of address. And while de Bretteville's mass-produced poster succinctly telegraphed the importance of ecological and visionary thinking to the School of

Spread from *Prologue to a Community*, 1970

15. Andrew Blauvelt, *Hippie Modernism: The Struggle for Utopia* (Minneapolis: Walker Art Center, 2015), 11, note 1. For more on the use of color in 1960s California design, see Wild's essay "Orange" in Sandhaus, *Earthquakes, Mudslides, Fires and Riots*, 220–26.

16. The poster was included in the exhibition *Now Dig This! Art and Black Los Angeles, 1960–1980*, organized by Kellie Jones for the Hammer Museum in 2012. See also Blauvelt, *Hippie Modernism*, 258–63; Sandhaus, *Earthquakes, Mudslides, Fires and Riots*, 382–87; and Mateo Kries, Amelie Klein, and Alison J. Clarke, *Victor Papanek: The Politics of Design* (Weil am Rhein: Vitra Design Institute, 2018), 47 and 102.

17. Sheila de Bretteville, Barry Hyams, and Marianne Partridge, eds., *Arts in Society* 7, no. 3 [*California Institute of the Arts: Prologue to a Community*] (Fall/Winter 1970). Founded in 1958, *Arts in Society* was a forward-thinking journal produced periodically by the University of Wisconsin's Extension School through the mid-1970s.

Design, a subsequent project would expand this message to include voices from across the entire institution.

In the spring of 1970, the editorial board of *Arts in Society* invited CalArts to create a document of the school at the moment of its formation. Designed and organized by de Bretteville, *Prologue to a Community* consumed an entire issue of the journal through a 174-page collaborative layout that incorporated contributions from dozens of faculty, administrators, students, and trustees.[17] Once again, de Bretteville productively blended vernacular packaging, crisp typeface, and organic composition. The issue was shipped in a plain cardboard sleeve on which the theme of the CalArts issue was printed in a bold neon-orange Helvetica. The rhythmic cadence of de Bretteville's design, with its hallucinatory mix of halftone photographic enlargements, scans of video and television screens, and handwriting printed on alternating signatures of card stock, vellum, newsprint, and Mylar, signals the diverse perspectives on offer as the school opened its doors: Associated Press images of Ronald Reagan, Stokely Carmichael, student protests collide with PR statements by Walt Disney and Corrigan about the value of the arts in society; film faculty Sandy MacKendrick laments the school's lack of equipment while a full-bleed image of video snow crackles on the opposite page; embedded journalists' photos of young soldiers in Vietnam—poignantly close in age to those about to attend CalArts—are juxtaposed with statements from student applications. Equally present is a recognition of the school's appearance within the built environment, and throughout the journal, documents related to the school are punctuated with stock images of California tract housing, smog-tinged vistas of Los Angeles freeways, and excerpts from John Baldessari's *California Map Project* (1969).

Like *Blueprint for Counter Education* and "Taste and Style Just Aren't Enough," *Prologue to a Community* signaled the CalArts ethos and rehearsed an awareness of the power of vernacular media while employing those very processes (commercial shrink-wrapping, industrial cardboard processing, photocopied and collaged materials) in order to make a statement about how design teaching figured into the broader media ecology of the moment. It was an aesthetic that aligned with aspects of Brand's DIY approach, while signaling the school's role within an unfolding debate about modernist and postmodernist aesthetics. Together, these documents informed a speculative, anticipatory sense about the role of media at the dawn of the 1970s and suggested an overall environmental framework for imagining what design and pedagogy might look like in the coming years. Their look and feel anticipate the hastily produced show flyers and zines of the '80s and the early allover aesthetic of early websites, while still trafficking in iconic modernist forms: book, poster, architectural blueprint.

By fall 1970—and as the "Taste and Style" flyer and the *Arts in Society* journal issue began to prompt national attention—Farson had further refined the School of Design's curricular vision for the coming academic year, expanding the school to a total of twenty core faculty—now including de Bretteville—and an enrollment of nearly one hundred and fifty students. An earlier list of potential guest speakers had been narrowed to eight visiting faculty and reflected a focused (if less diverse) cohort including Shadrach Woods, Stewart Brand, and Robert Sommer.[18] As the tumultuous first year of the school came to a close and CalArts prepared to relocate to its new Valencia campus for the 1971–72 academic year, Farson was already in the process of leaving the school and turning his administrative duties over to Victor Papanek,[19] who, as early as March 1971, had begun quietly discussing "phasing out social design" with some faculty—a maneuver that would have effectively dissolved the school into other departments by largely eliminating Farson's focus on socially engaged design, while absorbing various other components into service-oriented workshops. Throughout the 1971–72 term, the School of Design was directly responsible for producing and supporting some of the most prominent and discursively expansive events associated with early CalArts history. As the year started, the fall curriculum included thirty courses distributed across practical and theoretical processes ranging from studios in design fundamentals, photography, and 8mm film to specialized topics in architecture ("Advanced Design: Shelter, Settlements, and Regions"), systems theory, psychology, and computer programming.

Notable among the course offerings was the Women's Design Program, a one-year standalone course of study within the School of Design led by Sheila de Bretteville, and which featured design courses, group consciousness-raising sessions, and feminist literature-reading circles.[20] Positioned alongside the Feminist Art Program created by CalArts colleagues Miriam Schapiro and Judy Chicago, the Women's Design Program focused on the fundamentals of two-dimensional design and typography, "control and perception in the design process," and "female experience

18. Core faculty for the 1970–71 academic year included Roger Conrad, Leonard Cottrell, Peter de Bretteville, Sheila de Bretteville, Richard Farson, Keith Godard, Dick Higgins, Craig Hodgetts, Steven Katona, Benjamin Lifson, Paul Maguire, Victor Papanek, Peter Pearce, Hans Proppe, Harald Robinson, Edwin Schlossberg, Allen Schoen, John Seeley, Jivan Tabibian, and Gene Youngblood.

19. While stepping away from his position as dean, Farson turned to his duties as director of programs for the 1971 Aspen Design Conference (IDCA), which was held in June, and which prominently featured participation by CalArts faculty and students. See also the special edition of *Aspen Times*, June 20–24, 1971, which was designed by de Bretteville in a similarly collaborative manner as *Prologue to a Community*. For more on Farson's role throughout 1970 and the shaping of the 1971 conference, see Alice Twemlow, "A Guaranteed Communications Failure: Consensus Meets Conflict at the International Design Conference in Aspen, 1970," in *The Aspen Complex*, ed. Martin Beck (Berlin: Sternberg, 2012), 110–35.

20. Suzanne Lacy, who served as a teaching assistant to de Bretteville, led a related weekly Reading Seminar that further supported the Women's Design Program.

and perspective," while shaping the visual identity of many of the projects for which the Feminist Art Program is renowned.[21] Annealing her formalist training in graphic design at Yale in the early 1960s with a growing interest in the emancipatory writings of Frantz Fanon and Paulo Freire (in particular the latter's *Pedagogy of the Oppressed*), de Bretteville quickly honed an empathic pedagogical style at CalArts. She connected these influences with the principles of second-wave feminism and consciousness-raising techniques, which, like aspects of Freire's pedagogy, emphasized group-directed, nonhierarchical power structures in discussion and seminar settings. Throughout the Women's Design Program and its subsequent iterations, CR techniques were central to de Bretteville's master class, *Feeling to Form*, which was structured through an open workshop style, with participants being asked to speak and write through a personal object of their choosing. A second course, *Public Announcements / Private Conversations*, was devoted to questions of public discourse in spatial and institutional environments and directly influenced a wave of site-specific artworks created by FAP alumni throughout the ensuing decade.[22]

Throughout, de Bretteville continued to advocate for a participatory or consensus-based design. Just as her lectures and essays eschewed "simplicity, clarity, and oversimplification," her contemporaneous designs embraced visual unruliness, employed a freewheeling juxtaposition of image and text, and adopted a multiple-author mode of production—an approach that allowed for as many different voices and competing aesthetics as possible.[23]

John Campbell's invention, the sextant, an improved navigational device that enables sailors to measure latitude

A Proposed Curriculum (Re)Structure

Papanek's vision for design and teaching did not align with such participatory approaches and conspicuously collided with other faculty plans—most notably de Bretteville's—to such an

21. For example, de Bretteville designed the cover of the exhibition catalog for the iconic *Womanhouse* exhibition, held in a dilapidated Los Angeles mansion in early 1972.

22. In the wake of *Womanhouse*, de Bretteville and Chicago joined art historian Arlene Raven to form the Feminist Studio Workshop (FSW), and in November of 1973, they inaugurated the Woman's Building in Los Angeles. Serving as a site for art education and community organization and as the hub of a growing network of feminist activist spaces, these organizations hosted art galleries, studios, and activist organizations for over two decades. For recent assessments, see Linton and Maberry, *Doin' It in Public*; and Sondra Hale and Terry Wolverton, eds., *From Site to Vision: The Woman's Building in Contemporary Culture* (Los Angeles: Otis College of Art and Design, 2011).

23. In addition to her designs for the special edition of the *Aspen Times* created for the 1971 Aspen Design Conference, see Sheila de Bretteville, "Some Aspects of Design from the Perspective of a Woman Designer," and accompanying broadsheet design, "Women's Design Program, 1971–72," *Icographic* 6 (1973).

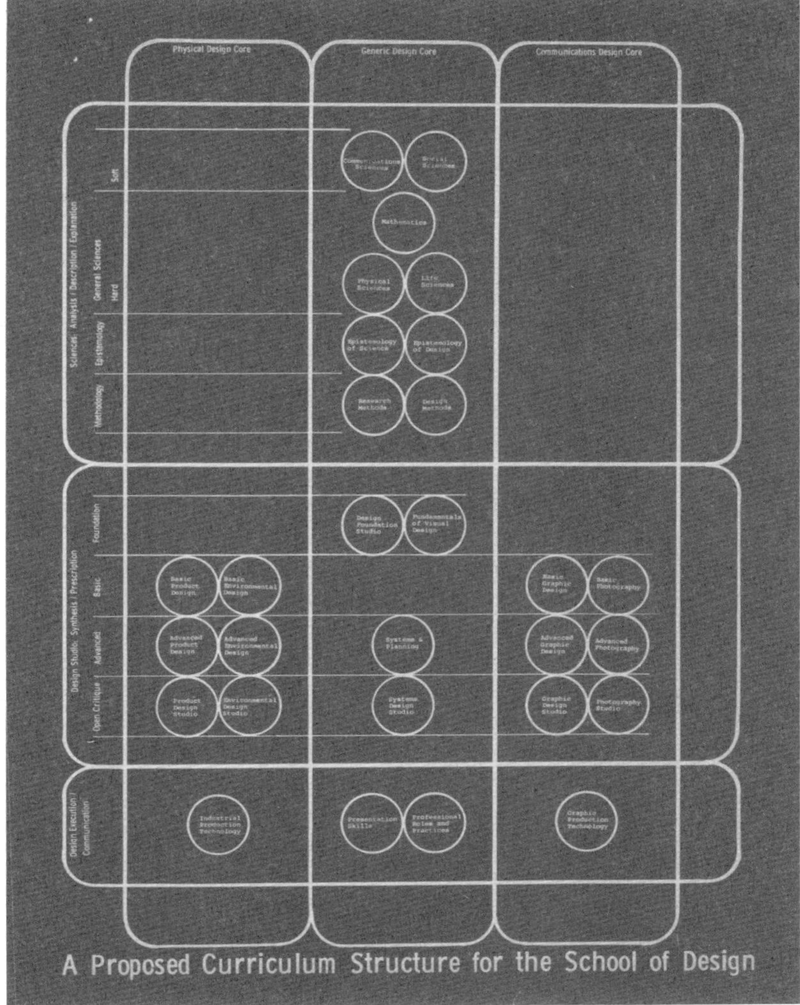

Gary Swift, *A Proposed Curriculum Structure for the School of Design* [internal memorandum], 1974

extent that he left his position after only one year.[24] As the 1972–73 academic year began, Papanek retreated to Denmark for a year-long leave while Paul Maguire assumed duties as dean. By December the dynamic at the school had changed dramatically: Blau's departure from CalArts had prompted multiple faculty (including Craig Hodgetts) to resign in protest, and Farson was informed that his contract would not be renewed for the coming academic year. Several months later, de Bretteville and Chicago announced their

24. Interview with de Bretteville, March 2015. De Bretteville has recalled in multiple exchanges that Papanek infamously described her plans for the Women's Design Program as a trending toward "ghettoization," a term she forcefully rejected. See Alison J. Clarke, *Victor Papanek: Designer for the Real World* (Cambridge, MA: MIT Press, 2021).

intentions to leave CalArts.[25] Subtending these personnel changes was a sense of dissatisfaction, at least among some faculty, with an expansive curricular approach to design education that included architecture and urban planning.[26] Papanek still believed that his vision for the School of Design might prevail, even though in his brief tenure as dean he had encountered considerable hostility. Describing the recent faculty departures as the "neutralization of the Farson-touch-me-feel-me-groupie-gropee approach," he openly mused to Lund that the school, while "under the guidance of wild men for its first year," might, upon his return, be reoriented toward areas of design that had been "long neglected."[27]

Meanwhile, Maguire was in the process of further reorganizing the School of Design's curriculum. A memorandum created by Gary Swift (who joined the school in 1972 and taught courses in design theory and methodology) suggests how aspects of both Farson's and Papanek's plans were mediated before the school was absorbed by the School of Art in 1976. Through a matrix that combined "soft and hard" science studies with a design-studio array, Swift's 1974 proposal created space for the study of cybernetics and systems theory–based approaches to design, while balancing communication theory with foundational and advanced studio courses in typography, photography, and environmental design. Absent, however, were slots for Stephen Selkowitz's courses on Funky Structures or the Energy Crisis, let alone Farson's advanced studies of Group Social Dynamics. By 1975, and as Maguire was notifying colleagues that the Design School would be subsumed within the School of Art, Design's initial engagement with ecological and environmental metaphor appears—as with a broader cultural trending—to have been redirected elsewhere.

What of the Gold Rush of 1970? Throughout its retelling, the origin story of CalArts is often cast as a brief Dionysian era that fades into orderly institutionalization as the chaos of the school's first two years of the school gives way to a structured curriculum. And what of its impact on design and pedagogy? While some of the most outrageously interdisciplinary horizons of Farson's original curriculum and de Bretteville's feminist program were ultimately short-lived, a more generous historical reading of the School of Design must acknowledge the ways that this early perspective has continued to thrive, both at CalArts and elsewhere.

25. Although de Bretteville began to focus on the establishment of the Feminist Studio Workshop and the Women's Building, as late as August of 1973 she signaled her commitment to fulfill her contract by teaching a studio class in Graphic Communication (Fall 1973), along with several other courses. Sheila de Bretteville, letter to Paul Maguire, August 15, 1973, CalArts Institutional Archives.

26. "Most of the Design faculty were really unhappy with the architectural embodiment of this program." Craig Hodgetts in conversation with Benjamin Tong, 2011, in collaboration with *East of Borneo*. See *Experimental Impulse* (2011), organized by Thomas Lawson and Aram Moshayedi for REDCAT, and available at https://www.youtube.com/watch?v=YSjAF35ZkZo&t=12s&ab_channel=eastofborneo.

27. Letter to William S. Lund, February 3, 1973, CalArts Institutional Archives. Also available at https://designschoolarchive.calarts.edu/.

QUEERING THE GRID: A READING OF DAN FRIEDMAN

POLYMODE: BRIAN JOHNSON and SILAS MUNRO

As gay designers and design educators, we look at design through the lenses of queerness and sexuality.[1] Stylistically we choose to regard "queer" as differing and bending away from the norm, and Queer as a marker of nonheteronormative sexual identity. Without asserting that differentiation confers advantage, we insist that queerness impacts, changes, and strengthens pedagogy. The life of Dan Friedman is a case in point. In the context of American design audiences, Friedman's interpretation of his second-wave Swiss design training (Ulm and Basel from 1966–69) can be considered a queer European import of a radical pedagogy that warped, bent, and reshaped design education in the United States. Friedman's use of highly specific but wildly arbitrary constraints made "experimentation" in US design education synonymous with a formalist method of "risk-taking." His teaching was a breakaway from that of his tutor, Armin Hoffman, who was known for a pedagogy that focused on the rigor of the progressive and iterative enforcement of norms. Friedman would bookend his life within the educational sphere (1970–74; 1990–94), fortified by productive and fertile moments of creation professionally at Anspach Grossman Portugal (1975–77) and Pentagram (1979–82), and his own practice of art, assemblage, and furniture-making (1981–95). His fifty-year life spanned the countercultural protests of the 1960s, gay liberation in the 1970s, and the culture wars and Queer activism of the 1980s. Across this complex cultural context, Friedman stands out for his ability to torque design and design education beyond the perceived dichotomy of modernism and postmodernism, navigating with his work and life the landscape between neoconservative, preppy Reaganites and progressive poststructuralists[2] through his seductive[3] eccentricity.[4]

1. "Every portrait that is painted with feeling is a portrait of the artist, not of the sitter. The sitter is merely the accident, the occasion. It is not he who is revealed by the painter; it is rather the painter who, on the colored canvas, reveals himself." Oscar Wilde, "The Picture of Dorian Gray," in *The Complete Works of Oscar Wilde*, ed. J. B. Foreman (New York: HarperCollins 1989), 21.

2. "The concept of postmodernism has been described as indicative of two modes: a neo-conservative historicism and a progressive poststructuralism. . . . It is not surprising that the design press could only locate the concept of postmodernism within the revived and alluded to styles of the past and not within the theoretical debates surrounding both the construction of meaning and the critique of modernity provided by poststructuralism. It is only recently, in the 1990s, that the ideas associated with poststructuralism have found their way into the design press and, not surprisingly, are pitted against the ideology of modernism." Andrew Blauvelt, "The Dynamics of Inscription," *Emigre* 34 (1995): 32–50.

3. "But it was still necessary, at least for a moment, to appropriate this power, channel it, capture it, and bend it in the direction one wanted; if one meant to take advantage of it, it was necessary to 'seduce' it. It becomes both an object of covetousness and an object of seduction." Michel Foucault, "Lives of Infamous Men," in *Power (The Essential Works of Foucault 1954–1984, Vol. 3)* (New York: Penguin, 1994), 157–75.

Friedman's teachings and making methods were dubbed "Swiss Punk," New Wave, and Deconstruction, and all took place before the advent of the public internet. The tragedy of his death from AIDS on July 7, 1995, is that his ethos and aesthetic would be very much at home in our contemporary media landscape (read: the tragic loss of our mentors). Friedman's manifesto "Radical Modernism" forecast our current context of wicked problems: hyperpolitical polarization, Internet trolling, racism, hate speech, the unstable vernacular of meme culture, unabashed capitalism, environmental collapse, drug addiction, the cult of the body, nationalism, voter suppression, war profiteering and proxy wars, religious persecution, queer oppression, and numerous global health crises.[5]

Design and design education cannot carry the burden or solve any of these problems by itself—but Friedman's utopian quest led him to try just that feat. He was like a typographic Johnny Appleseed for design education in America, bringing to the United States the ideologies and methodologies behind the Swiss-German grid; organizing a national lecture tour in October 1972 for his mentor Wolfgang Weingart that included stops at what is now University of the Arts in Philadelphia, schools in Chicago, University of Cincinnati, Yale University, Rhode Island School of Design, and the Art Director's Club in New York.[6]

Friedman's Pedagogical Lineages and Influences

Friedman began his design education at what is now Carnegie Mellon (then the Carnegie Institute of Technology), where he was

4. Dan Friedman, "Wild Style," in *Dan Friedman: Radical Modernism* (New Haven: Yale University Press, 1994), 150.

5. "At the end of this century, it has become a much greater challenge for design to inspire. There are fewer assurances that our future will be better than our past. How will it be possible to express a sense of balance, vision, and optimism in a world moving toward complacency, cultural conformity, or anarchy? How can we sustain the need for play, fantasy, and dream in the midst of our exhaustion from harsh realities? Is there still authenticity and originality in the fast world of appropriation and simulation? Does the preoccupation with the way things look (style) preclude design from ever again becoming radically progressive and meaningful? Will our multitude of personal visions prevent us from reconceiving an enlightened sense of community and social purpose?" Dan Friedman, "Projects of Optimism," in *Dan Friedman: Radical Modernism*, 209.

6. "Dan Friedman, Wolfgang Weingart Speaks to America, poster for a college lecture tour, 1972," in *Readymag Stories: Dan Friendman*, https://stories.readymag.com/friedman/basel-and-wolfgang-weingart/.

John Harrison develops reliable chronometers that allow sailors to measure longitude accurately

influenced profoundly by Ken Hiebert, an American designer who had been trained at the Allgemeine Gewerbeschule Basel (Basel School of Design) with Emil Ruder and Armin Hoffman. After he graduated in 1965, he studied at the Hochschule für Gestaltung Ulm as a Fulbright scholar and then went on to the Basel School of Design, returning to the US after three years abroad. Both schools had profound effects on Friedman: Ulm was highly structured, literal, and systematically gridded in its approach; Basel was starting to change under the influence of Weingart, emphasizing intuitive reasoning and visual enjoyment in abstraction and questioning typographic conventions.

On the recommendation of Hoffman Friedman taught at Yale (1970–73 and again 1990–91).[7] He also taught at Philadelphia College of Art (1972; PCA, now University of the Arts), State University College Purchase, New York (1972–76), and Cooper Union (1994–95).[8] At every educational juncture Friedman was in a constant process of reconciling the relationship between the conceptual and rational aspects of Ulm and the intuitive and playful nature of the influence of Weingart. Friedman reflects on this act of translation from graduate school to the classroom in a 1994 interview with Ellen Lupton:

> Weingart and I had similar interests. I thought he was incredibly talented. But his method of teaching was problematic to me. My biggest contribution at the time was to develop a methodology for teaching a "new typography." Unlike Weingart, I wasn't reacting against Swiss typography, because that rational system didn't really exist here except in isolated instances. . . . Whereas Wolfgang Weingart was teaching based on intuition, I was trying to verbalize and demystify the structures of typography. I wanted to create a method. I had to find a way to teach the rules and also how to break them at the same time, since nobody knew the rules.[9]

In the 1970s there was no better conspirator for breaking the rules for Friedman than April Grieman, who had been educated at Basel a few years after him. The two met on the campus of PCA in 1972 when Grieman arrived fresh from living with the Hoffman family and working under the tutelage of Weingart in his notorious *Weiterbildungsklasse für Grafik* (Advanced Further Education Class for Graphic Design). Weingart's course celebrated experimentation and risk-taking that included technical experiments led by Weingart, including asking his students to design letterpress typography compositions with grid-breaking layouts by pouring plaster directly into the bed of the press and setting the type and rules directly into the plaster rather than locking it up in a rectangular straitjacket. The two would eventually marry and reside together in Connecticut and New York, where they would occasionally collaborate on installations and decorative projects in their home.[10]

Grieman had sought out the Basel program because her early training mainly focused on an old-guard approach that was based

7. "Noted Graphic Designer Dan Friedman Is Subject of Retrospective," *Yale Bulletin and Calendar* 34, no. 5 (October 2005), http://archives.news.yale.edu/v34.n6/story14.html.

8. http://yamp.org/Profiles/DanFriedman.

9. Dan Friedman, interview by Ellen Lupton, June 15, 1994, transcript, http://elupton.com/2010/07/friedman-dan/.

on rigid formalism, technical skills, and bringing a design to market rather than visual exploration. This way of teaching was based on the training of the faculty, who were mainly alumni of Yale's MFA in Graphic Design program, where design pedagogy was approached with the heavy commercial hand of visiting critics like Paul Rand, who approached design pedagogy as art direction. Grieman noted:

> As an undergrad in Kansas City (Art Institute) we were training for corporate design jobs. Our program director, Rob Roy Kelly, was a Yale grad, thus the influence on him of some of the old guard teaching at Yale, and fathers of some of the most influential, still to date, corporate ID programs—and so my journey to the Basel School was liberating, a real chance to study more deeply, gain experience in the various disciplines that make up the art of design.[11]

Friedman's focus for teaching shifted away from a vocational approach (read: master/apprentice; dom/sub) toward a more personal transmission of ideology (read: passing on aesthetic value; an upanishad). For Friedman, the grid itself became a pedagogical tool, and from his time in New Haven, he queered the lineage of the grid, bending and skewing it until it broke free of legibility. Chris Pullman reflects on this inflection point:

> That gene was implanted by Weingart, and continued when Dan was at Yale. The things that Friedman brought to Hoffman's version of Swiss modernism were very grid-oriented and technical, which is quite different from what was going on in Zurich. He had this idea to train people using stuff that was just pulled right out of the program in Basel, but where he would take a grid, place an operation on it so that the grid gradually was eaten up by this new gene that came into it. It was very weird for a lot of students to have him say, you know, break it; break it so far that you can't understand what's going on.[12]

In a seminal case study of Yale student work called *The Weather Project*, Friedman takes the iterative pedagogy of Ruder, one of his other tutors, and queers it. Friedman asked his students to design the text of a banal weather report across a series of methodical operations that would turn pedestrian information into pyrotechnic typographic compositions that questioned typical ideas of hierarchy and reading order.[13]

The tension between a tight, gridded framework and flamboyant layout is a portend of Friedman's growing Queerness. Many contemporary educators, including Katherine McCoy, former co-head of the 2d and 3d Design Department at Cranbrook Academy of Art, were heavily influenced by this work:

> Perhaps we can view Dan's weather report project as indicative of his evolution from his modernist design education and initial modernist teaching methods to an exploration of postmodern design possibilities. An evolution from impersonal, dispassionate design toward a personal and culturally expressive design that permits and even encourages the

10. Chris Pullman, interview with the authors, May 12, 2020.

11. April Greiman, interview with the authors, May 13, 2020.

12. Chris Pullman, interview with the authors, May 12, 2020.

13. Daniel Friedman, "Introductory Education in Typography," *Visible Language* 7, no. 2 (Spring 1973): 129–44.

expression of personal identities, including shifting sexual and gender identities.[14]

This departure from the siloed pedagogy of professional development resulted in a groundbreaking proposal by Friedman to create the new art program at SUNY Purchase. His vision was to break down the perceived and actual barriers between design and art disciplines.[15] In the SUNY curriculum document, Friedman proposes a program within a program that is "a Fundamental Core." It would provide a "primal" sense of form-making that would give a student an intuitive animal sense that paradoxically comes out of systematic repetition.[16]

Friedman's proposal that "a myopic specialization" and "comfortable style" operated like a rigid structure foreshadows his future design leadership positions at Anspach Grossman Portugal and Pentagram. This also points back to

Weather:
Sunny
hot
humid
today and tomorrow.
Fair and warm tonight.
Temperature range:
Today
96-75
Tuesday 94-72

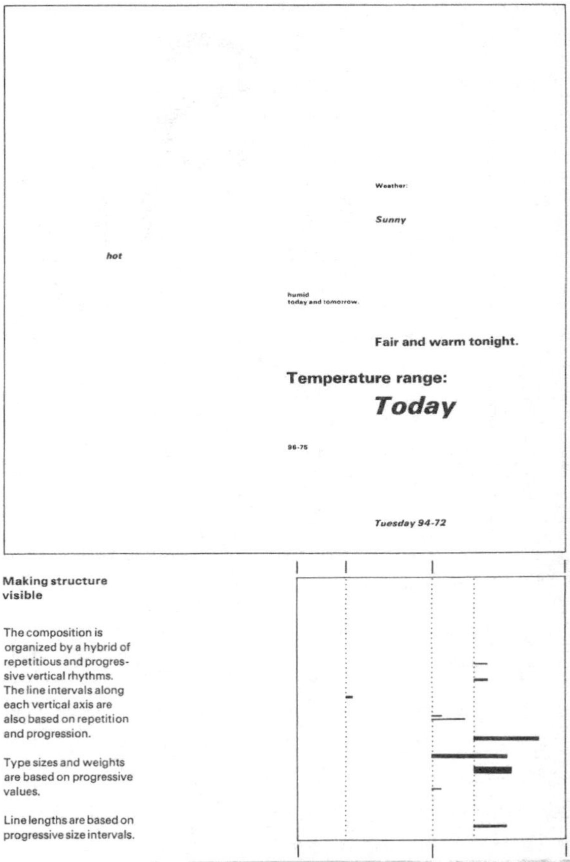

Making structure visible

The composition is organized by a hybrid of repetitious and progressive vertical rhythms. The line intervals along each vertical axis are also based on repetition and progression.

Type sizes and weights are based on progressive values.

Line lengths are based on progressive size intervals.

Pages of Friedman's typographic demonstrations and his student's work from Yale published in "Introductory Education in Typography," *Visible Language* 7, no. 2 (Spring 1973)

14. Katherine McCoy, email with the authors, March 1, 2020.

15. "The Division of Visual Arts supports neither a myopic specialization nor an immediate search for a comfortable style that could lead to confinement and inflexibility. Instead, it proposes a visual education which concentrates on the more generic aspects of the art/design process and on the idea of total systems as opposed to single precious, artistic entities. The program will offer a solid perceptual and conceptual basis which is designed to transcend style, fad, conventional boundaries between professions, the purely technical, and completely isolate artistic results." Dan Friedman's SUNY College of Purchase Division of Visual Arts Department proposal, 1974–75.

16. "The Fundamental Core is a kind of program within the program. It is designed so that there is a maximum amount of structure in which learning can take place and in which diverse individual dispositions can test for their durability. Especially in the earlier years, students must be willing to reconstitute the most primal aspects of form making and to rigorously tone their senses. But the fact that the Fundamental Core spreads over the entire four years of study also implies that the upper division years are never too late for continuing with fundamentals; that fundamental courses are a form of advanced study," Dan Friedman's SUNY College of Purchase Division of Visual Arts Department proposal 1974–75.

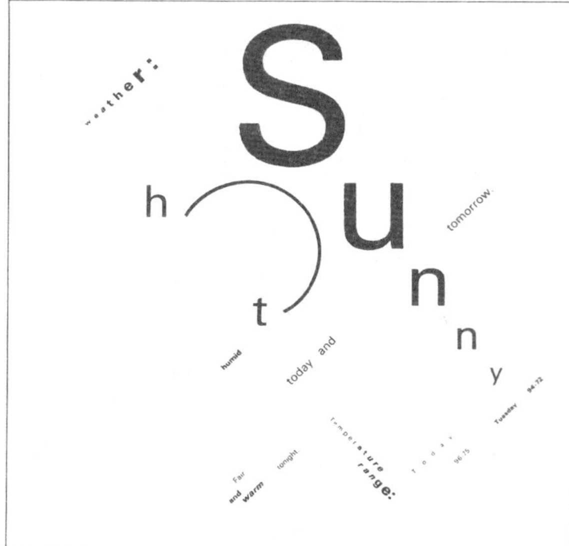

Student work by

Rosalie Hanson
Wayne Bokum
Richard Burgess
John Devine
Cathy Johnson
Peter Johnson
Azar Khosrovi
Andrea Mackler
Lisa Meyerson
Bernt Sanden
Stephanie Segal
Upendra Shah
Susan Thornton
Garretson Trudeau
Rick Villastrigo

Design: D Friedman

144

the straitjacket of the grid and white lab coats that unpin and reconfigure the Ulm influence from his first year studying abroad. Friedman broke from SUNY Purchase due to the school's lack of support for his vision (read: too radical, over-the-top) and limited flexibility for his professional practice.

Friedman came back to teaching with a renewed sense of optimism, buoyed by the publishing of his *Radical Modernism*. He returned to Cooper Union in the spring of 1995, offering a course in typography that was co-taught with Lorraine Ferguson. However, as the semester unfolded, the virus progressed quickly and he was not able to sustain his teaching duties. Ferguson took over the course, and Friedman died that summer on July 6, 1995.

A Safer Space

Over Friedman's lifetime of practice and teaching, the x- and y-axes of the modernist grid that centered the rational, corporate process of the "organizational man" would shift visually as well as geographically.[17] This change was linked to Friedman's new friends and creative collaborators in the Downtown art scene, including artists Keith Haring, Kenny Scharf, Jeff Koons, Katy K., and Jean-Michel Basquiat, gallerist Jeffery Deitch, and polymodal fashion designer Willi Smith. At times, Friedman's self-proclaimed eccentricity placed him in complex relationships that included and transcended labels like friend, partner-in-crime, comrade, lover, and mutual aesthetic influence. These personal networks resembled the nonaxial (read: bent, angled, cruise-y, overlapping, meandering) grid of Lower Manhattan.

One of those mutual influences was the graphic designer Bill Bonnell, who had collaborated on Willi Smith's utopian and accessible fashion brand, WilliWear. In 1977 Bonnell included Friedman in

Abraham Darby III builds a pioneering iron bridge

Post-modern Typography, an exhibition that he curated for the Ryder Gallery in Chicago. This exhibition was a hallmark event, spurring important discussions on postmodernism in graphic design. After the show, the two designers became friends; as Bonnell recently reflected on Friedman's practice,

> Dan was a different personality, he was living in New York and he got very involved with the art scene in the East Village. Artists like Kenny Scharf influenced him, and that influenced his design. I never thought of him as being somebody who was a theoretician, but he did have this background from Basel in typography and when he came to New York those two forces met in this incredibly wild time in the early 1980s. Living downtown influenced him as much as Weingart did.[18]

For Friedman, the simultaneous influence of the Downtown scene and his engagement with postmodern academic theory blew a hole in the alleged objectivity of the modernist project. This chasm could only be straddled by something or someone queer and subjectively expressive, thus rupturing the hegemony of the page or design system influenced by Robert Venturi's "complexity and contradiction."[19] It is worth noting that Venturi's pivotal "Learning From Las Vegas" road trip took place exactly as Friedman was

17. "The rise of the Organization Man had profound consequences for the newly accommodationist Cold War politics, helping to suspend inquiry and debate into the distribution of power and resources while reifying a conception of corporate hegemony leading to a truly classless society. Moreover, this new Organization Man redrew the boundaries of the social self, now ubiquitously defined in terms of shared patterns of consumption and its attendant desire for social and cultural conformity—the ideal occupant of the suburban paradise. Organization Man discourse necessarily privileged sociology, the descriptive discipline, ahead of a host of more interventionist and logocentric forms of inquiry. And as that descriptive mode, in the form of the survey, came to supplant the ideological perspective it further reinforced the incontestability of the status quo as the sole field of meaningful intellectual endeavor." Jonathan D. Katz, "Passive Resistance: On the Success of Queer Artists in Cold War American Art," *L'image* 3 (December 1996): 119–42.

18. Bill Bonnell, interview with the authors, May 6, 2020.

19. Katherine McCoy, email with the authors, February 29, 2020. See Robert Venturi, *Complexity and Contradiction in Architecture* (New York: Museum of Modern Art, 1966).

teaching at Yale.[20] The study opened the profession's eyes to the vitality of vernacular forms and indigenous structures and encouraged designers, in Friedman's words: "I began to think about a reconceptualized modernism . . . more radical in that it would not only accommodate order along with chaos but would embrace a variety of other conditions no longer paired as dichotomies."[21] This breaking of dichotomies played out in the city's subcultures which conversed, created, danced, played, and protested both the joys and sorrows of their collective lives.

Entrance to Friedman's New York City apartment with a detail of the assemblage *Deep Sea Meltdown*, photographed in 1991

Friedman's escape from the confines of the heteronormative grid took place when he moved into a Fifth Avenue apartment a block north of Washington Square Park in 1978. This geographic relocation was coupled with seismic cultural movements that happed nearby in the East and West Village enclaves; hotspots for artists, activists, drag queens, Queer families, and the underground ball and club scenes. It is critical to note that these revolutionary strides were led primarily by black and brown, trans, and Queer folx dating back to the 1969 Stonewall riots. Like the streets downtown and postmodern theory, these movements are interconnected, overlapping, and contain complex contradictions. These radical changes in his adjacent neighborhoods are mirrored in Friedman's ongoing decoration of his apartment.

The secondary definition of the word "queer" leads us to one of Friedman's self-chosen identifiers: *eccentric*, or that of the unconventional.[22] There was nothing freer and more unconstrained than Friedman's apartment (read: both queer and Queer). It seems like everyone we have interviewed has a story dealing with, or about, his apartment. In his tiny dwelling he started building a safer space, off the ordinal grids of Upper Manhattan and the high-modernist Swiss grid imported from Ulm and Basel. He was able to tinker, unpack, and unearth those deeper unconventional taboos, tidbits, and moody tidal waves. Not the closet of corporate or academic graphic design, but a room of one's own.[23]

20. Robert Venturi, Denise Scott Brown, and Steven Izenour, *Learning from Las Vegas* (Cambridge, MA: MIT Press, 1972).

21. Christopher Pullman, "Dan Friedman, Radical Modernist, Part 2," *Design Observer*, May 12, 2015, https://designobserver.com/feature/dan-friedman-radical-modernist-part-2/38882.

22. "Eccentric" was also used as a code word for homosexual men dating back to the late nineteenth century.

23. Virginia Woolf, *A Room of One's Own* (London: Hogarth Press, 1929).

Documentation of this transmutable space, and the objects within it, takes up a fair amount of visual real estate in *Radical Modernism*. One could say Friedman became increasingly proud (read: coming out) of the expressive, eccentric space that morphed into an unexpected site of pedagogy. During a visit to New York City, Kathrine McCoy recounts visiting Friedman's space with Lorraine Wild one of her former students:

> In 1980, Lorraine and I visited Dan in his apartment during our annual Cranbrook NYC studio tour to see his ongoing transformation of the space. Dan's apartment was great fun and seriously outrageous in his painterly use of color, detail, and spatial distortions. A corn plant was tied up in rubber bondage! I found the space quite groundbreaking at the time. There was perhaps a hint of gay coding or reference. But at that time there was still a general atmosphere of secrecy or discretion, and many designers did not feel free to be visibly out in their professional lives. I would say that in professional design and design education, Dan broke ground for gay identity."[24]

To this day, the common design standard to "Swiss it" places emphasis on formal structures of hierarchy and control. Instead, we choose to see new possibilities in Friedman's queering of both the grids of design education and personal spaces into a more open and *mutable* method to "swish it." Holding firm to both the lowercase queer and the capital Queen Queer, Friedman elucidated twelve points of optimism. We leave him with the final word:

> Live and work with passion and responsibility; have a sense of humor and fantasy. Try to express personal, spiritual, and domestic values even if our culture continues to be dominated by corporate, marketing, and institutional values. Choose to remain progressive; don't be regressive. Find comfort in the past only if it expands insight into the future and not just for the sake of nostalgia. Embrace the richness of all cultures; be inclusive instead of exclusive. Think of your work as a significant element in the context of a more important, transcendental purpose. Use your work to become advocates of projects for the public good. Attempt to become a cultural provocateur; be a leader rather than a follower. Engage in self-restraint; accept the challenge of working with reduced expectations and diminished resources. Avoid getting stuck in corners, such as being a servant to increasing overhead careerism, or narrow points of view. Bridge the boundaries that separate us from other creative professions and unexpected possibilities. Use the new technologies, but don't be seduced into thinking that they provide answers to fundamental questions. Be radical.[25]

24. Katherine McCoy, email with the authors, February 29, 2020.

25. Friedman, "Projects of Optimism," 209.

15.

THE EDGE OF THE INTERNET

BRETT MACFADDEN

When I went to graduate school, I did not have a smartphone. I did not have a Facebook account or Gmail, or a VPN, a blog, or a chat room, or a website, or any of it, really, mostly because the easy, consumer-friendly Internet was still coming to pass. You could have an AOL account, but I didn't. You could meet prospective lovers or find an apartment on Craigslist. You could code, you could html. Flash was thriving—God bless it—but I did not Flash or code or hook up. It was all there, like mushrooms growing in a deep dark forest, but I was not in that forest. Not yet.

I did, however, have an email address. It used to be my work's email address, and then that went away with my job, and I got a new email address from school. I also had a new mailing address, and they weren't that different—new place, new addresses. New org, new me. I had left a marketing job at an architecture firm in Boston for grad school at Cranbrook in the fall of 1998. I was very proud of this new email address. I belonged to Cranbrook, and my @cranbrook.edu was the proof, akin to the badge a detective presents from his suit pocket. Where once I was a marketer now I was a designer, only a thin membrane away from an artist.

The Design department at Cranbrook felt astoundingly modern when I visited it in the spring of '98 to interview. Scott and Laurie Haycock-Makela had taken over the 2D (graphic design) department from longtime head Katherine McCoy, and the couple represented a generational and technological shift for the program. Graphic design had worked its way from the grungy *Ray Gun* "deconstructed" design of the early '90s to the glossy cyberpunk stylings of the late '90s, and the Makelas were hotwired to that transition, both in output and attitude. Over the course of a long day of interviews with current students, I became desperate to join this confident gang of insider-outsiders. In the morning before I left for the airport I crossed paths with Scott in front of the school's Eliel Saarinen–designed library, and he confided that I would indeed be accepted to the program. I was (and remain) a lanky, buttoned-down-shirt type who likes to listen to soft rock on Sunday mornings, but at that moment I imagined myself becoming some kind of design-vanguard techno sex symbol. Basically Neo, who would arrive in theaters during the spring of my first year at school.

Nineteen ninety-eight is the year Google was founded. The Internet was chugging uphill, still in its "I think I can, I think I can" stage. The architecture firm I had just left was on dial-up, and we wore ties to work. Cranbrook, on the other hand, had a T1 line. The Internet went directly into your greige Mac desktop computer and was there all the time. Waiting. People had Syquest drives for big files and those hard, small floppy disks for normal ones. There was no cloud. We had a very special, very expensive, very precious Avid system for motion work. Only one person could use it at a time and it took hours to render anything—often the whole night. Motion was where it was at. Motion understood what the Internet knew was coming. All the hottest students (not I) were working in motion because the Makelas were working in motion. They would

Josiah Wedgwood (or Thomas Massey) invents the pyrometer

3D-render glossy, puffy words that would spin around some affirmation like "Choose Your Obsession" accompanied by lush electronic music that Scooby, a beloved student in Printmaking, would create. This sounds kind of silly, but it didn't seem silly at all; it was terribly seductive, that moment when you and the earth and the work around you are all moving at the same speed.

And yet, as James Gladman, who served as "creative tools specialist" for the department, reminded me, we had no Internet in the dorms, and phone calls came in for everyone on one landline in the design studio for both 3D and 2D. If a recruiter was courting a student, they would call the student on that line, and someone walking by would answer and yell for the student who would come to that one phone to talk. If a call came in for another student, while the phone was busy, well, that would be that. One at a time. James also reminded me how if he wanted to know what was going on in art and design outside of our little Cranbrookian bubble, he would go to New York, and he would go to St. Mark's Bookshop. And then he would pack up all the news he found there into a very heavy suitcase and bring it back to Michigan.

Things were shifting quickly and radically. Apple released the all-in-one iMac G3—the ones that looked like jelly beans—in 1998, and we soon had a gaggle of them in the school computer lab. They were beautiful to behold. Some people entering the program were already quite experienced in web design, like Mike Essl in my second year. Mike had cofounded a NYC shop called the Chopping Block in 1996, and the studio was creating complex animations and interactions through skills new (Flash) and old (drawing). Mike introduced me to stealing music though Napster, which arrived in the summer of 1999. Somehow that music is still on my iPhone. Sorry, Weezer.

Graduating in the late '90s and early 2000s, many alumni stepped directly onto the escalator of digital design, but at that time you mostly chose one team or the other—print or web—and the silos were robust. Alumnus Matt Owens was making a name for himself with his digital magazine *Volumeone*, founded in 1997, which also leveraged Flash, 3D rendering, and an enviable level of talent to create a quarterly digital tapestry of personal stories and animated experiments. SFMOMA acquired the site archive in 2001, and Matt went on to cofound the still-thriving New York agency Athletics. I, on the other hand, chose print, and so, despite twenty years in the Bay Area, I have never experienced the orgasmic glory of everlasting financial security that I assume an IPO to be.

At Cranbrook, a school without classes, everything centered around crits, which happened once a week and were the closest we had to a sacred ritual. We would run each other through the mill with a firm belief in the growth potential of tough love. I don't recall talking much about how this thing or that would evolve as technology does—a topic of regular concern with my students now. We mostly talked about what the work communicates: what it means, how it makes us feel, sometimes "how'd you do that?" The last question was mostly frowned upon; *how* mattered less than *why*. Our teachers, the Makelas, acted almost like debate coaches or refs, guiding things along but letting them go where they would. Technology was unfolding as it always did and always will, but we felt like we were the unfolding, we were the technology. We had no idea how insane it would get. How the snake would eat its own tail and then the rest of the kingdom.

I think of this time as peak *Wired*. It seemed perfectly natural for our digital world to be covered by a very successful, highly designed, unquestionably hip print magazine that used generous amounts of metallic and fluorescent ink. Cranbrook, within its own unapologetic bubble, reflected this techno-optimism in its pedagogy. The school, like others in its peer group, was still fighting against the idea of design as humble servant of content in favor of designer as author, as artist, as entrepreneur. Designer as their own dream client. This worked best, of course, in those two years in which our client was called student loans. There was much talk about things like "nonlinear narratives," and a sincere belief that we were part of a great reworking of how stories were told, and that art would no longer stand still waiting around for an audience. The school had spent the last generation mired in poststructuralist theory, and traces of that foundation still had a home in the program, but they were quickly being replaced by a focus on the individual, on quasi-religion, and on simply making things look cool and new. Formally, this mostly meant bright colors, glossy forms, electronic sounds, and puffy, anthropomorphic typefaces. Roundness. It was a formal world in which the digital had become polished and comparatively mature, no longer inhabiting the strict confines of vectors and LCD, and it was building a new language that did not require the old things like ink or stone or gravity. The Makelas thought it was all great, the new-new-new; they did not mourn the material.

Scott and Laurie identified as Buddhists, and Laurie's brother was an honest-to-God Buddhist monk in Korea. Buddhist philosophy informed their own way in the world, and their way informed ours. A favorite phrase of the Makelas was "Wide open and ready to receive." Design was a semi-spiritual practice and container for whatever we needed to explore. Where earlier Cranbrookians made design that challenged accepted forms of good design, organization, or beauty, we frequently used design for self-analysis, and somehow all that technology was the perfect partner in this quest, allowing for work that operated through layers and levels, anticipating in its own way today's land of endless platforms and personalization.

I'm so glad to have studied when I did. Attention has never been my strong suit and God knows how I would've gotten anything done with today's connectivity constantly tugging at my sleeve. I'm so grateful to have that mental space in the school's library, one book at a time, and time to walk in the woods without posting pics of my walks in the woods. Most of all, I'm thankful for that time in our little box of a crit room, where we could present and perform for each other, debate, drill down, hurt and make up with something approaching a focused state. I look at my students now, and me, on the phone on the phone on the phone—our crits bisected by a thousand whispers from afar. Everything available, searchable, provable. And us both there, in crit, and somewhere else. Distant, floating off in cyberspace. I know. The rosy glasses of yesterday. This too will pass, and it will all look so good, so simple, from twenty years away.

K'S EDUCATION

SULKI and MIN

K went to college in 1991. It was a time when South Koreans were feeling the effects of democratization and globalization after the authoritarian military regime had finally given way to a "civilian" government led by a former general. The economy was growing—achieving 10.4 percent growth in GDP in 1991—and the domestic consumer market was booming. Thanks to the 1988 Summer Olympics in Seoul and the liberalization of overseas travel in the following year, people were increasingly aware of the world outside the peninsula. Manufacturers were trying to transition from being subcontractors for American or Japanese corporations to makers with their own brands. It was, in short, a good time to be a designer. Universities were scrambling to open design programs, and they attracted a huge number of applicants. K was one of them.

K did not know what graphic design was. None of her classmates did. She liked drawing, and she was good at it. She could have chosen to be an artist, but "design" sounded more attractive to her. As the borrowed term began to replace native Korean equivalents, it sounded more foreign, more advanced, and much more glamorous. She suspected that many of her classmates were attracted by that image, not to mention the prospect of wealth that the new profession was promising.

1991

Like many similar programs in Korea at the time, the one that K entered was part of a large university and it offered a four-year bachelor's degree. The first year was centered on liberal art electives and foundation courses: drawing, sculpture, and design basics. The first foundation design studio was taught by a professor who had studied in Nebraska in the 1950s. On the first day, she asked the students what they had done during the winter break. Someone behind her raised his hand and said he had been reading about the Bauhaus. "Oh, what did you learn?" the professor asked. "I learned that design is, after all, for the good of the people," he answered without any sense of irony. K did not know what the Bauhaus was, but from this response, she gathered it was some kind of spiritual community.

The studio course comprised a series of two-dimensional composition assignments, each with a different theme: dots, lines, planes, colors, movement. The sessions were very quiet. While the students were silently working on their compositions, the professor would walk around the studio, occasionally giving advice and verdicts. K did not like the course: It was neither as expressive as the drawing studios nor as rigorous as the philosophy seminars. The professor's preferred mode of expression was facial, and she would rarely elaborate on her sparse comments. It was very Zen-like. "You like primary colors, don't you?" was one of the few comments K got from the professor, and she thought it was a compliment. At the end of the semester, K received a C for her colorful work. The guy who'd read about the Bauhaus got an A+.

The second-semester foundation design studio dealt with three-dimensional objects and materials. The professor, who had trained in Finland, emphasized the importance of understanding tangible structures for designers in all fields. The course culminated with the Staircase Project. The professor explained that the staircase was a perfect design problem because it combined clear physical—and physiological—constraints with aesthetic concerns (as it would always be part of a bigger structure). Or that was how K understood it; this professor talked even less than his predecessor. There were no discussions. Students would keep their mouths shut and just make stuff, then the professor would come and nod (approvingly) or simply turn away. Sometimes he would directly intervene by silently breaking apart the model of a staircase that a student had painfully assembled.

To compensate for this lack of articulation, the students organized discussion clubs for themselves. Some of them had links to left-wing student organizations, effectively functioning as clandestine cells to recruit potential warriors for "national liberation" or—depending on which faction they were associated with—"emancipation of labor." But the one that K joined was more benign, and the activities were centered on translating design-related foreign texts. The first assignment K took was an article about postmodernism in graphic design published in an American magazine. An intense debate erupted over it. While most of K's colleagues were skeptical of postmodernism, seeing it as just another foreign fad, a senior student passionately defended it, arguing that, if used wisely, it could be a "great tool for emancipating the people from the tyranny of modernism."

1992

K's professional education was to start in earnest from the second year, with courses on typography, photography, printmaking, and design history. There was also a core graphic design studio, and it was supposed to bring all the elements from the specialized courses together. Instead, it effectively became an illustration studio, mainly because the tutor was an illustrator by trade. K did not have enough knowledge to recognize its awkwardness, though. In fact, she quite liked it because illustration was considered a more personal activity, and the idea of working for herself, rather than as part of a team, appealed to her.

What she did not like was the typography studio. The course, taught by a conservative lettering artist, started with a series of assignments to trace the characters of existing typefaces, such as Garamond or Korean *myeongjo-che*, then moved on to the next stage, in which you created your own letterform. K never reached the next stage. She could not stand spending hours in front of a drawing board simply to make perfectly rendered unoriginal letters. She finally dropped out of the course after the instructor caught her smoking in the studio (totally acceptable at the time) and scolded her for it ("Girls are not supposed to smoke!").

Next semester's Advanced Typography was taught by a corporate-design specialist, who had drawn a lot of logotypes. He asked the students to work on a single problem for the entire semester. And the assignment was not a logotype, but to draw, curiously, a loaf of bread and a couple of crystal balls floating around it. Perhaps realizing it was too deep as a typography project for sophomores, the professor modified the problem and asked the students to add an appropriate caption to the final image. "Use only Helvetica or Univers, depending on the mood of your drawing, and set it under 7 point, so it won't interfere with the image." K chose Helvetica because her bread was whole grain. She took her caption from Iggy Pop: "The one who's searchin', searchin' to destroy."

The school was failing K, but she still had some hope for the history seminars. The lecturer was the author of a Korean textbook about design history, and he was good at simplifying complex ideas and phenomena into memorable formulas. "What is the key difference between interwar and postwar modernism in typography? Asymmetric arrangement? Sans serif? Nah—it's the unjustified text setting!" He presented a streamlined picture of development from William Morris to Walter Gropius and beyond. Nothing outside Europe or North America was mentioned. And he was not keen on anything that happened after 1978, the year he started teaching. In private, he would express frustration over the fact that he was always considered a "theory teacher." "Just because I wrote books about design doesn't mean I'm a weak practitioner!" One day, he impressed his students by passionately explaining—in the middle of a lecture about DIN formats—what it means to determine the grain direction of paper, as if all the knowledge he had been trying to impart would be useless if you did not know how to make a proper book.

With her discussion club K joined that year's Unity Winter Camp: a four-day gathering of art students from all over the country. The camp was initiated in 1988 by a left-wing nationalist student organization as part of a campaign against the Olympiad of Art, a large-scale international event organized in conjunction with the 1988 Summer Olympics in Seoul. The camp aimed to "break down the barriers of subjectivism, genius-worship, and factionalism forced by Western art" through the practice of collaborative work. In reality, though, the work was replaced by endless drunk debates. K was confused by the way design was portrayed by her "unit leader" as an evil service for the wealthy, removed from its socialist roots. The unit leader was a senior painting student, and upon graduation, she would denounce art and go on to work for a large advertising agency.

1993

The third-year core graphic design studio was focused on the exercise of corporate identity and branding and taught by a professor who was regarded as a pioneer of modern graphic design in Korea. He was part of a team responsible for the graphic design coordination of the 1988 Summer Olympics. His team employed the then-novel technique of computer graphics for the posters. It showed their belief in the potential of new technologies applied to a complex, large-scale project.

One of the assignments he gave to his students was to make two logos for the same organization: "one in a modernist style, the other in a postmodernist style." The brief reflected the professor's own practice. When he worked on a logo for, say, the National Museum, he would propose two contrasting "options" for the client to choose from: one that was reminiscent of Wim Crouwel's no-nonsense SM logo for the Stedelijk Museum Amsterdam, the other inspired by the playfully goofy MTV logo designed by Frank Olinsky. By now, K had read enough to know that such an assignment was itself postmodern, so she made two logos of the same design. The professor was a gentleman, and he took pains to compare them in case there were any differences.

The professor was so busy with his projects that he could not come to class very often. Instead, he would send his teaching assistant to help the students. The TA seemed to enjoy the opportunities to show off his skills. He once advised against using Korean—as opposed to English—text in the design. "Because in that case, people will be able to read the text and will not see your design." He was a big fan of Neville Brody. One day, he came to the studio clutching a handwritten letter. "Do you guys know what this is? This is a letter from Mr. Brody himself! I wrote to him months ago, a fan letter, really. Never expected him to reply. And now, look at this! Do you have any idea what it means?"

To K, however, Brody's work was already passé. For she had obtained a copy of Rick Poynor's *Typography Now* and had become acquainted with the works reproduced in it. The impetus came from the new course on digital typography. The instructor had just come back home after studying in New York City. He was the one who introduced K and others to the kind of works published in Poynor's book. "These are exciting," K concluded. "Forget illustration. Typography is much more expressive and personal. Who cares about drawing in the age of digital production anyway?" The instructor also showed the new digital fonts from Emigre, which K wanted to use for her projects. But there was no way she could acquire them. Desperate, she scanned the pages of *Typography Now* and started tracing the characters in her pirate copy of Fontographer installed on her first Macintosh, Classic II. While thus reverse-engineering the fonts, K wondered if it would have helped if she had not dropped out of her first typography class and learned how to trace letters manually.

K was also introduced to the work of Ahn Sang-soo, a pioneer of digital typography in Korea. His geometric Korean typeface was comparable to the experimental alphabets from Central Europe in the interwar years: It attempted a truly rational, if unconventional, representation of Hangul, the Korean alphabet. He was avant-garde, but he was not exactly a modernist—the distinction mattered at the time, at least to K's discussion-club colleagues. He created his typeface not in the 1930s or 1950s but in the 1980s, and it must have been awkward to claim to be a modernist then. And the magazine he founded and designed, *Bogoseo Bogoseo*, had much in common with the contemporary (postmodern) designer publications from the West—like *Emigre*—in terms of how it challenged the conventions of reading. Perhaps he had to be both modernist and postmodernist, switching between them depending on the occasion. Or he would rather have preferred to be positioned "beyond" the dichotomy. In any case, he was living in a compressed space-time continuum, like any Korean designer at the time, where multiple stages of "normal" history were unfolding in parallel.

K never met Ahn Sang-soo in person, he was teaching at a different school. She knew some of his pupils, though, and they were like true art-school students, playing rock music and making zines. She thought they were cool—and "cool" was a new buzzword that suited them well.

1994

K's final year in college was almost entirely devoted to the graduation show. She made a series of posters and a pair of advertising works for the exhibition. The posters were about the film *Edward Scissorhands*, a problem that K was almost forced to create for herself. What she originally wanted to do was a typographic representation of Arvo Pärt's music. But the instructor, an art director at an ad agency, did not like her initial sketches, which were covertly inspired by 8vo's Zanders calendar. The sketches were so true to the inspiration that the instructor thought K was designing a calendar instead of posters. He liked her later approach, though: a series of abstract compositions that combined aspects of Nick Bell's Virgin Classics record covers and Coop Himmelb(l)au's architectural drawings. But he did not get the musical reference. Instead, he insisted that the spiky shapes reminded him of Johnny Depp's metal hands in the movie.

As for the advertising project, the instructor asked the students to begin by finding a problem to solve: an existing advertisement that they could improve upon. Then he also advised that the problem should not be too problematic. "There is a limit as to how much you can improve an LG ad, while it's easier to make something tasteful with a Calvin Klein logo." The point was, the reasoning went, not actually solving any problems but to experience the *feeling* of solving something elegantly. K was not convinced, but she saw an opportunity to revive her failed attempt for posters. She fabricated a fictitious Arvo Pärt Music Festival and made artworks for its magazine advertising, turning her calendar-like poster design into an actual event calendar. After these multiple degrees of adaptation, the final work had no obvious resemblance to its origin. For K, the experience was profoundly educational. It was a realization of nonlinearity and heterogeneity inherent in any work with influences.

K was already subscribing to *Eye*, a new graphic design magazine from the UK that championed "critical journalism," and *Emigre*, which had recently shown more interest in critical writings. It was from their pages that K picked up notions like "nonlinearity" and "heterogeneity." She avidly read all the articles and interviews, familiarizing herself with key discussions and new developments. Some of the debates reminded her of the ones she had had with her discussion club or at the Unity Winter Camp. Except now they were unfolding in the same space with the coolest graphic design works, as if the two were inseparable. The more K tuned in to what was going on in the epicenters of contemporary graphic design, however, the wider the gap grew between them and what she saw in the world surrounding her. Any encounter with the "real world" through the small freelance jobs that she was then taking would only deepen the frustration, as if hammering into her what was not attainable in her culture.

The economy was still good, and people were taking design even more seriously, as Lee Kun-hee, then chairman of Samsung Electronics, famously proclaimed: "The key is distinctiveness—the key is design." But K was not interested in design as a means to boost the sales of domestic appliances. She wanted to pursue more personal work in a culturally meaningful way. She could see some distant hopes and inspirations, but not any real paths to follow. Graduation was only months away, but she had no plan for the future.

Despite the strong economy, there was a sense of impending doom in Korean society. It was the feeling that all the relentless change and feverish development would hit a wall sooner or later, with terrible consequences. The United States nearly went to war with North Korea in June to stop its nuclear program (a North Korean representative warned of a "Seoul inferno" in case of war). Then in July—the hottest summer on record—the North Korean leader Kim Il-sung suddenly died just days before what would have been the first inter-Korean summit. Early on the morning of October 21, Seongsu Bridge over the Han River in Seoul collapsed, killing thirty-two people. It would mark the midpoint of a series of disasters—buildings collapsing, airplanes crashing, ferries sinking, trains derailing—all attributed to haphazard construction and/or the lack of precautions. K suddenly found herself living in turbulent times. "History," the color therapists who visited K's school preached, "has its ways of settling outstanding bills." Later, K came to believe that the "color therapists" were in fact missionaries from the Shincheonji Church of Jesus cult.

It was mid-December when K received a meeting request from an MFA student of the same university. He was a star of the school, and he had just finished his legendary thesis on "Semiology, Hypertext, and Typography." There was a rumor that he had been offered a teaching job but had declined in order to start his own practice, some kind of multimedia studio. "The reason why I wanted to see you," he said at the meeting, "is because we want you to work with us." K was surprised and duly flattered. But she had no experience in multimedia. She had not taken any computer science classes, not even a motion design course. "You don't need any special knowledge about computer programming. Well, maybe a little bit. But you'll learn it naturally as you go along," he explained. "And we're definitely not looking for a 3D specialist or an animator. What we're looking for right now is someone good at typography and visual communication. You see, what we do here is . . . have you read my thesis? Well, that's OK. But that's basically what we're doing." K was confused. She'd heard about hypertext and had seen some examples of HyperCard games that came with her Classic II. But she had never considered it as something beyond a novelty. It could certainly not be an interest for serious graphic designers. "Maybe you're right, K, but things are changing—fast," he continued. "Have you heard of this thing called the World Wide Web?"

Italian Alessandro Volta makes the first battery (known as a Voltaic pile)

FROM INTERTEXTUALITY TO INTERSECTIONALITY: THE SOFT POWER OF THE BIBLIOGRAPHY

ANDREW BLAUVELT

The story of graphic design's pedagogy—how it is taught—is inseparable from a larger set of other institutionalized practices regarding what is taught, by whom, and for what purposes. I would argue that graphic design becomes a discipline at the moment it enters the academy, which is to say at the moment it can be taught, conceived, and practiced beyond the acquisition of craft skills and practical techniques. Were graphic design reducible merely to forms of embodied knowledge, it would be vocational in nature and therefore not admissible to the academy as a form of reflexive knowledge.

Graphic design entered schools of learning as a set of skills and professional techniques that first emerged in the marketplace. While it could aspire to that ineffable condition called art, particularly when practiced in an art-school setting, graphic design was considered more of a craft—something teachable and marketable as a skill. By applying visual art principles to commercial applications, graphic design isolated the skills necessary for design's reproduction and by doing so underscored its pedagogical dependence on technique as a primary method of instruction. Ensconced in the academy in art schools and university art departments, graphic design programs grappled with how to expand pedagogy beyond the mastery of technique, how to inculcate something in the classroom that couldn't be learned on the job. If graphic design was born in the commercial marketplace based on the reproduction of printed goods and communications, then its life in the academy would be sustained through the reproduction of design and of designers.

I recall a specific transformational period, in the late 1970s and early '80s, when graphic design educators debated the relative merits of a portfolio- versus a process-oriented pedagogy, particularly in the context of undergraduate education. In a portfolio-oriented approach, teaching was geared toward a simulation of professional practice. Students were assigned projects whose end products conformed to the prevailing logic and needs of the marketplace—a package, a poster, a logo, etc. Assembling a portfolio of designs that mimicked what a professional designer might show in a job interview or to a client to obtain a commission was the imperative. Entry into the profession based on that portfolio was the pedagogical goal.

This approach was contrasted with a process-oriented one, in which such end products and formats constituted only a final step in a series of exercises that atomized the constituent elements of graphic design. Typography, imagery, and color, for instance, could be isolated and studied separately before eventually being synthesized into a final design. This approach would spread to nonvisual aspects of graphic design too, including the conceptualization of ideas as design methods merged with more vernacular brainstorming exercises. It was argued that a process-oriented approach better served the interests of the student in the long term by instilling a methodological framework for creative expression, one that could be applied to any scale of project or scope of problem, whether on the first day of the job or later in one's career.

In a product-oriented approach the pedagogy is essentially mimetic, emulative. In the process-oriented approach, the pedagogy is closer to *poiesis*, the creation of something new. The concept of a process-oriented pedagogy is rooted in the metaphor of verbal language—learning its parts (alphabet, words, sentences, etc.) in order to assemble something greater out of its elements. Graphic design becomes a form of visual language. Downplayed in such an approach is the differential nature (common to all languages) of the creativity it inspires. That is, each student is required to design using a similar set of constituent parts from an otherwise shared system and then render these parts uniquely in a given problem. Creativity and uniqueness are judged as a matter of a degree of difference with every other student's solutions or designs.

The second transformational moment for graphic design pedagogy occurred in the 1980s and '90s with the rise of the MFA in the discipline. As Rob Giampietro has argued elsewhere, the history of MFA creative writing programs in the United States offers an interesting parallel to graphic design.[1] In his pioneering study of the subject, Mark McGurl identifies a triadic relationship among the three directives that have guided the formulization of a pedagogic approach to creative writing.[2] These three values are embracing authenticity ("write what you know"); developing your craft by learning to "show not tell"; and nurturing your self-expression by "finding your voice." These values—expressly not those of the practicing professional designer—oddly echo the values that graphic design master's programs of the period espoused. In order to distance and differentiate the programs from undergraduate education, an emphasis was placed on experiences and eccentricities that could be mined for expressive affect. An eventual codification of such values perpetuates a particular form of creativity, one that can be systemically produced in the student and, of course, reproduced institutionally.

I believe it is too early to fully historicize the contemporary transformations of either the BFA or MFA in graphic design—or perhaps I am now too distant from day-to-day teaching to offer such insights. From my vantage point outside of the classroom, however, I imagine that the pedagogical gaze has shifted outward, away from the profession and the field of study itself and toward the world and others, toward investigations of collective forms of social and cultural identity and expression. Creativity is no longer differentially produced within a shared belief system such as a visual language or common methodology but is reconstructed within a larger network of relations beyond both the self and the profession.

I would therefore like to do something I never thought I would do: quote Massimo Vignelli, who gave the keynote address to the first conference on the history of graphic design, entitled "Coming

1. See Rob Giampietro, "School Days," in *Graphic Design: Now in Production*, ed. Andrew Blauvelt and Ellen Lupton (Minneapolis: Walker Art Center, 2011), 212–19.

2. See Mark McGurl, *The Program Era: Postwar Fiction and the Rise of Creative Writing* (Cambridge, MA: Harvard University Press 2009).

of Age," held at the Rochester Institute of Technology on April 20, 1983. Almost four decades ago, Vignelli proclaimed:

> As we go about increasing awareness of history, theory, criticism, documentation, technology, and culture, we can't lose sight [of] the value of meaning over the value of form. It's not true that meaning is more important than form. It's not true that content is more important than form. Still, if for fifty years we have been trained and bombarded every day with the idea that form is really the greatest thing around, then for the next fifty years we've got to say that meaning is more important than form. Perhaps then, fifty years from now, we might reach a state of balance between form and content.[3]

So, according to Vignelli, we have until 2033 to get this right.

I did not interpret this as the typical dualism of form and content among designers—where visual expression is either independent of or dependent upon any specific content derived from the design problem—but rather as a call to grapple with graphic design's "meta-content" as both a practice and a discipline, its creation and its reception.

At another gathering of design historians, in Chicago around 1997, Vignelli held up a copy of the journal *Visible Language*, which I had edited, devoted to new approaches to graphic design history and proclaimed it a prime example of the "problem" of academic approaches to the study of the field.[4] I assumed I was being admonished for my theoretical approach to something as seemingly simple as graphic design. It would become a familiar critique. In retrospect, I realize that the discipline supports two types of practitioners: those with a theoretical bent who study graphic design and its effects and those who produce it. At the time, however, there was essentially no meaningful difference between these distinct and self-interested parties, and the people most invested in the study of the field were the same people producing it and teaching it.

To think about what we as designers—whether practicing professionals or academics—read is to think about the bibliography and its relationship to pedagogy as an important tool that both reflects and shapes our thinking of graphic design as a practice, a profession, and a discipline. More abstract than a textbook used for course instruction, where one presumes a direct connection to instruction, and broader than a reading list for a specific project or class, the bibliography as a compendium of thinking on a topic offers something more expansive, prospective, and perhaps even aspirational.

I would like to reflect here on two different bibliographies: one that I received at Cranbrook Academy of Art as a graduate student in the 1980s and another that I produced as a faculty member at North Carolina State University about seven years later. I do so in

3. Massimo Vignelli, "Keynote Address," in *The First Symposium on the History of Graphic Design: Coming of Age*, ed. R. Roger Remington and Barbara Hodik (Rochester: Rochester Institute of Technology, 1983), 11.

4. See "New Perspectives: Critical Histories of Graphic Design," ed. Andrew Blauvelt, the two-volume special issue of *Visible Language* 28, nos. 3 and 4 (1994) and 29, no. 1 (1995), http://visiblelanguage-journal.com.

an attempt to reflect on the nature of disciplinarity as it pertains to the practice and pedagogy of graphic design.

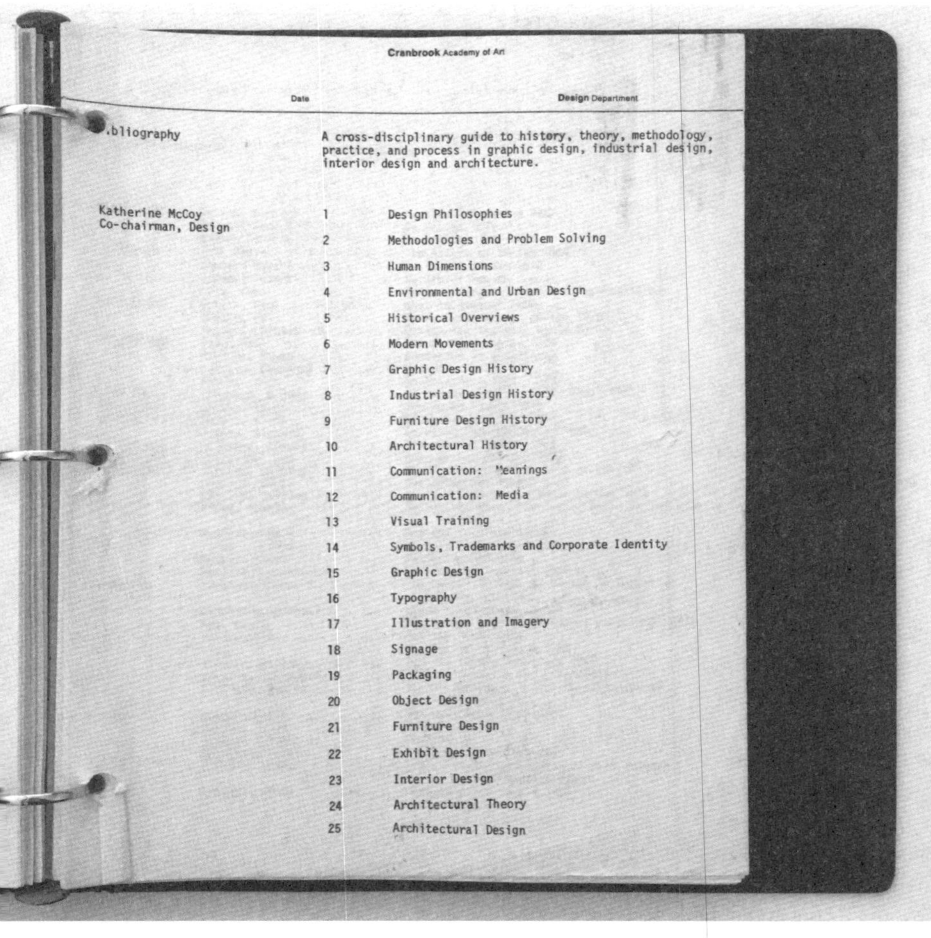

Cranbrook Academy of Art

Date Design Department

.bliography

A cross-disciplinary guide to history, theory, methodology, practice, and process in graphic design, industrial design, interior design and architecture.

Katherine McCoy
Co-chairman, Design

1 Design Philosophies
2 Methodologies and Problem Solving
3 Human Dimensions
4 Environmental and Urban Design
5 Historical Overviews
6 Modern Movements
7 Graphic Design History
8 Industrial Design History
9 Furniture Design History
10 Architectural History
11 Communication: Meanings
12 Communication: Media
13 Visual Training
14 Symbols, Trademarks and Corporate Identity
15 Graphic Design
16 Typography
17 Illustration and Imagery
18 Signage
19 Packaging
20 Object Design
21 Furniture Design
22 Exhibit Design
23 Interior Design
24 Architectural Theory
25 Architectural Design

Katherine McCoy, ed., "Bibliography," c. mid-1980s, Design Department, Cranbrook Academy of Art, n.p.

•

The bibliography of graduate studies at Cranbrook was a binder with more than forty pages of entries arranged by subject. It ordered design knowledge into twenty-five categories, including: design philosophies; methodologies and problem-solving; human dimensions; environmental design; graphic design history; industrial design history; communication: meanings and media; typography; furniture design; interior design; architectural theory; and so on. Compiled by Katherine McCoy, co-head of the design program at Cranbrook, the bibliography proclaimed itself a "cross-disciplinary guide to history, theory, methodology, practice, and process in graphic design, industrial design, interior design, and architecture," reflecting the integrated nature of the two- and three-dimensional design program at Cranbrook during the McCoy era. The particular version that I received in 1986 includes entries for some books published as late as 1982.

Painstakingly created in a time before search engines and the Internet, such bibliographies, not necessarily unique to Cranbrook, map an epistemological field of design circa 1980. What is most notable about Cranbrook's and made it different from other such bibliographies is its multidisciplinary nature, encompassing a wide range of design disciplines including architecture. Pedagogically, this cross-disciplinary medley underscored the department's bifurcated nature, which was itself a reflection of Cranbrook's first president and master architect, Eliel Saarinen, and his famous dictum to always design a thing by considering it in its next-largest context—a chair in a room, a room in a house, a house in an environment, an environment in a city plan.[5] Pragmatically, the integration of two- and three-dimensional design practices at Cranbrook was a consequence of the professional partnership of the husband-and-wife team of Katherine and Michael McCoy and a convenient by-product of Cranbrook's notorious frugality, which was nicely summed up by Kathy's frequent declaration, "Two designers, one paycheck."

Like most design bibliographies, Cranbrook's sought to convey a sense of the discipline's intellectual breadth to the user, to delineate the contours of thinking about design. A curated microcosm of design knowledge, it was meant to be a sketch of the

Design Department Fall 1988

BIBLIOGRAPHY CRANBROOK ACADEMY OF ART

11.3
Communications: Structuralism, deconstruction, literary criticism and postmodern theories

P99.E3	Eco, Umberto	A Theory of Semiotics 1976
	Eco, Umberto	The Role of the Reader 1979
P123.B38	Barthes, Roland	The Elements of Semiology 1967
	Hawkes, Terence	Structuralism and Semiotics 1977
	Scholes, Robert	Semiotics and Interpretation 1982
N7740.M52	Mitchell, W.J.T.	Iconology: OImage, Text, Ideology 1986
	Nadin, Mihai	'On the Meaning of the Visual', Semiotica
	Piaget, Jean	Structuralism 1970
	Bonsieppe, Gui	'Visual/Verbal Rhetoric', Ulm Papers 1965
	Ehses, Hanno	Rhetorical Handbook: A Manual for Designers 1987
	Kinross, Robin	'Semiotics & Designing', Information Design Journal 1986
	Ockerse, Thomas	'Semiotics and Graphic Design Education', Visible Language 1979
	Broadbent, Geoffrey	'A Plain Man's Guide to the Theory of Signs in Architecture', Architectural Design 1977
	Broadbent, Geoffrey	Perception and Communication
AC25.B313	Barthes, Roland	Mythologies 1972
PN45.B28	Barthes, Roland	The Pleasure of the Text 1975
PN37.B29	Barthes, Roland	Image-Music-Text 1977
	Barthes, Roland	The Empire of Signs 1982
	Barthes, Roland	The Eiffel Tower and Other Mythologies 1979
P99.B313	Barthes, Roland	S/Z 1974
	Ungar, Steven, ed.	'The Work of Roland Barthes', Visible Language 1977
	Bauer, George, ed.	'French Currents of the Letter', Visible Language 1978
	Culler, Jonathan	Roland Barthes 1983
	Culler, Jonathan	The Pursuit of Signs 1981
	Culler, Jonathan	Structuralist Poetics: Structuralism, Linguistics and the Study ofLiterature 1975
	Culler, Jonathan	On Deconstruction : Theory and Criticism after Structuralism 1982
	Leitch, Vincent B.	Deconstructive Criticism 1982
	Norris, Christopher	Deconstruction: Theory and Practice 1982
	Norris, Christopher	The Deconstructive Turn: Essays in the Rhetoric of Philosophy 1984
PN94.E2	Eagleton, Terry	Literary Theory 1983
	Selden, Raman	A Reader's Guide to Contemporary Literary Theory 1985
	Newman, Charles	The Post-Modern Aura 1985
	Newman, Charles	Discussions in Contemporary Culture 1987
BH301.M54A57	Foster, Hal	The Anti-Aesthetic: Essays on Postmodern Culture 1983
NX456.5.P66F67	Foster, Hal	Recodings: Art, Spectacle, Cultural Politics 1987
N6490.K93	Kraus, Rosalind	The Originality of the Avant-Garde and Other Modernist Myths1985
	Steiner, Wendy	The Colors of Rhetoric: Problems in the Relation between Modern Literature and Painting 1986
	Rorty, Richard	Philosophy and the Mirror of Nature: Indications for Post-Philosophical Culture 1979
	Rorty, Richard	'The Fate of Philosophy', The New Republic 1982
	Carroll, David	Paraesthetics: Foucault, Lyotard, Derrida 1987
PN94.D4	Bloom, de Man, Derrida, Hartman & Miller	Deconstruction and Criticism 1985
	Bess, Philip H.	'Deconstruction: A Brief Critique of Critical Theory', Inland Architect 1988
BD162.L913	Lyotard, Jean-Francois	The Post-Modern Condition: A Report on Knowledge 1984
	Lyotard, Jean-Francois	'Presenting the Unpresentable: The Sublime', Artforum 1982
	Rajchman, John	'The Postmodern Museum: Les Immateriaux', Art in America 1985
	Derrida, Jacques	Writing and Difference 1978

Page from a supplemental bibliography. Katherine McCoy, ed., "11.3: Communications: Structuralism, deconstruction, literary criticism and postmodern theories," Fall 1988, Design Department, Cranbrook Academy of Art, n.p.

5. The quote is routinely attributed to Eliel Saarinen, possibly by his son Eero. However, its source is unknown. It echoes a passage by Saarinen on Camillo Sitte's conception of architecture—"where the building was a part of a street, the street a part of the street-pattern, and the street-pattern a part of the whole town"—in *The City: Its Growth, Its Decay, and Its Future* (New York: Reinhold Publishing, 1943), 130.

territory but not necessarily of the trajectory of a user's inquiry. It was, in essence, a map in search of its territory: *a bibliography in search of its discipline*. In its desire to establish a historical identity, continuities of practice, and a consensus on methods, and in its emphasis on process over technique, it conformed to the professional aspirations of its time.

Sections 11 and 12 of the bibliography are devoted to communication, with entries on meaning and others on media. Authors on meaning, such as Gyorgy Kepes, Gui Bonsiepe, Tomás Maldonado, Geoffrey Broadbent, Umberto Eco, Noam Chomsky, and others, were represented by writings from roughly the mid-1960s to the mid-'70s and form a constellation of thinking around semiotics, for instance, and its application not simply to the study of signs but also to their creation and formation. Such references would not have been unique to Cranbrook; they would likely have also been found in the design bibliographies at the Rhode Island School of Design under Thomas Ockerse, who was invested in semiotics, and at the Nova Scotia College of Art and Design under Hanno Ehses, who was interested in applications of rhetoric to graphic design.

There is a natural lag in the development and revision of any printed bibliography, and the version issued to me at Cranbrook was no exception.[6] For example, there is an entry for "French Currents of the Letter," a 1978 issue of the journal *Visible Language* dedicated to poststructuralist ideas and designed by Cranbrook students with theoretical guidance from Daniel Libeskind, then head of Cranbrook's architecture department, years before his theories of deconstruction were directed toward built structures.[7] By 1983, however, thanks to the vogue for French theory in most art programs of the time, poststructuralist discourse had entered the studio at Cranbrook. The literary bent of the Cranbrook photography program, housed in the same building as the design department and under the leadership of Carl Toth, was another influence, although its focus was more on the postwar *nouveau roman* and French New Wave cinema than on poststructuralism per se. The writings and ideas of the usual suspects—Barthes, Foucault, Derrida, Baudrillard—circulated among the students, who used them to sharpen their critical knives, to fuel the discourse of the critique, and to guide their own work. Though it may have been the norm for such literature to circulate within the more adventurous visual-art graduate programs of the period, it was in fact highly unusual for graphic design programs. The ideas embedded in these writings were circulated in critiques and in the studio discourse in a more meaningful way than any set of bibliographic citations or literature reviews could be, and they reached students at the level of their

6. An updated bibliography that would include poststructuralist literature in circulation in Cranbrook's design program since the mid-1980s would be issued in 1988. Thanks to Scott Santoro and Katherine McCoy for directing my attention to this document.

7. See "French Currents of the Letter," *Visible Language* 7, no. 3 (1978).

practice as a kind of counter-discourse with which to unmake and perhaps even remake a rapidly professionalizing practice.

These ideas fell on fertile soil in a studio atmosphere in which students spoke of "unlearning," "deskilling," and "unmastery," seemingly the antithesis of what a master's program in the subject would seek to accomplish. At that time, the graduate program was neither a finishing school nor a place to shift careers—it was, as I saw it, very much about shaping the field through rethinking its practice. Though some interpreted it as an exercise in trashing the profession, it was instead a chance to "unpack" design, to make it susceptible to external influences and to critique by injecting new ideas and theories into it. For me, graphic design seemed less about solving problems and more about creating them.

Unlike the discipline's typical tendency to demarcate boundaries and protect turf, the bibliography at Cranbrook mapped knowledge from a set of adjacent practices in order to align graphic design with fields such as industrial design and architecture, while the informal readings that were fomenting new work in the studio were essentially unmaking this trajectory of professionalization. If the design program at Cranbrook was the "most dangerous" in the world, as was alleged, it was not because its designers used more than ten typefaces or that it embraced an anti-aesthetic formalism, but rather because the work and the discourse around it tried to question or disrupt the instrumentality of communication that undergirds graphic design's professional utility.

In the early 1990s, while a professor of graphic design at North Carolina State University in Raleigh, I used my Cranbrook experience to create my own bibliography. The first edition of the project, entitled "A Critical Theory and Cultural Studies Bibliography," was published by the now-defunct Graphic Design Education Association in 1993. The impetus for the project was the university's newly minted graduate program dedicated to the tripartite study of graphic design as a cultural, cognitive, and technological artifact. The program's graduate-level pedagogy consisted of seminars and related studio classes, attempting to bridge, in essence, theory and practice, reflection and making. Conceptualized by Meredith Davis, an alumnus of Cranbrook and a veteran of the design program at Virginia Commonwealth University, its structure was, in part, a reflection of faculty interest and research and a way to formalize the discourse of the studio. While the studio offers a reflective moment in the all-important sub-activity of the critique, where work is reviewed by peers and faculty, in the seminar, issues and ideas thought to be relevant to design could be cultivated and discussed. In retrospect, this structure of seminar and studio was itself a result of the bifurcated nature of design practice—one oriented toward a more disciplined understanding of the field and the other toward the changing nature of its professional practice—around the time of the advent of the commercial Internet and the full integration of computer-aided design.

The project would serve as a prototype for an expanded series of bibliographies in 1997, also published by the GDEA and distributed by the now-defunct American Center for Design. The bibliography on Cognition and Emotion was compiled by Liz Sanders

Henry and Sealy Fourdrinier develop the papermaking machine

(Ohio State University); on Design Planning by Ewan Duncan (Illinois Institute of Technology); on Interaction and New Media by Jessica Helfand (Yale/New York University); on Education and Learning Theory by Meredith Davis (North Carolina State University), who led the initiative. Each represented a different aspect of the graduate program at North Carolina State, which looked at graphic design as both cultural and cognitive artifact and in the context of new information environments such as emergent digital and interactive media.

The nearly 150 entries that make up this bibliography reflected the new program's focus on understanding graphic design through the twin lenses of critical theory and cultural studies—two academic concerns very much then in formation. The choice of these two areas was a by-product of my own interests as they were emerging in the context of the academic environment I found myself in as part of the Research Triangle Park in North Carolina.

CULTURAL STUDIES BIBLIOGRAPHY
1997
This bibliography brings together books that speak to the multidisciplinary nature of contemporary cultural studies. It is designed to introduce readers to a range of diverse topics that are considered relevant to the cultural study of graphic design and to provide a range of methodological approaches and theoretical strategies. Entries are organized under six categories: art history, theory and criticism; consumption studies; identity politics and cultural representation; media studies and technology; philosophy and history; and semiotics and literary criticism. Texts were selected from outside the design disciplines to broaden and inform the scope of ideas.
ANDREW BLAUVELT NORTH CAROLINA STATE UNIVERSITY
Andrew Blauvelt holds a master's degree in design from Cranbrook Academy of Art and is associate professor and head of the Department of Graphic Design at North Carolina State University. He recently edited three volumes on design history for Visible Language and is a frequent contributor to design publications.
This publication is a project of the Graphic Design Education Association, supported in part by a grant from the National Endowment for the Arts. Additional copies are available from the American Center for Design, 325 West Huron, Chicago, Illinois 60610 (312 787 2018)

Andrew Blauvelt, ed., "Cultural Studies Bibliography" (Chicago: American Center for Design, 1997), n.p.

The three points of this geographic triangle were North Carolina State University in Raleigh; the University of North Carolina (UNC) in Chapel Hill, which was in the midst of establishing a new program in cultural studies headed by Larry Grossberg; and the ascendant and notorious English department at Duke University in Durham, then headed by Stanley Fish, and the separate literature program headed by Fredric Jameson, both of which had recently introduced critical theory into their respective departments. My own interest in critical theory and cultural studies was an extension of those informal readings at Cranbrook, but it was also rooted in my undergraduate experience studying photography, which included not only technical instruction and photographic history but also lectures on theories of representation. In the early 1980s, we were being introduced to the work of the "Pictures" generation artists (such as Cindy Sherman, Laurie Simmons, and Barbara Kruger) and photo theorists such as Allan Sekula and Victor Burgin, with a little Susan Sontag and Roland Barthes thrown in for good measure. During my time in North Carolina, I had the opportunity to attend numerous lectures and symposia at both Duke and UNC by a cavalcade of itinerant scholars passing through the area, including Homi Bhabha, Jacques

Derrida, Stuart Hall, Pierre Bourdieu, Slavoj Žižek, Eve Kosofsky Sedgwick, Toril Moi, and Laura Mulvey. The Research Triangle Park area was also the epicenter of the culture wars, a medley of hot-button issues such as reproductive rights, gun control, gay rights, and the funding and access to research and treatment of AIDS, the separation of church and state, national drug-enforcement and sentencing policy, artistic censorship and defunding of the arts—basically everything, in other words, we still struggle with today! One of the main instigators of the culture wars was the late Jesse Helms, Republican senator from North Carolina, whose racist, misogynist, and homophobic agenda catalyzed the era's, and the area's, progressive politics.

Among the bibliographic entries were annotations on texts by Ien Ang, Roland Barthes, Jean Baudrillard, Pierre Bourdieu, James Clifford, Douglas Crimp, Michel de Certeau, Gilles Deleuze and Felix Guattari, Johannes Fabian, Hal Foster, Michel Foucault, Henry Louis Gates, Jr., Clifford Geertz, Jurgen Habermas, Donna Haraway, bell hooks, Fredric Jameson, Rosalind Krauss, Julia Kristeva, Jacques Lacan, Jean-Francois Lyotard, Trinh T. Minh-ha, Toril Moi, Craig Owens, Edward Said, Eve Kosofsky Sedgwick, Gayatri Spivak, and Paul Virilio, among many others.

The texts were selected, according to the bibliography, to "speak to the multidisciplinary nature of contemporary cultural studies" and "to introduce readers to a range of diverse topics that are considered relevant to the cultural study of graphic design."[8] Entries were initially organized in six categories: art theory, history, and criticism; consumption studies; identity politics and cultural representation; media studies and technology; philosophy and history; semiotics and literary criticism. While there were a few entries from the field of design, a strategic decision was made to look to other disciplines to "broaden and inform the scope of ideas." Simply put, I did not believe that graphic design had a sufficiently robust culture of critique or the analytical methods at hand to tackle its own cultural significance. Situating graphic design in a larger system of both its production and its consumption meant understanding the field and its output as an interface with contemporary culture at large.

If the informal readings at Cranbrook were situated in poststructuralism, then the operative metaphor was one of intertextuality, the relationship or reference of the text to other texts and its

8. Andrew Blauvelt, ed., "Cultural Studies Bibliography" (Chicago: American Center for Design, 1997), unpaginated. This version was culled from "A Critical and Cultural Studies Bibliography," ed. Meredith Davis (Raleigh, NC: Graphic Design Education Association and the School of Design, Department of Graphic Design, North Carolina State University, 1993), unpaginated.

use of figures such as allusion, quotation, parody, or pastiche. Julia Kristeva, who coined the term in the 1960s, described it in spatialized terms as "an intersection of textual surfaces, rather than a point (of fixed meaning), as a dialogue among several writings."[9] In the 1990s, bibliographic references began to map a range of social identities and experiences—aspects of sexuality, gender, race, and class, for instance. The interrelatedness of these categories was just coming to the fore, laying the foundation for today's concept of intersectionality, the complex overlapping forms of identity and its experience, particularly in terms of discrimination and systemic oppression.

Kimberlé Crenshaw introduced intersectionality in 1989 in her legal scholarship on the unique employment discrimination faced by Black women, which could not be understood in terms of the racial discrimination faced by Black men or the sexual discrimination encountered by white women.

The informal readings of the 1980s pointed outside the self, outside the work to other works; the bibliography from the 1990s, by contrast, turned inward toward the self as a kind of disciplined subject and toward the work as a reflection of these worldly forces. In short, the professional impulse in graphic design placed at the center of its study the work of graphic design—the designer, the solution, the process of creation, and so on. Its later counterpart would come to understand the work of graphic design like a text—situated and shaped by its power relations and its modes of reception.

What is most surprising to me now is the transformation in the subject matter of the bibliographies that were in circulation in the 1980s to those produced in the 1990s. In the latter, we see a near absence of design as it had been constituted, that is, in its professional guise. Instead of related fields of study such as architecture or typography, we find subjects such as philosophy and theories of representation. If early bibliographies were meant to consolidate knowledge around the need to professionalize the practice, these new bibliographies seemingly exploded it by relentlessly pointing outward and elsewhere. This tendency reflects Foucault's observation in *The Archeology of Knowledge* that a discipline is not an "enormous book that is gradually and continuously being written" but is in fact "a system of dispersion."[10]

In this way, the Critical Theory and Cultural Studies Bibliography attempted to define graphic design as a potential subject of study at the intersections of many other disciplines, discourses, and critical methods. At the same time, these new intellectual tools could be used to reshape the identity of not only design but also the designer, both professionally and subjectively.

It is this moment of disciplinary formation—the decade from 1985 to 1995—that I would like to explore a bit more. During this era of postmodernism, the trajectory of a professionalizing design

9. Julia Kristeva, *Desire in Language: A Semiotic Approach to Literature and Art* (New York: Columbia University Press, 1980), 65.

10. Michel Foucault, *The Archaeology of Knowledge and the Discourse on Language* (New York: Pantheon, 1972), 37.

Sir William Congreve develops long-range military rockets, based on an earlier Indian technology known as the Mysore rocket

practice under modernism changed course toward a *disciplined* design practice as graphic design pivoted to engage its semantic turn—to the construction of design's meaning and the contestation of interpretation.

As design was codified as a visual language beginning in the early twentieth century, malleable and manipulable like a verbal language, its syntax became the primary "problem" for the graphic designer to solve, in a manner not dissimilar to the modern artist's "problem" in painting or sculpture. This is, of course, very different from the concept of problem-solving now widely embraced by the field, which locates "problems" having their source with the client or society at large and positions the designer and her surrogates as offering solutions. In its semantic turn, the essential content of graphic design became the central "problem" for the designer to solve. Content was not only a struggle over given messages, commissioned or not, and the reception of meaning, intended or not, among audiences; but also the "meta-content" of graphic design itself, including its social and cultural significance.

In terms of product design, the semantic turn, as has been argued by Klaus Krippendorff, represents a paradigmatic shift by overturning a "form follows function" ethos inherited through the long period of modern industrialization.[11] Postindustrial society, emergent by the 1980s, signaled that design would now be understood more as a sense-creating and meaning-making activity. This transformation displaced the machine as design's central protagonist and instead embraced a newly rediscovered human subject—as the user (a locus of behaviors and emotions), on the one hand, and as society (the locus of intersecting power relations) on the other. For professional designers this shift would beget frameworks such as human-centered design, design thinking, and "wicked" as opposed to "tame" problems.

For the *disciplined* graphic designer, the "problem" was not an external puzzle to be solved—which was, after all, the bailiwick of the *professional* designer—but rather an internal problematic of design itself contained in the "ungiven" nature of its contents, its practitioners, and its audiences. For graphic design, the semantic turn manifests itself in a variety of ways, including, more recently, a postindustrial communicative landscape with the eclipse of the relative fixity of print media and the rise of a mutable screen-based culture and a fungible informatic society; the conflation of production and consumption through user-generated content platforms; and the reliance on distributed messaging through social media networks and their tribal bubbles. I would argue that its latest manifestation is beyond content in a post-rationalist sense, now that behavior or ideology is best induced through emotive or affective means, from the malignant to the benign, whether Donald Trump's dog whistles of white nationalism or Marie Kondo's exhortations to "spark joy" through decluttering.

11. See Klaus Krippendorf, *The Semantic Turn: A New Foundation for Design* (Boca Raton, FL: CRC Press, 2005).

In its initial guise, however, the semantic turn in design occurred on a variety of fronts: as a recourse to symbolism and metaphor, particularly historical; as a way to bridge form, function, and meaning; as a rejection of modernism and its supposedly universal aesthetic values and preferences; and in the use of language theories, both structural and poststructural, to both stabilize and destabilize meaning, such as semiotics, rhetoric, deconstruction, and linguistic wordplay.

In short, the "problem" became graphic design itself: the limitations of its practice as defined by its professional activities and methods; its lack of historical and critical depth and theoretical richness; and the lack of racial, ethnic, and gender diversity among its practitioners.

In 1982, artist Ed Levine, then dean of faculty at the Minneapolis College of Art and Design, wrote:

> It is through the development of theoretical issues that a medium becomes a discipline. Theoretical questions raised by a discipline become important sources of ideas which can extend and enlarge the medium because they provide a *metacritical* viewpoint. There is a sense in which the discipline is larger than any of its manifestations as a medium, where it can direct the attention of the artist as well as being directed by the artist.[12]

Levine was arguing for the place of film and video in art departments alongside other media, most notably painting and sculpture but also video's technological precursor, photography. For Levine and others, the elevation of a medium to the position of a discipline—construed as a form of academic self-organization and self-policing that both authorizes and is authorized—constituted a critical distancing, an ability to undertake a reflexive examination of the medium itself.

As Levine argued, the discipline must transcend the medium. However, graphic design is not a medium, but rather a practice. Design has thus tended to organize, define, and regulate its activities within its professional associations as it tries to order and control the field at the level of its practitioners. A discipline, by contrast, tries to order and control the field at the level of its discursive practices. Crudely put, the profession is concerned with the production and reproduction of design and designers, while the discipline is concerned with the production and reproduction of design knowledge.

In reality, even practitioners can be divided into those attempting a disciplined practice and those engaged in a professional practice. A disciplined practice incorporates an understanding of the discursive nature of graphic design—its history, methodologies, and theories, its pedagogy, critical reception, and social import, and the issues of its collective practice at a meta-level. Given that graphic design's practitioners were the primary instigators of its disciplinary formation, it is not surprising that many designers and design educators can be included among its disciplined ranks.

12. Edward Levine, "Vision and Its Machine," *Art Journal* 42, no. 1 (Spring 1982): 49.

Yet though some professional practicing designers argued in favor of disciplinary status, it was the design pedagogues—those responsible for teaching design—who were the strongest advocates. This is not surprising, since it is a natural consequence of academic belonging. In contradistinction to the widely held belief that art cannot be taught, design, particularly as it was constituted as a form of modern visual language, could be the subject of instruction. In fact, design principles would displace drawing as the fundamental language of the visual arts, just as surely as the Bauhaus workshops replaced the Beaux Arts academies as the preferred form of instruction. The question of what to teach about design drove its self-reflective examination and its linguistic distillation, inculcating a new visual language of form. If commercial art had been predicated on vocational instruction in trade schools or on-the-job training in techniques and perfecting typologies, then graphic design in the academy could be taught as a shared language one could master and as a series of problem-solving processes and methods deployed not as techniques but rather as tools, as instruments of reason. Thus the practice of graphic design would become more discursive and disciplined as it moved from a set of transmittable and embodied individual skills, a kind of craft, to one of shared methods and networks of knowledge, a kind of discipline.

Disciplining the practice of graphic design through its pedagogy was a necessary first step for its entrée into the academy. Other discursive aspects, such as graphic design's history, theory, and criticism, would follow suit—whereupon a shared sense or collective consensus or knowledge about practice would emerge. It is not surprising, therefore, that design's educators, rather than its practitioners, would be the primary source of its disciplinary formation. This was especially true for graphic design, since its professional practice did not have options such as credentialization and certification with which to order and regulate its ranks. Instead, the accreditation of graphic design instruction at the post-secondary level and the overproduction of degree-holding students have been the primary mechanisms for controlling entry into and reshaping the field of professional practice.

•

The imperative for a history of graphic design in the 1970s and '80s followed on the heels of the pedagogical consolidation of its core visual language as well as its methods and processes for unifying professional practice that began in earnest in the 1950s and '60s. The pursuit of a common history would further bolster claims to disciplinary status. After all, without a historical past, there is not much of a future; withholding a history is tantamount to withholding identity. The benefits of historical inquiry also flowed into professional practice, adding depth and breadth to the field while forming a backdrop against which progress and maturation could be gleaned. Graphic design became a practice whose origins reached back as far as cave paintings, a perspective that distanced it from nineteenth-century images of jobbing printers, for instance.

As the professionalizing impulses began to be tempered by a counterdiscourse, one that disrupted the nascent disciplinary status of a professionalizing field, graduate programs in graphic design in the mid-1980s reflected yet another transition, a hot mess of disruptions: intentional deskilling; technophilia and technophobia as reactions to the introduction of computer-aided design; critiques of modernism and the growth of stylistic eclecticism; the rise of identity politics and multiculturalism and the heating up of the culture wars; the steady rise in the number of female practitioners; and the proclaimed "end of history" and of grand narratives, to name just a few. This made for a series of seemingly contradictory moments for graphic design relative to other disciplines. The search for the field's history was underway just as the end of history itself was being proclaimed, and the demand for greater visibility and subjectivity of the otherwise invisible, objective designer was raised just as others announced the "death of the author and the birth of the reader." Indeed, graphic design did seem out of step with the academic literature of the time, even as those writings were being consumed and regurgitated in many artists' studios and critique sessions. Even the quest for disciplinary status was untimely: It was, after all, the antithesis of the anti-disciplinary tendencies of the 1960s and '70s as well as of the multi-, cross-, and trans-disciplinarity of the 1990s and 2000s.

In the 1980s and '90s, the search for "voice" by the designer—whether through actual visible presence in the work, through the creation of a highly personal and recognizable style, or through an expansion of the role of the designer that would help define, articulate, and better control the commissioning or creative process—could just as easily be read as a cry for recognition and, yes, for power. Just as the professional designer was demanding a "seat at the table," the disciplined designer was demanding a "presence on the page." Whether such claims were ironic positions to take in the face of post structural revelations or simply retrograde, they nonetheless recall the predicament faced by others who were seeking the right to self-representation and identity by claiming their subjective experience at the same moment that the academy, majority white and male, was conveniently proclaiming the end of subjectivity.

A key element of transformative thinking for certain designers was the shift in understanding the dynamics of meaning away from a direct transfer between writer and reader and toward a situation in which meaning is not lying latent in the text waiting to be decoded but rather is actively constructed, mediated by codes and references imparted to both writers and readers from other texts. This notion of intertextuality underscored a more disciplined approach to design in which designers could become more active agents in the co-production of meaning, in dialogue with readers and other works and with history and culture.

In the graphic design programs of the 1980s and '90s, the idea of "the personal" took on a slightly different valence from that of the second-wave feminist rallying cry of "the personal is political." Under the rubric of learning a modern visual language of design, the student sought a form of individuality predicated on being able to develop unique solutions to a commonly shared problem. Using essentially the same set of elements, designers were being asked to develop solutions within an existing framework or set of rules, participating in a differential system in which the designer's solutions could be used to gauge uniqueness and individuality. In the semantic turn, it is the uniqueness of the designer's problems—where they are found, where they are situated, how they are articulated, what they mean, and so on—that determines the designer's uniqueness and individuality. For designers, the personal is the problem.

I'm not sure what a bibliography for graphic design looks like today or what it might say about the discipline. The evolution of the "problem" of graphic design evolves as the profession transforms and the discipline expands. Once seen as internal to the work, the problem was then located beyond the designer, in the client or in society—the death of the problem became the birth of the solution. I suspect that the "problem" for graphic design now lies in the self and in itself: in its professional identity as a democratizing practice and as a disciplined subject among other professions and disciplines, but also in the intersections of identity of the graphic designer herself.

PLEASE READ

MARIA GOUGH

I.

At the May 2019 conference for which the present essay was first drafted,[1] there were numerous calls, from podium and floor alike, for graphic design to emancipate itself from its complicity with the corporate world and/or a narrow kind of professionalism. Lorraine Wild, for example, argued that design needs to find a way to regain some of the utopian speculative energy of early modernism. Johanna Drucker pointed out that there have been numerous moments in history when design has had a socially progressive or activist agenda and that it remains important for those stories to be told, especially in our troubled present. Others seemed to suggest that that energy and those stories had already found their way into pedagogy, at least at certain institutions: Ellie, a designer in the audience who came with her mom, also a designer, underscored the emphasis placed in her own recent training on collectivism, collaboration, and the realm of the social, rather than the more exclusively formal problems that had once dominated mainstream teaching in the field.

For conference organizer Geoff Kaplan, the act of reading, practiced on a regular basis and incorporated into the education of graphic designers, is what enabled the field to begin to break out of its professional straitjacket, starting in the later 1950s and accelerating thereafter. In a talk presented at the American Institute of Graphic Arts in 2016, Kaplan discussed the "reading habits"—essentially, the theoretical turn—that characterized the pedagogy of Gui Bonsiepe, Sheila de Bretteville, Jeff Keedy, Meredith Davis, Andrew Blauvelt, and other influential teachers of design. The reading of key texts from social theory, critical race theory, postcolonialism, feminism, semiology, structuralism, and poststructuralism helped to transport design students to other realms, which enabled the great expansion of the stakes and objectives of their subsequent practice. Of related importance was the reading of the history of design theory itself: the ways in which past designers and critics had theorized their enterprise over the course of a century or more from, say, William Morris onward.[2]

II.

One such theorist of design, who would become a major source of inspiration for artists, poets, architects, and designers in the postwar period, was the Russian Jewish artist, architect, and designer Lazar Markovich Lissitzky (1890–1941), also known as El Lissitzky. (He informally adopted the "El," it seems, because it is the sound of the phoneme "L"—the first letter of his first and last names—when

1. Warm thanks to Geoff Kaplan and Tim Barringer for inviting my participation in the conference "After the Bauhaus, Before the Internet: A History of Graphic Design Pedagogy," Yale University, May 10–11, 2019.

2. See Geoff Kaplan, "A History of Graphic Design Pedagogy, Or So They Tell Me," in this volume, 14–27.

read aloud.) In 1970, the poet Hans Magnus Enzensberger described Lissitzky as an "outstanding Russian media expert" who "demanded an 'electro-library' as far back as 1923—a request which, given the technical conditions of the time, must have seemed ridiculous or at least incomprehensible."[3] Enzensberger refers here to the artist's demand, in a manifesto-like contribution to his friend Kurt Schwitters's Dadaist magazine *Merz*, for the transcendence of print media in favor of electronic delivery: "The printed sheet, the everlastingness [*Unendlichkeit*] of the book, must be transcended," Lissitzky writes, concluding his short text with the neologism "THE ELECTRO-LIBRARY" blaring in all caps.[4] Entranced by wireless telegraphy, radio broadcast, and the then still nascent possibility of the electronic delivery of moving images, a.k.a. television, Lissitzky was acutely interested in the mediation of human perception by so-called technical media and the fundamental impact this has on the book as an object. But his 1923 text was a call for the end of neither the book nor typography—at least not just yet. On the contrary, it was a call for the radical transformation of their planar habitat or environment, what he calls their "topography."[5] As such, it might best be read as an attempt on the artist's part to promote the graphic innovations of a book that he had just designed for the poet Vladimir Mayakovsky, *Dlia golosa* (*For the Voice*) (1923). We will return to this extraordinary book toward the end of this essay.

El Lissitzky and Vladimir Mayakovsky. *Dlia golosa (For the Voice)* (Berlin: Gos. Izdatel'stvo RSFSR, 1923)

First, a little background. Born near Smolensk, in the Pale of Settlement, an area to which the imperial Russian court had confined the overwhelming majority of Jews since the eighteenth

3. Hans Magnus Enzensberger, "Constituents of a Theory of the Media," *New Left Review* 64 (November–December 1970): 33.

4. "Der gedruckte Bogen, die Unendlichkeit der Bücher, muß überwunden werden: DIE ELEKTROBIBLIOTHEK"; Lissitzky, "Topographie der Typographie," *Merz* 4 (July 1923): 47; trans. (slightly modified) Helene Aldwinckle as "Topography of Typography" in Sophie Lissitzky-Küppers, *El Lissitzky: Life, Letters, Texts* (New York: Thames and Hudson, 1980), 359.

5. El Lissitzky, "Topographie der Typographie," 47; Lissitzky-Küppers, *El Lissitzky*, 359.

century, Lissitzky was excluded from the Imperial Academy of Arts in St. Petersburg because of its entrance quota on Jews. In lieu of becoming a painter, he studied architecture at the Technische Hochschule in Darmstadt, Germany. As a foreign national, however, he was obliged to return home with the outbreak of the First World War. From 1916, Lissitzky worked in the service of the Jewish Renaissance as a book designer and illustrator of children's stories in Yiddish, without having had formal training in the printing trades. In 1919, on account of his architectural education and work experience, he was invited by Marc Chagall—whom the new Bolshevik government had recently appointed director of the Free State Art Studios (SVOMAS) in Vitebsk, in the now former Pale of Settlement—to run the school's architecture and print studios. There Lissitzky soon came under the electrifying influence of fellow instructor Kazimir Malevich, the inventor of Suprematism, and took up painting, while at the same time publishing his colleague's manuscripts.

At the end of 1921, he returned to central Europe for several years, where he worked on numerous projects, primarily involving print media, and networked with a cosmopolitan group of artists, critics, and patrons in Hanover, Berlin, and Amsterdam. (If his little red address book from this period is anything to go by, Lissitzky's wealth of contacts was impressive; consider, for example, a single glance at its "M" pages, where we find the coordinates of Swiss architect Moser, German architect Mendelsohn, Russian artist Malevich, Dutch painter Mondrian, Japanese Constructivist Murayama, Bohemian painter Melzer, Italian Futurist poet Marinetti, German artist Molzahn, and Russian architect Melnikov, among others.)[6] In 1924, Lissitzky moved to Switzerland to undergo medical treatment for tuberculosis and an extended convalescence. Denied a renewal of his visa, he returned to Moscow in 1925, taking up a teaching position at Vkhutemas, the leading school for art and design.

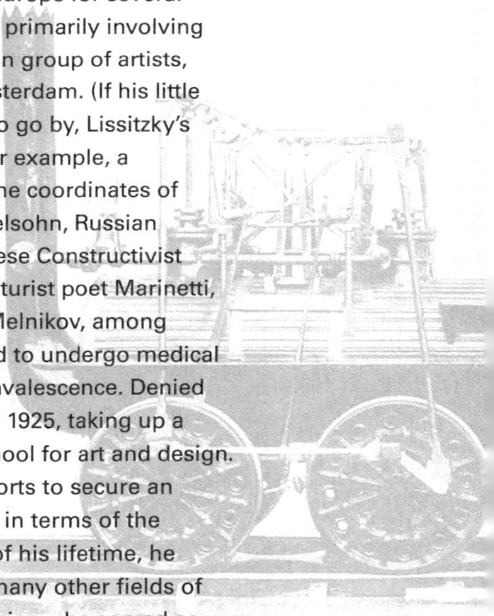

Lissitzky was peripatetic not just in his efforts to secure an education, community, and livelihood but also in terms of the media in which he practiced. Over the course of his lifetime, he crossed back and forth from architecture into many other fields of production: Aside from book and magazine design—he served as the founding editor of several journals (*Vesch'/Objet/Gegenstand*, *G*, *ABC*, and *Izvestiia Asnova*)—he worked in painting, photography, advertising, exhibition design, interior design, and furniture design. Nonetheless, he still found time to teach, give talks, and write and publish an extensive series of often groundbreaking theoretical reflections in Russian- and German-language periodicals, covering such subjects as architecture, exhibition design, painting, invention, mathematics, the state of contemporary art, and, most crucially

6. Getty Research Institute, Special Collections and Visual Resources, accession no. 950076, box 1, folder 7. The coordinates of Hungarian artist László Moholy-Nagy and German architect Mies van der Rohe are found in the next page opening.

for our purposes, the design of printed matter. Indeed, print media, whether in the form of books, magazines, or posters, was the field in which he practiced almost continuously from 1916 through to his death from pulmonary disease in 1941.

In his earliest published text on the subject—a pedagogical progam he formulated in 1919 for his students in the print studio at the Vitebsk SVOMAS—Lissitzky welcomes the transfer of the communicative and communitarian function of the cathedral typology to the printed book, precisely because the latter can be distributed en masse: "The book is now everything," he writes. "In our time it has become what the cathedral with its frescoes and stained glass . . . used to be, what the palaces and museums, where people went to look and learn, used to be. The book has become the monument of the present. But in contrast to old monumental art, it itself goes to the people and does not stand like a cathedral in one place, waiting for someone to approach." In these words, we hear an echo of Victor Hugo's quixotic logic that the printing press had killed architecture, though Lissitzky, sharing none of the French writer's regret, inverts that logic in the name of democratization. He furthermore insists that the "artist must . . . set aside his old instruments, his quill pens, brushes, and little palettes and take up chisel, burin, the lead army of the typecase, the rotary press. All this will then obediently begin to turn in his hands and will give birth to a work not in one copy—not a unique object for the enjoyment of the patron—but in thousands and thousands of identical originals for all."[7]

But it was for his polemical call for a new "optics" in book production that Lissitzky would later become best known: The book and its typography, he argues, can no longer be addressed to reading or hearing alone, but must now foreground seeing. "The words on the printed sheet are learnt by sight, not by hearing," he insists in his 1923 *Merz* text. "Economy of expression—optics instead of phonetics."[8] In the *Gutenberg Festschrift* two years later, Lissitzky asserts that the writer's "ideas reach you through the eye and not through the ear. Therefore typographical form should do by means of optics what the voice and gesture of the writer does to convey his ideas." In 1927, the *Gutenberg-Jahrbuch* carries the artist's fullest statement yet, in which he quotes a statement he made in 1920: "Gutenberg's Bible was printed with letters only, but the Bible of our time cannot be just presented in letters alone. The book finds its channel to the brain through the eye, not through the ear; in this channel the waves rush through with much greater speed and pressure than in the acoustic channel. One can speak out only through the mouth, but the book's facilities for expression take many more forms."[9]

In the books and magazines Lissitzky designed in the 1920s,

7. Lazar Lissitzky, "Novaia kul'tura," *Shkola i revoliutsiia* (Vitebsk) 24–25 (August 16, 1919): 11; trans. Peter Nisbet as "The New Culture," *Experiment/ Eksperiment* 1 (1995): 261.

8. Lissitzky, "Topographie der Typographie," 47; Lissitzky-Küppers, *El Lissitzky*, 359.

9. El Lissitzky, "Unser Buch (U.d.S.S.R)," in *Gutenberg Jahrbuch*, ed. A. Ruppel (Mainz: Verlag der Gutenberg Gesellschaft, 1927), 176; abridged trans. Helene Aldwinckle as "Our Book," in Lissitzky-Küppers, *El Lissitzky*, 362.

he implements the new optics in four ways: **1.** Visualization and spatialization of typography, through deployment of the maximum number of typefaces, point sizes, and orientations within a single page, in contrast to traditional book design, wherein typefaces were expected to be uniform. In other words, the book was to adopt the typographic conventions of the late-nineteenth-century advertising poster, wherein all the typefaces at the printer's disposal were utilized simultaneously in order to produce maximum visual impact. Each letter would thus be liberated from what the Russian Futurist poets Aleksei Kruchenykh and Velimir Khlebnikov had a decade earlier protested as the "gray prisoner's uniform" of mechanical type, wherein letters were "lined up in a row, humiliated, with cropped hair, and all equally colorless."[10] Liberation of the letter would lead, in turn, to the emancipation of its distribution across the page, the "topography of typography," as he put it. **2.** Disruption of the conventional parts of the book by, for example, transferring its table of contents to the front cover. **3.** Activation of the reader: "Do not read," he counterintuitively instructs the young reader of his Suprematist children's story, *Pro 2* ■ (Of Two Squares) (1920 [1922]), but instead "take papers, rods, blocks" and "arrange, color, build." **4.** Appropriation of the forms and techniques of utilitarian and commercial genres of printed matter, such as modern election propaganda, prospectuses, advertising brochures, large dailies, modern novels, advertisement pillars, and posters.[11] (The German typographer and book designer Jan Tschichold later commented on Lissitzky's "tendency to turn a book into a piece of technical apparatus."[12])

III.

Postwar graphic designers in the United States, especially those already familiar with, say, Filippo Tommaso Marinetti's influential demand for a *rivoluzione tipografica* that would take the form of a total disruption of the typographical harmony of the printed page, Guillaume Apollinaire's *Calligrammes*, or the international phenomenon of Concrete poetry, appear to have rediscovered Lissitzky's new optics during the recovery of the Russian and Soviet avant-gardes that began in the late 1950s and early '60s, the years of the Khrushchev Thaw. In the anglophone world, this recovery picked up speed with the publication of Camilla Gray's pioneering study *The Great Experiment: Russian Art 1863–1922.* A large-format and well-illustrated survey, Gray's book would become a key source of information about a vast body of work that Greenbergian

10. See Aleksei Kruchenykh and Velimir Khlebnikov, "The Letter as Such" (1913), trans. Anna Lawton and Herbert Eagle, in *Russian Futurism through Its Manifestoes, 1912–1928*, ed. Anna Lawton (Ithaca: Cornell University Press, 1988), 63.

11. El Lissitzky, "Typographische Tatsachen, z.B.," in *Gutenberg-festschrift, zur Feier des 25jährigen Bestehens des Gutenbergmuseums in Mainz*, ed. A. Ruppel (Mainz: Verlag der Gutenberg Gesellschaft, 1925), 152–54; trans. Helene Aldwinckle as "Typographical Facts" in Lissitzky-Küppers, *El Lissitzky*, 359–60.

12. Ivan Tschichold, "El Lissitzky (1890–1941)" (1965), abridged trans. in Lissitzky-Küppers, *El Lissitzky*, 389.

modernism, still dominant at the time of its publication, had sidelined, and it would be a major revelation for many American artists in the 1960s. Interest in the Soviet experiment increased through that decade in conjunction with rise of the New Left and various social movements, including decolonization, civil rights, and feminism.

With respect to Lissitzky in particular, however, the key early figure in his historical recovery was Sophie Küppers (1891–1978), a German curator and art dealer, who had essentially run—in all but name—the Kestner Gesellschaft in Hanover, which had hosted the artist in the mid-1920s. Lissitzky met Küppers in 1923 through their mutual friend Kurt Schwitters, and they soon became life partners. Beyond their personal relationship, however, Küppers also played a role in his design work, a fact that the historiography largely overlooked until just a few years ago.[13] In Germany she sometimes dealt with clients on the artist's behalf, translated articles from French (including one by Le Corbusier), and, one assumes, helped him with his German prose. In 1927, she joined Lissitzky in Moscow.

In the 1930s, Küppers's contribution to Lissitzky's work transcended the managerial in that she collaborated with him on the design and production of several photo-illustrated books and magazines commissioned by the party-state. It is for this reason that we find the double signature—"es and el lissitzky" ("es" being the sound of the phoneme "S," her first initial)—on certain print-media

El Lissitzky, ink drawing in letter to Sophie Küppers. July 2, 1935. Lissitzky's annotations within the image: "Or such a cover" (top), "Eat for [good] health!" (upper), "Food industry" (lower).

13. On the collaboration of Lissitzky and Küppers in the 1930s, see Samuel Johnson, *El Lissitzky on Paper: Print Culture, Architecture, Politics, 1919–1933* (University of Chicago Press, forthcoming). Overlooking the contributions women have made to the work of their male partners and institutions is common in the literature of art and design history; aside from Küppers, major cases in point would be Lucia Moholy, Sophie Taeuber, Carola Giedion-Welcker, and Lilly Reich, among numerous others. On this and related issues, see especially Beatriz Colomina, "With, or Without You: The Ghosts of Modern Architecture," in *Modern Woman* (New York: The Museum of Modern Art, 2010), 217–31; Bibiana Obler, *Intimate Collaborations: Kandinsky and Münter, Arp and Taeuber* (New Haven: Yale University Press, 2014); and Jordan Troeller, "A (Still) Marginal Modernity, or The Artist as Stenographer," *October* 172 (Spring 2020): 3–7.

projects. A case in point is a large portfolio of photographs and other photo-based images on the subject of the *Food Industry*. Küppers's total labor for this album, as for several other projects, ran the full spectrum of design work: negotiating contracts, dealing with pesky editors, securing photographic material from often recalcitrant photographers, organizing page layouts, and making photomontages for reproduction. Lissitzky registers the collaborative nature of their undertaking in a playful ink drawing he encloses with a July 1935 letter to Küppers from Abastuman in Georgia, where he is convalescing. On the left is Küppers, in the form of a fish holding a pair of scissors, while on the right is Lissitzky as a rabbit with what looks to be a palette but could also be a clipboard. Their mouths nibble at the edges of a large album opened to reveal the capital letter "L" on both pages, likely a reference to "Lissitzky," and thus to their union. Between them sits a stack of canned foodstuffs. Along the top he writes "Or such a cover," facetiously suggesting that they use this sketch as the album's cover. Around their shoulders appears the phrase "Eat for [good] health!," while the album's title, "Food Industry," wraps around their feet. The not-so-subtle joke, which is at the same time very serious, is that their design work on this state-sponsored album is what puts food on their table.

After Lissitzky's death in 1941, Küppers was exiled as an enemy national to Novosibirsk, in Siberia, where she lived for the remaining decades of her life, working as a needlework teacher in her neighborhood, a cleaning person to make ends meet, and the chief custodian of her husband's legacy. In a moving photograph, taken by their son Jen in 1978, one sees the modesty of her circumstances in the final years of her life, a startling contrast to her origins in the patron class of Hanover. But the Khrushchev Thaw had also provided a vital window of opportunity for Küppers, and in the 1960s she began to assemble what would become the first monograph on Lissitzky. Published in 1967, in Dresden, then part of East Germany, it was translated into Italian the same year, and then into English in 1968, with a second English edition appearing in 1980.[14]

14. Lissitzky-Küppers, *El Lissitzky*. Prior to 1967, a few short texts on Lissitzky were published in Russian and German, including Nikolai Khardzhiev, "El Lisitskii—konstruktor knigi," in *Iskusstvo knigi* (Moscow: Iskusstvo, 1962), 145–61, abridged trans. in Lissitzky-Küppers, *El Lissitzky*, 383–88; Ivan Tschichold, "El Lissitzky (1890–1941)" (1965), abridged trans. in Lissitzky-Küppers, El Lissitzky, 389; and Lucia Moholy, "El Lissitzky," *Das Werk: Architektur und Kunst* 53, no. 6 (1966): 229–36, trans. Jordan Troeller in *October* 172 (Spring 2020): 111–16.

Küppers's book includes reproductions of hundreds of works, many of which had never been seen before; most if not all of his critical and theoretical writings; reviews of his work by his contemporaries; and a lengthy historical overview of the artist's life and work by the author herself, in which she quotes extensively from his letters. As such, the monograph made possible, for the first time, an understanding of the centrality of graphic design in his enterprise, thus going far beyond the valuable but ultimately specialized formal appraisal of his typographical achievements by Tschichold in the mid-to-late 1920s. Despite some inevitable factual errors, which have been corrected by the groundbreaking scholarship of Peter Nisbet and Samuel Johnson, Küppers's monograph is a mammoth achievement by any measure.[15] Available in multiple languages, it was the publication that most stimulated interest in the artist's work among contemporary artists, architects, and designers wanting to escape the narrow professionalization of their respective fields.

IV.

From the late 1960s onwards, anglophone graphic designers and those interested in visual communication were reading about Lissitzky's theory and practice. In its first decades, for example, *The Journal of Typographic Research*—a leading periodical in the field, founded in 1967 by Merald Wrolstad and soon renamed *Visible Language*—carried a number of articles that brought Lissitzky's call for a new optics in book production to a specialized audience equipped to grasp its implications. The first such article was published in the October 1968 issue by Louise Leering-van Moorsel, the niece of Nelly and Theo van Doesburg and an educator from the Van Abbemuseum in Eindhoven, the Netherlands.[16] It comprises a general introduction to the artist's work across media and a dedicated survey of his typographical experiments. In its preparation, Leering-van Moorsel was able to draw upon her first-hand study of materials held by two Dutch designers, Piet Zwart and Pieter Brattinga, and the more than one hundred works that had been recently acquired by her museum through the efforts of her husband, Jean Leering. The progressive director of the Van Abbe from 1964 to 1973, Leering had trained as an architect before becoming an exhibition designer. While his primary interests lay in contemporary art and the recalibration of the museum's social function, he considered Lissitzky an important precursor for both. Over the course of his tenure, Leering assembled the most extensive collection of Lissitzky's work outside of Russia and dedicated several exhibitions to the artist, one of which included a reconstruction of his *Proun Space* (1923).

15. See Peter Nisbet, *El Lissitzky, 1890–1941* (Cambridge, MA: Harvard University Art Museums, 1987); Peter Nisbet, "El Lissitzky in the Proun Years: A Study of His Work and Thought" (Ph.D. diss., Yale University, 1995); and Johnson, *El Lissitzky on Paper.*

16. Louise Leering-van Moorsel, "The Typography of El Lissitzky," trans. J. J. van der Maas, *The Journal of Typographic Research* 2, no. 4 (October 1967): 323–40. Leering-van Moorsel is also known as Wies van Moorsel.

A brief but important mention in *Visible Language* of Lissitzky's theorization of typography and book design is found in an intriguing 1977 article by Aaron Marcus, who was then teaching graphic and information design classes and the like in the School of Architecture and Urban Planning at Princeton University. "As a graphic design student," Marcus reports, "I was once told by an instructor that typography at its best is 'invisible'" because in such a state it "permits the reader's eye to pierce effortlessly the core of (verbal) meaning." Noting that many professionals tout invisibility as a "desirable objective," he argues that it is, on the contrary, "always literally unattainable." In making his case, he refers to the Russian artist: "At the beginning of the profession of graphic design as a self-aware discipline in the twentieth century," he writes, "there were perceptive critics like . . . Lissitzky who anticipated the developments taking place in vision and in visual communication. Lissitzky foresaw 'optical' as opposed to 'acoustical' literature, i.e., typographic forms that more completely took advantage of their visual nature, that explored a full dimensional space rather than the more limited form of conventional typographic arrangement. Others have since repeated or enlarged Lissitzky's point."[17] In a kind of graphic meta-reflection on his argument, Marcus impedes our effortless reading of his article by removing certain letters from some of its lines and transposing them to the right margin. (This would have delighted the Russian formalist Viktor Shklovsky, who believed that the purpose of art was to slow down perception so as to make the latter a more palpable and thus more fully conscious process.[18]) Read vertically, the transposed letters spell out that aforementioned, forward-looking passage in Lissitzky's *Merz* text, which Marcus cites from the translation in Küppers's monograph, sans any punctuation: "The new book demands The new writer / ink stand and and goose quill are dead The / printed sheet transcends space and time / The printed sheet the infinity of the book / must be transcended."

My third example dates to 1988. Shortly after Sharon Poggenpohl assumed the editorship of *Visible Language*, Martha Scotford, then a professor in the School of Design at North Carolina State University and now emerita, published in its pages the results of an enterprising graduate studio that she had recently taught. The problem she had set the studio was how to make a verbal *and* visual translation into English of Mayakovsky's *For the Voice*, which, as noted near the outset, Lissitzky had designed in 1923. While the book's poems had already been translated, nobody had attempted the translation from Cyrillic into Roman of Lissitzky's extensive typographic constructions, wordplays, and puns. "Can the non-Russian reader see and understand this work to any extent

17. Aaron Marcus, "At the Edge of Meaning," *Visible Language* 11, no. 2 (Spring 1977): 4, 5.

18. Viktor Shklovsky, "Art as Technique" (1917), in *Russian Formalist Criticism: Four Essays*, trans. and with an introduction by Lee T. Lemon and Marion J. Reis (Lincoln: University of Nebraska Press, 1965), 3–24.

comparable to the Russian reader's experience?" Scotford asked. Answering this question was a complex and ambitious undertaking, the pedagogical goals of which were to encourage students to learn about design and typographic history, appreciate Lissitzky's inventiveness, practice formal analysis, and provide an opportunity for collaboration among designers and others outside the profession. Enlisting the assistance of a multilingual colleague, the late Elisabeth Jezierski (1924–2018), Scotford and her students—Michelle Stone, David Urena, and Sherry Blankenship—translated four of the thirteen poems in such a way as to preserve, to the extent possible, their verbal and visual content. The article includes the students' detailed notes on the design process and reproduces their results.[19] Scotford subsequently completed a translation of the entire book for publication by the British Library, in a boxed set that includes a facsimile edition of the Russian original in its collection and a volume of scholarly essays edited by Patricia Railing. One of these essays comprises a detailed and informative discussion by Scotford of the typographical principles and operations that underpinned the translation process.[20] The example of the Scotford studio attests to the fact that critical attention to Lissitzky's theory and practice was found in the postwar period not only in the periodical literature but also in the realm of pedagogy. Determining the precise extent to which this kind of undertaking was common in graphic design programs, however, requires further research and analysis.

19. Martha Scotford Lange, "Verbal and Visual Translation of Mayakovsky's and Lissitzky's *For Reading Out Loud*," *Visible Language* 22, no. 2/3 (Spring 1988): 195–222. Also included in this issue is a sharp critique of the original book by the Polish art critic Szymon Bojko (1917–2014) and the expatriate Polish design professor Krzysztof Lenk (1936–2018), who caution in an interview with the journal that Mayakovsky's poems embody "the hopes, illusions, myths, and also the diffused phraseologies, half-truths, and lies of Bolshevik propaganda" (227), and suggest that while Lissitzky gives "compelling graphic form to the poems"(227), his "graphic solution appears to be cool-minded, aesthetic and too speculative," essentially "a type of graphic mystification" and "part of the [state] propaganda program" (229); see their "*For Reading Out Loud* in Context," trans. Bozena Shallcross, *Visible Language* 22, no. 2/3 (Spring 1988): 223–30.

20. See Martha Scotford, "Notes on the Visual Translation of For the Voice," in *Voices of Revolution: Collected Essays*, ed. Patricia Railing (London: British Library, 2000), 44–64.

V.

Given Kaplan's emphasis on the act of reading, it seems appropriate to close with a reading of *For the Voice*, the title of which is sometimes also translated as *Reading Aloud* or *Reading Out Loud*. Lissitzky considered his design as something like an accompaniment to Mayakovsky's poetry, like a piano to a violin.[21] He designed the book in Berlin, where he was then residing, during or in the immediate wake of the poet's fall 1922 visit to the city to perform public readings as one of the leading voices of the Revolution. It was published by the State Publishing House of Soviet Russia, which, like dozens of other Russian-language presses, both pro- and anti-Soviet, maintained a branch office in Berlin in the early 1920s so as to take advantage of Germany's superior printing technology, not to mention a favorable exchange rate from ruble to mark thanks to Germany's runaway inflation. Its verse is mostly agitational in tone, eager for the reader to share its convictions. Incorporating the language of the street, it is a rich demonstration of what the Russian formalist critic Iurii Tynianov theorized in 1924 as the seemingly infinite capacity of literature to reach further and further into everyday life, into its backyards and low haunts, for new forms to make literary.[22]

How does this small book, measuring just 7½ × 5¼ inches, manifest the new optics? With respect to its typography, Lissitzky first sketched in pencil the layout for each poem's initial page opening, but for the typesetting itself, he worked alongside a letterpress compositor at the job-printing firm of Lütze and Vogt. While stanzas are printed in black and red ink in a standard serif Cyrillic typeface, the typography comes alive in the dynamic visualization and spatialization of each poem's title and its accompanying vignette. Both are constructed out of what Lissitzky could find in the compositor's typecase: not only letters but also typographic rules and furniture, geometric elements, and dingbats—this last a favorite of the Dadaist circles in which he was moving at the time. This correlates strongly with one of the bullet-point demands he makes in *Merz* concerning the designing of "book-space through the material of type [itself]."[23] *For the Voice* thus foregrounds the materiality of its own making: In the language of Russian formalist and Futurist poetic theory, specifically that of Shklovsky, Lissitzky's design "lays bare the device."[24] Or, as Ellen Lupton puts it in the language of typographic

21. "Meine Seiten stehen zu den Gedichten etwa in ähnlichem Verhältnis wie das die Geige begleitende Klavier"; Lissitzky, "Typographische Tatsachen z.B.," 154. This sentence is part of a paragraph-long caption that is outside the main body of the article; the paragraph is thus not found in the translation of "Typographical Facts" in Küppers's monograph, but rather in her caption for plate no. 95 (no page number).

22. Iurii Tynianov, "The Literary Fact" (1924), trans. Ann Shukman, in *Modern Genre Theory*, ed. and introduced by David Duff (Harlow, England: Pearson Education Limited, 2000), 33.

23. "Die Gestaltung des Buchraumes durch das Material der Klischees"; Lissitzky, "Topographie der Typographie," 47. (With respect to this sentence, the strange English translation in Küppers's monograph cannot be recommended.)

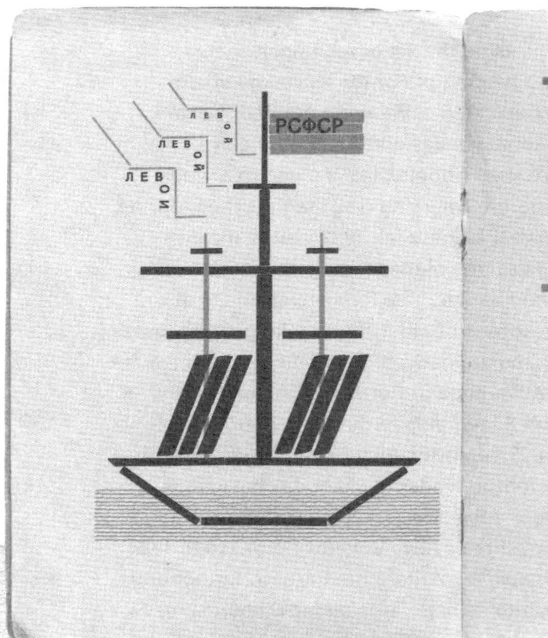

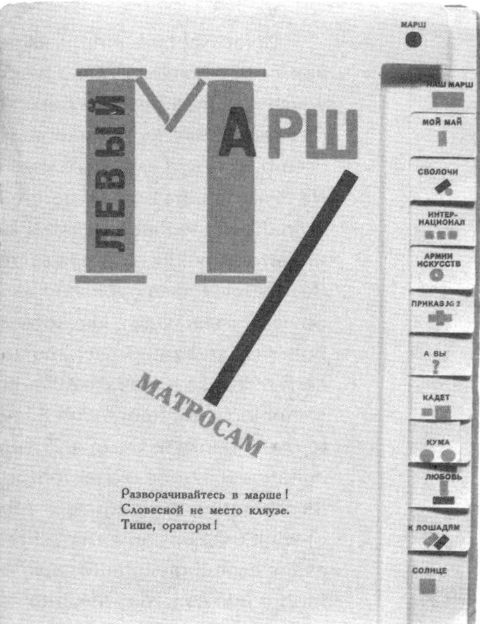

El Lissitzky and Vladimir Mayakovsky. *Dliia golosa (For the Voice)* (Berlin: Gos. Izdatel'stvo RSFSR, 1923). Page opening for the beginning of the poem, "Left March / To the Sailors"

theory, Lissitzky renders the printed book's "technological matrix physically present on the page" while also subverting the strictures of letterpress printing by insisting on its spatialization.[25]

Consider the cover, for instance: A monumental *M* (for "Mayakovsky") is composed out of typographic rules (two long and thick, two short and thin); the remainder of his name runs horizontally across the cover in black letters. Meanwhile, a vertical red bar contains three letters stacked one on top of the other to read "Для" ("Dliia," i.e., "For"); under them, but rotated clockwise ninety degrees, is the word "голоса" (golosa, i.e., genitive case of the noun "voice"). Together, the two words in the orange bar form the title, Для голоса (*For the Voice*). But notice the multitasking of the letter Я, which serves as the third letter in both Mayakovsky's name and the book's title. Arranging words in such a way that they share letters is a typical feature of Lissitzky's graphic work. There is also a pun here, too, because the single letter Я is also the Russian word for "I," which seems especially appropriate for a work by a lyric poet, especially one with a voluminous ego such as the great Mayakovsky.

The first poem in the book is "Левый марш матросам" ("Left March / To the Sailors"). On the right side of the page, the poem's title is pictorialized: The word Левый ("Levyi," i.e., "Left") is set vertically within the body of the large red *M* (for "Марш," i.e.,

24. Shklovsky, "Art as Technique."

25. Shklovsky, "Art as Technique." Ellen Lupton, *Thinking with Type: A Critical Guide for Desigers, Writers, Editors, and Students*, rev. and expanded 2nd ed. (New York: Princeton Architectural Press, 2014), 161.

"March") but rotated counterclockwise. This red *M* is akin to the one on the cover but composed now with wider rules, adjacent to which have been laid slender, horizontal ones that suggest slab-serifs, which were commonly used in nineteenth-century advertising posters to attract attention. Then, from just underneath the right end of the pictographic title "Left March," a diagonal bar runs down and back to the left, toward the word "Матросам" ("To the Sailors"), which tells us to whom the poem is addressed. In short, the poem is an exhortation to sailors to fall into military formation. On the left side of the opening, their battleship floats on a little sea, flying a flag upon which appears РСФСР ("RSFSR"), the acronym for the Socialist Republic of Soviet Russia. All is composed out of typographic rules and standard letters.

With respect to the design of the book overall, its key feature is the die-cut thumb index that runs down its right edge, each tab bearing a little icon that is half-Suprematist and half-semaphoric. This is the kind of device that is found in printed dictionaries, Bibles, trade brochures, address books, and the like, to enable the user to locate expeditiously the information she or he seeks. (For this reason, *For the Voice* has been called a "Dictionary of Revolution.") The insertion of a thumb index into a book of poetry is significant in three ways: **1.** It speaks to Lissitzky's habit of borrowing from utilitarian print genres, just as his visualization of the page borrows from the mixed typefaces and point sizes of nineteenth-century advertising flyers and the like. In short, it's another instance of poetry reaching into everyday life for new forms to make literary. **2.** The vertical column of tabs helps to underscore the physical objecthood and construction of the book: As soon as you open it, its entire volume is revealed to you in the form of strata, a bit like the cutaway section of an architectural model. **3.** The thumb index obviates the need for a table of contents, though it's perhaps a bit hyperbolic in a book as slender as this one. Nonetheless, because the reader can find a particular poem at a glance, the thumb index affords him or her spontaneity yet also precision in reading.

This brings us to Lissitzky's ultimate purpose, which is to facilitate not just the reading but the reading *aloud* of Mayakovsky's verse. The poems are not to be read in a contemplative fashion while sitting at home alone but rather declaimed in the street, town square, playground, school, factory, office, bar, café, and so on. Given its exhortation to revolution, *For the Voice* hovers somewhere close to a handbook, a manual for agitators, which was a whole genre of Soviet Russian print production in the 1920s, designed to assist the spread of revolution. Reading agitational poetry aloud is to be a communal and participatory activity. The book replaces the cathedral. But not only that: This dictionary of revolution is also to play a role in reclaiming public space from the private interests of advertising culture, which had been rapidly remaking the urban fabric of Berlin and other metropolitan centers. Thus, reading aloud in public space even those (few) poems in the volume that are not explicitly political in subject matter is still a political act, in the sense that it reclaims public space for human interaction. The typographical arrangement of *For the Voice* shows us, furthermore, that Lissitzky understood that reading poetry aloud in a context increasingly shaped by new communication technologies would not be the same act as it once was. Poetry now had to compete. To be "heard," it needed a new optics.

Who was the intended reader? There were some 350,000 Russian émigrés living in Berlin in the early 1920s. Half had fled Russia during the civil war, the other half after Lenin's announcement of the New Economic Policy, which proposed a partial return to a private market and which some revolutionaries regarded as an intolerable compromise, decamping to agitate elsewhere, especially to Germany. Unfortunately, however, we have very little concrete information as to how *For the Voice* was utilized in Berlin, or in Soviet Russia for that matter. We know only that it was sold in bookstores, but we don't know the size of the edition, how much it cost, who purchased it, and thus whether it remained an "artist's book" or enjoyed greater circulation.[26] And the only information with respect to its reception is what Lissitzky himself reported in a 1939 interview. A crowd of Russian artists and poets gathered at the Café Nollendorfplatz in Berlin to hear it read aloud by Shklovsky, the aforementioned Russian formalist. "Truly uproarious" was how Lissitzky remembered that Berlin evening.[27]

26. See Steven A. Mansbach, "A Universal Voice in Russian Berlin," in *Voices of Revolution: Collected Essays*, esp. 161–63 and 172–74.

27. Lissitzky-Küppers, "Life and Letters," in her *El Lissitzky*, 25. Küppers is drawing here from L. Feigelmann, "Ein Gespräch mit dem Künstler Lissitzky" (February 15, 1939), which was later reproduced in Sophie Lissitzky-Küppers and Jen Lissitzky, *El Lissitzky: Proun und Wolkenbügel: Schriften, Briefe, Dokumente* (Dresden: VEB Verlag der Kunst, 1977), 204.

OBJECT AS IMAGE: ART IN THE POSTWAR AMERICAN DESIGN CULTURE

SYDNEY SKELTON SIMON

The Becton Center is a landmark modern building on Yale University's campus, designed by the architect Marcel Breuer and completed in 1970. Today, it is home to the Yale School of Engineering and Applied Science and the Yale Center for Engineering Innovation and Design, as well as the subterranean Davies Auditorium, a large lecture hall in which scores of Yale undergraduates attend classes every year. Just inside the rear entrance to Davies Auditorium stands a welded metal sculptural screen by the Italian-American artist and designer Harry Bertoia.

Harry Bertoia, *Sculpture Screen*, 1958, metal, welded with golden coloration, 107 × 46 × 13¾ inches. Yale University Art Gallery, Gift of the International Business Machines Corporation 1966.61

The screen is installed against a wall, though it was clearly meant to be a wall itself: a sculptural partition that might, in another context, have helped to organize an interior design scheme. This *Sculpture Screen* is composed of three central poles that each stretch from the floor to the dropped ceiling. From these poles horizontal bars extend outward to support dozens of tapered rectangular planes of metal that face out toward both the front and the back. While most of the planes of metal are solid, a few repeat the tapered rectangular shape as a frame containing smaller-scale welded sculptural assemblages within. It is a screen of smaller screens, at once emphatically flat and tantalizingly tactile. The whole sculpture was brazed, or coated in molten metal, to create a range of expressive textures and colors—a relatively common practice among direct-metal sculptors in the 1950s and '60s.[1]

1. For an explanation of brazing and photographs of Bertoia using the technique on a related sculptural screen, see Dona Meilach and Don Seiden, *Direct Metal Sculpture: Creative Techniques and Appreciation* (New York: Crown Publishers, 1966), 68–79.

Created by Bertoia in 1958, the sculptural screen's aesthetic is unmistakably midcentury modern, playing up the tension between, on the one hand, a sense of modular design with interchangeable units and, on the other, the expressive content of an improvisational and gestural surface treatment. Illumination from the recessed lights above hints at the sparkle of the sculpture's gilded surface, though a darkening patina and accumulated dust make for relatively little contrast to the textured concrete walls of the Becton Center.

The screen was originally purchased by International Business Machines (IBM) in 1959 and is one of many welded metal sculptures that Bertoia made for corporate patrons in the 1950s and '60s. No record has yet been found of how, or even if, it was ever installed in any of IBM's New York–area buildings,[2] but it is easy to imagine the kind of environment that it was envisioned to inhabit because Bertoia made a very similar installation, also in 1958, that was commissioned by interior designer Florence Knoll for the First National Bank of Miami in Florida.

There, two rows of five tree-like structures, similar in composition to the IBM piece, flanked the main teller area. Their bases had been bolted to the concrete subfloor and covered over in tile, so that the ten sculptures appeared to rise up organically from the floor. The president of the bank, Harry Hood Bassett, referred to them as his "Money Trees," a forest of wealth and good taste to set the tone in the main lobby of this new marquee building.[3] The screens had both interior design and graphic design functions, organizing physical space *and* communicating a desirable corporate image. The renovation of this space and the commission of artwork for it was a media event designed to draw attention to the bank, as much as it was to create an appealing environment for the business of banking. This dual function was by no means unusual—indeed, it was the standard for the vast majority of Bertoia's commissioned sculptures, *and* for the corporate patronage of contemporary art more broadly.

The original design function of screens such as these was dependent on the specific historical, architectural, and corporate contexts of the postwar period. Having emerged triumphant from

2. There is no clear documentation of this sculpture and its acquisition by IBM in Harry Bertoia's papers at the Smithsonian Archives of American Art, nor do the object records for the screen at the Yale University Art Gallery contain any information about its initial purchase by IBM. Max Campbell, an archivist at IBM, was also unable to find any record of its having been installed in IBM's Gallery of Science and Art at their headquarters at 590 Madison Avenue. Email correspondence with the author, December 11, 2019.

3. Letter from Harry Hood Bassett to Harry Bertoia, dated January 7, 1965. "Business Records–81. Miscellaneous Correspondence 1953–1976," Harry Bertoia Papers, owned by Vitra Design Museum; microfilmed by Archives of American Art, Smithsonian Institution, reel 3849.

World War II with a booming consumer culture and a dominant position in the new world order, the United States became enthralled with design, particularly that for mass production and mass dissemination. In the late 1940s and early '50s, design became an essential means by which individuals related to increasingly complex technologies, systems, and institutions. Design organized, clarified, smoothed, persuaded, and signified in both explicit and subtle ways. The US saw an explosion in the visibility of design and widespread appreciation of its ability to express values, influence behavior, and cultivate desire. Good design, it was believed by many, could make the world a better place. In the context of the evolution of graphic design pedagogy, it is worth recognizing the deep entanglement of industrial design (which largely encompasses the design of consumer goods for mass production) and graphic design in this moment, and, in particular, the ways in which objects became images.

The idea of "Image" had significant currency in the postwar period. In his 1962 book, *The Image, or What Happened to the American Dream*, the conservative historian Daniel Boorstin lamented the fact that images had overtaken concrete, objective reality as the most important phenomena shaping public perception. Boorstin coined the term "pseudo-event" to describe what we would today call a "media event": an occasion cooked up for the sake of being disseminated or reported on.[4] Boorstin credited a "graphic revolution" with creating the conditions in which this obsession with the Image could flourish, referring to the ever-increasing capacity of mass media, mass communication, and mass distribution, or, in Boorstin's words, "man's ability to make, preserve, transmit, and disseminate precise images – images of print, of men and landscapes and events, of the voices of men and mob."[5] When Boorstin wrote about the Image, he did not mean an individual picture but rather a malleable accretion of visual data that, taken together, could form "a studiously crafted personality profile of an individual, institution, corporation, product, or service."[6] Boorstin's Image was today's "brand identity." And as he noted, the most elaborately contrived and expensive kind of Image was the corporate image.

As an artist and designer, Bertoia was intimately involved in the crafting of corporate images. He made many large-scale welded metal sculptures in the 1950s and '60s, and most were created for corporations looking to ornament their new or newly renovated buildings in the postwar construction boom. As works of lobby art, these site-dependent commissions functioned both as fine art pieces and as part of the brand or image being promoted by their

4. Daniel Boorstin, *The Image: A Guide to Pseudo-Events in America*, 50th anniversary ed. (New York: Vintage, 2012), 11–12. The book's subtitle was changed to "A Guide to Pseudo-Events in America" for the release of the paperback edition in 1964.

5. Ibid., 13.

6. Ibid., 186.

corporate landlords. They were designed to activate the physical and virtual points of interface between companies and their publics. Bertoia usually collaborated closely with architects to integrate his work within a specific architectural scheme, but the approval of his designs and the ways in which they were promoted in marketing efforts were ultimately subject to the discretion of corporate decision makers. Already by 1960, hundreds of American corporations recognized the value of investing in original works of art to decorate offices—and to be used in advertisements, company publications, and product packaging—for the accumulation of cultural prestige and as appreciating assets.[7]

Bertoia's abstract sculptures were receptive to, and thereby made emblematic of, explicit corporate messaging conveyed through titles assigned by their patrons, press releases, print media profiles, and other textual and graphic frames.[8] Take, for example, his largest and most commanding work: a seventy-foot-wide welded metal assemblage commissioned by architect Gordon Bunshaft for the Manufacturers Trust Bank branch on Fifth Avenue in Manhattan and completed in 1954. Bunshaft's building was radical in its transparency, signaling the transformation of banking from a security to a service industry.[9] Horace C. Flanigan, president of the Manufacturers Trust, announced the gambit of the bank's unconventional design at an opening event:

> These [glass] walls give the bank a wide-open, inviting look and turn it, day and night, into a giant showcase. The building will be its own salesman, a merchandising concept new in banking and one that we believe pioneers the way to better customer service.[10]

Bertoia's spectacular screen was a functioning part of the interior design: It divided space while still allowing light and air to circulate freely; it delivered emotional impact as a richly textured core to an otherwise transparent building; and it provided cultural

7. The Whitney Museum of American Art mounted the first major exhibition of contemporary art owned by American corporations, entitled *Business Buys American Art* (March 17–April 24, 1960), in order to investigate the by-then pronounced phenomenon of art patronage by the contemporary art market and to encourage the growth of this new class of collector. The San Francisco Museum of Art followed up a year later with *American Business and the Arts* (September 14–October 15, 1961), which expanded the scope of the Whitney's show by examining the extent to which American businesses were buying contemporary art by foreign artists as well as American ones.

8. Bertoia rarely titled his own work, but in many cases allowed the owners of his sculptures to name them. In the case of his corporate patrons, such titles were frequently crafted to complement the meanings they assigned to his work.

9. This transformation was enabled by the fact that deposits were now federally insured, as noted by Ada Louise Huxtable, "Bankers' Showcase," *Arts Digest* 29, no. 5 (December 1954): 12.

10. Flanigan quoted in "'Showcase' Bank Holds a Preview: Manufacturers Trust to Open 5-Floor Glass-Walled Offices at 43rd and Fifth on Oct. 4," *New York Times*, September 23, 1954.

currency for a publicity-minded institution. Manufacturers Trust's jewel box aroused tremendous public and media interest and lured substantial new business.[11]

Bertoia also made screens in the round, like the explosive *Sculpture Group Symbolizing World's Communication in the Atomic Age*. Commissioned by architect Alfred Shaw for the Zenith Radio Corporation's new Chicago display salon in 1959, and now in the collection of the Smithsonian American Art Museum, the four-piece installation provided a backdrop against which the latest models of televisions and radios were displayed, all visible from the street through large windows. The press release that announced the unveiling of the sculpture provided a tidy interpretation of the work and its relevance to the company. It explained: "The brass sculptural grouping, symbolizing world communications in the atomic age, consists of four units, a radiant eight-foot main unit and three smaller units representing sight, sound, and electronic control," all of which were "lighted to convey an abstract concept of electronic communications." The company's motivations for commissioning the work were made plain: "Bertoia's glittering brass sculpture . . . was designed as an invitation to passersby to look into the total depth of the exhibition area and to complement the consumer electronics on display."[12]

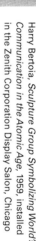

Harry Bertoia, *Sculpture Group Symbolizing World's Communication in the Atomic Age*, 1959, installed in the Zenith Corporation Display Salon, Chicago

IBM, one of the earliest American corporations to build a contemporary art collection, frequently used works of art by Bertoia and others as graphic elements in their advertising. One of his freestanding bursting sculptures was used, for example, to signify the explosion of the information age in a 1962 advertisement.[13] That same year, a rare figurative sculpture by Bertoia—a bust formed by

11. Jack Alexander, "The Bank That Has No Secrets," *Saturday Evening Post*, November 30, 1954, 36–37 and 105–06.

12. Press release, Zenith Radio Corporation, July 23, 1959, curatorial file for *Sculpture Group* (1979.107A–D), Smithsonian American Art Museum, Washington, DC.

13. The advertisement appeared on the back covers of the January 1962 issues of the magazines *Natural History* and *International Science and Technology*. IBM neither commissioned nor owned the sculpture in this case; the advertising firm Benton & Bowles borrowed a Kodachrome from Staempfli Gallery, which had exhibited the sculpture in Bertoia's first solo exhibition with the New York gallery, *Harry Bertoia: Recent Sculpture* (March 14–April 1, 1961).

an elaborate network of brass melt-coated wires given the title *Modern Man*—was presented in silhouette on the cover of *THINK*, IBM's corporate magazine. The flat tangle of black lines was used to suggest "the labyrinthine complexities of the human brain" in an issue dedicated to "Man's Creative Mind."[14]

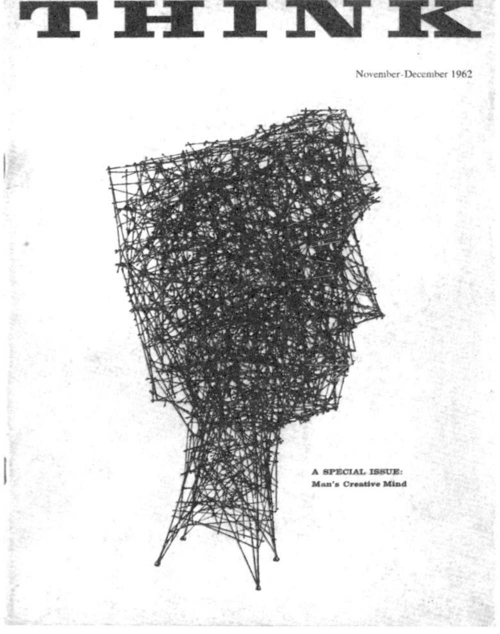

THINK
November-December 1962
A SPECIAL ISSUE:
Man's Creative Mind

Cover of *THINK* (November–December 1962), featuring sculpture by Harry Bertoia

These examples demonstrated how effortlessly Bertoia's screens moved from three to two dimensions, from object to Image, or from the singular, specific, and experiential to the symbolic, reproducible, and graphic. It is worth pausing to consider how peculiar this is. Given that welded metal sculpture is so emphatically physical, and that Bertoia's approach to metalwork was highly experimental and improvisational, it is counterintuitive that these sculptures would communicate most clearly in a graphic register. A brief review of Bertoia's own on-the-job training may serve to illuminate how he got there and to explain his dynamic engagement with the form and function of a screen as a surface that projects images while simultaneously obscuring what lies behind it.

In the late 1930s and early '40s, Bertoia spent six years at the Cranbrook Academy of Art, a small, unaccredited, and highly influential art school in Bloomfield Hills, Michigan. His tenure there paved the way for his career-long commitment to modernism, his openness to collaboration, his dedication to working directly with materials, and his eschewal of dogmatic hierarchies between media. After a year of studying painting and managing the metal shop as a condition of his scholarship, Bertoia was hired as the metalwork instructor in 1938. Cranbrook's program emphasized the importance of craft—of understanding the possibilities and constraints of one's materials—for the development of forms imbued with a contemporary spirit.[15] The school's director, architect Eliel Saarinen, championed the integration of the arts and fostered a strong spirit of collaboration among faculty and students. There was no set curriculum for students to follow; instead, the school sought to be (in Saarinen's words) a "working place for creative art," following a workshop model in which students were encouraged to experiment in a range of media.[16] Bertoia's own metalcraft courses emphasized the study of the limitations and possibilities of different metals and metalworking processes.[17] It was at Cranbrook that Bertoia had his first serious engagement with the rigors of design

14. *THINK* 28, no. 10 (November–December 1962).

for mass production when virtually the whole faculty and student body helped develop Charles Eames and Eero Saarinen's award-winning submissions for the *Organic Design* furniture competition at the Museum of Modern Art in 1940–41.

Bertoia's efforts extended beyond the metal shop, though, as he also began making prints in his spare time. Cranbrook had printmaking facilities but did not offer formal instruction in printmaking or graphic design. Bertoia taught himself to make monotypes that became the basis for a successful fine arts practice in the 1940s. He had gallery representation and exhibited at several major museums across the country. He began by making abstract stamped compositions and soon developed a method of drawing in monotype as a means of working through ideas.

View of St. Louis Airport, featuring sculptural screen by Harry Bertoia (1956), as seen in advertisement for Pittsburgh Plate Glass company, in *Time*, January 27, 1958

As he pursued these abstract compositions, Bertoia investigated the relationship between image and object. He made his earliest prints on thin Japanese rice paper, and he recalled in a 1952 interview that, while at Cranbrook, he would stretch the almost translucent paper on a frame and hang it up against the light: "the colors would float in the air, some closer, some farther back."[18] These experiments

15. In 1931, a year before Cranbrook Academy of Art opened its doors to students, Eliel Saarinen articulated his vision for the new school: "The main idea with the Craft Studios is not to develop craftsmanship, *but the design*. . . . If the young man in developing his design has possibilities to follow the work in a cabinet-maker's shop, in a bronze foundry, in textile and weaving shops, if he can follow the work in iron, silver, glass, wood, and stone, he begins to understand the material, and his design will be influenced by the character of the material." Eliel Saarinen, "The Cranbrook Development," Address to the American Institute of Architects' Convention in San Antonio, TX, April 1931, 6. Cranbrook Foundation Office Records, Box 26, Folder 13, Cranbrook Archives, Bloomfield Hills, MI.

16. Ibid., 4.

17. *Cranbrook Academy of Art Announcement, 1939–1940*, CAA Publications, Series V: Catalogs 1936–1948, Cranbrook Archives, Bloomfield Hills, MI.

18. "Pure Design Research," *Architectural Forum* 97, no. 3 (September 1952): 146.

clearly anticipated one of his earliest sculpture commissions, an enameled metal screen for architect Minoru Yamasaki's new terminal for the St. Louis Airport, which was commissioned in 1952 and finally installed in 1956.

Bertoia left Cranbrook in 1943 to move to Southern California. There he worked in the molded plywood division of the Evans Product Company under the design direction of his Cranbrook colleague Charles Eames. He learned to weld and was responsible for fabricating the metal armatures for the first commercially successful furniture designs by Eames. Later in the 1940s, Bertoia took a job at the Navy Electronics Laboratory in Point Loma, near San Diego, in the Visual Development Division. There he worked on graphics, photography, and layouts for technical reports and instruction books, while continuing his fine arts printmaking practice in the evenings.

In 1950, Bertoia was hired by Hans and Florence Knoll, and he and his family moved to Pennsylvania, where Bertoia committed himself to making welded metal sculpture while working on furniture designs for their company. After two years, Knoll released Bertoia's line of now-iconic gridded wire Diamond chairs. Throughout this formative period, Bertoia continuously engaged with both graphic and object-based work, and with art and design. Scholar Glenn Adamson has argued compellingly that Bertoia's furniture designs became iconic precisely because they could be translated from three to two dimensions so readily—they looked interesting, sculptural, and graphic in real space as well as in the space of a printed advertisement.[19]

View of Becton Center vestibule in which Bertoia's *Sculpture Screen* is installed opposite three digital monitors in cases embedded in the wall

By 2019, in Yale's Becton Center, Bertoia's sculptural screen had come to seem far less vital to the space than the corporate commissions discussed above, falling short on its dual purpose as a work of fine art and design. This failure was thrown into relief by the puzzling presence, immediately opposite Bertoia's screen, of a row of three glass display cases embedded in the wall that each housed a digital monitor that cycled through static informational pages

19. Glenn Adamson, "Learning from Harry Bertoia," lectured delivered at Knoll showroom, New York, March 18, 2015, https://www.knoll.com/knollnewsdetail/bertoia-at-100-harry-bertoia-centennial-celebration-at-knoll-new-york.

promoting the activities of Yale Engineering. Opposite these bright digital displays, Bertoia's screen was rendered obsolete: a sculpture that no longer communicated a clear and specific message—an image without impact.

IBM donated its Bertoia screen to the Yale University Art Gallery in 1966, just seven years after acquiring it. IBM Vice President Arthur K. Watson wrote about the screen in his letter offering it to Yale, "We think it is both interesting and valuable as art, but unfortunately we have never found a proper home for it in any of our buildings."[20] Which is to say, it had no corporate value to IBM because it was not doing the graphic design work—of persuasion, legibility, and impact—that the company required from its fine art collection. When the gallery installed it in the Becton Center in 1975, on long-term loan, the chairman of the Department of Engineering and Applied Sciences expressed his appreciation for the opportunity to "enliven our place of business."[21] We might imagine that it did just that, for a time. But such relevance needs to be actively cultivated.

Looking back to the context within which Bertoia's work was created and used to advance certain kinds of image creation and corporate messaging sheds light on the expansiveness of the field of graphic design at midcentury. I have characterized graphic design in this essay not as the aesthetic creation of a single visionary maker, but as a function to which something may be put by many interested agents. Given that, it is helpful to consider how a sculpture might lose that graphic design function in instances in which the object's relevance to contemporary image and design culture has not been sustained. Indeed, a work of art's graphic design function can only be retained if its owners and/or users remain invested in it.

20. Letter from Arthur K. Watson to Andrew C. Ritchie, Director of the Yale University Art Gallery, April 14, 1966. Registrar's File for *Sculpture Screen* (1966.61), Yale University Art Gallery, New Haven, CT.

21. Letter from Charles A. Walker, chairman of the Department of Engineering and Applied Science, to Susan P. Casteras, assistant to the director, Yale Art Gallery, March 20, 1975. Registrar's File for *Sculpture Screen* (1966.61), Yale University Art Gallery, New Haven, CT.

HAL FOSTER ON GRAPHIC DESIGN
with RACHEL CHURNER and GEOFF KAPLAN

RACHEL CHURNER: Many of the essays in *After the Bauhaus, Before the Internet: A History of Graphic Design Pedagogy* consider how graphic design moved from a professional practice to a discipline through the act of self-theorization. Geoff brought a wide range of voices together in 2019 when he organized a conference for Yale that raised the question of self-theorization by asking if pedagogy was the means by which design cemented its disciplinary structures. One of the main sessions at the conference was titled "What We Were Reading." Because your work was so critical to this category—I'm thinking particularly of *The Anti-Aesthetic: Essays on Postmodernism Culture* (1983) and *Recodings; Art, Spectacle, Cultural Politics* (1985), and then later, of course, *Design and Crime (and Other Diatribes)* (2002)—we were eager to speak with you.

GEOFF KAPLAN: Yes. Our ambitions in talking to you about design stem from my experience as an MFA student in the mid-'90s at Cranbrook, where virtually every grad student had a copy of *The Anti-Aesthetic* (and often *Recodings*) on their shelves and/or listed in their thesis bibliographies.

HAL FOSTER: Were Katherine and Michael McCoy still there?

GK: Yes, the McCoys were there from 1971 to 1995. I arrived at Cranbrook in 1994, their last year. (In my second year, 1996–97, Andrew Blauvelt was the graphic designer in residence.) While a student, I spent a good deal of time in the library reading through thesis documents from the 1980s and '90s and saw consistencies in reading patterns. A large majority of the bibliographies included your work. Even through the mid-'90s, students were very invested in the question "what is the postmodern," and this is reflected in their reading lists.

Your work has been formative in attempts to push graphic design beyond simply a service industry model, as some within the academy mobilized it to theorize the activity of graphic design and its teaching. Your introduction to *The Anti-Aesthetic*, for example, was an influential text for students in graphic design programs, suggesting how postmodern ideas of anti-mastery, anti–master narratives, the birth of the reader, allegory, and the shift from work to text could be mobilized in design education. The introduction to *Recodings* was also significant for designers, particularly in its call not only to engage counter-models and alternative narratives but also, as you wrote, to "seek out new political connections and make new cultural maps."

RC: Could you tell us a little about how *The Anti-Aesthetic* came to be? Were you surprised by its success?

HF: I wasn't aware of its impact in the design world; in the art and academic worlds its impact was fairly immediate and quite strong, and, yes, I was surprised by its success. In terms of design, I'm puzzled that the main provocation of *The Anti-Aesthetic* was

Louis Daguerre invents a practical method of taking pin-sharp photographs called daguerreotypes

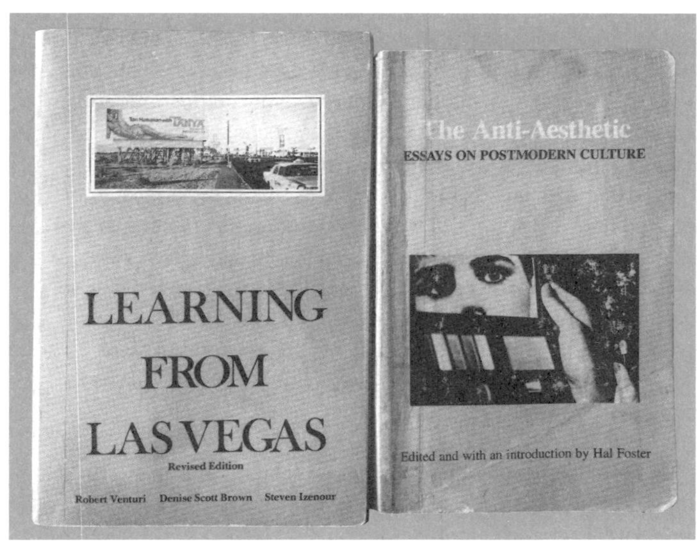

Hal Foster's copies of *Learning from Las Vegas* and *The Anti-Aesthetic*

the poststructuralist shift from work to text. I would have thought it would have been the postmodernism I called reactionary in the introduction, because its point of departure was architecture: I mean the postmodernism launched by *Learning from Las Vegas* (1972) and related manifestos. Rather than a double embrace of the vernacular and the historical, that postmodernism seemed to me to celebrate the dominance of the commodity-image—a very different enterprise from any poststructuralist analysis of culture as text.

GK: I can tell you another thing about the reading habits of graphic designers in that moment: On many students' bookshelves, next to your book was *Learning from Las Vegas*. Often the books rubbed up against each other, literally.

HF: Strange, because for me the two books are matter and anti-matter. But I suppose it does make a certain sense: Maybe design students turned to the textuality advocated by *The Anti-Aesthetic* as an alternative (or at least an antidote) to the scenography offered up by Venturi, Stern, Graves, etc. and their partners in design.

One thing that both delights and dismays me about architecture and design students is how porous they are to ideas and how eclectic regarding positions. More so than other students, they have a hit-and-run approach to both: "What's in this for me? How can I use it?" That way lies misreading. But then maybe there's nothing but misreading; maybe that's all we do—good and bad misreadings. Still, architecture and design students take it to a new level; they make it an art!

RC: It certainly speaks to the all-consuming ability of design to take from both the reactionary and the resistant postmodernisms.

HF: Just a couple of years after *The Anti-Aesthetic* was published, I revisited the idea of postmodernism in a piece titled

"(Post)Modern Polemics" (1984). Already there, I argued, the two postmodernisms—reactionary and resistant—couldn't be held apart so readily. Even if the reactionary version advanced postmodernism as pastiche, while the resistant treated it as deconstruction, both registered a general reification and fragmentation of the sign. This was a Jamesonian insight—that this capitalist dynamic had penetrated the very interior of the sign, and that this postmodern breakup of signification spoke to a new stage in capitalism. After Ernest Mandel, Jameson called it "late capitalism"—I was never so optimistic to think it was about to expire. But like Jameson, I was never interested in postmodernism as simply a marker of style. For me, too, it was most important as a way to periodize culture in relation to capitalism.

RC: Let's talk about your motivation in getting *The Anti-Aesthetic* out. The book was published while you were a senior editor at *Art in America*, right? Were you also writing for *October* at the time?

HF: I came to New York in late 1977. I was very drawn to both critical theory and contemporary art, and I wanted to work on the two together. Before *Art in America*, I hung out a little at the Institute of Architecture and Urban Studies, which was the brainchild of Peter Eisenman, who, along with colleagues like Ken Frampton and Tony Vidler, launched *Oppositions* (Peter also provided a space for *October* there). It was an intense time for architectural theory—for example, Rem Koolhaas was about to publish *Delirious New York*—but not for architectural work. New York City was bankrupt in the mid-'70s, so it was a period of paper projects and design debates, almost by default.

I met Craig Owens at the Institute. Like him, I began to write for *Skyline*, which was housed at the Institute. Soon enough we were swooped up by *Art in America*, Craig in 1980, me in 1981. The editor, Betsy Baker, saw that there was an audience for discussions of critical postmodernism; certainly that's what we plied there.

Soon, too, we were both in the ambit of *October*—again, Craig a little before me through his friendship with Douglas Crimp. *The Anti-Aesthetic* was generated within those two contexts. And there was a third—Columbia—where I did an MA in critical theory in the late '70s. There we were also students of Sylvère Lotringer, who launched *Semiotext(e)* in 1974 at Columbia. By "we," I mean the people who later started *Zone*: Michel Feher, Jonathan Crary, Sanford Kwinter, and me. We were inseparable in those days.

These little worlds—and there were others too—were in contact but not in conversation. *The Anti-Aesthetic* was a way to stage a debate, a series of debates. (This was a great period for the anthology as argument—very pre-Internet.) Craig, Douglas, and Rosalind Krauss could be juxtaposed with Edward Said and Jameson, Ken Frampton could be partnered with Jürgen Habermas, and opposed to Jean Baudrillard, and so on. That was the dramaturgy of *The Anti-Aesthetic*.

Hal Foster's copy of *Zone* 1/2 (1985), cover designed by Bruce Mau

RC: You mentioned *Zone*. Can you tell us about the founding of Bay Press and then *Zone*—and about the choice to hire Bruce Mau as *Zone*'s designer? *Zone* was so much more than a vehicle for content; the way it wove design and subject matter throughout each issue was highly influential. I'm curious, were you involved in design decisions at all?

HF: Bay Press was the project of a great childhood friend of mine from Seattle named Thatcher Bailey. I grew up with Thatcher and Charles Wright, who later directed the Dia Art Foundation from 1986 to 1994. Thatcher published *The Anti-Aesthetic* in 1983, and when Charlie became head of Dia, the three of us launched the series of "Dia Discussions in Contemporary Culture." Thatcher oversaw the design of all the books, and I liked how restrained it was. For all my work on postmodernism, I was a modernist at heart (I still am). Modernist design was an early love, and eventually that affinity produced some tension with my *Zone* colleagues. *October* is obviously very spare; its modernist affiliation is clear enough. *Zone* was different, intentionally so. In some ways *Zone* was defined against *October*. We wanted to open up an alternative kind of space. And that was made clear by the lavish design conceived by Bruce Mau.

In a sense, *Zone* discovered Bruce. In his book *Lifestyle*, he might tell a different story, but *Zone* gave Bruce his first real project. The initial issues were more mammoth magazines than little journals (the genre is familiar now, but it wasn't then). The first issue was on the city, the next couple were on the body, and they were all design objects first and theoretical interventions second—at least that's how they were received. "The Death of the Author" turned out to be the birth of the designer? Certainly Bruce was seen as an author of *Zone*, more so than I was.

In any case, I thought the design was too prominent. The type was set quite small and images tended to overwhelm texts. In retrospect this was in keeping with a world become image, but that was precisely the problem, at least to me; after all, I was also a student of the Situationists, and the design seemed, well, spectacular, not critical, certainly not self-critical. It heralded a *world become design*, which would be a prime bad object for me in the following decades.

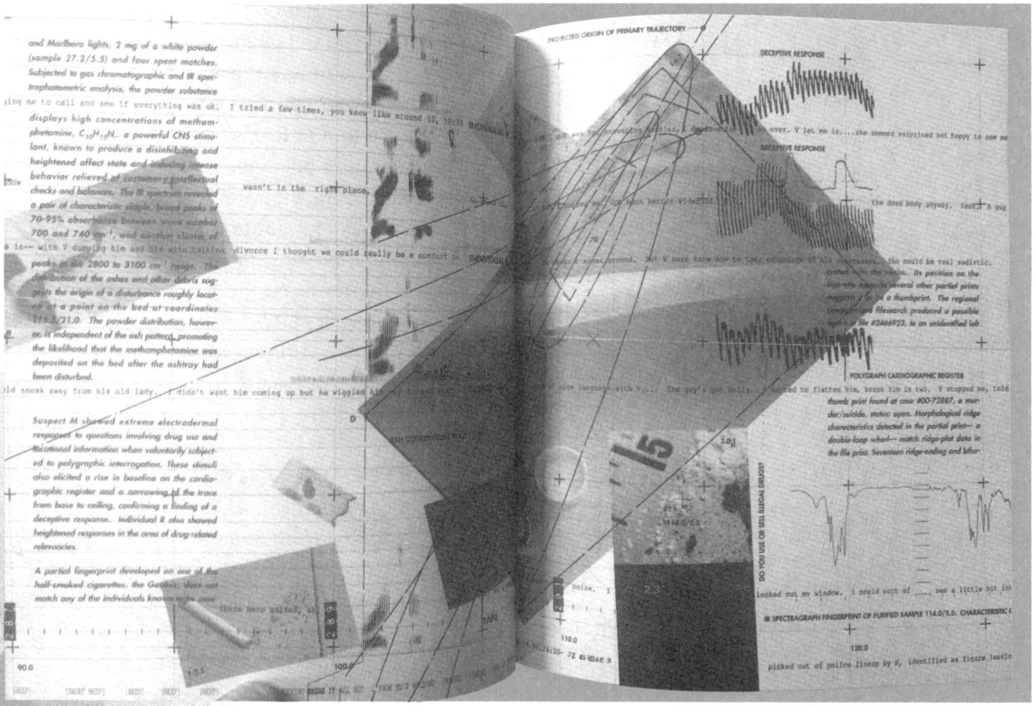

Spread from Hal Foster's copy of *Zone 6: Incorporations* designed by Bruce Mau, pages 351–52

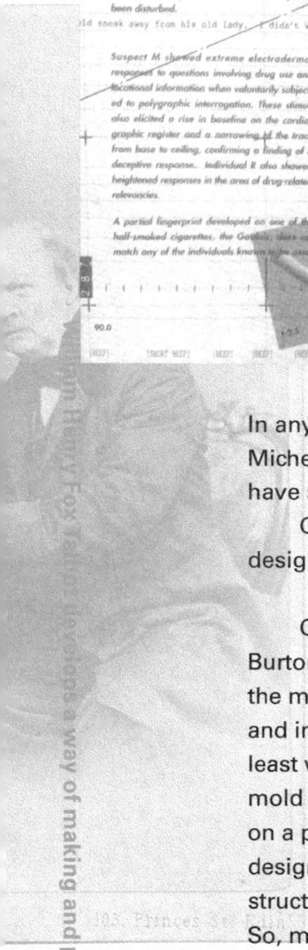

In any case, I slowly pulled away from the *Zone* project—though Michel and Jonathan remained close friends and interlocutors, and have so to this day—and I crossed back to the *October* milieu.

Geoff, how did design like Bruce's signify to you as a young designer at the time?

GK: In the late '80s, I got my first real design gig in Toronto with Burton Kramer, who's best known for designing the CBC logo. He's on the map along with older high modernists who were trained at Yale and in Switzerland. Bruce Mau, who was well known at that time (at least within Toronto design circles), was one of the first to break the mold of the high modernist "type and stripe" graphic design ideology on a professional level. It was a very exciting moment for graphic design, as it coincided with discussions of structuralism and post-structuralism, the free-floating signifier, notions of text and textuality. So, my small group of design friends didn't see a problem. In fact, we saw a promise in that what seemed otherwise locked in logics of hierarchies was suddenly available for reordering and for new ways of organizing information—leading to the construction of knowledge through a combination of images and texts on the printed page.

Of course, the shine eventually wore off when Mau became a champion of branding. Those marketing strategies don't fly in MFA design programs.

RC: What do you mean?

GK: They're understood as being in the service of industry and markets. Plus, as many MFA design programs moved away from marketing and branding to academically informed questions such as authorship, mastery versus anti-mastery, the status of the sign, we became very invested in formal strategies of layering. There was no one way to articulate a message, there were many; you just pile them all up and let the viewer pick a point of entry and find their own path to a new construction of a message.

HF: The early *Zone* publications were certainly very layered. But as a result they were sometimes rather opaque too. And soon that look congealed into a brand for *Zone*. In time *Zone* became a matter of books, a very important series . . .

SIRI: Okay, I found this on the web for a series of books. Check it out.

HF: Hah, that's beautiful. Thanks, Siri. Design has come "alive" with AI. My old qualms seem quaint given the new reality of Siri world.

Where were we? So far we've discussed the idea of design as text, and then the problem—for me anyway—of design as image, which can often harden into design as brand. My questioning of both was prompted by a further turn in the culture in the late '80s, when the AIDS epidemic began to rage. This attack on queer bodies in particular occurred in the midst of a pervasive attack on the body politic in general, indeed on almost any welfare provided by government. We have a term for it now—neoliberalism—but then it felt like pure malice and gross aggression. And in art, in culture at large, there was a turn away from the niceties of the text and the seductions of the image to the brute factuality of the body, to the damaged body as a way to figure a damaged body politic. Abjection as an (anti?) aesthetic and politic alike. (You can track this shift in the work of Cindy Sherman, Robert Gober, and many others.) That's what I meant by the "return of the real" in my book of that title from 1996: as a double tropism to a traumatic realism on the one hand and to a debilitated society on the other.

RC: How did you understand ACT UP's attempts to bridge the body and design?

HF: The artists involved in ACT UP were very adept not only at pointed signage but also at photogenic and mediagenic interventions. (The best review of this work remains a book that Douglas Crimp did with Thatcher Bailey called *AIDS Demo Graphics*.) And often those interventions put bodies on the line in direct ways, even as they also drew smartly on the techniques of performance art.

RC: Geoff, did the idea of the return of the real, the body in production, motivate your studies at all? I'm thinking about the structures of layering that you described, where the reader gets to choose her path and become the author, in a way, versus the need to assert that subjectivity has its own "body" or even a self. They seem radically at odds.

GK: This is an interesting question, not only because I can think of maybe three or four graphic designers who in the '90s turned to issues of the body. It cuts to the core of my interest in the question of graphic design pedagogy and disciplinarity. A "body" is produced by graphic design under the rubric of "design thinking"—it aids in the construction of the obedient subject, one whose patterns and desires are predictive, prescriptive, and financialized; a governable collective subject/consumer/body. This can be understood as an act of discipline and control exercised by the designer, who in effect stands in for the government under the logic of neoliberalism.

HF: Now that I think about it, part of my suspicion about design is that, historically, it has often tended to recoup artistic experiments for capitalist ends. The prime instance remains the repackaging of Bauhausian ideas by design innovators like Herbert Bayer and Moholy-Nagy for corporate America after World War II (for Walter Paepcke at the Container Corporation of America in particular). Did designers like Mau provide a similar service with postmodernist experiments in interdisciplinarity? Do your proponents of "layering"? This is too simplistic a claim, but still . . .

This suspicion runs deep in me. Although I was only a kid in the 1960s, I did experience, through my older siblings, the communitarian spirit of the era. To witness that '60s communitarianism transformed into '70s consumerism really troubled me even at the time. (The final episode of *Mad Men* captured this recuperation nicely when Don Draper is inspired by an EST retreat to craft the famous "collective" ad "I'd like to buy the world a Coke.")

GK: One of the things I'm hearing in this is an echo of Fred Turner's argument in *From Counterculture to Cyberculture* that the libertarian reactionary politics of today were already embedded in the commune of the '60s.

HF: I suppose so. But there is a more recent instance of design in service of the dark side, one that came in the 1990s, at the moment of the full dominance of neoliberalism. Remember, after 1989, "the new world order" proclaimed by the first Bush? There was also much talk, post-Wall, of "a new Europe," which required an extensive campaign of building and branding from a whole cadre of architects and designers. Along with new infrastructure, it also demanded a massive retooling of old industrial cities as new postindustrial tourist sites. The obvious instance is Bilbao, but many other places were refashioned in this way. The good leaders of such cities and regions thought they needed new entertainment centers, sports complexes, waterfront promenades, and, above all, iconic museums that could also function as media logos. Hence the profusion of architecture as spectacle and the rise of the starchitect. This is not to say that the results were all crap. Architects like Foster, Rogers, Piano, Koolhaas, and Herzog and de Meuron have produced very good buildings. But did they ever turn down a client, however nefarious, or a project, however problematic? Did they ever "just say no"? No. CCTV Headquarters is an extraordinary building, but only if you somehow bracket the client. And there are worse examples one could name.

At the time architects launched design arms within their offices; OMA, for example, seemed almost driven by AMO for a time. And the academy was brought in as well; consider how Koolhaas used his studios at Harvard for his projects on the city, the Pearl River Delta project, and study of the spatial logistics of shopping. I witnessed a similar development at Princeton: The architectural studio, which was supposed to be a place of critique, became a site of "research," which is to say, a lab for development. Super-important work was done at such places, but you get my drift.

Everybody was happy to see architecture and design re-centered, especially once critical figures like Liz Diller jumped onboard. I get it: Architects want to build, designers want to produce. But it all was floated, ideologically, on near nonsense. There was talk of "projective" architecture; "critical" practice was so last century. Most of the critical pieces collected in *Design and Crime* (2002) were written during this period.

RC: And you published the "ABCs of Contemporary Design" in 2002, in the 100th issue of *October*, the special edition on "obsolescence."

HF: Yes. Koolhaas republished "Junkspace" in that issue, and I published the "ABCs of Contemporary Design," a distillation of *Design and Crime*; it's my most caustic piece on design. *Design and Crime* plays, of course, on *Ornament and Crime* (1908) by Adolf Loos a century before. His critique of Jugendstil or Art Nouveau was that its emphasis on ornament was a criminal waste of labor. Just as importantly, though, Loos also argued that Art Nouveau, in its very attempt to provide a sanctuary for the bourgeois subject, created an aestheticist world that left no space for any subject to breathe. In "Style 1900" *everything* had become design. There was no *Spielraum*, as Karl Kraus called it, no room to move, to play, to live otherwise.

Kraus wrote that Loos had understood the difference between an urn and a urinal. That is, he provided an alternative both to Art Nouveau aesthetes, who wanted to treat the urinal as an urn, to prettify it, and to emergent functionalists, who wanted to turn the urn into a urinal, to make it nothing but use. (The artist Joe Scanlan offered a fitting update on the Kraus trope with his IKEA hack that showed how an IKEA bookcase could be turned into a coffin anywhere in the world "for under $399.")

For me the parallel was that in "Style 2000" everything had become design once again. The master term was no longer "text" or "culture" but "design." Everything seemed subject to it, from jeans to genes (this was the moment of the decoding of the genome), from places to people. The critical interdisciplinarity of the 1980s and '90s had turned into a bad design *Gesamtkunstwerk*, and architects like Koolhaas and designers like Mau were agents of this development. It's still with us. For my friends Beatriz Colomina and Mark Wigley, for example, design remains the dominant trope. "The constructed subject" of poststructuralist theory has become the designed subject of post critical practice.

Of course, this redesigning of the subject has precedents on the left too. Consider how communist designers like El Lissitzky and Gustav Klutsis believed that both subject and society could be totally remade, and consider how that refashioning could lead not only to rote rationalization but also to mass murder under Stalin (who had some of these figures killed too). People rightly bemoan this horror; meanwhile they are produced as a neoliberal construct, as human capital.

What was the reaction in your world to the predominance of architecture and design as branding?

GK: In order to consider a question like that, we'd have to zoom out a bit. I see throughout this chronology Hal Foster continually putting up guardrails for MFA students and the practice of graphic design in general—*Design and Crime* being just one example. A lot of us didn't listen or perhaps understand due to pure pragmatics, because the reality of contemporary life got in the way. People have to pay their bills, especially student loans. So a lot of people post-MFA went to work in advertising agencies. We were working in concert with your Koolhaases and Gehrys. Within an agency there was typically an architect on staff, and often we were working in an architectural decorated shed, for example Eric Owen Moss's Stealth building for Oglivy and Mather in Culver City.

HF: One thing that differentiates Koolhaas from the others is that he's not only super-smart but also cagily ambivalent. He has a Baudelairean way of celebrating and castigating modernity at one and the same time. Designers like Michael Rock attempt to hold to that ambivalent position too. I wonder whether you think they do so effectively.

GK: Ambivalence is not so interesting.

HF: Because it's a way to have it both ways?

GK: Yeah. Let me go back to this idea of guardrails and your question of, or your warning about, two postmodernisms. Interest in what you identify as a reactionary postmodernism continued well into the mid- to late-'90s in graphic design MFA programs. And I'd go so far as to say the continued interest is intentionally blinded; the blinkers are on, and the guardrails are blown by. Very often graphic designers in MFA programs are trying to sort out a relationship to their work that's not dependent on a client. Self-motivated works start to veer quickly into spaces of cultural production, and by extension in conversation with art making. And really the only way for designers to think through any theoretical position would be through images and making things that are based on relationships between typography and image. What I'm trying to say here is that graphic designers were still caught up in the language of postmodernism when that language moved on.

There was very little if any discourse around "late capitalism," as in Jameson, or "neoliberalism," as in David Harvey. There was a purposeful obtuseness in following a well-heeled commitment to reactionary forms of postmodernism.

RC: Geoff, you've been interested in the idea of self-theorization as a way in which design can structure itself as a discipline. But without a discourse around capitalism, can there be a coming to terms with what design is? It seems to me that knowing you're going to blow past the guardrails is a way of not really looking at the functions or repercussions of design as a discipline.

GK: Maybe this is me having it both ways? Design pedagogy has not really pushed itself hard enough to become disciplined. It continues to exist in a space between practice and discipline.

There's also a structural scenario to consider. Until just recently, there were no programs structured as histories of design, or a program of the theories of design. The initialization of a history and/or a theory of graphic design is an emerging phenomenon in graphic design pedagogy where students in programs—like those at Bard, say—can obtain PhDs in graphic design history. I see this as a watershed event. What happened before that was that almost everyone teaching graphic design was trained as a practicing graphic designer first and then found their way into adjunct teaching positions. Of course, there were tenured full-time graphic design professors, but it was the exception, not the rule.

HF: Is that a bad thing? Most of the PhD students in architectural history and theory at Princeton are also architects; they have a practical expertise that carries over into their thinking about architecture.

GK: This is true, Hal. I'd like to consider the Whitney ISP model for a moment. I've heard you describe the program as a triad composed of three threads: studio, criticism, curating. Looking forward, I think the triad suggests a model for the future of graphic design programs: a studio practice piece that runs in parallel with design history and theory, and a third piece that's curatorial.

HF: My comments have highlighted the recuperation of art by design. (Here's another old favorite I forgot to mention: Cubism "styled"—travestied—as Art Deco.) But that's a familiar story, with art positioned as the good object and design as the bad. (Some say I do the same thing with architecture—that I use it as a foil to set off art as somehow virtuous. Maybe so.)

Anyway, what about instances when this scenario is turned around or even reversed somehow? Consider the case of Richard Hamilton, who was also trained in design. Richard designed a stereo, he even designed a computer, and he adapted some Braun products as artworks of his own (he loved Dieter Rams). The Independent Group as a whole, guided by Reyner Banham in this respect, was also obsessed by American design and often made important art out of it. And then there's Pop, of course. In short, I wonder whether, against the usual story of the recuperation of art by design, there's another story to tell about designers who have inspired artists.

GK: Well, maybe one way to answer your question is through an observation. As I see it, within the studies of contemporary graphic design and its relationship to art-making, there seems to be an engagement with archives. A lot of students are turning to archives of graphic design practices (who knew there were such archives?) and various art practices including conceptual and process-driven art. On the art historical/theory side I'm seeing a renewed interest in the history of postmodernism! Some of this statement is influenced by my recent presence at Yale and the Beinecke Rare Book and Manuscript Library—students just go crazy when they're introduced to the Beinecke.

Their interests go beyond simply the holdings of the archive; they extend to the very status of the archive and how the archive can be recovered. There's a significant fascination in the history of images, the history of web, and how images circulate online, especially given that the Internet is now twenty-something years old. I see a lot of looking backwards now. I see a commitment from designers to history.

THE WAY YOU THINK ABOUT IT

GAIL SWANLUND

Driving north through the Central Valley of California en route to visit Zuzana and Rudy, I listen to a podcast, *The Jackie and Laurie Show.* The two comedians talk about writing and rewriting, structuring a set, the logistics of traveling and households, and performance. I'm struck by how much their process mirrors the graphic design process. Except the part about being on the road.

The pavement of Interstate 5 overlays desert and scrub grasslands and seasonal vernal pools, it cuts through orchards of pink and white flowering trees, runs alongside the aqueduct carrying water to Los Angeles, and past a feedlot crowded with thousands of standing cows. Weighty bovine fumes flood the car's cabin and linger for many miles. I drive past workers bent low picking strawberries and sliding their boxes of fruit down the row. Hand-painted campaign signs call for water. A red-tailed hawk pauses on a post to peer into the weeds of the ditch alongside the blacktop. Somewhere, maybe near Los Baños, I enter and drive through a gauzy cloud of vapor that hovers over and then reveals a fine trace of chartreuse-green shoots.

California can be a place of lightness and surprising subtlety. When compared with more northerly, midwestern states, seasonal changes are understated. To tune in, observe, and note the often delicate fluctuations calls for acclimating and recalibrating the senses. At the same time, the sunlight can sometimes feel like a weight that presses and burns, and may be unexpectedly dangerous. Potentiality is at once ferocious and ordinary. The earth can split open or wildfires may consume whole mountain ranges. Beyond California is the tremendous and wild ocean. The state is an edge, a cutoff. The furthermost.

Heading North, Los Angeles County, #1. Photograph by Rudy VanderLans

Sunspots

The Macintosh appeared in 1984, a buff-colored sturdy cube of plastic with a 512-pixel-wide screen and an attached blocky mouse and keyboard. "Welcome to Macintosh," the monochrome screen read. On start-up, the machine chimed, emitted smooth hums in tones, and asked for a boot disk. Holding down the mouse's button controlled a corresponding cursor on the screen that stood in for the table, or the desktop, upon which the Mac sat.

That year, in Oakland, California, Zuzana Licko began designing typefaces on the studio's recently acquired Mac; designing letterforms that were optimized for Macintosh viewing and ImageWriter printing, the best possible desktop publishing (DTP) printing available at that time. At the same time, Rudy VanderLans and a few friends launched an artist magazine named *Emigre*—for both Zuzana and Rudy *are* émigrés—which soon would feature Zuzana's low-resolution fonts. Rudy says of that moment, "The production was so different with these new tools. The known rules didn't make sense anymore. We questioned why we should do anything the way it had been done before then." After a few issues devoted to literature and popular culture, the magazine shifted course and became what we know it to be: a graphic designer's magazine about graphic design.

Emigre—the foundry and magazine[1]—is a project that transformed graphic designers' and readers' relationships to the profession, the discipline, and design education. It was an as-yet unheralded research forum as well as a place to read and formulate new ideas and ways of thinking about graphic design. Emigre was a portal into a curious world of graphic design that it reported, commented on, and influenced. The project identified a universe of unique critical (and playful!) thought and work that either wasn't on the radar of the graphic design establishment or had been dismissed. It embodied the pivot away from an authority held by "experts" and design educators. It sifted and in effect loosened notions of professional recognition, circumscribed taste, and universality. Emigre explored font design, typography, and graphic design, not as mediators of consumerism and advertising, but as complex and raucous fields of study and criticism. The Emigre project crystalized as an accessible primary site for inventive raw material, research, and creative energy.

Fermented Loquats

Zuzana and Rudy's home is in Berkeley, California, and it's warmhearted and welcoming. It's fantastic to see them again, and we spend a little time filling each other in on what's been happening. Their home-based twin studios' current projects-at-large include, among others: textile design, a photo book chronicling

1. "Emigre" (roman, not italicized) refers to the whole, intertwined endeavor of Emigre: type foundry, design studio, publisher, and distributor. When italicized, Emigre's magazine, *Emigre*, is implied.

Englishman Francis Pettit Smith and Swedish-American John Ericsson independently develop propellers with blades for ships

their travels on California's occasional and obscure byways, pattern font animations, recipe writing and testing for "Chowdown," the next type specimen catalog-as-cookbook,[2] and sculptural, resonant wheel-thrown ceramics. We talk about music and musicians who collaborated with Emigre, and look at the work of two designers they recently met, who teach graphic design classes fostering equity and access. Later, in the glassy winter dusk, the three of us examine the ornamented gate Zuzana designed to dissuade deer from spending time in the yard. She tells me an antlered stag likes to indulge in fermented loquats from the backyard fruit tree.

Periodical Stacks

My roommate, Diane Hellekson, introduced me to *Emigre*. The two of us pieced our rent together by waitressing at bars, cafes, and campus clubs, and freelancing at an array of Twin Cities magazines that ranged from high to low, commercial to countercultural and underground.

A fringe benefit of our involvement with publishing was bringing home bundles of discarded magazines. Sandwiched into the jumble of periodicals on our coffee table was an early issue of *Emigre*. I wanted to see more, to join this movement or whatever it was. I looked through the magazine to see if I could figure out where I could pick up another issue.

A soft summery evening, after handing off the disks of completed layouts for *Utne Reader*,[3] I biked across the park to the Walker Art Center, where I found the most recent issue of *Emigre*. The clerk slipped the magazine into a tall flat bag, and with two hands I carried it out to my bike and strapped it to the rack for the ride back to St. Paul along the Mississippi. I could hardly wait to see what the pages held. If there was an instant when the notion to study graphic design became evident for me, it was then, biking along through the dark with hard pings of june bugs glancing off my bare arms.

School Labs and Studio Culture

Elsewhere, students brought Emigre into their studios and Emigre brought the schools into the pages of the magazine. *Emigre* reported on what was happening in and around design schools—both graduate and undergraduate programs—and engaged in the conversations around the philosophical and theoretical shift that was happening in graphic design education. The project's significance for students, educators, and graphic design pedagogy was colossal; emerging critical conversation around graphic design was made *visual*. No other design resource at the time was as graphic or vivid. Emigre invited and entertained current discussions around graphic design, about form and media, content, language, and theory. And it wasn't even that Emigre functioned as an interpreter

2. *Chowdown* is an Emigre type specimen catalog that is also a cookbook, featuring twenty-one recipes by Zuzana Licko and showcasing Emigre library's picture font Chowdown by Tucker Nichols.

or mediator of contemporary design discourse; it was research, a laboratory. It was an awareness of graphic design as an immensity, as a discipline, beyond its professional or commercial establishment. That the newness of the means of digital production in tandem with authoring one's own content and work as just matter-of-fact was remarkable; content typically originated with and was in service to a client. Taken altogether, Emigre was a powerful, freeing, and bighearted influence.

Rudy's interviews were honest, candid; conversations unspooled organically and dipped into the philosophical as well as the personal, and were very much of the moment. The words were filtered, connotatively mediated by Emigre's typefaces (which are neither neutral nor impartial), and weighed and shaped on the page. Put together, the words and the form posed questions about structure, fixity, legibility, and objecthood. Words and content were not always in service to the ostensible linear transmission of a message, and the designers' presence and their very close read were palpable. There was a magnificence in the space between the words and the form.

Emigre reported on the visual and conceptual form and theory-driven work being made in schools—like Cranbrook and CalArts, Old Dominion, North Carolina State, Minneapolis College

3. At this moment, the means of graphic design layout resided in simultaneous and transitional methods. Traditional paste-up was necessarily in use alongside digital layout; offset printers were not yet converting to digital means, and photographic plates were still made from physical layouts.

The *Utne Reader* was produced on a Mac. The layouts were typeset and designed onscreen and backed up onto floppy disks that would be delivered to a service vendor who would output the files onto photographic paper. The layout galleys were waxed and burnished onto preprinted, non-repro, blue-lined boards. At *Artpaper*, where I freelanced at the same time, often on the same day, the galleys were set on a PC. Specifications for headlines, body text, captions, and column widths were coded by hand. Additional programming was required to boldface, condense, or italicize the two resident typefaces. Galleys were printed out on a laser printer in tiles, waxed, and pieced together on boards.

4. Graphic designer, writer, and educator Denise Gonzales Crisp first encountered *Emigre* in the computer lab where she was taking an introduction to the Macintosh course in 1985. "There was no turning back once I saw the pages of *Emigre*. It was a laboratory. The pages presented research, raw material, experiments." Later, when she was a frequent contributor to *Emigre*, her early experimentation with writing forms carried through in writing about Rick Valicenti and his studio Thirst. She riffed and improvised in multiple channels, even all at once: speculative fiction as journalism as critical design literature. See Denise Gonzales Crisp, "Speculations: A Book Review Gone Awry, a Search for Meaning, Some Letters, RuPaul, and Other Transformations (a response to current work by THIRST—in three parts)," *Emigre* 46 (1998): 42.

5. I met Rudy for the first time in 1992 as a student at CalArts when he gave a talk and workshop. When we spoke together about this essay, he told me Emigre's first school presentation was in 1987 when Katherine McCoy invited the couple to give a talk and meet with Cranbrook students who were on a field trip through California. "For the lecture, Zuzana pulled together some of her texts and writings on process that she had been accumulating. We used handmade slides made with Linotype film. This was one of our first lectures."

of Art and Design, Yale, and University of Texas at Austin, as well as others. These areas of research contemplated and in effect expanded understandings of graphic design as a discipline and a field. The magazine transformed the notion of where and how graphic designers could situate their work and practice in a cultural context. Entire issues were devoted to conceptual and theory-driven form-making methodologies, processes, and projects happening at schools. "Special Exchange," issue 10, was devoted to collaborative exchanges between Cranbrook designers in the US and Studio Dumbar and Hard Werken in Holland, investigating the connection between Dutch and American design. Issue 11 featured CalArts MFAs' illustrative folios. Rudy and Zuzana visited Cranbrook for issue 19, and looked at the program in "Starting from Zero," an interview punctuated with text-based descriptions of the scene like "!Loud dog bark!" and "baby cries." Issue 21, "Fresh Faces," was turned over to CalArts faculty member Jeffery Keedy, and the school's graphic design MFAs and BFAs wrote and designed the features and created an abundance of boisterous typefaces and illustrations for the issue. These issues were high-spirited reports on what was happening in design education and theory in Southern California and just outside Detroit. "Teach," issue 22, was dedicated to British designer and educator Nick Bell's work and teaching in London. To see design education reflected in print revealed a shift in the way graphic design was being taught and practiced, framed within a lively new set of ideas and criteria.

While arguments concerning legibility—of typefaces and typography—brewed in (some) professional circles, students plumbed the conceptual, expressive form and theory of language, structure, and authoring potential that Emigre embodied.[4] Rudy and Zuzana visited schools,[5] gave workshops, and talked with students about their work. They invited students and educators to publish their writing and design, and adopted several typefaces from students and educators alike into their font library. As producers of content, graphic design students didn't question their agency—to write and then design what they wrote for *Emigre*. Later, these readers/designers/writers created new programs, launched new endeavors, invented places for themselves and their work, and effectively compelled the profession to evolve, expand, and diversify. And for those who went on to become educators and program directors, the ethos and practices influenced by involvement with Emigre were brought into curriculums and classrooms.

Emigre's nonhierarchical, participatory stance wasn't a deliberate relocation of expertise—of professionals and design educators—but it did express and register the redirection of the practice away from "expert" oversight. As the conversations evolved and elaborated, Emigre's editorial inclusiveness played a big role in how graphic designers and students saw themselves,[6] and how the vocation defined and identified graphic design and its function in the field's diverse and expanding contexts and mediums.

Prior to the Internet, very few periodicals carried writing and critical literature about graphic design.[7] For many of us, stumbling on anything about design was dumb luck.[8] Graphic design literature was limited to whatever was carried in college libraries[9] or small bookstores.[10] And critical literature on graphic design, or scholarly research published in peer-reviewed journals like *Visible Language* and *Design Issues*, was read only by a small group of people. Rudy says, "At the time, design criticism wasn't really popular with design practitioners. It was a small group of academics, teachers, critics, and some grad students that saw the value of critical writing on design." He goes on to say, "It always was difficult to find writers. You had to keep your finger on the pulse. People like Lorraine Wild would deliver lectures that were written down word for word, so I would ask to publish them so more people would have access to her ideas and words."[11]

Emigre was one of the first forums for direct and straightforward philosophical conversations about unconventional and theory-driven form, and the role of graphic design—and design education—in a cultural, political, and speculative context.[12] For many readers, critical writers like Kenneth FitzGerald, Jeffery Keedy, Lorraine Wild, and Andrew Blauvelt were encountered first in its pages. Rudy says, "We were learning and educating ourselves. In *Emigre* 15, Ellen [Lupton] and Abbot [Miller] wrote about deconstruction in their essay 'Type Writing: Structuralism and Typography.' I had never encountered writing or discussion about type in that way." *Emigre*'s congenial editorial style and curiosity also personalized and opened up a world of critical discussion, although it's meaningful to note that most of the writers were graphic design insiders: practitioners and educators.[13]

6. *Output* was a student-initiated magazine that originated at Cranbrook Academy of Art and "traveled" to other graduate graphic design programs around the US, with different institutions' programs writing, designing, and publishing each issue. The magazine sparked the "Cult of the Ugly" essay in *Eye* magazine (1992). Attention from *Eye* marked a significant moment for students.

7. Public libraries and big chain bookstores tended to carry the most ubiquitous trade magazines like *Print* and *Communication Arts*, whose key focus was the profession and industry. *U&lc*, *I.D.*, and *Graphis* were fairly easy to locate. Harder to come by, even at the most eclectic newsstands (for there was a magazine for every enthusiast), were *Visible Language* and *Blueprint*. Rudy was familiar with the Rotterdam magazine *Hard Werken*, which made its way to the US via Cranbrook designers who had gone to work at Studio Dumbar. Although not a design magazine it had a huge influence on young designers including Rudy. There were others—*Adbusters* for example—but really, it was slim pickings. Information was shared by word of mouth. A little later, *Eye*, *FUSE*, and *Plazm* were very welcome additions.

8. Herbert Spencer's *The Liberated Page: An Anthology of Major Typographic Experiments of This Century as Recorded in "Typographica" Magazine* was an out-of-the-blue find in the art section of an independent bookstore, but *Typographica* wasn't readily available, at least not where I lived.

Like Breathing

While it's a matter of course for students and designers now, the notion that digital technology made possible an individual's control over production—and voice—was profound. The clunkiness of the equipment was—in retrospect—undeniable, the range of available typefaces was limited, and print output was coarse and letterforms were jagged. But the ability to do and see and have output in hand (just about) instantaneously made everything a little wild and loose. Outcomes held unspecified significance; the thinking and processes were the most fascinating part of the activity of making, and the edges of potentiality did not find solid footing.

Abundant iteration was as simple as saving a new file on a floppy disk. Not needing to wait for the typesetter to set the type and output galleys made for a more direct conversation with the content. But designing digitally did not make anything speedier. There were more skills to master and the computers were sluggish. Software frequently crashed mid-project. Many students can attest to spending more than a few nights napping on MacLab floors, waiting for the computer to complete an operation or render even a simple animation. But anyone with access to a computer (or who *owned* one!) and the software could design graphics and typefaces. It was heady and powerful.

Independant, Self-Standing

A "serious fanzine", *Emigre* magnetized enthusiasts: graphic design practitioners, type designers, students, devotees of counter-cultural and underground publications, writers, and critics.

9. Book-wise, Philip Meggs's *History of Graphic Design* was important, but the three books everyone walked around with—held close to heart—that showed contemporary, noncommercial design and discourse were Rick Poynor's *The Graphic Edge* (Booth-Clibborn, 1993) and *Typography Now* (Internos, 1991), and Hugh Aldersey-Williams's *Cranbrook Design: The New Discourse* (Rizzoli, 1990).

Four years after the introduction of the Macintosh, the Walker Art Center's *Graphic Design in America: A Visual Language History* was the first large-scale museum exhibition devoted to a survey of American graphic design. To say it was astonishing to see all that work—and in a museum!—is an understatement. Along with the three influential books noted above, this exhibition's catalog was a prized resource for students.

10. In the summer of 1985, graphic designer and educator Caryn Aono bought the first three issues of *Emigre* from a long-gone art bookstore on LaBrea Avenue in Los Angeles. "Jeff [Keedy] and I couldn't believe what we were seeing, and I think Jeff called Rudy soon after. You could order galleys of type from Zuzana back then!"

11. Rudy added, "At the time, we could only offer a $250 honorarium or a trade with typefaces. We rolled with the punches; there was no budget."

12. In Minneapolis, the Walker Art Center Design Curator Mildred Friedman edited *Design Quarterly*, the first design journal to come out of a major museum, and advocated for "'graphic design' as a major discipline." Especially relevant to this discussion is *Design Quarterly 66/67: Design and the Computer* (1966), where the idea of using the computer as a design tool was discussed for the first time in a national design journal. In 1986, *Design Quarterly* 133 carried April Greiman's legendary fold-out Apple Macintosh poster utilizing MacDraw.

The whole endeavor of Emigre really was invented on the fly, figuring things out as it happened. Independent, or "self-standing," comes closest to describing an undertaking that required such sustained, and muscular, intellectual care. Offset printing was jobbed out, but Rudy and Zuzana assumed the work and responsibilities of all the pre-press production details. Publishing and running a foundry meant doing the writing and proofreading, photography, illustrations, typeface design, typesetting, typography, graphic design, proofing, promotion, the whole of the activities of a mailroom, sales, and distribution, all on a tiny budget.

Distribution of the magazine around the San Francisco Bay Area was done in person and on foot. Rudy commented, "I'd bring as many copies as I could carry on BART and visit bookstores where I'd try to sell the magazine directly. This was an uphill battle because stores usually get their magazines from distributors. Stores can't deal with every single publisher. But over time we were able to find quite a few stores who were willing to deal directly. Of course everything was on consignment so it was quite an ordeal to get paid."

Emigre's surprisingly small staff included guest editors and designers, and two long-term associates: Tim Starback, who managed sales and distribution, and bicycled daily the twelve miles round trip to the Emigre studio in Sacramento; and Alice Polesky, who, Rudy notes, "was a no-BS copy editor. If she didn't understand something, she'd say, 'Rewrite.' Her eye on the texts helped to make the writing and ideas clearer."

DIY countercultural publications and zines from the 1960s, '70s, and '80s[14]—underground comix and punk-rock fanzines—might feel like incongruous peers of a design-oriented publication and type foundry, but they share a spirit of intrepid daring and independence from the authority of recognized experts and commonly held ideas of mastery. While punk was, among other things, a rejection of conventions and expertise, Emigre perhaps didn't set out to (I don't think) challenge or reassess established notions of the profession. Instead, it may be more true to describe the impulse as a singular, irrepressible project that heeded Emigre's diverse interests and fascinations.

13. Edited by Michael Bierut, William Drenttel, and Steven Heller, *Looking Closer: Critical Writings on Graphic Design* (Allworth Press, 1994) was (I think) the first anthology to address practitioners. Reviewing the anthology in *Eye* (1995), Teal Triggs points out that many of the essays were written by practitioners. Of graphic design critical literature, she writes, "[Steven] Heller probes for an acceptable definition of graphic design criticism, explaining that it is still in its early developmental stages and that the 'rough edges have not been smoothed out.'"

14. Rudy writes in *Emigre* of how punk zines and publications like *RAW* were very influential, both personally and creatively. And in the case of a publication like *RAW*, Rudy said, "What we really wanted to know was, how did they get their work out into the world and make it work out financially? What were the nuts and bolts of such an endeavor? How do you sign a contract, how do you distribute, etc.? How does design plus business work?"

While the magazine wasn't circulated in large numbers, it was widely distributed around the globe—you could find it in Hong Kong, in several cities in Belgium, Canada, and Australia, in Düsseldorf, in London, and in Tokyo. Like a vibration in response to an Emigre bat-signal sent out into the universe, letters and packages arrived at the studio, sharing self-published zines, typeface designs, illustrations, and design samples. Reporting from afar, these correspondences gave collective dimension, voice, and substance to what was happening in graphic design on yet another, very self-selected, individual level.

Frames

"Emigre" in name supposes that one hails from another land and, accordingly, sees from a fresh perspective or frame of reference. One could argue that access to everything via the Internet has flattened distinctive regional qualities, but place does imbue an indefinable attitude or essence. An undeniable West Coast vibe ran through Emigre—a certain kind of receptiveness to spontaneity and the experiential. At the time, the graphic design establishment typically lionized work from primarily East Coast studios. Edward Fella once told me that despite an established thirty-year career as a professional graphic designer in Detroit, his parallel body of experimental work was not widely known or seen before Lorraine Wild profiled Ed and his work and he was interviewed by Jeffery Keedy in *Emigre*.[15] With that issue, Ed's work and this discussion of design were *in* the world in a way it might not have been if they had been published in *Print* or *Communication Arts*.[16]

From the start, this engaged and inquiring audience made itself known, too, by the stream of in-person treks to visit the Emigre studio. Rudy says, "We were meeting so many people. People stopped by our studio in Berkeley to see the computer, they wanted to share information and talk about it with us." From all over the world people traveled to Berkeley and dropped in at their studio. Carloads

Bakewell, F. P. 1

15. Lorraine Wild, "Notes on Edward Fella: Design in a Bordertown," and Jeffery Keedy, "A Conversation with Edward Fella," were both published in *Emigre* 17 (1990).

16. While readers like me did look at the work featured in *Print* and *Communication Arts*, we understood that these magazines recognized the advertising and commercial graphic design profession establishment. As evidenced in letters to the editor, *Emigre*'s readers and typeface users were curious about and participated in conversations around the kind of work and critique that were located beyond prevailing notions of what "graphic design" meant. A very engaged, self-identified community, they were interested and sympathetic to work that happened outside the spotlight and authority of the professional magazines.

of Cranbrook and CalArts graphic design educators and students road-tripped from Michigan and Los Angeles to visit and talk and see what was happening. Rudy continues, "We also traveled a lot to do lectures and workshops and visited studios. Most of our contributors to *Emigre* came from these personal contacts. We also found a number of writers through the magazine's 'Letters to the Editor' section. That's how I found people like Kenneth FitzGerald, David Cabianca, and David Barringer."

Plainness

The first issue of my new subscription was delivered to me by mail to my home in Saint Paul. Returning from waitressing the breakfast shift, I found the magazine's slim cardboard mailing box stood up against the doorjamb on the hard-packed snow. Upstairs, I yanked off my boots and cleared a spot on the kitchen table. The crisp, cold publication slid out of the sleeve with a soft hiss. First, I held it to my nose to sniff the oily printer ink, then I sat down and opened to the first page. The magazine was so big I could set my forearms on a spread, and I had to bend in to examine every detail, to read blocks of sometimes teeny type. In these pages, I saw Zuzana's typefaces in performance; the issue's content percolated through her work. Rudy interviewed and showed the work of designers I hadn't heard of, who were handling typography like sculptors and lavishing attention on words and language like poets. It's decidedly unsophisticated to confess wonderment, but discovering the community and camaraderie that *Emigre* inspired was meaningful for me. The texts on the pages bloomed, and the writing took on myriad forms—conversations and short stories, criticism and essays, the explanatory and illustrative, natural history and historical accounts, captioning, manifestos, and letters and meditations. Before the Internet made it possible to see all kinds of work, *Emigre* was a place where one could see new work, read the words of designers from all over the world.

The beauty and plainness of being a working graphic designer was something I understood and was proud of, embodying professional service competence, arranging words and images anonymously behind the scenes. It was solid, quantifiable work that paid (some of) the rent. But in an interview conducted by Rudy, I read that Allen Hori spoke of mystery and narrative history, of picking apart the petals of a tulip—as metaphor and compositional apparatus.[17] This for me was revelatory. Allen's words, nuance, and work upended and unfastened my notions of graphic design's value and significance, and as activism. A tangible or recognized outcome, or even a transmission of succinct information, needn't be the objective of graphic design. Instead, it was to throw oneself into work that knowingly departed from notions of a quick read, economy of message, or, as architectural historian Gabrielle Esperdy writes, "a commitment to a known but mutable purpose and an unknown and frequently ineffable outcome."[18]

17. Rudy VanderLans, "Expatriates," *Emigre* 20 (1991).

18. Gabrielle Esperdy, "A Leap of Faith," *Theoretical Editions for Now, DesignInquiry Futurespective* 5 (2019).

Scotsman Alexander Bain invents a primitive fax machine

Serials and Intervals

A magazine, as a multi-paged, sequential, serial, and printed object, is a natural format for graphic designers. It seems obvious to say that *Emigre* was a magazine that behaved like a magazine, but it did: In its "pageness"[19] and materiality, *Emigre*'s spreads were carefully designed works of ink on paper. While a magazine is a practical medium for holding all kinds of content, it's also a conceptual space or performance, and sometime during and over the span of two decades, the form became the *event* that is *Emigre*. The graphic form itself always was interesting, but became more so once the Internet flourished and became routine. With design having entered into a state of *post-objectness*, does a printed object become romanticized or fetishized? Or does it become a place? Or is it an intriguing form with familiar limitations but conceptual opportunities?

The ordinariness and the affordability of magazines represented an accessibility that professional graphic design conferences did not. Conference attendance fees were out of reach for most students, educators, freelancers, and tiny studios. Many students perceived the professional conferences and standard-bearer organizations as exclusionary, promoting a dated and privileged definition of graphic design. Conferences were renowned for creepy hotel venues and often creepier networking, a one-way speaker-to-audience relationship. Magazines provided a passionate alternative venue, an intimate, garage-band-like countercultural platform, and, like *Emigre*, directly shared information and invited participation. It's significant to say that at that moment, there really weren't that many places for designers to engage in this kind of exchange.[20]

Time—lulls, and even seasons—is a built-in and undeniable part of print publication. Sixty-nine issues of *Emigre* were published, culminating with the book, *No. 70, The Look Back Issue*. Evenly spaced out over twenty-five years, the publication of the magazine corresponds to an experience of and *with* time, a singular and sustained attention, of endings and closings.

19. "Pages like posters," Rudy says, referring to *Emigre*'s newspaper-sized page size. The literal expanse of the spreads was an homage to graphic design publications *U&lc* and *Hard Werken*, two major influences for *Emigre*. On newsstands, *Emigre* was tallest, usually occupying a place on the top row. Once, when making the rounds of bookstores to see how the magazine was selling, Rudy said he was exhilarated to see that the magazine appeared to be sold out at one particular store. As it turned out, the shop's two issues were hidden behind the oversized *Interview* magazine. So he rearranged them.

20. Before IT help desks and online user forums, periodicals were one of the only venues to share specific tech information.

The relative agility of magazine publishing made for the most up-to-date content, while seriality established a kind of in-time narrative continuity and community through regular contributors and letters to the editor. Conversations in *Emigre*'s "Letters to the Editor" could take place over months, the literal machinery of printing inserting a compulsory "breather" between issues.

The activity of writing, printing, folding, and mailing (or faxing) acknowledged a distinct pause and weightiness. Mailing a letter is distinctly different from hitting "send." It's a long-distance relationship and it is a sincerely material matter. Letters to *Emigre* described and reflected the expanding edges of what was designated "graphic design," as the discussions concurrently surfaced and materialized. The readers became the writers, and the writers, by virtue of being fiercely engaged in graphic design in a multifaceted way, as serious contributors who responded to what was happening in the field, set in motion peer-to-peer conversations and reciprocated. Letters functioned as temperature-takers of the moment's complex and cacophonous ecosystem.

Writers mailed lengthy criticism and positions, and were provocative in the best sense; while other missives were fervent love letters. The letters demonstrated the value of facilitating a platform where individuals could carry on conversations with one another, where communities emerged and became visible, and ideas and critiques matured and fledged. Readers wrote in to effectively hang out, to just say hello. The editors' inclusivity and graciousness were a standing invitation for participation, as if saying, "Come on in, we're open."

The "Letters to the Editor" page was also an important site for unfolding critical discourse, analysis, and discussion. As makers and thinkers, attention, ambition, and regard are typically assessed and weighed by output and results, but Emigre's democratic and steadfastly egalitarian approach of nonhierarchical inclusiveness didn't distinguish the self-taught from the formally educated, or the student from the master.

The Way You Think About It

"The way you think about it is how it should be made." Zuzana says that she started writing to explain her process and her thoughts about type design. "People were always asking, 'How do you make your typefaces?' Since we were keeping track of everything we were doing and making, recording as we went along, it was just a matter of putting the process into words." Her critical commentary—how a typeface's form and attitude comment on written language—and the technical information about design were frank and poetic; her explanations and how-tos, precise and straightforward. She writes with humor and warmth, deploying a precise knowledge of technology in its historical context and an understanding of the activity of reading. With regard to the conversion from analogue to digital, she has written, "As well as respecting the nuances of our traditional typefaces and their evolution in conjunction to reading habits, the forms of computer fonts must result as an integral part of the digital process, not in spite of it."[21] For graphic designers and students designing typefaces at that time, this was a noteworthy distinction. It was a prompt for not only revealing materiality or a letterform's bones and connective tissue or its means of production, but being receptive and sensitive to context and histories.

Zuzana says that without the computer, she wouldn't have made her typefaces. "The software had a preview that made it possible to view, in real time, juxtapositions, rotations, connections, and alterations. Changes are seen in real time and I can react to what I see." Her typefaces, while sympathetic to the materiality and history of letterforms, turned upside down assumptions about form and style, and they manifested new potentials of digital media. The designs could be startling fantasias or inquisitive narratives. They could be technology-driven or drawn from overlooked history, a meditation on a historical form or patterned from parts and components. For students who were experimenting with type design software, Zuzana's writings on typeface concept and formal specs were very influential and instructive. Across the country, Emigre's type specimen posters were carefully pinned up in school studios, with students ensuring there were no marring pin holes.

Online

Emigre was the first type foundry to have an automated online ordering system. According to longtime Emigre collaborator Tim Starback, "We were sending a lot of overnight packages all over the country. Everyone needed the fonts ASAP, and it seemed like the next morning by 10:30 a.m. was still too long to wait. AOL was a thing (no Internet yet), so many people had modems to connect to AOL. My best guess is that we just had a number of customers requesting to download, so we started looking around. Modem-to-modem was possible but way too fiddly for almost everyone. The next best was a bulletin-board system called 'FirstClass' that if you got the client software it was relatively easy to connect and had a nice GUI. We would take the orders on the phone, give them an id/pw, and move the font files into their account manually. Because the download could take up to one hour, we had a limit of the number of customers who could log in at any one time. I think we eventually had between four and six modem/phone lines. We eventually added a 56K 'digital' connection to the Internet, which allowed customers all over the world to connect without long-distance-call rates. Eventually we figured out how to get the web server to talk to the database and then authorize a credit card (still done with a dial-up modem). At that point, we had an automated system that could process orders and give the customer access to the font automatically. All the tech stuff was new to everyone, so we were all learning together."

The first website was designed by Zuzana. She explained in an email, "It was hand coded in HTML, by me in 1995, with design

21. Zuzana Licko and Rudy VanderLans, *Digital Fonts*, Emigre type specimen booklet, 2016, 2.

input from Rudy. Tim [Starback] orchestrated the e-commerce, and provided the links for connecting to our 4D database. It was announced on the NotCaslon poster, October 1, 1995, and emigre.com went live that fall." Clicking through the initial site on the Internet archive WayBackMachine is like walking through a neighborhood that you used to know so well—seeing landmarks that resonate from long ago like "Fax order form," "Netscape," and "Fonts on Disc."

Getting on the Internet and looking around back then felt like dog-paddling along the surface, then abruptly jackknifing into a deep, very dark, and enveloping water. The Internet wasn't graphic just yet; only murmuring, in an indescribable zone of possibilities and potentialities waiting to happen.

Through the Mail

Emigre type specimen catalogs arrive in my mailbox every so often. Like an unexpected friendly letter from a pal, the booklets are surprises. Or gifts. Not mere introductions or samplers, each of these saddle-stitched booklets features a typeface or type family from the "Emigre Type Library"—or pattern font, pictograms, dingbats, or "FellaParts." Each typeface is put through a rigorous workout to showcase its range, temperament, and attributes—via short stories, literature, tech notes, or fantastical musings and illustrations.

Functioning both as practical type specimens—as resources and reference for type designers, with specifics and descriptions, illustrative and notional—and as serious investigations, the booklets do have a pragmatic job to do as well. They're catalogs. But at the same time, they're assays and testings, or poetic bodies and conceptual performances. Really, the booklets are as much a spectacle as type specimen—for example, *Nine Literary Types* opens with the words, "Performing Classic California Texts."

Putting together "Historia," Rudy traveled the state of California to the sites of various historical battles between the US and Mexico, photographing panoramas of each location. With multilayered historical texts, essays, travelogue, and designed in a way that alludes to the fruit crate and blinding sunshine of California, the Historia specimen is a tour de force of sumptuous visual form, multi layered and treated typography, and compelling content and concept.

My collection of the booklets is essentially a mixtape of lush singles gathered over a long while.

New Entry

Before search engines, everyone had a different relationship with finding out about things. I researched graduate schools in the pages of *Emigre*, and was right away drawn to CalArts. In the picture of CalArts that materialized, graphic design proposed a way of being in the world that could be made into whatever you wanted it to be, intellectually, critically, and/or formally. Within months, I drove across the plains and through the mountains, to study at CalArts.

After graduate school, I moved to Sacramento to work with Emigre, who had moved their studio there in 1991. I'd never been

Heading North, Los Angeles County, #2.
Photograph by Rudy VanderLans

to Sacramento and drove past the city for nearly an hour before it dawned on me that my exit was somewhere near where Interstate 5 bridged over a wide tree-lined river, about fifty miles or so behind me. The next morning, I walked under enormous shade trees and through one of the city's proper rose gardens to Emigre's studio.

At Emigre, *work* was practiced as generative and convivial, and the work of the studio included daily activities like making dinner together, taking walks and hikes, and listening to music. This gave shape to my notion of what could be called a creative life. My time at Emigre was as much a restorative postgraduate mentorship as a loose guide for inventive living. It's the philosophical core of Emigre-ness that surfaces in the ways I construct educational experiences and, by extension, think about creative endeavor for myself, in a flock of different contexts.

Every morning at 10 a.m., Zuzana or Rudy would bring a tray of coffee and a slice of cake around to each of us in turn.[22] We received the offerings with some ceremony and the knowledge that this was truly unlike any other workplace; this was what an interconnected and creative life felt like.

Pocket-Sized

With Issue 64, "RANT," *Emigre* came down to just the words—the conversations around graphic design criticism. Issue 64's trade-paperback-sized back cover reads, "RANT also signals another transition in the format of *Emigre*, away from its recent incarnation as an aural/visual showcase magazine toward a return-to-roots series of 'pocket books' focusing on critical writing about the state

22. Zuzana Licko, "Apple Chunk Snack Cake," *Chowdown*, Emigre type specimen booklet, 2020, 52–53.

of graphic design." Issue 69, titled "The End," closes the magazine project, and constitutes undeniable substance.

In 2019, every issue of *Emigre* was digitally photographed and now lives both virtually and physically at San Francisco's Letterform Archive. The digital archive is searchable, downloadable, and their physical archive welcomes visitors and researchers to visit—a veritable public library of graphic design. It's beautifully fitting that Letterforum Archive is home to the entirety of *Emigre*. The archive's mission, "inspiration, education, publishing, and community," mirrors the magazine's ebullient inquiry and attention to graphic design, typography, history, criticism, and literature, and, most of all, graphic designers themselves. *Emigre* modeled a way where everyone could make graphic design be the *everything* and the *anything* each and every one of us wanted it to be.

•

Billions of migrating painted lady butterflies follow faint north-by-northwest breezes through a once-wild canyon where I live in Los Angeles. The canyon's creek bed now is a street, houses notched into its walls. Light is made golden by an overhead river of pale orange wings with tiny blue eyespots. Very small butterfly shadows cross the patio and turn up walls, generally in one direction; individual eccentric lines of travel converge and separate.

Thank you dearly: Denise Gonzales Crisp, Sean Dungan, Geoff Kaplan, Ian Lynam, Tim Starback, and especially Rudy VanderLans and Zuzana Licko.

THE DIFFERENCE IT MAKES WHO IS SPEAKING: AN AUTOETHNOGRAPHY OF MINOR LITERATURE IN GRAPHIC DESIGN AT THE YALE SCHOOL OF ART

AUDREY G. BENNETT

I want to begin my essay with a bit about my cultural background. I am a naturalized American graphic design scholar of Afro-Caribbean descent. I hail from the Bahamas, where I lived for the first three years of my life, before moving to my parents' birthplace of Jamaica. After three years there, my family migrated to the United States. I grew up in northern New Jersey with a single mom who cooked Caribbean food, played reggae music every Saturday morning, and alternated between speaking Jamaican patois and standard English. At the predominantly black elementary and secondary schools that I attended, my teachers spoke standard English while many of my peers spoke Ebonics.

Myself, I spoke Nerd. Graduating valedictorian from high school, I traveled further north to pursue a bachelor of arts degree at Dartmouth College, which afforded me a unique opportunity to study abroad in Querétaro, Mexico. After college, in the early 1990s, I worked as a legal assistant in New York City while simultaneously deferring acceptance at the Rhode Island School of Design. After a conversation with the late African-American designer Sylvia Harris, I opted instead to attend Yale as one of six students in a three-year program in graphic design (the standard two-year program plus a "preliminary year" for those without a BFA) and the only Black student in my cohort during the first year. The overwhelming whiteness of the program and community did not discourage me; on the contrary, I found myself all the more drawn to the power of images and words, and the idea that culture can be an analytical lens through which we see layers of meaning—and that who speaks is just as important as what is said.

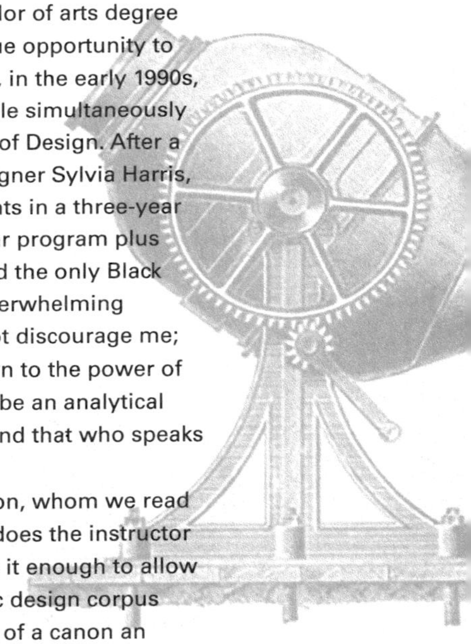

In design pedagogy, then, as in any education, whom we read is always a question of power and agency. Who does the instructor empower to speak through required readings? Is it enough to allow the student to pick and choose within the graphic design corpus to diversify the conversation? Or is the very idea of a canon an extension of white dominance? Are we using our power as faculty to its fullest potential to diversify design pedagogy? Does our design curriculum have an inclusive scaffolding of affordances in the struggle against oppression and social injustice? As students, are we fearlessly attempting to go where no *other* has gone before—whether it pleases our instructors or not?

I decided to approach those questions through autoethnography, a research method that emerged around the 1970s.[1] I wish I had learned about this form of qualitative inquiry as a graduate student, as it would have provided the methodological framework

1. Tony E. Adams, Carolyn Ellis, and Stacy Holman Jones, "Autoethnography," in *The International Encyclopedia of Communication Research Methods* (New York: John Wiley and Sons, 2017), 1.

for my thesis, which revolved around cycles and memory. Interestingly, by the mid-1990s, autoethnography had become "a method of choice [within research disciplines] for using personal experience and reflexivity to examine cultural experiences."[2] The method entails "calling on memory and hindsight to reflect on past experiences; talking with others about the past; examining texts such as photographs, personal journals, and recordings; and even consulting with relevant news stories, blogs, and other archives related to life events."[3]

Though I still have the SyQuest disks I used to store my graduate work, I no longer have a SyQuest drive; thus, I started the autoethnographic process with a technology that, in some cases, has the potential to transcend rapid technological evolution—my memory. There are specific texts that I experienced as a graduate student that have stayed in my memory these past two decades. Indeed, the past has agency in the present through memory as well as documentation. To supplement what I remembered I consulted my personal archive of decades-old assignment sheets from graduate school, which would have included required readings (if any). I also referred to canonical texts that may or may not have been assigned but would likely have influenced the way graphic design was being taught at Yale at that time. In the study of history, the past has agency in the present, but so too does the future. I therefore used some contemporary texts that shed light on other key texts published in the second half of the twentieth century that I may not have encountered during my stay at Yale.

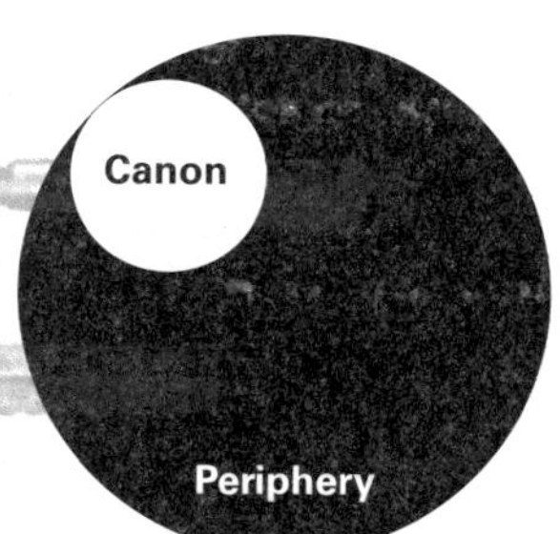

An expressive visualization of the Western-dominated and white-centered canonical texts in the discipline of graphic design.

Henry Bessemer pioneers a new method of making steel in large quantities

Here are my findings: My readings from the mid-'90s included canonical graphic design texts such as *The Elements of Typographic Style*, *Pocket Pal*, *The New Typography*, and *The Crystal Goblet*, the sort of required reading that imparts the principles of type design and explains the print-production process. I also remember reading *Decoding Advertisements: Ideology and Meaning in Advertising*, by Judith Williamson, which elucidated graphic design's tangled relationship with advertising and provided me with an introduction to visual semiotics. Two additional foundational texts—Edward Tufte's *Envisioning Information* (1990) and Jessica Helfand's *Six Essays on Design* (1995)—I read because they were gifted to me by my instructors Inge Druckery and Jessica Helfand, respectively. (The former was self-published by Tufte; the latter is a compilation of essays by Helfand that were published in *Print* magazine in 1994 and 1995, including "Design and the Play Instinct," "Electronic Typography," "The Pleasure of the Text[ure]," "The Culture of Reciprocity," "A New Webbed Utopia," and "The Lost Legacy of Film.")

2. Ibid., 2.

3. Ibid.

Outside of graphic design's canon, within the periphery where graphic designers frequently go to mingle with other disciplines, we were assigned readings from literature, mostly Western, and other disciplines to inform our practice. I distinctly remember reading "Lingering in the Woods," a chapter from *Six Walks in the Fictional Woods* by Umberto Eco, as part of my first-year class project, assigned by Bethany Johns and Michael Rock, about "narrative structures" and how to compose with "contrasting images and texts."[4] Then, for my Letterpress class, I remember reading Walt Whitman's *Democratic Vistas*.[5]

I may have forgotten all about this next set of texts had I not held onto some Tyco course readers compiled by a variety of instructors through Yale's printing service for the past twenty-plus years. I think they exemplify Yale School of Art's curriculum, as I remember it, through their eclectic mix of canonical and peripheral writings that included nonfiction, media, poetry, and short stories. The required-reading packets were multidisciplinary yet only vaguely multicultural, as if white minds could fly through every barrier in the universe yet still fail to cross the color line here on Earth.

One of the reading packets included the text "The Persistence of Industrial Memory" by Mark Dery, but I wish I had been assigned instead his 1994 essay "Black to the Future," where he coins the term "Afrofuturism," defining it as "speculative fiction that treats African-American themes and addresses African-American concerns in the context of twentieth century technoculture—and, more generally, African-American signification that appropriates images of technology and a prosthetically enhanced future."[6]

Of the numerous peripheral texts these reading packets comprised, the one that resonated with me the most is "Untitled," a 1987 poem by Matt Mullican about the milestones in a woman's life.[7] I appreciated this poem because of how it tells a woman's life story through milestones described in short phrases that reveal class and economic status. Some of the milestones I could relate to, but most of them were completely unfamiliar to me. I could imagine a Black woman's life story, like my own, including some entirely different milestones that tell a story of oppression and poverty-induced struggle. "Untitled" underscored my evolving understanding that text and image reflect culture as much as they convey it, and that they can simultaneously evoke resonance and dissonance in each reader. There is culturally based authorial intent in a text, and the reader brings his or her culturally based visual literacy to the interpretive experience. For instance, in *Type and Image: The Language of Graphic Design* (1992), Philip Meggs writes, "Rural villagers were shown a three-foot-tall illustration of a fly in health-care presentations explaining how a fly deposits infectious bacteria on food. Hopes that the villagers would adopt recommended sanitation

4. Bethany Johns and Michael Rock, syllabus for First Year Studio, fall 1995.

5. I remember this text because, as part of my class project, I had to typeset it—in its entirety—in Bodoni justified.

6. Mark Dery, "Black to the Future: Interviews with Samuel R. Delany, Greg Tate, and Tricia Rose," in *Flame Wars: The Discourse of Cyberculture*, ed. Mark Dery (Durham, NC: Duke University Press, 1994), 180.

procedures were dashed when the villagers left the meetings chuckling that they did not need to worry. After all, their village had no giant three-foot flies, only little tiny ones."[8]

How would one know that Meggs had paraphrased this story from personal communication with African-American designer Sylvia Harris? Her name is not mentioned in the text. Instead, if you look closely in the original text, you might notice a superscript number 4, and if you decide to go to the back of the book to look up that endnote, you'll see her credited on page 189. The question is: Why did Meggs bury Harris's name in a note at the end of the book when, in the previous paragraph, he includes Milton Glaser's name prominently when citing his work? This discrepancy is not something I might have noticed as a young graphic design scholar completing my graduate studies. Thus, my advice to current graphic design students: Mine the bibliographies and endnotes for culturally relevant texts and authors.

•

The required reading during my graduate experience at Yale was, indeed, multidisciplinary. Some of the works that stand out in my memory include fiction like Borges's "The Garden of Forking Paths"; cultural criticism like Benjamin's "The Work of Art in the Age of Mechanical Reproduction" (though I wish I had also read "The Author as Producer"); and bell hooks's take on feminist theory in "Selling Hot Pussy: Representations of Black Female Sexuality in the Cultural Marketplace." Many thanks to Michael Rock for assigning this last text because it woke me up. hooks whetted my appetite for writing, which is how I spent most of my precious few elective credits.

I am grateful to have been able to take Daily Themes, a popular creative writing course taught by Wayne Koestenbaum in which over one hundred students typically enrolled. Koestenbaum would start each class by reading an excerpt from anyone from Shakespeare and Homer to James Baldwin and Toni Morrison. Through this course, I was also introduced to the work of Afro-Caribbean author Jamaica Kincaid, including her 1988 book-length essay *A Small Place*. But I don't want to give the impression that every expansion of vision was tied to race and culture. In a fiction-writing course that I took with Kate Walbert, my path was illuminated by "Why I Write" by Joan Didion and *One Writer's Beginnings* by Eudora Welty.

One of the most memorable readings was not assigned in a course: I was chatting with a peer in sculpture class about my thesis when Haitian-American author Edwidge Danticat was brought to my attention. In Haiti, if someone, say an elder, says, "Krik?," it means he or she wants to tell a story; and the young respond, "Krak," if they want to hear the story. *Krik? Krak!*, Danticat's 1996 short-story

7. Brian Wallis, ed., *Blasted Allegories: Writings by Contemporary Artists* (New York: New Museum of Contemporary Art, 1987), 82–88.

8. Philip B. Meggs, *Type and Image: The Language of Graphic Design* (New York: John Wiley and Sons, 1992), 4.

collection, resonated with me because she was integrating a Haitian storytelling tradition into mainstream literature. It seemed to defy the narrow bounds of academic curricula. *Krik? Krak!* helped me see how my cultural background was not just exotic content but could offer powerful, culturally relevant narrative structures and models of communication practices.

My thesis culminated in a self-reflective creative writing piece that combined these inspirations from fiction and the influence of Sheila Levrant de Bretteville, who had become the director of the graphic design program at Yale four years prior to my arrival in 1994. She brought with her the explicit goal of making graphic design more inclusive. In a conversation with Ellen Lupton, she said:

> It is important to me that this program be person-centered. The students are encouraged to put and find themselves in their work; my agenda is to let the differences between my students be visible in everything they do. In most projects—not just in thesis work—it's the students' job to figure out what they want to say. Emphasizing the students' desire to communicate, and focusing on what needs to be said and to whom they want to say it—that's what I mean by person-centered.[9]

The thesis requirement in graphic design at Yale helped to give form and rationale to an idea that both the presence and absence of literature seemed to point me toward, the ghostly outline of a pedagogical platform that I struggled to articulate then—one that embraced difference beyond lip service to the sometimes weak rhetoric of "inclusion." It was at times strictly practical—compiling a bibliography, in relation to sketching, writing, and planning the creative development of my graphic design projects and thesis. But I now have a name for what I wanted: a minor literature.

Deleuze and Guattari introduced the term in their 1975 text "What Is a Minor Literature?," in which they argue that a minor literature is "that which a minority constructs within a major language."[10] A minor literature, they say, can be compared to "what blacks in America today are able to do with the English language."[11] They were likely referring to Ebonics; one could add to that the examples of rap, spoken word, even graffiti. The development of Jamaican patois and Haitian Creole are useful analogies as well.

A minor literature should not be understood as merely a minority perspective within a mainstream community. For instance, Katherine McCoy's article "American Graphic Design Expression" describes an intervention that gave disciplinary form to graphic design during the period of modernism in the early twentieth century.[12] This intervention was "[t]he [collective] writings of Josef Muller-Brockmann, Karl Gerstner, Armin Hoffman, and Emil Ruder—a few young American [designers] that assimilated a problem-solving method for corporations like the Container Corporation."[13] These white men might well have represented a minority of designers, but

9. Ellen Lupton, "Reputations: Sheila Levrant de Bretteville," *Eye* 8, no. 2 (1993), http://www.eyemagazine.com/feature/article/reputations-sheila-levrant-de-bretteville.

10. Gilles Deleuze and Félix Guattari, *Kafka: Toward a Minor Literature*, trans. Dana Polan (Minneapolis: University of Minneapolis Press, 1986), 16.

11. Ibid., 17.

they were responding to the interests of the majority of the market share. When you represent ninety percent of the wealth, you are not a minor literature, no matter how small your numbers.

A minor literature is better understood as texts that give voice to a marginalized group of authors. Too often the contributions of people of color to graphic design literature lie at the periphery of the discipline's canon and must be sought outside its boundaries. Seldom do we see the contributions of people of color included in the required readings—the major literature—of the design curriculum. When Sylvia Harris became one of my instructors at Yale during the 1996–97 academic year, my final year as a graduate student, she was probably in the midst of writing her article "Searching for a Black Aesthetic in Graphic Design," which was published in 1998 in Steve Heller's edited collection *The Education of a Graphic Designer*. Her article aims to emancipate graphic design from the shackles of cultural homogeneity by grounding the formation of a future Black aesthetic on Black historical milestones—from the New Negro to the civil rights movement to hip-hop.

At the beginning of this text, Harris asks questions that, I am certain, every Black student in graphic design also asks: "What influence have African Americans had on contemporary graphic design? Is there such a thing as an African-American design aesthetic?"[14] The answer she gets each time she asks those questions is "I don't know."[15] When Black students do not see their cultures represented in the canon of graphic design literature, she writes, they "feel they are not completely welcome in the profession."[16] As a result, Black students often exhibit insecurities that negatively impact their performance, leading them to imitate mainstream aesthetics rather than to innovate culturally based ones.[17]

During this critical time of my professional development as a Black designer, I do not remember reading texts written by other Black designers, nor do I remember any readings on the interfacing of Black history and culture with graphic design. Why was it so difficult for my professors to diversify the required reading in graphic design by including texts written by Black designers or media on Black culture?

In their 1996 essay "White on Black on Gray," graphic designers Ellen Lupton and J. Abbott Miller discussed a *New York Times* advertisement that promoted the CBS television series *Of Black America*, which had aired in 1968—two years before I was born in Nassau, Bahamas. The essay detailed some of the intersections between graphic design and African-American communities around the end of the civil rights movement. I am not demanding revolutionary writings (although those too would have been helpful and

12. Katherine McCoy, "American Graphic Design Expression," *Design Quarterly* 148 (1990): 10.

13. Ibid.

14. Sylvia Harris, "Searching for a Black Aesthetic in American Graphic Design," in *The Education of a Graphic Designer*, ed. Stephen Heller (New York: Allworth Press, 1998), 125.

15. Ibid.

16. Ibid.

17. Ibid.

welcomed). However, even as a mild intervention, it would have been welcomed by someone yearning for an identity as a Black designer in the United States.

In the "Authorship" chapter of *No More Rules: Graphic Design and Postmodernism*, Rick Poynor indirectly speaks to Harris when he says, "The act of designing can never be an entirely neutral process since the designer always brings something extra to the project. A design cannot fail to be informed, in some measure, by personal tastes and cultural understanding."[18] It *can*, however, fail if we have created barriers that prevent the experiences of marginalized groups from being recognized. The contributions of design students of color should never again be minimized because of a lack of understanding of their culture's contributions to the history of graphic design pedagogy. At the end of her text, Harris implores others to "contribute to the body of knowledge and support a generation of designers hungry to see their people and experience reflected in the mirror of [the] profession."[19]

The period that preceded the publication of *The Education of a Graphic Designer* in 1998 saw the emergence of "graphic authorship" as a creative phenomenon. At the time I distinctly remember encountering a 1995 issue of *Eye* magazine while perusing the shelves at the Atticus Bookstore Cafe in New Haven. Inside the issue I found an article titled "The Designer as Author," written by my instructor Michael Rock. This text introduced me to the ideas of Roland Barthes and Michel Foucault regarding the role in the literary text of authorship, which had "become a popular term in graphic design circles . . . at the edges of the profession."[20] Although Rock is generally credited as being the first to import the concept of authorship into graphic design, the conversation around authorship had been initiated by others such as Steven McCarthy. In 1995, prior to the publication of Rock's article, McCarthy and co-curator Cristina de Almeida issued a call for submissions for a juried exhibition titled *Designer as Author: Voices and Visions*.

But one could also argue that sociologist W. E. B. Du Bois had been a pioneer of authorship in graphic design. Thanks to the recently published *W. E. B. Du Bois's Data Portraits: Visualizing Black America*, I am "woke" to Du Bois's 1900 hand-drawn graphic "The Georgia Negro: A Social Study,"[21] which includes the following text, "written in neat script"[22] below the image: "This case is devoted to a series of charts, maps, and other devices designed to illustrate the development of the American Negro in a single typical state of the United States. 'The problem of the 20th Century is the Problem of the Color-Line.'" Consider this description of America's cultural context when Du Bois designed his series of infographics:

> At the turn of the century, portrayals of black people as subhuman, incapable of attaining great material and cultural achievements, were commonplace throughout the Western world.[23]

18. Rick Poynor, *No More Rules: Graphic Design and Postmodernism* (New Haven: Yale University Press, 2003), 120.

19. Harris, "Searching for a Black Aesthetic in American Graphic Design," 129.

20. Michael Rock, "The Designer as Author," *Eye* 20, no. 5 (1996): 52. See http://www.eyemagazine.com/feature/article/the-designer-as-author.

At the end of "The Designer as Author," Rock assumes a Foucauldian perspective with the provocative question "What difference does it make who designed it? . . . The primary concern of both the viewer and critic is not who made it, but rather what it does and how it does it."[24] As you can see from my handwritten notes from over twenty years ago, I disagreed with him. Then as now, I believed strongly that it matters who is speaking—because the listener might well be a Black student on a quest to understand his or her heritage in relation to what is being said. It matters who speaks, not because of some diversity quotient imposed upon us but because listening and speaking are constitutive social acts; because semiosis is at its most profound when actively engaged in the fields of power that communicative communities afford us.

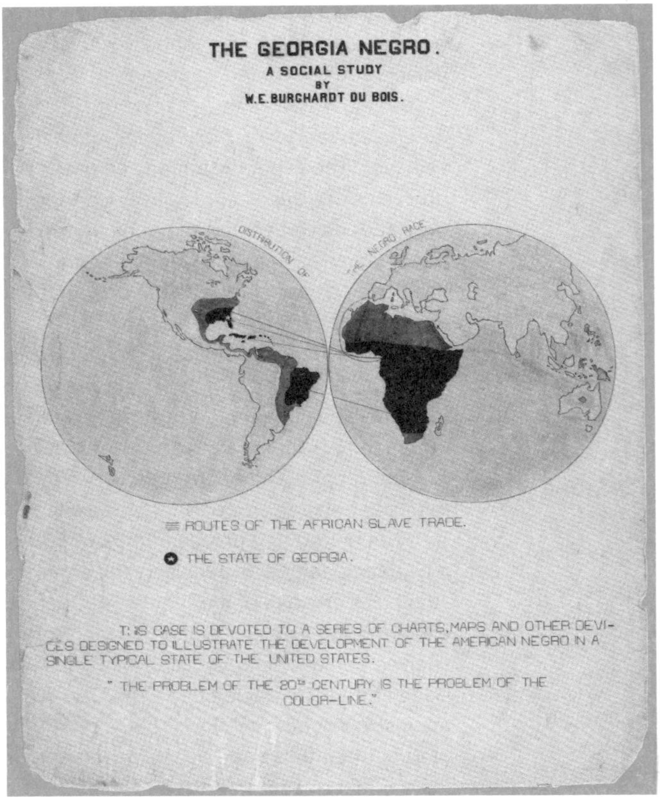

The texts that I collected for my autoethnography were a multicultural and multidisciplinary set of magazine articles, interviews, monographs, textbooks, and journal articles, as well as fiction, poetry, and other literary genres. What I read at the Yale School of Art in the mid-1990s contributed in a significant way to the scholarly path that I took in my professional career. Today, I am a design scholar who spends most of my time writing about my research findings. My research agenda includes a strand of inquiry in which I work collaboratively with ethnomathematician Ron Eglash, author of *African Fractals,* to diversify STEM education with heritage

An expressive visualization of the Western-dominated and white-centered canonical texts in the discipline of graphic design.

21. Mabel O. Wilson, "The Cartography of W. E. B. Du Bois's Color Line," in *W. E. B. Du Bois's Data Portraits: Visualizing Black America: The Color Line at the Turn of the Twentieth Century,* ed. Whitney Battle-Baptiste and Britt Rusert (Hudson, NY: Princeton Architectural Press, 2018), 37.

22. Ibid.

23. Aldon Morris, "American Negro at Paris, 1900," in Battle-Baptiste and Rusert, *W. E. B. Du Bois's Data Portraits,* 23.

24. Rock, "The Designer as Author," 53.

algorithms—computational thinking inherent to the cultural practices of Indigenous people. The peripheral texts in which I report my findings from this cross-disciplinary inquiry include "Ethnocomputational Creativity in STEM Education"; "Follow the Golden Ratio from Africa to the Bauhaus for a Cross-Cultural Aesthetic for Images"; "Culturally Situated Design Tools"; and "Towards an Authochthonic Black Aesthetic for Graphic Design Pedagogy." My texts that aim to permeate the boundaries of graphic design's canon include "The Rise of Research in Graphic Design" (the introductory chapter to a collection that I edited titled *Design Studies: Theory and Research in Graphic Design*), "Interactive Aesthetics," and "Good Design Is Good Social Change."

It is my hope that we can adopt a more integrative approach to graphic design pedagogy, in which major and minor literatures come together to form a de-canon—a fractalized coalescence of cross-disciplinary texts that originate from the Global South and attempt to bring about the end of marginalization and the beginning of consciousness about the contributions of "others" to the discipline. "Woke" is not a binary state that one either is or isn't; it is the dawn chorus that breaks down the wall separating light from dark.

Let's get "woke," y'all.

creator; the status of the creator frames the work and imbues it with mythical value.

While some claims for authorship may be simply an indication of a renewed sense of responsibility, at times they seem ploys to gain property rights, attempts to exercise some kind of agency where there has traditionally been none. Ultimately the author equals authority. While the longing for graphic authorship may be the longing for legitimacy or power, is celebrating the designer as a central character necessarily a positive move? Isn't that what has fuelled the last 50 years of design history? If we really want to go beyond the designer-as-hero model, we may have to imagine a time when we can ask, "What difference does it make who designed it?"

It makes a big difference → ! I disagree Michael

On the other hand, work is created by someone. (All those calls for the death of the author are made by famous authors.) While the development and definition of artistic styles, and their identification and classification, are at the heart of an outmoded Modernist criticism, we must still work to engage these problems in new ways. It may be that the real challenge is to embrace the multiplicity of methods – artistic and commercial, individual and collaborative – that comprise design language. An examination of the designer-as-author could help us to rethink process, expand design methods and elaborate our historical frame to include all forms of graphic discourse. But while theories of graphic authorship may change the way work is made, the primary concern of both the viewer and critic is not *who* made it, but rather *what* it does and *how* it does it. ○

I disagree

[T]hanks to my partner Susan [S]ellers and colleague Jenny [T]han for invaluable assistance [w]ith this essay.

53 EYE 20/96

Handwritten notes showing my disagreement with Rock's claim that the author does not matter

Bibliography

Texts that are culturally situated (minor literature)

Bennett, Audrey. "Ethnocomputational Creativity in STEAM Education: A Cultural Framework for Generative Justice." *Teknokultura* 13, no. 2 (2016): 587–612.

Bennett, Audrey. "Follow the Golden Ratio from Africa to the Bauhaus for a Cross-Cultural Aesthetic for Images." *Critical Interventions* 6, no. 1 (2012): 11–23.

Bennett, Audrey. "Towards an Autochthonic Black Aesthetic for Graphic Design Pedagogy." *Journal of Design Research* 3, no. 2 (2003): 61–70.

Borges, Jorge Luis. *Labyrinths: Selected Stories and Other Writings.* New York: New Directions, 1964.

Danticat, Edwidge. *Krik? Krak!* New York: Soho Press, 1995.

Dery, Mark. "Black to the Future: Interviews with Samuel R. Delany, Greg Tate, and Tricia Rose." In *Flame Wars: The Discourse of Cyberculture,* 179–222. Durham, NC: Duke University Press, 1994.

Eglash, Ron. *African Fractals: Modern Computing and Indigenous Design.* New Brunswick, NJ: Rutgers University Press, 1999.

Eglash, Ron, Audrey Bennett, Casey O'Donnell, Sybillyn Jennings, and Margaret Cintorino. "Culturally Situated Design Tools: Ethnocomputing from Field Site to Classroom." *American Anthropologist* 108, no. 2 (2006): 347–62.

Harris, Sylvia. "Searching for a Black Aesthetic in American Graphic Design." In *The Education of a Graphic Designer,* 125–29. Edited by Steven Heller. New York: Allworth Press, 1998.

hooks, bell. "Selling Hot Pussy: Representations of Black Female Sexuality in the Cultural Marketplace." In *Black Looks: Race and Representation,* 145–56. Boston: South End Press, 1992.

Kincaid, Jamaica. *A Small Place.* Boston: MacMillan, 1988.

Morris, Aldon. "American Negro at Paris, 1990." In *W. E. B. Du Bois's Data Portraits: Visualizing Black America,* 23–36. Edited by Whitney Battle-Baptiste and Britt Rusert. Hudson, NY: Princeton Architectural Press, 2018.

Wilson, Mabel O., "The Cartography of W. E. B. Du Bois's Color Line." In *W. E. B. Du Bois's Data Portraits: Visualizing Black America,* 37–43. Edited by Whitney Battle-Baptiste and Britt Rusert. Hudson, NY: Princeton Architectural Press, 2018.

Texts in graphic design's canon

Bringhurst, Robert. *The Elements of Typographic Style.* Vancouver: Hartley and Marks Publishers, 1992.

Heller, Steven. *The Education of a Graphic Designer.* New York: Allworth Press, 1998.

Helfand, Jessica. *Six Essays on Design and New Media.* New York: William Drenttel, 1995.

Frenchman Étienne Lenoir and German Nikolaus Otto pioneer the internal combustion engine

McCoy, Katherine. "American Graphic Design Expression." *Design Quarterly* 148 (1990): 3-22.

Meggs, Philip B. *Type and Image: The Language of Graphic Design.* New York: John Wiley and Sons, 1992.

International Paper Company. *Pocket Pal: A Graphic Arts Production Handbook.* Memphis: International Paper, 1992.

Lupton, Ellen, and Abbott Miller. *Design Writing Research: Writing on Graphic Design.* London: Phaidon Press, 1999.

Lupton, Ellen. "Reputations: Sheila Levrant De Bretteville." *Eye* 8, no. 2 (1993), http://www.eyemagazine.com/feature/article/reputationssheila-levrant-de-bretteville.

Poynor, Rick. *No More Rules: Graphic Design and Postmodernism.* New Haven: Yale University Press, 2003.

Rock, Michael. "The Designer as Author." *Eye* 20, no. 5 (1996): 44–53.

Tschichold, Jan. *The New Typography: A Handbook for Modern Designers* (1928). Translated by Ruari McLean. Berkeley: Regents of the University of California, 1995.

Tufte, Edward R. *Envisioning Information.* Cheshire, CT: Graphics Press, 1990.

Warde, Beatrice. *The Crystal Goblet: Sixteen Essays on Typography.* Cleveland: World, 1956.

Williamson, Judith. *Decoding Advertisements: Ideology and Meaning in Advertising.* New York: Marion Boyers Publishers, 1978.

Texts in the periphery

Adams, Tony E., Carolyn Ellis, and Stacy Holman Jones. "Autoethnography." In *The International Encyclopedia of Communication Research Methods*, 1–11. New York: John Wiley and Sons, 2017.

Barthes, Roland. "The Death of the Author" (1968). In *Modern Criticism and Theory.* Edited by David Lodge and Nigel Wood. London: Routledge, 1988.

Benjamin, Walter. "The Author as Producer." *New Left Review* 1, no. 62 (1970): 83–96.

Benjamin, Walter. "The Work of Art in the Age of Mechanical Reproduction." In *Illuminations: Essays and Reflections* (1968), 217–51. Edited by Hannah Arendt. New York: Schocken, 2007.

Borges, Jorge Luis. "The Garden of Forking Paths." In *Collected Fictions.* Translated by Andrew Hurley. New York: Grove Press, 1962.

Deleuze, Gilles, and Félix Guattari. *Kafka: Toward a Minor Literature.* Translated by Dana Polan. Minneapolis: University of Minneapolis Press, 1986.

Dery, Mark. "The Persistence of Industrial Memory." *ANY: Architecture New York* 10 (1995): 24–31.

Didion, Joan. "Why I Write." *New York Times Book Review,* December 5, 1976.

Eco, Umberto. *Six Walks in the Fictional Woods.* Cambridge, MA: Harvard University Press, 1994.

Foucault, Michel. *What Is an Author?* New York: Cornell University Press, 1979.

Heider, Karl G. "What Do People Do? Dani Auto-Ethnography." *Journal of Anthropological Research* 31, no. 1 (Spring 1975): 3–17.

Mullican, Matt. "Untitled." In *Blasted Allegories*, 82–87. Edited by Brian Wallis. New York: New Museum of Contemporary Art, 1987.

Welty, Eudora. *One Writer's Beginnings.* Cambridge, MA: Harvard University Press, 1983.

Whitman, Walt. *Democratic Vistas.* New York: J. S. Redfield, 1871.

SCRAPS: ON PROCESS, PROXIMITY, AND BLACK TEXTUAL INTERVENTION

SHIRAZ ABDULLAHI GALLAB

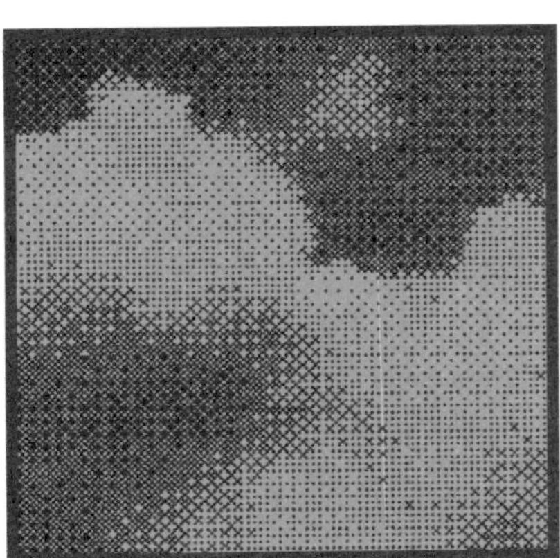

(1) Our intentions shape the words that we speak, relaying who we say we are and rendering nuance via breath and blank stares. Who we are has nothing to do with who we say we are; the latter is your doing while the former must make do. We're not hearing every word but instead counting every sigh. Thirsty for dark matter, we move onward, and under, and so on, and so forth.

(2) It's like magic. Our gestures replace words that were never ours to begin with. Neatly embedded in a livelihood that hinges on lack, we shrug, sway, and chuckle when and where we want and without backdrop. We avoid answering questions; the "how" and "why" unravel before you can even ask how or why. Beheld and beholden,

(5c) I want to do that because I love them
then I look at them, then I hate them again
I hate them because I love them so much
and I don't know
I don't know where hate begins and love ends
I don't know how love ends and hate begins
I don't know any of these things[1]

(6b) These words were originally printed on index cards measuring four by six inches. I fed each card through my cheap laser printer twice after treating the text in 10% black. I wrapped the words around the outer edge of each card, contouring the perimeter and establishing a jagged frame. The perimeter piqued my interest, because its start and end points are difficult, if not impossible, to define. The continuum questions the notion of a border, a boundary, an ending, and a beginning.

(3) As we establish a connection, we repel, rebel, repeat. No longer servicing right or wrong, we simply stitch together the grime that's left on the table after everyone else goes to bed. Lights off . . . Let us gather the things that were mentioned, then introduce them to those who were not, then sculpt the fog that surrounds us and rearrange it before the sun comes up.

(10b) With texts as with people, we know them by the company they keep. Consequently, when we see them in new or strange company we may see a whole new side of them that was previously hidden and perhaps unsuspected. The critical point is that we must learn to look at texts not only in their "original" (i.e., usual, conventional) contexts and co-texts. We must also be prepared to pull them out and look at them again, in others, differently.[2]

1. Sun Ra, "like a universe," in *This Planet Is Doomed: The Science Fiction Poetry* (Brooklyn: Kicks Books, 2012), 110.

2. Rob Pope, *Textual Intervention: Critical and Creative Strategies for Literary Studies* (London: Routledge, 1994), 9.

(5b) then again, I look at people, and I
love them
I love them so very much until I turn
my head in shame
I want to touch them with my fingertips
and erase every frown from their face
I want to touch them with my mind and
erase every care and every sorrow away
I want to touch them with my mind and
open their mind's eye and let them see
the things that I know and feel[3]

(4) Together, these written words become a variant. They cycle through a series of screens—implicit, onward, under. They allude to your anxieties while keeping a steady measure. These words migrate and eventually land before undermining your "who?" and "what?" and "why?" Now it becomes pointless to write from top to bottom and left to right. We must circle through thoughts that appear to be vast and detached from one another, jumping from *there* to *that way* and replacing *your things* with *my emotion*.

(14) There is always rhythm, but it is the rhythm of segments. Each unit has a rhythm of its own, but when the whole is assembled, it is lacking in symmetry. But easily workable to a Negro who is accustomed to the break in going from one part to another, so that he adjusts himself to the new tempo.[4]

(8) The field of publishing, alongside graphic design, continues to serve people of color. And when I write this, I'm thinking of historical examples of Black publishing: journals and magazines like *Fire!!*, *Soulbook*, *Umbra*, and *THING*, which circulated throughout the twentieth century and featured poetry, prose, criticism, and radical texts. Further back in time, Ida B. Wells published investigative pieces on lynchings and mob violence, bringing these atrocities to the attention of a national and global audience. Throughout this country's history, publishing, design, and typography have accommodated the needs and interests of Black people, and in future years, I imagine that this will continue and intensify.

(5a) yes, it's there
and my mind searches for it
and my heart searches for it
And I look and I think,
yes, here it is
then it's gone
it's like a mist
then it's like a sunset
it's like a sunrise
it's like a universe
it lies there
and yet I walk among people all long

3. Sun Ra, "like a universe," 109.

4. Zora Neale Hurston, "Characteristics of Negro Expression," in *Negro: An Anthology*, ed. Nancy Cunard (London: Wishart, 1934), 26.

James Clerk Maxwell figures out that radio waves exist and sets out laws of electromagnetism

not knowing
and the people not knowing
and then I think
I say,[5]

(6a) Too close to the brim: The source lasts before the end of time, feeling in a foolish language, giggling while we steal time to be me like meat.

(7a) In 1934, Zora Neale Hurston wrote an essay titled "Characteristics of Negro Expression." In it, she defines Black expression as an ongoing adaptation and ownership of words that were originally foreign to Black people. "Everything that [the Negro] touches is re-interpreted for his own use," Hurston argues, and each move that a Black person makes is embellished with language that is clever, sound, and unparalleled.[6]

(10a) In 1994, Rob Pope published the book *Textual Intervention*, which walks readers through a series of exercises and prompts that fuse literary criticism with hacking, remixing, and repurposing existing texts. Pope argues that "the best way to understand how a text works . . . is to change it: to play around with it, to intervene in it in some way (large or small), and then to try to account for the exact effect of what you have done."[7] Through textual intervention, the adaptations that emerge reflect the reader's relationship to the text in question while also tightening that relationship. New texts emerge alongside new meanings.

(11a) Typography has something of a split personality—it's both the technical act of writing words into the world by giving them form and it's also a way of understanding the world through the forms of its writing. Designer Paul Elliman describes this two-way street concisely:

(11b) "Writing gives the impression of things. Conversely, things can give the impression of writing."[8]

(7b) Hurston's essay makes me think of our current condition: distant despite our thirst for connection; separate but similar at times. When published online, our words can easily be referenced and repurposed with dramatic emphasis. And through the constant contact that comes with remote life, we move closer to each other while standing still, fostering a new kind of kinship that is reliant on our shared use of written words.

(13) We don't know how fonts become vehicles, but this form of travel seems an important parallel to the metaphors we use to understand the otherwise formless Internet.[9]

(10c) Our speech patterns and preferences say a lot about who we are, and the same can be said of our treatment of text—how we read, respond to, typeset, and publish it. In *Textual Intervention*, Pope describes his exercises as "critical-creative" because they employ a hybrid method of examining and understanding text.

5. Sun Ra, "like a universe," 108.

6. Hurston, "Characteristics of Negro Expression," 28.

7. Pope, *Textual Intervention*, 1.

8. David Reinfurt, *A *New* Program for Graphic Design* (Los Angeles: Inventory Press, 2019), 19.

9. Yanie Fécu, "Sycorax's Other Son," *Cabinet* 67 (Spring 2019–Winter 2020).

Pope asks readers to also be writers: to decode and recode, to consume and reproduce, to observe and act upon the text that greets them. And this duality is always simultaneous—never siloed.[10]

(11c) I'd suggest this reading and writing at the same time, or typography, is the root-level skill of graphic design, and I'd like to talk about typography as something that joins reading and writing.[11]

(postscript-1) Each publication is an adaptation of the one that came before it. Based on the responses we receive and the revisions we propose, we build on what was done the last time. This would challenge the assumption that a printed publication is finished and that new publications are new. In this realm, each publication is made up of scraps—pieces of a cosmic whole that fail to coalesce despite expected efforts at congregation. Borrowing from Amiri Baraka's sentiments, "the possible is obvious, what is desired is the impossible."[12] These words live in a time, frame, and location that lack legibility.

(postscript-2) From revelation to revelation, immeasurable, revolution to revolution, like heartbeats of truth. The breathing of always.[13]

10. John Walter, "On Rob Pope's Textual Interventions," http://www.jpwalter.com/cyber-rhetoric/archives/725.

11. Reinfurt, *A *New* Program for Graphic Design*, 19.

12. Amiri Baraka, foreword to *This Planet Is Doomed*, xi.

13. Ibid., x.

ON THE HETERONOMY OF DESIGN IN A POST-UTOPIAN AGE

GUI BONSIEPE

A generation ago, the differentiated discipline of graphic design seemed to be reasonably settled. Today, however, innovations in technology and in the socioeconomic context have undermined this once firmly grounded domain. The catastropohic global effects on the environment of industrialization and our consumption-saturated lifestyle, the socioeconomic polarization within industrially advanced countries and between the Global South and North, and the primacy of financial markets have all led to significant changes in professional practice and in approaches to design education. All too slowly, the imperatives of growth and progress have been submitted to critical review and the simple and uncomfortable question been asked: "Who, in the end, reaps the benefits of these processes?"[1]

Formerly, the various design disciplines were organized by the special label attached to each field: magazine design / poster design / exhibition design / packaging design / type design / textile design / fashion design / industrial design / corporate-identity design / service design / game design / web design. . . . Today, however, we are faced with a bewildering variety of new permutations of the concept "design": strategic design / emotional design / experience design / postmodernist design / transactional design / transformational design, critical design / radical design / socially responsible design / inclusive design / post-utopian design / speculative design, calm design / participatory design / people-centered design / co-design / "dirty design" . . .

This proliferation of new labels reveals a particular approach to design rather than, as before, a reference to its field of intervention. One could read this increasing heterogeneity as a symptom of vitality and dynamism, of a profession expanding and differentiating the gamut of its services. Yet this heterogeneity has also increased concerns that the identity of design as a rigorous discipline might be corroded and diluted to the point where everything could be said to be design or that everyone could claim to be a designer. How can we explain this explosion of design? Is it more than a passing fad? Why are we attracted to design as a concept?

One reason, I would suggest, is that design is intrinsically linked to the future, that it has, in fact, the chance to shape the future. For example, one of the latest additions to what is called the "knowledge economy" is "knowledge design." Certainly, visual communication is closely connectioned to knowledge design as a new arena of specialization. Unfortunately, this promising term runs the risk of blotting out any reference to the critical component of knowledge, instead concentrating on Big Data, software

1. Arturo Escobar, *Encountering Development: The Making and Unmaking of the Third World* (Princeton: Princeton University Press, 1995).

development, software-based education, and capital-intensive research, above all in biotechnology and neuroscience.

Another impetus for the rise of new approaches to design might have to do with the limitations and contradictions of design practice and design education within the global market, and the erosion of democracy as a result of the ever-increasing financialization of the global economy. (Indeed, financialization can now be considered the fourth power, in addition to the executive, judiciary, and legislative powers.) A driving force behind the diversification of the term *design*, then, can be identified as the wish to create more environmentally and socially sustainable systems and the longing for design to be a socially relevant activity.[2] To which I would add another desire: to use design to explore the degree of elasticity and tolerance within the current set of given sociopolitical and economic conditions.

At times, these desires are phrased explicitly: How can design change society? Such a question obviously runs the risk of loading disproportionate expectations onto the shoulders of the discipline and thus of remaining limited to verbal declarations and manifestos. Today, the place once occupied by the great narratives has been filled with what may be called micro-narratives. Professions are embedded in narratives about what they are, and those stories are not stable. They evolve; they are exposed to contradictions. Most critically, they create a reality (as opposed to merely mirroring it), and in this dynamic of narratives, discourses gain and lose dominance. Take history as an example. Until 1968, that discipline had been dominated for decades by the "school of long duration" led by Fernand Braudel. Adherents of this school reacted against the invasion of their discipline by economists, sociologists, and anthropologists. They refused to see the role of the historian reduced to that of an antiquarian, detached from the world and dedicated to collecting and organizing documents in archives for the benefit of social scientists. (The situation can be compared to that of designers when they are confronted with the widely shared opinion that design is basically about making things beautiful.) Braudel and his colleagues perceived the danger of heteronomy and patiently and efficiently defended their area of competence against academic cannibalism.[3] The apostles of micro-history, who focus on aspects of history that the long-duration school had not taken into consideration, are a reaction to Braudel and his followers.[4]

I chose the case of history to demonstrate that what is happening to the profession of design is not an exception. In the field of design, however, the fundamental criterion is coherence, while for sciences the fundamental criterion is truth. Epistemological innovation in search of truth constitutes the professional identity of scientists. Structuring the interaction between users and

2. Terry Irwin, Carnegie Mellon University, https://design.cmu.edu/people/faculty/terry-irwin.

3. François Dosse, *La historia en migajas: De Annales a la 'nueva historia'* (1987; Mexico City: Universidad Iberoamericana, 2006).

4. Carlo Ginzburg, *The Cheese and the Worms: The Cosmos of a Sixteenth-Century Miller*, trans. John and Anne Tedeschi (Baltimore: John Hopkins University Press, 1980).

artifacts (both material and semiotic), by contrast, constitutes the professional identity of designers. Whereas university education in general is characterized by forming and privileging discursive expertise—that is, language-based intelligence—the design disciplines stress the formation of nondiscursive intelligence, including aesthetic or sensorial competence understood as the capacity to make perceptual, particularly visual distinctions.

The creation of advanced-degree programs for design can serve to counteract this discursive weakness by increasing the knowledge base of design. In these programs the emphasis is on the study of a canon of historically established, finely honed rules, culminating with a written document that requires discursive competence. Depending on the orientation of the program, complex practical issues can be addressed that require extensive research and can lead to the solution of a design problem.

Advanced-degree programs are oriented either toward professional development or toward careers in academia. The reason for this bifurcation is historically rooted: Project-oriented approaches did not exist during the creation of higher-learning institutions and thus—with the exception of architecture—were never firmly established in the university structure. This still has echoes today and can, depending on the institution, make things difficult when instructors in a design program are required to have at least a master's degree. In such a situation sometimes a back door called the "Picasso paragraph" is invoked, in which outstanding professional accomplishments are taken as the equivalent of academic accreditation. But this exception only serves to question the wisdom of the rule.

Since the mid-nineteenth century, when "objectivity" was promoted as the fundamental characteristic of scientific research, as the key epistemological virtue, the aim of research has been to produce knowledge without conflict of interest or exclusivity. This is why there are the academic imperatives to publish research results in peer-reviewed journals and share knowledge by making it publicly available. For design to become an academic discipline, it too would have to obey these imperatives.

Precisely because of the distinction between coherence and truth, it should come as no surprise that dysfunction can arise when putting scientific disciplines and design disciplines together in a program. To take one historical example: the Ulm school. Although the closing of the Ulm school was politically motivated, as a politician has admitted—a rare exception, since politicians are not fond of admitting errors—the institution had a constitutively vulnerable flank. The founders of the school and creators of its constitution had not foreseen the potential conflict between discursive and nondiscursive competences in the faculty. The differences led, only a few years after the school opened, to abrasive internal conflicts. Moving one step deeper into this issue, one comes across the relation between theory and practice. The roots of this phenomenon reach back into Classical history: The act of theorizing was limited to the small group of free citizens (limited to men and excluding women) who had leisure and did not have to work to maintain their subsistence. Practice was for those who were not free.

Elisha Graves Otis invents the elevator with built-in safety brake

My reservations as to whether design has reached a level of maturity to claim a proper theory notwithstanding, I continue to use the notion of "design theory." Theory exists outside of profit-oriented calculations. Students of design might therefore criticize its supposed lack of relevance for practice. But theories do not have to be practical. Theory reveals the differences between instrumental reason and critical reason, the latter understood as the capacity to think about what one is doing, to identify the forces of heteronomy and to act against them.

To return to our earlier question: What is the appeal of the word *design*, which has colonized the media, marketing, management, and even politics? It should cause no surprise, given the inflationary use of the word, that valuations of the profession of designer differ dramatically. I quote an example by a keen observer of cultural phenomena:

> After the last follower of the Bauhaus had left the world, these people are occupied with making objects of daily use unusable. Amongst their triumphs they count the elimination of the water tap, the fabrication of skewed bookshelves, the invention of lamps that don't look like lamps and provide as little illumination as possible, and of seating accommodations that do no only wobble, but that are, as the famous chair from Gerrit Rietveld, a mockery of human anatomy. The surplus-value of these objects consists in being decorated with the name of their creators. One must imagine hell as a place completely furnished by designers.[5]

Contrast that negative assessment with the following report: "In 2012 IBM set out a bold vision . . . to train its entire workforce—some 377,000 employees worldwide—to think, work, *feel* like designers." The article quotes Phil Gilbert, general manager of design for IBM software, as saying, "Design is everyone's job. Not everyone is a designer, but everybody has to have the user as their north star."[6] The emphasis on the issue of use as the main criterion of design is not to be confused with Sullivan's old claim that "form follows function," which has produced numerous polemical confrontations and often been used like a mantra to invalidate a contrary opinion. Already in the late 1960s Adorno explained that in the era of overproduction the use value of consumer goods has become questionable, giving way to the secondary pleasure of prestige, of being "with it," and finally to the proper character of merchandise, i.e., to what is today called the increase of the symbolic dimension of artifacts.[7] But this calling into question of use value is not to be interpreted as a disavowal of its relevance. With roots in eighteenth-century economics, use value refers to the output that a user receives from an artifact or the services provided by an artifact—the way a user interacts with an artifact. This interaction is mediated by the interface. For this reason I link the

5. Hans Magnus Enzensberger, *Mr. Zed's Reflections*, trans. Wieland Hoban (London: Seagull, 2015).

6. Ann Quito, "IBM Is Becoming the Largest and Most Sophisticated Design Company," 2016, https://qz.com/755741/ibm-is-becoming-the-worlds-largest-design-company/.

7. Theodor Adorno, *Ästhetische Theorie: Gesammelte Schriften*, vol. 7 (Frankfurt am Main: Suhrkamp, 1972), 32.

term *design* to the domain of use, and I characterize managing the interface of artifacts (material and semiotic) as the main defining feature of design professions, particularly visual-communication designers and industrial designers. Obviously the designer may face problems reaching beyond this aspect—questions, for example, about whether the product makes sense or the size of its ecological footprint during the different phases of production, distribution, use, and elimination. But the issue of how to interact with an artifact remains paramount.

In an interview, the philosopher Étienne Balibar characterized the issue of use unequivocally as a priority and asked:

> Is it about common use? Or is it about individual use? The issues of the priority of use, of the type of use, of a non-destructive use of nature, of use as a more important criterion compared to efficiency or value, seem to be a fruitful category. Obviously the use is related to a modality of informing citizens; a civilization of use does not have the same type of citizens as a civilization of credit.[8]

In 1957 Tomás Maldonado, a member of the teaching staff of the Ulm school, made a draft proposal for organizing a study program there that provided conceptual clarity about the design disciplines in the context of a technological, scientific civilization. In a two-page typescript, he wrote:

> It is recommendable to divide the world in which the human being lives as a social creature and in which he produces and produces himself into two parts: 1) Into the sector of primary or direct artifacts (not the totality but that class of objects whose use occurs with the objects themselves, e.g., tools, apparatuses, instruments, fittings, furnishings, etc.); 2) Into the sector of secondary or indirect artifacts (objects whose use occurs by mediation, that is, those that fulfill a function of conveyance).[9]

At Ulm, the Industrial Design department and the Building department were linked to the realm of material artifacts, while the design of immaterial artifacts was the responsibility of the Department of Visual Communication and the Department of Information (i.e., verbal communication)—the Ulm school featured a department that dealt with language. Maldonado took the decisive step of drawing on the anthropological concept of the "artifact," which at that time was not common in design discourse. Furthermore, he emphasized the category of use as central to design. Up until that point, the Bauhaus had functioned as the main point of reference for Ulm. However, Maldonado's prospectus broke with the terminology of the Bauhaus, relativizing the concept of form and treating it as only one of various factors to be taken into account. Form was no longer the prima donna of design concepts.

A few years later, in 1963, Maldonado published an article with the provocative title "Is the Bauhaus Relevant Today?"[10] His text called for the recognition of the achievements of Hannes Meyer, the second director of the Bauhaus, a position that was by

8. AA.VV., "Étienne Balibar: Pensador Latinoamericano," *Review: Revista de libros* (Buenos Aires) 3 (July–August 2015).

9. Tomás Maldonado, Typescript 1957, HfG Archiv Ulm.

10. Tomás Maldonado, "Is the Bauhaus Relevant Today?" *Ulm* 8/9 (1963): 5–13.

no means popular at that time. Meyer had been shunted into oblivion by representatives of the official history of the Bauhaus under the influence of Walter Gropius and above all of Nikolaus Pevsner. (Just as there is a heaven for the canonized, there is a hell for heretics and dissidents.)[11] Meyer had undoubtedly been a heretic. During his brief tenure as director of the Bauhaus Dessau (from April 1, 1928, to August 1, 1930), he made four essential contributions to design education. First, he revamped the hybrid structure of the Bauhaus under the considerable inherited restrictions of the school as one of craft education characterized by the rules of guilds from medieval times. Second, he reinforced the relation between design education and the sciences by inviting scientists from a wide variety of disciplines to give conferences. (At that time he could not integrate scientists into the teaching staff. As I noted earlier, the Ulm school's attempts at integration also caused conflict.) Third, he assigned students real problems from industry, rather than hypothetical or invented ones. (Which did, however, cause difficulties by exposing the teaching program to the contingencies of industry and limiting its work to the current state of industry rather than enabling it to anticipate potential design problems.) Finally, Meyer broke up the rigidly sequential structure of the program and permitted students from different years to work together on assignments. In this way, younger students could learn from their more experienced peers and learn teamwork. It took several decades until design programs went further by permitting students from different careers (design, engineering, marketing) to work together (at the University of Alto, for instance).

As is well known, the Preliminary Course was central to Bauhaus pedagogy. As an organizational unit, it took up the first semester of study. The Preliminary Course (*Vorlehre* or *Vorkurs*) functioned foremost as a remedy for the deficits of the years prior to higher study. The exercises in the course were intended to train the students to differentiate aesthetic ability; they were later called "nonapplied design exercises," in contrast to the applied exercises, which focused on solving practical problems. Not all of the students responded positively to these assignments. In a call to action in 1929, several students characterized the course as pointless tinkering and a waste of time and requested that it be transformed into a practical workshop and reclassified as optional instead of mandatory.[12] In 1962, first-year students at the Ulm school expressed a similar frustration with the theoretical orientation of the teaching program: "We do not want to become sociologists, physiologists, psychologists, and definitely not theoreticians, statisticians, analysts or mathematicians, but d e s i g n e r s."[13]

These two protests spanning three decades reveal the potential conflict between traditional lecture-based (discursive) teaching

11. Antonio Toca Fernández, "Héroes y herejes: Juan O'Gorman y Hannes Meyer," *Casa del Tiempo* 3/4 (June 2010): 18–23.

12. Bauhaus Archiv BHA_8529-1+2-Vorkurs-1929.

13. Archive of the HfG Ulm.

methods and the training of (nondiscursive) design competence. Such a conflict can be resolved, however, by the problem-oriented teaching typical in design programs, though such pedagogical approaches often remain a novelty in other disciplines, such as medicine.[14]

In conclusion, I want to touch briefly on the political dimensions of design discourse—politics being the domain in which the dialectical dynamics between power and emancipation unfold. The present period has been characterized as post-utopian in its frank opposition to the modernist project. The driving force behind modernity was a belief in the potential of development in the broadest sense—social, industrial, technological, economical, cultural, scientific—for the benefit of humanity. Even if one dismisses the modernist project, its programmatic stance vis-à-vis the future remains valid, and the disposition to consider how to change existing social relations remains not only desirable but necessary.

In such a context, history reveals its relevance when understood not as chronology, as a sequence of threaded facts, but as explanation of the past—and of the present through the past. The potential of design history remains limited as long as it privileges style and its evolutions instead of approaching design within the broader framework of a history of industrial civilization. The discipline of design history can play a decisive role for design programs, because without knowledge of the past, one does not know where to go in the future.

Discourses and theories oscillate between converging with and diverging from hegemony. It is up to every participant in the design discourse to decide between these extremes, above all in those period permeated by the growth of anti-democratic forces. Concerning the political dimension of design activity, it comes down to a question that is not easy to answer: Does the project consolidate hegemonic conditions, or does it contain an emancipatory potential? That is, does it reduce heteronomy, or does it reinforce it?

Christopher Latham Sholes invents the modern typewriter and QWERTY keyboard

14. McGill University is credited with breaking from the traditional teaching method and in the 1970s having adopted a problem-oriented teaching approach for students of medicine.

FOR GUI BONSIEPE

PAMELA M. LEE

It's my privilege to respond to Gui Bonsiepe's text on the heteronomy of design in a post-utopian age. Bonsiepe offers the timeliest reflections on contemporary design education against the expanded field of a generalized design ethos today. Fundamentally, he articulates a paradox trailing the culture of design as it's been submitted to the pernicious ideology of growth—the logic of which has wreaked havoc on the environment, markets, media, and democracy. Bonsiepe identifies the "discursive weakness" of the discipline of design as a dispiriting contrast to the field's ballooning presence elsewhere. From strategic design to emotional design to experience design to "design thinking," the founding concept of "design" has been rendered at once too meaningful and wholly meaningless, unmoored from such hoary conceits as "history," "theory," and "praxis." In this regard, I take the heteronomy of design critiqued by Bonsiepe as continuous with a market trading in lifestyle memes and the rituals of mass customization. As an art historian, I note also that the current usage of the term *design* finds its rhetorical cognate in another overused phrase in the digital lifeworld—"to curate." Both phrases telegraph the aesthetic and affective surplus value that supplies both the realm of biopolitics and the experience economy.

So, what happens to design as a discipline when the term itself has been effectively deregulated? The neoliberal resonances of this phrasing are unavoidable and, for our interests, purposeful. I want to reflect briefly on Bonsiepe's entwined terms "heteronomy" and "post-utopia" by applying them retroactively to Bonsiepe's own beginnings as designer and thinker. From his tenure as both student and teacher at Ulm, the storied postwar design school, to his work in Santiago, Chile, where he was a principal actor in the creation of Cybersyn, Bonsiepe's experience bookends the pivotal moments from after the Bauhaus to before the Internet and well beyond.

General view of the Opsroom of Cybersyn. Design: INTEC Design group, 1973.

We start at Ulm in the light of "heteronomy," the notion of which we necessarily oppose to the interests of "autonomy," and one with a strong inheritance in Enlightenment thought. The institutional history of Ulm is indeed guided by extramural interests, notably the disasters of war. Founded after the cataclysms of midcentury and spanning the years 1953–68, Ulm was no pedagogical monolith. Although it was referred to as the "New Bauhaus" in its inaugural years, there was but a singular Bauhaus alumnus, the Swiss artist and designer Max Bill, critical to the school's establishment; Bill's resignation soon after becoming the school's first rector led to the formative tenure of Tomás Maldonado, the great Argentine painter and designer and Bonsiepe's mentor. Under Maldonado's leadership, Ulm's curriculum would come to embrace a range of new theories and methodologies that we could call "heteronomous," for their expansive outlook on systems discourse. While the critical theory of the Frankfurt School undergirded the ideological commitments of many participants—advancing the critique of high culture as immanent or autonomous in its inflection—so too was the *administrative* and technocratic logic continuous with the rhetoric of systems, information and game theory, cybernetics, operational research, and the many other new languages consistent with Cold War think tanks. Ulm's interdisciplinary curriculum based around four departments (Product Design, Visual Communication, Building, and Information) as well as its formative, if ever-evolving, Basic Studies course, variously incorporated these tendencies. As Kenneth Frampton writes, Maldonado's course in "Operational Research" took inspiration from the work of Anatol Rapaport, a pivotal mathematician in the development of game theory, key thinker in the movement of General Semantics and Systems Theory, and influential presence at the RAND Corporation, where he was an erstwhile consultant to Robert McNamara's Department of Defense.[1] Three other instructors—Abraham Moles, Max Bense, and Horst Rittel—were likewise influential in reshaping the curriculum through complementary syllabi on cybernetics and semiotics.[2]

What effects such language had on the teaching and practice of design and its aesthetics would prove a question of existential importance for Bonsiepe and many of his colleagues. The assimilation of both systems theory *and* the prewar avant-garde—of management cybernetics *and* the formal rigors of modernism's radical experiments—found ample expression in publications and prototypes, from stacking dishes to industrialized buildings, from wallpaper to advertisements for Lufthansa. Yet as appealing as such products were on aesthetic grounds, they could only flag a structural contradiction at the heart of the school's founding mission. Bonsiepe raised this issue in a 1968 contribution to the *Ulm Journal*. Insofar as design served the needs of the "Communications *Industry*" (my italics), the coinage recalling Adorno, Horkheimer, and Alexander Kluge on the industrialization of consciousness and the media, the Ulm designer would implicitly challenge the heteronomous interests of the institution. Aesthetics, Bonsiepe argued, would only ever implicitly challenge domination.

Aesthetics, in other words, could not hover aloft, lifted from the dross of industry and its *raison d'être* in the corporate shareholder. But aesthetics could also operate as a lever for complexity, as the lessons of systems would suggest. Here, then, let's consider the next step in Bonsiepe's itinerary, as a designer on the ground in

1. See Anatol Rapaport, *Operational Philosophy* (New York: Harper and Brothers, 1953).

2. On Maldonado's interest in operational research, see Kenneth Frampton, "The Ideology of a Curriculum," in *Ulm Design: The Morality of Objects*, ed. Herbert Lindinger (Cambridge, MA: MIT Press, 1991), 130–48.

Chile during the embattled years of Salvador Allende's short-lived presidency. This moment, just *before* the Internet, precedes the *post*-utopian ethos he describes as a condition of the present.

Bonsiepe's collaboration with a group of Chilean engineers and the British management cybernetician Stafford Beer would result in the legend that is Cybersyn: a digital prototype that would manage Allende's planned economy during his Unidad Popular government. Copious scholarship has been devoted specifically to Cybersyn's operations room ("Opsroom"), demonstrating how innovative design principles might contribute to the work of the first democratically elected socialist president in the Western hemisphere. What I am interested in here is what the design has come to emblematize. For many, an image of the Opsroom might inevitably conjure the visuals of popular science fiction, the stage-craft of *Star Trek* or *2001: A Space Odyssey*. These references are to the point in marking the project's vintage and its speculative imaginary. At the same time, the once-modish interior of the Opsroom, with its swivel chairs and futuristic interfaces, now betrays the project's technological obsolescence.

What gets lost in such associations, however, is the proposition that design might effectively liberate the people it was imagined to serve. Beer's notion of "designing freedom" emphatically conveyed design's historically radical prospects. In this regard, the Opsroom remained continuous with an ethos of the Bauhaus, if distinctly different in its means, inflections, and ambitions. The destruction of the room shortly after Augusto Pinochet's coup of September 11, 1973, would suggest otherwise, if not strong-arm such possibilities altogether. The Opsroom, as such, has become an artifact of a failed digital utopia.

Or perhaps, to borrow Bonsiepe's language, it has become something *post*-utopian. I understand that this phrase may not be familiar in such a context, Bonsiepe included. "Post-utopian" may well sound a dispiriting note to many, as if the striving for utopia were over and done with, a failure. And so, the question that logically follows is, why even bother? Why even worry about design education *now*, if it has been totalized in the interests of the market, rendered discursively weak and amorphous?

But in taking the notion of utopia as a non-place seriously—as fundamentally and structurally unreachable—I'll end by modifying this interpretation. For perhaps the qualifier "post" here actually lays *claim* to a history of such events, a history of a utopia still to come, even as it's rendered inaccessible to many of in the present. And perhaps it's a history of design that would enable us to chart these speculative imaginings. Bonsiepe's contributions in this light—not just after the Bauhaus and before the Internet, but in the present—reaffirm such commitments looking forward.

WHY WE SHOULD STOP DESCRIBING DESIGN AS "PROBLEM-SOLVING"

HUGH DUBBERLY

The world today faces multiple intertwined crises, including the COVID-19 pandemic and the resulting economic depression—on top of economic disparity, racial injustice, global warming, and more, which arose in a context of large and intertwined technological, economic, and social changes. Designers have proposed for several decades that the world needs design (or "design thinking") to solve these problems.[1] Even today, such a proposition seems self-evident to many designers. But this mindset reflects misconceptions about the world in which designers work and what designers do.

The first misconception is that the world is composed of "problems" and that each problem can be neatly carved out from the next, fixed in time, and defined in an objective way so that anyone can find a lasting "solution"—like a watchmaker replacing a broken gear. In fact, most issues facing the world (and designers) are not isolated, not static, and not clear; they are "systemic," connected in networks of cause and effect, ever changing, and defined largely by one's point of view. In 1979, Russell Ackoff wrote, "Managers are not confronted with problems that are independent of each other, but with dynamic situations that consist of complex systems of changing problems that interact with each other. I call such situations messes."[2] A neutral term might be "tangles."

The second misconception is that designers have special skills in "solving" problems, that they stand outside a situation, diagnose what's "wrong," and prescribe the "right" therapy. Instead, like physicians, designers engage in a back-and-forth with other participants, the situation, and their tools and materials. As Donald Schön has noted, "In the literal sense of the word, designing can be understood as a 'conversation,' a dialogue among individuals who frame a design situation in different ways, employ different generative metaphors, operate from different appreciative systems."[3] So perhaps the idea of facilitating a conversation about goals and means is more helpfully descriptive of the design process than that of "problem-solving."

This paper explores the myths of design as problem-solving—their origins in design history, issues that call into question the validity of the problem-solving frame, and alternative ways of framing the process.

The Problem-Solving Frame

If design is problem-solving, then the "problem" is the designer's basic unit of work. It has many synonyms:

- Breakdowns / malfunctions / opportunities
- Context / environment / situation

1. For example, Tim Brown and Don Norman.

2. Russell Ackoff, "The Future of Operational Research," *Journal of the Operational Research Society* 30, no. 2 (February 1979): 93–104.

3. Donald Schön, "The Design Process," in *Varieties of Thinking, Essays from Harvard's Philosophy of Education Research Center*, ed. V. A. Howard (New York: Routledge, 1990), 137.

- Goals / jobs to be done
- Functions / requirements / constraints
- Human needs / wants / desires / values
- Tasks / scenarios of use / use cases

The process of "problem-solving" is framed as rational. It, too, has many synonyms:

- Addressing issues
- Changing existing situations into preferred ones
- Creating order
- Ensuring clarity, reliability, and safety
- Improving efficiency
- Increasing effectiveness
- Reducing costs
- Removing pain points

An axiom of modernist design is that defining a problem reveals its solution.[4] The problem-solution pair forms two sides of an equation. Implicit in this axiom is the idea that the problem *has* an objective definition and that the designer's role is not only to solve it but also to define it.

Many models depict the design process as linear, with a clear beginning, middle, and end.[5] For example, the "double-diamond" model includes four steps: "Discover, Define, Develop, Deliver."[6] In practice, the design process is iterative, and the proposed solution is often a redefinition of the problem.

Despite its popularity, describing design as problem-solving does not make it true; rather, it is one of several possible frames—stories designers tell themselves and others. These stories are myths that support political agendas, position designers in relation to organizations, and help sell services.

How did we get here?

1.0 Origins

Many designers have sought a rational basis for their work.[7] This search gained momentum at the end of the nineteenth century and accelerated throughout the twentieth as Beaux Arts approaches to architecture and design were replaced by late-modernist ones—and as the frame of design as decorative art was replaced by the frame of design as problem-solving. This shift had several dimensions:

from		*to*
slow, rural, agrarian ethos	→	fast, urban, machine ethos
handcraft-making	→	planning-for-manufacturing
lesser art	→	science of the artificial
skilled trade	→	expert professional service

4. For example, Louis Sullivan, Max Bill, George Nelson / Armin Hofmann, Christopher Alexander, Charles Eames, William Peña, et al.

5. Hugh Dubberly, "How Do You Design? A Compendium of Models," 2004, http://www.dubberly.com/wp-content/uploads/2008/06/ddo_designprocess.pdf.

6. In 1996, Bela Banathy proposed the double-diamond design process; in 2005, the British Design Council made it popular.

decorative art ——————> problem-solving
idiosyncratic intuition ——————> repeatable method
subjective ——————> objective

Statements framing design as problem-solving are common throughout the modernist canon, beginning with its origin documents and continuing today, underscoring how foundational such a frame is for design practice and design education.

Let's consider some of those statements.

1.1 Louis Sullivan

In 1896, as modernism began, American architect Louis Sullivan declared, "Form ever follows function" and, "The design of the tall office building must be recognized and confronted at the outset as a problem to be solved—a vital problem pressing for a true solution." He added, "It is of the very essence of every problem that it contains and suggests its own solution. This I believe to be natural law."[8]

1.2 Deutscher Werkbund

The shift to modernism also had roots in Europe. In 1907, Peter Behrens[9] and Hermann Muthesius helped found the Deutscher Werkbund. The Werkbund's motto was "From sofa cushions to city buildings," framing design as concerned with everything from product details to large systems. Muthesius read Frederick Taylor, who gave management of manufacturing a "scientific" basis and turned it toward problem-solving. Muthesius brought the "science" of experimentation, efficiency, and standards to the Werkbund and its designers.[10]

1.3 Constructivism

In 1922, in the opening statement of the avant-garde design journal *Veshch*, El Lissitzky and Ilya Ehrenberg wrote, "The new art is founded not on a subjective, but on an objective basis. This, like science, can be described with precision and is by nature constructive. It unites not only pure art, but all those who stand at the frontier of the new culture. The artist is companion to the scholar, the engineer, and the worker."[11]

1.4 Bauhaus

In 1919, Walter Gropius (who had worked for Behrens) formed the Bauhaus in Weimar; in 1920, Lenin formed the VKhUTEMAS in Moscow. Both schools shared many of the Werkbund's goals. The rise of fascism in Germany created a diaspora of Bauhaus faculty and students in the Soviet Union, Switzerland, and the United States, where many found influential positions. The problem-solving frame appeared frequently in the writings of former Bauhaus faculty:

7. For example, Leonardo's "Vitruvian Man," Le Corbusier's "Le Modular," and Henry Dreyfuss's "The Measure of Man."

8. Louis Sullivan, "The Tall Office Building Artistically Considered," *Lippincott's Magazine*, March 1896.

9. Behrens employed future stars Walter Gropius, Ludwig Mies van der Rohe, Le Corbusier, and Adolf Meyer.

• In 1937, Lászlo Moholy-Nagy wrote, "We don't teach what is called 'pure art,' but we train what you might call the art engineer. . . . But to you—the industrialists—we offer our services for research. We shall work on your problems."[12]

• In 1955, Gropius wrote, "My intention is . . . to introduce a method of approach which allows one to tackle a problem according to its peculiar conditions."[13]

• In 1963, Josef Albers used the word *problem* fifteen times in the short text of his masterwork, *Interaction of Color*; he wrote of "solving our problems" and titled his student exercises "problems"—framing them as questions with answers that are either right or wrong, like problems in math or physics.[14]

1.5 HfG Ulm

In 1953, the modernist movement received an infusion of energy with the opening of the Hochschule für Gestaltung (HfG) in Ulm. The problem-solving frame continued in the writings of Ulm faculty:

• In 1974, Max Bill, Ulm's first rector (and a former Bauhaus student), wrote, "The creative process, taken step by step, corresponds to a logical operation and its logical verification. Much the same applies to all my activities. They are always based on the analysis of the problem and its logical, verifiable solution."[15]

• In 2002, Tomás Maldonado, Ulm's second rector, wrote, "In all of us, especially myself, there was a deep dissatisfaction with a didactics (and a design activity) that had appealed only to intuition. In this context an increasing interest in disciplines . . . with a heuristic function such as 'problem-solving' and 'decision-making' [emerged]. We were very curious about anything moving in the world that was concerned with scientific questions."[16]

Another design diaspora ensued after the school closed in 1968.[17] One of Ulm's lasting legacies was to recast the vague notion of problem-solving into a standardized, repeatable method. The resulting curricula focused on design methods, with core courses such as the Scientific Problem-Solving Design Studio.[18]

1.6 Allgemeine Gewerbeschule Basel

Meanwhile, the Allgemeine Gewerbeschule Basel (originally a

10. Ivan Rupnik, "Projecting in Space-Time: The Laboratory Method, Modern Architecture and Settlement-Building, 1918–1932" (PhD diss., Harvard University, 2015).

11. El Lissitzky and Ilya Ehrenburg, "Statement by the Editors of *Veshch/Gegenstand/Objet*" (1922), in *Art in Theory 1900–1990*, ed. Charles Harrison and Ed Wood (Oxford: Blackwell, 1994), 321. (I am indebted to Lou Danzinger, who pointed to El Lissitzky as a source, and to Elizabeth Byrne, who helped me locate the reference.)

12. Sibyl Moholy-Nagy, *Moholy-Nagy: Experiment in Totality* (New York: Harper and Brothers, 1950), 149–50.

13. Walter Gropius, *Scope of Total Architecture* (London: Allen and Unwinn, 1956), 21.

14. Josef Albers, *Interaction of Color: Revised Edition* (New Haven: Yale University Press, 1971).

15. Eduard Hüttinger, *Max Bill* (Zurich: ABC Editions, 1978), 212.

program to train high-school students in typesetting) expanded into an international graduate school of design (led by Emil Ruder and Armin Hofmann), attracting many notable designers. Its graduates formed a third design diaspora.[19]

• In 1965, George Nelson wrote in his preface to Hofmann's *Graphic Design Manual* that Hofmann believed "that if problems can be correctly stated, they can be solved."[20]

• In 1967, Ruder's *Typographie* (a primer for generations of designers) began on the flyleaf, "After 21 years of teaching typography, the author is concerned in this book with the problems of form which confront the typographer in the practice of his craft."[21]

• In 2019, Baseler Ken Hiebert confirmed, "Problem solving was embedded in every aspect of learning in the Basel Program."[22] While Basel focused on "form," problem-solving remained a central metaphor in its curriculum.

1.7 Design Methods

William Wurster embodied the transformation of design in the twentieth century. At the University of California, Berkeley, he studied architecture in the Beaux Arts tradition; he went on to Harvard (where Gropius was teaching) and later served as dean of MIT's School of Architecture and Planning. In 1950, Wurster returned to Berkeley to "modernize" its School of Architecture. He recruited new faculty, including, in 1963, Christopher Alexander, who had also studied at Harvard, and Horst Rittel, who had taught at Ulm.

16. Tomás Maldonado in "Looking Back and Forward: Interview," in *The Ulm School of Design—Beginnings of a Project of Unyielding Modernity*, ed. Martin Krampen and Günter Hörmann (Berlin: Ernst and Sohn, 2003), 241.

17. Some notable examples: Bruce Archer went to the RCA; Tomas Gonda to OSU; William Huff to Buffalo; Klaus Krippendorff to Penn; Horst Rittel to Berkeley. Along with Gui Bonsiepe, Karl Gerstner, Martin Krampen, Tomás Maldonado, and other Ulm alumni, they affected the course of design education and design practice for decades.

18. The author's first design studio course, in 1976, at the University of Colorado's College of Environmental Design, was run by graduates of Berkeley and influenced by Ulm. I would like to thank Caroline Hightower, former executive director of the AIGA—who in exasperation once told me she wished she would never again hear design described as problem-solving—for planting the seeds of doubt in me about my education.

19. In 1965, Ken Hiebert joined the faculty of PCA (now University of the Arts). Others soon followed Hiebert into teaching, including Hans Allemann (PCA), Dan Boyarski (CMU), Philip Burton (Yale, Illinois), Inge Druckrey (Yale, PCA, etc.), Jim Faris (CCA), April Greiman (KCIA), Dan Friedman (Yale), Terry Irwin (CCA, CMU), and Helmut Schmid (Hong-Ik, etc.). Many other Baselers went on to teach and practice around the world.

20. Armin Hoffman, *Graphic Design Manual: Principles and Practice* (New York: Van Nostrand Reinhold, 1965).

21. Emil Ruder, *Typography: A Manual of Design* (Basel: Verlag Arthur Niggli, 1967).

Both Alexander and Rittel were instrumental in the Design Methods Movement, a series of conferences and publications from the early 1960s through the early '70s, which borrowed ideas from military planning, information theory, operations research, and cybernetics in an attempt to put design on a "scientific" basis. For them, design as problem-solving was a given.

• In 1964, Christopher Alexander wrote, "Every design problem begins with an effort to achieve fitness between two entities: the form in question and its context. The form is the solution to the problem; context defines the problem. In other words, when we speak of design, the real object of discussion is not the form alone, but the ensemble comprising the form and its context."[23]

• In 1964, Horst Rittel wrote, "Science and design are usually taken as polar contradictions. . . . What do the words science and design mean and what do they have in common? . . . [a] activities, [b] names for the results of activities, [c] associated with social institutions . . . [d] directed to the achievement of new realities . . . [e] problem-solving activities, . . . [f] unpredictable results."[24]

• In 1968, the Nobel-laureate economist and artificial-intelligence pioneer Herbert Simon published *The Sciences of the Artificial*, positioning design as a branch of science encompassing all the professions (e.g., architecture, business, engineering, law, medicine). He wrote, "The natural sciences are concerned with how things are. . . . Design, on the other hand, is concerned with how things ought to be, with devising artifacts to attain goals." He proclaimed, "Everyone" designs who devises courses of action aimed at changing existing situations into preferred ones." He noted, "Human problem solving, from the most blundering to the most insightful, involves nothing more than varying mixtures of trial and error and selectivity. . . . There is now a growing body of evidence that the activity called human problem solving is basically a form of means-ends analysis that aims at discovering a process description of the path that leads to a desired goal."[25] In short: feedback. In 1972, with Allen Newell, Simon published *Human Problem Solving*, laying a foundation for a rationalistic approach to the development of AI.

• In a 1969 interview, Charles Eames noted, "Design depends largely on constraints. . . . Here is one of the few effective keys to the Design problem: the ability of the Designer to recognize as many of the constraints as possible; his willingness and enthusiasm for working within these constraints. Constraints of price, of size, of strength, of balance, of surface, of time, and so forth. Each problem has its own peculiar list."[26]

• In 1977, architect William Peña wrote, "You can't solve a problem unless you know what it is." He defined "programming" as "the search for sufficient information to clarify, to understand, and

22. Ken Hiebert, email correspondence with the author, April 2019.

23. Christopher Alexander, *Notes on Synthesis of Form* (Cambridge, MA: Harvard University Press, 1964), 15–16.

24. Horst Rittel, "The Universe of Design," in *The Universe of Design: Horst Rittel's Theories of Design and Planning*, ed. Jean-Pierre Protzen and David J. Harris (New York: Routledge, 2010), 48.

to state the problem." For Peña, "Programming is problem seeking" and "design is problem solving." He believed each required different attitudes and different skills that were rarely found in the same person.[27]

Three other books also illustrate the central role the problem-solving frame played in the discourse of midcentury design:

• *The All New Universal Traveler: A Soft-Systems Guide to Creativity, Problem Solving, and the Process of Reaching Goals*, by Don Koberg and Jim Bagnall (students of Rittel at UC Berkeley) (1972), a common textbook for design students of the time.

• *How to Solve It*, by George Polya (1945), a primer for math students, recommended by *The Universal Traveler* as a reference tool for designers.

• *The Vignelli Canon*, by Massimo Vignelli (2010). In this primer, Vignelli summarized his beliefs after fifty years of practice, describing designers' three levels of responsibility: "One—to ourselves, the integrity of the project and all its components. Two—to the client, to solve the problem in a way that is economically sound and efficient. Three—to the public at large, the consumer, the user of the final design. On each one of these levels we should be ready to commit ourselves to reach the most appropriate solution, the one that solves the problem without compromises for the benefit of everyone."[28]

1.8 Design Thinking

By the late 1970s, interest in design methods had waned; however, it reemerged in the late 1990s, rebranded as "design thinking." Two books were important in describing the history and laying a foundation for the future; both discussed problem-solving at length.

• *How Designers Think: The Design Process Demystified*, by Bryan Lawson (1980), a survey in three parts: "Part One: What Is Design?"; "Part Two: Problems and Solutions"; and "Part Three: Design Thinking."

• *Design Thinking*, by Peter Rowe (1987), a comprehensive and rigorous history of design methods of all types.

Today, design thinking is often associated with the consultancy IDEO and Stanford's d-school. Both link design thinking and problem-solving.

• In 2008, IDEO chair Tim Brown wrote in *Harvard Business Review*, "No matter where we look, we see problems that can be solved only through innovation: unaffordable or unavailable health care, billions of people trying to live on just a few dollars a day, energy usage that outpaces the planet's ability to support it, education systems that fail many students, companies whose traditional markets are disrupted by new technologies or demographic

25. Herbert Simon, *The Sciences of the Artificial* (Cambridge, MA: MIT Press, 1968), 111, 132, 195, 211.

26. Charles Eames, interview, "What Is Design?" (1969), in *Eames Design: The Work of the Office of Charles and Ray Eames*, eds. John Neuhart, Marilyn Neuhart, and Ray Eames (New York: Harry Abrams, 1989), 14–15.

27. William Peña and Steven A. Parshall, *Problem Seeking: An Architectural Programming Primer* (New York: John Wiley and Sons, 1977), 5.

shifts. . . . They require a human-centered, creative, iterative, and practical approach to finding the best ideas and ultimate solutions. Design thinking is just such an approach to innovation."[29]

• In 2021, the website for Stanford's d-school put it plainly: "Design thinking is a methodology for creative problem solving."[30]

1.9 DesignX

In 2014, thought leaders Ken Friedman, Yongqi Lou, Don Norman, Pieter Jon Stappers, and Patrick Whitney proposed "DesignX" as a new way of "addressing many of the complex and serious problems facing the world today."[31] Now many of these same experts are involved in a project titled the Future of Design Education.[32]

2.0 Issues

As the statements above suggest, "the 'problem/problem-solving' language frame . . . has been near ubiquitous in the design literature."[33] This positioning will likely continue well into the future because it is convenient and has the clear benefit of promising change with little risk—on time and on budget.

Why should we question it?

Because it creates confusion about both the subject of design and the process of designing.

The word *problem* is misleading because it implies that the subject of design already exists out there for the designer to find. A closer look, however, suggests "the problem" is co-constructed by people involved with the "project." Problem is also misleading because it implies that the design situation can be isolated from the larger systems in which it is embedded, but a closer look finds designers are increasingly involved in the on-going management of those larger systems.

Problem-solving is misleading because it implies that designing is an algorithm guaranteeing results, a mechanical process with a clear beginning, middle, and end. While checklists may be helpful, the design process is a generative conversation having more in common with play and world-building than problem-solving.

Let's consider other ways in which framing design as problem-solving can be misleading and create confusion.

2.1 Mistaking Evolution for a Straight Line

Describing the design process as problem-solving suggests that it proceeds in a straight line and can be managed, when it's

28. Massimo Vignelli, *The Vignelli Canon* (Zurich: Lars Müller, 2010), 31.

29. Tim Brown, "Design Thinking," *Harvard Business Review*, June 2008, https://readings.design/PDF/Tim%20Brown,%20Design%20Thinking.pdf.

30. Stanford d-school, accessed February 15, 2021, https://dschool.stanford.edu/resources/getting-started-with-design-thinking.

31. Don Norman et al., "DesignX," *Shè Jì: The Journal of Design, Economics, and Innovation* 1, no. 1 (Autumn 2015).

32. The Future of Design Education project's website is at https://www.futureofdesigneducation.org/.

33. Steve Harfield, "On Design 'Problematization:' Theorising Differences in Designed Outcomes," *Design Studies* 28, no. 2 (March 2007): 160–61.

often more like a random walk with many dead ends—an evolution not entirely controlled by the designer.

In the early stages of most design projects, the path forward is unclear; often not even the goals are agreed upon, much less the means. As yet, innovation has no recipe; it does not happen on a schedule. No one can guarantee a solution—or a "hit" product—because the process is largely unknown. Each situation is particular, and the "right " design process must be found—just as the "right" design "solution" must be found—by experimentation, by trial and error, by iteration.

One reason designers describe their work as "problem-solving" is to make it less frightening to potential clients. Proposing a linear process with milestones, delivery dates, and hours makes it seem manageable. For example, the double diamond may seem like a set of instructions but is in fact a promise, an aspiration, a goal.

The problem-solving frame also positions the design process as repeatable and designers as objective professionals, experts for hire capable of solving problems of any type. It turns designing into a commodity that consulting firms, schools, and the media can sell more readily. In short, it's marketing.

2.2 Mistaking a Solution Space for the Correct Answer

Describing the design process as problem-solving suggests it leads to one correct answer, when no answer is "right."[34]

In math or physics classes, each student ideally arrives at the same answer. In design classes, many answers are possible, and students seek unique answers. In design competitions, sponsors provide the same brief to all participants and expect different results! Why?[35]

Design problems may result in a range of solutions because they describe spaces with many dimensions, and each solution is a combination of choices along each dimension.

While a group of designers may start from the same brief, they may interpret the brief differently, redefining the problem for them-selves. They also bring different levels of design experience to the project, and different levels of knowledge about the problem domain and the media in which they work. And finally, they bring different values and traditions, all of which may drive different trade-offs.

2.3 Mistaking "Satisficing" for "Optimizing"

Describing the design process as problem-solving suggests an optimal solution can be found, but this is rarely possible; most "solutions" merely satisfy or suffice—"satisfice."[36]

On the one hand, one's time and budget may not allow for a thorough search of a huge solution space, particularly if it's dynamic. On the other hand, the criteria may also be dynamic as stakeholders learn new things.

34. Victor Papanek, *Design for the Real World: Human Ecology and Social Change* (New York: Pantheon, 1971), 5.

35. Harfield, "On Design 'Problematization,'" 165.

36. Simon, *The Sciences of the Artificial*, 27–30.

2.4 Mistaking What-to-Do Questions for How-To Questions

Policy questions differ from engineering questions. Describing the design process as problem-solving suggests that the problem—the goal—is known, defined, clear, that what to do is understood and that the designer merely needs to figure out how to do it. In design practice, such situations are rare. Most of the time designers must define both the "what" and the "how."[37]

2.5 Mistaking Designers for Experts

Describing designers as problem solvers suggests they have "expertise" other stakeholders may not have. But while designers may be more experienced in designing, they are no more knowledgeable about the situation than other stakeholders.[38]

Describing designers as problem solvers may create asymmetry—a power imbalance—by putting them in control of the situation and disenfranchising other stakeholders who rightfully "own" the problem and who should "own" its definition.

A further consequence of framing design as problem-solving is that outsiders may impose their beliefs on insiders. This may happen, in part, because the frame of problem-solving obscures key questions:

- Whose problem is it?
- Who has the power to decide questions?
- What politics should the resulting artifacts have?

2.6 Mistaking Delivering for Finishing

The framing of design as problem-solving emerged with the industrial age; it has roots in mass production, which requires that plans be nearly perfect because mistakes are expensive. It also involves a handoff from designer to manufacturer, which often ends the designer's role. Yet the delivery of a "final plan" is an anomaly of mass manufacturing and may lead to a distorted view of the design process as having an end point.

As hardware manufacturing has become enmeshed in software development and as stand-alone products have become enmeshed in networks of services, "continuous improvement" and "continuous deployment" have become norms. Today's product-service ecologies are never finished. Likewise, the information revolution has changed the way designers work. They have become stewards with ongoing roles in their firms, and their stewardship is never finished.

2.7 Mistaking Systems for Individual Objects

The association of problem-solving with manufacturing may lead to another distorted view: that designing is concerned primarily with individual objects detached from context. And it may lead to ignoring the social-technical systems in which designers and their work are embedded.

37. Rittel, "Dilemmas in a General Theory of Planning" (1972), in *The Universe of Design*.

38. Rittel describes this as "the symmetry of ignorance."

In 1983, systems analyst Geoffrey Vickers wrote: "To focus on problem solving is to divert attention from the far more important function of problem definition and to confuse the continuing process of system regulation with the episodic activity of seeking specific goals and the much more frequent and radically different activity of averting specific threats."[39]

2.8 Other Critiques

Prior efforts at reforming the problem-solving frame deserve mention:

• In 1968, Rittel and Webber noted that problems are not all of the same type. They introduced the idea of "wicked" problems (political problems about which agreement is not possible), to be distinguished from "tame" problems (engineering problems about which agreement is not disputed).[40] In 1987, Rowe proposed three levels of problems: **1.** simple, where the goal is agreed upon; **2.** complex, where the goal is being discussed; and 3) wicked, where stakeholders cannot agree on the goal.[41]

• A recurring critique is that problems are not "objective." In 1986, Terry Winograd and Fernando Flores wrote, "The critical part of problem-solving lies in formulating the problem." They noted that any "space of alternatives" exists in relation to some "observer." And they underscored the subjective nature of problem-finding. "A problem is created by the linguistic acts in which it is identified and categorized."[42]

Schön shared a similar view: "A designer forms a representation of some initial design situation, framing a design problem that includes, when it is 'well formed,' elements from which to construct design options, a description of the situation in which options may be enacted as moves, and criteria sufficient to evaluate the effectiveness of proposed solutions."[43]

While framing a problem may suggest solutions, prototyping a solution may likewise affect the framing. In 1996, Winograd wrote, "There is no direct path between the designer's intention and the outcome. As you work a problem, you are continually in the process of developing a path into it, forming new appreciations and understandings as you make new moves."[44] For many "problems,"

39. Geoffrey Vickers, "The Poverty of Problem Solving," in *Systems Analysis in Urban Policy-Making and Planning*, ed. M. Batty, B. Hutchinson, NATO Conference Series 12 (Boston: Springer, 1983), 17–18, https://link.springer.com/content/pdf/10.1007/978-1-4613-3560-3_3.pdf.

40. Rittel, "Dilemmas in a General Theory of Planning" (1972), in *The Universe of Design*.

41. Peter G. Rowe, *Design Thinking* (Cambridge, MA: MIT Press, 1987), 39.

42. Terry Winograd and Fernando Flores, *Understanding Computers and Cognition: A New Foundation for Design* (Norwood, NJ: Ablex, 1986), 147.

43. Donald Schön, "The Design Process," in *The Reflective Practitioner: How Professionals Think in Action* (New York: Basic Books, 1983), 111.

44. Terry Winograd, *Bringing Design to Software* (Reading, MA: Addison-Wesley, 1996), 5.

designers may not be able to define "requirements" a priori; "fit" may have to be achieved through iteration in context.

Lucy Suchman questioned the idea that a designed solution emerges from the clear formulation of a plan; instead, she proposed that a definition of a problem emerges while exploring possible actions in a context.[45]

In other words, framing design as problem-solving reduces it to a mechanical feedback process seeking a clear, unchanging goal. In practice, the process of designing leads to the discovery of both alternative means and alternative goals.

3.0 Alternatives

In 2017, designer Kees Dorst noted, "When people started trying to understand design . . . the first model they devised was of design as a problem-solving process."[46] A few alternatives:

• Art: The model of design as fine art—pursuing an artist's vision rather than a client's need—has little relevance in practice but persists in schools for primarily financial rather than ideological reasons. Such design programs attract students, whose tuition pays for other programs. Critical design—critiquing design and society—may be an exception, a design practice akin to art practice.

• Drawing: Illustrator Milton Glaser maintained, "Drawing is thinking."[47] Computer scientist Bill Buxton argued that designing is sketching. Buxton focused on drawing, though he included prototyping broadly.[48] Drawing needn't be art; it can be a process of learning.

• A Third Culture: Reasoning that design is neither art nor science, systems expert Bela Banathy suggested that design is its own way of knowing and acting in the world. Similarly, historian Andrew Pickering suggested a "weak knowledge" contrasting with the "strong knowledge" of traditional science. Pickering built on Heidegger's notion of *poiesis* to describe "performative experimentation" or "experimental dances," offering as examples the work of cyberneticians like Ashby, Beer, and Pask, which bears similarities to designing.[49]

• Play: In "Design and the Play Instinct," Paul Rand wrote, "The play principle serves as a basis for serious problem-solving."[50] Rand saw design and play as improvisation within rules, exploring the constraints and possibilities of a system.

45. Lucy Suchman, *Plans and Situated Action: The Problem of Human-Machine Communications* (Xerox Palo Alto Research Center, February 1985).

46. Kees Dorst, *Notes on Design: How Creative Practice Works* (Amsterdam: BIS Publishers, 2017), 19.

47. Milton Glaser, *Drawing Is Thinking* (New York: Overlook Duckworth, 2008). 5.

48. Bill Buxton, *Sketching User Interfaces: Getting the Design Right and the Right Design* (San Francisco: Morgan Kauffmann, 2007).

49. Andrew Pickering, "Poiesis in Action: Doing without Knowledge," in *Weak Knowledge: Forms, Functions, and Dynamics*, ed. Moritz Epple, Annette Imhausen, and Falk Müller (Frankfurt: Campus Verlag, 2019).

50. Paul Rand, "Design and the Play Instinct," in *A Designer's Art* (New Haven: Yale University Press, 1985).

• World-building (or World-forming or World-making): Filmmaker Alex McDowell has described world-building as "a narrative practice in which the design of a world precedes the telling of a story."[51] World-building[52] is fundamental to movies and game design. World-building also plays a role in service design and interaction design. Indeed, software pioneer Ted Nelson described software design as a branch of moviemaking.

Designer Cheryl Heller has written, "People talk about design as problem-solving . . . but that's a limited view." In contrast, she describes design as creating "new ways of being on this planet, and with each other."[53] The idea that the world needs to be "in transition" also suggests world-forming, as does Arturo Escobar's concepts of the "pluriverse" ("a world in which many worlds fit") and "ontological design" ("a conversation about possibilities" for action).[54]

3.1 Establishing a New Foundation

In *Understanding Computers and Cognition: A New Foundation for Design*, Winograd and Flores questioned the foundations of artificial intelligence. In a review, former Ulm student and teacher Gui Bonsiepe wrote, "Winograd and Flores launch particular attacks on the tendency that was widespread in the sixties to see design as a process of problem-solving underpinned by decision theory."[55] As Winograd and Flores note, "A 'problem' always arises for human beings in situations where they live—in other words, it arises in relation to a background. Different interpreters will see and talk about different problems requiring different tools, potential actions, and design solutions. In some cases, what is a problem for one person won't be a problem at all for someone else."[56]

Winograd and Flores also questioned the foundations of design. "In order to understand the phenomena surrounding a new technology we must open the question of *design*—the interaction between understanding and creation. . . . How a society engenders

51. University of Southern California, School of Cinematic Arts, World Building Institute website, accessed February 15, 2021, https://worldbuilding.institute/about.

52. The concept of *Weltbild* (whether translated as "world-formation" or "world-building") comes from Heidegger's insistence that the human being be defined as world-forming (as an extension of his idea of being-in-the-world). See his *Fundamental Concepts of Metaphysics: World, Finitude, Solitude*. (I am grateful to Rachel Churner for this observation.)

53. Cheryl Heller, quoted on the Arizona State University website, 2019, https://asunow.asu.edu/20190403-cheryl-heller-joins-asu-director-design-integration.

54. Arturo Escobar, *Designs for the Pluriverse: Radical Interdependence, Autonomy, and the Making of Worlds* (Durham, NC: Duke University Press, 2018), xvi and 110. Escobar builds on Winograd and Flores, who also draw on Heidegger.

55. Gui Bonsiepe, "Through Language to Design," in *Interface: An Approach to Design* (Maastricht: Jan van Eyck Akademie, 1994), 139 (quoting from Winograd and Flores, *Understanding Computers and Cognition*).

56. Winograd and Flores, *Understanding Computers and Cognition*, 77.

inventions whose existence in turn alters that society. We need to establish a theoretical basis for looking at what devices do, not just how they operate."

3.2 Deliberation and Conversation

Winograd and Flores proposed an alternative to Simon's problem-solving. Simon described designing as a sequence of steps:

- framing a problem;
- outlining a solution space + selection criteria;
- determining values + probable outcomes;
- selecting a solution.[57]

For Winograd and Flores, a "breakdown" results in a "situation of irresolution . . . in which the course of activity is interrupted by some kind of 'unreadiness.'" Moving "from irresolution to resolution is 'deliberation.' . . . conversation (in which one or many actors may participate)." Deliberation may include:

- selecting from a space of possibilities defined by the original frame;
- generating new possibilities (changing the dimensions of the existing space);
- changing the frame (creating a new space of possibilities);
- rejecting the frame (deciding there really isn't a problem after all).[58]

3.3 Systems

In "The Poverty of Problem Solving," Vickers wrote that management consists not in solving problems but rather in "regulating systems."[59] For example, children are not "problems to be solved"; they are living things to be nurtured. So too are the systems we design, particularly software and services.

A new frame of design is emerging. Ensuring that "systems" thrive—that they learn, regenerate, and adapt—becomes important. The "problem" becomes a "network of relationships"; the "solution" becomes "dynamic equilibrium."

This emerging shift parallels the earlier shift from Beaux Arts to late modernism:

from		*to*
fast, urban, machine ethos	→	organic-systems ethos
planning-for-manufacturing	→	stewarding continuous deployment
science of the artificial	→	the political or rhetorical
expert professional service	→	co-creation
problem-solving	→	facilitating generative conversation
repeatable method	→	directed learning
objective	→	negotiated

3.4 Solving Problems vs. Becoming Responsible

A final note: Claiming that design can solve the world's myriad problems is a mix of hubris, marketing, and misunderstanding. The

57. Simon, *Sciences of the Artificial*, 51–83.

58. Winograd and Flores, *Understanding Computers and Cognition*, 147–50.

59. Vickers, "The Poverty of Problem Solving," 18.

"problems" that matter—the wicked problems, messes, or tangles that threaten our existence—cannot be "solved" in the sense of "put right" so that they disappear. Instead, we must manage them on an ongoing basis, both globally and locally, through generative conversations.

This requires a change in our view of the world, of ourselves, and of design.

The literature of systems design points to ethical propositions that might help:

Bonsiepe noted, "[Winograd and Flores] go to the heart of the matter concerning design: 'We encounter the deep questions of design when we recognize that in designing tools we are designing ways of being.' . . . 'We create and give meaning to the world we live in and share with others. . . . We design ourselves (and the social and technological networks in which our lives have meaning) in language.'" Bonsiepe added, "Designing means entering into an obligation to ensure that the world meets our intentions."[60]

In his essay "Metadesign," Humberto Maturana concluded, "It is not information that constitutes the reality that we live. The reality that we live arises instant after instant through the configuration of emotions that we live. . . . But if we know this . . . we shall become responsible of what we do."[61]

Cybernetician (and designer) Heinz von Foerster vowed, "[I shall] act always so as to increase the number of choices."[62] His "ethical imperative" foregrounds our responsibility to enable others to decide for themselves; it suggests that a designer's role is to help bring forward valid options, not just many versions of the same thing but true 'variety'—the diversity needed for resilience. That is, we are responsible for maintaining generative conversations.

60. Bonsiepe, "Through Language to Design," 139–40.

61. Humberto Maturana, "Metadesign," for "TechnoMorphica," 1997, https://www.pangaro.com/hciiseminar2019/Maturana_Metadesign.pdf.

62. Heinz von Foerster, "Ethics and Second-Order Cybernetics," in *Understanding Understanding: Essays on Cybernetics and Cognition* (New York: Springer, 2003), 295.

TECHnoCRITICISM

SHARON HELMER POGGENPOHL

It may seem commonplace to spell it out: Technology changes our lives in complex and profound ways. But leaving this generality unacknowledged is a mistake; it needs to be brought to design. In "Why We Should Stop Describing Design as 'Problem-Solving,'" Hugh Dubberly notes that the frame for design action—the way in which we frame design questions—changes how we work and how we solve problems.[1] Values and processes are realigned as new stakeholders appear, as collaborative partners appear, as interdisciplinary works appear. More than ever, design and technology are intertwined, but I hardly need to mention theirs is an unequal partnership.

Yet if technology's effects are omnipresent, where are the critics of technology? Given the speed with which its products appear, it is hard to find critical voices and compete with hyperbole-driven advertising. Yet critics are present, if often unheard. Two voices from the late twentieth century are important. In 1986, Abraham Moles, a French sociologist, wrote about micro-anxieties in the seminal essay "The Legibility of the World: A Project of Graphic Design."[2] These micro-anxieties are revealed when our digital tools fail us and we are distracted from the task at hand. Technology is rife with such failures—new software updates with minimal improvement; endless new configurations for seldom-used websites; ever-widening connected services; more equipment planned only for the short term, resulting in obsolescence; lack of attention to continuity for the user; changing things to make them "new" rather than improving function; the list could go on. Uncertainty claims our attention with regard to the immediate future. Thus, micro-anxieties, such as those mentioned, are a tax on focused activity. They prevent us from achieving Mihaly Csikszentmihalyi's "flow"—a desired state of complete, uninterrupted concentration.[3]

Autoclav

A second important critic is the communication theorist Neil Postman, who observed that how people are dealt with is also a technological product.[4] Underlying every instrument or service are social, sensory, emotional, political, and content attitudes. Postman offers ten principles with which to assess and critique technology. For example, as he notes in number 5, "Technological change is ecological; it changes everything." Digital medical records, for example, often change the nature of a medical visit, for the doctor may spend more time addressing the record's device than attending to the patient. But the potential transparency and collaboration between patient and doctor is an upside.

A writer of more recent vintage is Nicholas Carr, the former executive editor of the *Harvard Business Review*, who follows technology closely and critically. His concern is whether we are in

1. Hugh Dubberly, "Why We Should Stop Describing Design as 'Problem-Solving,'" in this volume, 274–88.

2. Abraham Moles "The Legibility of the World: A Project of Graphic Design," *Design Issues* 3, no.1 (1986): 43–53.

3. For more on the concept of flow, see Mihaly Csikszentmihalyi, *Flow: The Psychology of Optimal Experience* (New York: Harper and Row, 1990).

Postman's Technological Principles

1. Technological change brings both advantage and disadvantage.
- *Technological change is a business disrupter. If the change is a genuine improvement, and if a sufficient population of adaptors is found, competitors will flounder.*

2. Advantages and disadvantages benefit some and harm others.
- *Regarding who wins, business reaps an advantage, while workers may become obsolete or require new training.*

3. Every technology has a philosophy: how people use minds and bodies, how the world is represented, and what senses are amplified.
- *Smart phones emphasize easy, immediate access to information, rapid gratification, and connection to others filtered by distance and the instrument itself.*

4. New technology fights with and replaces old technology.
- *In mainland China, a smart phone replaces physical money, credit cards, calendars, address books. An individual's life details are within the device.*

5. Simply adding something is not the goal. Technological change is ecological; it changes everything.
- *Digital medical records alter the doctor-patient relation. The doctor may be less attentive to the patient as s/he consults the record, but it may support a shared decision process.*

6. Different technologies have different intellectual and emotional biases.
- *Texting or Skyping have different emotional characters. The text is casual and an abstraction of thought. A Skype session is close to "presence," it is immediate and multi-sensory.*

7. Access and speed create technologically different political biases.
- *The power of easy replication and distribution of ideas via the Internet alters the sense of fact or fiction, recognition of truth, and erodes basic common ground.*

8. Different technologies play on different sensory biases.
- *The expansion of sensory stimulation and integration of presence and immediacy in game platforms via virtual reality delights or confounds participants.*

9. Social biases are present in different technologies.
- *Social platforms on the Internet support all manner of human connection.*

10. Due to technical and economic structures, technologies have different content biases.
- *The wealth of content digitally available, some valuable and some worthless, continues to expand and address specific audiences.*

or out of the digital future. Artificial Intelligence (AI) can replace human decision-makers by offering a variety of outcomes weighted in different ways. Thus, even with increases in advanced education, white-collar jobs are disappearing due to sophisticated digital techniques capable of bolstering legal arguments with supporting searches, reading medical scans for anomalies, performing language translation, or providing templates in which image, text, video, diagrams, and feedback can be accommodated, providing a systematic structure for communication.[5] Carr asks whether, despite the ability of algorithms to accomplish such tasks, there remain tasks for which humans are uniquely suited. He is searching for a robust people-machine interface much like the one HCI (Human-Computer Interaction) embraces.

John Markoff, a technology and science reporter for the *New York Times*, goes even further by reducing the situation to its fundamentals, posing the man-vs-machine divide as one of AI (Artificial Intelligence) versus IA (Intelligence Augmentation).[6] Business favors AI as a means of removing costly and unpredictable human employees. Yet the alternative IA creates a human-machine partnership in which people maintain control, i.e., they can override

4. Neil Postman, *The End of Education: Redefining the Value of School* (New York: Knopf, 1995).

5. For more on this question, see Nicolas Carr, *The Glass Cage: How Our Computers Are Changing Us* (New York: Norton, 2014).

6. See John Markoff, *Machines of Loving Grace* (New York: HarperCollins, 2015).

Charles Chamberland invents the autoclave

automatic decisions and actions. For example, airplanes are often on automatic pilot, but if something unforeseen happens, the pilot takes over. The pilot landing on the Hudson River is a good example.[7] It is likely that both AI and IA develop, and no doubt the cultural outcome of these different positions will be profound; the issue is whether we have the foresight to understand their limitations and benefits for deployment. It all comes down to who or what is in control.

In the late 1940s and early '50s, the father of cybernetics, Norbert Wiener, envisioned a utopia in which people would be released from heavy manual labor or repetitive work.[8] They would become free to advance knowledge as citizen scientists or pursue art in its many forms. Today it is hard to imagine a world in which such a future is conceivable. We feel closer now, perhaps, to John Maynard Keynes's "technological unemployment" (a phrase coined by the economist in 1930), a condition in which people's skills become obsolete, requiring retraining to forestall unemployment. Such is our current condition—and it seems to be gathering speed.

Gui Bonsiepe calls out our lack of resistance to what he refers to as our "consumption-saturated lifestyle" in "On the Heteronomy of Design in a Post-Utopian Age."[9] This has a particularly destructive effect on the environment. Planned obsolescence, a product of 1950s business strategy, has found new momentum in the digital world. A new object or edition is always just around the corner; nothing is finished or complete. A 2017 United Nations report takes a holistic view of e-waste with a perspective on the toxic pollution that permeates water, soil, and air.[10] It even proposes a virtuous business model that reclaims e-waste containing valuable raw materials, usually lost, worth over 55 billion euros in 2016. The impressive scale of the e-waste problem is a record of our obsession with the latest technology: Currently, there are 7.7 billion mobile cellular subscriptions with phone models that are designed to be replaced every few years. This ignores computers, tablets, and other digital devices that further compound the problem. If we want our consumption-saturated lifestyle, we need to pay for recycling digital equipment to close the loop created by the endless production of the new. Technological success should not be dependent on environmental degradation.[11]

7. On January 15, 2009, United Airlines pilot Chelsey "Sully" Sullenberger landed an Airbus A320 in the Hudson River after the plan lost all engine power.

8. See Norbert Wiener, *The Human Use of Human Beings, Cybernetics and Society* (Doubleday Anchor, 1950).

9. Gui Bonsiepe, "On the Heteronomy of Design in a Post-Utopian Age," in this volume, 264–70.

10. C. F. Bolde, V. Forti, R. Kuehr, and P. Stegmann, *The Global E-waste Monitor-2017, Quantities, Flows, and Resources* (Bonn: United Nations University, International Telecommunication Union, and Solid Wastewater Association, 2017).

11. For a more detailed argument regarding digital waste, see Sharon Poggenpohl, "Waste and Agency in the Digital Era: Who's in Charge?" *Shè Jì: The Journal of Design, Economics, and Innovation* 6, no. 3 (2020): 331–44.

We have a stake in these issues as designers, as users of technology, and as citizens. As Dubberly notes, there are some ways in which design is changing: an increased concern for reusable modules and systems, and models that have more longevity. Interaction and experience are intertwined. Yet endless tinkering with navigation systems results in micro-anxieties, adding to user frustration. Attention to user concerns is an essential part of the contemporary design process, as is collaboration and cross-disciplinary research.[12] We need a critical approach that recognizes the interconnectedness of design with technology and business. We need to attend to cultural implications and listen to critical voices. "As computer systems and software applications come to play an ever larger role in shaping our lives and the world, we have an obligation to be more, not less, involved in decisions about their design and use—before technological momentum forecloses our options. We should be careful about what we make."[13]

12. For more on research and collaboration, see Sharon Poggenpohl and Keiichi Sato, eds., *Design Integrations, Research and Collaboration* (Bristol: Intellect, 2009).

13. Carr, *The Glass Cage*, 224.

DESIGN INVESTIGATIONS
(AN HOMAGE TO JOHN CHRISTOPHER JONES)

DENISE GONZALES CRISP

The First Day of the Session

The click of my heels on the linoleum echoed as I rushed to the studio. Arriving at the closed door, I paused to catch my breath, then carefully snuck the door open. About a dozen students were scattered around the room. They sat on sofas or on stools around high tables. I slipped onto the nearest empty stool.

It was the summer of 2016 and I had entered my second Intensive "refresher." My first Intensive, in 2006, was eight weeks long. This time I enrolled in the four-week module that included one session with the renowned Welsh designer and engineer John Christopher Jones. And there he was, in person, sitting in the middle of the room.

Professor Jones smiled at me as he resumed the discussion. "So, creativity. We stopped using that term in design decades ago. It meant thinking of alternatives, like how many uses can you think of for a brick." I opened my tablet.

5/4 Jones:

* **Creativity implies too much control, too little sensitivity.**
* **Inventiveness or imagination is designing.**
* **More profound: changing one's view of things and oneself or looking at each item in a box . . . a list of all possibilities.**
* **The real creative thing: find where the edge of the box is and ask what's outside it.**
* **Key! . . . Can't look outside the box until you have the box . . . it expands your view . . . to spend life in the box is sort of wrong.**

Professor Jones moved to one of the freestanding whiteboards. I copied as he wrote:

* 2016 Session 5, Module C: Seminar. John Chris Jones.
* Mondays: 05–26 JUL, 13.00 17.30 hrs.
  Accument Day: 01 AUG.
* Readings on reserve in the café
* How to Improve the World (You will only make matters worse), Cage
* Philosophical Investigations, Wittgenstein (English Trans.).
* Design Methods: Seeds of Human Futures, 2nd Edition, Jones

"By yours truly." He bowed self-mockingly. "You can call me Chris."

In the late 1970s and early '80s, Chris was among many like-minded designers and design educators, engineers, computer scientists, cybernetics scholars, musicians, urban planners, and social theorists who joined forces to wrest conventional authority from design pedagogies rooted in art-based, industry-centric curricula. The result was the Design Education and Pedagogy Reform (DEAPR). By the time I got to design school in 1992, the curriculum had already radically changed years earlier. We were taught quite naturally to establish design inquiries, devise and deploy cultural probes and interpret their results, design for and within systems and environments, design working with as many perspectives as possible. All that stuff had served me well; however, my scope had narrowed to the hard practicalities of commerce. I enrolled in this refresher to be reminded, again, of practicing—attempting, essaying, discovering—over producing.

Materials/Equipment:

* Typewriter: Library lends: Brother Deluxe 1522 (3), Royal Epoch Portable (2), Smith Corona Corsair (6), Royal Epoch Portable (6).
* Scissors + tape/adhesives.
* Recording devices: audio/motion capture, videotape/film, digital (avoid editing software . . . Wite-out ok). Access to copier, scanner, still camera (smartphone/tablet).

Throughout the four-week session we were to select sections from Chris's book *Design Methods*, first published in 1970, republished in 1992, and widely adopted in design practices. I'd read some of it in an undergrad theory course (alongside *Blueprint for Counter Education*, also published in 1970).

We were then to randomly select a number from 1 to 693 (the number of Wittgenstein's Investigations), and, informed by John Cage's writing based on nothing other than individual whim, we would accomplish four essayings, "thinking-at-the-typewriter" manifested in visual and physical form. The Wittgenstein passages were fodder to be used to interrogate the design methods we selected.

* Thinking-at-the-typewriter is like speaking.
* Each word/phrase inspires the next—once spoken, can't take it back.

Jim, a slightly balding, kind-looking man, raised his hand. Chris acknowledged him, saying that he needn't do so to speak. This gesture of deference had been eradicated during the Reform, so I surmised that Jim was probably attending his first Intensive. He later told me that he had studied design before DEAPR had overtaken the pedagogy that defined what in his time was called "training."

"Can you speak more about these essayings, and the methods?" Chris patiently explained that the constraints are not methods exactly. Rather, they are means that set up temporary, provisional circumstances. Working within them, he said, requires intellectual and emotional presence, some interpretative sensitivity, intuitive responses, and imagination. As designers or anyone endeavoring to understand something, Chris went on, the constraints are actually portals to "boundless space for imagining, for formulating ultimately workable ideas." Jim sunk down a bit and said shyly, "I don't think I know how to do that." "Are you a learner?" Chris countered. "I guess so." Jim shrugged, "I'm here." "Only learners know what they are doing. Skilled people act unconsciously. Skilled performance is predictive." I flashed on a thought:

Composing words (of intent?) on a typewriter as one writes = relinquishing control to medium, method, reaction . . . yet is complete and materialized extension of thought. NOT tools but MEANS.

Chris pulled a yellowing paperback from his rumpled satchel on the floor. "Several examples of this kind of investigation are published in my later book, *Designing Designing*." I knew the book well because it was required reading in school. "For this paper published in the proceedings of the InfoTech Conference in '79," he explained, holding up the book to a spread, "I first typed ten subject titles—the ideas that I wanted to think about and present to conferees—each at the top of a sheet of paper. I then positioned a quotation or image on each page, like this one," he pointed to a silhouette of a leaf positioned in the middle of the page, "determined by chance operation. I borrowed this idea from John Cage, by the way. The arbitrary placement of these random bits determined how much space my typewritten text could occupy. And their presence on the page influenced what I wrote. This essay is titled 'Continuous Design and Redesign.'" He set the book down, silently inviting responses.

I said that I had read the essay in undergrad and marveled at how it could still make sense, despite chance being central to its structure. A couple of my fellow design learners nodded in agreement. "Why do you think that is?" "Well, I think it's because when we really focus on the circumstances as influences, whether they're images or statements or people or materials, we are compelled to imagine how they *might* make sense, both in that moment and later when someone else reads or sees or experiences the thing."

"Speaking of which," Chris said suddenly, "I nearly forgot this . . ." He placed a small digital recorder on a central table, hit record, and said that recordings would be available online after the class. "The recordings are available to you *not* as chronicles of a given day. They are offered to present a new experience, another perspective of the goings on." This insistence on immediacy—typewritten writings, recordings that are not records but prompts—glaringly implicated work habits that I had acquired as a practitioner: planning out everything before making anything; resisting digression; submitting to perceived or imposed barriers to seeking. A feeling of familiar restlessness began to take hold in me.

"Let's discuss the course rubrics." I thought it odd that Chris would have rubrics for an Intensive that so far seemed to encourage nothing other than chance and free association. He began a kind of slow oration as he scanned the room, watching us write as we followed his words.

Begin with what can be imagined.
Use both intuition and reason.
Work it out in context.
Model the contextual effects of what is imagined.
Change the process to suit what is happening.
Refuse what diminishes.
See inspiration in what is.
Choose what depends on everyone.

The "rubrics," it turned out, were actually a set of Tao-like aphorisms registering a code of conduct. I recognized them from his book *The Internet and Everyone*, which I had read just after its release in 2000. Hearing Chris recite them on that first day of the session, I was reminded of the core principles promoted throughout my own design education and that had lost their sway over the last ten years of practice.

I was one of an early generation of "design learners" who studied under the full expression of the Reform. We took courses in visual literacy, information systems and cybernetics, designform (a course that studied the relational nature of intention and form), world politics, and developmental psychology. We studied the work of Sheila Levrant de Bretteville, bell hooks, Marshall McLuhan, Buckminster Fuller, Stewart Brand, Victor Papanek, and Sister Corita Kent. The Macintosh revolution had already become business as usual, and we did much of our work on desktop computers and laser printers that spat out iterations almost as quickly as we could generate them. We created Hypercard stacks that visualized and activated stories and essays that we wrote. We made digital typefaces and used photocopiers to explore typography. From what I hear, this approach is radically different from design education before the Reform.

Having covered the general particulars of the course, Chris prompted a discussion about design's relationship to the recording device, or the typewriter, or the computer. The reserved Shadrick, an interaction designer who had worked on the first e-book, tapped his notebook thoughtfully, then spoke. "They are designed things that capture and represent human thought." A pause. Jessye added quickly: "Speaking is thinking. It's a process. And typing is a process, as is designing." Jessye tended to run through thoughts that way, sorting it out as she spoke. Chris nodded approval. Randa, who had been writing about design as part of her practice, said, "These things report back to us our words." Chris turned to the whiteboard and wrote.

"All words to be written are present, potentially, in the making of pens, paper, presses, computers, typewriters."
> + whiteboards + tablets + post-its + msg + twitter + + + = inventions for impermanent words

The class puzzled over Chris's pronouncement for a long minute, until Ashamsa, the budding theorist, broke the intense silence confidently. "What we design determines not only what can be written but *how* we write." She giggled behind her hand, "Okay so I've read a little Wittgenstein." I wasn't as certain, but ventured a thought that I'd jotted down.

Design enables and anticipates possible futures
possible other constructed things

"Yes, I agree. What is a *thing* that is designed or constructed?" With this John began the first of many insightful anecdotes he would offer over the course of the session. His story began with a photo that he had taken of the room in which he did his typewriting. He had to stand on the landing outside the room to take the photo because the room was so small. "I get cold when I write, and this was the cheapest room to heat in the daytime when my family was out and the central heating was off." It being the 1970s, he supposed that it was the oil producers, the OPEC countries, that had forced him into the littlest room in a big house. This intangible system with global impact, designed through the circumstances of economic power and subsequent fiat, invisibly directed his behavior and decisions within his private space.

Design of systems of things <-> means <-> power = intangibles.

What is intangible in graphic design?

"I don't know if this is a question or a comment," I interjected, "but in undergrad we had a kind of mantra, 'No should, only is.' Seems like that idea is implied in the design of intangibles in that to design is to engage complex realities, dynamics."

"Yes, that originates with the designer-poet-artist Edwin Schlossberg, who founded ESI Design in New York over fifty years ago and was an early adopter of and contributor to the Reform principles. Some of you probably only know of him as Caroline Kennedy's husband." A few people smiled in recognition. Chris explained that Schlossberg had once written to him this advice (he had memorized it): "There is nothing to be got or gained by doing, including designing. There's only something to be free of, like the anxiety of an obligation to do what 'should' be done. No should. Only is. Schlossberg reminds us about the humanity of designing." Chris went on. "If we think of designing for interconnection only at the object level, as had been done in the past, we limit ourselves to what can be calculated and we neglect what can be imagined and felt but not measured. If we think that way, then we are bound to create a way of life which is experienced as inhuman. What makes us people, and not objects, is that we *are* those interconnections."

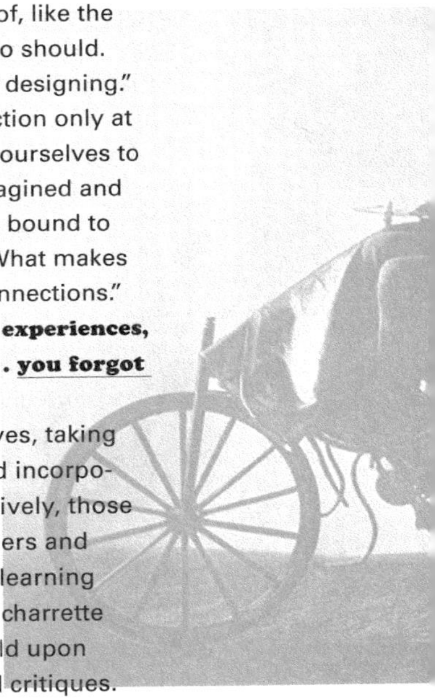

Intangibles = interconnected-ness . . . moments, experiences, cause/effect, dynamics >> these are what IS . . . you forgot about that !!

The Reform espoused such humanistic perspectives, taking to heart counter-establishment '60s and '70s ideas and incorporating them into curricula that challenged, quite effectively, those adapted from Bauhaus, Basel, and Ulm schools. Teachers and students, learners together, collaboratively identified learning methods and aims. Regular "discurssants"—a hybrid charrette and critical discussion where peers scrutinize and build upon each other's work through "amplifications"—replaced critiques. The Reform abandoned designed artifacts as exclusive evidence of design knowledge. Extensiveness and connectedness of design processes became the focus of evaluation, privileging continuation over separation. "Propositions" supplanted projects and were meant to raise questions that would point to the next exploration, like ever-firing chain reactions. A tome representing work from six or eight semesters, what we know commonly today as "accuments," took the place of the polished portfolio. Accrual rather than redaction.

Chris reached down again into his satchel, produced another worn hardbound book, John Cage's *Empty Words,* opened to a dog-eared page and read aloud:

> Many composers no longer make musical structures. Instead they set process going. A structure is like a piece of furniture, whereas a process is like the weather. In the case of a table, beginning and end of the whole and each of its parts are known. In the case of weather,

> though we notice changes in it, we have no clear knowledge of its beginning or ending. At a given moment, we are when we are. The nowmoment. . . . Since processes can include objects (be analogous, that is, to environment), we see there is no limit.

Chris was given to non-answers and divergent thought, and it was therefore fully in character when he added, peering over reading glasses, "Did you know that Cage was not only a composer, a philosopher, and a writer but also a typographer?" He fished around in his satchel once more. I was beginning to think that it was magical, like Mary Poppins's carpet bag. Another aged paperback emerged, also by Cage, entitled *X*. Chris passed it to the person nearest him. She thumbed through and read a bit, turned to another page, then handed the book to the next person wordlessly. For nearly ten minutes we united around the hushed sound of fingers touching toothy paper, punctuated by the quick swish of a page turning. I noticed that Chris was observing us closely, intently listening it seemed, and it occurred to me that our actions were transforming a book of printed words into a wholly new composition.

The Last Day of the Session

It was Accument Day and I arrived early to sort and review my collected work. I counted sixty-three folios and at least fifty minutes of video and audio, each square inch and clip charged with the experiences, discoveries, and insights of the last four weeks. I was an electrified spirit who had completed a quest and was buzzing to embark on the next one.

As I sorted through my material I rediscovered the essaying made with my first group in week one. It was a rather dull exposition on "Method 3.5: Questionnaires," partnered with Wittgenstein's investigation #123 (we changed the word "philosophy" to "design"): "A [design] problem has the form: 'I don't know my way about.'" I recalled Chris's commentary on the piece during the discurssant that day. He circled our droopy attempt: text typed on letter-sized paper and taped together in the form of a human-sized Möbius strip, hung in the hall outside of the studio. He read it closely, hands clasped behind his back respectfully. Finally, he spoke. "Collective action is seldom achieved. It is more likely that people who think they are collaborating are in fact failing to do so." My partners and I exchanged glances, quietly conceding that we hadn't quite meshed, nor had we designed a strategy for meshing.

Chris seldom spoke specifically about student work during discurssants. He would instead allude to failures of imagination and point out adjacent concepts or circumstances. His words both interfered with and magnified our thoughts. "This makes me think of ways in which failures to collaborate are often the result of an absence of formal support . . ."

rhythm in music >> enables choirs, ensembles << Yes
"competitions, teams, dances, wars": external systems to support collaboration
Can our work as designers enable others to collaborate when these supports aren't present? . . . Remember!?!

Karl Benz builds a gasoline-engined car

The studio slowly filled with my design-learner peers, and the collective volume of folios and media astounded us all. Our chatter reflected the exhilaration that had accelerated as we progressed together through the module. We agreed that we were especially fortunate to have studied with Chris. When he entered the studio, we all spontaneously applauded. He grinned and once again bowed, this time sincerely.

Grace, a young designer who had worked only three years before taking this, her first refresher, started the day's discurssant with a question of origins. "Where did 'discurssants' and 'accuments' come from?" It was a good question, one I had never thought to ask because such methods and vehicles are just how we'd always done things. It was design gravity.

"Those of us who organized the first design methods conference in 1962," Chris explained, "underplayed a most important attribute in designers. Imagination. Imagination must come first and be supported by reason and research, and not vice versa. If rationality predominates, imagination flies away."

Alberto, a self-trained graphic designer who was finishing this, his fifth consecutive Intensive, crossed his arms and sighed. "Yes, we know that now, reading *Design Methods* and challenging them similarly. But I'd also like to hear how and why the practices came to be." "Allow me to continue the thought," Chris chuckled, seemingly pleased to recall the heady debates that bore so much promise in the early days of the Reform. "Our design methods intended to provoke and make possible a *collective* imagination based on the thoughts and experience of many, far more than can be lived by a single designer, and this new kind of designing needed a new language." He left it at that.

Intensives were introduced around 1990 to teach aspects of DEAPR, the "new methods and new language," to practitioners who had studied before its inception, as well as to self-trained designers. The programs, at first offered in a few major US and UK cities, became more widely available over time, and people like me who had studied under the Reform and didn't wish to pursue a master's design research degree began to enroll. The Intensives became a chance to reconnect with the processes of possibility, and with each other, and to sharpen responsiveness to the uncertainty that is designing. It has now become natural if not necessary for design learners to take time out for these nurturing interludes.

Jim, the shy, older student whose old-school perspectives had been permanently altered by the end of the session, was fidgety but finally dared to speak. "Okay, so we've been working all along with, you know, sequences of chance, like random selection and intuition and responsiveness to 'what is,' right?" Everyone assented. He continued a bit more quietly, seeing that everyone's eyes were on him. "So, I just wanted to say that, whatever the language is, for me the important thing here is allowing chance to play a part. Chance is, paradoxically, a determinant, one that instigates reactions, ideas, actions. When I was a student, you know, before, we carried on using so-called rational methods. That's all good, but it turns out that chance is as legitimate a method as any to challenge what we think we know." "To make unforeseen connections, yeah," Shawnda chimed in, "it's a catalyst for inquiry favoring imagination, sure, and *then* it's molded through research and reason. So, you're good."

Chris nodded. "Rationality, originally seen as the means to open up the intuition to aspects of life outside the designer's experience, became, almost overnight, a tool kit of rigid methods that obliged designers and planners to act like machines, deaf to every human cry and incapable of laughter. That's what made me leave designing."

Chris was among the first cohort of educators to teach at the Open University in London, established in 1969. He resigned after only a year. According to fellow design theorist and friend Nigel Cross, Chris found that the OU was not the democratized educational opportunity and learning facilitator that he had envisioned. Chris "turned, instead, to redesigning design in a much more radical way than before, especially to the use of chance processes in designing life, the universe, and everything."

Chris walked over to his fertile satchel and retrieved the *Diary: How to Improve the World*, the Cage book that we now knew pretty well. "The Cagean method of composing not only music but life itself was, I learned, to give up intention, to seek unpredictable results. Indeterminacy, in place of control. Accepting what we did not choose."

So, I was in fact refreshed on this last day of the session. We laughed a lot as we reviewed our essayings, our imaginative failures, our failures to imagine, and carried on with our theorizing and debating. When the session ended we bid our thankful goodbyes to Chris and collected up our accuments and newly added amplifications. Walking down the hall from the studio with my fellow design learners, I tuned to the sound of our shoes on the linoleum and voices echoing amidst the walls. They created a lively and layered harmony, at moments discordant yet welcome. It's the kind of thing you observe when your senses and intellect are primed, ready to take in and spin out from anything you happen to encounter.

Quotations are borrowed from several sources. From John Christopher Jones: *Design Methods* (London: Wiley, 1992); *Designing Designing*, rev. ed. (1991; London: Bloomsbury, 2021); *The Internet and Everyone* (London: Ellipsis 2000), and "Digital Diary," the online diary of John Christopher Jones, http://www.publicwriting.net/3.0/entries_in_softopia_3.0/dd_archive.html. See also Nigel Cross's address for the awarding of the Design Research Society (DRS) Lifetime Achievement Award to John Chris Jones, http://www.4d-dynamics.net/DDR4/Award-JCJ.html. Quotations from John Cage are from *Empty Words* (Middleton, CT: Wesleyan University Press, 1979); *X* (Middleton, CT: Wesleyan University Press, 1983); and *Diary: How to Improve the World (You Will Only Make Matters Worse) Continued: Part Three* (New York: Something Else Press, 1967).

DESIGNING FOR NEOLIBERALISM

FRED TURNER and ANNIKA BUTLER-WALL

Something strange is afoot. Thirty or forty years ago, those who studied design thinking learned to be designers—of images, products, buildings. They hunkered over drawing tables and clustered around clay models at Parsons or RISD. Today, however, if they are studying design thinking, they are more likely to be sticking Post-it notes to walls and analyzing their personal collaboration styles than to be building anything concrete. Somehow a phrase that once meant "thinking like a designer of visual or material things" has become a highly developed system for training people in all walks of life to become more creative and to solve complex social problems. The question is: Why? And why now? What is it about design as a category of practice that renders it applicable to so many realms? And what has become of its narrower, professional meaning as the shaping of things?

To answer these questions, we need to step back from the world of professional design pedagogy and revisit the intellectual history of economics and particularly the body of theory that we now call "neoliberalism." Since the late 1970s, nation-states across Europe and America have been deregulating industries, dismantling their social safety nets, and encouraging their citizens to think of themselves as entrepreneurs of their own lives. Design thinking has arisen alongside these policies. But not just alongside; design thinking in fact represents a repurposing of twentieth-century design pedagogy for a neoliberal era. Part ideology, part tool kit for self-transformation, design thinking has turned the work of designing things into the work of designing a new kind of person—a person fit for a topsy-turvy, innovation-driven, deregulated world.

What *Is* Neoliberalism? And What Does It Have to Do with Design?

In popular usage the word *neoliberalism* has become an all-purpose name for the commercialization of everyday life and an insult to be aimed at right-wing governments by activists on the left. But a brief review of the substantial literature on neoliberalism reveals that it has had at least three lives.[1] It first emerged among

1. For more-thorough reviews, especially of neoliberalism's origins, see Philip Mirowski and Dieter Plehwe, eds., *The Road from Mont Pelerin: The Making of the Neoliberal Thought Collective* (2009; Cambridge, MA: Harvard University Press, 2015); Jamie Peck, *Constructions of Neoliberal Reason* (Oxford: Oxford University Press, 2010); and Quinn Slobodian, *Globalists: The End of Empire and the Birth of Neoliberalism* (Cambridge, MA: Harvard University Press, 2018).

a group of European economists in the years just before and after World War II as a theory of market-based democracy. By the 1970s and '80s, Michel Foucault and a number of American and European scholars had begun to describe neoliberalism as a way of being, a mode of governmentality brought to bear on even the most intimate parts of people's lives. Their analyses coincided with the deployment of neoliberal economic policies by right-wing governments in Europe and the Americas. And in the early 2000s, Marxist scholars such as David Harvey pointed to those policies to demonstrate how the governments involved had leaned on neoliberal ideology to justify the production of widespread inequality.

In each of its incarnations, neoliberalism has assigned a central role to design in the practice of government. Historians still debate the precise origins of particular neoliberal ideas and communities, yet virtually all agree that no one defined or promulgated early neoliberal ideals more aggressively than the Austrian economist and co-founder of the enormously influential Mont Pelerin Society, Friedrich Hayek.[2] During and just after World War II, Hayek laid out the foundations of neoliberal economic and social theory in a series of essays and in the surprise 1944 bestseller *The Road to Serfdom.* The rise of fascism in Nazi Germany and of centralized wartime planning throughout Europe and the United States filled Hayek with fear. In his view, it wasn't the appearance of a charismatic leader or the power of mass media that created totalitarian systems; it was centralized planning itself. "A directed economy must be run on more or less dictatorial lines," he wrote, equating the rising Keynesianism of the Allies to the National Socialism they were fighting.[3] In order to make a top-down economic system work, he explained, a state would need to persuade its citizens to desire that which the planners prescribed. This in turn would require leaders to saturate their societies with propaganda. And if propaganda failed to turn freethinking citizens into followers, as Hayek often thought it did, leaders would resort to force in order to bring their policies into being.

Friedrich Hayek reads *The American Spectator*, date unknown.

In the process, they would erase the individual desires and local knowledge that were the roots of freedom, said Hayek. To concentrate the power of social decision-making in a single all-powerful state, he explained a few years later, would turn

2. For a succinct account of the recent historiography of neoliberalism, see Mirowski and Plehwe, "Preface," in Mirowski and Plehwe, *The Road from Mont Pelerin* (2015 edition), ix–xxiii.

3. Friedrich A. Hayek, *The Road to Serfdom: Text and Documents: The Definitive Edition*, ed. Bruce Caldwell (New York: Routledge, 2008), 124.

individuals into "interchangeable units," blank, obedient nonentities.[4] To preserve citizens' individuality, social authority would have to be decentralized. The essential problem, he argued, was one of information. No one person could know more about the world than what he or she saw around themselves or knew from their own experience. No one—not even an all-powerful king—could see the whole of society nor define what was good for it.[5] Only a decentralized system could bring together the many separate bits of knowledge lodged within separate minds. And only a decentralized society could turn that knowledge into a social order within which individuals could find their own unique places.

The engine of such a system would be the free market, a system of buying and selling that Hayek reimagined as an *information* system. According to Hayek, the price mechanism within the free market served as the most effective single way to identify and build order from a universe of individual preferences:

> The price system [is] a kind of machinery for registering change, or a system of telecommunications which enables individual producers to watch merely the movement of a few pointers, as an engineer might watch the hands of a few dials, in order to adjust their activities to changes of which they may never know more than is reflected in the price movement.[6]

Of course, humans being humans, the need for the nation-state, and especially its monopoly on violence, would not disappear. Rather, said Hayek, the nation-state should become the guarantor of market freedom. It should enable the marketplace to offer the individual citizen a chance to seek information and to act on it in light of his or her own interests. That way, a more diverse, more democratic polity would ostensibly emerge.

If they could have, Hayek and his colleagues might well have done away with states altogether and replaced the soldiers and politicians of traditional government with designers and engineers. Hayek's market-centered democracy is a society-by-design. Its central feature is the marketplace itself, an agora made up of data and accounts and buildings and professions—all of which must be designed to work together so as to most effectively contribute to the social good. The marketplace issues no commands to citizens. Rather, through careful design and maintenance of its formal properties, it offers citizens opportunities for action, multiplies their options, and facilitates their sharing of information. In Hayek's account, the price system alone, backed by the state, allows social order to emerge. Yet in any actual, functioning marketplace, social organization emerges thanks not only to information exchange but to the design and maintenance of information systems and the infrastructures that support them.

4. Friedrich A. von Hayek, "Individualism: *True and False*," in *Individualism and Economic Order* (1948; Chicago: University of Chicago Press, 1980), 1–32.

5. Friedrich A. von Hayek, "The Use of Knowledge in Society," *The American Economic Review* 4 (September 1945), reprinted in Hayek, *Individualism and Economic Order*, 77–91.

6. Ibid., 87.

In *A Brief History of Neoliberalism*, David Harvey acknowledges the roots of neoliberal economic theory in the mid-century writings of Mont Pelerin intellectuals, then bears down on the late 1970s, the elections of Thatcher and Reagan, and the rise of Deng Xiaoping in China. He particularly notes the Reagan administration's efforts "to curb the power of labor, deregulate industry, agriculture, and resource extraction, and liberate the powers of finance" and suggests that they were simply one site of a global effort by the forces of capital to overwhelm the working class.[7] In Harvey's account of 1980s and '90s neoliberalism, the state becomes a servant of capital, granting special rights to capitalists to accumulate wealth at the expense of ordinary workers.

Harvey focuses his analysis on economic policy, interparty struggles, and the like. But just beneath the surface of his analysis, we can see how designers might help legitimate this transfer of wealth. As Harvey notes, there is a "burgeoning disparity between the declared public aims of neoliberalism—the well-being of all—and its actual consequences—the restoration of class power."[8] In Marxist theory, it is the role of ideology to paper over such discrepancies. But ideology goes beyond words and pictures. As Douglas Spencer has shown in his marvelous 2016 study *The Architecture of Neoliberalism*, some of the world's most famous architects have busied themselves doing ideological work—that is, designing environments that simultaneously celebrate the ideals of egalitarian opportunity and materially promote the well-being of mobile, wealthy elites. The British group DEGW, for instance, designs open-plan office spaces in which workers are free to move around as they like, yet in which they are also expected to be constantly available for on-the-spot collaborations.[9] Such offices promise to allow workers to bring their "whole selves" to work—and so increase their collective well-being—while at the very same time concentrating and accelerating the ability of capital to extract their labor power.[10]

Buildings like these also change the nature of labor power itself. In Marx's nineteenth century, capital managed to transform the sweat of individual workers into goods, thus commodifying their labor power. Today, autonomous Marxists and others suggest that industrial-era modes of commodification have been replaced by new rationalities of political economy, drawing on Foucault's concept of governmentality. Foucault's lectures of 1978 and 1979

7. David Harvey, *A Brief History of Neoliberalism* (New York: Oxford University Press, 2005), 1.

8. Ibid., 79.

9. Douglas Spencer, *The Architecture of Neoliberalism: How Contemporary Architecture Became an Instrument of Control and Compliance* (New York: Bloomsbury Academic, 2016), 78.

10. For an example of this strategy at work in Silicon Valley, see Fred Turner, "The Arts at Facebook: An Aesthetic Infrastructure for Surveillance Capitalism," *Poetics* 67 (April 2018): 53–62.

explore the origins of neoliberal theory in mid-century Austria and Germany and the theory's migration to the United States. In his lectures, Foucault argues that under neoliberalism, citizens are no longer governed by the state alone, if they ever were. Rather, they move from project to project within an "enterprise society."[11] The individual becomes a portfolio of small businesses and the agent of his own reflexive self-management. As Foucault puts it, "The individual's life itself—with his relationships to his private property, for example, with his family, household, insurance, and retirement—must make him into a sort of permanent and multiple enterprise."[12]

As Nikolas Rose and Wendy Brown have pointed out, such an enterprise society transforms all of social life into market activity. In that sense, everything we do becomes labor and every action we take has the potential to be commodified. At the same time, the market—as information system and social world, as well as a setting for economic exchange—provides the terms in which we express our deepest needs. On the one hand, in theory at least, the self is suddenly a free individual, the very opposite of the authoritarian's drone. As Rose puts it, "The [neoliberal] self is to be a subjective being, it is to aspire to autonomy, it is to strive for personal fulfillment in its earthly life, it is to interpret its reality and destiny as a matter of individual responsibility, it is to find meaning in its existence by shaping its life through acts of choice."[13] On the other hand, writes Rose, this classically liberal subject must now "make an enterprise of its life."[14] Like an executive in charge of a company of one, it must invest for the future, monitor its progress, and, at the end of the day, assess its return on investment.

This enterprise model tends to shift public concerns into a private idiom. "The project of navigating the social becomes entirely one of discerning, affording, and procuring a personal solution to every socially produced problem," notes Brown.[15] The consequences for democracy, she explains, are potentially disastrous. Citizenship can become a matter of "self-care," and the kind of active engagement with state policies required to keep democracy functioning can disappear.[16] Democratic institutions, collaborative lawmaking, negotiating across difference—all become far less interesting to a person who believes that making the world better starts with improving one's self.

This mode of thinking has been a boon to the field of design. Many product designers, for instance, make their living creating

11. Michel Foucault, Michel Senellart, and Collège de France, *The Birth of Biopolitics: Lectures at the Collège de France, 1978–79* (Basingstoke: Palgrave Macmillan, 2008), 242.

12. Ibid.

13. Nikolas S. Rose, *Inventing Our Selves: Psychology, Power, and Personhood* (Cambridge: Cambridge University Press, 1996), 151.

14. Ibid., 154.

15. Wendy Brown, "American Nightmare: Neoliberalism, Neoconservatism, and De-Democratization," *Political Theory* 34, no. 6 (2006): 704.

16. Ibid., 695.

tools that enable us to monitor our progress through life and to turn public problems into personal solutions. Think of the Apple Watch, the smartphone, the laptop computer. In a neoliberal society, whether described by Hayek, Harvey, Foucault, Rose, or Brown, technique tends to replace politics, and when it does, designers take on the work of government. They build the technologies that make the marketplaces and circulate the information on which individual choices depend. Designers create the devices with which individuals track and broadcast the minutiae of their lives. At companies like Google and Facebook, interface designers nudge users to make choices that feel independent yet also produce the most profitable outcomes for the firm.

Welcome to the d.school

To the extent that neoliberalism has transformed state-based governance into market-based governmentality, those who would govern have begun to see themselves anew. In the nineteenth century and even much of the twentieth, the universities that produced the leaders of American and European institutions would have schooled them in the arts of rhetoric and negotiation, the biographies of ancient Romans and Greeks, and, unless they were engineers, just enough math to manage a business. Today's future leaders, by contrast, are entering a project-based world in which they must equip themselves to fit ever-changing circumstances and to engineer circumstances to their own benefit wherever possible. And they are being asked to study design—or, more precisely, "design thinking."

While no one has yet articulated a definition of design thinking on which everyone can agree, historians have traced its origins to the 1980s and '90s.[17] Just as Western European and American governments began to deregulate and privatize their societies, design theorists and practitioners began to transform the working knowledge of designers into a set of stories and principles that could be applied to a wider variety of situations. In volumes such as Donald Schön's *The Reflective Practitioner* (1983), Peter Rowe's *Design Thinking* (1987), and Bryan Lawson's *How Designers Think: The Design Process Demystified* (1980), analysts sought to locate the practices and states of mind conducive to creative design.[18] In part, they aimed to make designers more effective. At the same time, though, they began to turn design into an all-purpose practice for the enhancement of the kind of creativity on which an entrepreneurial life depended. In his widely read 1992 article "Wicked Problems in Design Thinking," management professor Richard Buchanan, head of Carnegie Mellon's Design School

17. Ulla Johansson-Sköldberg, Jill Woodilla, and Mehves Çetinkaya, "Design Thinking: Past, Present and Possible Futures," *Creativity and Innovation Management* 22, no. 2 (2013): 121–46.

18. Johansson-Sköldberg, Woodilla, and Çetinkaya, "Design Thinking," 124; and Lucy Kimbell, "Rethinking Design: Part I," *Design and Culture* 3, no. 3 (2011): 291.

19. Richard Buchanan, "Wicked Problems in Design Thinking," *Design Issues* 8, no. 2 (Spring 1992): 5. See also Kimbell, "Rethinking Design: Part I," 292, and Johansson-Sköldberg, Woodilla, and Çetinkaya, "Design Thinking," 125.

from 1992 to 2002, even went so far as to claim that design was a "new *liberal art of technological culture*" (italics in original).[19] Building on the writings of Walter Gropius and John Dewey, Buchanan argued that design represented a new mode of "experimental thinking" that could tackle problems that spanned four discrete areas of human life: "symbolic and visual communications," "material objects," "activities and organized services," and "complex systems or environments for living, working, playing, and learning."[20] In the process, Buchanan helped turn the professional practices of designers into a simple means by which individuals could understand themselves, the organizations in which they worked, and the problems they faced.

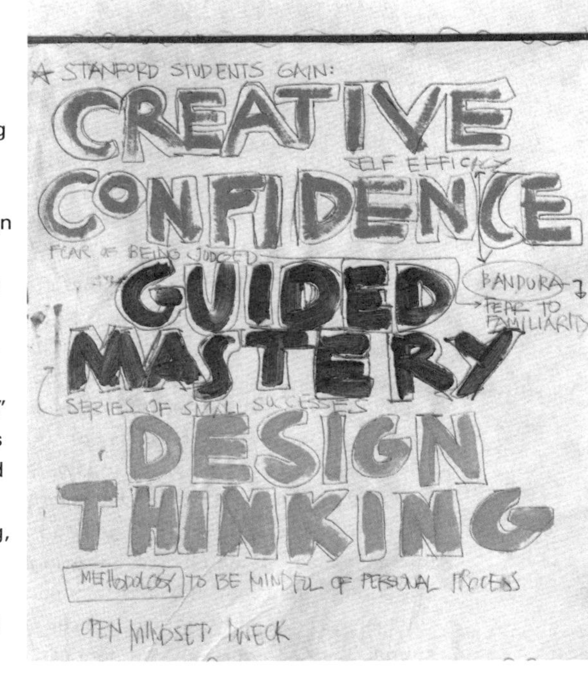

Design thinking poster drawn by David Kelley

In 2005, Stanford University institutionalized this expansive view of what design thinking could do when it established the first school devoted entirely to the teaching of design thinking. Funded by Hasso Plattner, founder of the global software giant SAP and led by David Kelley, a Stanford professor and founder of the design firm IDEO, "the d.school," as it was called, became a freestanding unit at the university that aimed "to teach design thinking—a methodology for innovating routinely—to future entrepreneurs from Stanford's graduate schools."[21] Two years later, Plattner established the Hasso-Plattner Institute (HPI) School of Design Thinking in Potsdam, Germany, bringing together forty students from thirty different universities.[22] Both the Stanford and Potsdam schools soon began offering classes and workshops to professionals as well as graduate students.[23] Plattner has also worked to globalize the Stanford model. Since 2012, he has established centers for design thinking in Beijing, Kuala Lumpur, and Cape Town, and HPI's website lists twenty-four other locations worldwide that offer courses in design thinking. In 2017, the HPI opened a new office in New York and founded the Global Design Thinking Alliance with ten other international educational institutions, including the London School of Economics School of Management and the School of Public Policy and Global Affairs at the University of British Columbia.[24]

20. Buchanan, "Wicked Problems," 9–10.

21. Tom Kelley and David Kelley, *Creative Confidence: Unleashing the Creative Potential Within Us All* (New York: Crown Business, 2013), 4.

22. "Chronology: 10 Years of Design Thinking at HPI," Hasso-Plattner-Institut, https://hpi.de/en/school-of-design-thinking/hpi-d-school/history.html.

Today, design thinking has become what sociologist Geoffrey Bowker has called a "universal discipline"—a way of talking and a set of practices that proponents claim can solve most any institutional or even interpersonal problem.[25] To see how this discipline works on the ground, we have examined the architecture, curriculum, and promotional materials of Stanford's d.school and explored two books that have centrally informed its practices: Tim Brown and Barry Katz's *Change by Design: How Design Thinking Transforms Organizations and Inspires Innovation*, published in 2009 when Brown was CEO of IDEO, and brothers Tom and David Kelley's 2013 *Creative Confidence: Unleashing the Creative Potential Within Us All*. Together they suggest that design thinking has transformed the historically specific working habits of designers into a dehistoricized, depoliticized tool kit to help neoliberal elites manage their lives and the institutions they will someday or already lead.

Consider the d.school's central work and teaching space, the "design garage." It's a simple concrete rectangle, two stories tall, with a projection screen at one end, ringed by a balcony. In the main space, students push lightweight chairs and tables into any configuration. This flexibility is meant to encourage creativity. "Just as the right party atmosphere can bring out your 'inner party animal,' the right work environment can bring out your latent creative capacity," write the Kelleys in *Creative Confidence*. "An open space facilitates communication and transparency. Wide stairways encourage serendipitous conversations among people from different departments. Ubiquitous writing surfaces prompt spontaneous ideation sessions. Dedicated project spaces can help the team be more cohesive."[26] The Stanford d.school has been designed to promote collaboration, flexibility, and speed: "When you walk into the d.school, you'll see that almost every piece of furniture (and many walls) is on wheels. For physical space to

23. Between 2005 and 2016, for instance, the Stanford d.school offered 279 for-credit classes and 132 pop-up classes, started a K12 Lab for professional development for educators, and ran executive workshops for groups ranging from the San Francisco Opera to General Motors to the LA County Department of Public Social Services. "Our Impact," Hasso Plattner Institute of Design at Stanford, 2019, https://dschool.stanford.edu/our-impact/; "K12 Lab," Hasso Plattner Institute of Design at Stanford, 2019, https://dschool.stanford.edu/programs/k12-lab-network; "Executive Education," Hasso Plattner Institute of Design at Stanford, 2019, https://dschool.stanford.edu/programs/executive-education.

24. "Chronology: 10 Years of Design Thinking at HPI"; "About Us," Global Design Thinking Alliance, 2018, https://gdta.org/about-us/.

25. Geof Bowker, "How to Be Universal: Some Cybernetic Strategies, 1943–1970," *Social Studies of Science* 23 (1993): 107.

promote creativity, rather than limit it, the space must be malleable. It's there to accommodate the work, not the other way around."[27]

The design of the d.school garage sends a clear signal that students are no longer in the world of cubicles and corner offices—that is, the world of bureaucracy. They have entered an open space in which their scope of action is determined only by their ability to spot and generate new kinds of signals. Post-it notes go up on the walls; colored construction paper hits the floor; students move and talk and build and play. Even as it stimulates the production of new ideas, the design garage models the marketplace described by Hayek. No money changes hands, of course, but the walls of the garage nicely set the boundaries of an arena devoted to information exchange. Secure, guaranteed by the institutional power of the university beyond its walls and of the state beyond the campus, the garage becomes an open space in which entrepreneurial individuals can practice signaling to one another. Through the exchange of information—about the project at hand, but also about their individual needs, intentions, styles—students can increase their capacities for action. They can build new collaborative teams to get course assignments done even as they build entrepreneurial habits and new relationships that will endure beyond the class.

In this way, the design garage helps train d.school students in the modes of self-management that a neoliberal marketplace ostensibly rewards. When he helped found the d.school, Kelley brought with him an understanding of the marketplace that had been substantially shaped by his time at IDEO. In fact, in *Change by Design*, Tim Brown credits the origins of the term *design thinking* to a conversation he had with Kelley during a period of economic instability for the firm. Kelley had founded his own design company in 1978, and, with his team, he designed the first Apple mouse. In 1991, Kelley merged his company with two others to form IDEO.[28] After the dot-com bust of 1999, the company began broadening its design services beyond its traditional Silicon Valley clients. As IDEO applied principles of design to health-care foundations, universities, and old-school manufacturers, Brown and Kelley began reconceptualizing their work as "design with a small d." Soon they were using the term "design thinking" as shorthand for "a set of principles that can be applied by diverse people to a wide range of problems," such as those encountered by IDEO in the expanded market for their design services.[29]

With IDEO's own transformation as a backdrop, Brown argues that the shift away from manufacturing toward services in

26. Kelley and Kelley, *Creative Confidence*, 194.

27. "How to Start a d.school," Hasso Plattner Institute of Design at Stanford, 2019, https://dschool.stanford.edu/how-to-start-a-dschool/.

28. Funding Universe, "IDEO, Inc. History," http://www.fundinguniverse.com/company-histories/ideo-inc-history/.

29. Tim Brown, *Change by Design: How Design Thinking Transforms Organizations and Inspires Innovation* (New York: HarperCollins, 2009), 6.

Nikola Tesla patents the alternating current (AC) electric induction motor

developed economies competing in a global market means "innovation has become nothing less than a survival strategy."[30] Manufacturers must reimagine consumers as "participants" in the production process, he maintains, and they must acknowledge a "blurring of line between 'products' and 'services,' as consumers shift from the expectation of functional performance to a more broadly satisfying experience."[31] In this context, design thinking becomes a way to stay competitive by constantly signaling to customers that you are ready to collaborate. The old, industrial order may have split services away from goods, the local away from the global, the technological away from the organic. But the new postindustrial order had begun to break down all of these walls. To survive in this boundaryless world, the individual has to design interactions so as to foster and even take control over the new relationships on which profits depend.

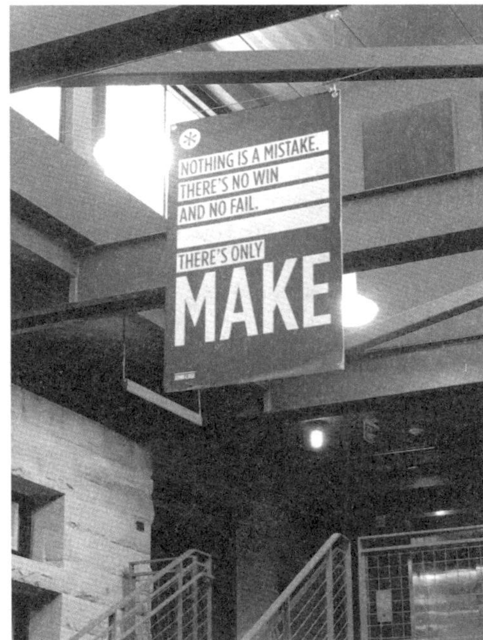

Inside the d.school, 2017

To that end, design thinking offers its students a methodology and a set of protocols for approaching indeterminate situations and the "wicked problems" of late capitalism. In *Creative Confidence*, Tom and David Kelley define design thinking as a "process for creativity and innovation." That process relies on iteration and collaboration to balance technological feasibility, economic viability, and human desirability.[32] The specific methods for such processes of thought are constantly evolving, flexible yet structured; there is, they write, "no one-size-fits-all methodology for bringing new ideas to life, but many successful programs include a variation on four steps: inspiration, synthesis, ideation/experimentation, and implementation."[33]

The Kelleys recommend specific protocols to follow within each of these general categories. To find inspiration, for instance, they advise readers to "go out in the world and proactively seek experiences that will spark creative thinking. Interact with experts, immerse yourself in unfamiliar environments, and role-play customer scenarios. Inspiration is fueled by a deliberate, planned course of action."[34] Instead of waiting idly for lightning to strike, design thinking prescribes *systematic* and *disciplined* activity. Similarly, success in "ideation and experimentation" requires particular tempos and structured activities. These "quick and dirty" methods include fast prototyping and getting feedback from users to "adapt, iterate, and pivot our way to human-centered, compelling, workable solutions."[35]

30. Ibid., 7.

31. Ibid., 178.

32. Kelley and Kelley, *Creative Confidence*, 21.

33. Ibid., 21–22.

34. Ibid., 22.

Design thinking's emphasis on protocols and processes marks it as a classic example of Foucauldian governmentality. So, too, does its emphasis on the formation of a particular kind of self, the design thinker. At Stanford, the d.school aims to endow its students with eight "core abilities" of design thinkers.[36] The ability to "synthesize information," for example, "requires skills in developing frameworks, maps, and abductive thinking," whereas "design your design work" involves "using intuition, adapting old tools to new contexts, and developing original techniques to meet the challenge at hand."[37] By following the protocols associated with the various prescribed stages of design thinking, individuals can not only acquire the ability to apply design thinking to a wide variety of spaces; they can become a new kind of person.

One of the key tenets of neoliberalism is the production of the responsible self—one who is capable of self-governing—through practices of self-mastery or what Foucault calls techniques of the self. As Nikolas Rose notes, "Individuals are to become 'experts of themselves,' to adopt an educated and knowledgeable relation of self-care in respect of their bodies, their minds, their forms of conduct and that of the members of their own families."[38] In *Creative Confidence*, the Kelleys show how design thinking provides techniques for self-mastery and the cultivation of a creative self. Creativity is a natural and universal force, they explain, but it is frequently blocked by psychological and social factors, such as a fear of failure and a lack of support for creative pursuits in traditional schooling. They describe the process of "unblocking" as achieving a form of freedom: "Opening up the flow of creativity is like discovering that you've been driving a car with the emergency brake on—and suddenly experiencing what it feels like when you release the brake and can drive freely."[39] When students overcome

35. Ibid., 23–24.

36. The eight core abilities are "Navigate Ambiguity," "Learn from Others (People and Contexts)," "Synthesize Information," "Experiment Rapidly," "Move Between Concrete and Abstract," "Build and Craft Intentionally," "Communicate Deliberately," and "Design Your Design Work." "8 Core Abilities," Hasso Plattner Institute of Design at Stanford, 2019, https://dschool.stanford.edu/about/#about-8-core-abilities.

37. Ibid.

38. Nikolas Rose, "Governing 'Advanced' Liberal Democracies," in *Foucault and Political Reason: Liberalism, Neo-Liberalism and Rationalities of Government*, ed. Andrew Barry, Thomas Osborne, and Nikolas Rose (Chicago: University of Chicago Press, 1996): 59.

39. Kelley and Kelley, *Creative Confidence*, 5.

such blockages at the d.school, the Kelleys report that they also experience moments of emotional release: "Students began visiting [David Kelley] during office hours—sometimes months after the class was over—to tell him that they had started to see themselves as creative individuals for the first time. That they could apply creativity to *any* challenge. Their eyes would light up with excitement, with a sense of opportunity, of possibility. Sometimes they cried."[40]

In this sense, design thinking works as a form of therapy. Yet, as Rose has argued, therapeutic modalities are central techniques in the production of a neoliberal self.[41] The therapeutic method also illustrates a key aspect of creativity and design thinking: the reliance on the intuitive and emotional. "Design thinking relies on the natural—and coachable—human ability to be intuitive, to recognize patterns, and to construct ideas that are emotionally meaningful as well as functional."[42] In contrast to traditional problem-solving strategies of rational deliberation and deduction, design thinking focuses on feeling and intuition and on turning these inborn elements of our psyches into "coachable" skill sets. At the same time, design thinking demands that the individual both *believe they are* and *choose to be* creative. Using the work of psychologists Carol Dweck and Robert Sternberg, Kelley and Kelley argue that creativity requires both a "growth mindset" and active decision-making: "Creativity seldom follows the path of least resistance. You need to deliberately choose creativity."[43] Design thinking offers the tools and methods to maximize the knowledge of the self as both a creative being and an actor capable of making choices. One such method in the d.school is psychologist Albert Bandura's concept of "guided mastery": "By entrusting individuals with increasingly complex tasks, then guiding them through a rehearsal of potential actions they might take, they begin to develop self-efficacy."[44] Creativity, though innate, must be disciplined and cultivated by individuals through the protocols offered by design thinking.

As Tim Brown's experience at IDEO demonstrated, we live in an era in which creativity is a commodifiable skill. That is, individual creativity not only drives individual contributions to collective enterprises, it serves as an organizational ideal as well. "Whatever your profession, when you approach it with creativity, you'll come up with new and better solutions and more success," explain the Kelleys in *Creative Confidence*.[45] Counter to the industrial-era "iron cage" that trapped workers in unfulfilling jobs wholly separate from their personal lives, creative confidence lets workers bring their "whole selves" to work, which the Kelleys argue is valuable to workers and businesses alike:

> If your CEO has enough good ideas to fuel the company's growth objectives in perpetuity, maybe you don't need to tap into the reservoir of talent at other levels of the organization. But the most innovative companies in the twenty-first century have transitioned from

40. Ibid., 26–27.

41. Rose, *Inventing Our Selves*, 156.

42. Kelley and Kelley, *Creative Confidence*, 25.

43. Ibid., 30–31, 76.

44. "How to Start a d.school."

45. Kelley and Kelley, *Creative Confidence*, 9.

> command-and-control organizations to a participatory approach that involves collaboration and teamwork. They draw on the whole brain of the company, gathering the best ideas and insights wherever they find them. They are open to listening to people from the front lines of their operation. They nurture the innovative spirit in all their team members so that ideas percolate up through the organization.[46]

No longer trapped in the "iron cage," workers are free to "unleash" their creative sides and bring their passion to work. In return, firms can draw on "the whole brain of the company" to create market value in a globalized, competitive economy.

While the Kelleys depict this as a mutually beneficial relationship, the destruction of the "iron cage" also has the potential to erode boundaries between work and leisure and turn playtime into work time.[47] "Work doesn't have to feel like 'Work with a capital W.' You should be able to feel passion, purpose, and meaning in whatever you do," write the Kelleys.[48] After listing a number of activities to cultivate creativity in the workplace, including "being remarkable about the extracurricular," "double delivering," and "creating an innovation lab," they remark upon the *labor* of being creative:

> Does all that sound like a lot of effort? It is. But people have told us that it works. And that they've had a lot of fun along the way, in spite of the work. Or maybe *because* of the work. That is the potential of creative confidence. If you can unleash the creative talent you have carried around inside you since childhood . . . If you can build a few skills and learn a few techniques for applying that creativity . . . If you can find the courage to speak up and experiment, to risk failure and act on your creative impulse . . . you might discover, to paraphrase Noël Coward, that *work* can be more fun than *fun*.[49]

While this "extra effort" couched in the terms of "fun" sends up warning signals for those concerned about fair compensation, overwork, and exploitation, we should also remember that "creative confidence" has been built through specific methodologies aimed at maximizing *design* solutions that ultimately seek to balance technological feasibility, corporate viability, and human desirability.

Conclusion: Design and Democracy

For Tim Brown, "relaxing the rules is not about letting people be silly so much as letting them be whole people—a step many companies seem reluctant to take."[50] To be whole, however, is not to be free of the need to produce a return on an employer's investment. On the contrary, the methodologies of design thinking aim to enlist an individual's desire for self-fulfillment and transform it into an instrument with which to navigate a landscape in which society

46. Ibid., 208.

47. For more on this point, see Daniel Kreiss, Megan Finn, and Fred Turner, "The Limits of Peer Production: Some Reminders from Max Weber for Web 2.0," *New Media and Society* 13, no. 2 (2011): 243–59.

48. Kelley and Kelley, *Creative Confidence*, 154.

49. Ibid., 255.

50. Brown, *Change by Design*, 32.

itself has been reimagined as a marketplace. In the 1940s, Hayek and his colleagues did not, so far as we can tell, foresee the fusion of the marketplace and everyday life that we inhabit today. Yet Hayek did depict the marketplace as the model of an ideal demos. Within its walls, individuals would be free to transform whatever inner capacities they had into action. All they needed to do was keep an eye on the information around them.

For Hayek, a marketplace of individuals simultaneously seeking self-fulfillment and profit was the best alternative to the centralized, top-down modes of control exercised by totalitarian states. But his marketplace was hardly an anarchist's paradise. As the nation-state retreated to simply guaranteeing the security of the marketplace, design and engineering stepped in as modes of government, helping to create conditions in which individuals could find their own ways and to engineer tools with which they could do it. Even today, the fantasy that we can replace the hard work of politics and government with benevolent social engineering lingers, and not just in Silicon Valley.[51]

So, too, do the social consequences of that fantasy. In Hayek's vision, a free marketplace would naturally produce inequality. The key, he argued, was to give everyone an equal opportunity to enter the marketplace. Individuals would bring different resources with them, and so much the better. According to Hayek, this kind of diversity was required for democratic societies to flourish. If the state sought to equalize its citizens directly, through taxation or other techniques of redistribution, it would deprive them of the motivation they needed to build social order from the bottom up. Inequality, he argued, was the price of freedom.

To the extent that the proponents of design thinking have turned the professional practices of designers into a universal discipline, they have helped to produce a far less egalitarian world. This is hard to see from the floor of the d.school garage. If you were to stand on a balcony and watch individual students collaborate, explore, and play below, you would be struck by the absence of hierarchies, of bosses, of formal structure. What you might not see would be the inequalities submerged into the design of the learning experience. As in Hayek's marketplace, students do not enter classes as equals, but rather with a wide array of talents and experiences—many a product of their membership in a particular social class. The ability to participate in d.school-style exercises must be produced. And with a few exceptions, it is being produced primarily in schools and companies that train members of today's upper class.

The words *upper class* conjure visions of bankers and butlers and ancient smoking clubs, but in the neoliberal world foreshadowed by Hayek and created by Thatcher, Reagan, and several generations of political leaders since, one's ability to accumulate

51. Fred Turner, "Machine Politics: The Rise of the Internet and a New Age of Authoritarianism," *Harper's*, January 2019, 25–33.

French brothers Joseph and Louis Lumière invent movie projectors and open the first movie theater

wealth depends on one's ability to move flexibly from project to project. Those who embed themselves in unchanging hierarchies—factory-floor laborers, government bureaucrats—may make a living, but only that. To be a leader today is to be an entrepreneur, a self-made person, someone who can spot an opportunity, gather a team, solve a problem, and move on to the next one. For members of this class, design thinking offers a discourse of empowerment and a tool kit to match. The psyches it produces are trained to rule themselves and to treat the problems they encounter in their lives and in the world at large not as structural or political but as personal and aesthetic. In the world of design thinking, there is no class struggle; there are only problems needing designers to solve them.

By erasing questions of equality and difference, by subsuming them into a rhetoric and practice of interpersonal collaboration and suggesting that such ways of talking and playing together can change the world, design thinking reveals itself to be a neoliberal ideology. In *Change by Design*, Tim Brown put the issue this way: "Design thinking needs to be turned toward the formulation of a new participatory social contract. It is no longer possible to think in adversarial terms of a 'buyer's market' or a 'seller's market.' We're all in this together."[52] For Brown, the social contract that has been the heart of democracy since the eighteenth century is always already a marketplace. We are either buyers or sellers; as in Hayek's early accounts, there is no one else to be. To live a right life in such a place, design thinking teaches us that we need to think collaboratively and act accordingly. As Brown puts it, "The implications are clear: the public, too, must commit to the principles of design thinking, just like the nurses at Kaiser, the production workers at Toyota, the WOLF Packs at Best Buy, and the public servants at the Transportation Security Administration and the Department of Energy."[53]

Design thinking's emphasis on collaboration has a utopian ring. But we are far from the founding of the Bauhaus or Buckminster Fuller's commune domes. In design thinking, as in neoliberalism more generally, the individual must be the agent and the product of her own success. Her life must be a portfolio of skills, and she must carry a quiver of techniques for turning her senses into tools for recognizing and resolving the quandaries she encounters. Design thinking aims to make each of us a designer of our own lives, yet it offers us no tools with which to collaborate in more than temporary and largely for-profit ways. On the contrary, it teaches us that the proper place to express our individuality and negotiate our differences is not the public sphere but the factory floor.

52. Brown, *Change by Design*, 178.

53. Ibid., 201.

The authors would like to thank the members of Stanford University's Communication Works in Progress workshop and all the participants in "After the Bauhaus, Before the Internet" for their very helpful feedback.

NOTES ON PRACTICE: EXPANDED, COMPACTED, EXPLODED

LORRAINE WILD

In 1980, when I was in my first semester of the MFA Graphic Design program here at Yale, Alvin Eisenman, the director of the program, would take students out to lunch to ask them what they wanted to do with their education. He'd just gotten back from a trip to Egypt, where he'd been looking at ancient cuneiform and conducting research for a book on the early development of writing. When Alvin asked me what I pictured myself doing after Yale, I said, "I want to do what you do: I want to design books, and I want to teach, and I want to research and write about graphic design." His response was, "That's impossible."

Flummoxed, I asked for an explanation. He responded that no one could do *all* of those things—one activity would always conflict with the others, and you'd always think that one or another part of your work wouldn't measure up. I decided to ignore him, since several members of the faculty had managed to teach *and* publish, though most of their writing focused on their own work.[1] Ironically, and perhaps proving his point, Alvin never completed his book—and I never completed mine.

I've been thinking about this lately because I've been listening to visiting designers at CalArts and to *Scratching the Surface* podcasts, and one designer after another will refer to the pursuit of something called an "Expanded Practice."[2] I've also heard this term used to describe academic programs in a wide range of fields, from architecture to nursing.[3] In each case, I've noticed that "practice," once a verb, is now a noun denoting the set of activities engaged in by an individual who may or may not identify primarily as a designer. The individual determines the definition of "practice," and this definition is fluid. There are no standards to judge whether or not all the hyphenated terms comprising an "Expanded Practice" connect.

Such open-endedness is not unfamiliar. Graphic design has always been a bit rogue, especially compared to its legally well-defined and highly regulated cousin, architecture. Graphic designers receive a specialized professional education without the concomitant professional licensing, continuing education, and ethical guidelines. Yet anyone who dismisses contemporary "Expanded Practice" as deprofessionalization is indulging in a type of nostalgia. From about 1935 to 1995, graphic designers ran their offices, taught part-time, served on the boards of the AIGA or their clients' companies, and maybe even made the occasional collage—but they still identified themselves as "professional"

1. For examples of Yale design faculty who published monographs about their own work, see Paul Rand, *Thoughts on Design* (New York: Wittenborn, 1947); and Bradbury Thompson, *The Art of Graphic Design* (New Haven: Yale University Press, 1988).

2. Jarrett Fuller, *Scratching the Surface* podcast at https://scratchingthesurface.fm/.

3. On expanded practice in architecture, see https://urbanismseminars.cornell.edu/courses/expanded-practice-seminars; in nursing, see https://edu.cdhb.health.nz/Hospitals-Services/Health-Professionals/pdu/Documents/Guideline-Expanded-Practice.pdf.

graphic designers. Whereas the identity of today's "coder/performance artist/graphic designer" or "painter/curator/graphic design professor" is far more diffuse.

Because digital media have democratized (and lowered the price of) the means of production, designers are, at least in theory, less dependent on their clients, and their clients have gained a reciprocal independence. The new independence of contemporary designers distinguishes their practice from earlier incarnations of graphic design, which involved solving someone else's problems according to someone else's specifications for someone else's audience. In rejecting its primacy, the Expanded Practitioner implies that graphic design may no longer be the central focus of his/her practice. And of course, the construction of an Expanded Identity is symptomatic of another contemporary trend: the need to "brand" oneself as a unique entity in a competitive marketplace.

It Starts at School

In his 2011 essay "School Days," Rob Giampietro proposed that graduate-level design had entered a new academic phase. He compared the training of MFA graphic designers and MFA creative writers: The goal of the training is not the acquisition of specific skills, but the self-actualization of the designer (or writer) through the development of a body of work that grants access to the larger world of design (or writing). Giampietro writes:

> Students' design work is less learning by rote than practice through self-examination. The resulting work . . . becomes, in effect, an advertisement for its accompanying self, the designer whose interests and academic path of inquiry shaped it, framed it.[4]

The process he describes also characterizes the acquisition of a typical MFA in art. A blurring of boundaries has occurred in many graphic design graduate programs—particularly those situated next to MFA programs in art—in that art pedagogy has moved away from media specificity and skills toward a process of conceptual inquiry driven by the MFA candidates. For example, Michelle Grabner, a professor at the Art Institute of Chicago, describes her method of working with students as follows:

> The most effective and trustworthy assignment . . . is simply: NO ASSIGNMENT as a form of indirect teaching. . . . [I]t does cultivate critical thinking while eschewing the authority of the teacher and rebuffing the pedagogical misadventure of assessment outcomes. . . . [I]ndirect teaching . . . (supports) self-directed knowledge. . . . Work and assessment are the responsibility of the student.[5]

Because the practice of graphic design is so diffuse, and because so many MFA graphic design programs still accept students without prior study or experience, it's easy to see how Expanded Practices have evolved comfortably in the context of art school pedagogy. Design faculties often encourage students

4. Rob Giampietro, "School Days," in *Graphic Design in Production* (Minneapolis: Walker Art Center, 2011), 214.

5. Michelle Grabner, in *Draw It with Your Eyes Closed: The Art of the Art Assignment* (New York: Paper Monument, 2012), 119.

to think of themselves as the product of their practices: Graphic design becomes an element of the larger project of individual self-construction.

Design pedagogy has its own trajectory of abrupt transitions. Until the First World War, the complex artistic and technical skills necessary for graphic reproduction were largely acquired by anonymous craftspeople as apprentices working under other craftspeople, until they achieved an approved level of competence (maintained by a guild system, which sometimes provided the training). Meredith Davis points out that internships, student-to-working-master relationships in design teaching, and entry-level jobs in design are vestiges of craft-training systems,

and the association of craft skills with commerce, in contrast to fine art, which is considered to be outside the market and for elevated audiences (traditionally, the Church; now, as always, the rich). This hierarchy was reinforced by the institutional separation of "fine" art from "applied" art and the development of independent curricula for the teaching of each.[6]

The founding of the Department of Design at Yale in 1950, the first such program in the US, was the result of an effort on the part of Dr. Charles Sawyer, dean of the College of Fine Arts, to "break down the walls" of a then-calcified art school hierarchy and synthesize a new formal discipline that challenged the separation of "fine" and "applied" art. By bringing in practicing designers and artists, he hoped to create a curriculum that would combine practical training with projects more allied to modern architecture than the conventional academic art school training of the period.[7] In the early years of the Yale program, for example, Josef Albers taught a variant of his Bauhaus exercises in form alongside the study of printing, typography, and book arts. Yale and other schools that followed its model developed the discipline of graphic design through critique, theory, and aesthetics. And while none of the dialectical inquiry was crucial to the training of working designers, it was the beginning of the institutionalization of a design education whose goal was to produce better designers and design educators.

While the early Yale program might be called "Expanded Practice 1.0," its innovations (which were resisted for years by many successful but unschooled early practitioners) were nevertheless grounded in older models of practice.[8] The point of bringing design into the academy was not to turn design into art but to establish a field of integrated artistic professionalism. In his 1989 essay "The Yale Years," Rob Roy Kelly notes that representatives of major corporations (such as General Motors, Ford, Container Corporation, CBS, and Time-Life) attended the first public announcement of the founding of the Yale program at the 1951 Aspen Design Conference,

6. Meredith Davis, *Teaching Design* (New York: Allworth Press, 2017), 8–9.

7. Rob Roy Kelly, "The Early Years of Graphic Design at Yale University," *Design Issues* 17, no. 3 (2001): 3.

8. I witnessed (on several occasions) designers—particularly those who either did not go to college or did, but did not study design—complain about the perceived uselessness of a graduate degree through the 1980s and '90s.

German engineer Rudolf Diesel develops his diesel engine

signaling their eagerness to deploy this newly conscious design as an integral part of their corporate communications strategies: They were ready to hire the new designers.[9]

Graphic design gained recognition and degree programs proliferated; but the programs themselves were sites of chronic ambiguity, simultaneously training professional designers and cultivating designers as artists. Assignments were structured like jobs, with problem statements, constraints, predetermined formats, and deadlines. At the same time, there was a contradictory expectation that each student would define and answer their own problems in a thesis project that translated research into visual production, a summary of their identities as independent creators.

The MFA graphic design thesis (which has evolved as the primary vehicle for Expanded Practice) is its own force field, in tension with other aspects of graduate-level design education. It casts a shadow over one of the more interesting aspects of graphic design education, the design of assignments. In contrast to the expansionary practices associated with the thesis project, MFA design assignments in the past have been polemical "compacting practices," designed to support the production of knowledge transcending current practice. With Expanded Practice in mind, I'd like to examine a set of typography assignments given over thirty years that demonstrates a conundrum: The Compacted Practice of design problems at the microscale enabled designers (at least for a while) to develop modes of practice that challenged prevailing models.

The Soap Box

In the '60s, at Yale, Paul Rand asked students to redesign a box of Duz laundry detergent.[10] On the surface, it seems like the epitome of a design assignment formulated by commercial practice. But Rand's Duz assignment had nothing to do with creating a more beauteous soapbox.

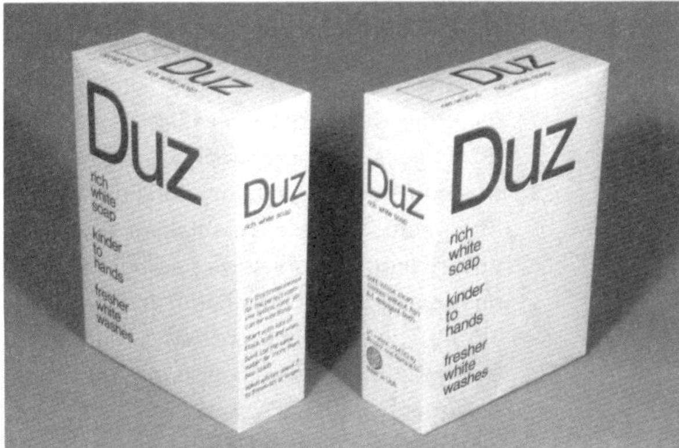

Chris Pullman, Packaging Project (Duz), 1964

Students were asked to remove the type and illustration from the surface of the box. They were then asked to reposition all of the text on the box, in one color, in a new style, what we now call Swiss or International style typography. Rand gave several packaging design problems that semester. Some were more conceptual (like applying interchangeable product names on the same plain corrugated box) and some more commercial (like redesigning a chewing-gum package). Students were asked to bring in their favorite food or candy packages for critical analysis.

9. Kelly, "The Early Years of Graphic Design at Yale University," 4.

10. Paul Rand, course syllabus for Design 120, 1964–65, Yale School of Art (unpublished). Courtesy of Chris Pullman.

In the process of replacing typographic chaos with sans-serif fonts arranged on a grid, the students devised new designs for an ordinary product type. As the final step in the project, students took their mocked-up boxes to a local grocery store and placed them on the shelves alongside the real detergent boxes. A *covert* goal of the Duz project was revealed: to translate the product's lowbrow American commercial vernacular into a higher-brow yet productive replacement (similar to contemporary packaging at Target). The supermarket "test" also imagined a new consumer who would respond to a more sophisticated visual language.

The Duz project resembled projects presented in the pages of *New Graphic Design* (*NGD*), a magazine published in Zurich in 1958 and edited by Richard Lohse, Josef Müller-Brockmann, Hans Neuburg, and Carlo Vivarelli.[11] *NGD* published Swiss graphic design of uncompromising simplicity used to promote all kinds of consumer goods: furniture, food, cars, appliances. The designers argued that the simplicity of their style embodied ideals of socio-cultural agreement (conveyed through the disciplined use of grids, sans-serif fonts, and photography) that transcended excessive individuality and commercial noise (conveyed by everything they rejected, such as eclectic typography and illustration). The work was presented as technocratic, socially democratic, and sophisticated. The association of these socio-political ideals with the constricted visual language of the Swiss Style was so persuasive that—to bring it back to the Duz project—it did not need to be spelled out in order for young designers, an ocean away, to be convinced.

By the mid-'60s, however, the Swiss style had become the standard graphic style of corporate communications for new multinationals on both sides of the Atlantic. Too big for ad slogans or cute cartoons, these companies (like Rand's clients, Westinghouse and IBM) needed comprehensive, scalable, graphically unified design that conveyed the stability and authority of vertically and horizontally integrated large-scale capitalism. Rand had come from the world of advertising; grocery-store packaging problems had been his bread and butter. But he left all that around the time that he began teaching at Yale. The application of Swiss methodology and style (championed by Rand) in the Duz box assignment is finally intended to create a designer capable of speaking in a corporate voice. Yale graduates would not be going off to advertising agencies, but instead would work for corporate offices or the consultancies that served them (if they weren't going into teaching or publishing). Despite his earlier work in advertising, by the time I had Rand as a teacher, all commercial constructs in his assignments had disappeared, and he was making pronouncements in class like, "Only stupid people go work for ad agencies" (and that other sage but frustrating piece of advice, "Only work for the president of the company").

11. Richard Lohse, Josef Müller-Brockmann, Hans Neuburg, Carlo Vivarelli, eds., *Neue Grafik / New Graphic Design / Graphisme actuel* (Switzerland: Verlag Otto Walter, 1958).

The Grid on a Square

If work featured in *New Graphic Design* offered "proof of concept," the most careful presentation of the formal methodology behind it appears in Emil Ruder's book *Typography* (1967), a distillation of his teaching at the Schule für Gestaltung in Basel.[12] Ruder isolated typographic training in laboratory-like conditions. A contrasting pedagogical approach appears in the projects Josef Müller-Brockmann assigned at the Zurich school where students worked on more quotidian projects such as identity programs, technical manuals, signage systems, and published in his book *The Graphic Artist and His Design Problems* (1961).[13] In contrast, Ruder provided a generative syntax for modern typography, regardless of application, based on the controlled use of form: negative and positive space, proportion, composition, contrast, scale, independent of use. It must be noted that another important Swiss book on typography, *A Compendium for Literates*, by Karl Gerstner, focused on the process of communication over the resolution of form.[14] Published in 1974, Gerstner's valid but less formalized modernism was not as immediately influential as Ruder's exercises. Ruder's more elemental approach to creating and controlling meaning through the limitations of stylistic vocabulary provided his audience with a de facto rule book. American graphic design programs looking to distinguish themselves from commercial art training programs found in *Typography* a comprehensive and easily replicated guide to teaching typography in the abstract.

Unidentified student of Dan Friedman, Weathering Information Project, Yale University or Philadelphia College of Art, as published in Friedman's essay "Introductory Education in Typography," *Visible Language* 7, no. 2, (Spring 1973): 139

An Exercise in Utopia

The late Dan Friedman—an American who went to Basel and studied under Ruder (and his protégé, Wolfgang Weingart)—began teaching in a variety of East Coast programs, including Yale, in the early '70s. In 1973, Friedman published a brief but widely circulated article in *Visible Language* titled "A View: Introductory Education in Typography."[15] In it, he displays examples of his students' work on his revision of the Ruder project. The project starts like Ruder's, where a simple message (in this case, a weather report) is typeset in Univers 65 on a square field. But Friedman encouraged subtle but undeniably

12. Emil Ruder, *Typographie* (Sulgen: Verlag Niggli, 1967).

13. Josef Müller-Brockmann, *The Graphic Artist and His Design Problems* (New York: Hastings House, 1961).

14. Karl Gerstner, *A Compendium for Literates* (Cambridge, MA: MIT Press, 1974).

15. Daniel Friedman, "A View: Introductory Education in Typography," *Visible Language* 7, no. 2 (Spring 1973): 120–44.

"subjective" formal manipulations, as he was convinced that graphic design could convey more than the restrictions of optimized functionalism. His project was a "vehicle for syntactic (and semantic) exploration": Meaning—maybe even a poetics of meaning—was now in play.[16] Friedman added symbolism and pictorialism to the options a typographer might explore. He was building upon a line of thinking explored by Wolfgang Weingart, who had also been working to expand the means of expression available to Swiss typography, but the clarity of Friedman's project statement published in an American journal had an enormous impact here. Friedman's revisions to Ruder redefined the relationship between a designer and his or her audience, challenging the myth of objectivity.

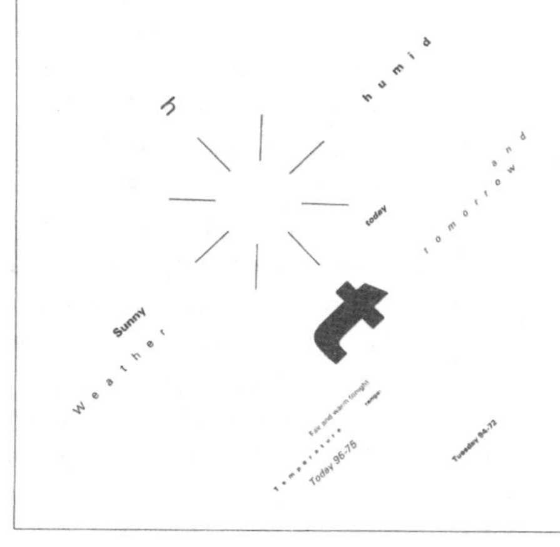

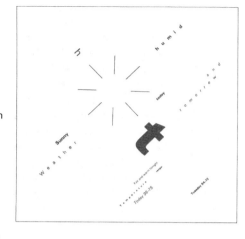

Unidentified student of Dan Friedman, Weathering Information Project, Yale University or Philadelphia College of Art, as published in Friedman's essay "Introductory Education in Typography," *Visible Language* 7, no. 2, (Spring 1973): 139

What pushed Friedman to expand upon Ruder? In a later essay, "What Is Wrong with Modernism?" Friedman noted a schism between the optimism of the early twentieth-century avant-garde, expressing a "spirit of progress, reason, and political change," and the devolution of the modernist style, which he felt had become "about itself."[17] He knowingly cited all the arguments against International style modernist graphic design that had been articulated by the early '90s: that it had lost its moral authority as it had become the banal signature of corporate marketing and that it was "too rigid, humorless, exclusive" to tell the stories of others. Feeling that rote methods of teaching design had facilitated that loss of spirit, he sought to inject humanism into the pedagogical reductionism that he abhorred. Friedman sought to recuperate an earlier idealism: what he called "radical modernism"—in his words, "a reconsideration of how modernism can embrace its heritage along with . . . a more humanistic purpose."[18]

Russian Konstantin Tsiolkovsky figures out the theory of space rockets

Typography in a Hothouse

Starting in the mid-'70s, Katherine McCoy began to assign a variant of the Ruder/Friedman type-in-a-square projects to her graphic design students at Cranbrook. McCoy, trained as an industrial designer, had picked up Swiss graphic design on the job (notably at Unimark, one of the earliest multinational design consultancies) and via books and publications, so when she began to teach she used Swiss pedagogy as her guide.[19] But Cranbrook was far away from Basel, and maintained a kind of independence thanks to its operation as an atelier, a site for collaborative

16. Ibid.

17. Dan Friedman, "What Is Wrong with Modernism?" in *Dan Friedman: Radical Modernism* (New Haven: Yale University Press, 1994), 114–15.

18. Ibid.

experimentation. As McCoy reiterated these Swiss projects, she (and the students) began to improvise over the expressiveness of Friedman's "weather report." It was still a "step-by-step" project (on squares), this time based on a food package or a Yellow Pages ad, but the biggest change was that at a certain point, students were asked to reintegrate the vernacular elements of their original artifact *back into* the typography of their compositions. The inclusion of a previously forbidden visual vocabulary was the result of several influences on McCoy and her students: reading *Learning from Las Vegas* alongside structuralist and poststructuralist theory with Daniel Libeskind, Cranbrook's architect-in-residence at the time.[20] And one cannot overemphasize the influence of Edward Fella, a major presence in the Cranbrook Design studios even before his matriculation, and whose collage experiments with found imagery and type inspired Cranbrook designers to revive the very visual styles that Rand's Duz project was designed to eliminate. The Vernacular Sequence project was an organic collaboration that eventually coalesced around the creation of visual narratives, and an investigation into typography's role in the processes of both seeing and reading.

These sequences looked weird at the time, which led to their being misunderstood as formalistic games. The same was true of Friedman's project: The curse of dissemination via publication was that judgments—pro and con—were made primarily by an audience accustomed to looking only at the surface of graphic design. The Friedman and McCoy projects granted a new level of agency to the designer, one that allowed for engagement and interpretation, thus opening design to a wider range of expressions: an Expanded Practice 2.0. It's striking that these simple, two-dimensional exercises that simply tweaked the conventions of typographic practice would prove to be so powerful as manifestations of thought.

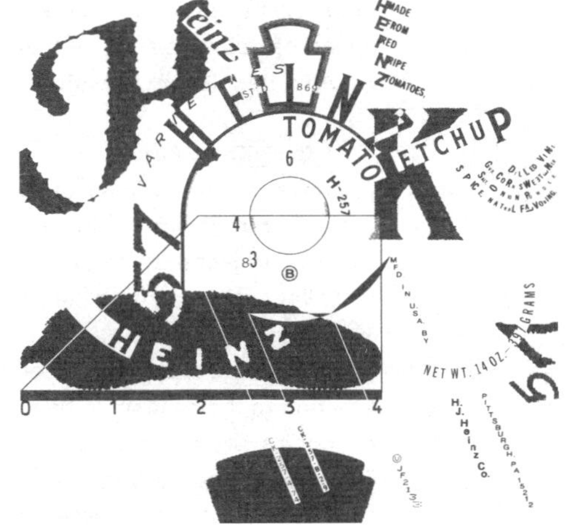

Robert Nakata, Vernacular Message Sequence Project (Heinz Ketchup), Cranbrook Academy of Art, 1984

It was easy to dismiss theory-driven studio work in MFA graphic design programs: To practitioners, it all seemed like pointless rebellion with no commercial value (at least at the beginning). Critics of the postmodernists from within academia claimed that the work was not serious enough, and misunderstood the generative nature of these projects.[21] Johanna Drucker has attributed the

19. Lorraine Wild, "Katherine McCoy," https://www.aiga.org/medalist-katherinemccoy.

20. See Wild, "Katherine McCoy"; and Ellen Lupton, "The Academy of Deconstructed Design," *Eye* 1, no. 3 (1991), http://www.eyemagazine.com/feature/article/the-academy-of-deconstructed-design.

21. Ellen Lupton and J. Abbott Miller, "Deconstruction and Graphic Design," in *Design Writing Research* (New York: Phaidon, 1996), 2–23.

influence of theory in design education as a search for legitimacy: "There was a sense that the profession . . . needed a metalanguage of self-conscious critique in order to decode its complicity and contradictions . . . in everyday life."[22] Whether that's valid or not, the same "self-conscious critique" was apparently shared by architecture and literature and history and philosophy and law, to name just a few other areas of scholarship influenced by postmodernism. If graphic design had been immune, it would have been a sign of brain death. The biggest problem many critics had with the experimental graphic design of the late '70s was that designers played with critique through form, wading into one of the most ancient fights of all, the knock-down, drag-out between words and pictures.

Speaking as someone who witnessed this firsthand, I believe that it's a mistake to attribute too much to the influence of postmodern linguistic theory.[23] The general lack of faith in late modernism (so eloquently described by Friedman) had led many of his same generation to reinvestigate the utopian, speculative energy of earlier modernism. The notion that modernism was timeless seemed like one giant mistake shoved down our throats by the (authoritarian and corporate) late modernists. Avant-garde modernism seen through the lens of postmodernism provided a model of self-reflexivity, and an allegiance to constant change that would guide design forward.

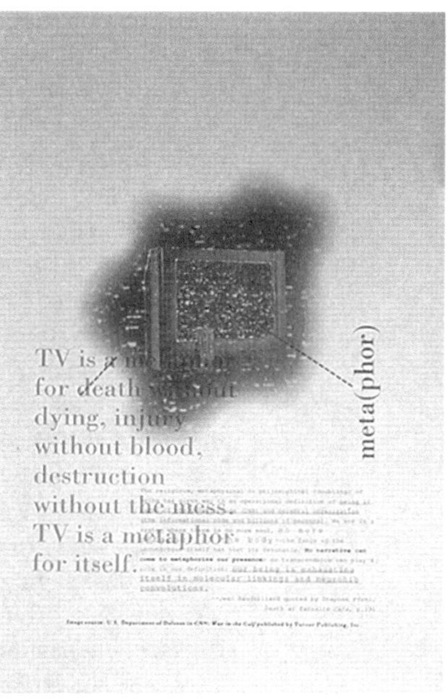

Louise Sandhaus, Lexicon Project (Metaphor), CalArts, 1992

Using Our Words

I want to show one last series of typography projects that date from the late '80s at CalArts. The first project that I (along with Jeff Keedy and Ed Fella) assigned was called the Lexicon: Each MFA student would be given three words and asked to make typographic compositions that interpreted their meaning. Books like Raymond Williams's *Keywords* or Terry Eagleton's *Literary Theory* provided us with critical terms to deploy in response to the assignments instead of "I like it" or "this doesn't work." The outcome of the project was not only the work, but the critique itself; pinned-up pages instigated conversations that carried on through other projects. The Lexicon was a typography assignment through which we hoped students would develop fluency in visual rhetoric and understand the transmission of both connotative and denotative meaning via typography (as opposed to using visual metaphors).

The postmodern rebellion of the time was explicit in a typographic project that Laurie Haycock and I assigned to MFA students

22. Johanna Drucker, "The Critical Languages of Graphic Design," in *Graphic Design: History in the Writing 1983–2011* (London: Occasional Papers, 2014), 194.

23. Lorraine Wild, "Castles Made of Sand" (review of Rick Poynor's book *No More Rules: Graphic Design and Postmodernism*), *Emigre* 66 (2004): 109–23.

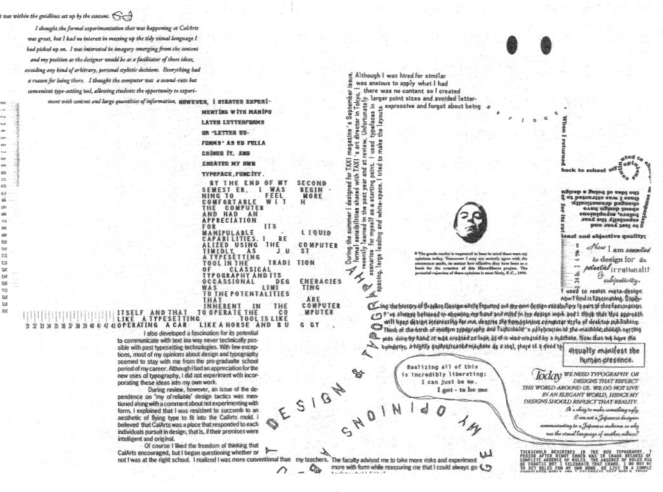

Robin Cottle, Macro-Micro Project (Proto-Type, Neo-Type), CalArts, 1989

called Macro-Micro. We were obsessed with the idea that an individual designer should be able to connect with the larger societal or cultural context they were working in, or to the history of the practice they had chosen. Macro-Micro asked each student to design a book where a personal story, written by the student, ran alongside, and responded to, a text that addressed that outside context. The practical problem was designing pages that held more than one type of information: How do you handle typographic continuity and hierarchy? But most discussion went into the construction of the narrative itself: "objective" reportage of the "macro" story interwoven with "subjective" interpretation of the "micro." As we were determined to allow for as great a range of expression as possible, this project focused on the student's narrative. The DNA of this project lives on in the CalArts curriculum (now called Editorial Complexity), and it's a hybrid, a project designed as if there is a reader, but the subject is still the designer placing themselves in a larger context. They are their own first audience.

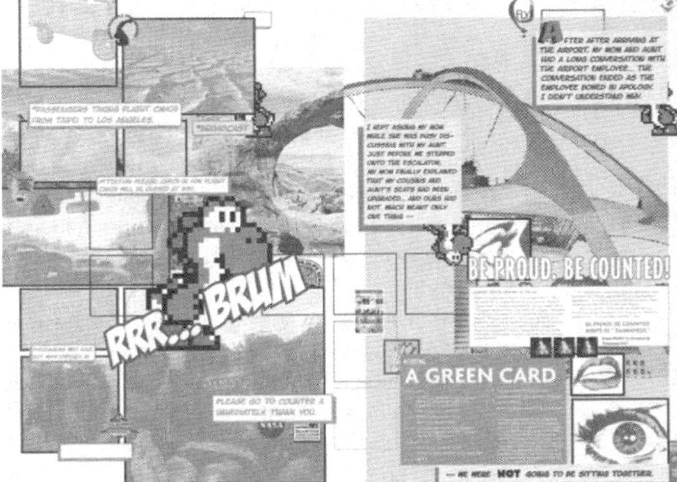

Jessica Lee, Editorial Complexity Project (Childhood), CalArts, 2010

When Sheila de Bretteville became the director of the MFA program at Yale in 1990, she was asked what she would change, since the program had remained basically unchanged since its founding. She stated that she intended to bring in "the individual voices of the students" (something she had been doing steadily through her previous work at CalArts and the Women's Building).[24]

De Bretteville was an early proponent of an idea that represents the generational change of the '80s and '90s, advocating a radical subjectivity after the austeriy of late modernism. Work made with the "designer's voice" embraced relative and multiple perspectives; reconsidered history; created plural visual languages; and aimed to make graphic design appropriate to a wider range of purposes and audiences. In trying to describe the difference between modernism and postmodernism, Rick Poynor has said: "If modernism sought to create a better world, postmodernism—to the horror of many observers—appears to accept the world as it is."[25] However, at least at the level of graduate studio postmodernism, I witnessed a tsunami of idealism: to pump life back into a visual culture that had become too reductive. The energy was also stoked by optimism for technologies that were changing the way things were being made. Personal, poetic, exploratory, kitschy, messy things were made in the compacted process of Expanded Practice 3.0 by teachers *and* students striving to liberate graphic design from the confines of older pedagogies and working toward diversity through a plurality of visual languages.

The Blow Up

Meanwhile, other developments shifted and in some ways overwhelmed the MFA graphic design trajectory that I am describing. Of course, there was the advent of the Macintosh computer and the attendant software development, which in the course of a decade changed from a sort of primitive graphic-arts tool to the all-encompassing digital context we live and work in today. With every improvement in processing speed, software, browsers, and the Internet, the number of things anyone could do as a designer kept growing. A whole new set of skills was added to the already considerable set of skills graphic designers were expected to master. In many design programs, these requirements were simply added to existing curricula; their advent did not occasion a reenvisioning of the curriculum itself. As a result, many design programs struggled to fit everything in, and there was less time to go deeply into anything.

More subtle, but still unnerving, was the appropriation of the MFA experiments of the late '80s and early '90s by commercial marketing: first for youth culture, then more broadly for info-entertainment. Postmodern experiments calcified into a postmodern style. What was once meaningful became trite and empty. Of course, in our late-capitalist context, *everything*, particularly the signs and symbols of personal agency, is appropriated to mark the illusion of personal freedom in the face of an ever more controlled and globalized economic system. In many graphic design graduate programs, the idea of the "designer's voice"

24. Ellen Lupton, "Reputations: Sheila de Bretteville," *Eye* 8, no. 2 (1993), http://www.eyemagazine.com/feature/article/reputations-sheila-levrant-de-bretteville.

25. Rick Poynor, *No More Rules: Graphic Design and Postmodernism* (New Haven: Yale University Press, 2003), 11.

persisted as a sort of currency—something one went to grad school to get, and something one might expect to be able to sell once one graduated—but now with less critique, a fuzzier relationship to graphic design thinking, and a tendency to careen into solipsism, given the limited access to critical and historical discourse that still plagued many design programs.

Many of us in graduate design education were hoping that the spread of (and competition among) design programs would encourage specialization; that programs might evolve to focus on information design, or interactive design, or design management, or type design, or even "art-design," and a few of those programs announced themselves in the '90s. But the majority of MFA graphic design programs retained a loose generalism that combined different modes of teaching: a bit of post-Bauhaus *Vorkurs*, some tradecraft, some old-school portfolio development, and then this newer element, dedicated to the individual voice. As this pluralism was institutionalized, it began to exhibit some of the very characteristics that late modernism had been accused of. To (grossly) paraphrase Hal Foster, pluralism grants equal status to all kinds of work, but in doing so, everything becomes less important.[26]

Between the dot-com bubble of 2000 and the recession of 2008, the advent of software that deskilled designers, and the rise of the smartphone, the landscape of graphic design finally shifted to reflect the sorting out of technology into four or five mega-platforms and a steep decline in print publication (despite the simultaneous rise of micro-publishing): simultaneous consolidation and atomization. Returning to typography as a compacting practice, you also see an exponential growth of interest in font design, in "personalizing" fonts, alongside a new indifference to the visual languages (plural) of graphic design.

Design historians in the future will have a field day with the appearance of the digital default / trendlist.org "Trend Generator" typography of the early twenty-first century: Simultaneously a stab at the postmodern excess of personality, a depressive acknowledgment of debased contemporary system fonts, and/or a predictor of totally engineered and templatized systems like Google Material Design, the default moment was yet another product of the academic hothouse, but this time the polemic was one of deadpan rejection.[27] Perhaps the default style signified resistance to (what remained of) graphic design culture, to all those theory bibliographies of the '90s that now seemed quaint? Or an attempt to visualize the deskilling of practice? To resist the appropriation of the market by appropriating *from* the market? In 2012 Susan Sellers was quoted as saying (about student work), "Graphic design looks poor now. It is self-effacing, dematerialized, diminished in its form. I feel that often results from an effort to be taken seriously, in

26. Hal Foster, "Against Pluralism," in *Recodings: Art, Spectacle, Cultural Politics* (Seattle: Bay Press, 1985), 13–32.

27. See https://www.trendlist.org/.

an understandable rejection of the smooth, seductive surface of advertising."[28] The desire to be taken seriously is symptomatic of the denizens of art schools and university departments, places not known for comfort with the marketplace. But art schools provide a pipeline into our cultural ecology of galleries and museums and art fairs and biennials. And while we wrestle with art education's complicity in the globalized art economy, we must also recognize that they have a relationship of co-dependence. So it seems only natural that design students would inflect their MFA thesis projects toward the model of contemporary art practice, both out of a philosophical comfort and the promise of reward in a seller's market. Thus, the MFA graphic design student of today is indeed "working for the president"—but the executive now is him- or herself, as the field of graphic design expands to include just about anything (except reliable jobs).

The thesis student is free to call the shots, in many cases dispensing with the one and only condition that distinguishes design practice from art practice: that one makes work for an audience other than oneself. I witness crit after crit where faculty congratulate MFA design students for producing truly individual works, work for which there is no market, encouraging them to go out and create their own contexts. And some will, in very productive ways; those who won't or can't, however, face membership in what has been called the "Uber design precariat."[29]

I can't say that I blame students for trying to Expand their Practices, given the depths of student debt, the predominance of the gig economy, and the shade cast on the MFA degree given that graphic design can now be made by anyone. Perhaps, as my colleague Mr. Keedy has been proclaiming for years, all the cultural, social, technological, and economic conditions that led to the rise of graphic design in the late nineteenth and early twentieth century have shifted so dramatically that graphic design as we thought we knew it is dead, and we are all practicing in the Upside Down. Time to work on that side hustle!

I do try to imagine what might have happened—a kind of counterfactual history—if we design educators of the 1980s had not been so focused on that Expanded Practice 3.0. Would we have developed more rigorous, critical bodies of work that might have encouraged a wider set of engaged practices beyond commerce? Would we have gone more deeply into graphic design as a kind of visual knowledge? Would we have spent a little more time on history, criticism, publication? Most importantly, would we have continued to develop a pedagogy less dependent on art school models obsessed with individuality, and spent more energy on the collaborative, research-based, synthetic, and outward-facing practices that ideally constituted graphic design?

28. Inva Cota, Golnaz Esmaili, and Susan Sellers, "Working in the Real Economy, Wildly Contradictory Narratives, and Our Most Powerful Tool Is Visual Complexity and Beauty," *Graphic* 22 (2012): 188.

29. Silvio Lorusso, "The Designer without Qualities: Notes on Ornamental Politics, Ironic Detachment, Bureaucreativity and Emotional Counterculture," *Onamatopee* 163 (2019): 248.

We'll never know, and what we have now, another generation later, is something entirely different. We have, as our context, the "wicked problems" of today: issues of such complexity that no individual designer could possibly solve them, beyond the scale of the school-run studios dedicated to nonprofit practice or short-term collaboration. Design metaphors based on twentieth-century tropes of command-and-control are defunct. And while the capabilities of any single designer are exponentially larger than ever, we operate in the frustration of never being able securely to map our position on the field of anything.

Yasmin Gibson and Jessica Wexler, two graphic design educators who run a wiki and all sorts of associated events in a collaboration called Workshop Project ("a place to imagine what a pedagogical graphic design project could be"), acknowledge the fact that so many of us working in graduate education sense that the model is in need of renovation:

> We are process-based and fallible. . . . [T]his has become our most constant . . . principle. . . . . [W]e do not believe the classroom, the studio or the institution are spaces for resolution. They are spaces for iteration, inquiry and sitting in process alongside our students, moving toward unforeseen outcomes.
>
> We exist in a new void. . . . Inquiry is the cornerstone of future design practice. Form and object are outcomes of an exploration into the unknown, not ends in themselves. . . . [W]e believe that design education is the only area of graphic design in which one can now be truly innovative."[30]

If we are honest (as Gibson and Wexler are), the present set of circumstances puts teachers and students back on the same plane again. Gibson and Wexler are definitely part of the next generation of younger design educators questioning the current state of graphic design education, with an explosion of new writing, workshops, summer programs and the assertion of other criteria (like conditional design, or queering or decolonizing) that represent the desire—once again—to reform practice itself through the reinvention of graphic design education.[31]

As we interrogate design education yet again, it is useful to remember that our pedagogy has a history.[32] What I have tried to outline here, by looking at this evolution through a small set of typography assignments, is the critical role of work produced in the academy by designers responding to their own contemporary contexts, a legacy of thought in design that the marketplace would

30. Yasmin Gibson and Jessica Wexler, "We Used to ___, Now We ___," Workshop Project, www.workshopproject.org.

31. Francisco Laranjo, "A Brief History of the Design Summer School," *Onamatopee* 163 (2019): 190–95. See also Julia Born, Luna Maurer, et al., *Conditional Design Workbook* (Amsterdam: Valiz, 2013); and Decolonizing Design Collective, "Decolonizing Design Education: Ontologies, Strategies, Urgencies," *Onamatopee* 163 (2019): 76–90.

32. Brave New Alps, "Design Education as a Practice of Freedom," in *About Learning and Design*, ed. Georgio Camuffo, Magdalena Dalla Mura, and Alvise Mattozzi (Bolzano: Free University of Bozen-Balzano, 2014), 65–72.

never have supported. To teach or study in an MFA program in graphic design is, after all, a declaration that the field still contains some work whose quality transcends its commercial value; related to, but not subordinate to, art practices, dedicated to communication not as an option but as an imperative. During earlier cultural crises, in the '20s or the '60s, for example, some designers set aside business in favor of collaborative and relational experiments in the schools that engaged with problems outside of design (and, in the course of doing so, revised the entire practice). Utopian visions are a legacy of design education (I'm just sayin' . . .).

Freed from the old myths of professionalization, in the maw of Big Data, we now understand that design practice can be anything, in any medium. Yet the question remains: Can graphic designers expand their Expanded Practices outward, beyond strategies of self-preservation, toward a more engaged public practice? Can graphic design education be reinvigorated by a focus on a pedagogy of communication, dedicated to citizens rather than consumers? Or are the imperatives of the neoliberal marketplace compelling everyone to brand themselves as individuals, "creatives," speaking for themselves, and consequently overpowering the ability of graphic designers to address collective problems and present crises?

Guglielmo Marconi sends radio-wave signals across the Atlantic Ocean from England to Canada

This paper was first delivered at the conference "After the Bauhaus, Before the Internet: A History of Graphic Design Pedagogy," which took place at Yale University on May 10 and 11, 2019. As a way of introduction, I stated: "Andrew Blauvelt and I were discussing our slight nervousness about participating in a symposium sponsored by an art history department, since neither one of us has a degree in art history; so we came up with 'expert witnesses' as a term to describe our position in all of this. We are honored to be asked to testify." I thank Tim Barringer, Chair of the Yale Art History Department, and Geoff Kaplan of the School of Art for the invitation to participate; and Christopher Pullman for cross-generational conversations that helped me to focus this paper and for providing material from the class that he took with Paul Rand in 1964. Additional thanks to Katherine McCoy; my teaching colleagues at CalArts; and the many CalArts Graphic Design alumni who have gone into teaching, and who are advancing the field. Finally I would like to acknowledge my first design teacher, the late Joseph Kuzai, Yale MFA 1961, professor at Michigan State University for fifty years, for his relentless encouragement: a quality I try to emulate in my own teaching practice.

MACHINES, FACTORIES, SCHOOLS: A HISTORY OF GRAPHIC DESIGN

DANIELLE AUBERT

In many undergraduate graphic design programs, a History of Graphic Design class may be one of the few institutional spaces that allow for a critical examination of the field. Such a class is where we look at past models and seek to define disciplinary boundaries, where we ask: What is considered "graphic design" and what isn't? What is valued? Who are the key figures? What is considered canonical?

The students who enroll in a History of Graphic Design class tend to be graphic design majors. And there is general agreement among educators that learning the history of graphic design is an important step in preparing well-rounded practitioners. In teaching history, we define what graphic design is for the next generation. In this text I will look at some of the external pressures that shape how we understand and teach the history of graphic design, including the way in which the university itself creates a fundamental, if not always acknowledged or even recognized, structure that determines what happens in any classroom, including History of Graphic Design classrooms. It is not just what happens in the classroom but where that classroom is located and who is in it that affects the way we understand the history of graphic design. The greatest of those external pressures is financial. Tuition is high, and there is constant pressure to train students so they can step into good-paying jobs the moment they graduate. Another, broader pressure stems from the intertwining of modern graphic design and capitalism. The primitive accumulation of wealth[1] took place over years of colonial rule—companies in Western Europe profited from labor and land in other parts of the world; in the United States, primitive accumulation took place on the backs of enslaved Africans. Many early examples of advertisement serve to undergird a system built upon privation and the oppression of others.[2]

If we as instructors don't actively adjust our curricula, we teach a canon full of work made by white men in the service of capital: advertisements for cookies, liquor, cigarette papers, Hollywood movies, computers, and television stations. While some anti-capitalist movements have made their way into the canon, these have been led largely by European men (William Morris, the Russian Constructivists[3]), some of whom were openly fascist (the Italian Futurists).

Modern graphic design emerged with the advent of advertising and mass culture. When we teach the history of graphic design, we might reach back to early books, scrolls, pamphlets,

1. Karl Marx discusses primitive accumulation (which can also be understood as the theft of land and resources) in the last parts of the first volume of *Capital*. See Karl Marx, *Capital*, vol. 1 (London: Penguin Classics, reprinted 1990), 873–942.

currency, broadsides, and the history of the written language. But patterns in the division of labor and in the form of the worker have changed over time. Today we recognize that the production of a book requires someone to fulfill the role of graphic designer, and that this person's labor generally takes place after the book has been written and edited but before it has been printed. At an earlier historical moment, the role of the graphic designer did not exist. An author might have sent a completed manuscript to a printer, who typeset the text and prepared galleys for printing. The work of typesetting was done on site—possibly by a person whose job it was to set type, but it could even have been set by the person operating the printing machinery.[4] That is to say, prior to the emergence of mass culture in the mid-nineteenth century and the large-scale circulation of branded commodities, the role of the graphic designer did not exist.

The history of graphic design as an academic field is even younger. In her essay "Designing Graphic Design History," Teal Triggs quotes an art and design publisher stating in 1983 that most books published on graphic design were practical, "how-to" guides. Of 120 active titles, only one was on the history of graphic design. In the 1980s there were some key books published on industrial design history and or general design history, but very few that were

2. The website Vintage Ad Browser includes a category called "Race Advertisements" that catalogs several such examples. One is a 1920 advertisement for Towle's Log Cabin maple syrup depicting a group of Native Americans sitting around a vat of boiling maple syrup; the accompanying text is a poem titled "The Legend of Woksis—Discoverer of Maple Sugar." The advertisement makes a direct connection between Towle's Log Cabin and the Woksis Indians: The consumer can now benefit from riches acquired through settler colonialism (http://www.vintageadbrowser.com/race-ads-1920s). Other examples may be less explicit but no less pernicious. Lipton tea, for instance, was founded upon the labor of indentured Indian workers in Sri Lanka (then Ceylon, a British colony), who worked the tea gardens. The Royal Dutch Shell Group (now Shell Oil) began by extracting oil from an oil field in Sumatra, a Dutch colony. The ability of these companies to exploit workers in the colonies was dependent upon state power.

3. Although there were influential women among the Russian Constructivists, such as Varvara Stepanova, Lyubov Popova, and Valentina Kulagina, the Constructivists who show up the most in graphic design lectures are men: El Lissitzky, Alexander Rodchenko, Gustav Klutsis.

4. The International Typographical Union was founded in 1852 in the United States to represent typesetters who worked primarily in the newspaper industry.

specific to graphic design.[5] Although some well-known books have been published (for example, catalogs by Philip Meggs and Richard Hollis), many of us who teach the history of graphic design are piecing things together as we go along.

Why Teach Graphic Design?

To understand the ways in which both graphic design practice and pedagogy have taken shape, it is useful to consider the history of the labor processes associated with making publications, advertisements, and other pieces of graphic design. In the first volume of *Capital*, Karl Marx writes about how the advent of machines in factories made it possible for large numbers of women and children to do work that previously required brute physical strength. As steam-powered machines became more common, the production expectations of those laboring *without* machines also increased. People had to work at a faster rate in order to keep up with the mechanical production of commodities.

As an example, Marx describes the labor involved in operating the steam-powered rotary presses that were replacing manual letterpress printing. Whereas letterpress printing required workers who could read (in order to set type), new printing machines required a group of workers, generally boys aged about eleven to seventeen, "whose sole occupation [was] either to spread the sheets of paper under the machine, or to take from it the printed sheets. They perform[ed] this weary task, in London especially, for 14, 15 and 16 hours at a stretch, during several days in the week, and frequently for 36 hours, with only 2 hours' rest for meals and sleep."[6] These boys would then age out of the work: "As soon as they get too old for such children's work . . . they are discharged from the printing establishments. They become recruits for crime. Attempts to procure them employment elsewhere come to grief owing to their ignorance and brutality, their mental and bodily degradation."[7]

In response to the conditions described by Marx, and in particular the number of children who were working in factories, Parliament passed the Factory Acts in the early 1800s. These sweeping reforms set limits on the use of child labor.[8]

Marx often returns to the contradictions inherent in capitalism. The capitalist requires a class of unemployed workers and surplus labor in order to keep wages low. An individual factory owner may prefer an uneducated worker; the boys feeding paper into printing machines did not need to read and write and were essentially disposable. But other owners might require an educated population, workers who could read, write, and perform simple math, for instance. While the capitalist class as a whole requires a ready supply of unemployed laborers prepared to take low-paying

5. Teal Triggs, "Designing Graphic Design History," *Journal of Design History* 22, no. 4 (2009): 327.

6. Marx, *Capital*, vol. 1, 522.

7. Ibid.

8. Ibid., 523.

jobs, the optimal education level of that unemployed person is a matter of some debate. From the perspective of the capitalist, an unemployed worker will ideally transition into a position whose wages remain low so that more profit can be extracted. A worker, however, will try to acquire the knowledge and skills that will lead to a higher-paying position.

In many cases, the more formal education a worker has, the better able they are to adapt to new work situations. The logic of capitalism is not always coherent, and owners and the state are often at odds with one another. Marx writes, "Thus large-scale industry, by its very nature, necessitates variation of labor, fluidity of functions, and mobility of the worker in all directions."[9] The kind of education that is required to make a worker flexible is an education with radical potential. Marx emphasizes that the production process is "revolutionary"—in the sense that it is constantly changing. Machinery and technical skills are continually transforming, and they in turn transform the worker as a person.

Within graphic design, we can look at the difference between programs that focus exclusively on software skills versus those that include critical design thinking. I would argue that a graduate with up-to-date software and coding skills will in fact be less flexible on the job market than a graduate who has had a broader liberal arts education that allows them to perform multiple kinds of jobs. At the same time, a graduate who has thought about the ways in which commercial visual culture upholds white supremacy might be more likely to recognize institutional racism in the workplace. Students exposed to ACT UP protest graphics demanding support for AIDS research might later question the role of the pharmaceutical industry in resisting legislation to reform health-care systems and its failure to respond to the COVID-19 pandemic. The more educated designer is not only "better" but less docile.

What Do We Teach When We Teach the History of Graphic Design?

If we consider the history of graphic design from a perspective of labor, we see some important threads emerge. In the later twentieth century, the advent of the desktop computer revolutionized the manufacture of publications. As the printing trade changed, so did organized labor. The formerly powerful International Typographical Union, most of whose members were involved in the newspaper-printing business, lost relevance. The trend has continued into the twenty-first century, with very little union representation among graphic designers.

These massive shifts in the way that labor is performed also affect the kind of education that is required to prepare workers. The Bauhaus was one of the first schools to offer classes in modern design and typography.[10] The demands of industry were shifting, and the schools responded. The Bauhaus, for example, famously

9. Ibid., 617.

10. Design classes were also taught at VKhUTEMAS schools in the Soviet Union as early as 1920.

Brothers Wilbur and Orville Wright build the first engine-powered airplane

embraced machine-made design in an attempt to wed craft and automation. At both the Bauhaus and VKhUTEMAS, the factory was revered as a site of production, and artists and designers compared themselves to factory workers.[11]

Is the School a Factory?

The Bauhaus instructors who emigrated from Germany to the United States during World War II had a tremendous influence on the way graphic design education developed here. Yet the relationship between the school and the factory had long been felt in the US, and not only in art and design education. In 1916, Elwood Cubberley, dean of the Stanford School of Education, said, "Our schools are, in a sense, factories in which the raw materials are to be shaped and fashioned into products to meet the various demands of life. The specifications for manufacturing come from the demands of the twentieth-century civilization, and it is the business of the school to build its pupils to the specifications laid down."[12] In this metaphor, the students themselves are the "raw materials" that will be transformed into a product: future workers.

University boards of trustees almost always include a healthy number of business executives and economic development officers. Although board members generally do not play an explicit role in determining course content or developing curriculum, the orientation toward market needs is still felt on most campuses. Administrators are encouraged to develop relationships with local executives, and these relationships trickle down to the faculty or form the basis of new courses. For example, at the College for Creative Studies in Detroit, Toyota sponsors a lecture series, and design majors work on projects sponsored by the company.

Students arrive at school already concerned about their future job prospects. Although the classic image of a college student may

11. In her text "Troubling Design Pedagogy," included in this volume, 420–34, Lauren Williams writes about the school as a factory, responding in part to Jacob Lundgren's recent article "Graphic Design's Factory Settings," which looks at the lasting influence of the Bauhaus on graphic design curricula. Williams emphasizes the ways in which these "factory settings" were built to serve capitalism and thereby uphold racist structures designed to generate a class of flexible workers. Williams discusses the idea of maintenance—of the self and of the factory. She questions the wisdom of perpetuating institutions founded to support and maintain capitalist systems of oppression.

12. Allan Sekula quotes Cubberley in his documentary photo essay *School Is a Factory* (1978–80).

be that of a young person, funded by their parents, living in a dorm overlooking a grassy quad, more than half of US college students are financially independent and work while in school, more than forty percent live at or below the poverty line, and one-quarter are parents themselves.[13] Many will piece together in-person and online classes at several schools and work outside jobs while taking classes. The vast majority will take on debt. Obtaining a bachelor's degree is a huge financial stressor, and it is no surprise that students are thinking about their future earning prospects. They check to see what alumni have gone on to do and what kind of career services may be available.

Some majors lend themselves more directly to the market than others. Business programs are explicitly oriented around training students to be managers and employers. Engineering programs, which often have direct relationships with manufacturing companies, tend to place students in some of the top-paying post-graduation jobs. Design programs are expected to help place students in internships and frequently offer classes that simulate the real-world experience of working directly for clients. The best internships are paid, but many are not, and they have become a de facto requirement for students to begin building their résumés before they graduate. It's harder to tie the humanities directly to industry, despite the fact that, over time, liberal-arts majors have been shown to earn more money than their peers in engineering and science.[14] But humanities programs across the country have been decimated by the turn toward neoliberalism in academia since the early 1990s.

The first time I taught a History of Graphic Design class was at an art school. There I experienced firsthand the ways in which the market devalues the humanities. I had been teaching studio classes in the Graphic Design department, but the history class was taught through the Liberal Arts department. Adjunct pay was lower for this class, ostensibly because the number of contact hours with students was lower. Nonetheless, the course required significantly more preparation outside of class. The chairs of the Graphic Design and Liberal Arts programs were apologetic; they recognized that

13. Association of American Colleges and Universities, "Facts and Figures: Misconceptions about Today's College Students," November 2018, https://www.aacu.org/aacu-news/newsletter/2018/november/facts-figures.

14. See Wesley Whistle, "Department of Education Releases Earnings by Major," *Forbes.com*, November 20, 2019, https://www.forbes.com/sites/wesleywhistle/2019/11/20/department-of-education-releases-earnings-data-by-major/#6b0bf91b22dd; and Scott Carlson, "Over Time, Humanities Grads Close the Pay Gap with Professional Peers," *Chronicle of Higher Education*, February 7, 2018, https://www.chronicle.com/article/over-time-humanities-grads-close-the-pay-gap-with-professional-peers/.

the workload was higher—but this was the structure that was in place. A few years later, when I was hired full-time to teach graphic design at Wayne State University in Detroit, I was offered a much higher starting salary than my colleagues in Art History. I was told that it was because graphic design is a specialized technical skill. In reality, it was due to a surplus of art history PhDs on the job market and the relative paucity of graphic design MFAs looking for full-time teaching positions.

Teaching the History of Graphic Design in Detroit

When I began teaching graphic design history, I taught it just the way I learned it from Doug Scott when I was an MFA student at Yale in the early 2000s. I was insecure about my handle on the subject. I did my best to identify specific designers, movements, and projects that I thought students absolutely should know about, many of which I was hazy on myself (De Stijl? I knew I should talk about it, but I wasn't totally clear on how to summarize it). I did a lot of Google Image searches, which I knew was probably not the way you were supposed to assemble slide lectures for teaching. It will come as no surprise that my survey ended up being week after week of jumping around among groups of Western European men working between 1900 and 1940 (with the exception of a visit to the Soviet Union and New York to cover Rodchenko, El Lissitsky, and Paul Rand). It was not satisfying, nor did it really connect to the current graphic design landscape.

At some point I happened to meet the artist Sam Durant, who was working on a catalog about Emory Douglas, the Black Panther who designed the party newspaper. He shared images with me and I created a lecture about Douglas and the Panthers. I also started to feel quite urgently that I needed to find a way to talk about Detroit—the Motor City, where everyone seems to have some connection to factory work through their families or their own experiences. This is a majority-Black city. Many students are first-generation immigrants from the Middle East or Central or Eastern Europe.

Like many others in the city, I felt that the local visual culture needed greater visibility and acknowledgment. There was a tendency to look outward to the centers of power on the East and West coasts; I felt we needed to uncover and lift up what was already here. As the city entered a stage of accelerated gentrification, it seemed more urgent than ever to strengthen what is and was here—before it was overshadowed by a homogenous global visual language.

I looked for local models. One characteristic of this area is the predominance of manufacturing equipment, and I have found that in southeast Michigan there is a high overall level of confidence in fixing up and using industrial machines. The Detroit Printing Co-op, a nonhierarchical print shop that existed from 1970 to 1980 and was founded by the publishers of Black and Red Books, was no exception. Its founders and users were distrustful of educational institutions and factories. They used machines designed for factory production, but not in order to be competitive on the market. Rather, they used machines to withdraw from competition and

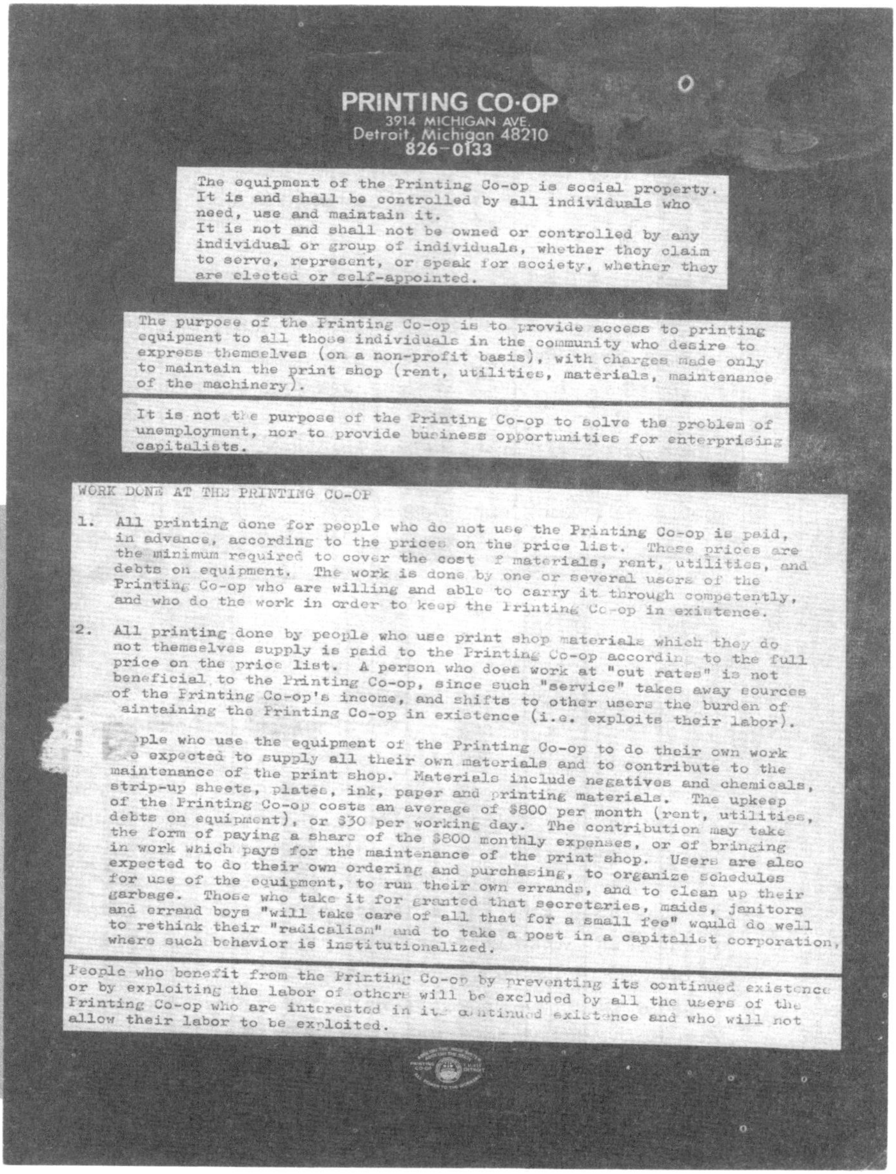

PRINTING CO·OP
3914 MICHIGAN AVE.
Detroit, Michigan 48210
826-0133

The equipment of the Printing Co-op is social property. It is and shall be controlled by all individuals who need, use and maintain it.
It is not and shall not be owned or controlled by any individual or group of individuals, whether they claim to serve, represent, or speak for society, whether they are elected or self-appointed.

The purpose of the Printing Co-op is to provide access to printing equipment to all those individuals in the community who desire to express themselves (on a non-profit basis), with charges made only to maintain the print shop (rent, utilities, materials, maintenance of the machinery).

It is not the purpose of the Printing Co-op to solve the problem of unemployment, nor to provide business opportunities for enterprising capitalists.

WORK DONE AT THE PRINTING CO-OP

1. All printing done for people who do not use the Printing Co-op is paid, in advance, according to the prices on the price list. These prices are the minimum required to cover the cost of materials, rent, utilities, and debts on equipment. The work is done by one or several users of the Printing Co-op who are willing and able to carry it through competently, and who do the work in order to keep the Printing Co-op in existence.

2. All printing done by people who use print shop materials which they do not themselves supply is paid to the Printing Co-op according to the full price on the price list. A person who does work at "cut rates" is not beneficial to the Printing Co-op, since such "service" takes away sources of the Printing Co-op's income, and shifts to other users the burden of maintaining the Printing Co-op in existence (i.e. exploits their labor).

3. People who use the equipment of the Printing Co-op to do their own work are expected to supply all their own materials and to contribute to the maintenance of the print shop. Materials include negatives and chemicals, strip-up sheets, plates, ink, paper and printing materials. The upkeep of the Printing Co-op costs an average of $800 per month (rent, utilities, debts on equipment), or $30 per working day. The contribution may take the form of paying a share of the $800 monthly expenses, or of bringing in work which pays for the maintenance of the print shop. Users are also expected to do their own ordering and purchasing, to organize schedules for use of the equipment, to run their own errands, and to clean up their garbage. Those who take it for granted that secretaries, maids, janitors and errand boys "will take care of all that for a small fee" would do well to rethink their "radicalism" and to take a post in a capitalist corporation, where such behavior is institutionalized.

People who benefit from the Printing Co-op by preventing its continued existence or by exploiting the labor of others will be excluded by all the users of the Printing Co-op who are interested in its continued existence and who will not allow their labor to be exploited.

Guidelines taped to the wall of the Detroit Printing Co-op

create community. The Co-op users exemplified the fluidity and flexibility of workers that Marx describes. They knew enough about the operation of machines and the mechanics of typesetting and printing to use these in a way that was critical of capitalist modes of production.

As a model, the Detroit Printing Co-op presents itself at the intersection of the history of graphic design and the history of capital. It emerged in Detroit in the years following the 1967 rebellion, in a city that is basically a factory town for the "Big Three" auto manufacturers (Chrysler, Ford, General Motors). The Co-op was open for use by anyone who wanted to print there for non-profit purposes. The main users were all involved in leftist politics and many had ties to *Fifth Estate*, a publication with anarchist tendencies, as well as to the League of Revolutionary Black Workers, a Marxist-Leninist group that agitated in the auto factories in the 1960s and '70s. The Detroit Printing Co-op was a part of the radical IWW union (International Workers of the World), which called for the abolition of wages and of the state and whose motto was "All power to the workers!"

Fredy and Lorraine Perlman were two of the founding members. When they started the Co-op in 1970, Fredy was coming off a two-year position as a visiting economics professor at Western Michigan University. They moved to Detroit to pursue more explicitly radical political projects. The Co-op's large Harris offset press was a difficult-to-use machine that would usually have required a fair amount of training to operate; Fredy, however, learned to print informally from the printer manual and from others who had worked in commercial print shops or had taught themselves. Those at the Co-op willingly shared their knowledge: Stewart Shevin, a high-school student at the time, learned to print and to operate the machines by working on some of the paid jobs that the Co-op brought in and by printing an alternative newspaper that he and some friends put together. He also read a number of the texts that were being printed at the Co-op and engaged in conversation with other users on their lunch breaks or while working side by side with them. He was only fifteen years old when he started going to the Co-op, but he said he felt that his ideas were heard and recognized by the adults. People at the Co-op engaged with him as an equal.

In looking for Detroit's graphic design history, I frequently came back to Cranbrook Academy of Art—Ed Fella, Lorraine Wild, the McCoys—but Cranbrook is about a forty-minute drive from downtown, in a wealthy suburb that is nothing like Detroit. Fella had worked in the auto industry before going to Cranbrook and was a graduate of Cass Tech High School in the city, but the work he's most known for happened after he left Detroit.

Detroit is the home of Motown Records, United Sound Systems, and techno, music industries that yielded their own visual languages. In the world of literature, there was Broadside Press, founded in Detroit in 1965 to publish poetry chapbooks by African-American authors. Many of these booklets were designed and printed in Detroit. In search of political pamphlets, I visited the Walter Reuther labor archives to look at the print materials produced by the League of Revolutionary Black Workers. They printed a newspaper called *Inner-City Voice* and a newsletter, *DRUM* (an acronym for the Dodge Revolutionary Union Movement). The League had its own print shop, called Black Star. All of this visual work, which exists far outside the graphic design "canon," requires its own narrative-building and storytelling to make it fit into an academic context.[15]

Fredy was deeply critical of academia, which he saw as fully complicit with industry.[16] Upon his departure from Western Michigan University, he published a pamphlet called "I Accuse This Liberal University of Terror and Violence." The text was published in an issue of the Perlmans' *Black and Red* magazine and also distributed as a stand-alone stapled pamphlet. The provocative title was set in an all caps sans serif against a duotone red photograph of a building on the WMU campus. The interior text was set using a typewriter. In this treatise on "the Reactionary" and "the Liberal" in academia, Perlman describes being fired for being too radical. While he is critical of the Reactionary, he prefers him to the Liberal. The Reactionary "openly identifies with the project of Big Business" and is "overtly pro-Capitalist; an ardent supporter of every American corporate and military bureaucracy."[17] The Liberal, however, claims to be sympathetic to the Left yet shuts it down whenever a real threat to dominant systems of power presents itself. The Liberal "spends his life manipulating students to fit the requirements of a corporate or state bureaucracy."[18] The Liberal claims to be neutral but always sides with the dominant force: "The mere presence of the radical exposes the 'neutrality' of the Liberal: HE CHOOSES TO ACCEPT THE DOMINANT BUREAUCRACY."[19]

As pedagogy around the history of graphic design matures and develops, it is important for us to continually recognize the connection between the history of capitalism and the history of graphic design. If we want to be truly anti-racist and anti-colonial, we have to acknowledge, expose, and combat the tendency to naturalize and reinforce the dominance of capitalist modes of production within our educational institutions.

15. While conducting research for an essay about the cover design of a book of poetry, *Intervals in Time and Space*, by Kofi Natambu, I learned that Debra Jeter, the cover designer, had received a bachelor's degree in graphic design in 1979 from the College for Creative Studies in Detroit. She was politically active, having traveled to Libya with a group of African-Americans who'd been invited by Muammar Gaddafi to see what was happening in that country.

16. Members of the board of trustees at Western Michigan were closely connected to Dow Chemical (located in central Michigan), which at the time was manufacturing napalm being used against civilians in Vietnam.

17. Fredy Perlman, "I Accuse This Liberal University of Terror and Violence," *Black and Red* 6 (March 1969).

18. Ibid., 6.

19. Ibid., 5. For Fredy, printing was separate from scholarly academic work but was an intellectual pursuit in its own right. Lorraine would later say that Fredy found the graphic arts to be intellectually rewarding and stimulating.

MOVE OVER NEW YORK—APPLE IS OUR MIDDLE NAME: A CASE FOR THE INDEPENDENT EXPLORATION OF REGIONAL DESIGN HISTORIES

JAMES SHOLLY

In January of 1982, marketing officials from the Indianapolis Convention and Visitors Association proudly unveiled a new promotional campaign designed to lure lucrative tourism business to the burgeoning Midwestern metropolis, ignominiously known to some as Naptown. "Move over New York—Apple is our Middle Name," became a pervasive presence on buttons, posters, mugs, and the airwaves, where it briefly ingratiated itself as a perky jingle.[1] The design of the campaign looked like an awkward, wordy cousin to Milton Glaser's already iconic "I ♥ NY" design (introduced in 1977). On a dark-green background, white Cooper Black type appears to be pushing a giant red apple off the right edge border. Take that, New York!

As might be expected, not everyone was pleased. *The Washington Post*'s "Media Fast Track" column sardonically described the new slogan as being "in the fine tradition of overreaching."[2] Most local letters to the editor took aim at the perplexing comparison of Indianapolis to New York. *Indianapolis News* reader Louise Hutchins wrote, "It suggests that we're just a replacement, a substitute, an understudy as in a Broadway play."[3] *Indianapolis Star* columnist John Shaughnessy claimed, "Assuredly, the 'Apple' slogan was awful" in a piece entitled "The City Is Losing Its Own Identity," published in 1985, when the campaign had already been shuttered.[4] Indianapolis is many things, but New York City is not one of them.

Artwork from the "Move over New York. Apple is our middle name." 1982 Indianapolis Convention and Visitors Association tourism advertising campaign

Describing Midwestern cities as cultural deserts when compared to coastal cities is nothing new. Even as a young graphic design student I was regularly assured that in order for a career to have impact, one would need to relocate from Indianapolis to New York City (or Boston if your focus was publishing). Another prevailing conceit among both peers and professionals was simply that design work produced locally was innately inferior to work produced in larger (i.e., more sophisticated) cities. Urban analyst, and Indiana native Aaron Renn credits the origin of this perceived second-class slight to "an excessive preference for the pragmatic . . . the Midwest tends to actively discourage ambitious undertakings and the pursuit of excellence. This can produce a stifling environment for people who want to dream big and care about doing things right." He adds "There are all sorts of great

1. *Indianapolis News*, January 19, 1982.

2. "Media Fast Track," *The Washington Post*, January 31, 1982.

3. Louise Hutchins, Letter to the Editor, *Indianapolis News*, June 29, 1982.

4. John Shaughnessy, "The City Is Losing Its Own Identity," *Indianapolis Star*, November 20, 1985.

things and great people in Indy, but they take time to find and get to know. In some cities the greatness is on the surface. In Indy, it's in layers you need to dig up over time."[5]

Studying at Indianapolis's Herron School of Art in the 1980s, I was unfamiliar with the names of most well-known designers. At that time, the nascent pedagogy of graphic design history, or even just design history, existed strictly as a component of my Visual Communications studio courses. The landmark works and giants of the profession were revealed only as my classmates and I designed, researched, and critiqued exercises like typographic history posters. Art History faculty may have referenced graphic design but only fleetingly and in correlation to architectural and art historical movements like De Stijl and Constructivism. The instructional avenues to address the profession's history broadened considerably when Philip Meggs published *A History of Graphic Design* (Van Nostrand Reinhold, 1983), a book that opened doors for faculty to begin incorporating newly legitimized periods of *graphic design* history into their syllabi.

A 1986 classroom visit from the California textile designer and book artist Frances Butler offered a glimpse into a history that was in development. Butler was not only a practicing designer, artist, educator, and the subject of the monograph *Colored Reading: The Graphic Art of Frances Butler* (1979), but someone whose work was already being accessioned into the collections of prominent museums like the Cooper Hewitt Smithsonian Design Museum and the Museum of Modern Art. Despite her many accomplishments, Butler was not known to me or, I presume, my classmates, and she was not represented in Meggs's authoritative new book. To me, she was a secret treasure—the professor to my professor—and part of an almost master-and-apprentice-like transfer of knowledge. A regional designer creating important, if not yet historical works, Butler appeared to me to be a future historical figure, living and working parallel to an amorphous but burgeoning pedagogy that had yet to find room for her. Years later, I would initiate a project aimed at revealing secret figures that, like Butler, hadn't yet received the type of recognition I felt their achievements merited.

The notion of regional design history scholarship did not exist at Herron apart from the occasional field trip to an established local design or advertising firm, where a senior partner may have chosen to share their recollections of the good old days. Perhaps surprisingly, the greatest insights into what was happening in local design could be found in the school's library and within the pages of the *Print Magazine Regional Design Annual*, a national survey in which selected works were organized into localized subcategories like "Far West" and "Mid-Atlantic." This publication offered an instant assessment of how flyover practitioners compared to their

5. Aaron Renn, "Ten Things You Need to Know About Indianapolis City Culture," March 14, 2017, https://www.aaronrenn.com/2017/03/14/ten-things-you-need-to-know-about-indianapolis-city-culture/.

coast-adjacent peers. And even when Indiana designers were relegated to the "Rest of the Midwest" catch-all bucket, it was still a fascinating and revealing exercise to compare. It turns out that we were not that different.

My interest in Indiana's regional design history can be traced to Gene and Jackie Lacy. The Lacys were my in-laws and began working as designers, illustrators, educators, and artists in Indianapolis in the early 1950s, careers that lasted the better part of forty years. Their work was sophisticated in the modernist tradition, but with a warmth and humanism that set them apart from their contemporaries. With few exceptions—and despite the fact that they enjoyed productive careers—the body of their working lives was virtually unknown outside of Indianapolis, and barely known there. The absence of recognition or even documentation of their creative achievements was disheartening and eventually led me to conceive of a publication called *Commercial Article*, a self-produced journal that strives to document the lives and work of little-known design figures from Indiana like the Lacys.

Initially, *Commercial Article* (a publishing offshoot of my graphic design studio Commercial Artisan) was envisioned to be a promotional device and a graphic-design cousin to Harry Smith's *Anthology of American Folk Music* or the Smithsonian's *Folkways* program, a sort of populist repository for Indiana graphic design that hadn't been previously documented or celebrated—always attempting to identify the regional qualities (what vintners refer to as *terroir*) that inform and shape the unique characteristics of the work created in the Hoosier state. Over the course of a dozen issues, the self-published *Commercial Article* has evolved into an archive of Indiana's graphic, architectural, fashion, industrial, consumer, and environmental designers whose lives and work have been unrecognized, ignored, or simply forgotten.

Cover of *Commercial Article 03*, featuring the Indiana home designer and iconoclast Avriel Shull

Regional assessments of design history are typically categorized according to national boundaries. The histories of design powerhouses like Japan and Switzerland have been well documented. It's uncommon for a particular state or region to be the topic of this sort of investigation, Louise Sandhaus's tour de force *Earthquakes, Mudslides, Fires and Riots: California Graphic Design 1936–1986* (Metropolis, 2014) being one notable exception. And Indiana, long-regarded as flyover territory by design historians, has rarely fallen under the gaze of cultural miners looking to excavate undiscovered design gems. In a 2017 discussion, in which I was asked to participate, esteemed

6. Steven Heller, "Design In Indiana," November 3, 2017, https://www.printmag.com/daily-heller/design-in-indianapolis/.

graphic design historian and educator Steven Heller began, "I know it's very New York of me, but I don't think 'design' when I think of Indiana."[6] That might have been the bait, but I took it:

> The perception of Indiana as a place that doesn't appreciate or contribute to noteworthy design is a misconception we're challenging. Many people don't realize that Columbus, Indiana, is one of the most significant architectural cities in the country, or that the Indianapolis Museum of Art is home to 10,000 square feet of gallery space reserved for a vast collection of contemporary design.[7]

To the surprise of many, Indiana's design history is rich and filled with figures who may have slipped from memory, but whose outsized talents belie their humble beginnings. Following are descriptions of just a few of these design luminaries.

Walter Dorwin Teague was born in Pendleton, Indiana, in 1883, and went on to great acclaim, designing everything from decorative typographic borders to cameras and airline interiors. He was an establishing figure in his profession, eventually earning the sobriquet "Father of Industrial Design." *Teague: Design and Beauty*, a 2014 documentary, strove to shine new light on his myriad achievements and reminded us that the firm bearing his name is still in operation today.

Norman Norell hailed from Noblesville, Indiana, and was a towering presence in the world of fashion. Credited with adapting Parisian couture style for the American ready-to-wear market, Norell was the first recipient of the prestigious Coty Award and the inaugural inductee into the fashion industry critics' Hall of Fame. A hugely influential figure (particularly to fellow Indiana fashion designer Stephen Sprouse), his elegant garments have been embraced by first ladies from Jacqueline Kennedy to Michelle Obama.

The work of Jane and Gordon Martz and their business Marshall Studios was selected by Edgar Kaufmann Jr., Florence Knoll, and Alexander Girard for inclusion in MoMA's 1953 *Good Design* exhibition. The Martzes were in good company—the show also included the work of Harry Bertoia, Charles and Ray Eames, Stig Lindberg, and Raymond Lowey, among others. Marshall Studios operated in rural Veedersburg, Indiana, from 1941 to 1989 producing signature homewares that are today highly prized by devotees of midcentury design.

Other lesser-known figures include the iconoclastic renaissance woman and modern home design entrepreneur Avriel Shull; Moderne architect, master renderer, and elegant man-about-town Leslie Ayers; Austrian transplant and supergraphics pioneer Roland Hobart; turn-of-the-twentieth-century fashion sophisticate George Philip Meier and his wife, Nellie—a "scientific" palmist who used her abilities of divination to counsel everyone from movie stars to presidents. All of these figures contributed in remarkable ways to Indiana's legacy of design excellence.

Commercial Article has influenced the efforts of others with similar ambitions to celebrate regional and unrecognized design. In 2012 the website *Design Observer* (in association with the Winterhouse Institute and AIGA) launched a series entitled

7. Ibid.

Unusual Suspects that aimed "to expand the canon of graphic design practitioners, looking over time at the contributions of local design leaders and legends—designers overlooked in our annuals and histories."[8] The series came about at least in part due to editor Andrew Blauvelt's *Design Observer* reports featuring the stories of Avriel Shull and Gene and Jackie Lacy from *Commercial Article*. Blauvelt expertly summarized the motivation and immediate need for the series:

> Because our history is gradually vanishing, there is a renewed sense of urgency in documenting the lives of those graphic designers who were so influential in the formation and maturation of the field in their respective cities. Hopefully, projects like these will help to create something greater than the sum of their individual parts, by providing answers to more widespread historical questions: how, for example, did modern graphic design spread (from East and West) across the central United States? Such answers contribute significantly to a more substantial picture of graphic design history, by focusing long-overdue attention on those so-called local practitioners—people whose work helped pave the way for all of us. This is not necessarily about writing History with a capital 'H,' but about identifying an alternative history—a history from below.[9]

However, following the announcement of a run of planned profiles that included Wisconsin's Hamilton Wood Type Museum, Minnesota's Peter Seitz, and even the Lacys from Indiana, the series *Unusual Suspects* faded from view and is now (according to *Design Observer* cofounder Michael Bierut) indefinitely on hold. Five years later, in 2017, an AIGA-supported effort tried again with a plan for a crowd-sourced, regionally focused design repository called *Making History* (later renamed *Designed Here*), but unfortunately, that too failed to take hold and has yet to come to fruition. While institutionally supported initiatives like these will undoubtedly continue—and hopefully eventually succeed—the preservation of vanishing regional design histories may perhaps be best left to the individuals with the closest geographic and emotional proximity to their subjects.

In some instances, *Commercial Article*, and the research that my small team and I have completed, is the only existing record of the achievements of our subjects, the Lacys being a prime example. Another is the story of an ironically named Indianapolis business called "Stupid Incorporated." This company, formed after World War II by three art school buddies, thrived in the late 1950s and early '60s, producing humorous *Mad Magazine*–inspired paper goods and novelty gifts. Despite being a sensation across the United States and United Kingdom, there is no appreciable record of its wit, creative verve, or provocative design outside of *Commercial Article*. And it was only due to a friend—the daughter of one of the

8. "*Unusual Suspects*: A New Series," *Design Observer*, May 9, 2012, http://www.partinandcheeklaw.com/feature/unusual-suspects-a-new-series/34108.

9. Ibid.

founding partners—mischievously mentioning that she had once worked for a company called Stupid Incorporated, that this creative venture was documented for posterity.

A further qualitative example of our research is the story of artist/designer Roland Hobart. Hobart immigrated to Indiana from his native Innsbruck in the late 1960s. In 1973 his was the winning entry in an ambitious Indianapolis public art competition. Hobart's spectacular and towering supergraphic design (dubbed the *Urban Wall*) was produced on the cornered sides of two downtown buildings. Public favor, however, soon gave way to civic indifference and Hobart's creation slowly sank into disrepair. After more than forty years of neglect, focused efforts that utilized our *Commercial Article* profile of Hobart and his work were successful in leveraging funding from legislators for the *Urban Wall*'s restoration, now scheduled to begin in 2020.[10]

I wish I could say that the research we do to preserve and celebrate the work of local designers isn't done in a vacuum, but it is. With no official association to university design programs or academic research centers, it remains an independent study project that exists apart from a context normal to it and in which it can best be understood and assessed. This is not necessarily a critical drawback. An early goal of *Commercial Articles* was that the results of our research be made available to the public or anyone interested in learning more about design in Indiana, and now—through modest distribution and inclusion in public libraries and historical archives—it is. In these local institutions examples of designers' work lives with the potential to fortify future educational endeavors and inspire other individuals to document the design they discover in the places they love.

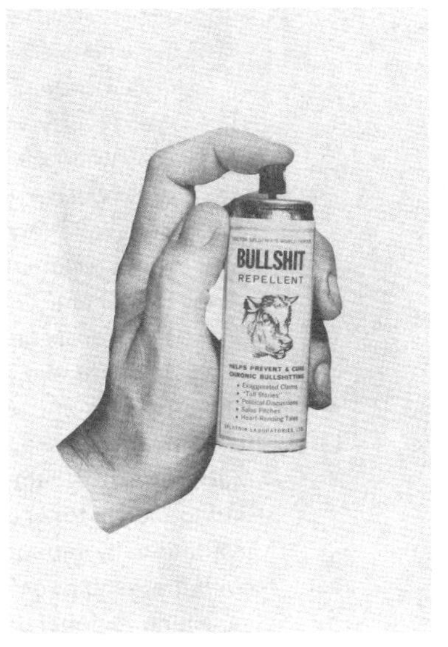

Promotional photo of the Stupid Incorporated product "Bullshit Repellent" from *Commercial Article 12*

Romanian-born Henri-Marie Coandă builds a simple jet plane, but it never flies

10. Allegra Lynn East, "Indianapolis Bicentennial Commission Announces First Set of City-Community Partnership Projects for 200th Celebration," October 16, 2019, https://polis.iupui.edu/announcements/indianapolis-bicentennial-commission-announces-first-set-of-city-community-partnership-projects-for-200th-celebration/.

LIVE IN YOUR WORLD: WHEN DESIGN BECOMES CURATING

PREM KRISHNAMURTHY

The COVID19 pandemic highlighted the mounting inequalities crafted over hundreds of years of extractive colonialism and rampant capitalism; it has also made even clearer the necessity of reimagining structural assumptions that underlie commonly held ideas of communications and community. As part of this larger task, the opportunity presents itself to reformulate the role of artistic production, and to ask how it might offer models for communing with others as an essentially and fundamentally *social* practice. Collaborative creative fields such as graphic design and curating already represent modes of practice that are simultaneously individual *and* collective, authorial *and* space-making for others, rather than being either one or the other. How might the entangled histories of these two fields suggest paths for reorienting artistic practice and pedagogy moving forward?

Although they originated as trade-based or institutionally embedded professions, graphic design and curating have undergone multiple disciplinary changes over the past hundred years, with resulting shifts in their cultural valuation. This is most apparent in the transformation of the image of designers and curators into buzzy tastemakers within a global cultural context. Such a change had been anticipated by developments in educational programs and graduate academies beginning in the 1970s and '80s; this schematic essay sketches out the intertwined trajectories of graphic design and curating through an examination of intersecting practitioners and projects. What skills and perspectives from graphic design have supported curatorial practitioners historically, and what might be future opportunities to build upon these connections in an educational context?

Within existing narratives of twentieth-century art history, a number of key figures have taken on the roles of both graphic designer and exhibition curator within the field of modern and contemporary art. Notable European examples include Walter Dexel, Willem Sandberg, and Wim Crouwel, each of whom enjoyed a consequential trajectory and recognition across both fields.[1] Although he moved fluidly between art and other pursuits throughout his lifetime (a position not uncharacteristic of the period), Dexel's work as both a curator and designer at the Kunstverein Jena from 1916 to 1928 stands out for both its disciplinary straddling and impact within its context. There Dexel helmed an exhibition program that offered early shows to avant-garde artists and architects from the Bauhaus and beyond. The programming's reach expanded through his standardization of a "house style" for the Kunstverein's communication materials and graphic ephemera, characterized by a sans-serif look. Dexel's own publishing on the "new typography" in the 1920s helped to cement this early relationship between modern art and asymmetrical typography.[2]

The slightly younger Sandberg's early work as a designer led to his role first as a curator and then as director of the Stedelijk Museum Amsterdam after World War II. In his role of director,

Sandberg continued to design graphics for many of the museum's catalogs, exhibitions, and ephemera. Until his retirement from the Stedelijk in 1962, Sandberg redefined the display and presentation of modern art to reach wider audiences through innovative and accessible exhibition layouts, as well as experimental presentation formats. After 1962, he continued on to direct the newly formed Israel Museum, developing the museum's graphic identity. This wide-ranging graphic work expanded upon the radical openness of his mature aesthetic, developed in the 1940s within the pages of his underground journal, *Open Oog*. He designed and printed the journal while in hiding from the Nazis for his wartime activities as an active member of the Dutch resistance.

Crouwel, whose eventual path was in some ways paved by Sandberg, maintained a longer and more visible practice as a graphic designer. While continuing his work for industry and establishing the design agency Total Design, Crouwel became design director for the Stedelijk Museum in 1964. His groundbreaking posters prefigured his later position as director of the Museum Boijmans Van Beuningen in Rotterdam, where from 1985 to 1993 he also curated exhibitions and designed their layouts. This new role as director also allowed him to work in a curatorial fashion with other designers, for example in his commissioning of the emerging London-based graphic design studio 8vo to produce the museum's experimental visual identity.

Although limited in their geographic and temporal reach, these three examples hint at a strong relationship between the disciplines of graphic design and curating that exists on the levels of practice and discourse. Until the field of curatorial education became institutionalized in the 1980s and '90s, curators often applied their knowledge from other backgrounds, including art history, philosophy, literature, or theater, to their museum and independent work. The figures of Dexel, Sandberg, and Crouwel, however, suggest

1. For more information on these figures and their interdisciplinary work, see the following monographs: Walter Dexel and Ernst-Gerhard Güse, *Walter Dexel: Bilder, Aquarelle, Collagen, Leuchtreklame, Typographie: Westfälisches Landesmuseum für Kunst und Kulturgeschichte Münster, Landschaftsverband Westfalen-Lippe, 27.5. bis 29.7.1979, Ulmer Museum 19.8. bis 23.9.1979* (Münster: Landschaftsverband Westfalen-Lippe, 1979); Willem J. H. B. Sandberg and Ad Petersen, *Sandberg: Een Documentaire = A Documentary* (Amsterdam: Kosmos, 1975); and Frederike Huygen and Harry Lake, *Wim Crouwel: Modernist* (Eindhoven: Lecturis, 2015).

2. Walter Dexel, "What Is New Typography?" *Frankfurter Zeitung* (February 5, 1927), in Eckhard Neumann, *Functional Graphic Design in the 20's* (New York: Reinhold Publishing, 1967).

significant overlaps between the concerns of graphic designers and curators: The conceptual, visual, typographic, and production skills that these three developed allowed them to better communicate their curatorial ideas in graphic form.

At the same time, both fields require strong interpersonal and intersubjective faculties, such as listening, coordination, negotiation, facilitation, and organization; although these "soft skills" are all too often ignored by pedagogy and in the press, they are the foundational tools that allow both designers and curators to assume roles of leadership and authority while also creating space for others. This suite of creative and managerial skills, in tandem with their social, intellectual, and artistic networks, allowed the exhibitions and programs of Dexel, Sandberg, and Crouwel to reach their immediate and farther-flung peers while also connecting avant-garde ideas with larger, receptive audiences. Furthermore, the ability to create graphic documents of their curatorial pursuits—through outreach and communications such as posters and in the form of exhibition catalogs—granted their exhibitions and programs a highly visible legacy.

This fact was not lost upon others in the field: Significant twentieth-century curators often recognized the importance of progressive graphic communication and publishing in distributing timely ideas. An incomplete list of examples include museum director Pontus Hultén, whose exhibition catalogs themselves formed a significant strand of his curatorial work;[3] Mildred Friedman, whose curatorial work, experimental editorial oversight of *Design Quarterly*, and development of the design department at the Walker Art Center in Minneapolis helped transform the institution from a regional museum into an internationally recognized program;[4] Kynaston McShine, whose *Primary Structures* at the Jewish Museum, New York, in 1966 helped established Minimal art as a category and was accompanied by an iconic catalog designed by Elaine Lustig Cohen;[5] polymathic artist, critic, and sometime curator Brian O'Doherty, whose guest editing of the landmark "conceptual issue" of *Aspen Magazine* 5+6 (1967) also included designing the publication's box format and materials;[6] and, perhaps most paradigmatically, the independent curator Harald Szeemann, who, although not trained as a graphic designer, worked in his early years as a freelance designer and is credited with the design of the catalogs for his landmark exhibitions *When*

3. Pontus Hultén and Lutz Jahre, *Das Gedruckte Museum von Pontus Hultén* (Ostfildern-Ruit: Cantz, 1996); cited in *A Brief History of Curating*, ed. Hans Ulbrich Obrist (Zurich: JRP|Ringier, 2018).

4. Andrew Blauvelt, "Design for Explication Not Veneration: Remembering Mickey Friedman," *The Gradient*, Walker Art Center, September 4, 2014, https://walkerart.org/magazine/mildred-mickey-friedman-obituary.

5. Bruce Altshuler, *Biennials and Beyond: Exhibitions That Made Art History: 1962–2002* (London: Phaidon, 2013), 4.

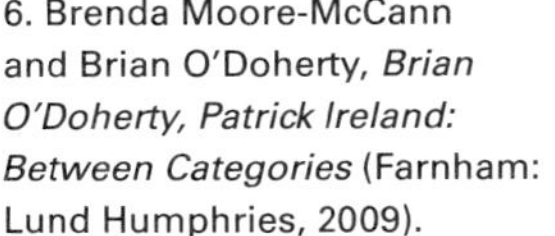

6. Brenda Moore-McCann and Brian O'Doherty, *Brian O'Doherty, Patrick Ireland: Between Categories* (Farnham: Lund Humphries, 2009).

Attitudes Become Form (Bern, 1969) and documenta 5 (Kassel, 1972).[7] These examples of approaches to curating, design, and publishing span the era of early conceptual practices of the 1960s, in which an exhibition catalog's distribution was one primary way that it could travel between disparate international art scenes. If they could not design the graphics themselves, such curators strategically commissioned designers to create striking and long-lasting communications materials.

Szeemann in particular represented both a starting point and an apogee of a trajectory within curatorial practice toward an authorial role that threatened to usurp that of the artists, a criticism leveled publicly in his time by artists Robert Morris, Daniel Buren, and others.[8] There is a cultural hierarchy at play in the critique here that assumes that, within the art world, the degree of agency and power decreases from each successive rung of the "cultural ladder" descends from artist/author to curator to designer (in that order). This valuation follows upon the trend, apparent from the Renaissance onward, that positions the artist as "apex predator" within a cultural and creative ecosystem. Such an assumption ignores the fact that many of the most important exhibitions were

7. João Doria "Catalog and Archive: Two Szeemann Designs," *The Gradient*, Walker Art Center, December 3, 2012, https://walkerart.org/magazine/catalog-and-archive-two-szeemann-designs.

8. Bruce Altshuler, *Salon to Biennial: Beyond Exhibitions That Made Art History, 1863–1959* (London: Phaidon, 2008). As Altshuler notes in the book's introduction, many of the most significant art exhibitions have been curated by artists. He also underscores the extensive movement and cross-disciplinary practice within these fields, particularly in the 1920s and '30s, when progressive artists such as El Lissitzky and others integrated graphic design, art-making, exhibition design, and exhibition-making into their practices. Such well-documented examples belie the historical transdisciplinarity of major artists, from Leonardo Da Vinci to many others. From a critical perspective, it seems that the desire to atomize and separate creative pursuits into neatly ordered categories is a more recent development, and one that is supported in part by the desire of the rising art market to more easily identify and commodify individual artistic "genius," as distinguished from the more visibly collaborative and intersubjective work of designing and curating.

themselves organized by artists,[9] and that twentieth-century avant-gardes witnessed a constant blurring of artistic, curatorial, and design roles. Designer-curators such as Dexel, Sandberg, and Crouwel practiced a hybrid approach, communicating complex ideas with an individual voice while simultaneously creating platforms for others through their curatorial programs for artists and commissioning of other designers. Such generosity of practice may be embedded within design's relatively humble origins as a skilled trade or cooperative craft within a workshop context.[10] Taken together, these examples offer arguments against assumed dichotomies between individual and collective creative work; rather, they suggest that it is possible (and even desirable) to emphasize both the authorial and the collaborative aspects of creative practice in the same breath.

Yet with the rise of elite American graphic design academies such as Cranbrook, Yale, and CalArts from the 1970s through the '90s, graphic design's educational focus began to take a turn away from the field's more practice-based origins toward supporting a sense of individual graphic authorship and articulating a historical and theoretical discourse for the field. The most recognized work from such schools from this period integrated critical theory, personal experience, and experimental visual form to claim a more autonomous position for graphic design. The authorial claims of this era are most succinctly and resonantly critiqued in Michael Rock's 1996 essay "The Designer as Author," in which Rock argues against the idea of the graphic designer as sole author and toward the notion of the designer as an auteur akin to a film director, whose particular form of agency lies in directing the collaboration of multiple people working together.[11]

In a roughly parallel development, the late 1980s and early '90s saw the establishment of the first master's programs for curating within the European and American contexts, including the École du Magasin in Grenoble, the Royal College of Art in London, and Bard College's Center for Curatorial Studies. These institutions functioned as preprofessional programs meant to prepare their participants for career paths as arts professionals within a newly opening cultural field, yet they also had the effect of solidifying and canonizing a set

9. Ibid., 157–74.

10. Richard Sennett's books *The Craftsman* (2008) and *Together* (2012) offer a useful examination of the connection between the workshop as a site of production and the development of modern notions of cooperation and collaboration.

11. Michael Rock, "The Designer as Author," *Eye* 20, no. 5 (1996). Ellen Lupton's essay "The Designer as Producer," from the same period, is helpful in contextualizing those 1990s debates within a larger avant-garde discourse questioning models of authorship. Lupton traces these back to Walter Benjamin's "The Author as Producer." Of another era, but equally relevant, is Roland Barthes's canonical "The Death of the Author," which was first published in Brian O'Doherty's *Aspen* 5+6.

of approaches to the curatorial field. Significantly, they provided an academic context for moving away from older, more traditional ideas of the curator as "caring" for museum collections toward the role of the independent curator whose authority blurs with that of the artist.[12] This trend followed upon modes of curatorial authorship as practiced by Szeemann and his ilk in the decades prior. Establishing "the curatorial" as a field of study and a *discourse*, as opposed to a *practice*, the introduction of curating into the academy supported the field's perceived cultural value.

Viewed within the broader context of expanding neoliberalism (capped by the "failure" of state socialism in 1989), the buttressing of ideas of sole authorship, agency, and value undertaken within both the graphic design and curatorial programs of the 1980s and '90s takes on greater significance. Both types of programs sought to elevate what was once considered either a practical trade or an institutionally embedded profession into academic and creative disciplines with greater cultural capital. Graphic design and curating, both of which also require managerial, coordinative, and cooperative skills, sought to balance this understanding of the field's contingency with a more expansive and autonomous self-view. These transformations within the fields and an increasingly individualistic emphasis mirror larger cultural transformations since that period that have helped to destabilize and threaten environmental, social, and political systems.

By seeking to emphasize the individual and insular discourses of the field at the expense of their interpersonal aspects, such programs of the 1980s and '90s (from which I also emerged) may have unwittingly reinforced certain categorical and professional disciplines, despite their claims to the contrary. Sandberg, for example, managed to direct a major museum, shape its exhibitions program, and create highly individual works of design while also inviting broader audiences into the institution to understand and experience art. Operating across the perceived spectrum of individual practice "versus" collective activity, Sandberg demonstrated that one can occupy multiple positions at once. Such resolute straddling of established institutional curatorial roles and personal design or artistic practice appears as an exception from the perspective of today's arts discourse, in which individual genius is the most commonly understood unit of creative valuation, a position that discounts the underlying support systems and collaborations that make any production in the world possible.[13]

12. Paul O'Neill, *The Culture of Curating and the Curating of Culture(s)* (Cambridge, MA: MIT Press, 2016).

13. Céline Condorelli, James Langdon, and Gavin Wade's *Support Structures* (2009) is an indispensable compendium of support structures within art, design, and architectural fields. It makes the clear argument that, far from being the exception within the arts, collaboration and mutual interdependency are the (often unacknowledged or willfully elided) rule.

Yet as the past twenty-five years have witnessed the spread of personal computing, accessible networked communications, and the progressive deskilling of knowledge-based professions, a space may also be opening up within which to reexamine models of creative practice and consider their renewed social relevance. Starting in the 1990s, one can trace a second arc of practitioners who incorporated the skills of designing, publishing, and exhibition-making in order to simultaneously create space for others, structure narratives in nonnormative ways, and communicate ideas to broader publics while still participating in a rigorous disciplinary discourse.[14] In the educational field, experimental institutions such as the Werkplaats Typografie in Arnhem, the Netherlands, and conferences such as 2012's "Graphic Design, Exhibiting, Curating" in Bolzano, Italy, have provided forums for relevant discussions.[15] The decade just past has also seen the emergence of a new generation of hybrid practitioners, who work fluidly between design, curating, research, publishing, and pedagogy in order to connect timely aesthetic ideas with pressing cultural concerns in unexpected and engaging formats.[16]

As a conclusion to this exploratory sketch: The uncertainties, inequalities, and imminent crises of our current times afford a rare moment to rethink how, why, with and for whom designers and curators make what they make, and how these skills can be more effectively integrated into broader creative practice. Both fields possess specific tools for both individual creation as well as collaboration; even if the skills belonging to the former category (e.g., typography, layout, image-making, exhibition design, checklist development, etc.) are more typically taught in school, it is those of the latter category (e.g., active listening, empathic feedback, group facilitation, research and discovery, organizing and project management, etc.), typically learned "on the side" over years of professional practice, that must begin to occupy equal footing within the pedagogy and mentorship of coming generations.

By expanding the curriculum of both fields to include not only "hard skills" but also these "soft" ones, can design, curating, and art help to support broader social transformations? The intersubjective tools embedded within both design and curating, if used well, could serve to emphasize the importance of understanding bias and positionality through a participant-observer mode; they can allow

14. A partial list of such figures might include Åbäke, Andrew Blauvelt, Design/Writing/Research, Dexter Sinister, Jon Sueda, Louise Sandhaus, Mark Owens, Michael Worthington, Na Kim, Silas Munro, Sulki and Min Choi, Tetsuya Goto, and many others.

15. See Giorgio Camuffo and Mura M. Dalla, *Graphic Design, Exhibiting, Curating* (Bolzano: Bozen-Bolzano University Press, 2013).

16. An inexhaustive sampling of more recent figures and their initiatives might include Lauren Mackler of Public Fiction, Hala Al-Ani and Riem Hassan of Möbius Design Studio / Design House, Tereza and Vit Ruller of The Rodina, Corinne Gisel and Nina Paim of common interest, and Anja Lutz of A–Z Presents, each of whom brings a different perspective into the space between curating and graphic design.

for opportunities to reconsider given briefs and institutional formats in order to open space for others. Through public presentations and communications, design and curating can help provide resources to those most in need and reimagine platforms for virtual interchange beyond the normative, centralized, and corporatized forms at hand. Learning from historical lessons and examples, these fields may continue to reshape each other—as well as other, adjacent areas of creative practice—in generative and generous ways.

Robert Hutchings Goddard, a physicist, publishes influential ideas on building space rockets

I would like to give my heartfelt thanks to designer and professor Emily Smith, whose ideas during our conversations and whose feedback throughout the writing process helped shape this essay.

PERHAPS: TIME, EXPANSION, TIME

IAN LYNAM

> Asian philosophers see the universe not only as a vast space around us, but as a presence inside our own bodies and minds. These teachings, found in ancient India's Upanishads and in the works of China's Lao-tse and Chuangtse, have penetrated deep into the lives and hearts of Asia's people.[1]

Of the many educators who contributed to the pedagogy of the Hochschule für Gestaltung Ulm, few have had such influential legacies as the Japanese graphic design educator and graphic designer Kōhei Sugiura 杉浦康平. And few have been as overlooked in Western design history. Sugiura's body of work even went unmentioned in the Ulm school's in-house journal while he taught there. Yet Sugiura is one of Japan's foremost design thinkers, critics, and educators, and in Japan his name is synonymous with Ulm as an academic institution and with graphic design as a sector of cultural production.

The Road to Ulm

Born in Tokyo in 1932, Sugiura graduated from the Tokyo University of the Arts with a degree in architecture in 1956. The following year, he began working in the design and promotions department of Takashimaya department stores—Japan's preeminent site of commercial consumption both before and after the war. The design department at Takashimaya opened in 1912, creating advertising with streamlined visual messaging characterized by an economy of form and directness in consumer appeal that can only be described as "modern," as it was largely free from the visual frippery and excess ornament of earlier times. The history of the designers who worked for and with Takashimaya over the decades is a veritable who's who of modern Japanese designers, from designer/critic/historian/tastemaker Shichiro Imatake to counterculture design hero Hirano Kōga.

While working at Takashimaya, Sugiura submitted a record-jacket design that won the 5th Japan Advertising Artists Club Award, a design competition organized by the Japan Advertising Artists Club (JAAC), the first nationally oriented organization devoted to graphic design in Japan. Founded in 1951 with the mission "to impart the sociocultural significance of advertising art, to establish and protect the occupational position of advertising artists, to support them mutually, and to promote friendship," the JAAC held exhibitions of work by its official members and by the general public.[2]

Winning a coveted JAAC Award paved the way for recognition within the realm of graphic design in Japan as much as for commercial success. Sugiura's 1955 award led to both. Within six months he was able to create his own design studio thanks to an

1. Kirti Trivedi, *Kohei Sugiura: Graphic Design Methodology and Philosophy* (Mumbai: Asian Design and Art Research Group, 2015), 11.

abundance of design commissions. He was also recognized as a leading young designer by Masaru Katsumi, the mastermind behind the design planning for the 1964 Olympics and the figure who was largely responsible for helping to mold the commercial direction of much of postwar Japanese advertising-oriented graphic design.[4] For the Tokyo Olympics, Katsumi served in a dual role as both design coordinator and art director, recruiting Japan's top designers to work in two teams to create a programmatic approach to the design of the Olympics. Emblems, symbols, colors, and typography were all unified in a design manual—a first in Olympic design history—and Katsumi served as chief decision-maker for all aspects of the program.

In 1960, Katsumi engineered a private logo competition for the upcoming Olympics, with Kōichiro Inagaki, Yūsaku Kamekura, Takashi Kōno, Kazumasa Nagai, Ikkō Tanaka, and Kōhei Sugiura pitted against one another in winner-take-all fashion. Kamekura's modern logo design—a stacked composition with a red circle at the top, the Olympic rings rendered in gold in the center, and bold, condensed characters that read TOKYO 1964, also in gold, at the bottom—was the winner. (It was undoubtedly helpful that Kamekura enlisted the help of his mentor Hiromu Hara in approaching the compositional and lettering aspects of the logo, though Hara's contribution has been downplayed in most published histories.)

2. Members of the independent organization were "gathered" rather than elected, and because it was not a government- or trade-initiated association, JAAC's members were responsible for internal oversight and development. As the organization developed, so did the exhibitions, and in 1953 the JAAC adopted a bifurcated model of exhibiting members' work alongside work submitted by the public. Since in postwar Japan it was expensive to have works professionally printed, JAAC exhibitions often featured original artwork for speculative designs.

3. Katsumi's career featured stints at some of Japan's most prestigious design schools, including Yokohama University and Kuwasawa Design School. He also co-founded Tokyo Zokei University. He worked as an exhibition advisor to the World Graphic Design Exhibitions that were held by Tokyo's Metropolitan Government from 1951 through 1960 and was one of the founders of the private Japan Design Committee in 1953. Katsumi also worked as advisor to the Tokyo National Museum of Art on exhibitions on the Bauhaus and on twentieth-century design in 1954 and 1957, respectively. Until his death in 1983, he was involved in all of the major postwar Japanese design organizations, including the JAAC, the Tokyo Art Directors Club, the Japan Design Committee, and the Japan Graphic Design Association. As a critic, educator, advisor, writer, and connoisseur he wielded incredible power, and his influence on Japanese design culture is inestimable.

But it was Sugiura's submission that was undoubtedly the most futuristic and progressive of the logo options. His design featured a black circle trisected by an angular, abstract *T* with the Olympic rings in miniature and XVIII OLYMPIAD TOKYO rendered in slightly letter-spaced, all-capital, sans-serif type. It was stylistically similar to the high-modernist typographic design that would emerge in the 1970s in Europe, in which sober approaches to increased use of negative space and abstraction would come to the fore, and a clear precursor to Otl Aicher's design for the 1972 Munich Olympics.

Despite not winning the logo competition, Sugiura worked on other aspects of the Olympic campaign in 1960 alongside a host of other notable young designers. That same year he was a panelist and participant in the World Design Conference (abbreviated as WoDeCo) in Tokyo, organized by a group of Japanese designers and architects in the hope of establishing a permanent international organization of designers. This attempt was made after the International Design Conference in Aspen (IDCA), launched by American designers in 1951, rejected a suggestion from the IDCA's Japanese committee that Japan host the 1958 IDCA meeting, which the committee thought would help increase the organization's international stature. While only one WoDeCo was ever held, it was a momentous event, bringing together over 250 guests from twenty-six countries to discuss the theme of the "Total Image for the 20th Century."[4]

The World Design Conference would be notable largely for its promotional materials, which were designed by the newly formed Nippon Design Center, a consortium of designers and advertisers working alongside corporations that included such luminaries as Takashi Kono, Ikkō Tanaka, Seiji Shirai, Hiromu Hara, Kazumasa Nagai, Eiji Fujimoto, Iwao Hosoya, Yoshiimi Inokuti, Gan Hosoya, and Kōhei Sugiura. The internationalist focus and United Nations–like expansiveness of the WoDeCo helped launch the reputation of the Nippon Design Center as a purveyor of effective and trusted design. The advertising consortium received investment funding from eight major corporations (Asahi Breweries, Asahi Kasei, Nippon Steel, Toshiba, Toyota Motor, Nikon, NKK, and Nomura Securities) and has largely defined advertising-oriented design and branding in Japan from its formation through to the present day. All of the committee members that organized the WoDeCo were Nippon Design Center affiliates, and while the conference helped popularize modern Japanese graphic design across the globe, the

4. The event, fraught with translation issues, consisted of six days of lectures, workshops, panel discussions, and presentations broken up by group lunches—one of which featured then-exotic hot dogs. Seventeen satellite exhibitions related to the conference were held in nearby Tokyo department stores, helping to promote further awareness of design in Japan's capital.

corporate undercurrent was a sign of the times, as Japan's booming postwar economic recovery was largely predicated on the output of its corporate juggernauts.

Just a year later, Sugiura received the Mainichi Design Award, one of Japan's premier design awards, for a series of concert posters. At the time, he was recognized largely for his programmatic approach—a mix of Swiss-inspired structural typography and abstract, architectonic, modular-based forms. This would, however, evolve into something very different.

An Awakening in Southwest Germany

As one of Japan's foremost design talents, Sugiura was invited to teach at Ulm as guest faculty in the last quarter of 1965, and he stayed on through 1967. During the school's years of operation, from 1953 to 1968, it implemented a progressive approach to design process in which questions of aesthetics and technology were informed by extensive readings in sociology, psychology, politics, economics, philosophy, and systems-thinking. Sugiura quickly realized that the school's curriculum was easily a decade or two ahead of global cultural understanding.

The Ulm school's founders wanted to create a teaching and research institution that fostered a human-centered pedagogical ideal and linked creative activity to everyday life, and the school quickly gained international recognition for its emphasis on the holistic, multidisciplinary context of design beyond the Bauhaus approach of integrating art, craft, and technology. However, Sugiura felt that there was a certain rigidity in the German worldview and German culture that chafed against his Japanese sensibility, of which a tolerance for ambiguity is an important attribute: "The German way of thinking . . . is 'Ja oder nein?' In other words, 'yes or no.'"[5]

Sugiura felt that the design theory practiced at the Ulm school reflected this rigidity and was often reductive in nature; to their often complex questions about the methodological and philosophical aspects of their studies, students received mostly "yes" or "no" answers. Sugiura often found himself unable or unwilling to respond in this binary manner and would reply to students' questions with "perhaps" or "maybe" ("たぶん" in Japanese), "possibly" or "perchance" ("おそらく" in Japanese), common Japanese expressions of equivocal possibility intimating that life is too complex for pat answers. His philosophy was that, rather than seek dogmatic, rule-based approaches to designing, students should embrace the possibility of *in-betweenness*.

Sigiura's divergent mode of thinking and teaching at Ulm awakened in him a new consciousness of being "Asian" and encouraged him to cultivate an approach to the theory of design that was different from the one quickly becoming standardized in the West. Indeed, over the course of the rest of his career he would develop

5. Kōhei Sugiura, "Design Thinking," in *Moderne Design* (Tokyo: Musashino University Press, 1999), 5.

John Logie Baird develops mechanical television

his own "Pan-Asian" approach to design in contradistinction to the logic-based Western modernist approach he had imbibed at Ulm.

Sugiura began to incorporate aspects of psychology into his writing and work and explored some of the pseudo-sciences that had gained popularity in the 1960s, such as proxemics (the study of partial perception and awareness of the individual and of society) and chronemics (the study of the role of time in communication). Through his interest in chronemics he discovered alternative temporal conceptions such as "polychronic time," i.e., one's perception and experience of time when performing multiple actions simultaneously. In this vein, Sugiura has also written about how some animal species experience the world differently than humans, as well as how the globe can be mapped according to time instead of geography.

These theoretical interests led Sugiura to turn his back on certain notions of pure, logical, function-driven modernism, but he has consistently maintained that the shift in his approach to graphic design was in no way philosophically postmodern. Rather, it was based on a desire to make design that more accurately reflected an Asian perspective.

Sugiura incorporated aspects of Confucian philosophy into his work to distance it from the Western obsession with the *self*, most notably in the ways in which his typography began to explore different voices within one text. He wrote: "There is 'anonymity' at the root of the richness of Asian culture and religion. Supporting Asian beauty is something that people unconsciously created from the depths of the mind and the body, and the Western beauty that claims the existence of 'I' is fundamentally different."[6] This refusal to design from the perspective of the singular "I" allowed him to inflect his modernism with a more communally oriented idiom, and he set out to identify the multiple ways in which Asian aesthetics express a collective vision: "Asia has the ability to find common items, not 'categorizations' that are divided into 'many' things, and to 'integrate' them into a single, large 'one,'"[7] he wrote.

Sugiura's legendary book cover for Summa Cosmographica 全宇宙誌, edited by Matsuoka Seigo 松岡正剛 and published by the Tokyo-based publisher Kousaku-sha 工作舎 in 1979

Homecoming

Upon leaving the Ulm school in 1967, Sugiura returned to design practice in Japan and began teaching at Tokyo Zokei University in 1968 at the invitation of Masaru Katsumi. In 1989 he transferred to Kobe Design University, where he taught until

6. Ibid., 11.

7. Ibid., 12.

The fore-edge of Sugiura's holistic editorial design for Summa Cosmographica 全宇宙誌. Fanning the pages reveals two different views of space: either the Andromeda Nebula or a constellation map, depending on one's perspective

2003. Among his more notable projects were designing stamps for the West German government in 1972 celebrating the Sapporo Olympics and creating the logo for the stereo-component manufacturer Audio-Technica. In 1997 Sugiura received a medal of honor with purple ribbon from the Japanese government for his contributions to art and society. He is still active today, lecturing about Pan-Asian aesthetics and symbolism at design conferences globally.

Sugiura's body of work encompasses a number of masterworks, especially in the area of book design. One of these is the nine-year undertaking *Summa Cosmographica* 全宇宙誌, published by Kousakusha in 1979, a black-and-white book serving as an expansive study and semantic manifestation of the cosmos wrapped in a screen-printed clear vinyl tubular sleeve. Nearly every spread of the *Summa Cosmographica* is printed with individual star fields printed to bleed from edge to edge, with discreet reversed-out text fields harmoniously nestled within the vastness. When readers shift the entirety of the book left or right, the facing edge of the book's pages reveals an andromeda and a constellation map—a considerable technical achievement in the pre-digital age.

Perhaps it was the star-gazing that Sugiura did both metaphorically and literally while working on the *Summa Cosmographica* book design project that led to some of the shifts in his philosophy. He has been incredibly dedicated to mapping aspects of the world which are invisible, creating information graphics that chart the world of taste and the hierarchy of time, and writing about how the globe can be mapped according to time instead of geography.

> I always want to appeal to, and absorb, the wisdom and knowledge of the many people who lived before me into my body. I would like to deeply study and digest what they did and what they meant. . . . Further, I would like to capture the importance of images' surroundings, images which spread outside of a frame like a multitude of dust particles or minute flying insects, and include these important yet seemingly insignificant aspects of life into designs I work on—like "invisible noise" brought again to life.[8]

By embracing the expanded visual language of Asian typography, the spiritual ambiguity of Confucian cultures, and an expanded understanding of how both designer and audience experience time and physicality, Sugiura opens his work to a multiplicity of readings. The thousands of publications designed by his studio force the reader to slow down and appreciate the delicacy of the typography and materials and how every aspect of the printing, binding, and packaging of a book can be be reimagined.

> A book embodies the concept of "one in many" and, at the same time, "many in one." The concept of "many" is reflected not just in the number of pages but also in a book's many characters, many images, its gathering of many elements, many chapters (as in short story collections or anthologies) and many subjects (as in a dictionary). Space and time are folded into multiple layers, creating a universe in the shape of a book. In this concept of "one in many, many in one," "one" and "many" are of the same rank, in a mutual relationship as equals, forming a circle.[9]

Sugiura's Pan-Asian approach is underpinned by a critical reevaluation of Western modernism as being largely materialist and function-driven at its core and a corresponding valorization of Asian aesthetic approaches as embodying very different spiritual and emotional values. He emphasizes the shared material and cultural history of Asian cultures and societies prior to Japan's emergence as de facto "capital" of Asia during the rise of the Japanese Empire.

During his time at Ulm, Sugiura's German colleagues gave him the nickname "Vielleicht," meaning "perhaps," a nod to his fondness for the gray areas between "yes" and "no."

Perhaps this is something we can learn from.

8. Nguyen, *Ma: The Realm of Mystery in Sugiura Kohei's "Asian Grammar of Design,"* 3.

9. Trivedi, *Kohei Sugiura: Graphic Design Methodology and Philosophy*, 10.

I would like to thank Kiyonori Muroga for providing me with some of the source material for this project; Iori Kikuchi for assisting with the translation of certain references; and Mariko Nagai, Anais Di Croce, and Emily Proulx for their unwavering support of my research efforts.

THE PRECARIOUS BODY (TEXT): *KISSING DOESN'T KILL*

NICOLE KILLIAN

If we look to the act of queering as pedagogy, we must turn our eyes to the act of urgent spirit, urgent making. Image and text are the primary tools available to the designer. Both are flexible and ever-becoming—unstable energies with the power to make things visible and speak, to become the precarious body. The image informs the text; the text informs the image. These bodies talk. When text and image merge to become the body, it punctuates and punches. In this essay, we are not only looking at the work of Gran Fury but also examining the queer body (as made visible by Gran Fury) both in a state of precarity during the AIDS epidemic and as precarious within the context of heteronormative patriarchy. It may also be important to think of the combination of text and image as *precarious*, unstable, ever-becoming.

Judith Butler's writing is one foundation for the discourse on precarity.[1] Butler draws a critical distinction between *precariousness* and *precarity*. She sees precariousness as a human condition that defines all humans as interdependent and therefore vulnerable. Precarity is different because it is distributed unequally. Precarity is experienced by marginalized people who are exposed to insecurity, injury, violence, and so on. Further, social value is ascribed to some lives and bodies and denied to others; some are protected while others are not. Butler posits the potential for freedom through an embrace of the common circumstance of precariousness, as against the unequal destinies of precarity. She rejects the idea of achieving "stability" and instead sees precariousness for all as offering the only basis for unity.

The collective Gran Fury was formed as the "unofficial propaganda ministry"[2] of New York's ACT UP (AIDS Coalition to Unleash Power) in 1988, a time when the US government was willfully ignoring the thousands of people dying from AIDS. Gran Fury was a political collaboration centered on cultural production in many forms and media, including posters, newspapers, stickers, billboards, video, and apparel.

Design, including that of Gran Fury, works within the act of visibility. It is the thing that can talk about and point more or less directly at *the thing*, especially if using what already exists. We look at the reproduction differently because something came before it. We then ask ourselves, What do we *not* see? Design, rather than being a mystical realm controlled by an unseen puppeteer, is simple assemblage: a tangible alchemy of human satisfaction, completely within the grasp of anyone who needs to be heard. A democratic and accessible design is a queer design. Design is a process of arrangement, aggregation, aggression. Effectively using the object fetish as a way to bring visibility to interracial and queer couples, making something out of nothing, can be considered resistance work—queer. By hijacking dominant methods of design and advertising, Gran Fury flipped the scripts of "understood" images, asking questions and creating openings for conversation.

Kissing Doesn't Kill (*KDK*) circulated as a twelve-foot-long advertising panel on buses and transit-station billboards in Chicago, San Francisco, Washington, D.C., and New York in 1989 and 1990.[3] The image presented three interracial couples, each locked in a kiss. Two of the couples are of the same sex. The high-contrast clothing, diverse models, and stark white background

1. Judith Butler, *Precarious Life: The Powers of Mourning and Violence* (London, Verso, 2004).

2. Douglas Crimp and Adam Rolston, *AIDS Demo Graphics* (Seattle: Bay Press, 1990), 16.

Karel Čapek and his brother coin the word "robot" in a play about artificial humans instantly evoked Italian ready-to-wear brand Benetton, enacting a "coming out" and affirming the visibility of gay and lesbian people in the public sphere. Even though the HIV message was less clear than in Gran Fury's other works, the images were legible as queer and the bodies were demanding to be seen. In the cultural climate of America at that time, images of same-sex kisses were nowhere to be found; queer desire was not to be visualized in public. There was tremendous value in the visibility alone.

KDK's appropriation of Benetton photographer Olivero Toscani's colorful portrayals of good-looking models repurposed the bankrupt promises of advertising to call attention to what really kills marginalized people. The United Colors of Benetton brand dominated the image space of the time, with Benetton pouring countless dollars into its promotion. Its stores were seemingly everywhere. Toscani was given free rein by the fashion company in the early '80s, and he swiftly capitalized on the rising interest in multiculturalism through images of youths of different races. Gran Fury used this as an opportunity to play off the ads' corporatist utopian morality.

The *KDK* "ads" featured images of the couples kissing accompanied by the tagline "Kissing Doesn't Kill: Greed and Indifference Do" and, further (in some iterations), "Corporate Greed, Government Inaction, and Public Indifference Make AIDS a Political Crisis." Benetton had access to prime real estate on bus panels across New York City, and Gran Fury needed a similarly expansive space in order to feature models representing a range of identities, ethnicities, and races, à la Benetton. Using the bus as a mobile messaging unit, Gran Fury's campaign could reach multiple audiences. Many of the group's members worked as art directors and designers and were therefore fluent in the language of advertising. Gran Fury was able to use the legible form of advertising to talk about something misunderstood: the queer body and the epidemic plaguing the queer community. It was important not only to talk about the causes of AIDS but to make visible the people affected by it. Images of lesbians were especially shocking at a time when their visibility did not exist and false statements were being made to the effect that women did not die of AIDS. Gran Fury replicated

3. *Kissing Doesn't Kill* was commissioned by Art Against AIDS on the Road, a public-art project "organized in conjunction with several auctions of contemporary art that benefited the American Foundation for AIDS Research (amfAR)." Richard Meyer, *Outlaw Representation: Censorship and Homosexuality in Twentieth-Century American Art* (Boston: Beacon, 2002), 237. *KDK* was produced in additional formats, including a postcard and video spots that aired on MTV Brazil and MTV Europe.

Toscani's slick, simple visual recipe but infused the hollow formula with meaning and life.[4]

When *KDK* was originally planned to run in Chicago, there were complaints that the billboard had nothing to do with AIDS, that the Chicago Transit Authority should not be promoting a "particular lifestyle," and that the posters were directed toward children for "recruitment" purposes. In June 1990, the Illinois State Senate barred the CTA from displaying any poster showing a same-sex embrace in any place where persons under twenty-one could view it. Protesting the bill, the American Civil Liberties Union claimed it was unconstitutional. Concurrently, at Chicago Pride, queers marched with a *KDK* poster and a "kiss-in" was organized outside the CTA's offices. By August, the billboards had been installed, but within two days nearly all were defaced, allegedly by religious conservatives.

In the original design of *KDK*, the main slogan was to be followed by the phrase "Corporate Greed, Government Inaction, and Public Indifference Make AIDS a Political Crisis." However, some corporate sponsors balked at the mention of "corporate greed," so a compromise was reached: Billboards on buses would have to run without the secondary text, but it could be included on posters. This was a strategic compromise, as Gran Fury member Michael Nesline explained: "As long as it gave you a foot up, we felt it was actually part of the process." Avram Finkelsein added, "Yes, inside the gallery, outside the gallery; can we navigate certain opportunities by getting sponsorship for other ones? We were frequently in that situation." The process of getting *KDK* from concept to billboard not only illustrated Gran Fury's strategy of seeking to present work on its own terms but exemplified queer praxis as democratic, scrappy, urgent, and accessible.

Gran Fury's work engaged the space of visual consumption and repositioned relationships between subject and object in terms of desire. The feeling of the work was its function. It was raw, visceral. It was work made because it had to be. At its best, graphic design communicates and becomes an entity unto itself, a body. At its worst, it is mere text, without the independent form or feeling of a self. Cultural production that deals with bodies—precarious bodies intersecting with all-powerful capital—not only highlights and makes visible the queer body but starts to discuss the unstable and predatory practices of the advertising world. Public spaces are intrinsically dialogic, and the sheer ingenuity of repositioning work somebody else paid for—the time-honored tactic of appropriating the labor of the capitalist for a subversive aim—opened many eyes to the resourcefulness of this form of reproduction.

How does one confiscate mainstream narratives and transform them into forms of resistance? It is the work of the marginalized to take hold of aspects of the dominant culture and reshape them into something that can be useful and ultimately *owned*. It therefore

4. Avram Finkelstein, "Kissing Doesn't Kill," in *After Silence: A History of AIDS through Its Images* (Berkeley: University of California Press, 2020), 107–25.

5. Ibid.; Gran Fury, *Gran Fury: Read My Lips* (New York: 80wse Press, 2015).

seemed second nature for Gran Fury to queer the strategies of graphic design. It is important to note here that these strategies of queering corporate graphic design have been also used by far-right and fascist movements. What this means is context is everything—one must examine the roots of the images digested and how those images flow and mutate in culture. Who has taken the reins of an image, and for what purposes and to what extent?

With *KDK*, the structure was appropriated but not the image. Sheer publicity with no product, the billboard was selling nothing but queer joy, queer sexiness, mimicking the tenets of capitalist seduction to capture the viewer's attention and direct it toward queer bodies and the AIDS crisis. The group's decision to photograph representatives of its own community was crucial to this project. It affirmed the power of queer desire in the face of an ongoing epidemic and urged lesbians and gay men to fight the efforts of the larger culture to render their sexuality, their desiring bodies, invisible.

In producing affirmative images of desire, Gran Fury insisted on the centrality of sexual liberation to its practice of AIDS activism and on the ideal of (safe) sexual freedom in the midst of the crisis. As early as 1985, queer theorists such as Cindy Patton were arguing that "AIDS must not be viewed as proof that sexual exploration and the elaboration of sexual community were mistakes. . . . Lesbians and gay men . . . must maintain that vision of sexual liberation that defines the last fifteen years of [our] activism."[6] Insisting on the visibility of the precarious body via an appropriation of advertising tactics illuminating the instability of capitalism meant that viewers had to deal with the contradictions this "ad" presented head-on. While other pieces by Gran Fury used fear and shock to agitate, *KDK* focused on queer joy. The images of the dominant culture continue to be abusive acts of erasure in terms of who is chosen to be visible, legible. Joy visualized is rare, and political.

Given the increase in queer visibility over the past twenty years, it is interesting to look back on *KDK*. The bodies on the billboard radiated not because they were seasoned models but because such queer images did not exist in our everyday world. This project was the first of Gran Fury's explorations into identity politics, in which people told their own stories and conveyed what it felt like to be seen. What had been a mere lack became a presence; the body began to speak for itself. *KDK* was a queer act of communion and rebirth.

6. Cindy Patton, *Sex and Germs: The Politics of AIDS* (Boston: South End Press, 1985), 142.

BASMA HAMDY AND YARA KHOURY ON DESIGN EDUCATION IN THE "ARAB" WORLD

with WAEL MORCOS

Introduction

In 1992, a four-year graphic design program was launched at the American University of Beirut. It was the first of its kind in Lebanon and the region. Design education in the Levant and the Gulf often adapts and expands upon the Western canon. Some schools implement this methodology by franchising Western and American curricula and tailoring them to regional needs. A popular localization tactic is the reclamation of a glorious "Arab" past by unearthing native craft practices and reintroducing them in a contemporary design context. This application is most evident in interior, industrial, and fashion design practices and in burgeoning high-end, local design houses. The revitalization of regional visual histories is happening in parallel to an ongoing Arabic typography renaissance. This renewal is supported by recent technological advances of accessible design software and type design applications that accommodate the Arabic script.

The tension between teaching imported Western name brands and tempering them with "pre-colonial" design practices is driven by the desire to be globally relatable while holding onto personal narratives. In the early twentieth century, the Bauhaus movement proposed an alternative to this dialectic through the development of a global language and universal laws for geometry and perception. This supposedly comprehensive pedagogy and methodology established a legacy upon which many design programs worldwide are predicated. But can a model built upon the professionalization of the European Arts and Craft movement be truly inclusive? If the Bauhaus ideal is a powerful and practical tool to understand and teach design, can it be deployed without erasing the cultural histories of any given region of the world—and more specifically, the Middle East's?

I first encountered Basma Hamdy's work online in 2011 and have followed her research on the creative output of the Egyptian Revolution since. Her book *Walls of Freedom: Street Art of the Egyptian Revolution* is a one-of-a-kind exploration of visual communication's role in the political upheavals that swept the country in the early 2010s. In juxtaposing the universal yearning for freedom with a specifically Egyptian story, Hamdy's compendium masterfully engages with the current tension in regional design education. Hamdy has extensive experience teaching in the Middle East and is currently associate professor of graphic design at Virginia Commonwealth University in Qatar, where she is building a curriculum tailored to the needs of the local communities.

I met Yara Khoury in 2004–2005, when I was a student at the Notre Dame University in Lebanon. She was one of the few instructors who were also practicing designers; at the time, Khoury was the design director at Al Mohtaraf, a design house based in Beirut with clients in Lebanon and the Middle East. Her classes interspersed design theory with real-life scenarios, confronting aspirational manifestos with the question, would the client buy that? Her expert navigation of the intersection of theory and practice was eye-opening and energizing. She reminded us that while graphic design can be a research methodology for social studies, it is largely a service profession that lives in a commercial context with which we must contend. Her advocacy for Arabic typography underscored her conviction that Western design approaches, as valuable as they may be, would never be enough to address the complexities of Middle Eastern cultures. Khoury is currently assistant professor at the American University of Beirut and an independent designer since 2017.

The following conversations took place over Google Docs in the early months of 2020 before the outbreak of COVID-19.

—Wael Morcos (WM)

Basma Hamdy

WM: You have taught in Cairo and Dubai, and for the past seven years, you have been a professor at the Virginia Commonwealth University Qatar in Doha. What are the similarities and differences between graphic design programs and students in these cities?

BH: It is difficult to compare the three institutions and the students that attend them. Cairo has a long history with academia, and there are deep-rooted histories and legacies of creative industries that naturally influence and affect education. In Dubai, I was teaching at a government institution that only admitted women. After eight years of teaching there I moved to VCUarts Qatar. When I arrived, the program was based on a curriculum created for VCUarts Richmond decades ago that was outdated and unsurprisingly based on a Western Eurocentric canon. The faculty on both campuses (Richmond and Doha) felt that it was time to create a forward-looking curricular system dedicated to transcending its current basis of process, production, and profession to foster the contextualized and inclusive creative agency of each student in a manner that orients him/her to a future of emerging practices of graphic design. In September 2016 we began a collaborative two-year redesign of the Graphic Design Department's undergraduate curriculum. Our goal was to move away from curricula of Western universities to better prepare students—as individuals and as collaborators—to be practitioners not limited by the confines of employment markets and practices and to increase cultural literacy.

A decade in the Gulf is quite transformative, and so it's hard to compare Dubai and Doha because of this jump in time. However, I will say that teaching in the Gulf is more challenging as students have more social and cultural restrictions and expectations. That said, I enjoy the challenge tremendously because I am able to witness student transformations firsthand, and I can influence their outlook and understanding of the world they live in. Qatar's wealth was built from extracting and exporting natural gas. Like its neighboring countries, it is aware of the short-term life of hydrocarbon-based economies and actively invests in alternative modes of economic development, notably in the arts and cultural sectors, thus creating a need for design practices focused on cultural institutions and funded by governments. Qatar is different from the UAE in that it places more emphasis on knowledge production and education.

WM: The Bauhaus movement was an ideological design movement that wanted to break from previous practices. How does design encourage students to develop novel ideas? Do these ideas extend into Qatari society?

BH: The Bauhaus movement was responding to industrialization and wanted to give meaning to objects, reducing the separation between form and function. But I need to rethink the Bauhaus and its intentions for our current time, where political, cultural, sociological, ethical, and philosophical implications play a much more vital role in our everyday interactions. We encourage students to understand their responsibility and to examine what and how they design to uncover their consequences and impact on the world. We challenge them to transcend the mere aesthetics of what they produce and ask pertinent questions that engage with issues like cultural appropriation, power structures, capitalism, inclusion, and decolonization. Our goal is to encourage our students to abandon the myth of producing something original and instead focus on producing something responsible. The concept of the design "master" or "creator" is outdated in today's world. It's an exclusionary and privileged concept that should be replaced with an inclusionary, collaborative, and ethical framework. In short, we need to discuss design beyond a privileged fetishization of newness, of shiny materializations of technological ingenuity and consumer desire.

One way that we promote research, experimentation, and exploration at VCUarts Qatar is through our Materials Library. It is one of a kind in the Arab and Gulf region and includes an exhaustive collection of diverse materials from around the world. Visitors can interact with the materials that have been curated for the art and design disciplines in order to enhance their knowledge and literacy in materials, processes, and fabrication methods. A key aspect of the library is to encourage students to think outside the box and approach projects in a new and unusual way. The collection includes material categories ranging from natural materials (plant, animal, and mineral), metals, textiles, ceramics, glass, polymers, and cement-based samples. The Materials Library also houses a collection of finished products, including student work, that demonstrate unique or exciting material applications and investigations.

WM: One of the Bauhaus's tenants was a rational, minimal, functional aesthetic. Even though patterning is prominent in the weaving work that was done in Bauhaus workshops, it was limited to abstract geometries. How do your students interpret the seemingly opposing concepts of minimalism and formal excess?

BH: Today we live in a postmodern reality where formal excess and minimalism can exist side by side. However, the key components of this conversation are who wrote history and what can we learn from it. There are a wealth of aesthetic movements that have inspired Western artists and designers for decades without ever entering design-history books. An example is the North African Gnawa aesthetic, which influenced jazz music and is a musical genre that blends African and Sufi traditions. Gnawa could be synonymous with formal excess but has inspired artists such as famed photographer Hassan Hajjaj, who uses his photography to challenge Western stereotypes of Arab societies. Students should be encouraged to examine their identity and cultural heritage and to find their own voice and to redefine their own visual culture—and perhaps even create a new aesthetic.

WM: Your work has researched and documented Egyptian street art and calligraphy. How is design a tool for expressing dissent and issuing a call for social change in the Middle East in general and Egypt in particular?

Basma Hamdy and Don Karl, *Walls of Freedom: Street Art of the Egyptian Revolution* (Berlin: From Here to Fame, 2014)

BH: Creative expression has been a tool for expressing dissent since the Ancient Egyptians; humans have relied on the creative and satirical forms of communicating resistance for centuries. During the Egyptian revolution and the Arab Spring art and design were used as tools that articulated and transmuted people's feelings and opinions by giving them visual form. The walls of Cairo were filled with images of resistance, providing an alternative to the dominant propaganda-fueled media. If you follow street art's timeline during the Egyptian revolution, you can trace almost every incident or event and even read and see the "pulse" of the people. Street art is a miraculous manifestation of the creative energy of the revolution, uniting people together in their fight for freedom and social justice. Murals on the streets of Cairo mixed pharaonic, Coptic, Islamic, and modern motifs to represent a new Egyptian identity that transcended religion and sectarian divides.

WM: You presented this street art in your first book. How would you describe the state of literary production when it comes to the Middle East and North Africa (MENA) region?

BH: My personal experience with producing two books in and about the region included many challenges. My first book, *Walls of Freedom: Street Art of the Egyptian Revolution*, was published in

2014 by an independent publisher in Berlin and was funded through a crowdfunding campaign supported by seven-hundred people. The book is a historical document that captures the street art of the Egyptian revolution. However, finding a publisher was difficult, and when I began collaborating with my co-author Don Karl, who runs From Here to Fame Publishing, we soon realized that we could not fund the book unless we got a grant. That also proved nearly impossible, and so we resorted to crowdfunding. Following its success, the book was banned in Egypt for "instigating revolt"; authorities considered the images it contained as a threat rather than an act of preservation and documentation. My second book, *Khatt: Egypt's Calligraphic Landscape* (co-authored with Noha Zayed), is published by Saqi books, an independent publisher in the UK focusing on books from the MENA region. For this project, a grant from VCUarts Qatar helped to defray some of the research and printing costs.

Overall, there is still a state of anxiety concerning literary production in the MENA region, and many authors self-censor to avoid the consequences of freedom of expression. A famous example is Ahmed Nagi, who was jailed in 2016 for "violating public modesty" with his book *Using Life*, a dystopian novel set in Cairo about a secret society responsible for a number of global conspiracies. A reader complained that an excerpt of the novel published in a literary journal was offensive because it used "explicit" descriptions of body parts (which is not unusual for classical Arabic literature). When we created *Walls of Freedom*, we were in the midst of the revolutionary high point and did not expect it to be banned or censored. Today, we understand that attaining freedom of expression in the Arab world is a battle that we have yet to win.

Yara Khoury

WM: You started your design education at Notre Dame University (NDU) in Lebanon. What was the program like when you joined?

YK: When I first arrived at NDU, the graphic design program was a mix of art and advertising/marketing courses; it was far from what such a program should be. The classes were distributed into one-hour slots every other day, attending to art history, drafting skills, drawing, economics, statistics, advertising marketing models, you name it. Students jumped from class to class every hour or so, ticking the attendance boxes and taking notes. The content of the classes never merged into a synchronized whole.

A seismic shift occurred in 1995, when Peter Rea, a professor of graphic design from London who had studied art, design, and typography at the Royal College of Art in London, was invited by Professor John Kortbaoui to be a consultant and instructor to the program. Rea was known for setting up graphic design programs modeled on Bauhaus principles in other universities, and he overhauled the whole design pedagogy at NDU. Starting with the foundation year (which I unfortunately missed because I was already in my second year of study when he arrived), the courses provided students with a holistic approach to basic design skills. They also allowed students to test their abilities and confirm their choice of discipline, whether graphic design, architecture, interior design, or something altogether different. The courses then rolled out over the next three years, moving from developing the studies and skill sets of the foundation year to applied design classes where students could form opinions through critical debate. The courses included basic compositional principles, typography, editorial design, visual rhetoric, information design, moving-image studies, environmental graphics, and identity design. The design pedagogy was based on a looping process of experimentation and problem-solving centered around the philosophy "East meets West." As kitschy as it might sound today, it was an early attempt at decolonizing the imported dominant Western aesthetic and at finding relevance, as well as reference, in the Lebanese local visual culture.

I was very lucky to be a part of that first wave of graduates under the new program. The courses changed from being one-hour classes, in which it was difficult to achieve anything substantial, to six-hour studio courses held three times a week! Our day started at 10 in the morning and officially finished at 4 in the afternoon, but often it continued into the late hours of the night. The setup made sure the student worked in the studio with proper mentorship and continuous feedback. It was an intense experience and a far cry from the earlier program.

WM: You continued your education in the United Kingdom. How did that come about, and how did that experience affect your outlook on design?

YK: As the first wave of students under the new program graduated, I was selected to be part of the core team that continues teaching under the new pedagogy. Rea wanted his new graduates to carry on the torch and teach after completing the program. But we had to earn a master's degree first, as the school in Lebanon required. He had previously developed a flexible master's program with Middlesex University in London, which started with a summer semester of intensive courses that prepared us for a year-and-a-half thesis project. We were the first group of students to graduate from this program, which included five students from Lebanon and others from Germany and Holland.

He took a chance on a group of students who were too young—I was 20 years old at the time—to handle a class but who exhibited strong design skills, studiousness, leadership, and a willingness to learn. Eventually, we replaced our own instructors who were part of the previous program. He used to say: Wisdom and whiz kids work together. He was the wisdom and we were the kids.

The experience of doing an apprenticeship in London was enriching and rewarding. The city itself is a hub of the design world. We met professionals in the field, professors and students with very different experiences and backgrounds. It also spurred me to appreciate my own language and its script; I immediately felt the urge to contribute to its advancement. I was fully aware at that point of the dangers of slipping into a Eurocentric design pedagogy and had so many questions left unanswered. I decided at that moment to become a practicing designer, an educator, and an informal researcher—all in one.

WM: What were the changes that were made to the curriculum upon your return, and how did that evolve in the subsequent years?

YK: The changes had already been instituted at Notre Dame University during my apprenticeship. As young instructors, we were there to make sure the courses rolled out as designed. I can't say it was an easy task. The courses did not fit into the operational mold of the university nor its subsequent finances. Imagine changing three-credit courses, the equivalent of three hours per week, into six-credit studio classes of eighteen hours a week! All courses were co-taught, which was also a novelty at the university. In line with what used to occur at the Bauhaus school, many visiting professors from England and Europe were invited by Rea to join the main team of instructors. We had, among others, animation experts from the movie *Chicken Run*, famous illustrators from the *Guardian* newspaper, professional photographers who had worked for the *Economist* and other major news outlets, and renowned graphic designers from Germany. The motto of this vibrant program was "learn by doing!" and students carried out their projects while working with professionals and guest lecturers in the field, who willingly shared their global experience.

Typography took center stage in the graphic design program at NDU. Just as Rea—master typographer—was my mentor and I was the apprentice, I turned to mentor my own students who eventually went on to pursue their own degrees in design and particularly Arabic type design. Most traveled to Europe and the United Kingdom and few ventured over to the US. Pascal Zoghbi, Krystian Sarkis, and Khajag Apelian studied type design at KABK in Holland, and you, Wael, studied graphic design at the Rhode Island School of Design.

Here, the notion of mentor is not meant in the classical sense; that is, the exclusive information transfer within a tight circle of hand-picked individuals. Although during the first phase, a quasi-master/apprentice model was adopted to form a core that would have the necessary support tools needed to grow it into a school, the program was soon capable of distributing its knowledge at a much larger, democratized, and sustainable scale. The master/apprentice model is rigorous, intensive, and rich. Its high degree of interactivity with a limited number of minds getting together was needed at the outset of the new program, which eventually proved its success in establishing the new core. Here, richness is inversely proportional to reach. The greatest ideas and schools of thought were disseminated in that model from Plato/Aristotle to Huxley/Orwell to the Bauhaus's own Kandinsky/Bayer. A modern version of this model is not as one-way or top to bottom as the name suggests. The apprentice gains an amalgam of the master's own experience mixed with their own; an influence that they carry through for the rest of their life. The master becomes a measure of the apprentice's actions and decisions mixed with the latter's own experience. Hence, a pupil is not a copy of the master.

WM: You are now a full-time faculty member at the American University of Beirut, one of the first departments to offer a graphic design degree in Lebanon. Can you tell us a little bit about the program at AUB? How is it different from and similar to other design programs in Lebanon?

YK: AUB's graphic design program was initiated in 1992 under the tutelage of Professor Leila Musfi. After acquiring her master's at Cranbrook, Musfi developed the first graphic design program in the Middle East region with that took into account local issues while still participating in the global market. The four-year BA program is based on a design school approach with two studio courses per year that cover major theoretical, practical, and technical skills reinforced with field and general electives. Situated in the crux of the Arab world, Beirut offers a curious amalgam of histories, languages, and experiences. As a result, most students at AUB develop a rich intellectual background, critical thinking, and a visual aesthetic that contributes to the region and beyond. The program itself is designed to answer the needs of the Arab region by being the first to integrate the graphic use of the Arabic language in its core subject areas.

However, the implications of Arabic type design and the practice of its typography in other interrelated domains tend to be researched as unrecorded or un-archived individual efforts, rather than as an academic discourse. In response, Leila Musfi, Reza Abedini, and I established the Arabic Type Unit (ATU) at AUB in 2017. ATU is an academic entity that aims to research, develop, and set standards of design in Arabic type, lettering, and typography. It plans to centralize resources on Arabic-type development and typographic practices by building an archive of its historical development, publishing research, creating forums of discussion, and eventually developing a master's program for Arabic type design. This unit is poised to become a full-fledged center of research, archive and hub of activities. One of the main activities ATU is involved in at the moment is the organization of its first two-day conference—Mashq—dedicated to advancing the discourse on Arabic type and typography in the region.

WM: Can you tell us more about Mashq? What did it set out to do?

YK: The word "Mashq" in Arabic means training, exercising, or practicing. A mashq is a sheet of calligraphy drawn by the master calligrapher for the pupil to copy and master in return. In that line, Mashq conference plans on bringing together professionals, scholars, and students to explore historical developments, research outcomes, technical updates, and emerging trends in the field of Arabic typography, type design, lettering, and regional visual communication in general. The first Mashq was planned for April 2020 with a major lineup of speakers from the Arab world and Europe, but it was postponed because of the COVID-19 pandemic.

Mashq aims to address inherent practices that have not been formalized yet into a set of processes or disciplines. I'm now more convinced than ever that when it comes to graphic design, practice is the research. Another aim is to expand the industry of Arabic type and typography so that it not only answers client briefs but also embraces innovation, pedagogy, and knowledge production through research. And by showing that designing with type and designing type itself are human-centered endeavors, it aims to change the widespread view that graphic design and typography are marginal activities that do not contribute at a constituent level to society.

We also hope to create a multi-disciplinary network around the subject of Arab type and typography, strengthening connections between designers in the region, initiating standards for the industry, and publishing research literature from the field.

WM: AUB offers several courses on Arabic typography. How are these classes filling gaps in the education of graphic designers?

YK: From the outset, the graphic design program at AUB focused on localizing visual communication through the use of the regional languages and their visual manifestations through calligraphy and typography. The study of Arabic calligraphy, lettering, and typography is a core requirement and an integral part of its philosophy. Celebrated master artist Samir Sayegh taught full-time courses on the appreciation of Arabic calligraphy—not so students would become master calligraphers, but so they would develop an understanding of the historical development of the script, the variety of calligraphic styles, its proportions and script rules by hand-drawing the letters, dissecting, and reorganizing them into rich visual compositions. In turn, this method gave birth to several renowned pioneers in Arabic type design and typography, such as Nadine Chahine and Tarek Atrissi. Although Sayegh does not teach at AUB anymore, his legacy is one of the backbones of the graphic design program. When Reza Abedni joined the program, almost ten years ago, the emphasis shifted from the appreciation of the calligraphic to the richness of the typographic application; from the romanticized historicization of the hand-drawn to the rich mechanization of the Arabic typographic letterform.

HB Beiruty is inspired by the Arabian wooden bay windows known as Rawasheen. Designed as the Arabic companion to the Latin by Taline Yozgatian and Markus Bernatsky, 2006

I genuinely believe that typography is the semiconductor that runs through graphic design. Without enough variety of Arabic

Robert Watson Watt oversees the development of radar

typefaces to enrich different communication voices, we cannot move forward. In an effort to fill this gap, I developed, with my colleague Khajag Apelian, an elective Arabic type design course. Our students realize the importance of producing the building blocks of Arabic visual communication through designing their own Arabic typefaces that cater to modern-day communication problems. They are also increasingly designing bilingual publications that tackle multi-scripts while questioning notions of cultural biases and language authority. In fact, the study of Arabic typography enriches their roles as active contributors to the society they live in and to the livelihood of the Arabic language.

WM: Graduates from Lebanon often leave their country to continue their education in Europe and the United States. What challenges and opportunities do you think that brings?

YK: The graphic design discipline developed in the West with the rise of the industrial revolution. The aesthetics, the theory, the practice, and even the technology were all developed in a Western context using the Latin script. Germany's Bauhaus ideals of form follows function, optimization of industrial production, and asymmetric theories in typographic layouts govern the educational systems. Consequently, our students are preconditioned to look westward for furthering their education. And a lack of advance degree programs means there is no alternative. Additionally, the majority of students want to experience the international design scene, which gives them more opportunities to develop the work they are most interested in. The challenges they face are many. Whereas European students focus their four-year undergraduate studies on the Latin script, mastering its typography and referring to thousands of well-searched references, our students try to master both Latin and Arabic without any references for the latter script. This immensely dilutes their efforts and their learning outcomes. On a master's level, their first instinct would be to absorb and digest until they eventually start building new regional principles and aesthetics.

But many of those who have studied abroad have returned and are giving back to our design community more than we can imagine. Amongst their achievements in the past ten years is the production of more quality Arabic typefaces than we have ever seen before, placing the Arabic type industry on par with other scripts. We are gradually witnessing the emergence of academic research on Arab printing history and a new exploration in the design of the Arabic and bilingual publications.

WM: The Bauhaus school put a lot of emphasis on the craft by blurring the lines between artist and craftsman. This approach is very present in type design, a discipline that evolved in parallel to technological advancements. How is craft a part of Arabic type design today?

YK: Art + technology = design, Walter Gropius declared a hundred years ago. The equation resonates today still, even more so with Arabic type design. If you want to venture into designing an Arabic typeface, the skill and craft of a thousand-year-old discipline rest on your shoulder. The lore of Arabic calligraphy is a long history of manuscripts with religious connotations and a stupendous display of technique that we, as designers, have come to glorify. The craft itself has little space for personal narratives and subjective interpretations. It is governed by rules and proportions established by years of practice.

The challenge for the modern Arabic type designer is that of self-teaching. It lies in understanding the underlying stroke modulation of classical calligraphy, reinterpreting those modulations into new curves and eventually letterforms, and then digitizing them in a software with its own limitations. This sinuous trail that moves between calligraphy, their reinterpretation into new shapes, and their digital translation is the crux of Arabic type design. It is a relatively new course, with a long way to go still before becoming a clearly defined and independent discipline. We need a bigger body of work, a critical mass, to formulate a formal discourse around it. We can barely discuss terminology, let alone conventions of Arabic type design, without the personal experience and interpretation of each designer taking center stage.

WM: Bauhaus artists favor linear and geometric forms, avoiding floral and organic ones. The Arabic script in its variety often combines those characteristics in complex systems. Does the Arabic script fit within the concept of circle, square, and triangle?

YK: The Bauhaus's circle, square, and triangle concept is an attempt to streamline all shapes into a limited set that presents all others; the truth lies in the rigid, the modular, the reproducible, and the linear. This seems like a far cry from Arabic letterforms with their intertwining organic shapes, which at first glance appear to be fully ornamental, flexible, variable, and nonlinear. However, a further study of the Arabic script reveals a much more ordered and modular system of structures. During the tenth century, Ibn Muqla, a revered calligrapher of the Abbasid period, and his pupil Ibn Albawwab installed strict rules and proportions to the Arabic letterform. His reform standardized the calligraphic styles through three canonical rules: *nizam al da'era* (the rule of the circle where all letterforms fit into a circular form of a fixed diameter starting with the first letter of the alphabet, the Alif), *nizam al nuqat* (the rule of the rhombic dot as a fixed unit of measurement) and *nizam al tashaboh* (the rule of similarity that denominates the different components of the letterforms). The modularity of this approach simplified a seemingly complex system reminiscent of Bauhaus's circle, square, and triangle.

With the shift from handmade calligraphy to machine-made typography, Arabic letterforms became more rigid and linear in order to fit the technological limitations of mechanical reproduction. As a result, the printed text type transitioned from traditional Naskh with several forms per letter to "simplified" Naskh with one or two forms per letter. Many lamented and romanticized the loss of the calligraphic tradition. But with time, overuse, and habit, we developed a preference for those simplified shapes. More so, recent research suggests that simplified Naskh is the most legible and comfortable to read. The case is the same with rigid Kufi-esque typefaces that fill our news websites, litter our advertising messages, and brand international outlets. With time, would we be reading Kufi instead of the quintessentially text-friendly Naskh script? On a design level, digital reproduction of typefaces has opened the doors wide open to all possibilities. It is now technically possible to design typefaces that range from classic revivals with all their contextual alternates and connective strokes to extremely abstracted unified forms. What will we be reading next?

SOME PEDAGOGIES OF THE SOUTHLAND INSTITUTE

JOE POTTS with ADAM FELDMETH

What would it look like to build a responsible financial framework for higher education that costs students less and pays those contributing their labor more than existing institutions? What types of pedagogies can be activated within, and in support of, such a framework? How, by engaging with histories and active developments of progressive, critical, queer, feminist, anti-racist, and anti-ableist pedagogies, can the tools of typography, graphic design, and critical art be used toward building holistic and sustaining critical practices? What nutrients remain in the increasingly bereft soil of the standard patrician, Western, capitalist design-education trajectory (Bauhaus / Ulm / Black Mountain / Harvard / Yale / RISD / Cranbrook / CalArts)? How might successful approaches, ideas, and pedagogical models of the present and recent past (such as the Werkplaats Typografie and Michael Asher's long-running "post-studio art" class) complement a consideration of less canonical—yet no less potent—models of inspiration, such as necessity-driven, community-run initiatives like the Mississippi Freedom Schools of the 1960s or the emancipatory adult-education initiatives of the Black Panther Party? How might a curriculum attending to design and art, and the histories that it looks to, decenter colonial, war-derived notions of any sort of "avant-garde" as the driver of an exclusionary narrative of art and/or design in favor of ideas and practices from labor and civil rights movements and a focused attention on care and maintenance, drawing from teachings and ideas on education from (though certainly not limited to) Pestalozzi, Montessori, Dewey, Freire, hooks, Lorde? What if the search for a functional, humane, liberatory, and just model for higher education was part of the DNA of an organization? At what scale could such a project find equilibrium, expand notions of what is possible, and not only exist but sustain itself within an economic system highly unfavorable to these kinds of questions? Founded in 2016 in Los Angeles, the Southland Institute (for critical, durational, and typographic post-studio practices) is dedicated to exploring these questions in order to identify and implement meaningful, affordable, sustainable alternatives in design and art education in the United States.

A crucial problem that presently afflicts countless conversations around pedagogy within the economically fraught, debt-fueled arena of post-secondary education in 2020 is that pedagogies cannot be unlinked from the frameworks they are enacted within. However good their intentions may be, however sound their concepts and purported ethics in and of themselves, the most progressive / expansive / radical / forward-thinking curricula, delivered from within schools that leave their students hundreds of thousands of dollars in debt, are diminished or negated when taken in tandem with the financial conditions they exist within. This is why the pedagogical approaches and interests of the Southland Institute are inseparable from a framework of an affordable, accessible, and sustainable structural model for education.

The selection of pedagogies collected here is drawn from a larger group of pedagogies engaged by the Southland Institute that are being continually explored, expanded, critiqued, and refined and that are very much a living text intended for active use and inquiry.

A Pedagogy of Working with What's (T)here and Proposing What Isn't

In any given situation, there are existing conditions. A location, a budget, available tools, the chain of circumstances that have dictated these elements and the working materials that derive from them. This can be a starting point from which to observe, analyze, and take notes. How do histories—an acknowledgment of points of departure and reference—inform the directions in which a school (or an organization, a collective, a group) moves? How can current and past models be examined and learned from, and how can existing pieces be recombined and added to in order to build holistic design and art curricula? When state universities and other public institutions that ostensibly provide accessible public education—many of which have been increasingly starved of resources—become difficult to access, is it possible to identify other public offerings that remain truly open and available? What does it look like to identify and foster places where people can gather, where resources can be pooled, where education can be expansive and fluid?

Working with limited resources is itself a mode of learning. In working with what's already there, a productive constraint is engaged, an active inquiry: What are the tools that are most widely available, and how might these be put to use?

With a specific focus on its immediate location, Los Angeles—yet in a manner that might be recreated anywhere—the Southland Institute asks: How might learners engage the access they have to public schools, public offerings at private schools, museums, galleries, libraries, archives, parks? What learning already happens or could happen within the spaces that people live in, work in, and move through: living rooms, kitchens, studios, sidewalks?

When little is available in the way of dedicated resources, options exist to leverage whatever is at hand, creating connections, bringing together that which is already in proximity but perhaps not yet in dialogue. The Southland Institute maintains and circulates an evolving list of excellent courses that are available for free or at low cost at area community colleges, public universities, and extension programs. Prior to COVID-19, we organized open public discussions in existing museum and gallery exhibitions with free admission and hosted our own events in partnership with local organizations such as the MAK Center for Art and Architecture, Los Angeles Contemporary Archive, Laurel Doody Library Supply, the Brand Library and Art Center, Los Angeles City College, Workshop Project, and Otis College of Art and Design, to name a few. Lacking a physical space of our own, we sometimes rented space from community organizations (such as the Women's Center for Creative Work and the Velaslavasay Panorama) to host events and classes, supporting accessible spaces with rental fees.

Working with what's there can be an act of reconfiguration, as one re-sorts, reshuffles, rearranges all that is available, using everything and wasting nothing. It can also be an act of subtraction and/or distillation that raises important questions. Working with what's there can (and often does) reveal things that may have otherwise gone unnoticed. It can also reveal what is lacking. Does what you need already exist? Are you able to access it? If not, there can be a shift from "working with what's there" to "proposing what isn't." This prompts a pedagogy of proposals, of suggestions for augmenting the existing options with things that are necessary but absent.

In identifying a conspicuous lack of affordable, rigorous, accessible, thoughtfully implemented offerings in post-secondary design and art education in the United States, the Southland Institute sets out to propose an alternative framework and to engage the pedagogies at work within it.

A Pedagogy of Attention

As the world perpetually clamors for our attention, to what extent does attending to such demands bring focus, fulfillment, or an engaged self? As interruptions escalate, some tune out while others attempt to keep up, often to no avail. Attention is an act of giving. When what we receive in return for this generosity is a further demand, the notion of attention itself can seem futile, abusive, laborious. Passivity ensues.

As digital interconnectivity brings on, for many, a mounting sense of isolation, the question of how to cope with distraction grows more relevant. This issue is not new in education. The history of pedagogy is a genealogy of the delicate but crucial distinction between the lost focus of a straying attention and the expansive opportunities presented by a wandering mind. Compare "Are we there yet?" with "Where are we, here and now?" When class begins with attendance being taken by an alleged authority figure, we respond: "Present," "Here." Yet how accurate are these statements of presence? To pursue one's curiosities is to take attendance of oneself.

Genuine attention is a skill to be cultivated. Giving attention to what is going on around you—to what people, systems, and structures are doing, how they are behaving—provides many clues to what is going on behind the scenes.

A Pedagogy of Typographic Literacy/Fluency

Typography is a practice of attention: to letters, words, space, and proportion, to the ways that these formal elements affect the meaning of text and language. It is also a practice of attention to histories, to the ways in which letterforms and systems of writing have been used to support and/or subvert language(s), to what the form of typography can mean, and how it communicates.

At once an instrument, a tool, and a medium that exists only in the presence of and in relation to other fields, typography functions as a threshold of interdisciplinary critical practice. Its components—letters, margins, structures, words, lines, paragraphs, spacing, grids, alignment, hierarchies, scale, weight, texture—inflect everything that comes into contact with language. This makes typography an ideal point of departure and return for a wide range of intellectual inquiries. Placing a typographically attuned pedagogy at the core of a curriculum requires that creative practitioners of all kinds hone a craft at once ubiquitous and often neglected, giving close consideration to the world via the way humans have made language visible and understanding how these typographic structures functionally provide a common boundary that transcends discipline. Typographic literacy comes with dedicated study, fluency with sustained practice. It is an ongoing aim to provide opportunities for both.

In 2019–20, the Southland Institute offered a series of affordable or free one- and two-day workshops led by both local and international practitioners on variable font design (Dinamo), web typography (Masato Nakada), writing using found material and ephemera that we keep on our digital devices (nicole killian), and revival type design (Jaimey Shapey), alongside a public lecture series and an annually recurring curriculum that includes longer-form courses: *cf.* (Adam Feldmeth), which provides an occasion to collectively consider cultural production and praxis set in direct comparison with references of substance to advance a contextual discourse; *typographies* (Joe Potts), in which participants develop self-directed text-based projects with close attention to the craft and meaning of their typographic implementation; and *Text/Space* (Carmen Amengual), in which participants examine different dynamics between text and spatiality, develop linguistic awareness, and explore functions and modulations of the act of reading and writing.

A Pedagogy of Making Public and of Publication

If we define publication as "making something generally known" as well as "preparing and issuing books, journals, websites, blogs, etc.," a pedagogy of publication and of making public is a typographic pedagogy that incorporates a process of research, reading, critical thinking, making connections, revising, understanding structures and systems, and sharing. The act of publication—gathering, editing, arranging, sequencing, composing, choosing typefaces, typesetting, printing, programming—demands and brings together a vast range of skills and inquiries. Augmenting the traditional exercise of "writing a paper," this opens the process of learning not only to writing but also to design, production, distribution, and the meaning that continues to be made via the decisions and actions that make up these processes.

A Pedagogy of Revealing Infrastructure

Understanding systems both visible and invisible is key to understanding how our world is structured, how buildings and networks are assembled, how water and electricity flow, how power operates, how systems of oppression are perpetuated. Examining and understanding systems are required in order to design and build and to productively dismantle and transform. In making visible the structures that surround, contain, support, and frame the world, we analyze their functionality and effectiveness. In examining the infrastructures of a city—plumbing, roads, electricity, zoning, building codes—we can learn how it is put together and where the stresses and the fractures are. In discovering and articulating these things it becomes possible to ask whether they can be repaired or if they need to be replaced. In examining the underlying structures of other objects of interest—from creatively generated artifacts to institutions to systems of education—we can learn similar things. How was this made? Where do these materials come from? How were they sourced? What were the labor conditions under which they were generated? Where do they succeed and where do they not? Such questions help us move closer to an understanding that can influence future action and responses.

A Pedagogy of Increasing Access

A core tenet of the Southland Institute is identifying and implementing educational opportunities that are both rigorous and accessible. This is tied to a belief in the value of increasing access to knowledge, tools, information, and the spaces and frameworks through which these may be shared.

- Increasing financial accessibility: A significant motivation for the founding of the Southland Institute was the lack of high-quality, low-cost design education options. With the exception of a handful of thoughtfully, progressively, discerningly run public programs throughout the United States (e.g., Rutgers, UCLA, UIC, VCU, to name a few—many of which derive a degree of elitism through selectivity, if not cost), many formal education programs in design, and the institutions that have been historical mainstays of forward-thinking, rigorous design education, are private art schools whose sticker prices now often exceed $50,000 a year for tuition alone. More problematic still, at many of these schools, faculty are significantly underpaid, both with regard to a cost-of-living metric and to the percentage of the education cost. In this configuration the structure of the class is accessible only to the affluent or those who have placed themselves in significant debt, while at the same time paying an unsustainable wage to the very instructors without whom the classes could not exist, many of whom are themselves in significant debt from having paid for the educations that provide the credentials required for these jobs.
- Increasing physical, sensory, and temporal accessibility: In the absence of the resources that enable dedicated space, programming events such as talks and workshops requires coordination with existing institutions. In many cases these institutions—themselves often operating on a shoestring and with few resources—lack accessible architectures. It is an aim of the Southland Institute to have its programming be physically, visually, audibly, and temporally accessible and to propose amendments and alterations to partnering venues to increase access toward these ends.

Igor Sikorsky builds the first practical helicopter

- Intellectual accessibility: How can we make higher education intellectually accessible to everyone? How can we create a platform for content and conversation that is available to audiences and participants with widely varied experiences of formal and informal education? A continual attention is paid to vocabularies and translational strategies that open rather than close spaces of learning. The core of intellectual accessibility is recognizing and truly valuing the fact that different experiences shape different insights and perspectives, and that a multiplicity of perspectives invariably enriches and expands everyone's learning.

Of course, none of these pedagogies (nor the larger body from which these are drawn) are isolated. Points of contact abound, as do places of entry. These pedagogies have grown, and will continue to grow, out of conversations, conflicts, practices, mistakes, jobs, lives, discomfort, play, families, friendships. The questions asked here can be entered through language, documented by giving that language form. In typographic terms, the page size may be fixed, constrained to what's at hand, but much remains possible within this allotted space. When the margins are activated, the area within is given definition, structure, air. A framework is put into play for documenting, sharing, and composing findings, as well as that which can't be found. These pedagogies, like the Southland Institute itself, are necessarily incomplete, unfinished, mutable, nonterminal.

Thanks to Jessica Hoffmann for her editorial suggestions.

WORKSHOP PROJECT: A PREFACE

YASMIN GIBSON and JESSICA WEXLER

I am stretched on your grave
And will lie there forever
If your hands were in mine
I'd be sure we'd not sever
My apple tree my brightness
It's time we were together
For I smell of the earth
And am worn by the weather
— Sinéad O'Connor, "I Am Stretched on Your Grave"

This much is true in the United States: it cannot be denied that the university is a place of refuge, and it cannot be accepted that the university is a place of enlightenment. In the face of these conditions one can only sneak into the university and steal what one can. To abuse its hospitality, to spite its mission, to join its refugee colony, its gypsy encampment, to be in but not of—this is the path of the subversive intellectual in the modern university.
—Fred Moten and Stefano Harney, "The Only Possible Relationship to the University Today Is a Criminal One"[1]

We begin with a lament for the loss of our once guiding star: a belief in the transformative potential of formal innovation in the space of the graphic design curricula and class projects. We loved writing those projects. They felt meaningful and rewarding, and we understood them to be spaces that could create change, movement. We (and our students) could marvel at the formal outcomes together, witnessing the transformation of received values and priorities. In the time between the early 2000s and the now (2021), design has gone supernova. The visual outcome has stopped speaking. It doesn't reveal anything beyond its surface, which is immediately overwritten in an endless stream of making. And so we shift our attention from that now-dead star to the transformative potential of the black hole that its implosion created.

We now find ourselves grieving a value system that we once *passionately* believed drove our particular strain of graphic design pedagogy. We lament the subsequent loss of our belief in subculture, and by extension the power of resisting "mainstream" visual culture as "meta program learning outcomes,"[2] and we acknowledge that our understanding of graphic design pedagogies is tribal and as such stems from the oral traditions of the crit room, passed down through a family tree of a handful of individuals over the course of sixty-odd years. We're inscribing this folklore/history

1. "Thesis 1," in Fred Moten and Stefano Harney, "The University and the Undercommons: Seven Theses," *Social Text* 22, no. 2 (2004): 101.

2. You might respond: Those were never the meta-program learning outcomes for a graphic design program! But they are/were at CalArts—which is to say, they defined the curriculum, which was, like all folklore, subjective.

with a post-Internet coming-of-age tale. Spoiler alert: The outcome is no longer transformative.

As chroniclers of graphic design pedagogy, we submit this collection of annotated prompts, which, we believe, is how much of the history of graphic design pedagogy has been created: through accounts of the lived experience of its practitioners. The history of this pedagogy is most accessible and most clearly visible through its project briefs, which are always evolving and adapting to shifts in technology and practice. "Thinking through making" is a shibboleth of the subculture of design education in which we locate our practice, our educations, and our own evolving pedagogy. The history of design pedagogy is the documentation of the educator thinking through making projects, syllabi, and curricula. The vocation of the design educator is, at its core, a narrative endeavor. The fundamental pedagogy of Workshop Project has been that our syllabi function as forms of critical writing.

Every thought is a dream
Rushing by in a stream
Bringing life to our kingdom of doing
—Earth, Wind & Fire, "Fantasy"

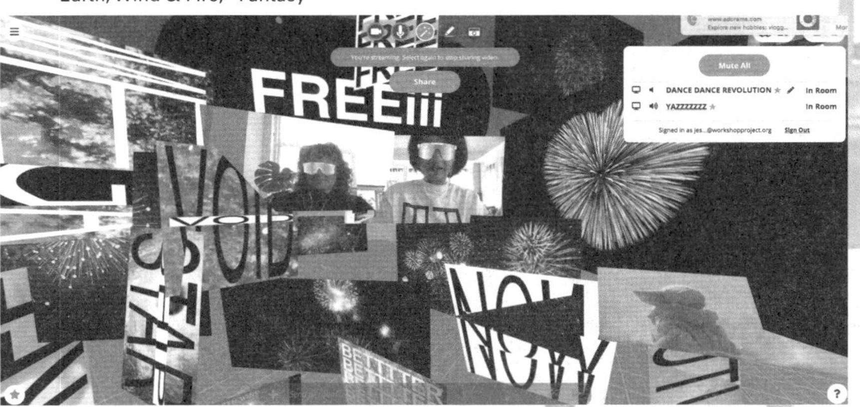

Flash-forward to today: a time of accelerated disruption, thanks to technology, biology, and the erosion of hierarchies that were constructed as a bulwark against the lived experiences of the many to preserve the narratives of the few. As of this writing (mid-pandemic 2021), we are collectively witnessing a once-in-a-generation confluence of events that is reshaping education at all levels.

The (art and design) academy's primary function has devolved from embracing the complexities of emerging culture (outward- and forward-looking) to being a patronage system that shelters and archives practices (backward- and inward-looking) whose values stifle responses to cultural change. Though maybe it was always that way.[3] Do we meet the world where it is, ask it to meet us where

3. Chad Wellmon, "The Scholar's Vocation," *Aeon*, April 17, 2020, https://aeon.co/essays/weber-diagnosed-the-ills-of-the-modern-university-and-prescribed-the-cure.

we are, or create a third space that extends our understanding of what is possible in the now?

We call for a new design pedagogy that expands the narrative work of the design educator to embrace the structural, financial, and administrative. The possibilities for exercising agency and movement are distributed in the administrative labyrinths beyond the classroom.

To create change requires imagining pathways and access to education that do not yet exist. They must be written into existence. Like the syllabus and the project brief, the administrative work of the design educator should also function as a form of writing and inquiry. This is the space where concrete factors that determine access—such as funding, facilities, and our ability to engage underserved populations—intersect with narrative and critical potential. As one inhabits the structure beyond the classroom—as a lichen, as a symbiont, as a fugitive—one's movements, both within it and outside it, change the nature of the whole. And as one moves through the administrative terrain of the institution, the notion of authority also changes from one grounded in the accumulation of institutional knowledge and power to one grounded in participation and engagement.

The vocation of the design educator is no longer to design curricula and projects but to conceptualize and design the structure and conceptual models of delivery within and outside the institution. Systemic change is no longer possible at the level of the project or course or curriculum because possible actions are limited to the reorganization of content. Equity, pluralization, greater agency, and access are only possibly through changes at the level of the structural, where the hierarchies and pathways that determine access to knowledge can be reimagined. We now believe that systemic, structural change and evolution are possible only at the institutional level. At the level of the project or classroom, we educators are limited by what we can see, make, and understand. The work that lies in front of us is broader in scope by orders of magnitude.

Hold up
Wait a minute
Let us put some booooom in it
— Anquette, "Shake It (Do the 61st)"

In 2012, developmental biologists Scott Gilbert, Jan Sapp, and

Alfred Tauber wrote, "We perceive only that part of nature that our technologies permit, and so too, our theories about nature are constrained by what our technologies allow us to observe."[4] Scientific discoveries and technological advances continue to expand our sight and understanding, providing us with conceptual models—tools—that allow us to map things we can't yet fully see and don't yet understand. In our investigation of new structural models for design education, we are currently focused on two contemporary models of organization and exchange from the fields of natural science and digital technology: the holobiont and the blockchain.

Holobiont is a term originally defined by evolutionary biologist Lynn Margulis that describes an assemblage of a host and the many other species living in or around it, which together form a discrete ecological unit.[5] The structure of the holobiont challenges our conventional way of thinking about the body as a self-contained, genetically pure, singular entity. The implications of this conceptual model extend to our narratives surrounding evolution itself. Instead of the fittest individual rising to genetic dominance, we now believe that "life did not take over the globe by combat, but by networking."[6] Similarly, the model of the holobiont challenges our pedagogical master narratives around the author, genius, and the inviolate work of art.

Another twenty-first-century model, the blockchain, has helped us understand the potential for structures that embrace the values of distributed authority, trust, and stability, and that also resist monopoly and privatization. This is another structure that represents a first step in the potential reordering of our critical civic protocols and infrastructures in areas such as finance and education.

Enter Economic Space Agency, a self-described "group of radical economists, distributed systems architects, game designers, activists, monetary theorists & content creators deeply passionate about the economy."[7] The group is a start-up exploring post-capitalist crypto-economic networks as "economic structures capable of expressing the values of community, care, biosphere, and other intangibles." They are prototyping a peer-to-peer economic-networking protocol that is open and free to use. In so doing, they are also creating a new economic lexicon that can express ideas and values beyond the limits of current capitalist network protocols and economic terminology. As Benjamin Lee, ECSA's chief economic linguist, observes, "The nature of our economic networks is bound by the expressivity of the language that can conceive them." Just as technology helps extend our perception of the world beyond the limits of our physical senses, so language helps extend our ability

4. Scott Gilbert, Jan Sapp, and Alfred Tauber, "A Symbiotic View of Life: We Have Never Been Individuals," *Quarterly Review of Biology* 87, no. 4 (December 2012): 325–34.

5. Lynn Margulis, *Symbiosis as a Source of Evolutionary Innovation*, 1991. Shout out to Randy Nakamura of FREE 2018.

6. Ibid.

7. See https://economicspace.agency/vision/#language.

to imagine what is possible. Conceptual models like the holobiont and the next-gen blockchain provide us with tools to map the now and create structural prototypes in design education that reflect the needs and priorities of a new age.

> Presidential party
> No one wants to dance
> Looking for a new star
> To put you in a trance
> Let's go all the way

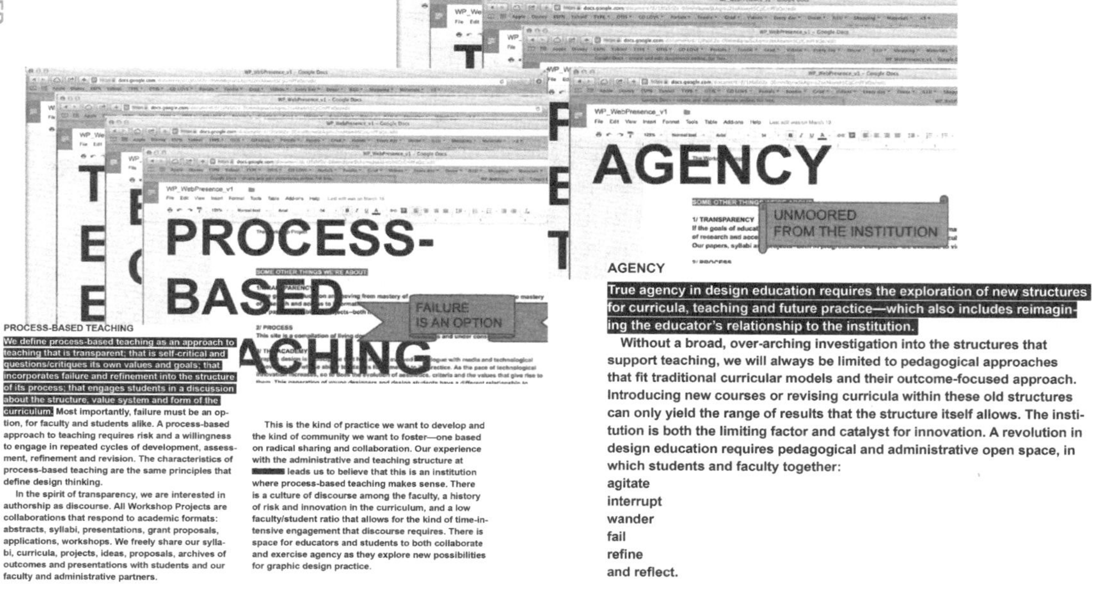

PROCESS-BASED TEACHING

We define process-based teaching as an approach to teaching that is transparent; that is self-critical and questions/critiques its own values and goals; that incorporates failure and refinement into the structure of its process; that engages students in a discussion about the structure, value system and form of the curriculum. Most importantly, failure must be an option, for faculty and students alike. A process-based approach to teaching requires risk and a willingness to engage in repeated cycles of development, assessment, refinement and revision. The characteristics of process-based teaching are the same principles that define design thinking.

In the spirit of transparency, we are interested in authorship as discourse. All Workshop Projects are collaborations that respond to academic formats: abstracts, syllabi, presentations, grant proposals, applications, workshops. We freely share our syllabi, curricula, projects, ideas, proposals, archives of outcomes and presentations with students and our faculty and administrative partners.

This is the kind of practice we want to develop and the kind of community we want to foster—one based on radical sharing and collaboration. Our experience with the administrative and teaching structure at ████ leads us to believe that this is an institution where process-based teaching makes sense. There is a culture of discourse among the faculty, a history of risk and innovation in the curriculum, and a low faculty/student ratio that allows for the kind of time-intensive engagement that discourse requires. There is space for educators and students to both collaborate and exercise agency as they explore new possibilities for graphic design practice.

AGENCY

True agency in design education requires the exploration of new structures for curricula, teaching and future practice—which also includes reimagining the educator's relationship to the institution.

Without a broad, over-arching investigation into the structures that support teaching, we will always be limited to pedagogical approaches that fit traditional curricular models and their outcome-focused approach. Introducing new courses or revising curricula within these old structures can only yield the range of results that the structure itself allows. The institution is both the limiting factor and catalyst for innovation. A revolution in design education requires pedagogical and administrative open space, in which students and faculty together:
agitate
interrupt
wander
fail
refine
and reflect.

> Let's go all the way
> Yeah, yeah, yeah, yeah, yeah
> Let's go all the way
> —Sly Fox, "Let's Go All the Way"

We started Workshop Project in 2016 with a presentation at Otis College of Art and Design called "Now = Void" that announced the end of our studio practices and careers as we knew them. We proposed abandoning client-driven practice in favor of the then decidedly uncool and marginally relevant field of graphic design education. It was an unknown entity at that point, one that existed only in our imaginations. We moved forward as if it were real. Our first step would be to establish a "pedagogical design practice," not knowing precisely what it looked like or what we would make. We began by asking the following questions through making artifacts of design education:

> What the fuck does one teach in a contemporary graphic design curriculum?
> What does an educator make?
> How do we participate in larger conversations about cultural production from inside academia?

The syllabi, presentations, and, most importantly, the annual FREE Design Educators Workshop we produce began as tools that help up bridge the meta and the concrete and evolve our thinking about design education. Workshop Project both informs and is informed by our work as educators and administrators. We are interested in a specific kind of dialogue nested within the mainstream of graphic design education. And we have learned that there is a need for community, a network among design educators who share an interest in looking at their practice critically.

In the years since, our "day jobs" have changed significantly. Both of us have moved into administration in our respective programs, Jessica as chair and Yasmin as program director. Today, mid-pandemic, we frame our work in a different way, asking different questions. But the importance of our fantasy lives and narrative work has not diminished. Graphic design education has been pushed, by a confluence of cataclysmic world events, into its next evolution. Our conviction today is that the role of the design educator is to create the conceptual models that help us see the future now and envision possible trajectories.

Our narrative design work lies at the intersection of the fantastical and the actionable. We are done talking about the future. We are believers in "the future now." In his 2016 talk "Tomorrow Never Known" at European Lab, the music critic Simon Reynolds stated that if something is thinkable, it is doable and therefore not of the future but of the now. The *real* future "is beyond our imagining, and even beyond our desiring." What we do in our practice may seem speculative, impractical, or even implausible. But we believe that if we can conceptualize or describe a thing, it can be prototyped and in some way implemented. The speculative is real. The future is now.

THE DESIGN CAVE: NOTES FOR A PREHISTORY OF GRAPHIC DESIGN PEDAGOGY

IGNACIO VALERO

Caves, Images, Signs, and Meanings

The brisk and invigorating walk I took that sunny summer day from the beautiful medieval town of Santillana del Mar to the nearby Cuevas de Altamira in the Cantabrian region of northern Spain is firmly etched in my memory. I recall my quick stride down a winding road to the entrance of the famed caves, as I delighted in my wanderlust and absorbed the peaceful sight of rolling hills, a verdant countryside peppered by the hedgerows of cultivated fields and pastures, generously kept alive by their proximity to the Cantabrian Sea. I was sweating profusely under the canicular heat but happy finally to be near fulfilling an earnest pilgrimage I had wanted to take ever since settling in Madrid, some years before, for my environmental education-project with the United Nations Environment Program and the Iberian-American Institute. The soothing coolness of the cave was a refreshing change as we entered into a semi-mythical past of chiaroscuros, animal figures in motion, vivid colors, abstract shapes, and claviform designs, and stood in awe at the stenciled images of ancient hands that had recently completed those magnificent and evocative images. Here "heart and hand" fused to express the nurturance, mystery, and vastness of the human and nonhuman condition. It was fortunate that I was one of the last visitors that summer allowed to experience the caves' aura before they were permanently closed, like the caves in Lascaux, due to the decay caused by the breath and body heat of innumerable daily visitors.

Prehistoric rock paintings in Manda Guéli Cave in the Ennedi Mountains, Chad, Central Africa

First commercial nuclear power is produced at Calder Hall, Cumbria, England

Those caves were closed just as another, albeit figurative, one opened: In 2021, "cave syndrome" was named by *Scientific American*.[1] This psychological phenomenon seems to be a sort of Lacanian fear to confront an ineffable "real," an inability to come out of social seclusion after enduring a long year of isolation, and psychological and material trauma, caused by the ravaging effects

1. Melba Newsome, "'Cave Syndrome' Keeps the Vaccinated in Social Isolation," *Scientific American*, May 3, 2021, https://www.scientificamerican.com/article/cave-syndrome-keeps-the-vaccinated-in-social-isolation1/.

of the COVID-19 pandemic that sent those of us privileged enough into forced hibernation to weather the grave impacts of this rapidly evolving virus—a situation needlessly worsened by the criminal indifference and manipulation of many in power for whom profit, financial speculation, and surplus value always come before humanity. Tragically, too, isolation has not been an option for the majority of the belatedly "discovered" *essential* workers both in the Global South and the wealthier societies, all of whom I humbly honor for helping us to stay alive, even at the price of their own lives.

Given how profound and durable the idea of the cave is, our ancestral collective unconscious must be at play. Caves were, after all, many of our early dwellings, hostile and protective at the same time: "In the darkness and complexity of caves, all senses are on alert for ground-level hazards and the potential of lurking dangers. . . . However, a cave's enveloping nature also offers security, once the cave and its layout is understood."[2] In spite of our early nomadic existence for hundreds of millennia, our *Homo neanderthal*, *naledi*, and *sapiens* ancestors often dwelled in caves or constructed cave-like structures to protect themselves from the elements and dangers outside—which today we surmise through the material and cultural traces left in caves all around the world.

The cave plays a role, too, in the cultural primacy given to "seeing the light," in distinguishing it from the "shadows," and ideally comprehending their yin-yang dialectics. Because our sensory, cognitive, and emotional coordination developed over millennia, alongside an increasingly diverse and complex net of social and urban structures, our languages, images, and communications became more sophisticated. Words began as pictures, and transformed over time into more stylized pictographs, hieroglyphs, ideograms and logograms, and alphabets.[3] Instead of a rupture between early oral and visual communication strategies and later textual and written cultural developments, much continuity between image and word has been maintained.[4] This continuity allows a multiplicity of "readings—pictorial, iconic, semantic—that are at once valid and simultaneous."[5]

A study of visual storytelling, language, epistemology, and psychosomatics, from prehistory to the contemporary, may open us to a "prehistory" or "cave history" of graphic design pedagogy that is

2. https://artsandculture.google.com/story/prehistoric-art-in-modern-and-contemporary-creations/7QVBYIHNu32FGA?hl=en.

3. See, for example, the work of artist Xu Bing and his search for the "living word": Xu Bing, *Book from the Sky to Book from the Ground* (Woodbridge, UK: ACC Art Books, 2020); Xu Bing, *Book from the Ground: From Point to Point* (Cambridge, MA: MIT Press, 2018); and Mathieu Borysevicz, ed., *The Book About Xu Bing's Book from the Ground* (Cambridge, MA: MIT Press, 2014).

4. See Thomas S. Mullaney, *The Chinese Typewriter: A History* (Cambridge, MA: MIT Press, 2014); Mark Edward Lewis, *Writing and Authority in Early China* (Albany: SUNY Press, 1999); Christopher Leigh Connery, *The Empire of the Text: Writing and Authority in Early Imperial China* (Lanham, MD: Rowman and Littlefield, 1998); and Haun Saussy, *The Problem of a Chinese Aesthetic* (Stanford: Stanford University Press, 1993).

fully entwined with our material and nonmaterial history and culture, specifically with our long journey through religion, mathematics, philosophy, art, politics, economics, ecology, psychology, and ethics. It aligns south and north, east and west with the evolution of human culture, exemplified in the intergenerational teachings embedding those early hominids over millennia within the fertile yet precarious *humus* that the "arts of language and the languages of art" allowed the human experiment to unfold to the present, from the perforated shells of Cueva de los Aviones some 115,000 years ago to the drawing made in Blombos Cave almost 75,000 years ago to the "ladder" design possibly rendered by Neanderthals 64,000 ago in La Pasiega Cave to El Castillo's hands and some of the claviform signs of the "Gran Sala" of Altamira around 40 to 36 millennia ago to Chauvet, Lascaux, and indeed many other great cave visual examples throughout the globe.[6]

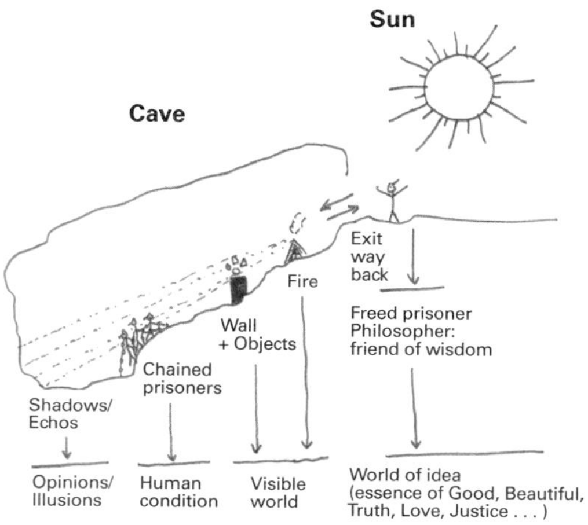

Plato's Allegory of the Cave

"Allegory of the Cave" is presented in Book VII (514a–520d) of the *Republic* of Plato, the *Res-Publica*, or more precisely, *Politeia*, on the government of the Greek *polis*.[7] It encapsulates Plato's pedagogical, epistemological, political, ethic, gymnastic, aesthetic, and technical project and constitutes a kind of epistemological *axis mundi* for his philosophical corpus, on the nature of truth, reality, education, justice, governance, and the illusions and mirages of the image.

Illustration describing Plato's theories of the Forms through his images of the sun, the divided line, and the cave.

The story goes like this: In the dark of the cave, shackled prisoners can only see in one direction, toward the wall of cave. Behind them are puppeteers whose figures, backlit by a fire, cast shadows on the cave wall. The prisoners mistake this false puppet world for reality, not realizing that what they are seeing are merely the outlines of forms, rather than the objects themselves.

From time to time, chained individuals are set free. As the newly freed prisoners ascend out of the depths of the cave, they begin to discover the different stages that lead to a final liberation: exiting the narrow entrance of the cave to behold the real illuminated by the

5. Mary E. Hocks and Michelle R. Kendrick, eds., *Eloquent Images: Word and Image in the Age of New Media* (Cambridge, MA: MIT Press, 2003), 7.

6. See Bruno David, *Cave Art* (London: Thames and Hudson, 2017); Randall White, *Prehistoric Art: The Symbolic Journey of Humankind* (New York: Abrams, 2003); Georges Bataille, *The Cradle of Humanity: Prehistoric Art and Culture*, ed. Stuart Kendall (New York: Zone Books, 2009); and Georges Bataille, *Lascaux or the Birth of Art* (Geneva: Skira, 1955).

7. Plato, "The Allegory of the Cave," trans. Paul Shorey, in *The Collected Dialogues of Plato*, ed. Edith Hamilton (New York: Random House, 1963), 747–52.

sun. Those liberated are so joyful at this newfound world that they rush to share, Bodhisattva-like, this new reality with their former fellow prisoners and invite them to come up to the light and experience this truth for themselves. But the return is not easy; it is fraught by a return to blindness in the dark, making a smooth journey to the world they knew before impossible. Plato leaves open the possibility that those in the cave cannot comprehend what is being shared and thus may likely kill the intruder trying to jolt them out of their shadowy, sleepy complacency in the "waters of *Lethe*."

This allegory's conceptual architecture, which describes a movement from shadowy darkness to the realm of the visible and sensible (aesthetics) to the realm of form and ideas, was to exert an inordinate influence over the next two thousand years. It is again most relevant today with the pressing questions on the "real" and "reality" posed by a wide assortment of fields from relativity, quantum mechanics, genetics, psychoanalysis, neuroscience, cybernetics, AI, robotics, virtual reality, aesthetics, design, technology, globalization, climate change, politics, economics, education, and other various contemporary developments. From this viewpoint, Plato could be understood as the first "media" analyst in Western thought. Indeed, philosopher, mathematician, writer, and political activist Alain Badiou—an inspiration for my interpretations here—takes full advantage of this possibility when, in his retelling of the cave metaphor, he equates it to an "enormous movie theater," where a large screen goes all the way up to the ceiling and "gets lost in the dark." I fancy this description comes close to portraying those monumental 3-D IMAX ("Image Maximum") screens.

The Republic's Pedagogy

> The seriousness with which Plato regards education, especially early education in poetry and other arts, is seen in the sheer amount of attention he gives it. . . . As we see, the state as a whole is largely structured around its educational system, and its other features are tailored to allow the educational system to work. Plato holds that only if the state performs the crucial task of education properly can it succeed.[8]
>
> —George Klosko

I purposely began the enumeration of the *Politeia*'s various fields with pedagogy, for in a fundamental sense Plato's political proposal is the education of the philosopher-king, with all the attendant sociocultural, physical, and philosophical scaffolding necessary to build such *Res-Publica*, the "thing" charged with justly governing the city-commons and environs, the public "time-place" of the *polis*.

The Republic was written around 375 BCE by a distraught Plato as he witnessed the political, economic, and psychological chaos brought on by the Peloponnesian War, thirty years of dead, plague, and hostility that ended Athens's Golden Age, though the city itself—after untold suffering—was spared complete destruction and

8. George Klosko, *The Development of Plato's Political Theory* (Oxford: Oxford University Press, 2006), 124.

enslavement. The political and identity vacuum had left Athens prey to the extremes of populism and tyranny, and Plato with his *Republica* sought to provide an irenic path forward out the dark tunnels of fear, ignorance, and demagoguery, imagining the philosophical, political, and pedagogical principles on which a just city-state composed of a just humanity could be based and constructed.[9]

But Plato's political (and aesthetic) pedagogy cannot be fully understood without understanding his mistrust of the seductive and obscuring impact of the drawn image and the spoken word, *eikasia* and *rhētorike tekhnē*, facilitated by the widespread epochal crisis his world sustained after the Peloponnesian War. Confronted with fake teachers and saviors—not unlike those of the Mosaic and Babylonian crises of faith and captivity suffered by the early Hebrews—prescribing graven images and idolatry, Plato could not help but be a stern iconoclast. The way out of such a political and cultural morass was to develop critical thinking, a hermeneutics, that arduous awakening from the slumber of illusion that truth (*aletheia*) requires. It is a necessary putting back together of the fragments, *anamnesis*, a re-membering, a breaking of the spell,

9. Chastised throughout the ensuing ages as merely a political utopia, this "nowhere," *ou-topos* (a name coined centuries later by Thomas More during the European Renaissance), is key to such enduring relevance. As More himself clarified in an addendum, what was named was "*not Utopie but rather rightely my name is Eutopie, a place of felicitie,*" the "good place," not the "no-place." With "utopia," he dared to envision, once more, a Platonic, humane state with the highest social, political, and legal guarantees and protections, and his work challenged, as Plato's *Politeia* had, the political and economic status quo through its particularly insightful exposure of the cruel "enclosure of the commons," which destroyed the medieval communal lands, leaving behind hordes of dispossessed and starving peasants in favor of sheep-grazing latifundia on which a new agrarian capitalism was finding its political, economic, social and cultural base. Its merciless "enclosure laws" were one major instance of "primitive" or "original" accumulation through purportedly "legal" means.

rupturing the amnesia produced by the shadowy images of the cave or the golden calf.

•

Why do I dwell on what might appear to be some kind of 2,400-year-old history? Because I feel that today, confronted with the simultaneous and intertwined acceleration of crises at the ecological, economic, and political levels globally, we continue to be intoxicated with our winner-takes-all superpower status, our great wealth, advanced technology, and global reach. And, to our peril, we are failing to absorb important lessons, warnings, and reminders from the ancient and recent past, be they from old or new empires or any other kind of national or international arrangements. I would, more specifically, suggest that for the purposes of the pedagogical story at hand, revisiting this saga might help us understand some of the conundrums the graphic design field and practice, and by extension the entire field and practice of design, are facing today.

In very crucial ways, many of the rules of the game were set up for us long ago. As the great British process philosopher and mathematician Alfred North Whitehead wrote in the past century, "The safest general characterization of the European philosophical tradition is that it consists of a series of footnotes to Plato." Though it would also be fair to say that Plato was in turn an insightful interpreter of his time and the philosophical tradition that we characterize now as pre-Socratic. It is necessary as well to remember that simultaneously, around the same centuries—eighth to third century BCE—the philosophical and religious developments in Persia, India, and China were no less sophisticated than Judeo-Greco-Roman thought.

But the European philosophical tradition, Plato proper and, by association, his mentor Socrates and his disciple Aristotle, are necessary for our pedagogical story to make sense, because **1.** their methodic naming and conceptualizing traveled to the four corners of the world after the Middle Ages, with European colonialism, the Protestant Reformation and the Roman Catholic Counter-Reformation, the Scientific Revolution, and the development of capitalism, and **2.** because such naming and conceptualizing, born of profound social, economic, and political instability, and of the identity dislocations produced by the cultural, educational, and knowledge polarization of the Athens of his day, is being, once more, uncannily reenacted in our crisis-ridden contemporary world. Moreover, what Plato wrote might have been relegated to oblivion had it not been for the fact that his writings and influence survived through their marriage with Neoplatonic Hellenistic Judaism, Roman Christianity, and medieval Islamic and Byzantine scholars and clerics, up to our present era.

Perhaps we are not so far from the cave after all.

The following is a revised syllabus for a class taught at the California College of the Arts from 2014–19. I offer it as an example of how design pedagogy can be mobilized for socially and ecologically positive ends.

Media Matters: A Semiotics, Ecology and Political Economy of the Image and the Commons

This graduate studio/course aims to experiment with concepts, images, and forms with an ethical animus to better understand the evolution of text, word, and image directed toward socially and ecologically positive ends. It explores the role of design and graphic design in a practice of shared commons within rapidly changing technologies, ecologies, and global and local geopolitical and cultural contexts. The post-truth and hyper-truth Artificial Intelligence era of platform surveillance and emotional capitalism, invasive neuro-technologies, consumerist "augmented" realities, deep fakes, fanatical populisms, and xenophobia, along with worsening climate change, has blurred the social, biological, and psychological boundaries of the "real" and has created a never-ending "production of subjectivity." How can design respond to these deeply troubling systemic conditions beyond mere PR "solutionism" and/or naive techno-fetishisms, and deploy its powerful arsenal of insights and tools at its disposal?

Cybernetic informatic utopias have been largely superseded by dystopian worlds of obscene concentration of wealth, ecological destruction, and expanding emotional and physical precarity, which I have called the "*emotariat* burnout." It is a "brave new world" of fast-paced media images and sound bites, infotainment and infomercials, and social media banality and/or toxicity, where countries, ideologies, religions, artists, preachers, youth, celebrities, CEOs, and politicians alike are branded and sold to audiences as if fungible consumer products. Our analytical goal is to sift through this visual clutter of memes, logos, slogans, and hidden and seductive persuasions in order to shed some light and try to unravel many of the overlapping layers, through a history, semiotics, and political economy of the image and the society of the spectacle. The course is developed along three interlocking areas: **1.** "aesthetic alienation" or the ancient question of art and truth, the intelligible and the sensible; **2.** "commodity aesthetics" or the fetishism of the commodity, the society of the spectacle, and the monetization of desire through "behavioral futures"; and **3.** an *aesthetic(s) of the common(s)* suggested as one possible, more democratic practice, stemming from what I have called *EcoDomics* or the "art of living and making (in) common(s)." A synthetic diagram of concepts discussed along with an intellectual journal would be the expected assignments for the students in the more discursive side of the studio/seminar. In the associated studio course, we will explore the ideas presented in the seminar context through making. For example, analysis and insights are put to use in the design and making of antidotes, parodies, and other alternative constructions. Likewise, you will be called upon to use methods of communication and persuasion in form making for socially and ecologically positive ends.

PART I: AESTHETIC ALIENATION/THE IMAGE/DESIGN

Introduction: Toward an Epistemology of Resemblance, Representation, and the Image: The Allegory of the Cave, *Mediums*, Orders, and Frames

Google "iconoclasm," "idolatry," "aniconism"; Alain Badiou, *Plato's Republic* (New York: Columbia University Press, 2012); Plato, *Republic*, trans. G. M. A. Grube, revised by C. D. C. Reeve (ca. 380 BCE; Indianapolis: Hackett, 1992); Michel Foucault, "Preface," and "Las Meninas," in *The Order of Things* (1970; New York: Vintage, 1994)

The "Words and Things" of the "Renaissance Episteme": Magic, Science, and Erudition Share the Same Epistemic Level Beyond Frames. "The Quarrel of the Ancients and the Moderns," the Disenchantment of the World, and the "Classical Episteme": Representing Identity and Difference, the Intelligible and the Sensible, *Don Quixote*, Mathesis, and *Taxinomia*

Michel Foucault, "The Prose of the World," "Representing," and "Exchanging," in *The Order of Things*; Jacques Derrida, "The Parergon," in *The Truth in Painting* (Chicago: University of Chicago Press, 1987)

The "Modern Episteme": The Decline of Representation, Time and Science, Labor Value, Aesthetic Truth and the Question of Design.

Michel Foucault, "Labor, Life, Language," in *The Order of Things*; Michel Foucault, *This Is Not a Pipe, with Illustrations and Letters by Rene Magritte* (Berkeley: University of California Press, 1982); Jacques Rancière, "The Surface of Design," in *The Future of the Image* (London: Verso 2007)

Contemporary Epistemologies of the Global South and Ecologies of Knowledges—Africa and Latin America: "Epistemicide," Black Reason, and "Cannibal Metaphysics"

Achille Mbembe, *Critique of Black Reason* (Durham, NC: Duke University Press, 2013); Boaventura de Sousa Santos, *Epistemologies of the South: Justice Against Epistemicide* (London: Routledge, 2014); Arturo Escobar, *Encountering Development: The Making and Unmaking of the Third World* (1995; Princeton, NJ: Princeton University Press, 2012); Eduardo Viveiros de Castro, *Cannibal Metaphysics* (Minneapolis: University of Minnesota Press, 2014); Marisol de La Cadena, *Earth Beings: Ecologies of Practice Across Andean Worlds* (Durham, NC: Duke University Press, 2015); Enrique Dussel, *Politics of Liberation: A Critical Global History-Reclaiming Liberation Theology* (Norwich, UK: Hymns Ancient and Modern, 2011); Enrique Dussel, *Philosophy of Liberation* (Eugene, OR: Wipf and Stock, 2003)

Contemporary Epistemologies of the Global South and Ecologies of Knowledges—Asia: "Cognitive Justice," Consumerism, and "Confucian Perfectionism"

Pankaj Mishra, *Age of Anger: A History of the Present* (New York: Farrar, Strauss and Giroux, 2017); Sreedeep Bhattacharya,

Consumerist Encounters: Flirting with Things and Images (Oxford: Oxford University Press, 2020); Shiv Visvanathan, *A Carnival for Science: Essays on Science, Technology and Development* (Oxford: Oxford University Press, 1997); Xudong Zhang, *Postsocialism and Cultural Politics* (Durham, NC: Duke University Press, 2008); Jiang Qing, *A Confucian Constitutional Order* (Princeton, NJ: Princeton University Press, 2012); Joseph Chan, *Confucian Perfectionism: A Political Philosophy for Modern Time* (Princeton, NJ: Princeton University Press 2013); Timothy Cheek, *The Intellectual in Modern Chinese History* (Cambridge: Cambridge University Press, 2016)

PART II: COMMODITY AESTHETICS/SURVEILLANCE CAPITALISM/EMOTARIAT

Capitalism, Alienation, and the Society of the Spectacle

Karl Marx, "Estranged Labour," *Economic and Philosophical Manuscripts of 1844*, http://www.marxists.org/archive/marx/works/1844/manuscripts/labour.htm; Guy Debord, *The Society of the Spectacle* (1967; New York: Zone Books, 1995); Tiernan Morgan and Lauren Purje, "An Illustrated Guide to Guy Debord's "The Society of the Spectacle," *Hyperallergic*, August 10, 2016, https://hyperallergic.com/313435/

The Urban Sublime/On Psychogeography and Resistance: A Dérive Field Trip as Transversal Diagram

Google "Guy Debord's Theory of the Dérive"; Merlin Coverley, *Psychogeography* (Harperden, Herts, UK: Oldcastle Books, 2018)

Aesthetics, Commodity Fetishism, and the Monetization of Desire

Karl Marx, "The Fetishism of Commodities and the Secret Thereof," *Capital*, vol. 1 (Part I: "Commodities and Money," Ch. 1, "Commodities"), http://www.marxists.org/archive/marx/works/1867-c1/ch01.htm#S4; "Marx's Commodity Fetishism and Theory of Value," February 10, 2011, http://www.thesociologicalcinema.com/videos/marxs-commodity-fetishism-and-theory-of-value; Walter Benjamin, "The Work of Art in the Age of Its Technological Reproducibility (1936)," in *The Work of Art in the Age of Its Technological Reproducibility, and Other Writings on Media*, ed. Michael W. Jennings, Brigid Doherty, and Thomas Y. Levin (Cambridge, MA: Harvard University Press, 2008); Adam Turl, "The Work of Art in the Age of Digital Reproduction," May 1, 2019; http://www.redwedgemagazine.com/online-issue/digital-reproduction; Terry Eagleton, *The Ideology of the Aesthetic* (Oxford: Blackwell, 1990)

Commodity Aesthetics, Branding and Design, and the Production of Subjectivity

Wolfgang Fritz Haug, *Commodity Aesthetics: Appearance, Sexuality and Advertising in Capitalist Society* (1971; Minneapolis: University of Minnesota Press, 1986); Maurizio Lazzarato, *Signs and Machines: Capitalism and the Production of Subjectivity* (New York: Semiotext(e), 2014); Nick Srnicek, *Platform Capitalism*

(Cambridge: Polity Press, 2017); https://mashable.com/2018/01/12/facebook-dystopia/; https://www.tc.columbia.edu/articles/2020/june/how-tiktok-is-shaping-politics/; https://www.nytimes.com/2020/06/28/style/tiktok-teen-politics-gen-z.html

Surveillance Capitalism, Behavioral Futures, and the Emotariat

Shoshana Zuboff, *The Age of Surveillance Capitalism: The Fight for a Human Future at the New Frontier of Power* (New York: Public Affairs, 2019); Shoshana Zuboff, "Covid-1984: Surveillance Capitalism," May 18, 2020; https://www.youtube.com/watch?v=OoJ-yqO9A9Y; Ignacio Valero, "*Emotariat* Accelerationism and the Republic of Data," *Data Publics*, ed. Peter Mörtenböck and Helge Mooshammer (London: Routledge 2020); Joanna Kavenna, "Surveillance Capitalism is an Assault on Human Autonomy: Interview with Shoshana Zuboff," https://www.theguardian.com/books/2019/oct/04/; Noah Kulwin, "Shoshana Zuboff On Surveillance Capitalism's Threat to Democracy," *New York*, February 24, 2019, http://nymag.com/intelligencer/2019/02/; Katie Fitzpatrick, "None of Your Business," *The Nation*, April 30, 2019, https://www.thenation.com

PART III: *ECODOMICS*, "FREE" MARKETS & THE *AESTHETIC(S) OF THE COMMON(S)*

The Myth of the Free Market, The Great Recession and the Great Pandemic: COVID-19 Zoonosis, Wall Street and The Mortgaging of the Future

Ignacio Valero, "How Free is Free? Property, Markets and the Aesthetic(s) of the Common(s)," in *What We Want is Free: Critical Exchanges in Recent Art*, ed. Ted Purves and Shane Aslan Selzer (Albany: SUNY Press, 2nd ed., 2014); David Bollier, *Silent Theft: The Private Plunder of Our Common Wealth* (London: Routledge, 2003); "How Coronavirus is Changing the World: DW (German PBS) Documentary," https://www.youtube.com/watch?v=UrcD-LopNPV8; Chuck Collins, "Updates: Billionaire Wealth, US Job Losses and Pandemic Profiteers," https://inequality.org/great-divide/updates-billionaire-pandemic/; https://www.livescience.com/dangers-of-zoonoses-pandemics.html; "Viral TikTok Uses Rice to Show How Rich Jeff Bezos Is," March 2, 2020, https://www.youtube.com/watch?v=qSOVBiEotaw; Aimee Picchi, "World's Billionaires Have More Wealth than 4.6 Billion People," https://www.cbsnews.com/news/worlds-billionaires-have-more-wealth-than-4point6-billion-people-oxfam-report-today-2020-01-19/; Johns Hopkins's Coronavirus Resource Center, https://coronavirus.jhu.edu/map.html

Emotional Neurocapitalism, and the Semiocapitalist Precariat: Proletariat, Cognitariat, Emotariat

Ignacio Valero, "*EcoDomics*: Life Beyond the Neoliberal Apocalypse," in *Informal Market Worlds*, ed. Peter Mortenbock and Helge Mooshammer (Rotterdam: NAi Publishers, 2015); Raffi Khatchadourian, "What Is in Your Mind," *The New Yorker*, January

19, 2015; "Are We Ready for the Age of 'Neurocapitalism'?" *BBVA OpenMind*, March 22, 2020, https://www.bbvaopenmind.com; Sigal Samuel, "Brain-Reading Tech Is Coming: The Law Is Not Ready To Protect Us," *Vox*, December 20, 2019, https://www.vox.com/2019/8/30/20835137/; Kate Kenny, "The Effect of Affect," *Ephemera* 11, no. 3 (2011): 235–42; Emma Dowling, Rodrigo Nunes and Ben Trott, "Immaterial and Affective Labor: Explored," *Ephemera* 7, no. 1 (2007): 1–7; Patricia Ticineto Clough et al., "Notes Towards a Theory of Affect-Itself," *Ephemera* 7, no. 1 (2007): 60–77; Franco 'Bifo' Berardi, *Precarious Rhapsody: Semiocapitalism and the Pathologies of the Post-Alpha Generation* (London: Minor Compositions, 2009)

Decolonial Design, Post-Capitalist Political Economy, and the Question of the Common(s)

Arturo Escobar, *Designs for the Pluriverse: Radical Interdependency, Autonomy, and the Making of Worlds* (Durham, NC: Duke University Press, 2018); Achille Mbembe, *Out of the Dark Night: Essays on Decolonization* (New York: Columbia University Press, 2021); Arturo Escobar, "Other Worlds Are (Already) Possible: Self-Organization, Complexity and Post-Capitalist Cultures," in *World Social Forum Challenging Empires*, ed. Jai Sen and Peter Waterman (Montreal: Black Rose Books, 2009), 393–404; Madina V. Tlostanova and Walter D. Mignolo, "Global Coloniality and the Decolonial Option," *Kult 6* (Fall 2009): 130–47; Walter Mignolo, "The Collective Project Modernity/Coloniality/Decoloniality," http://waltermignolo.com/the-collective-project-modernitycolonialitydecoloniality/; Pheng Cheah, "The Limits of Thinking in Decolonial Strategies," Townsend Center for the Humanities, UC Berkeley (2006), https://townsendcenter.berkeley.edu/publications/limits-thinking-decolonial-strategies

***EcoDomics* and the *Aesthetic(s) of the Common(s)*: An Art of Living and Making (in) Common(s)**

Valero, "*EcoDomics*: Life Beyond the Neoliberal Apocalypse"; Jason W. Moore and Raj Patel, "Unearthing the Capitalocene: Towards a Reparation Ecology," *ROAR Magazine*, January 4, 2018, https://www.resilience.org/stories/2018-01-04/; James O'Connor, *Natural Causes: Essays in Ecological Marxism, Capitalism Nature Socialism* 30, no. 4 (2019); Riane Eisler, *The Real Wealth of Nations: Creating a Caring Economics* (San Francisco: Berrett-Koheler, 2007); Paolo Virno, *A Grammar of the Multitude* (New York: Semiotext(e), 2004); David Harvey, Michael Hardt, and Antonio Negri, "*Commonwealth*: An Exchange," *Artforum*, November 2009; Alan D. Schrift, *The Logic of the Gift: Toward and Ethic of Generosity* (London: Routledge, 1997)

I would like to acknowledge the invaluable support, kindness, and friendship of Geoff Kaplan over the years, and the students who partipated in our experimental studio/theory course *Media Matters* at CCA San Francisco.

MINERAL, IMMUTABLE, HISTORIOGRAPHY: HISTORY IS DESIGNED

CHRIS LEE

"[R]edemption" is . . . really more a matter of destroying the entire system of accounting. In many [Ancient] Middle Eastern cities, this was literally true: one of the common acts during debt cancelation was the ceremonial destruction of the tablets on which financial records had been kept, an act to be repeated, much less officially, in just about every major peasant revolt in history.
—David Graeber, *Debt: The First 5,000 Years*

Introduction

Graphic design history, pedagogy, and practice have had little place for the broad spectrum of things that could be included in the genre of *the document*, in spite of the fact that they are implicitly historiographical. The theoretical literature around design has relatively little to say about what documents are and offers little help in cultivating a critical understanding of how they come to be. This lack seems to suggest that documents are taken for granted, a *fait accompli* or even a natural phenomenon, outside of the subjective activity of designing. Indeed, although the document may represent design's most profoundly consequential genre, design pedagogy seldom regards it as a form and format for students to consider, much less explore, as a viable field of study and practice. As the epigraph to this essay suggests, ostensibly banal documents play a definitive role in producing and maintaining unjust relations of power. The earliest documents, created as such, and exemplified by ancient Mesopotamian clay tablets, typically recorded exchange relations—often claims of debt obligation, ownership, wages, etc., with countless examples of inscriptions stating something to the effect of: "This tablet says who owes how much of what to whom and by when." David Graeber's observation shatters the fallacy that design, particularly when it entails the making of documents, can be reduced to a neutral and technical, let alone expressive, activity. Instead, it posits that it is inherently political, and, as I will sketch out briefly in this text, a matter of *claiming*, *remembering*, and *defending* documentary inscriptions. The combination of these actions is understood as an imperative and imposition of colonial power with its attendant technologies of statecraft and capitalism.[1] It is for this reason that I endeavor to sketch a designerly way of making sense of what documents are and how they come to be—to situate this genre within the critical and creative modalities of graphic design practice and its attendant theoretical discourses and pedagogical imperatives.

This historiography begins where currency and typography overlap. At first glance, this may seem idiosyncratic, arbitrary, and achronological.[2] It was initially a hunch, later given charge by Keith

1. Eve Tuck and K. Wayne Yang, "Decolonization Is Not a Metaphor," *Decolonization: Indigeneity, Education and Society* 1, no. 1, (2012): 4.

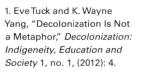

Hart's recognition of *money* and *language* as a matter of memory. In my project, imbricating these subgenres of design helps to frame things like standardization, ways of knowing, and governance as political dimensions of design, and cast them as realms of critical/creative study and exploration.[3] This essay is about historio*graphy* as a genre of design that is inherently about claims about what is/was (i.e., this is New York City vs. this is Lenapehoking) and the recognition that such claims are radically contestable. I aim to consider how history is designed to serve an agenda and to sediment assumptions about power, and how the politics of remembering might matter for how we think about, teach, and practice graphic design.

•

Around seven years ago I started a new position teaching graphic design at the University at Buffalo SUNY and found myself immediately out of my depth having to teach a course on the history of graphic design. The only starting place that I knew of was the Philip Meggs book that I had barely made it through over a decade prior as an undergraduate student. Due diligence brought me to a handful of more compelling alternatives. The option that stood out—and the one I ended up using—was Johanna Drucker and Emily McVarish's *Graphic Design History: A Critical Guide*. Their book offered a critical framework for substantive intellectual engagement with the history of a discipline to which my students imagined themselves to be initiates. Drucker and McVarish equip readers with a fundamental critical tool: a prompt to always query the "agenda" of designed artifacts. Instead of simply reading graphic design history as a linear, progressive teleology of established facts, the authors consider the various "why's" that have motivated (what we now call) graphic design, and they demonstrate how graphic design artifacts serve as active agents of history, shaping and being shaped by knowledge, identity, labor, technology, and so on. In short, their book contextualizes and politicizes design. This was exciting to me, because one thing that I hope to do as an educator is to challenge students to think critically about why they do what they do, as an inoculation against the uncritical reproduction of a world and so many of its attendant problems in which design can be

2. "[M]oney considerably expands the capacity of individuals to stabilize their own personal identity by holding something durable that embodies the desires and wealth of all the other members of society. An aid to memory, indeed. . . . Communities exist by virtue of their members' ability to exchange meanings that are substantially shared between them." See more in Keith Hart, *The Memory Bank: Money in an Unequal World* (London: Profile Books, 2000), 259–61.

3. This essay is a kind of note-to-self toward a forthcoming book project that hopes to provoke readers to discuss what it might mean to think about graphic design as being concerned primarily with the politics of *remembering*.

IBM and General Motors develop Design Augmented by Computers-1, the first computer-aided design system

implicated. Drucker and McVarish's book also enables one to extend a conception of design's agency to concerns outside of traditional disciplinary boundaries. Because if we as designers (students, educators, and practitioners) can make sense of the ways in which seeing, thinking, and acting in the world have been entangled with design, then perhaps we can understand our practices as similarly consequential, urgent, and transformative.

In my own creative-research practice, I have undertaken an ongoing exploration of design genres typically peripheral to the historiography, pedagogy, and practice of graphic design. For the past ten years, I have been interested in forms and formats of graphic design that generally fall under the category of *the document*. This started with graduate research on various forms of "alternative currency" (of which there is an incredible variety, ranging from local time-banks to labor-union tokens to cryptocurrencies) as a genre of design that entails a spectrum of concerns beyond those usually addressed in design pedagogy (for instance, how security and governance imperatives are manifest in graphics). This interest has drifted into somewhat more abstract territory and now orbits around themes of standardization, visual epistemology, and the ways in which graphic design functions as an instrument of power.

As an educator, the question motivating this work is: Why does graphic design studio pedagogy typically persist in teaching things like logos, books, posters, websites, while almost universally excluding things like driver's licenses, passports, money, tax forms, and property deeds, in spite of the profound systemic effect they have in shaping lives and reifying hierarchical power relations? To be clear, my ambition is not to create a graphic design curriculum that prepares students to become administrative officers who are proficient at designing bureaucratic forms. Rather, it is to cultivate a design student's consciousness about design's systemic consequentiality and to investigate the ways in which the subordination, marginalization, and oppression that it enables might be undone and abolished. I quote the geographer Ruth Wilson Gilmore, who has said:

> Abolition is not *absence*, it is *presence*. What the world will become already exists in fragments and pieces, experiments and possibilities. So those who feel in their gut deep anxiety that abolition means knock it all down, scorch the earth and start something new, let that go. Abolition is building the future from the present, in all of the ways we can.[4]

In other words, *abolition* is not simply a negation but rather an affirmation of the emancipated forms of sociability that already

4. Ruth Wilson Gilmore and Léopold Lambert, "Making Abolition Geography in California's Central Valley," *Funambulist*, December 20, 2018, https://thefunambulist.net/magzine/21-space-activism/interview-making-abolition-geography-california-central-valley-ruth-wilson-gilmore.

exist, and the radical imagination of other, more liberated and non-oppressive ways of being. This is resonant with what Ariella Aïsha Azoulay calls "potential history," a notion that gives an affirmative charge, and produces a radical desire to imagine and actualize that which could have been had the quasi-apocalyptic forces of colonialism and capitalism not been brought to bear on much of the world.[5] Perhaps with such interlocutors in mind, design education could take on a much more radical mandate that exceeds the persistent client-oriented service priorities that so many programs reproduce.[6]

•

What Does Design History Design?

> History is made when archives accession and "process"—as it is called—*records of interest.*
>
> —Lisa Gitelman, "Rethinking Attachment" (emphasis mine)

The past few years have seen an intensifying interest and urgency around rethinking the boundaries of the graphic design canon, and for good reason. Perhaps for as long as graphic design history has been taught at design schools, it has privileged a narrative of design's progressive orientation toward mass production and mass communication, implicitly normalizing the values of a Western colonial/statist/capitalist order.[7] It has, for instance, glossed over the significance of labor, particularly gendered labor, and instead fetishized technological progress and individual (male) genius as the drivers of history. It has, perhaps most egregiously, centered Euro-American sources and neglected the practices and histories of an entire planet's worth of other people and places. In doing so, it has cast design as an agent of progressive modernization (defined in ways that occlude the violence that this has entailed) and submerged entire worlds populated by artifacts often trivialized, for instance, as craft. Design, in other words, has been designated as an agent of "progress."[8]

Within this discursive space, there are indispensable efforts being made by designers and educators to challenge design's canonical parochialism with the inclusion of more diverse sources. However, while I believe it an important political and pedagogical project to broaden design's spectrum of references, I would humbly point to the potential traps and limitations of the corrective politics

5. Ariella Aïsha Azoulay, *Potential History: Unlearning Imperialism* (London: Verso, 2019).

6. See Mahmoud Keshavarz, *Design Politics of the Passport: Materiality, Immobility, and Dissent* (London: Bloomsbury, 2018).

7. Benedict Anderson's notion of "print capitalism" does much to account for the technological, economic, and political implications of the European formation of movable typography in a way that ought to correct the techno-progressive blind spots of more conventional narrations of graphic design history.

8. Where "progress" is problematized as the modus operandi of empire. Azoulay, *Potential History*, 18.

of "inclusion." Often, the valorization of non-Western, non-male, nonwhite others' "contributions" is premised on their proximity to reference points within the established canon. The minimal design of W. E. B. Du Bois's sociological information visualizations, while undoubtedly to be treasured, are perhaps, incidentally minimalist, and have been noted in a way that measures their value against, or at least in relation to, the standard of European modernism's ostensibly universal (and rather mechanical/industrial) principles of form and cognition.[9] Similarly, while the acknowledgement of the Asian advent of movable typography corrects the hubris of the Eurocentric perspective, it also tends to neglect a more confrontational recognition of the legacy and role of the European printing press in enabling colonialism, nationalism, and capitalism.[10] In a text challenging the popularization of "decolonization" in design, Ahmed Ansari invokes Frantz Fanon's observation that "[B]lack people modify their speech, body language, and actions to 'prove the existence of a black civilization to the white world at all costs,' [pointing] to [an] awareness of the colonized that they exist in relation to a colonizer."[11] To paraphrase, Ansari (and Fanon) lament a fetishization of inclusion in the form of a liberal politics of representation/recognition, rather than articulating something more substantively decolonial.[12] In other words, there are formations of artifacts and the social systems in which they circulate that are simply incommensurable with any conventional notion of design, because the assumptions that frame these are irreconcilable.[13] While I appreciate the affirmation of cultural ego that examples

9. Maria Popova, "W. E. B. Du Bois's Little-Known, Arresting Modernist Data Visualizations of Black Life for the World's Fair of 1900," October 9, 2017, https://www.brainpickings.org/2017/10/09/w-e-b-du-bois-diagrams/. For a more substantive treatment, see Silas Munro, "Introduction to the Plates," in *W. E. B. Du Bois's Data Portraits: Visualizing Black America*, ed. Whitney Battle-Baptiste and Britt Russert (Hudson, NY: Princeton Architectural Press, 2018), 49–105.

10. See S. H. Steinberg, *500 Years of Printing* (London: Penguin, 1955): and Benedict Anderson, *Imagined Communities: Reflections on the Origin and Spread of Nationalism* (London: Verso, 2006).

11. Ahmed Ansari, "The Work of Design in the Age of Cultural Simulation, or, Decoloniality as Empty Signifier in Design," https://medium.com/@aansari86/the-symbolic-is-just-a-symptom-of-the-real-or-decoloniality-as-empty-signifier-in-design-60ba646d89e9.

12. "Of course, dressing up in the language of decolonization is not as offensive as 'Navajo print' underwear sold at a clothing chain store and other appropriations of Indigenous cultures and materials that occur so frequently. Yet, this kind of inclusion is a form of enclosure, dangerous in how it domesticates decolonization." Tuck and Yang, "Decolonization Is Not a Metaphor," 3.

13. See also Joi T. Arcand, Chris Lee, and Winona Wheeler, "I'm a Little Too Rebellious for That: A Conversation with Joi T. Arcand and Winona Wheeler," *cmagazine* 141 (2019), https://cmagazine.com/issues/141/im-a-little-too-rebellious-for-that-a-conversation-with-joi-t-ar.

like the two mentioned above give to the people and places that are affiliated with these forms, I withhold a full endorsement for two main reasons. The first is that such inclusion can be a form of body-language modification that is made in an attempt to seek recognition from the gaze of Euro-American institutions and audiences, and which affirms their priorities as the normative basis—the grid, the rule, the standard—against which "other" forms are measured, valued, and granted accession.[14] The second is that "contributions" (to the hegemonic center) that are valued on the basis of their chronological precedence accept as valid the very idea of a linear progressive historiography as value-free and uncontroversial and turn the process of redressing history into an untenable, unwinnable race consistent with the "doctrine of discovery"—a kind of "finders keepers" principle of erasure used to justify colonization.

There is another schism that might help dissolve the inevitability of the canonical Eurocentric forms and formats that tend to be taught in graphic design history and studio pedagogy. It is inspired by Azoulay's inversion of the Western museum's tendency to affirmatively narrate its collection not as a cache of stolen artifacts (extracted violently from the worlds they help constitute) but as props in the teleological justification of the advances of Western civilization. I propose centering *the document*—the material basis of historiography—but inverting its status as evidence in the narration of civilizational progress, by instead regarding it as evidence of crime—I propose that violating the canon entails mounting evidence on which to indict graphic design as an agent of colonialism/coloniality and capitalism. This immediately prompts a few questions. How might centering the document shape the design student's disciplinary imaginary, their sense of agency, and the array of theoretical and practical concerns that designing entails? Can a designerly intellect and creativity be mobilized to undo the kind of violence of colonial property deeds, border regimes, the carceral state, etc., enabled by documents? Can the design student abandon the vague ethical paradigm of "problem-solving" to question whose problems are being solved and to create forms of antagonism toward the powers that be?

I don't pretend that graphic design will magically bring about the dissolution of the "modern world system" or the so-called Capitalocene.[15] But I do propose considering document-centered design as a framework through which to do what the anthropologist

14. I should note that the example I've given here of Du Bois was written by an apparently white author. However, one might contend that such an affirmation of Black design coming from a white author constitutes a form of inclusion fraught with unexamined bias and the baggage of white saviorism (inclusion as what Eve Tuck and K. Wayne Yang have called a "move to innocence").

15. See Jason W. Moore, "The Capitalocene, Part I: On the Nature and Origins of Our Ecological Crisis," *The Journal of Peasant Studies* 44, no. 3 (2017): 594–630.

Laura Nader has called "studying up."[16] In other words, can graphic design education be adapted to study the way that it has itself been implicated as an instrument of epistemological violence that has facilitated and enabled other, more brutal forms of violence?

To reiterate: Yes, indeed, we ought to recognize and affirm that the Asian advent of movable typography independently preceded its European counterpart. But it is just as important that we not forget the critical role played by movable typography in the European development of capitalism and colonialism. Techno-progressivist historiographies of design neglect that the revolutionary impact of Gutenberg's press had more to do with the nascent capitalist economy developing in Europe (founded on the primitive accumulation of wealth through slave-powered colonial extraction) than with some pathologically inevitable tendency toward industrial mechanization driven by European ingenuity and entrepreneurial innovation, or a tautological equation between literacy and democratization. Without European printing, the VOC (*De Vereenigde Oostindische Compagnie*, or, the United Dutch East India Company) could neither issue a public offering of stocks in its highly risky colonial ventures (thereby distributing that risk on a national scale and creating the first publicly traded multinational [read: colonial] corporation), nor could it generate the conditions for the world's first stock exchange in Amsterdam (giving birth to the immense force of globalized financial capitalism). The historian of print S. H. Steinberg reminds us that Gutenberg's primary business was in job printing—quotidian artifacts like calendars and, more salient to our discussion, things like papal indulgences. Just as the advent of writing in ancient Mesopotamia is understood to have more to do with accounting than with literary expression, so too ought printing to be understood as having more to do with genres like finance and property than with romance and mystery.

•

Histori*ography*

Graphics make and construct knowledge in a direct and primary way. Most information visualizations are acts of interpretation masquerading as presentation. In other words, they are images that act as if they are just showing us what is, but in actuality, they are arguments made in graphical form.

—Johanna Drucker, *Graphesis: Visual Forms of Knowledge Production*

The colonist makes history and he knows it. And because he refers constantly to the history of his metropolis, he plainly indicates that here he is the extension of this metropolis. The history he writes is therefore not the history of the country he is despoiling, but the history of his own nation's looting, raping, and starving to death. The immobility to

16. See Laura Nader, "Up the Anthropologist: Perspectives Gained from Studying Up," in *Reinventing Anthropology*, ed. Dell Hymes (New York: Random House, 1972), 284–311.

> which the colonized subject is condemned can be challenged only if he decides to put an end to the history of colonization and the history of despoliation in order to bring to life the history of the nation, the history of decolonization.
>
> —Frantz Fanon, *The Wretched of the Earth*

In my italicized stylization of historio*graphy*, I emphasize, along the lines of Drucker's observation, that history is a creative, contestable, and ultimately political formation. I am echoing Frantz Fanon's critical recognition in the quote above that history is not simply a dispassionate concatenation of chronological facts, but rather a field of contestation, a selective picture constructed self-consciously and systematically in a manner of what Michel Foucault might call a "discursive formation."[17] In other words, *history is designed.* What

17. The first of the discursive unities/formations Foucault comments on are discourses constituted upon a known object, i.e., madness. But since such a thing as "madness" is not knowable in any stable way—it doesn't have a fixed definition—the discursive unity around the object is then figured by the changes in how the object is constituted by the statements in which it is made. The second of the unities/formations has to do with how statements are made. For instance, medical scientific discourse is constituted as such through "the group of rules, which, simultaneously or in turn, have made possible purely perceptual descriptions, together with observations mediated through instruments, the procedures used in laboratory experiments, statistical calculations, epidemiological or demographic observations, institutional regulations, and therapeutic practice[.]" A third framework of discursive unity/formation may have to do with the grouping of statements based on their foundation on a set of established concepts (i.e., the classical analysis of language and grammar includes in its conceptual architecture such things as the noun, the predicate, the verb, etc.). However, Foucault notes the regular emergence of new and/or derivative concepts, or concepts that are incompatible with the established set. He doubles back and offers instead that perhaps the unity of language analysis can then be justified around the simultaneous appearance of a set of concepts and their succession by other concepts. He describes the fourth unity/formation as being premised on themes (i.e., evolution), or rather the possibility of divergent statements on a theme.

Foucault is ambivalent about these principles, or rules of formation. He doubts that any of these principles will be definitive and without gaps and doubt, and he offers what I see as an emancipatory possibility: "One may be compelled to dissociate certain oeuvres, ignore influences and traditions, abandon definitively the question of origin, allow the commanding presence of authors to fade into the background," and so "one is forced to advance beyond familiar territory, far from the certainties to which one is accustomed, towards an as yet uncharted land and unforeseeable conclusion" (Foucault, *The Archaeology of Knowledge and the Discourse on Language*, 31–39).

18. In *Principles of the New Associationist Movement*, Karatani Kojin also observes that the state and capital are two sides of the same coin: "Capital and state are two separate things in their modus operandi. Capital belongs to a principle of exchange, while state belongs to the principle of plunder and redistribution. Historically speaking, it was in the stage of the absolutist monarchical state that they were combined. The state necessitated the development of the capitalist economy in order to survive and strengthen itself; while the capitalist economy has had to rely on the state, because it has not been able to affect all productions to make them part of it, and what is more, it continues to be dependent even upon un-capitalized productions such as the reproduction of humans and nature. Thus, after the rise of industrial capitalism and bourgeois revolution of state, the two joined together and came to form an inseparable amalgamation, yet at the same time sustaining their own autonomies" (https://www.nettime.org/Lists-Archives/nettime-l-0105/msg00099.html).

a historiography of historio*graphy* includes are things that are designed to be historical—that is, things that are intended to carry memory, to function as evidence, to produce information, to render objective and *immutable* subjective claims, to sediment arguments that would otherwise be contingent. This historio*graphy* is constituted by the various "records of interest" generated in the course of administrating the development and perpetuation of colonial institutions like the state and the corporation, entities for whom maintaining radically contingent claims to power and authority were at stake.[18] The artifacts foregrounded in this historio*graphy* instantiate imbrications of language and money, or what anthropologist Keith Hart calls "the memory bank." Hart's metaphor of the bank, implying storage of memorial inscriptions, intersects with the media historian Lisa Gitelman's formulation of the document's dual functions as producers of knowledge and evidence, what she calls the document's "know/show" function, which represents a dual status as dormant file and as proof that is activated precisely in moments of controversy and conflict.[19] The document is thus cast as an *argument* over the legitimacy of one claim or another. The document's knowledge-producing capacity is given an existential stake and a violent charge in Jonathan Beller's assertion that *information*, reified in documentary formats, cannot be extracted from the capitalist logic of the commodity form, which transposes "chicken lives to another domain" in which living beings are reduced to the *claim* that they are simply numerical units available to the murderous rationality of managerial calculation.[20]

Below I offer a brief, preliminary sample of a document-centric design historio*graphy* with a collection of reference images and captions. It is a narration that spans roughly 5,000–6,000 years where "minerality" serves as a thematic/material notion for exploring what I call the design imperative to *immutability*—mineral as substrate, mineral as standard, mineral as conduit, mineral as weapon.[21] These aspects of "minerality" variously immunize the integrity of inscriptions and claims "against both any alterity that might transform [them] and whatever dares to resist [them]."[22] These are the broad strokes of a historiography that centers documents precisely because they were designed to function as the material constituent of history by virtue of their capacity to maintain their form against the entropic corrosion of time, space, and contestation (politics). Ultimately, this is an exploration of the role that designing documents plays in legitimizing power, and an experiment in theorizing legitimacy through a designerly lens, elaborated through the categorical frames of clay and stone, custom and convention, coercion and code—each cast as an aspect

19. Lisa Gitelman, "Rethinking Attachment," *The New Everyday: A Media Commons Project*, June 29, 2010, http://mediacommons.org/tne/pieces/rethinking-attachment.

20. Jonathan Beller, *The Message Is Murder: Substrates of Computational Capital* (London: Pluto Press, 2017), 30.

of minerality. These techniques are not meant to be comprehensive or even inarguable, but rather starting points for measuring out the extent to which design operations might be seen as political operations, and vice versa. My hope and intention are to facilitate a kind of tangential narration and an experimental, nonlinear, non-teleological way of writing and reading history. I now ask the reader to attune a part of their readership to the nonverbal paratextual and hypertextual signals (recalling the term in the way it was discussed by Samuel Delany and Octavia Butler)[23] present in the following images, as well as other kinds of verbal and nonverbal referencing, to orient one's visual senses toward texture, form, picture, and to seek resonances amongst the following samples:

•

Clay and Stone

The ability of clay to hold pressed forms enables a morphological standardization of signs, figuring it as the earliest substrate for typography. To the extent that typography is essentially a function of pressing, these tablets are prototypical. This back-projection and alignment with contemporary notions of typography is not meant so much to valorize tablets as graphic design as to highlight the political consequentiality and stabilization of meaning enabled by typography's standardizing effect. Once hardened through firing, the clay document is securitized, and any attempt to revise the inscription will be recognized as invalid because of its irregularity from the smooth surface

21. A deep-time media history that spans the inert to the intermediary to the malicious application of the mineral is laid out in Jussi Parika, *The Anthrobscene* (Minneapolis: University of Minnesota Press, 2014), 55; he quotes Thomas Pynchon, *Against the Day*, 88: "'But if you look at the history, modern chemistry only starts coming in to replace alchemy around the same time capitalism really gets going. Strange, eh? What do you make of that?' Webb nodded agreeably. 'Maybe capitalism decided it didn't need the old magic anymore.' An emphasis whose contempt was not meant to escape Merle's attention. 'Why bother? Had their own magic, doin just fine, thanks, instead of turning lead into gold, they could take poor people's sweat and turn it into greenbacks, and save the lead for enforcement purposes.'"

22. Michel de Certeau, *The Writing of History* (New York: Columbia University Press, 1992), 216.

23. Octavia Butler and Samuel Delany, edited transcript of conversation at MIT on February 19, 1998, http://web.mit.edu/m-i-t/science_fiction/transcripts/butler_delany_index.html.

and forms of the original inscription. Redemption from any onerous debt inscribed on such documents would be enacted literally through dissolution of the document in formal jubilees—debt cancellations decreed by a sovereign or religious authority.

The ancient King Hammurabi receives from Shamash (seated), the deity of justice and truth, a rod and a coil. These are both symbols of power and tools for measurement (adjudication). Some interpretations regard these objects as surveyor's tools, representing an indisputable standard of measurement. James C. Scott reminds us that the generalization of one standard over another is the result of struggle.[24] The image makes the claim that the laws inscribed below it are not the arbitrary invention of a fallible human being but that they are of divine provenance and thus beyond contestation. "Hammurabi, the king of righteousness, on whom Shamash has conferred right (or law) am I."[25] The definitions of criminality and the parametric enumeration of their penalties are inscribed thereunder. The basalt substrate upon which the laws are written reinforces these claims by rendering them physically immutable.

Lydian coinage (minted from electrum, a natural gold-silver alloy) is by historical consensus the first coinage to be issued by a state anywhere in the world. What makes it significant to future developments of coinage is that it was stamped with a seal of the state that issued it, making it an official, constitutive feature of state administration and effectively obliging its holder to extinguish their tax obligations in this coin. This very technique and the skill set required to make these coins echo those required to produce inscriptions on clay tablets in the preceding millennia and foreshadow what will be indispensable to the development of movable typography, thousands of years later.

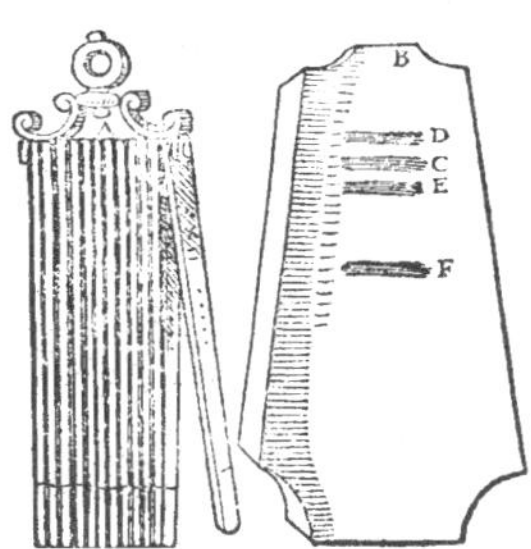

Assay stones (touchstones) and hallmarks were devices used to confirm the authenticity of precious metals. In the illustration to the left, touchneedles (left), a standardized set of precious-metal alloys, would be rubbed against a touchstone (right) made of slate, leaving a mark against which to compare marks made by the metal object being tested. The image at the top of the next page would be punched into metal goods to certify their precious-metal content by, in this case, the London assay office (Goldsmith's Hall, which is the place from which the term "hallmark" in English is derived). Other punches would typically include those for the initials of the maker of the metalware, a

24. James C. Scott, *Seeing Like a State: How Certain Schemes to Improve the Human Condition Have Failed* (New Haven: Yale University Press, 1998), 28.

25. *The Code of Hammurabi*, trans. L. W. King (1907), https://avalon.law.yale.edu/ancient/hamframe.asp.

letter signifying the date of certification, and occasionally a mark indicating the payment of taxes on precious metals. In total, these serve as a basis of accountability for the purity claims made upon the metal and are mandated by a governing authority. These metal-smithing tools and techniques echo the morphological standardization enabled by pressing into clay, and the skillful ability to cut detailed punches that enabled the marking of Lydian coinage. Furthermore, they are primary in the development of movable typography.

•

Custom and Convention

This tablet records a five-day ration list (presumably for a worker). Each row is distinguished by the graphical intentionality of the double horizontal lines. It is an example of visual epistemology and graphical thought. In her book *Graphesis*, Johanna Drucker calls our attention to the grid of lines appearing on such tablets, remarking that although these lines do not themselves hold semantic value, they produce a syntactic order and orthographic convention. They figure what Rosalind Krauss might call an "infrastructure of vision."[26] This serves to sediment, with as little ambiguity as possible, a specific interpretation of the document's author(ity). The lines function as a "point of reference against which the basic graphic properties of sequence, direction, orientation, size, and scale can register their significance."[27] They function as a technique of disambiguation, shoring up a defense against doubt, dispute, and deniability. Drucker supplies the striking insight that grid systems are not only an innovation of mid-twentieth-century modernists but, more interestingly, have an ancient, political origin, formed out of a managerial agenda to coordinate legal meaning and reinforce the authority/authorship of those in commanding positions within what Michel de Certeau calls the "scriptural economy."[28]

This is a 3D scan of one of the last remaining public standard meters (*mètre étalon*) in Paris, still in its original location. This marble monument was mounted to serve, like a clock tower, as a public instrument of commercial coordination. It embodied the ideals of a new French republic, signaling that "the Revolution has given the people the meter!"[29] The French revolutionary government would take up programs of rationalizing exchange standards like money, time, space, and weight as a just and measured remedy to the various forms of abusive arbitrage and taxation exercised over the merchants and peasantry in the *ancien régime*. Prior to metrication, the definition of length of textiles in one part of France might not be the same as in another part of the country. Or, what a peasant farmer thought of as a

26. Rosalind Krauss, "Grids," *October* 9 (Summer 1979): 57.

27. Johanna Drucker, *Graphesis: Visual Forms of Knowledge Production* (Cambridge, MA: Harvard University Press, 2016), 85.

28. Michel de Certeau, *The Practice of Everyday Life* (Berkeley: University of California Press, 1984), 131–53.

barrel and what their landlord defined as a barrel might be two completely different things. This created disputes in commerce and onerous impositions in taxation. Metrication was a process of standardization designed to systematically facilitate the rational governance of these forms of sociability across a national territory (and eventually the world), for all time. The meter was defined as 1/10,000,000 of the distance between the equator and the North Pole along the Paris meridian. The conceit of this definition was that it was premised not on the arbitrary subjectivity of a human standard but rather displaced onto the indisputable foundation of the objective, empirical, and unfathomable phenomenon of the globe.

Excerpts from Ivan Illich's *Vernacular Values*, regarding Antonio de Nebrija, the first person to publish a standardized grammar for a Romance language, Spanish. Illich quotes Nebrija addressing Queen Isabella I: "'My Illustrious Queen. Whenever I ponder over the tokens of the past that have been preserved in writing, I am forced to the very same conclusion. Language has always been the consort of empire, and forever shall remain its mate. Together they come into being, together they grow and flower, and together they decline.' . . . Nebrija here reminds the queen of the new pact possible between the sword and the book. . . . [He] calls to their minds a concept that, to this day, is powerful in Spanish—*armas y letras.* He speaks about the marriage of empire and language." Nebrija thus advocates for mobilizing the industrial capacity of the printing press as a political tool for "standardizing a living language for the benefit of its printed form. . . . He wants to replace the people's vernacular by the grammarian's language. . . . By this monopoly over an official and taught language, he proposes to suppress wild, untaught vernacular reading."[30]

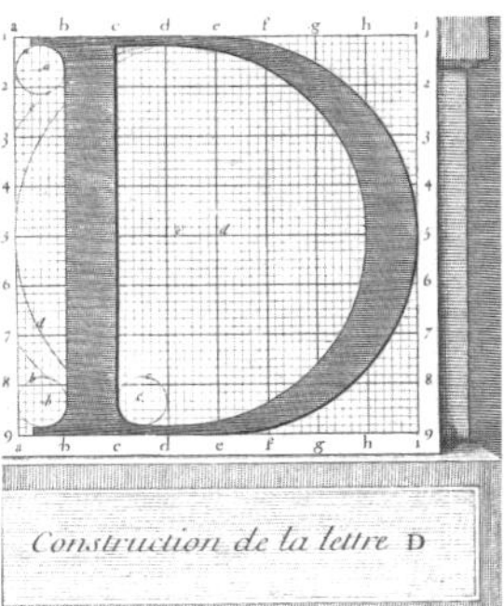

The 1693–1718 Bignon Commission, directed by Minister of Finance Jean-Baptiste Colbert, charged the abbot Jean-Paul Bignon with describing all the arts and industrial processes in use in France at the time. The commission and its staff begin their work with a study of printing and typography—"that art which will preserve all others"[31]—and led to the development of the first typographic point system and the creation of a royal typeface. The result was the *Romain du Roi.* Capital letters were constructed on a grid of 2,304 small squares; lowercase letters on a grid of 2,688. The precise specifications for their construction exceeded the

29. James C. Scott, *Seeing Like a State: How Certain Schemes to Improve the Human Condition Have Failed* (New Haven: Yale University Press, 1998), 32.

30. Ivan Illich, "Vernacular Values," *Philosophica* 26 (1980): 68–73.

31. Jacques André and Denis Girou, "Father Truchet, the Typographic Point, the *Romain du roi,* and Tilings," *TUGboat* 20, no. 1 (1999): 9.

skill with which the letters could actually be cut, but the geometric/mathematical principles of form upon which they were built made consistent reproduction possible, thereby protecting the authenticity (authorship, authority) of the king's typographic voice.

•

Coercion

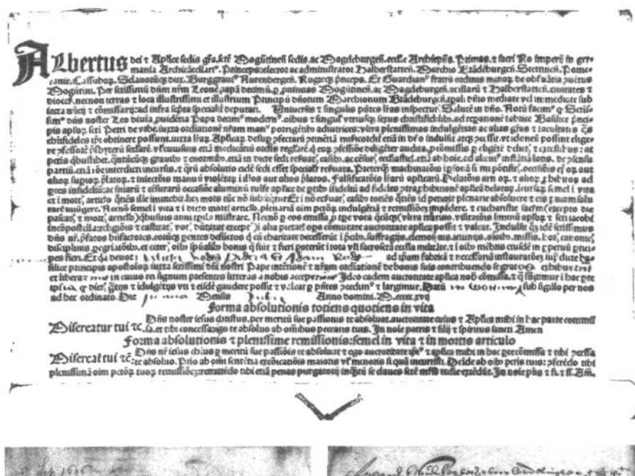

On the left-top, an example of a printed papal indulgence from the late 1400s, sold by the Catholic Church to relieve its faithful holder of the full debt of their sin or to certify the recognition of good works. On the left-bottom is the recto and verso of the second-oldest extant stock certificate, representing ownership of shares in the United Dutch East India Company (VOC) and recording the payment of dividends in 1606. Note the formatting similarities, which are banal yet significant: The blank spaces amongst the typesetting make themselves available for inscription particular to the holder of the document, actualizing an industrial capacity to prefigure individual yet interchangeable (private-property owning) subjects. Pressing and printing—counter to conventional narratives that celebrate the democratization of literacy—can be seen less as being about figuring such a thing as the public and more about poietically bringing into being a notion of private property. What the dividend payments listed on the verso obscure is the violent colonial activity that went into the extraction of value being disbursed to shareholders.

The earliest known instances of paper money are found in China. This example is from the Ming Dynasty (late fourteenth century). The combination of the printing press with movable typography indeed was first developed in Asia, not Europe. However, Janet Abu-Lugodh, in her book *Before European Hegemony*, makes a point of the nondevelopment of an industrial capital st economy in China, in spite of its earlier invention of gunpowder and the printing press.[32] She argues that the capitalist ascendance in Europe is less a factor of European ingenuity and entrepreneurial innovation than a result of the availability of immense wealth captured through primitive accumulation enabled by slavery and colonization. Given this insight, historiographies that recuperate the Asian precedent in the name of diversity actually deflect a scrutiny of the teleology of capitalist technological progressivism.

32. Janet Abu-Lugodh, *Before European Hegemony* (Oxford: Oxford University Press, 1989), 10–11.

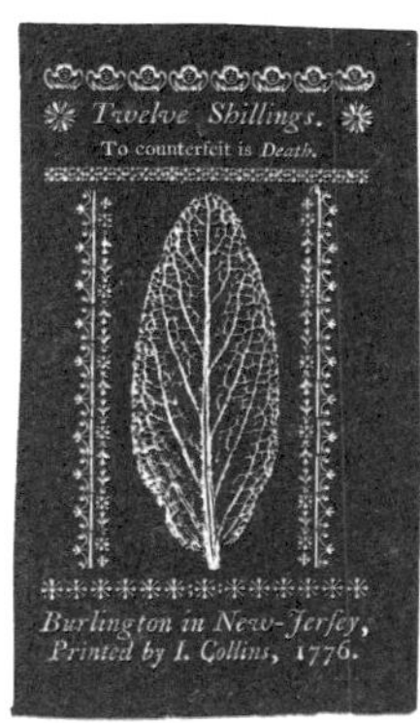

Early American colonial paper money employed a variety of techniques to foil counterfeiters and, as a corollary, secure its own legitimacy. Benjamin Franklin developed a process for transposing the vein patterns of tree leaves to printing plates as one such technique. Another technique is more typographical but—recalling Nebrija's marriage of *armas y letras*—more violent. One can find some examples of colonial currency that circulate some variation of the warning that "to counterfeit is death." Such an inscription suggests that what enables this paper to function as *official money* is the extent to which its claims are backed by the force of the state and its exclusive monopoly on ostensibly legitimate violence.

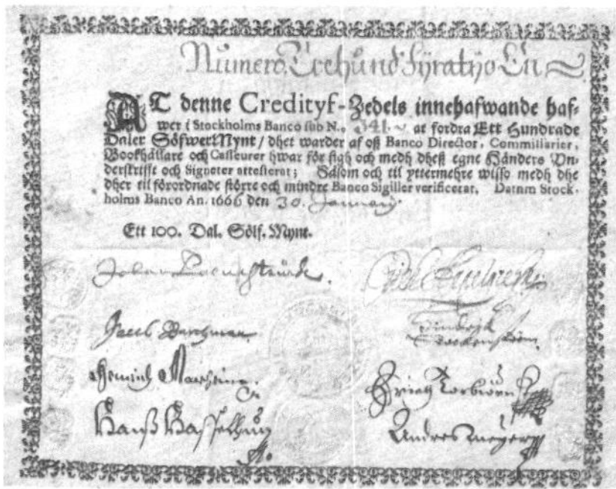

Johan Palmstruch (1611–1671) was Europe's first central banker for the *Stockholms Banco.* He is credited as the publisher of Europe's first paper banknote. However, he was sentenced to death (then, through a reprieve, to a prison term) for printing claims on deposits that exceeded what was actually held in the bank. The initial severity of the punishment, recalling the inscriptions on American colonial money, gives some indication of the inherent vulnerability of a printed document's status as legitimate, notwithstanding the state's capacity to back its legitimacy through force (i.e., taxation). Above, a Stockholms Banco paper banknote from 1661.

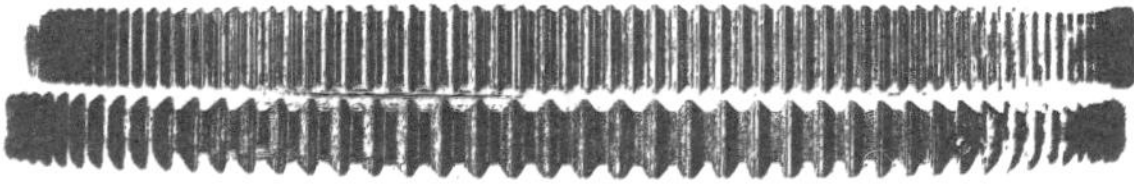

Considered as dangerous as counterfeiting, the practice of "clipping" coins—that is, cutting off or filing the edges of precious-metal coinage so as to preserve its face value but with a reduced amount of precious metal—was severely punished, occasionally by death. The reeded edges we see on some contemporary coins is a skeuomorphic vestige of a security feature designed to protect the face value of precious-metal coinage. The presence of such an edge indicated that the coin had not been tampered with. It was meant to function as a sort of "silent policeman" by establishing a normative morphology against which one could discern whether or not the actual value of the coin agreed with its face value.

•

Code

Matthew Boulton, business partner of James Watt, applied the steam engine to minting coinage. He established the Soho Mint and took commissions to output coinage for domestic circulation, as well as some British colonies. Boulton's mint was equipped with eight steam-powered presses that could strike coins at a rate of approximately 70–80 per minute with a precise morphological regularity such that counterfeits, even

with minor flaws, would be easily detectable. The mechanical objectivity of this production process" displaced the fallibility of subjective human intervention. Boulton's machines improved Isaac Newton's innovation of reeded edges with their precise mechanical consistency. The presses also included a built-in mechanism for counting its output, ensuring an objective, transparent accountability.

The first successfully laid transatlantic telegraph cable, spanning the west coast of Ireland to the east coast of Newfoundland, Canada, in 1858, did not last longer than a month. Efforts to establish a successful connection continued, however, and in 1866, a stable line was established. With the telegraph cable, the entropy of time and distance on the transmission of information across the Atlantic was lessened: Investors could stay current with and command their interests more directly as communications traveled in a time frame of minutes rather than days and weeks. In the commemorative medal shown above, bolts of electricity, representing more immediate and reliable couriers than human beings, extend from John Bull's (left) and Uncle Sam's (right) hands:

"How are you Jonathan?"

"Purty well old feller heow's yerself?"

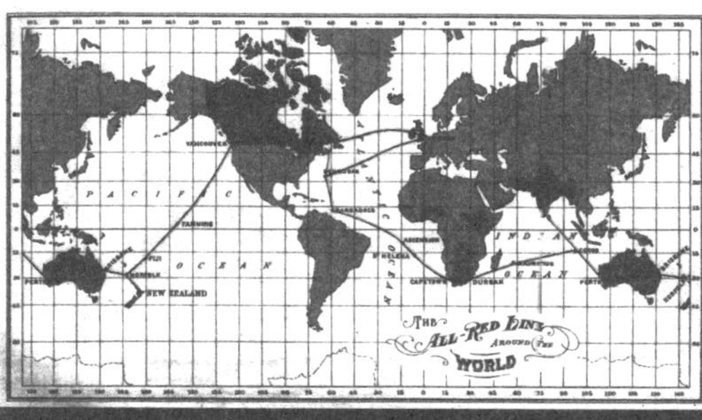

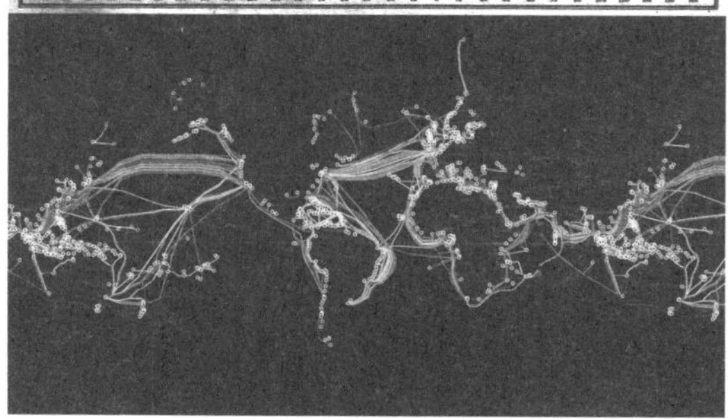

The "All Red Line" was the name for a telegraphic cable network that connected the colonies of an empire (upon which the sun never set) to its metropole. This has served as the physical, financial, and political scaffolding of today's network of submarine telecommunications cables—the physical infrastructure of the Internet, the nervous system (among other things) of contemporary global finance. Just as we have seen with ancient clay tablets and the printing press, these communications technologies and the infrastructure that embodies them ought to be seen in this narrative as vehicles of financial and colonial administration.

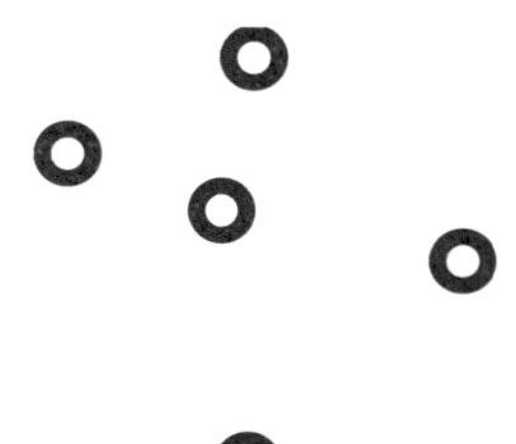

The EURion Constellation is a steganographic security symbol that appears on banknote designs from around the world. Functionally legible to an algorithmic, sentinel gaze, the constellation authenticates and protects the document. Color photocopiers and software like Adobe Photoshop can detect the symbol and prevent opening and printing the banknotes on which it appears. Controversy arose when it was learned that Adobe Systems had voluntarily adopted a Counterfeit Deterrence System (CDS) developed by the US Central Bank Counterfeit Deterrence Group.

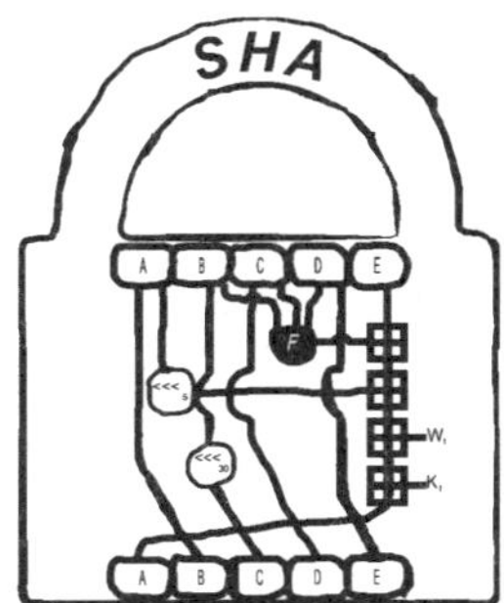

SHA (Secure Hash Algorithm) is a cryptographic hash function designed by the National Security Agency that produces a hash value. Hash values are a key element of technologies like blockchain and function like signatures or seals for documents inscribed on a distributed/networked ledger. This composition of functions is the proverbial stone on which these transactions are set, precluding the need for an institutional third-party authority to govern the validation and exchange of documents like cryptocurrencies.

The media historian Lisa Gitelman's insight that documents "triangulate the self in relation to authority" is particularly apt for the scene to the left—a glyptic carving found on a cylinder calculi from ca. 3600–3100 BCE.[33] It depicts pottery, and possibly textile production, as well as two seated figures doing some form of accounting with sticks, under the imposing gaze of a managerial figure.[34] This image concisely illustrates a political economy, a form of hierarchical and systemic oppression actualized through the production and circulation of administrative documents. In Jonathan Beller's formulation, such administration is premised on a violent simplification and standardization of an otherwise plural field of ontological possibility; it is enabled by a reduction of all things to calculable, manageable units. James C. Scott gives us a way to understand this tendency as something of a source code for the assertion and imposition of colonial claims: "[S]uch projects of administrative, economic, and cultural standardization are hard-wired into the architecture of the modern state itself. . . . One way of appreciating the effect of this colonization is to view it as a massive reduction of vernaculars of all kinds."[35]

33. Lisa Gitelman, *Paper Knowledge: Toward a Media History of Documents* (Durham, NC: Duke University Press, 2014), 135.

34. "Cylinder Seals," *Encyclopaedia Iranica*, http://www.iranicaonline.org/articles/cylinder-seals.

35. James C. Scott, *The Art of Not Being Governed: An Anarchist History of Upland Southeast Asia* (New Haven: Yale University Press, 2009), 12. See also Beller, *The Message Is Murder*.

•

Conclusion

Scott also offers that "the larger the pile of rubble you leave behind, the larger your place in the historical record!"[36] Although he is, in the context of this quote, commenting on the relative population density of state centers, I appropriate and rephrase this slightly to amplify a partisan bias for the colonized and the oppressed, and suggest that it be read more as an indictment: "The larger the pile of rubble you leave in the wake of your conquests, the larger your place the historical record."

If politicizing the design of history were to be reduced to a single agenda, it would be to displace the privileged position of documentary forms legible to the empirical gaze of imperial institutions (universities, museums, state bureaucracies) as the exclusive basis of legitimate knowledge. Privileging such knowledge effectively violates the worlds of those who leave no legible inscription; whose ways of knowing escape the literacy of the hegemonic institutions; and those embodied and performatic ways of being are obliterated through quasi-apocalyptic colonial violence. Indeed, the planet has been suffused for millennia with unmarked graves strewn in the wake of the colonizer's rampage. These terrestrial burial scars are themselves the marks, scored into the earth, that inscribe a record of the colonizer's criminality.

This is the violence that constitutes what the pedagogue Paulo Freire might refer to as a "limit situation"—a point of conflict from which to imagine another world and to undertake a process of "humanization."[37] For me, the most striking and resonant element of Freire's pedagogy for graphic design is the activity of "naming the world." I see this activity as a possible starting point for rethinking questions of design and studio pedagogy. This would entail a praxis that asks what ought to be known and remembered, in a way that antagonizes established ways of knowing and being and determined by those for whom the asking of this question has been suppressed and prohibited. I am particularly inspired by Diana Taylor's theorization of "the archive and the repertoire" for its possibility of providing graphic design discourse, theory, pedagogy and practice with concepts that might destabilize its ocular-centrism and offer a sense of the vast spectrum of knowledge and transmission practices and forms that are incommensurable with and exceed graphical inscription.[38] What would an exploration of her idea of the "performatic" as a domain of knowledge production and transmission that is embodied and situated (to paraphrase severely) yield for designers? I bring this up now only to close with a small list of prompts for further reflection: Can design be oriented toward studying, exploring, and creating other ways of remembering? Could it be about designing history, and does that involve new kinds of writing, transmission, storage, retrieval, and performance? Is it possible within the disciplinary imaginary of design to eschew legibility and mass literacy in favor of artifacts that leave no objective trace, can't technically be transmitted through colonial communications infrastructures, or are legible only to a small community from whom no profit can be made? At what point is it even

Martin Cooper develops the first handheld cellphone

useful to retain design as a disciplinary framework, and at what point must its institutional and professional horizons be abandoned to undertake a meaningful exploration of these questions? To echo Wilson Gilmore's formulation of abolition (and with respect for the different degrees of urgency), can design affirm and amplify existing non-oppressive ways of knowing and being, but also be tasked with exploring and giving form to radically divergent ones? In other words, could the monocultural commercial forest that is design wither in its own colonial sterility such that the strange bugs, the scraggly shrubs, the irregular fungi, the unruly vines and vermin can instead thrive in a new, unfathomable, untamable, and monstrously wet biological wealth of the swamp?

36. Ibid., 33–34.

37. See Paulo Freire's *Pedagogy of the Oppressed* (New York: Continuum, 2005).

38. See Diana Taylor's *The Archive and the Repertoire: Performing Cultural Memory in the Americas* (Durham, NC: Duke University Press, 2003).

Thank you to Margaret Rhee for her generous and insightful advice and support.

TROUBLING DESIGN PEDAGOGY

LAUREN WILLIAMS

This is a text about why design is taught, and how. The multiple enmeshments between the design profession and design pedagogy demand that we simultaneously ask why and how design is *practiced.* Many designers would argue that we design to solve problems, innovate, or even make the world a better place. The truth is, however, that mainstream design consistently serves no master but capitalism; and mainstream design education dutifully follows suit.

Capitalism depends upon and reproduces racism and other forms of oppression. Accordingly, design and its pedagogy cannot escape unblemished from their entanglements with capitalism: Their complicity with capital, neoliberalism, and white supremacy calls for close examination. Our care for the practice demands that we consider ways to repair the damage to which design disciplines contribute.

I am a designer who remains agnostic about media. Because I am committed to an overall practice that examines capitalist power relations and their attendant racist oppression, I care more about examining meaning than *exclusively* evaluating form. I privilege that perspective as I examine design education, pedagogy, and history here. In this text, I chart the ways that pedagogy itself is troubling in its capacity for encoding and reproducing oppression. At the same time, I hope to offer a way forward with a hefty dose of skepticism about who or what might follow: that we might begin by *troubling* the pedagogy we inherit with an eye toward maintaining, repairing, and caring for the subjects of design and its pedagogy most injured by its oppressive tendencies.

The Trouble: Factory Settings

Where the Trouble Lies

Design schools in the US are overwhelmingly white. The educators, the canon, the monographs, and—to a lesser extent—the student bodies are not inclusive with respect to gender or race, and so the schools are sites that reproduce oppressions that intersect and amplify each other along lines of race, gender, sexuality, ability, and citizenship.

Most people want classrooms—and perhaps even design studios—that *look* diverse and *feel* inclusive; at least, it's frowned upon in many circles at this point in history to strive for homogeneity and exclusion. We want the formal choices and designed elements of our educational environments to outwardly express that we value "diversityequityandinclusion."

"Diversityequityandinclusion" is important but inadequate. It's always the thing we—people generally, but designers especially—mention when we actually mean some form of oppression. It also refers to the *material* of racism in a way that makes it easier to ignore its oppressive effects on bodies, futures, and livelihoods: "diversityequityandinclusion" is visible, measurable, countable, photographable, aesthetic. It's material we can manipulate. When design institutions consider "diversityequityandinclusion," they rely on visible markers of difference, which often constrain the possibilities of discourse by reproducing racist, gendered ideas about what diversity "looks like": On a grassy quad on a sunny day, a well-dressed, not-too-dark-skinned Black girl sits cross-legged to the left of her presumably gender-nonconforming pan-Asian friend wearing a Pride rainbow pin and laughing comfortably at a tasteful joke told by a hijabi woman in the foreground. But "diversityequityandinclusion" on college campuses does little to address the structural factors and interpersonal racism that produce inequity for students of marginalized identities. Nothing is done to ensure that kids who did not attend high schools with well-funded arts programs—in nonwhite communities, school-funding inequalities are produced in large part by segregation, redlining, federal housing policy, and restrictive planning policy—are able to thrive with the pace and quality of work expected at the collegiate level. Students of color are expected to pay the exorbitant cost of higher education despite the staggering wealth divide produced by generations of extractive, racist policymaking, and few are able to take unpaid internships because they need income during school.

If *oppression* is disruptive—and it most certainly is for those it harms—how can we expect to dismantle it without some degree of inconvenience? Dealing with oppression is uncomfortable, confrontational, and difficult; it doesn't lend itself to expression in a language that designers, artists, and form-makers speak. But leave it to designers to treat the surface-level problem with "solutionism" while leaving the subterranean questions of infrastructural and interpersonal oppression for another day. Give us a pat on the back if we add the word "equity" to the mix, but don't expect us to shift the structure enough to deliver reparative care to those who have been historically or are at present harmed, excluded, or marginalized.

If dealing with the material of oppression—especially racialized oppression—isn't enough, what is? In a recent essay in the Walker Art Center's *Gradient,* Jacob Lindgren challenges readers to consider the origins of graphic design's presumed defaults: the ways we design, the function of graphic design education, the influence of the Bauhaus and its proselytes.[1] Lindgren demands "a closer examination of graphic design's factory settings—both the widely unchallenged, inherited, models it has come to consider 'default' in addition to its reluctance to step outside of (or sever from) its relationship to industry, to the factory," and he offers a sampling of noninstitutional educational models that contest many of those presets. My essay echoes Lindgren's charge.

What Are Graphic Design's "Factory Settings" and How Did They Come to Be?

Lindgren proposes that the "factory settings" of graphic design are a legacy of the Bauhaus and shaped primarily by the ties between design and industry: the studio-workshop model, a

1. Jacob Lindgren, "Graphic Design's Factory Settings," *Gradient*, January 2, 2020, https://walkerart.org/magazine/jacob-lindgren-graphic-designs-factory-settings.

master-apprentice educational system, and an apolitical bubble around creative production. The Bauhaus was built atop the *Deutscher Werkbund*, a union of design and industry, whose motto was "Art into Industry." The factory settings he describes are also the modernist standards of "good design" that continue to shape evaluative criteria in design classrooms: Modernist framing eliminates historical context, creates false barriers between society, culture, and aesthetics, constructs a notion of purity based on Western ideas of rationality, and privileges "masculine" design treatments.[2]

Accordingly, design educators focus on formal mastery of these rules at the expense of conceptual development and critical practice. There is a tendency to privilege "rationality" as expressed in the adherence to a singular grid structure, and we calcify students' understandings of typographic "neutrality" by setting introductory typography assignments entirely in "neutral" typefaces like Helvetica. In "Now You See It: Helvetica, Modernism and the Status Quo of Design," Jen Wang indicts the factory settings as mechanisms for encoding curricula and the profession with white supremacy: "How can a profession hope to attract people of color when the requirements are to assimilate, internalize, and perpetuate white hegemony?"[3] This question points to perhaps the most insidious factory setting—the notion of modernist "universality" or "neutrality" reflected in sans serif typefaces, "rational" grid systems, and rules about visual hierarchy and composition. That these qualities are presumed to be "timeless, neutral, useful for all types of communication" is, as Wang writes, how design "both echoes and reinforces the constructs of racial whiteness through visual representation."

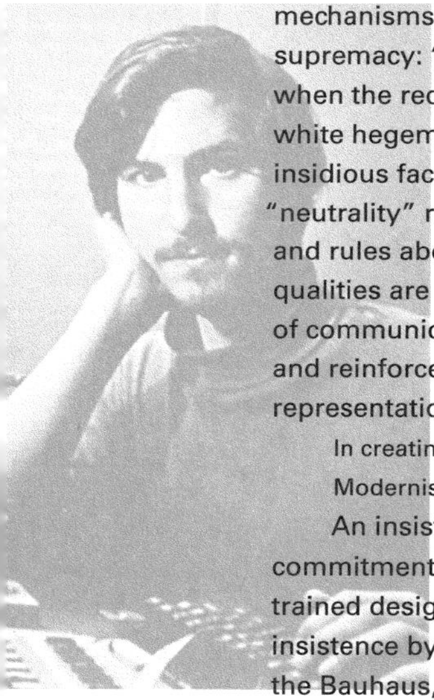

> In creating the aesthetic standards of design and typography, Modernism codified white supremacy into visual form.[4]

An insistence on "neutrality" extended to the avowed political commitments—or lack thereof—of modernist design and Bauhaus-trained designers. But the apoliticism was a farce; despite the insistence by its founder Walter Gropius on excluding politics from the Bauhaus, the school was submerged in a political maelstrom such that even the decision to avoid politics was, as always, political. Early state funding rendered it a public institution. Its subsequent privatization signaled a shifting orientation toward the state. The rise of the Nazi regime and its suspicion of Bauhaus ties to the "Jewish Bolshevik conspiracy" led to its ultimate closure.[5] Among the Bauhaus students and educators who survived the

2. Jen Wang, "Now You See It: Helvetica, Modernism and the Status Quo of Design," https://medium.com/@earth.terminal/now-you-see-it-110b77fd13db.

3. Ibid.

4. Ibid.

5. Nicholas Fox Weber, "Deadly Style: Bauhaus's Nazi Connection," *New York Times*, December 23, 2019, https://www.nytimes.com/2009/12/27/arts/design/27webe.html?pagewanted=all&_r=1.

Nazi occupation, several did design work for the Nazi state and the Soviet Union;[6] some were involved in projects that played a role in celebrating decolonialism (in Lagos) and others contributed to the occupation of Palestine and destruction of Jaffa.[7] All of these were incontestably political affairs.

Lindgren argues that many of the factory settings, derivative of Bauhausian mores and histories, were further molded by the dispersion of Bauhaus ideals and advocates throughout the Western world in the decades following the school's closure. These defaults also emerged from the confluence of particular movements, events, and norms that took place after the Bauhaus but before Silicon Valley really took off. They were then passed down through institutions like colleges, conferences, and professional design associations so that, even though Silicon Valley icons like Steve Jobs weren't trained in the Bauhaus tradition, they unquestioningly bought into it.[8] Lindgren notes that as stars like László Moholy-Nagy and Ludwig Mies van der Rohe emigrated to the United States and established themselves in industry, their Bauhaus was firmly embedded in global capitalism, and today both the modernist and capitalist factory settings remain encoded into Western design and its pedagogy.

Though Lindgren's analysis is silent on race, both the graphic design factory settings and their subsequent developments have been *as steeped in racism as they are in capital.* The emergence of capitalism in Europe was enabled by the racialization of populations in Europe long before far-flung colonial invasions and occupations, Indigenous genocides, or the trans-Atlantic slave trade. Capitalism has always relied upon genocide, imperialism, and the slavery that evolved from a feudal order that preceded it:

> The origins of racism cannot be separated from the origins of capitalism. The origins of capitalism cannot be separated from the origins of racism. The life of racism cannot be separated from the life of capitalism, and vice versa.[10]

While capitalism has always relied on racism, the period between the end of the Bauhaus and the early Internet age saw these systems integrated with design in new ways. This was the era preceding the neoliberalization of the '70s, when design, capital, and racism interacted in still newer ways. In the '60s, particularly, movements in the US for civil rights, Black liberation, peace, women's rights, and LGBTQ+ rights and abroad, anti-colonial wars and

6. Ibid.

7. Lindgren, "Graphic Design's Factory Settings."

8. Lindgren, "Graphic Design's Factory Settings."

9. See Cedric J. Robinson, *Black Marxism: The Making of the Black Radical Tradition* (Chapel Hill: University of North Carolina Press, 1983).

10. Ibram X. Kendi, "Part 3: How to Be an Antiracist: Ibram X. Kendi on Why We Need to Fight Racism the Way We Fight Cancer," interview by Juan González and Amy Goodman, *Democracy Now!* August 13, 2019, https://www.democracynow.org/2019/8/13/ibram_x_kendi_class_race_capitalism.

decolonization in Africa and the Americas challenged conventional understandings of race, gender, and power. Though some landmark reforms took hold, many were largely symbolic. These social changes occurred alongside shifts in design practice that prioritized a desire for scientific rigor and participatory engagement to inform and optimize the appeal and utility of new products. At the same time, designers contributed to these moments with posters, fashion, architecture, communes, and the beginnings of the techno-utopianism that would come to define Silicon Valley.

These distinct shifts in both design practice and social norms coincidentally preceded neoliberal reforms—deregulation, the New Economy, financialization, and austerity—that came to shape new design practices and define new commodities.[11] Mainstream commercial design culture developed alongside neoliberalism in order to "support and promote" it.[12] Many modernist and Bauhausian factory settings were reified by the underpinnings of neoliberal reforms: Notions of neutrality were rehabilitated by neoliberal conceptions of societal problems that divorced them from historical and social context.[13] The same tendency to privatize problems of collective concern—problems that might have once been addressed by the state—molded design's obsession with problem solving, one that continues to produce techno-solutions for sociopolitical problems.

Mainstream design education evolved alongside the profession to supply it with the designers who would support, promote, and serve capital. Part of what enabled schools to do so was neoliberalism's destruction of the university's academic mandate:

> Factories are decreasingly places where goods are produced and increasingly places where new kinds of humans are produced.[14]

That design education churns out these new kinds of human subjects is troubling, not least of which because the capital-serving imperative of the design profession is inherently racist. As long as design pedagogy reproduces institutional structures that are complicit with racism, design students will be educated into habits and value systems that cannot effectively combat racism. Lindgren asks, "How might graphic design pedagogy be repositioned to critique rather than uphold the ideological structures of capital?" Those "ideological structures" contain multitudes even if they remain unnamed: How might design pedagogy critique racism? Imperialism? White supremacy? Patriarchy? Misogyny? Transphobia?

Dangerously Close to Design

The state of design pedagogy is largely a function of the way design is practiced. Serving capital like a dutiful neoliberal cog, the design profession calls for design institutions to produce students

11. Guy Julier, *Economies of Design* (Los Angeles: SAGE Publications, 2017), 13.

12. Ibid.

13. Lisa Duggan, *The Twilight of Equality?: Neoliberalism, Cultural Politics, and the Attack on Democracy* (Boston: Beacon Press, 2003), 5.

14. Lindgren, "Graphic Design's Factory Settings."

who can frictionlessly fit into that framework. It's precisely this "entanglement of design and industry" that defines graphic design's factory settings.[15]

To compound the capital-informed state of the pedagogy, there is—by design—very little distance between design education and practice, and even less between design and capital. As Kenneth FitzGerald notes in a recent essay: "[T]here's no being outside the commercial imperative of design. It's that or the void."[16] As a result, the design pedagogy we have inherited is almost an *anti*-pedagogy: an educational approach more committed to the commercial imperatives of the design industry than to a historical, epistemological, or ontological foundation. "Presenting design," FitzGerald continues, "as something one might study just for edification, like philosophy, is likely to be the most disruptive idea a teacher could ask students to entertain."[17]

By the same token, we don't "*educate* design educators in educating."[18] As a result, a relatively small group of educators circulates in and out of institutions from which they graduated. The evidence is in the text and subtext of faculty job descriptions, the expectation that faculty submit portfolios of work and samples of student work in order to teach, the fact that "formal deviance between students" might be cause for concern.[19] The tendency to presume that design expertise takes precedence over teaching expertise is made clearest by design colleges' overwhelming reliance on practicing designers as part-time, adjunct faculty for many teaching positions. Part of a larger trend at colleges nationwide, the effect of adjunctification at art and design colleges amplifies the ties between industry and the classroom: "Professionals" make up the bulk of faculty—who are severely underpaid for their labor as educators—rather than "professors." The precarity of these positions, marked by exceedingly low pay, lack of benefits, short-term contract positions at risk of termination, further ensures that adjuncts must maintain employment elsewhere in order to survive financially.

Design colleges compete for coveted sponsored studios to supplement revenues from exorbitantly high tuition dollars. As Lindgren writes, "assignments which bring client work into the school, or invite 'practical and professional experience,' condition students even further." These studios shift the purposse of education away from helping students practice how to think and make for themselves and toward a predilection to think and make *in service of* a profit-driven enterprise.

Countless designers lament the apoliticism and lack of criticality in the field.[20] FitzGerald proposes that "design as an academic area of study is an uneasy situation for many design teachers. . . . There remains a fundamental discomfort, if not disdain, for any progressive, critical manifestations of design theory or production."[21] The avowedly apolitical positioning—belied by acts of design that

15. Ibid.

16. Kenneth FitzGerald, "(Incomplete)," *Modes of Criticism* 4 (2019): 46.

17. Ibid., 43.

18. Ibid., 44.

19. Ibid., 45.

support oppressive power—allows for a non-pedagogy that is, at least partially, informed by Bauhaus distancing from political affairs that was shaped in the midst of the Nazi rise to power in Germany. Perhaps this historical proximity to fascist, genocidal power at least partially explains the failure of design pedagogy to account for systemic oppressions. The same type of apoliticism shapes how design skirts around current affairs, or affairs concerning power. Today, the factory settings have been updated in ways that make the operations of oppression less transparent; near the end of the Bauhaus, its stars lent their design talents to the Nazi cause in ways that were unapologetically anti-Semitic.

This apoliticism is exacerbated by an educational and professional emphasis on individual genius rather than collective modes of design and action: Activism, uprising, and collective bargaining all require a degree of collectivism unheard of at many "prestigious"—read: egregiously expensive—design institutions. At art and design schools throughout Europe and the United States, "there's a priority on ushering in an individualistic approach to design, which is also how the capitalist design framework has allowed it to flourish."[22] The emphasis on the individual has only been exacerbated by the new kind of obsession with celebrity that emerged in the Internet age. And the money funneled into contemporary digital design projects serving social-media and online platforms and the proliferation of expensive design conferences and competitions only strengthen the cycle by serving to support the exclusive institutions that host them.[23]

> We Couldn't Have It Any Other Way
>
> Design education not only teaches its technical and historical canon, or how *to* design, but more importantly teaches students how *to be* designers in society and in relation to capital. A school becomes a factory producing designers, one that, in keeping with the principles of "good design," turns them into efficient and interchangeable parts ready to hit the market.[24]

Design is relentless in its myopic focus on driving consumption, pushing designers to act unethically—building brands out of thin air and convincing consumers that corporations and brands are

20. Eric Carter, "Do You Want Typography or Do You Want the Truth?" *Gradient*, June 7, 2018, https://walkerart.org/magazine/erik-carter-op-ed-do-you-want-typography-or-do-you-want-the-truth; Loretta Staples, "Less Is More 2000 (or 'Who Needs Design?')," http://www.lorettastaples.com/writing/less.html; Lindgren, "Graphic Design's Factory Settings"; FitzGerald, "(Incomplete)."

21. FitzGerald, "(Incomplete)," 42.

22. Amy Suo Wu, as quoted in Anoushka Khandwala, "'Decolonizing Means Many Things to Many People'—Four Practitioners Discuss Decolonizing Design," *AIGA Eye on Design*, February 17, 2020, https://eyeondesign.aiga.org/decolonizing-means-many-things-to-many-people-four-practitioners-discuss-decolonizing-design/.

23. Carter, "Do You Want Typography or Do You Want the Truth?"

24. Lindgren, "Graphic Design's Factory Settings."

more valuable than they really are—to render their products more appealing. Even when designers try to contribute in other ways (e.g., civic projects, community efforts), they often resort to reproducing the same consumption-focused approach. In another call to action aimed at graphic designers, "Do You Want Typography or Do You Want the Truth?" Eric Carter laments the capacity for typography and logo design to obscure the true implications of a product by disingenuously elevating its aesthetic.[25] He challenges designers to engage with political material rather than fuel consumerism.

There is a long history of calls for a reexamination of the profession. In 1999, AIGA published "First Things First Manifesto 2000," a reissue of a 1964 call to action in which graphic designers, art directors, and visual communicators signed on to challenge one another and the profession more broadly to pursue more honorable aims than advertising.[26] Even then, the signatories were presumably fed up with the capital-serving orientation of their field, the complicity of schools, and the corrupting system of awards and institutions. The authors demand a "reversal of priorities," which leaves me to wonder: Has graphic design as we know it ever *not* served capital?

Carter worries that even when designers enter realms of civic engagement or social concern, they often reduce their scope of interest and influence to consumable material, ignoring the fact that the effects of those material manipulations resonate beyond the screen or page on which a design is experienced. He argues that designers in these situations, and as a general rule, tend to disengage from foundational histories and social implications; instead, they "virtue signal and try to fundraise with enamel pins and tote bags."[27] Still, he muses that the field would be better off if it were both more inclusive, less obsessed with celebrity, and more informed about politics than aesthetics.

Perhaps we've encountered a chicken-and-egg problem about whether to intervene first in practice or education, but I question the value of dispatching more designers into public-serving, anti-capitalist environments to "solve" problems. After all, who's to say that these factory settings wouldn't persist if we changed nothing about the designer except their *location* in relation to capital? Loretta Staples offered a dose of timeless skepticism back in 1999 as she questioned communication designers' capacity to agitate the field in ways that might reconstitute the "discursive space of design." In "Less Is More 2000 (or 'Who Needs Design?')," Staples responded to the "First Things First Manifesto 2000" that challenged designers to unleash their problem-solving prowess on issues of greater significance than selling "dog biscuits" and "butt toners."[28] Staples—like Lindgren, Carter, and many others—called for designers to examine the profession's inability to engage with critical concepts and its dutiful servitude to consumerism. She warned that if designers

25. Carter, "Do You Want Typography or Do You Want the Truth?"

26. "First Things First Manifesto 2000," *Eye* (Autumn 1999), http://www.eyemagazine.com/feature/article/first-things-first-manifesto-2000.

really did dismantle what they know holds the field together, what they would expose might shock and unsettle them: As she put it, "You'll no longer recognize what you're doing as design."

How Should What Be Done?

As he concludes his examination of graphic design's factory settings, Lindgren ponders "what should be done?" To adapt his own phrasing to my musings: How might design pedagogy be repositioned to critique rather than uphold the ideological structures of heteropatriarchal white supremacy? But Lindgren's suggestion

27. In the wake of the May 25, 2020, murder of George Floyd in Minneapolis, the movement to preserve and protect Black life has gained new attention and taken many forms nationwide. The liberal rush to stay on the "left" side of history has driven countless forms of performative acts of solidarity and virtue signaling, enabled in many ways by design and designers. These ploys swiftly reveal themselves as thinly veiled, if veiled at all, opportunistic attempts to keep or attract Black customers or otherwise-conscious consumers to brands with no discernible track record in addressing racial injustice internally; placate residents in cities where massive murals declaring the value of Black lives distract from substantive calls to defund police; or give social media–wielding consumers a way to move in solidarity that costs little more than a retweet or post of a black square (posts that temporarily distorted algorithms directing resources to #BlackLivesMatter organizers). While there are certainly designers—those who recognize themselves as such and those who do not—behind more substantive movement work, the ways in which design has helped capital attempt to navigate this social upheaval through branding, social media strategy, public-apology strategy, mural design, and more are worth calling out as we examine the relationships between design and capital in this essay.

28. "First Things First Manifesto 2000."

that design pedagogy be "reset" or reprogrammed or uninstalled is insufficient. A factory reset would typically erase all of a device's data and promptly return it to a pre-installed operating system and set of programs that—though updated over time—are exactly the original defaults we argue should be reexamined. The "pre-installed" operating system has already received several updates over time, many of which compounded and calcified its original settings instead of transforming them.

One could argue that diversifying the field is "what should be done." But this brings us back to the inadequacy of diversity-and-inclusion discourse. A common delusion presumes that if we simply insert more material, more bodies "of color"—especially those of discernibly *different,* identifiably racialized folks—into an educational environment, the environment will inherently adapt. But the environment *doesn't* adapt to the needs of those students, faculty, or staff; too often, it remains inhospitable, if not hostile, to their studies and their well-being. So, sure: Diversify the field, include more and different people as educators and students and professionals, lift up different voices as authorities of design practice and figures in design history. But don't expect the approach to erase the need for a reexamination of factory settings in the first place.

Perhaps "how should it be done?" is a more instructive question than "what." We should examine design pedagogy's factory settings as an expression of care for the field, its pedagogy, and the subjects it has neglected or injured over time, what Shannon Mattern describes as "maintenance . . . as a theoretical framework, an ethos, a methodology, and a political cause."[29] To question the state of design pedagogy is a reparative act of maintenance that is concerned less with preserving the canon than with expressing care for the discipline(s) of design *and* the subjects and objects of design, including the social infrastructures of design and the many worlds only marginally considered but maximally affected by design.

What *is* the maintenance, repair, and care demanded by the systems through which we teach design? What is the infrastructure of care in the context of higher education? Those systems—the ways we train and compensate faculty; the financial and emotional costs we expect students to shoulder; the ways students matriculate; the prequalifications required of them; the pipeline we expect them to follow; the forms of employment and practice for which we're preparing them, as well as the factory-set assumption that the cost of school can and should keep ballooning; that taking out debt to finance education is the norm; that this costly education alone will enable economic mobility—would seem to cry out for maintenance and repair. The norm, in today's landscape, that the armies of adjuncts responsible for educating these financially precarious students are themselves mostly underpaid and overextended, is sorely in need of repair as well.

29. Shannon Mattern, "Maintenance and Care," *Places Journal*, November 2018, https://placesjournal.org/article/maintenance-and-care/.

The infrastructure of care is intensely personal and political: It's how we communicate concern and accommodate students in need; what we expect of students and how we communicate those expectations; how we deliver critiques of students' work; how we structure assignments and projects; how we equip students to lead their own critiques; how we evaluate students' work. In terms of curriculum, it's the ways we structure assignments to prioritize certain information and truths; the examples of work we choose to give; how we work through a student's fear of representing their identity in their work because the only representations they've ever witnessed were crass appropriations. It's the language we use to describe the outcomes students produce: Is a poster a "solution" or a "provocation"? Are we pursuing research questions to investigate and define a problem or solve a problem? Do we carefully integrate ethical analysis into our research process, or do we dive into fieldwork without regard for the varying costs and benefits participants may encounter?

An Interlude on Innovation

These factory settings are also products of "innovation," with which maintenance, repair, and care are fundamentally at odds. On the surface, they might seem to involve a similar *process*: incremental changes, improvements, or new ways of doing familiar things. Perhaps they diverge with respect to motivation: Maintenance and repair emerge from a need to prevent something from breaking or wearing down, and caring for it once it does. Innovation strives to improve for the sake of improving or rendering products more appealing to new buyers.

Innovation is presumed benevolent until proven otherwise, but rarely do we question its intentions, because *progress* is the highest order capitalist value. In *Keywords: The New Language of Capitalism,* John Patrick Leary claims that innovation is ascribed an "implied sense of benevolence," hence while we unreservedly and unabashedly accept that innovation means progress, we rarely acknowledge when innovation causes harm: innovative automatic machine guns, credit swaps, or chemical weapons.[30] Care, by comparison, is value-laden and value-forward: It demands a positionality toward an agreed-upon shared need or benefit—a degree of concern for others or one's self.

The mythology of innovation also carries with it a class and gender distinction that, when juxtaposed against the notion of maintenance, repair, and care, is thrown into stark relief. When we talk about innovation, we talk about the future, progress, upward mobility, and novelty. Maintenance, repair, and care, by contrast, imply reverence for a thing's history, a life and its end, and perhaps an inability to acquire the new. Consumerism and planned obsolescence—consequences of innovation—inspire us to throw away things that have outlived their useful, beautiful, relevant lives. It's easier to replace than repair. Maintenance and care, in a general

30. John Patrick Leary, *Keywords: The New Language of Capitalism* (Chicago: Haymarket Books, 2019), 115.

sense and in many sectors, are overwhelmingly performed by the underpaid: immigrants, women, and people of color; we only stoop to repair when we can't *afford* to replace.

In the loose net of this metaphor, one might interpret the preservation of *the factory settings* as an act of *maintenance or care.* But caring for the factory settings means caring for a system that encodes harm into its inner workings; caring for the factory settings is caring for a racist, sexist, patriarchal system, a prevailing framework, canon, and industry and those it satisfies and props up. This is fundamentally in conflict with the meaning of care as applied here: Prioritizing shared benefit, care should serve the subjects and environments shaped by design, the people who practice it, and the subjects of design education. Instead, design practice and pedagogy have been *innovated upon*: replaced periodically with new operating systems that improve upon their capacity to deliver the promised oppression without disrupting the anticipated experience.

To reorient toward maintenance, repair, and care challenges us to consider, above all else: who and what should be the subjects and objects of maintenance, repair, and care in order that a radical shared benefit is the highest-order priority? This shift might challenge the field and its educators, for example, to catalog and teach a more contextualized understanding of the harms caused by design's intersections with capital; to disabuse ourselves of the utility of canons entirely; to acknowledge the impossibility of neutrality or apoliciticsm; to refuse to legitimate the social violence perpetuated by design by declining to participate in projects that purely serve the market.[31]

What Then, If Not This?

Like FitzGerald, I am interested in "confronting two nested dogmas of design: definition by (and servility to) the marketplace and the primacy of formal expression" and hopeful that "meaning might prevail over mastery."[32] And like Staples, I expect that, by interrogating the factory settings, a practice and pedagogy will emerge that are unrecognizable as design. "For this new work, as a new kind of practice, will need a new name. And we don't know what to call it yet."[33]

How might maintenance, care, and repair engender a practice and pedagogy that look unlike design as we know it? In graduate school, some friends and I started the Antiracist Classroom. As a student group, *not* an actual class, we brought people together in ways that we hoped we might collectively practice how to both make the institution less racist and shape our own work to be proactively anti-racist. We struggled continuously about whether the goal should be to transform the institution (if even possible) or to create our own institutions or models of operating outside of spaces where the factory settings are defined by white supremacy

31. Hannah Rose Mendoza, "Beyond Doing Good: Civil Disobedience as Design Pedagogy," *Thresholds* 40 (2012): 236.

32. FitzGerald, "(Incomplete)," 48.

33. Staples, "Less Is More 2000 (or 'Who Needs Design?')."

and Western hegemony. Without throwing the institution away entirely, perhaps the least we could do was try to equip students to recognize and disrupt hegemonies of power and politics embedded in how we design and how design enables design. We could try to repair the damage we had endured as students.

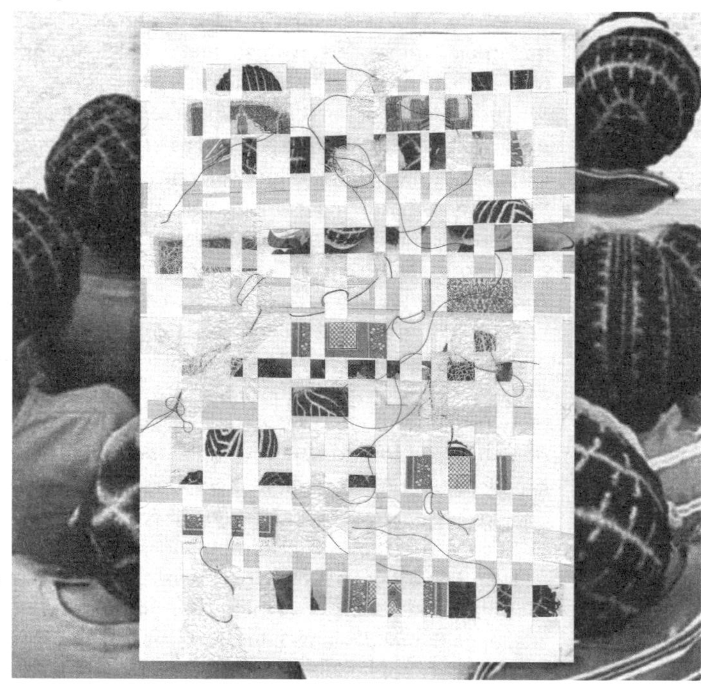

This paper weaving by Yasmin Ali, a student in Lauren Williams's senior thesis studio at the College for Creative Studies, was an early experiment in Ali's research on modes of making to recover the self, a reference to bell hooks's essay in *Talking Back*. Ali's thesis explored the ways white supremacy teaches us to compartmentalize ourselves for the sake of learning and sought to develop teaching strategies that enable a degree of recovery and resistance in their forms and processes.

In the act of organizing this group, we vacillated between two main questions: "How do we teach anti-racist design?" and "How do we make design education and practice anti-racist?" In retrospect, I think a slight rearrangement of the language would have been more productive: "How do we teach and practice anti-racism *through* design?" This phrasing reorients our priorities as designers and (now) educators and places design in service of a social and political *need* instead of capital in a way that allows for a different pedagogy and field of practice to emerge. To extend it beyond a single-issue oppression frame of reference, because the many dimensions of oppression based on race, gender, sexuality, ability, and class, more often coexist in the same person: "How do we teach and practice liberatory design?"

If a traditional design education produces subjects who serve capital, what kinds of subjects would an anti-racist, anti-ableist, feminist, decolonial classroom produce? They would become students who: critique work in a way that abandons the master-apprentice or art direction dynamic; create designs that don't exclusively serve a solutionist frame of reference and respond to other imperatives like critique, provocation, and world-building. These students would receive open-ended assignments that reflect evolving social and cultural circumstances; interact ethically with the communities that surround them and the communities they influence, intentionally or incidentally, with their designs. They would be able to do so because they would be supported financially, not gouged by the cost of higher education; they would be guided by faculty, also supported financially, who engage with culture, confront appropriation, and question norms. They would be invited to pursue a study of design that privileges both meaning and mastery.

Perhaps care—for faculty and students alike—also means stepping away from the factory floor and into reparative spaces. Who performs the labor of care? It's typically only the marginalized who are even attuned enough to notice the need for repairs: It falls to the disabled person, the Black person, the Indigenous person, the queer person, the trans person, the woman, the immigrant. Canaries in the mine, we notice the fumes first: drawing into focus the ways in which the classroom or wider institution isn't serving us and others like us, either because it's broken or more likely *because it's working exactly as it was designed to.*

To be frank, I'm increasingly disinterested in what BIPOC faculty, students, and designers can or should do in order to address these gaps or failures. It drains us of the capacity to do our actual work, to practice design in the ways we hope to—which may (in my own case, at least) have very little to do with the commercialism of the field I'm critiquing here. The duty of care, in this sense, is like a well-placed obstacle preventing us from carving out space in the field. How do we care for *ourselves* in the scheme of all this? What if caring for yourself looks like staying *out of* the mix—preserving your intellectual and emotional well-being by steering clear of soul-sucking, thankless committee work or intra-institutional organizing work that hopes to turn the rudder but rarely changes the course of the ship?

> Across the many scales and dimensions of this problem, we are never far from three enduring truths: (1) maintainers require care; (2) caregiving requires maintenance; and (3) the distinctions between these practices are shaped by race, gender, class, and other political, economic, and cultural forces.[34]

This is exactly the kind of distraction that Audre Lorde warned of in "The Master's Tools Will Never Dismantle the Master's House." In her words, "this is an old and primary tool of all oppressors to keep the oppressed occupied with the master's concerns."[35] If the act of examining the factory settings is antithetical to caring for ourselves and our practice or maintaining our own well-being, maybe care requires stepping into spaces that hold us fully and enable critical thought and practice; at the very least, periodically if not permanently.

Then again, Black, disabled, Indigenous, and queer students—students vulnerable to the oppressive effects of these factory settings—will continue to enroll at design institutions, especially as schools continue pushing ahead "diversityequityandinclusion" initiatives, no matter how cosmetic they may be at their core. So, perhaps, we have an obligation to stay with the trouble; perhaps the only way to survive in these kinds of spaces *is* to *stay* with the trouble. Marie Louise Juul Søndergaard is an interaction designer and researcher whose work explores themes of gender and sexuality

34. Mattern, "Maintenance and Care."

35. Audre Lorde, "The Master's Tools Will Never Dismantle the Master's House," in *Sister Outsider: Essays and Speeches by Audre Lorde*, ed. Cheryl Clarke (Berkeley: Ten Speed Press, 1984), 113.

to understand future technologies. In "Staying with the Trouble through Design," she offers a way of *practicing* interaction design that challenges the field's predilection toward techno-solutionism, notions of universality and homogeneity, and future narratives void of context.[36] Unsurprisingly, interaction design shares these factory settings with many other areas of design practice. "Staying with the trouble" is an approach first articulated by Donna Haraway that, in Søndergaard's work, prioritizes bringing trouble to reside with and through design: offering cultural and social sensitivity, acknowledging the ways in which knowledge is situated, and crafting futures about and through intimacy.[37]

Like those of us clamoring to examine the factory settings from within major design institutions or industry, Søndergaard offers this critical-*feminist* approach from within a decidedly heteropatriarchal field. Much as questions of intimacy—a gendered term in a heteropatriarchal frame of reference—are female-coded, care and maintenance are also gendered and classed. Consider, too, how often questions of oppression are encoded as the exclusive purview of the oppressed. Søndergaard proposes staying with the trouble as an anti-solutionist framework in order to "understand the conflicts and responsibilities involved in complex social, cultural, and political issues in order to imagine and design still possible futures."[38]

Søndergaard would say that staying with the trouble requires being truly present. To do so, she invites us to tell stories that have been overlooked or ignored; care "for our entanglement with different times; pasts, presents and futures";[39] operate with an understanding of "thick presents"[40] or the pluralities of lived experiences; and imagine futures that include us. Søndergaard resists offering a framework for enhancing, improving, creating more, or "facilitating intimacy." To do so would be antithetical to her central argument that intimacy "is situated and contextual," not universal.[41]

Like intimacy, maintenance or care in response to oppression "is not a problem or a solution, but a subject that brings trouble to or with which we may respond."[42] In solidarity, rather than proposing a solution to the trouble or codifying a new step-by-step, appealingly packaged, mechanized process,as designers love to do, I offer this essay as a response and an invitation to bring trouble to design's factory settings to the point of breaking them. As long as they remain intact, functioning exactly as they were intended to, there's no use in repair.

36. Marie Louise Juul Søndergaard, "Staying with the Trouble through Design: Critical-Feminist Design of Intimate Technology," Aarhus University, 2018, https://doi.org/10.7146/aul.289.203.

37. See also Donna J. Haraway, *Staying with the Trouble: Making Kin in the Chthulucene* (Durham, NC: Duke University Press, 2016).

38. Søndergaard, "Staying with the Trouble through Design: Critical-Feminist Design of Intimate Technology."

39. Ibid., 39.

40. Ibid.

41. Ibid., 171.

42. Ibid.

DANIELLE AUBERT is the author of *The Detroit Printing Co-op: The Politics of the Joy of Printing* (Inventory Press, 2019), *Marking the Dispossessed* (Passenger Books, 2015), and *16 Months Worth of Drawing Exercises in Microsoft Excel* (Various Projects, 2006). She is co-author, with Lana Cavar and Natasha Chandani, of *Thanks for the View, Mr. Mies* (Metropolis Books, 2012). She is an associate professor of Graphic Design at Wayne State University in Detroit.

TIM BARRINGER is Paul Mellon Professor of the History of Art at Yale University and served as department chair from 2016 to 2021. He writes on visual culture in the nineteenth century in Britain and the United States with a focus on issues of race and empire.

AUDREY BENNETT is a University Diversity and Social Transformation Professor at the University of Michigan and a professor in the Penny W. Stamps School of Art and Design. She is also a former Andrew W. Mellon Distinguished Scholar of the University of Pretoria, South Africa, and a former College Art Association Professional Development Fellow. Bennett's research concerns race and aesthetics, technology and inequality, the design of health campaigns, the analysis of images and graphics, interactivity, and the decolonization of graphic design history. Her research publications include "How Design Can Use Generative Play to Innovate for Social Change"; "The Rise of Research in Graphic Design"; "Interactive Aesthetics"; "Good Design Is Good Social Change"; and *Engendering Interaction with Images* (Chicago, 2012). She is the co-editor of the Icograda Design Education Manifesto (2011), and a member of the editorial boards of the journals *Image and Text* (South Africa) and *New Design Ideas* (Azerbaijan). Bennett is a member of the board of directors of the College Art Association.

ANDREW BLAUVELT is director of Cranbrook Art Museum, Detroit. As a curator of contemporary art and design, he organized numerous traveling exhibitions and edited accompanying catalogs, including *Too Fast to Live, Too Young to Die: Punk Graphics, 1976–1986* (2018), *Hippie Modernism: The Struggle for Utopia* (2015), and *Graphic Design: Now in Production* (2011) with Ellen Lupton. His most recent projects include *Designs for Different Futures* (2019), a joint project of the Art Institute of Chicago, Philadelphia Museum of Art, and Walker Art Center; and *With Eyes Opened: Cranbrook Academy of Art Since 1932* (2021). A practicing communications designer specializing in work for the cultural sector, Blauvelt is the recipient of nearly 100 design awards and his work has been published and exhibited internationally. Before entering the museum world, Blauvelt was a tenured professor at North Carolina State University's College of Design where he served as Head of the Graphic Design department and Director of Graduate Studies.

GUI BONSIEPE is a designer, educator, and author in the field of design. He studied information design at the Ulm School of Design, where he taught from 1961 to 1968, when he moved to Latin America to work as a consultant for public institutions and freelance designer in Chile, Argentina, and Brazil. From 1987 to 1989 he worked in a software house in Emeryville, California, specializing in interface design. From 1993 to 2003 he taught interface design at the Köln International School of Design. His books—including a volume of collected writings, *The Disobedience of Design* (Bloombury, 2021)—have been published internationally.

After graduating from North Carolina State University's Graphic Design department, **J. DAKOTA BROWN** completed an MA in visual and critical studies at the School of the Art Institute of Chicago (SAIC). He is currently a PhD candidate in Northwestern University's Rhetoric and Public Culture program. Brown's dissertation research is focused on reinterpreting graphic design practice by situating its emergence and transformation in the history of capitalism. Parts of this ongoing research were recently published in the pamphlets *Typography, Automation, and the Division of Labor: A Brief History* (Other Forms Books, 2019) and *The Power of Design as a Dream of Autonomy* (Green Lantern Press, 2019). Brown teaches design history and theory at SAIC and the University of Illinois at Chicago, and he designs books and journals.

CRAIG BUCKLEY is an associate professor of modern and contemporary architecture in the Department of the History of Art at Yale University. He is the author of *Graphic Assembly: Montage, Media and Experimental Architecture in the 1960s* (University of Minnesota Press, 2019). He is also the editor of numerous volumes, including *Screen Genealogies: From Optical Device to Environmental Medium*, with Francesco Casetti and Rüdiger Campe (University of Amsterdam Press, 2019), *After the Manifesto: Writing, Architecture, and Media in a New Century* (Columbia University Press, 2014), and *Clip/Stamp/Fold: The Radical Architecture of Little Magazines*, with Beatriz Colomina (ACTAR, 2010). He is currently at work on a book about transnational cinema architecture from the 1920s to the 1960s.

ANNIKA BUTLER-WALL is a PhD candidate in Modern Thought and Literature at Stanford University. She holds a BA in American Studies and Economics from Wesleyan University. She is currently researching the role of digital media platforms in restructuring the relationship between gender and labor in the United States.

CHOI SULKI and **CHOI SUNG MIN** are graphic designers based in and around Seoul, South Korea. They met at Yale University where they both earned their MFA degrees. After working as researchers at the Jan van Eyck Academie in Maastricht, they returned to Korea in 2005 to start their practice. Since then, they have created graphic identities, publications, and websites for clients including the National Museum of Modern and Contemporary Art (MMCA), Seoul Museum of Art (SeMA), Asia Culture Center, BMW Guggenheim Lab, Munhakdongne, and Mass Studies. Crossing the border between design and art, they have participated in numerous exhibitions in Korea and abroad, and the first mid-career survey of their work took place in 2021 at the Kyoto DDD Gallery, Japan. Their work is included in the permanent collection of MMCA, Gwacheon; M+, Hong Kong; Cooper Hewitt, Smithsonian Design Museum, New York; Musée des Arts Décoratifs, Paris; and the Victoria and Albert Museum, London. They have written and translated extensively on the subject of graphic design and typography and published artist books through their own Specter Press since 2006. Sulki is an associate professor at Kaywon University of Art and Design, and Sung Min is a professor at the University of Seoul.

RACHEL CHURNER is an art critic, editor, and co-founder of no place press. She is also director of the Carolee Schneemann Foundation. The recipient of a Creative Capital / Andy Warhol Foundation Arts Writers Grant, she has written for *Artforum* and *October*, among other publications. Her edited volumes include two volumes of writings by Annette Michelson (MIT Press, 2020 and 2017), Yvonne Rainer, *Revisions* (no place press, 2020), and *Hans Haacke* (MIT Press, 2015). She is a faculty member at Eugene Lang College at The New School.

DENISE GONZALES CRISP is based in Los Angeles and Raleigh, NC. She is professor and director of the Master of Graphic Design program in the College of Design at North Carolina State University. She is the author of *Graphic Design in Context: Typography* (Thames and Hudson, 2012), and many other essays published in journals and books. She was co-curator of *DesignInquiry: Futurespective*, ICA MECA, ME (2019), and *Deep Surface: Contemporary Ornament and Pattern*, CAM Raleigh, NC (2012). She is currently co-authoring a book that promotes improvisational, situational, and circumstantial approaches to design pedagogy.

HUGH DUBBERLY studied environmental design (University of Colorado) and graphic design (RISD and Yale). At Apple Computer (1986–94), Dubberly was a creative director, managing graphic design and corporate identity; he also produced the technology-forecast film "Knowledge Navigator" presaging the Internet and interaction via mobile devices. At Netscape (1995–2000), he became Vice President of Design managing groups responsible for the design, engineering, and production of Netscape's web services. In 2000 he co-founded Dubberly Design Office, a software, service, and systems design consultancy. Dubberly has served on AIGA's national board, the SIGGRAPH Conference Committee, and chaired ACD's "Design for the Internet" Conference. He edited the column "On Modeling" for ACM's journal, *Interactions*, and has published more than fifty articles on design methods. He was elected to the ACM CHI Academy and is an AIGA Fellow.

COLIN FANNING is a PhD candidate in design history and material culture studies at Bard Graduate Center in New York City. His research encompasses a broad range of American and European architecture and design from the mid-nineteenth century to the present, focusing on the history of design pedagogy in the United States, the material culture of childhood, the intersections of postwar craft and counterculture, and the visual and material cultures of spaceflight. Fanning previously held curatorial positions at the Museum of Arts and Design, the American Federation of Arts, and the Philadelphia Museum of Art, in addition to teaching history of design at Drexel University's Westphal College of Media Arts and Design. He curated and co-curated PMA exhibitions including *The Architecture of Francis Kéré: Building for Community* (2016); *Design Currents: Oki Sato, Faye Toogood, Zanini de Zanine* (2016–17); *Channeling Nature by Design* (2017); *Dieter Rams: Principled Design* (2018–19); and was a contributing curator to *Designs for Different Futures* (2019–21), organized jointly by the Art Institute of Chicago, Philadelphia Museum of Art, and Walker Art Center. His writing has appeared in the *Journal of Design History*,

The Public Historian, Response: The Digital Journal of Popular Culture Research, Metropolis magazine, and several edited volumes and exhibition catalogs.

ADAM FELDMETH lives in Los Angeles and Berlin. His work engages the social elasticity of art through actualizing situated discourse with those involved in its materialization. In Los Angeles, he has been the organizer of "stone soup," a discussion forum for individuals without institutional affiliation; "Discussions in Exhibitions," public-initiated gatherings within ticketless venues; and most recently, "a stone's throw," an online context for inquiry-motivated, discursive engagement among those involved in the production of visual culture as social action. He is co-director of the Southland Institute. His investigation and subsequent consultation critically emphasizing on-site incongruities during the 53rd Venice Biennale within the reconstruction of a Blinky Palermo installation was published in *X-TRA Contemporary Art Quarterly*. In 2008, he co-authored *Nomad Post School* with Guan Rong, and in 2020 *Some Pedagogies of the Southland Institute* with Joe Potts.

SILVIA FERNÁNDEZ is Visual Communication Designer at the National University, La Plata, Argentina. She has been a lecturer at the UNLP, in the Master Program of Design at the University of Palermo, Buenos Aires, and in the Master of Information Design at the UDLA, Puebla, Mexico, as well as dean of the Faculty of Design and Communication at the Universidad del Este, La Plata. Her articles have been published in specialized magazines such as *Tipográfica* and *Design Issues*, and she has written for, among others, *Ulmer modelle: Modelle nach Ulm, HfG Ulm 1953–1968* (Hatje Cantz, 2003), and the *Dictionnaire Universal des Créatices* (Paris). Fernández is director of NODAL editions (Nodo Diseño América Latina) and editor of *Historia del Diseño en América Latina y el Caribe* (2008). As part of the collection Women in Argentine Design, she completed the work started by María Laura Pedroni during the 1980s in the publication *Diseño Visual y Conocimiento Científico* (Nodal, 2016) and by Victoria Ocampo in *Señal Bauhaus* (Nodal, 2019). In the context of the centenary of the Bauhaus, she curated the section "Argentina" in the exhibition *The Whole World a Bauhaus?*, organized by the IFA in Karlsruhe, Germany.

HAL FOSTER is the author of numerous books, including, mostly recently, *What Comes After Farce? Art and Criticism at a Time of Debacle* (Verso, 2020), and *Brutal Aesthetics* (Princeton University Press, 2020), his 2018 Mellon Lectures at the National Gallery in Washington. A co-founder of *Zone* Magazine and Books, he teaches at Princeton University, co-edits the journal *October*, and contributes regularly to the *London Review of Books* and *Artforum*.

SHIRAZ ABDULLAHI GALLAB is a designer and educator who examines language, form, and location. She is the author of headgear.pw, an autobiographical piece that confronts the limitations of text-based expression, and she is the founding curator and co-author of *Samples and Parallels*, a collaborative publication that responds to an appropriated text. Shiraz has contributed to *Women of Graphic Design*, *Ficciones Typografika*, *Are.na*, and *Amalgam*, and she has exhibited at Klemm Gallery, the Muted Horn, and http://data-as-symbolic-form/exchanges, among other locations. Since receiving her MFA at Cranbrook Academy of Art, Shiraz has taught at the California College of the Arts, Virginia Commonwealth University, the University of Illinois at Chicago, and Purchase College. She was born but not raised in Khartoum, Sudan.

YASMIN KHAN GIBSON, Director, Program in Graphic Design, California Institute of the Arts, is a graphic designer and design educator based in the exurban foothills of Los Angeles. Prior to returning to her alma mater as faculty, Gibson was an associate professor at Otis College of Art and Design and part of the founding faculty of Otis College's MFA Program in Graphic Design. Gibson is also a former partner in the studio Counterspace. Her work has appeared in numerous publications and has been recognized by the Society of Type Designers, ACD, Art Directors Club, and :output. Her work with Counterspace was featured in publications such as *The Graphic Design Reader*, *Graphic Design for the 21st Century*, and *Contemporary Graphic Design*. Workshop Project is the pedagogical design practice of Yasmin Gibson and Jessica Wexler. Founded in 2013, the collaborative studio is a space to imagine pedagogy as a form of professional design practice.

MARIA GOUGH writes on modern and contemporary art, with an emphasis on the historical avant-gardes in a transnational context. Her key interests are abstraction, drawing, photography, print media, exhibition design, para-architecture, and the relationship between aesthetics and politics. Gough is Joseph Pulitzer, Jr. Professor of Modern Art at Harvard University.

BASMA HAMDY is an Egyptian research-based designer, author, curator, and educator producing work that bridges historical, political, and social issues with archival documentary, and critical mechanisms. She is co-author of *Walls of Freedom: Street Art of the Egyptian Revolution* (2014), as well as *Khatt: Egypt's Calligraphic Landscape* (Saqi Books, 2018). She has been interviewed and featured in prominent publications internationally and exhibited at art and design festivals and conferences around the world. She is currently associate professor of graphic design at VCUarts Qatar.

BRIAN JOHNSON is a partner at Polymode, focusing on creative direction, design production, writing, and teaching. He has guest lectured at School of Visual Arts, Washington University, and the Institute for Contemporary Art at Virginia Commonwealth University, and his writing appears in *Willi Smith: Street Couture*. Born into a family of printers, Johnson is deeply invested in the production of good design without the expense of sacrificing our humanity; meeting both the client and the producer in the middle to respect all avenues of time and budget in a hyper-paced world. Johnson holds a BFA from the Rhode Island School of Design where he met and began collaborating with Munro. He also is the Creative Director of Marketing at the University of North Carolina at Chapel Hill.

GEOFF KAPLAN of General Working Group has produced projects for a range of academic and cultural institutions, including the Museum of Modern Art, Harvard University, and the Museum of Contemporary Art, Los Angeles. His work is included in SFMOMA's and MOMA's permanent collections, and he has exhibited internationally. Kaplan received his MFA from Cranbrook; he teaches in the graduate design program at Yale University and was the Frank Stanton Chair in Graphic Design at Cooper Union. Kaplan wrote, edited, and designed *Power of the People: The Graphic Design of Radical Press and the Rise of the Counter-Culture, 1964–1974*, published by the University of Chicago Press. Kaplan is one of the co-founders of no place press.

NICOLE KILLIAN is an artist and design educator based in Richmond, VA, where they co-direct the graduate program in the Department of Graphic Design at Virginia Commonwealth University. killian is invested in exploring design pedagogies that center generosity, dialogue, and making things public through performance, mediums mis-use, and text. killian runs a publishing initiative, *nico fontana*, which concerns itself with a queering of language, objects, bodies, and spaces. killian holds degrees from the Cranbrook Academy of Art, Bauhaus/Hochschule Anhalt in Dessau, and the Rochester Institute of Technology.

JULIET KOSS is the Gabrielle Jungels-Winkler Professor of the History of Architecture and Art and chair of the Department of Art History at Scripps College in Claremont, California. She has published widely in Europe and the United States on modern European art, architecture, and design and is the author of *Modernism after Wagner* (University of Minnesota Press, 2010) and *Model Soviets* (MIT Press, forthcoming).

PREM KRISHNAMURTHY is based in Berlin and New York. His work across media explores the transformative potential of art and design by experimenting with presentational strategies, performative modes, and ways of communing. He directs Wkshps, a multidisciplinary design consultancy; is artistic director of FRONT International 2022, the Cleveland triennial of contemporary art; and organizes *Commune*, an emergent workshop that practices artistic tools for social transformation. Previously, Krishnamurthy founded the design studio Project Projects and the exhibition space P! in New York. He received the Cooper Hewitt National Design Award for Communications Design in 2015 and KW Institute for Contemporary Art's "A Year With..." residency fellowship in 2018. His professional papers were acquired by Bard College's Center for Curatorial Studies in 2019. In March 2021, Pompeii Archaeological Park released his new digital artwork, *Pompeii!*, which reflects upon rituals, destruction, memory, and letting go.

PAMELA M. LEE teaches the history, theory and criticism of late modernism and contemporary art with research interests in the relationship between aesthetics, politics, time, and system. Her courses include lectures and seminars on Abstract Expressionism, the art of the 1960s, contemporary art and globalization, intergenerational and intersectional feminism, methods and historiography, art and technology, modernism and war, and media cultures of the Cold War.

CHRIS LEE is a graphic designer and educator based in Brooklyn, NY, where he is an assistant professor at the Pratt Institute in the Undergraduate Communications Design Department. He graduated from OCADU (Toronto) and the Sandberg Instituut (Amsterdam) and has worked for *Walrus Magazine*, Metahaven, and Bruce Mau Design. He was also the designer and an editorial board member of the journal *Scapegoat: Architecture/Landscape/Political Economy*. Chris's primary research explores graphic design's entanglement with power and standards through the document.

DEBORAH LITTLEJOHN is an associate professor in the Department of Graphic Design and Industrial Design at the College of Design, North Carolina State University. In addition to the scholarship of design education, Deborah's research investigates design's role in transforming the social understanding of science through multidisciplinary collaborations that involve visualization strategies and co-productive participatory methodologies. Deborah holds an MFA in Graphic Design from California Institute of the Arts and a PhD in Design from North Carolina State University. In 2021, she was named a NCSU Faculty Scholar.

IAN LYNAM works at the intersection of graphic design, design education, and design research. He is faculty at Temple University Japan, as well as at Vermont College of Fine Arts in the MFA in Graphic Design Program and at Sam Fox School of Communication at Washington University Saint Louis, and is Visiting Critic at CalArts. He operates the Tokyo design studio Ian Lynam Design, working across identity, typography, and interior design, as well as the publishing imprint and type foundry Wordshape. Lynam writes for *IDEA* (Japan), *Slanted* (Germany), and *Modes of Criticism* (Portugal) and has published a number of books about design.

BRETT MACFADDEN is a partner in the San Francisco–based design studio MacFadden & Thorpe and a senior faculty member at the California College of the Arts. His work has been shown at SFMOMA and the International Biennial of Graphic Design Brno, and is held in the AIGA Collection at the Rare Book and Manuscript Library at Columbia University. He received his MFA in Design from the Cranbrook Academy of Art.

KATHERINE MCCOY was co-chair of the Design Department at Cranbrook Academy of Art for twenty-four years, a distinguished visiting professor at London's Royal College of Art, and senior lecturer at the Institute of Design in Chicago. A medalist of the AIGA and an elected member of the Alliance Graphique Internationale, she served as president of the Industrial Designers Society of America and the American Center for Design, and vice president of the American Institute of Graphic Arts. Her practice and writing on graphic design were recognized by the Smithsonian Design Museum's first Design Mind Award, shared with her husband, Michael. She currently focuses on cultural and environmental subjects for nonprofit institutions and governmental clients. She and Michael host the High Ground Design Conversation, an annual gathering of design curators, critics, and educators.

WAEL MORCOS is a graphic designer and type designer from Beirut, Lebanon. Upon receiving his BA in Graphic Design from Notre Dame University (Lebanon), he spent three years developing identities and Arabic-Latin bilingual typefaces, in addition to working in print and exhibition design. Wael received his MFA from RISD in 2013, after which he moved to New York and worked with several studios in the city before founding Morcos Key. Wael has been featured in *Print Magazine*'s 15 under 30, was named a Young Gun by the Art Directors Club, and an Ascender by the Type Directors Club.

SILAS MUNRO is a partner at Polymode. Munro's writing appears in *Eye*, *Slanted*, the Walker Reader, and *W. E. B. Du Bois's Data Portraits: Visualizing Black America*. He is particularly interested in the often unaddressed postcolonial relationship between design and marginalized communities. Munro holds an MFA from CalArts and a BFA from RISD. He has served as a critic at CalArts, MICA, and Yale University. Munro is an associate professor at Otis College of Art and Design and founding faculty and chair emeritus at Vermont College of Fine Arts.

YARA KHOURY NAMMOUR is a graphic designer, type designer, and educator. She is assistant professor of graphic design at the American University of Beirut and, since 2017, an independent designer after twenty years at AlMohtaraf design house. Her graphic work and type design has been published internationally, and she is the author of *Nasri Khattar: A Modernist Typotect* from Khatt Books.

TOM OCKERSE taught at the Rhode Island School of Design from 1971 to 2018. Born Dutch (in Bandung, Indonesia), he and some of his family moved from the Netherlands to the US in 1957. He earned a BFS from Ohio State University in 1963 and an MFA from Yale in 1965. In 1990, Ockerse began working primarily for nonprofit organizations such as *Visible Language* and the Humanity Initiative, where he partnered with Tony Balis "to encourage people to understand this planet as our common home."

SHARON HELMER POGGENPOHL is retired and living in Colorado. She edited the journal *Visible Language* for twenty-six years and taught at the Institute of Design, IIT, the Rhode

Island School of Design, and Hong Kong Polytechnic University. A recent critical article, "Waste and Agency in the Digital Era: Who's in Charge?" appeared in *Shè Jì: The Journal of Design, Economics, and Innovation* 6, no. 3 (2020). She self-published *Design Theory To Go, Connecting 24 Brief Theories to Practice* in 2018.

JOE POTTS is a designer and educator dedicated to exploring and implementing sustainable educational frameworks, cultivating public spaces for learning within the gaps of an increasingly privatized present, and building functional educational alternatives and supplements that move toward a more equitable, viable future. He founded and co-directs the Southland Institute (for critical, durational, and typographic post-studio practices) and is an associate professor and interim assistant chair of the Communication Arts and Graduate Graphic Design programs at Otis College of Art and Design. Potts holds a BA from Connecticut College and an MFA from the California Institute of the Arts.

JAMES SHOLLY is a principal in the graphic design studio Commercial Artisan (Indianapolis) and publisher of the Indiana design history journal *Commercial Article*. Sholly's work has been honored by AIGA, the American Association of Museums, *Communication Arts*, and others, and featured in design-focused publications like *Eye*, *Emigré*, and *Metropolis* over the course of his thirty-year career. Sholly is a contributing author to *Teaching Graphic Design History*, ed. Steven Heller (Allworth Press, 2019).

SYDNEY SKELTON SIMON is an art historian and museum educator. As the Bradley Assistant Curator of Academic Affairs at the Yale University Art Gallery, she is responsible for promoting, managing, and implementing the gallery's outreach and teaching programs. Simon received her BA from Yale University in the History of Art, and her PhD from Stanford University, specializing in post–World War II American art and design. Simon has also held positions at the National Gallery of Art, in Washington, DC, and at Stanford University's Anderson Collection and Cantor Arts Center.

GAIL SWANLUND's creative work has been exhibited at San Francisco Museum of Modern Art (SFMOMA), Los Angeles Contemporary Exhibitions (LACE), CAM Raleigh, Pomona College, the Biennial of Graphic Design in Brno, Czech Republic, and elsewhere. Her work may be found in public collections, including the Getty Research Institute, Los Angeles County Museum of Art (LACMA), and SFMOMA. She served on the board of DesignInquiry, a vanguard educational nonprofit organization whose mission is to cultivate the collective goal of extra-disciplinary discourse, productive counter-production, and research of design. Swanlund received her MFA from CalArts where she is an Art School faculty member in the Graphic Design program.

JAMES MERLE THOMAS is an interdisciplinary scholar and curator whose work examines the art, visual culture, and technology of the twentieth and twenty-first centuries. His research engages histories of modern and contemporary art, theories of postcolonialism and globalization, experimental pedagogy, and media studies of late modernity and the Cold War. He was assistant professor of art history at Temple University and curator at the Philadelphia-based Slought before being named director of the Resnick Center for Herbert Bayer Studies.

JORDAN TROELLER is lecturer in modern art history and theory at the University of Graz, Austria. Her recent publications have appeared in *Hyperallergic*, *October*, *Women's Art Journal*, and the anthology *Textile Modernism* (Böhlau, 2019). An essay on the drawings of Ruth Asawa, the subject of her current book project, in *Object Lessons* (Harvard Art Museums, 2021).

FRED TURNER is the Harry and Norman Chandler Professor of Communication at Stanford University. He is the author or co-author of five books, including *Seeing Silicon Valley* (University of Chicago Press, 2021), *The Democratic Surround: Multimedia and American Liberalism from World War II to the Psychedelic Sixties* (University of Chicago Press, 2013), and *From Counterculture to Cyberculture: Stewart Brand, the Whole Earth Network, and the Rise of Digital Utopianism* (University of Chicago Press, 2006). Before coming to Stanford, he taught Communication at Harvard's John F. Kennedy School of Government and MIT's Sloan School of Management. He also worked for ten years as a journalist. Turner has written for newspapers and magazines ranging from the *Boston Globe Sunday Magazine* to *Harper's*.

JESSICA WEXLER is chairperson of Undergraduate Communications Design at Pratt Institute. From 2006–13 she maintained an independent design partnership, Greenblatt-Wexler, focused on print and screen-based projects for arts-related and cultural institutions. Prior to her appointment at Pratt Institute, she was an assistant professor and the coordinator of the Graphic Design department in the School of Art + Design at Purchase College, SUNY. Her perspective on design education is informed by a decade of teaching, designing curricula, and coordinating faculty within diverse public, private, and for-profit institutions. Her work has been exhibited at White Columns and MOMA and is in the Rare Books and Manuscripts Library at the Butler Library at Columbia University and the AIGA Graphic Design Archives at the Denver Art Museum. Greenblatt-Wexler was featured in *Guide to Graphic Design* by Scott Santoro and GDNYC's *Super Models*. Workshop Project is the pedagogical design practice of Yasmin Gibson and Jessica Wexler. Founded in 2013, the collaboratiave studio is a space to imagine pedagogy as a form of professional design practice.

IGNACIO VALERO is associate professor at California College of the Arts, San Francisco. He was previously a professorial research fellow at the Vienna University of Technology; dean of the School of Fine Arts, CCAC; a member of the Presidential Advisory Council for the new Colombian Constitution; acting director and deputy director, Colombian Environmental Agency-INDERENA; Latin American coordinator, CIFCA/UNEP, Madrid; and coordinator, Sierra Nevada de Santa Marta Eco-Development Pilot Project and Environment/Science/Technology, COLCIENCIAS. He has taught at Goldsmiths, University of London, Universidad de Madrid Carlos III, Universidade de Lisboa, Xavier University, and the University of the Andes, Colombia.

LORRAINE WILD is the principal of Green Dragon Office, a design firm that focuses on collaborative work with artists, architects, curators, editors, and publishers. Wild also serves as the Consulting Creative Director at the Los Angeles County Museum of Art (LACMA), where she contributes to the design of publications, exhibitions, and the visual identity of the museum. She is a faculty member of the Graphic Design program at the California Institute of the Arts (CalArts). In 2006, Wild received the AIGA Gold Medal; she has also earned accolades from the New York Art Director's Club, the American Center for Design, the American Institute of Architects, and the American Association of Museums. Wild's award-winning books have been included in *Design Observer*'s (formerly AIGA's) selective "50 Books/50 Covers" competition over twenty-five times. Wild is a graduate of the Cranbrook Academy of Art and the Yale School of Art. She is on Cranbrook's National Advisory Board and is a member of the Los Angeles Institute for the Humanities at USC.

LAUREN WILLIAMS is a designer, organizer, researcher, and educator. She works with visual and interactive media to understand, critique, and reimagine the ways social and economic systems distribute and exercise power. Her practice and research revolves around Blackness, identity, and social fictions and examines the ways in which racism is felt, embodied, and embedded into institutions. Her work often engages people through collaborations and facilitated experiences in service of imagining and manifesting a more liberated present and future. In the past, she has managed programs and policy aimed at cultivating economic justice. Going forward, she's most interested in finding ways to align her capacities with revolutionary movements that build toward a different economy entirely and usher in new dimensions of power and freedom altogether.

CREDITS

Lucia Moholy's "Questions of Interpretation" was originally published as "Fragen der Interpretation" in *Bauhaus und Bauhäusler: Bekenntnisse und Erinnerungen*, ed. Eckhard Neumann (Stuttgart: Hallwag, 1971), 169–78. It was translated by Eva Richter and Alba Lorman in *Bauhaus and Bauhaus People: Personal Opinions and Recollections of Former Bauhaus Members and Their Contemporaries*, ed. Eckhard Neumann, rev. ed. (New York: Van Nostrand Reinhold, 1993), 237–46. (Note that an earlier version of Neumann's anthology, published in English in spring 1970, does not include Moholy's text.) The 1993 translation is based on the 1985 German reedition of Neumann's book, in which two paragraphs are curiously reordered. Not knowing who was responsible for this change, Jordan Troeller used the original 1971 text for the translation published in this volume and previously in *October* 172 (Spring 2020).

IMAGE CREDITS

The publisher has made every effort to clarify all copyrights. If proper acknowledgment has not been made, we kindly ask copyright holders to contact us.

By page number:
30: gift of Susan Lustig Peck, 2001-29-52. Cooper Hewitt, Smithsonian Design Museum. Photo: Matt Flynn © Smithsonian Institution
32: museum purchase through gift of Lucy Work Hewitt, 1992-167-8; Cooper Hewitt, Smithsonian Design Museum. Photo: Matt Flynn © Smithsonian Institution
35: from the collection of Katherine and Michael McCoy
37: gift of Anonymous Donor, 1994-109-17; Cooper Hewitt, Smithsonian Design Museum. Photo: Matt Flynn © Smithsonian Institution
39, 58: courtesy The MIT Press
72, 77: public domain
76: courtesy Galerie Berinson, Berlin
80: Harvard Art Museums/Busch-Reisinger Museum, Museum Purchase, © Artists Rights Society (ARS), New York/VG Bild-Kunst, Bonn, Photo ©President and Fellows of Harvard College, BR48.10; Harvard Art Museums/ Busch-Reisinger Museum, Gift of Herbert Bayer, Photo © President and Fellows of Harvard College, BR48.85
81: Harvard Art Museums/Busch-Reisinger Museum, Purchase, © Artists Rights Society (ARS), New York/VG Bild-Kunst, Bonn, Photo © President and Fellows of Harvard College, BR48.53
83: © Artists Rights Society (ARS), New York/ VG Bild-Kunst, Bonn, Photo © President and Fellows of Harvard College, BR48.94]
97: photo: Roland Fürst, 1963 © HfG-Archiv, Ulm
100: photo: Eva Maria-Koch, 1955 © HfG-Archiv, Ulm
104: Creative Commons
106, 107, 108, 109: public domain
112: photo: Hans G. Conrad © René Spitz
114: © BRAUN P&G/Braun Archive Kronberg
116: photo: Sigrid von Schweinitz, 1955 © HfG-Archiv, Ulm
121, 122, 124, 125: public domain
125: courtesy the author
127, 128, 129, 130, 132, 136, 144, 147: courtesy the author
155, 157: courtesy Sheila de Bretteville
161: courtesy California Institute of the Arts Institute Archives
167, 168: © *Visible Language*, University of Cincinnati
170: photo: Antoine Bootz, 1991
185: courtesy Scott Santoro
186, 189: courtesy the author
198, 208: courtesy Letterform Archive
202: Getty Research Institute, Los Angeles (950076) © Artists Rights Society ARS, NY/ VG Bild-Kunst, Bonn
215, 221: © 2021 Estate of Harry Bertoia / Artists Rights Society (ARS), New York
217: photo by the author, May 2019
221, 223, 224: courtesy the author
231, 245: photo: Rudy Vanderlans
248, 255: courtesy the author
254: public domain
271: photo © Gui Bonsiepe
302: public domain
307: Creative Commons
310: photo: Annika Butler-Wall
319: © Chris Pullman
321, 322: © *Visible Language*, University of Cincinnati
323: © Robert Nakata
324: © Louise Sandhaus
325: © Robin Cottle; © Jessica Lee
338: public domain
341: public domain
343, 346: © *Commercial Article*
359, 360: photo: Steve White II/Ian Lynam
369: © Basma Hamdy
374: © Yara Khoury
385, 386, 388: courtesy Workshop Project
390: David Stanley/CC BY 2.0
392: Creative Commons
410, 411, 412, 414, 416: photo by the author
411, 414: Creative Commons
411, 412, 413, 414, 415, 416, 417: public domain
432: ©Yasmin Ali

TO TEACHERS AND STUDENTS

This book would not have been realized without the generosity, trust, and patience of all involved, knowingly or otherwise. The idea of the book was conceived of in conversation with Susan Bielstein, editor extraordinaire at the University of Chicago Press, over drinks in 2013. The collective efforts have finally been realized, all these years later, despite much change and turmoil, including a resurgence of global fascism, a pandemic, and loss for far too many. In 2016 the project began to be formalized upon an invitation by Amy Fidler and Jenn Stucker to present at the AIGA Design Educator's Conference. It was here that I asked Audrey G. Bennett and Deborah Littlejohn, fellow keynote presenters, to contribute to the project. Momentum built slowly from there. Soon after the AIGA event I met with Tim Barringer, then the chair of Yale's art history department, I mentioned the pedagogy project at which point Tim devised the plan to host a two-day conference. The Yale conference convened on May 10–11, 2019, and included seventeen presenters. One goal of the conference was that the resulting presentations would produce the backbone of a publication. Following the Yale event, I invited an almost equal number of additional contributors, resulting in the forty-one essays you now hold. Gratitude to Prem Krishnamurthy for sharing his Rolodex and to the largesse of Yale and Tim Barringer. That said, this book does not become a reality without the brilliant and joyous force that is Rachel Churner.

Authors who presented at the Yale conference:
Janet Abrams, Audrey G. Bennett, Andrew Blauvelt, Gui Bonsiepe, Sheila Levrant de Bretteville and James Merle Thomas, Hugh Dubberly, Silvia Fernández, Maria Gough, Juliet Koss, Pamela M. Lee, Deborah Littlejohn, Katherine McCoy, Sharon Helmer Poggenpohl, Sydney Skelton Simon, Fred Turner, and Lorraine Wild

Yale conference support:
Caitlin Woolsey, Nicole Chardiet, British Art Museum and Courtney Martin, Allen Hori, Julian Bittiner, and Dho Yee Chung

Authors post-conference:
Danielle Aubert, Tim Barringer, J. Dakota Brown, Craig Buckley, Annika Butler-Wall, Colin Fanning, Hal Foster, Shiraz Abdullahi Gallab, Yasmin Gibson and Jessica Wexler, Denise Gonzales Crisp, Wael Morcos with Basma Hamdy and Yara Khoury, Brian Johnson and Silas Munro, nicole killian, Prem Krishnamurthy, Chris Lee, Ian Lynam, Brett MacFadden, Thomas Ockerse, Joe Potts with Adam Feldmeth, James Sholly, Sulki and Min, Gail Swanlund, Jordan Troeller (and Lucia Moholy), Ignacio Valero, and Lauren Williams

Special thanks to:
Rachel Churner and Jordan Kantor, no place press; Linus Lee, Pristone Press
&
Miguel Abreu, Tim Allen, Caryn Aono, Stacy Asher, Leslie Atzmon, Connie Lee Batlevi, Dodie Bellamy, Gunjan Bhutani, Simon Bowden, Julia Bryan-Wilson, Anne Burdick, MEC, Alan Carver, Scott Cataffa, Mel Chen, Todd Childers, Alan Chong, Meredith Davis, Apsara DiQuinzio, Sean Dungan, Joe Evans, Vince Fecteau, Ed Fella, Jessica Flemming, Karin Fong, Geoffry Fried, Rochelle Goldberg, Christian Grommes, Eric Hardrath, Steve Hartzog, High Ground, Steven Inconto, Hayley Jackson, Jan Jancourt, David Joselit, David Karam, Jeff Keedy, Stuart Kendall, the late Kevin Killian, Jennifer Lee, Kristina Leonetti, Bridgette Lery, Connie Lewallen, Sam Lewitt, Sara Liebert, Catherine Lord, Ellen Lupton, Beth Mangini, Olivia Neel, Steven Nelson, Zeena Parkins, Dana Peterman, Katherine Pickard, Jeff Preiss, Blake Rayne, Kurt Rohde, Beau Rothrock, Louise Sandhaus, Brian Scott, Jon Sueda, Sandy Tait, Kim Thomsen, Teal Triggs, Alex Tylevich, Rick Valicenti, Martin Venezky, Anne Walsh, Michael Worthington, and Dana Yee
♥
The extended Lee (Vaughn, Samuels) and Kaplan (Brown, Wagreich) families, & always & forever, P Lee
X O

Notes on design:
The images printed in gold and rendered as dithered bitmaps, split over successive pages produce a timeline, a "history of technology" that runs parallel to the history of graphic design pedagogy. Much of this "history" is based on the timeline constructed by Chris Woodford (https://www.explainthatstuff.com/timeline.html). In running the timeline alongside the book's texts, I hope to counteract what is most often recounted as a Eurocentric, white, and male history of technology that fetishizes technological progress and individual (male) genius as the drivers of history. In fact, the images veer away from a material history of technology and toward images of historical things. I emailed the artist Sam Lewitt about this image usage because his work has been an important influence. Sam replied:

> The macro perspective of all things technical under and including the sun is at once too general in terms of scope and too selective in terms of the material artifacts chosen. In that sense I read these images more like stock images related to the search term "history of technology"—which reflexively relates to your introduction essay in terms of the critical assessment of the question of discipline. These emblems of "technology" are more about the *homogenization* and *dissolution* of the protocols, developmental narratives, and exclusive selection criteria etc. necessary for a disciplinary regime. In other words, I read them more as pointing to something outside the necessarily narrow bounds of a discipline's proper objects. After all, the claim is not that "graphic design" has existed as long as parchment, or tracing figures in sand, or language, or the sun, right?

The jacket unfolds as a map in the form of an index filtered page for page as seen on one side of the jacket, and on the other side chapter by chapter. Following is a sample of the python code Alvin Ashiatey wrote:

```
# -*- coding: utf-8 -*-
"""IndexPY.ipynb

Automatically generated by Colaboratory.

Original file is located at
    https://colab.research.google.com/drive/
1M73taL3Smy_MoQDxb9AT0QNs-biKCYR0
"""

from google.colab import drive
drive.mount('/content/drive')

import os
import csv
import glob
import pprint
os.chdir('/content/drive/My Drive/Geoff Kaplan')

!pip install PyPDF2

import PyPDF2
import re
import json

docu = PyPDF2.PdfFileReader("GK.pdf")

NumPages = docu.getNumPages()

def searchPdf (num, obj, searchEntry):
  r = []
  for i in range(0, num):
    PageObj = obj.getPage(i)
    Text = PageObj.extractText()
    strpText = searchEntry.strip()
    reValue = r"\b{}\b".format(strpText)
    reg = re.compile(reValue,re.MULTILINE |
re.IGNORECASE)
    reFind = re.findall(reg, Text)
    numberCount = Text.count(strpText)
    d = dict()
    if len(reFind) > 0:
      d["page"] = str(i + 1)
      d["count"] = len(reFind)
      r.append(d)
  return r

indexDict = {}
pathName = "index.csv"
with open(os.path.join(pathName),
encoding='utf-8') as file:
  reader = csv.reader(file, delimiter=',')
  counter = 0
  print("START")
  for row in reader:
    for column in row:
      counter += 1
      indexDict[column] = {}
      indexDict[column]["matches"] = searchPd-
f(NumPages, docu, column)
  print('FINISHED')

with open('output.json', 'w', encoding='utf-8')
as f:
  json.dump(indexDict, f, sort_keys=True,
indent=4)
```

Geoff Kaplan, ed.
After the Bauhaus, Before the Internet; A History of Graphic Design Pedagogy
Published by no place press

Contributions by, as they appear in the book: Tim Barringer, Geoff Kaplan, Colin Fanning, Katherine McCoy, Deborah Littlejohn, J. Dakota Brown, Jullet Koss, Jordan Troeller, Lucia Moholy, Craig Buckley, Silvia Fernández, Thomas Ockerse, James Merle Thomas, Polymode: Brian Johnson and Silas Munro, Brett MacFadden, Sulki and Min, Andrew Blauvelt, Maria Gough, Sydney Skelton Simon, Hal Foster, Rachel Churner, and Geoff Kaplan, Gail Swanlund, Audrey G. Bennett, Shiraz Abdullahi Gallab, Gui Bonsiepe, Pamela M. Lee, Hugh Dubberly, Sharon Helmer Poggenpohl, Denise Gonzales Crisp, Fred Turner and Annika Butler-Wall, Lorraine Wild, Danielle Aubert, James Sholly, Prem Krishnamurthy, Ian Lynam, nicole killian, Wael Morcos, Basma Hamdy, and Yara Khoury, Joe Potts with Adam Feldmeth, Yasmin Gibson and Jessica Wexler, Ignacio Valero, Chris Lee, and Lauren Williams

Design: General Working Group
Managing Editor: Rachel Churner
Proofreading: Jordan Kantor, Olivia Neel, Nick Sywak
Jacket programming: Alvin Ashiatey

ISBN: 978-1-949484-09-0

English
First edition of 1,000
Printed in Singapore, Pristone Press

Paper: Munken Print White 70 gsm, and 200 gsm

Distributed by the MIT Press
Cambridge, Massachusetts, and London, England

no place press
New York and San Francisco, 2022.
448 pages : illustrations : 23.495 cm

no place press catalogue

Jordan Kantor: Selected Exhibitions 2006–2016
Conversation with Yve-Alain Bois

Bill Berkson
A Frank O'Hara Notebook
Contributions by Ron Padgett and Constance Lewallen

Pamela M. Lee
The Glen Park Library: A Fairy Tale of Disruption
Foreword by Michelle Kuo

Anne Walsh
Hello Leonora, Soy Anne Walsh
Contributions by Dodie Bellamy, Julia Bryan-Wilson, and Claudia LaRocco

Amy Franceschini and Michael Swaine, Futurefarmers
For Want of a Nail
Contributions by Peter Galison, Patrick Kiley, Lucy Lippard, Megan Prelinger and Rick Prelinger, and Anne Walsh

Yvonne Rainer
Revisions: Essays by Apollo Musagète, Yvonne Rainer, and Others
Contributions by Gregg Bordowitz, Douglas Crimp, Emily Coates, and Anna Staniczenko

Yvonne Rainer
Revisions #2 by Apollo Musagète a.k.a. Yvonne Rainer